The LATEX Companion

Integrating TEX, HTML, and XML

Addison-Wesley Series on Tools and Techniques for Computer Typesetting

This recently inaugurated series focuses on tools and techniques needed for computer typesetting and information processing with traditional and new media. Books in the series address the practical needs both of users and of system developers. Initial titles comprise handy references for LaTeX users; forthcoming works will expand that core. Ultimately, the series will cover other typesetting and information processing systems, as well, especially insofar as those systems offer unique value to the scientific and technical community. The series goal is to enhance your ability to produce, maintain, manipulate, or reuse articles, papers, reports, proposals, books, and other documents with professional quality.

Ideas for this series should be directed to the editor: mittelbach@awl.com.
All other comments and questions should be sent to Addison-Wesley: awcse@awl.com.

Series Editor

Frank Mittelbach
Manager LaTeX3 Project, Germany

Editorial Board

Jacques André
Irisa/Inria-Rennes, France

Barbara Beeton
Editor, TUGboat, USA

David Brailsford
University of Nottingham, UK

Tim Bray
Textuality Services, Canada

Peter Flynn
University College, Cork, Ireland

Leslie Lamport
Creator of LaTeX, USA

Chris Rowley
Open University, UK

Richard Rubinstein
Perot Systems, USA

Paul Stiff
University of Reading, UK

Series Titles

The LaTeX Companion, by Michel Goossens, Frank Mittelbach, and Alexander Samarin
The LaTeX Graphics Companion, by Michel Goossens, Sebastian Rahtz, and Frank Mittelbach
The LaTeX Web Companion, by Michel Goossens and Sebastian Rahtz

Also from Addison-Wesley:
LaTeX: A Document Preparation System, Second Edition, by Leslie Lamport

The LaTeX Web Companion

Integrating TeX, HTML, and XML

Michel Goossens
CERN, Geneva, Switzerland

Sebastian Rahtz
Elsevier Science Ltd., Oxford, United Kingdom

with Eitan M. Gurari, Ross Moore, and Robert S. Sutor

ADDISON WESLEY

An Imprint of Addison Wesley Longman, Inc.
Reading, Massachusetts • Harlow, England • Menlo Park, California
Berkeley, California • Don Mills, Ontario
Sydney • Bonn • Amsterdam • Tokyo • Mexico City

Many of the designations used by manufacturers and sellers to distinguish their products are claimed as trademarks. Where those designations appear in this book and Addison Wesley Longman, Inc. was aware of a trademark claim, the designations have been printed in initial capital letters or all capitals.

The authors and publisher have taken care in the preparation of this book, but make no expressed or implied warranty of any kind and assume no responsibility for errors or omissions. No liability is assumed for incidental or consequential damages in connection with or arising out of the use of the information or programs contained herein.

The publisher offers discounts on this book when ordered in quantity for special sales. For more information, please contact: AWL Direct Sales
Addison Wesley Longman, Inc.
One Jacob Way
Reading, Massachusetts 01867
(781) 944-3700

Visit A-W on the Web: http://www.awl.com/cseng/

Library of Congress Cataloging-in-Publication Data

Goossens, Michel.
  The LaTeX Web Companion: integrating TeX, HTML, and XML/Michel
Goossens, Sebastian Rahtz; with Eitan M. Gurari, Ross Moore, and
Robert S. Sutor
    p. cm.-(Addison-Wesley series on tools and techniques for
computer typesetting)
  Includes bibliographical references and index.
  ISBN 0-201-43311-7
  1. HTML (Document markup language) 2. XML (Document markup
language) 3. LaTeX (Computer file) I. Rahtz, S. P. Q. II. Title.
III. Series
QA76.76.H94G66 1999
005.7'2-dc21
                                                            98-48199
                                                              CIP

Reproduced by Addison Wesley Longman, Inc. from camera-ready copy supplied by the authors.

ISBN 0-201-43311-7

1 2 3 4 5 6 7 8 9 10–CRS–0302010099

First printing, May 1999

Contents

List of Figures

List of Tables

Preface

The aim of this book is to provide help for authors, primarily scientists, who want to invest in the Web or other hypertext presentation systems but are not living in the world of Microsoft Word or QuarkXpress. They have an investment in markup systems such as LaTeX and have special needs in fields like mathematics, non-European languages, and algorithmic graphics. The book will tell them how to

- make full use of the Adobe Acrobat format from LaTeX;
- convert their legacy documents to HTML or XML;
- make use of their math in Web applications;
- use LaTeX as a tool in preparing Web pages;
- read and write simple XML/SGML;
- produce high-quality printed pages from their Web-hosted XML or HTML pages using TeX or PDF.

LaTeX as a document repository for the Internet

The World Wide Web has invaded all areas of society, and science is no exception to this rule. This should come as no surprise since the Web paradigm was born at CERN, one of the largest scientific laboratories in the world.

The present ubiquitous Web interface is the result of basic research that took place in the first years of the 1990s at CERN. Before then use of the Internet had been mostly an affair of specialists. It needed the genius and insight of Tim Berners-Lee and collaborators to create a tool that allowed physicists participating in CERN's high-energy physics program but located all over the world to exchange data and information via the Internet in an intuitive and "user-friendly" way. Their work led directly to the development of the HTML language, the HTTP protocol, and the URL addressing scheme—the three basic pillars on which the Web is built. From the very beginning, the group took the farsighted decision to share their work freely with the Internet community. Then, thanks also to the appearance of the graphic interface of the *Mosaic* browser, the Web paradigm was received enthusiastically by developers and users alike. The growth of the number of Web sites and users became exponential, culminating in the "Woodstock of the Web" at CERN in May 1994. CERN, a scientific laboratory dedicated to basic research, did not have the resources to coordinate Web development further, and hence these responsibilities were transferred to the international World Wide Web Consortium [↪W3C], which at present consists of three main components: the Laboratory for Computer Science at MIT [↪MIT], USA; INRIA [↪INRIA], France; and Keio University [↪KEIO], Japan. The Consortium is supported by DARPA [↪DARPA] and the European Commission [↪EC].

One lesson to be learned from the history of the advent of the Web is that basic research, in completely unexpected ways, can lead to very important and wide-ranging spin-offs for society.

Although most people do not realize it, SGML (in the form of the ubiquitous lingua franca of the Web, HTML) is today without doubt the leading markup language for electronic documents. Similarly LaTeX has been used for over a decade for marking up scientific documents. Even today there is no viable alternative to print texts containing a lot of mathematics without using LaTeX. Therefore it seems reasonable to look for ways to find a (possibly) automatic procedure to translate LaTeX documents in a form that is exploitable on the Web. Conversely, documents marked up in XML and HTML should be able to benefit from the high typographic qualities of the TeX processor.

Therefore in this book we explain how LaTeX can be used as the central component of an electronic document strategy for the Web. We show how you can reuse your existing LaTeX documents on the Web by translating them into HTML, and how, by using some LaTeX extension packages, you can more fully exploit the hypertext capabilities of HTML. Today HTML and Web browsers cannot deal very well with nontextual document components, such as pictures (which are translated into bitmap images) or mathematics. We also address the translation of LaTeX into PDF and the possibilities of interpreting LaTeX commands directly by extensions of a browser.

We also introduce you to the secrets of XML, the extensible markup language, which uses a subset of SGML and which is set to replace HTML as it allows for application-dependent extensions. In particular, we look at MathML—the mathematical markup language—its syntax and how it can be generated, and what it can be used for.

Going in the other direction, we discuss various strategies to transform Web source documents marked up in XML or HTML into LaTeX or PDF for optimal printing, in particular using DSSSL and XSL style sheets.

Many tools for transforming TeX-based source files into HTML have been developed over the years. The programs described in this book are a representative sample chosen mainly because we were familiar with them and have used them ourselves. The absence of a description of other tools in this book in no way implies that we consider them to be less useful or of inferior quality.

Logical structure of the book

We suggest that all readers look at Chapter 1 before going any further, because this chapter introduces how we think—that the Web is not a threat to LaTeX, but an opportunity and why you should or should not continue to write in LaTeX. We also present a short introduction to the Web from the point of view of the LaTeX user.

Chapter 2 treats the subject of how to marry hyperdocuments with page fidelity using the Portable Document Format (PDF).

The conversion of LaTeX documents into HTML is tackled in Chapters 3 and 4. In Chapter 3 we discuss LaTeX2HTML, which uses Perl to interpret LaTeX source documents and to generate HTML code. Extension packages can be easily added in the form of Perl routines, while various extensions to the LaTeX language make LaTeX2HTML a real high-performance tool to generate hypertext documents.

We take a different approach in Chapter 4, where TeX4ht uses a redefinition of LaTeX's TeX macros to generate HTML or XML, possibly using also the MathML application for expressing the mathematics.

Recently we have seen the development of browsers (with plug-ins) that are able to interpret mathematical markup directly. Chapter 5 looks at implementations that can direcly interpret large subsets of native LaTeX code without prior translation into HTML, in particular techexplorer, a plug-in for Netscape and Internet Explorer developed by IBM, and WebEQ, a Java applet for rendering math.

Chapter 6 looks at the broader picture and gives a gentle introduction to SGML (Standard Generalized Markup Language); it explains how XML (Extensible Markup Language), a simpler and more "Internet and user-friendly" variant of SGML will become an important element in any future document strategy for the Internet. It is anticipated that XML, combined with object databases and other current object-oriented technologies, will revolutionize our document management at all levels. Tools for authoring and interpreting XML will be described, and we will spend some time building a LaTeX-like XML markup language.

TeX was originally developed by Don Knuth to print his math books in accordance with the highest standards of the typographic art. Therefore it should come as no surprise that TeX has been proposed as a typesetting engine for Web material. Tools to translate XML sources into various output formats are described in Chapter 7. The use of Cascading Style Sheets (CSS), Document Style Semantics and Specification Language (DSSSL), and Extensible Stylesheet Language (XSL) for controlling the translation process will be detailed.

Chapter 8 tackles the "hot" issue of how to take maximal advantage of LaTeX's optimal mathematical notation to translate LaTeX markup into XML and MathML (Mathematical Markup language), a companion to XML to present and work with math on the Web (see Foster (1999) for an overview of various ways to handle math on the Web).

The book ends with appendixes that contain technical information to complement the chapters in the book. We provide an introduction to Web namespaces, discuss internationalization issues, and review a few important XML DTDs.

History and authorship

When *The LaTeX Graphics Companion* was in its early stages, Sebastian Rahtz and Michel Goossens intended to include coverage of the Portable Document Format, SGML, and the Web in that book. It became apparent, however, that the hypertext and SGML material would require a whole book of their own, so as soon as the *Graphics Companion* was completed, work started on this *Web Companion*. Even more than is the case with most TeX work, the packages and programs related to the Web and TeX were changing very rapidly; it was decided, therefore, to ask the authors of three of the most important packages to work with Rahtz and Goossens, to make sure that the chapters would be up-to-date and accurate.

The chapter on LaTeX2HTML is primarily the work of Moore; that on TeX4ht the work of Gurari; and that on IBM `techexplorer` and WebEQ that of Sutor; Goossens and Rahtz shared the remaining chapters between them. Gurari, Moore, and Sutor also contributed significantly to the rest of the book by commenting on material, contributing sections, and discussing the issues involved.

It is, perhaps, a tribute to the Internet that the five authors never met in person as a group during the entire writing and editing process. The nearest they came was a pleasant dinner in Saint-Malo at the 1998 EuroTeX meeting, where all but Eitan Gurari were present.

Using, and finding, all those packages and programs

Unless explicitly mentioned otherwise, all packages and programs described in this book are freely available in public software archives; some are in the public domain, while others are protected by copyright. Some programs are available only in source form or work only on certain computer platforms, and you should be prepared for a certain amount of "getting your hands dirty" in some cases. We also cannot guarantee that later versions of packages or programs will give results identical to those in our book. Many of them are under active development, and new or changed versions appear several times a year; we completed this book in the winter of 1998–1999, and tested the examples with versions current at that time.

As regular users of the World Wide Web will know, keeping track of URLs is a tricky, error-prone process as sites continually disappear or change their structure. In this book, therefore, we do not give formal URLs in the text, but rather give pointers (typeset like "[↪ W3C]") to a catalog of URLs (starting on page 499). This catalog will be kept up to date and will be available in the directory `info/lwc` on the CTAN nodes, where the source code of most of our examples will also be made available. We have tried to clear up some of the fog of acronyms by providing a glossary of terms (starting on page 489).

Colophon

This book was prepared using LaTeX. The main text font is Adobe Janson, the sans serif font is Y&Y's European Modern Sans, the math is set in Y&Y MathTime Plus, and the literal typewriter text is set in Y&Y's European Modern typewriter.

The LaTeX style was refined and generalized by Frank Mittelbach from that developed by him and Sebastian Rahtz for *The LaTeX Graphics Companion*, which, in turn, was derived from the style by Frank Mittelbach and Michel Goossens for *The LaTeX Companion*.

Acknowledgments

We are grateful to Nelson Beebe (University of Utah), Tim Bray (Textuality), Mimi Burbank (Florida State University), David Carlisle (NAG), Hans Hagen (Pragma), Hàn Thế Thành (Masaryk University, Brno), T. V. Raman (Adobe Systems), D. P. Story (University of Akron), Michael Downes (American Mathematical Society), Peter Flynn (University College, Cork), Chris Maden (O'Reilly), Thomas Merz (Munich), and Chris Rowley (Open University) for advice, encouragement, and comments on draft chapters.

Sebastian Rahtz would like to take this opportunity to thank Tanmoy Bhattacharya, David Carlisle, Patrick Daly, Yannis Haralambous, and many others, for their help with the hyperref package, and Berthold Horn (Y&Y) for sponsoring part of the development.

Eitan M. Gurari is very thankful to Gertjan Klein and Sebastian Rahtz for their contribution to the development of TeX4ht. Gertjan's help came at early stages of the project, offering important code and advice for making TeX4ht a portable tool and providing numerous detailed comments and suggestions for configuring the output. Sebastian got involved in the project at later stages, providing an enormous amount of feedback, setting up challenging objectives, collaborating in the development of interesting configuration files, aggressively promoting the system, and heavily editing my contribution to this book. Aside and beyond the professional aspects, Gertjan and Sebastian were great Net associates!

Robert Sutor wants to express express his gratitude to Bill Pulleyblank, Marshall Schor, and Dick Jenks of the IBM Research Division for their support during the time `techexplorer` was developed.

Ross Moore would like to acknowledge first Nikos Drakos, for his foresight in designing a translator such as LaTeX2HTML and establishing its basic design principles. There is insufficient space here to list all those who have made significant contributions; we thank them all. Among them we especially wish to acknowledge Marcus Hennecke and Herb Swan, who were the most significant contributors when Nikos could no longer be involved. We also wish to acknowledge Jens Lippman, Scott Nelson, and Marek Rouchal who continue to supply the support necessary to develop, maintain, and distribute the latest revisions of the LaTeX2HTML program. Second Ross wants to thank Michel Goossens, Mimi Jett, Jerold Marsden, Robert Miner, and Kristoffer Rose for supporting visits to various places around the world, where ideas for extensions to LaTeX2HTML were discussed and/or developed; some of these visits have directly affected the contents of this book.

On the publishing side, Frank Mittelbach (series editor) did an excellent job of trying to keep us on the straight and narrow path, and Peter Gordon (Addison Wesley Longman, Inc.) provided all the encouragement, support, jokes, and help any authors could want. When it came to production, John Fuller, Helen Goldstein, and Maureen Willard were very patient with our idiosyncrasies, steered us safely to completion, and edited our dubious prose into real English.

Feedback

We would like to ask you, dear reader, for your collaboration. We kindly invite you to send your comments, suggestions, or remarks to any of the authors. We will be glad to correct any mistakes or oversights in a future edition and are open to suggestions for improvements or the inclusion of important developments we may have overlooked. We will maintain a list of errata in a file called `webcomp.err` in the LaTeX distribution, and this will contain current addresses for the authors.

Many of the Web applications that we describe in this book continue to evolve rapidly. The source code of the examples in the directory `info/lwc` of the CTAN nodes will be kept up-to-date to guarantee that the code will work with future versions of W3C specifications. This applies in particular to the XSL files of Sections 7.6, B.4.5, and C.3 since the syntax of XSL is not yet finalized.

CHAPTER 1

The Web, its documents, and LaTeX

In this chapter we will look at how the World Wide Web was born and the main components that make it into a genuine global cultural and language-independent communication tool. This includes a short introduction to HTML, the markup language used in most Web documents at present. Most of the tools discussed in this book generate HTML or, more generally, XML markup, so that an elementary knowledge of its syntax will come in handy later.

Then we will take a bird's-eye view of the various approaches that have been developed to deal with content-rich scientific documents focusing on the role of LaTeX as an input or output format in this environment. This will lead us to the conclusion that the development of the Web and its new view of an electronic document should be considered an enrichment of the toolbox available to scientists to communicate results and data.

*   *   *

The Internet, and in particular the World Wide Web, reached a peak of public visibility when President Bill Clinton mentioned them in his State of the Union address before the United States Congress on January 27, 1998 [↪SOTU98]:

> We should enable all the world's people to explore the far reaches of cyberspace. Think of this—the first time I made a State of the Union speech to you, only a handful of physicists used the World Wide Web. Literally,

just a handful of people. Now, in schools, in libraries, homes and businesses, millions and millions of Americans surf the Net every day. . . . But we also must make sure that we protect the exploding global commercial potential of the Internet. . . .

For one thing, I ask Congress to step up support for building the next generation Internet. It's getting kind of clogged, you know. And the next generation Internet will operate at speeds up to a thousand times faster than today.

And on January 19, 1999, President Clinton was proud to announce [↪ SOTU99]:

. . . We are well on our way to our goal of connecting every classroom and library to the Internet.

Nowadays not only does the White House take the Web seriously (the above quote was taken from one of the thousands of government documents available on its Web site), but every company, school, organization, public or commercial utility, and, before long, every individual will want a presence on the Web. It has become common practice in scientific (and not-so-scientific) publications to use URL addresses to refer to supplementary information, and in many cases scientific work is now available first on a Web site long before it is published in "paper" form in a recognized journal.

In the scientific world we have seen an extremely swift evolution from a kind of hesitation to embrace the new Web technology to the enthusiasm of using preprint databases to speed up the dissemination of information. The main problem that remains to be solved is *quality*, both in content and form. The quality of the content can be guaranteed by adopting the established peer review system, building upon the expertise of many of the existing publishing houses that find a new role as "information verification agents." The quality of presentation is a problem that is not yet fully solved. There have been many public debates about whether current computer screens can provide the necessary detail to represent faithfully the visual multidimensional information inherent in a mathematical or chemical formula. Several attempts have already been made to come up with ways to overcome the coarseness of the computer screen (at best a few pixels per millimeter), keeping the flexibility of interactive hypertext searching possibilities.

Consider also the situation in parts of the world, such as Russia, Southeast Asia, and Africa, that are facing severe financial constraints, and where it is often out of the question even to consider printing multiple copies of a highly technical document. Electronic dissemination via the Web is the only way, then, to publish. Thus the Web is not only an additional medium for the traditional publishing establishment, but a necessity for the larger part of the world to participate in sharing the information and benefit from the wealth and progress it creates.

What form will information on the Web take in future? The *World Wide Web Consortium* (W3C) was formed to encourage software companies to work together to come up with solutions that guarantee interoperability and statelessness of electronic documents and data on the Internet.

When we look at our own system (TEX), we see that the Web is not a threat to LATEX but an additional opportunity. We expect that scientists will continue to use the tools they feel most comfortable with for writing their documents (be it LATEX or other applications), but they will have new opportunities for making the results available.

We hope to convince you in this book that, thanks to the tools we describe in the following chapters, you do not have to choose between TEX's typographic quality and the global connectivity of the Web: You can have both.

1.1   The Web, a window on the Internet

The popularity of the Internet expanded greatly across national and subject barriers during the 1990s, and this is in great part due to the advent of the World Wide Web which was developed at the European Laboratory for Particle Physics (CERN) [↪CERN] in the early 1990s.

Before looking at the Web itself, let us say a few words about the Internet. The need for reliable countrywide communication channels for the United States military complex led to the development of a packet-switching network. *Arpanet* allows messages to reach their destination via different routes, thus guaranteeing delivery under adverse conditions. The work on Arpanet was the basis of Transmission Control Protocol/Internet Protocol (TCP/IP), a method that is now used almost universally on networks to divide messages into separate datagrams, each identified by a unique sequence number. The messages reach their destination via a variety of routes and are reassembled there to deliver the original message text (Tanenbaum (1996)). Since Arpanet, and subsequently the Internet, which replaced Arpanet around 1988, interconnect all kinds of computers and physical networks, TCP/IP has become the lingua franca of communication protocols.

In the 1980s, electronic mail (*e-mail*) was the most popular form of communication between users on a network, with File Transfer Protocol (*ftp*) and terminal emulation (*telnet*) serving as direct-connection applications when needed. However, a stateless, easy-to-use information distribution system, where the connection does not have to be kept alive, was long overdue.

By 1989 TCP/IP had also become well established internally at CERN, with the Internet replacing most of the proprietary homegrown communication protocols. It was in that year that Tim Berners-Lee put forward his first ideas of what would become the World Wide Web. He could build upon the expertise he had gained in the area of "distributed computing," in particular working on remote procedure calls. Tim also benefited from the "Mac" and "NeXT" cultures, two computer systems that offered a rich and user-friendly interface to (distributed) programming. These systems were very popular with many physicists in those days (the Mac still is). By mid-1990 Tim and a colleague (Robert Cailliau)[1] had finalized the three basic software protocols of the World Wide Web:[2]

1. *Hypertext Transport Protocol* (HTTP), the method that allows various WWW servers to communicate (see Section 1.1.1);

2. *Universal Resource Locator* (URL), a universal addressing scheme to locate all information on the Internet (see Section 1.1.2);

3. *Hypertext Markup Language* (HTML), the language for marking up the information (see Section 1.1.3).

By the end of 1990 a demonstration version of a Web client on a NeXT computer existed. It was soon to be followed by a linemode browser that could be easily interfaced to the many information formats available at CERN. Thus the open architecture (via the URL) allowed us to reuse the thousands of existing documentation pages and to integrate them neatly with the new WWW paradigm.

Although the Web was presented at a seminar in June 1990 and introduced to the whole of the High Energy Physics community in the CERN *Computer Newsletter* 204, by December 1991 not more than ten Web servers existed in the world and the physicists regarded the WWW as just one more of those computer gadgets that diverted them from doing physics. What was needed was a *killer application* that would really show the advantages of the Web as an interface to the global Internet. Although a few browsers offering a graphical user interface were available at the beginning of 1993, it was Marc Andreessen's Mosaic that got the ball rolling. For the first time users could "click away" and jump between documents comprising the information web in a simple and "visual" way.

In May 1994 the first World Wide Web Conference took place at CERN; it later became known as the "Woodstock of the Web." Indeed, 1994 can be considered a real turning point, with CERN handing over the development of the WWW to the World Wide Web Consortium [↪W3C] and the very influential Netscape Company being created. Since then Microsoft, and by 1998 all the other giants of the software industry, have become interested in the advantages of the global Web. Nowadays, there is hardly any company or government agency in the world that, alongside a fax number and an e-mail address, does not proudly display the URL of its home page on business cards and letterheads.

1.1.1   The Hypertext Transport Protocol

HTTP is the language which WWW servers use to talk to one another; technically speaking, it is an application-level protocol for distributed, hypermedia information systems. The first version (confusingly known as HTTP/0.9) was developed in

---

[1] Robert was a specialist in `Hypercard`, the Macintosh hypertext program that used a scripting language called `hypertalk`.

[2] For more details on the early history of the Web see [↪WEBHIST] and [↪RAGHIST].

1990 by Tim Berners-Lee and collaborators in the framework of the World Wide Web initiative at CERN. It was a simple protocol for raw data transfer across the Internet. In 1996 HTTP/1 0 introduced messages using a Multipurpose Internet Mail Extensions (MIME) [↪RFC2045] format. This allowed some semantic interpretation of the content thanks to elementary support of metadata. However, some problems remained, and this led to the definition of HTTP/1.1 in January 1997 [↪HTTPRFC]. It introduced "search," "front-end update," and "annotation." It also allowed for use of Uniform Resource Identifiers (URIs). Moreover, HTTP can now also be used as a generic protocol for communication between user agents and proxies/gateways to other Internet systems, thus allowing basic hypermedia access to resources available from diverse applications.

Since the World Wide Web is still growing extremely fast and further evolution depends very much on the efficiency of HTTP, some questions have been raised about the monolithic structure of the HTTP specification. Therefore, the Internet Engineering Task Force (IETF) [↪IETF] is at present preparing a *New Generation* specification for the HTTP protocol. It will take a modular approach, working outward from an efficient and small core, supplemented by message transport, general-purpose remote method invocation, and document processing layers. This should guarantee global scalability, network efficiency, and transport flexibility (see [↪HTTPNG] for more information).

1.1.2   Universal Resource Locators and Identifiers

A URL is the "postal address" of a document on the Web. The syntax and semantics of the Uniform Resource Locator (URL) for locating and accessing resources via the Internet were first developed in 1990 at CERN and later were formalized [↪RFC1738].

It was soon realized that the original URL syntax was a little too rigid to deal with moving resources, such as a change of the Internet address of the server where a document resides. Hence the idea of a unifying syntax for the expression of names and addresses of objects on the Internet was introduced [↪RFC1630]. The Web must be able to deal with objects accessed using an extensible number of protocols, present and future, with the access instructions of the protocol encoded into the form of the address string of the object.

A Universal Resource Identifier (URI) [↪RFC2396] is a member of this universal set of names in registered namespaces and addresses referring to registered protocols. A URL is a special case of a URI, which maps onto an access algorithm using network protocols. A Uniform Resource Name (URN) is intended to serve as a persistent, location-independent, resource identifier that can map other namespaces that share the properties of URNs into URN space [↪RFC2141].

The general structure of a URI is

```
scheme://hostname[:port]/path/filename[#fragment]
```

Using the HTTP protocol you can have, for instance,

```
http://info.internet.isi.edu:80/in-notes/rfc/files/rfc1630.txt
http://www.oasis-open.org/cover/topics.html#entities
```

while examples on a local file system (Microsoft Windows and UNIX) are

```
file:D:\lark\lark.html
file:/afs/cern.ch/user/g/goossens/hagel.html
```

You can also specify connection-type protocols, such as ftp or telnet, as follows:

```
ftp://ftp.jclark.com/pub/xml/xt.zip
telnet://mycomputer.cern.ch
```

1.1.3   The Hypertext Markup Language

HTML is a simple markup language for creating documents that will appear on the Web. It did not have a formal description (an SGML "Document Type Definition"; see Section 6.3.3) until 1995 [↪RFC1866]. It is a subset of this HTML Version 2 that we will review (another quick introduction can be found at [↪RAGHTML]). Nowadays, HTML Version 4 (see Section 6.2) offers a much wider functionality, although the basic principles remain the same. Furthermore, HTML is being recast in a form compatible with XML (see Appendix B.5 and [↪HTMLINXML]). Table 1.1 gives an overview of some basic HTML tags. Following we will review a few of them in more detail. This should allow you to understand the structure of an HTML source document if you ever see one. Most browsers will let you see the HTML source of the display with something like a "View source" menu item.

1.1.3.1   The minimal HTML document

A simple example of HTML is the following:

```
<TITLE>The simplest HTML example</TITLE>
<H1>A level one heading</H1>
<P>Welcome to the world of HTML!
<P>Let's have a second paragraph.
```

HTML uses *tags* primarily to tell the Web browser how to display the text. The example given uses

- the <TITLE> tag (which has a corresponding </TITLE> end tag) to specify the title of the document,
- the <H1> header tag (with corresponding end </H1>), and
- the <P> start-of-paragraph tag.

Table 1.1: Basic HTML tags

General structure of an HTML document

```
<html>
  <head>
    <title>...</title> document title
    <meta>...</meta> generic meta information
  </head>
  <body>...</body>
</html>
```

Elements used inside the body

Text elements

`<p>` start of new paragraph
`<pre>...</pre>` preformatted text (may include embedded tags—not all tags allowed)

Headers

`<h1>...</h1>` first-level header	`<h2>...</h2>` second-level header
`<h3>...</h3>` third-level header	`<h4>...</h4>` fourth-level header
`<h5>...</h5>` fifth-level header	`<h6>...</h6>` sixth-level header

Logical markup

`<em>...</em>` emphasis	`<code>...</code>` computer code
`<samp>...</samp>` sample output	`<kbd>...</kbd>` text entered at keyboard
`<var>...</var>` variable instance	`<cite>...</cite>` citation

Physical font styles

`<b>...</b>` **bold text**	`<i>...</i>` *italic text*
`<u>...</u>` underlined text	`<tt>...</tt>` typewriter text

Lists

`<dl>` begin definition list	`<ul>` begin unordered list	`<ol>` begin ordered list
`<dt>` *term* `<dd>` *data*	`<li>` items in list	`<li>` items in list
`</dl>` end definition list	`</ul>` end unordered list	`</ol>` end ordered list

Hyperlinks and anchors

`<a name="anchor_name">,,,</a>` define an anchor
`<a href="#anchor_name">...</a>` link to anchor in same file
`<a href="URI#anchor_name">...</a>` link to a target location in another file

Images

`<img src="URI">...</img>` include a graphic image

HTML[3] tags consist of a left angle bracket (<), followed by the *element type name* and zero or more attributes, and closed by a right angle bracket (>). Tags usually occur in pairs, for example, `<H1>` and `</H1>`, where the ending tag looks just like the starting tag except for the slash (/). In the example, `<H1>` signals the start of a top-level heading, `</H1>` its end.

---

[3] The syntax of markup based on the SGML standard will be discussed in detail in Chapter 6.

Many elements do not need to be used in begin/end pairs (such as the `<P>` start-of-paragraph tag in the example) since the start of the next tag often closes the previous one. Nevertheless, it is good practice always to provide close tags for those that are open (take into account the correct nesting, as explained in Chapter 6).

Note also that HTML tags (and attributes) are case *insensitive*, that is, `<title>` is equivalent to `<TITLE>`, or even `<TiTlE>`.

1.1.3.2 Titles and headings

Every HTML document should have a title that is generally displayed separately from the document and is primarily used for document identification (it is shown in the window title of most graphical browsers). Choose a meaningful title, since it will generally show up in Internet searches. The title should go at the beginning of the document and be enclosed between `<title>...</title>` tags.

HTML has six levels of headings, usually displayed using larger and/or bolder fonts than in normal body text. The first heading in each document should be tagged `<H1>`. The syntax of the heading tag is

```
<Hy>Text of heading</Hy>
```

where y is a number between 1 and 6 specifying the level of the heading.

1.1.3.3 Lists

HTML supports unnumbered, numbered, and description lists. No paragraph separator is required for list items. The tags for the items in the list implicitly terminate the previous list item.

Unnumbered lists

Unnumbered or unordered lists start with an opening list `<UL>` tag. You then enter the `<LI>` tag followed by the item text (the closing tag can be omitted) and terminate the list with a closing list `</UL>` tag.

HTML source with two items   Text generation

```
<UL>
  <LI>apples
  <LI>bananas
</UL>
```

- apples
- bananas

Browsers can display an unnumbered or unordered list in various ways, for example by using bullets, filled circles, or dashes to show the items. As explained in Chapter 7, style sheets should be used to control the rendering of HTML elements.

Numbered lists

A numbered or ordered list is quite similar in structure to an unordered list except that the <OL> tag is used instead of the <UL> tag. Items are tagged using the same <LI> tag. On the output medium the items will be numbered.

HTML source with three items   Text generation

```
<OL>
  <LI>oranges
  <LI>peaches
  <LI>grapes
</OL>
```

```
1.  oranges

2.  peaches

3.  grapes
```

Once again, the actual symbols used for ordering the items (Arabic or Roman numerals, alphabetical letters, and so on) can be controlled by a style sheet.

Description lists

A description list consists of a set of *description terms* (tagged <DT>) and *description data* (tagged <DD>).

HTML source with three items   Text generation

```
<DL>
<DT>URI
<DD>Universal Resource Identifier
<DT>URL
<DD>Universal Resource Locator
<DT>URN</DT>
<DD>Universal Resource Name</DD>
</DL>
```

URI Universal Resource Identifier

URL Universal Resource Locator

URN Universal Resource Name

The <DT> and <DD> entries can contain multiple paragraphs (separated by paragraph tags), lists, or other descriptive information. Note how we used an end tag for the last entry.

1.1.3.4   Hypertext links

The chief power of HTML comes from its ability to *link* regions of text (or images) to an "anchor" (location) in the same or an external document. These regions are typically highlighted by the browser to indicate that they are hypertext links. HTML's single hypertext-related directive is the <A> element.

Anchors can be used to move to a particular section in a document. Suppose you want to define a link from "documentA" to a particular section in "documentB." First, you need to set up a *named anchor* in "documentB" as follows:

```
<A NAME="myname">target text</A>...
```

Then, to link to the target text region, as defined earlier, create a link in "documentA." Include the name of the target document, as well as the name of the target region itself, as follows:

```
My link to the target is <A HREF="documentB.html#myname">here</A>.
```

When you click on the word "here" in "documentA," the browser will load "documentB" and position the top of the window at the start of the paragraph "target text."

1.1.3.5 Images

Browsers can display bitmap (usually GIF, PNG, or JPEG) images inside documents. You can include such an image by using an `<IMG>` tag (or more generally, in HTML4, an `<OBJECT>` tag; see Section 6.2.1). For instance, the following two ways of including the GIF image "mypict.gif" are equivalent:

```
<IMG SRC="mypict.gif">
```
and
```
<OBJECT DATA="mypict.gif" TYPE="image/gif">
```

Such images are inline components so that you might have to place them on the screen by specifying alignment details or by putting them in a separate paragraph.

In general, by using a URI as the `SRC` or `DATA` field, you can include an image residing anywhere on the Internet. You can also include the URI of the image inside an anchor so that it is up to the user to get the image or not (saving bandwidth if the image is large) by specifying something similar to the following:

```
My picture is <A HREF="http://host/path/mypict.gif">here</A>.
```

1.1.3.6 Special characters

Some ASCII characters are treated specially by HTML and, therefore, cannot be used directly in the text. These include <, >, and &. To produce such characters as part of normal text, you have to use a so-called entity reference[4] that consists of an ampersand as the start symbol, followed by the entity name, followed by a semicolon as a terminator. For the above three characters this would be `&lt;`, `&gt;`, and `&amp;`, respectively.

Several entity sets exist. An example is the Latin 1 (ISO8859-1) character set, where in addition to many others, the following entities are defined:

`&ouml;`	generates a lowercase o with an umlaut: ö,
`&ntilde;`	generates a lowercase n with a tilde: ñ,
`&Egrave;`	generates an uppercase E with a grave mark: È.

---

[4]See Section 6.5.4.3 to know more about the SGML entity reference mechanism.

Table 1.2. Comparison of HTML and LaTeX

Description	HTML	LaTeX equivalent
Document sectioning commands		
level 1	`<H1>`*text*`</H1>`	`\chapter{`*text*`}`
level 2	`<H2>`*text*`</H2>`	`\section{`*text*`}`
level 3	`<H3>`*text*`</H3>`	`\subsection{`*text*`}`
level 4	`<H4>`*text*`</H4>`	`\subsubsection{`*text*`}`
level 5	`<H5>`*text*`</H5>`	`\paragraph{`*text*`}`
level 6	`<H6>`*text*`</H6>`	`\subparagraph{`*text*`}`
new paragraph	`<P>`	`\par`
Highlighting text		
emphasis	`<EM>`*text*`</EM>`	`\emph{`*text*`}`
bold font	`<B>`*text*`</B>`	`\textbf{`*text*`}` `(\mathbf{`*text*`})`
teletype font	`<TT>`*text*`</TT>`	`\texttt{`*text*`}` `(\mathtt{`*text*`})`
Lists		
ordered list	`<OL>...</OL>`	`\begin{enumerate}...\end{enumerate}`
unordered list	`<UL>...</UL>`	`\begin{itemize}...\end{itemize}`
list item	`<LI>`*text*	`\item` *text*
description list	`<DL>...</DL>`	`\begin{description}...\end{description}`
description term	`<DT>`*term*	`\item[`*term*`]`
description data	`<DD>`*text*	*text*
Special characters		
accents (e.g., é)	`&eacute;`	`\'e`
umlauts (e.g., ü)	`&uuml;`	`\"u`
new line	` `	`\newline`

1.2   LaTeX in the Web environment

In the previous sections we described how the revolution of generalized access and of distribution of electronic documents on the Internet, in particular via the World Wide Web, has come about, and what the technical principles that underpin its success are.

But how does that new environment fit into the picture of producing and distributing scientific documents of the highest possible typographic quality—an area where LaTeX is still largely unchallenged?

First let us note the similarity of approach between HTML and LaTeX in areas of structural representation of the information. In Table 1.2 we present a comparison of markup in the two systems. At a basic structural level it is not too difficult to translate between LaTeX and HTML, thus allowing convenient reuse of our investment in LaTeX documents for display on the Web.

Present-day browsers do not always represent complex information (tables, mathematics, pictures) in a precise and acceptable way. As we explain later, in such a case the information can be represented in various ways, perhaps as inline bitmap images or as external files, using the PDF or PostScript formats. As an appetizer of what is possible with quite simple tools, consider the *Digital Library of Mathematical Functions* Project by the National Institute of Standards and Technology (NIST). They are planning to provide the complete contents of the *Handbook of Mathematical Functions* (Abramowitz and Stegun (1972)) in electronic form [↪NISTHMF], with interactive VRML graphs,[5] links to software to calculate functions, and so on. Figure 1.1 shows examples from the chapter about Airy functions.

1.2.1 Overview of document formats and strategies

Figure 1.2 shows various formats in which electronic documents for the Web can be prepared and ways to transform between them. In the upper left-hand corner we represent a LaTeX document. A standard and well-known procedure is to compile the LaTeX file with TeX, generating a DVI file, and from there to obtain a PostScript file with `dvips`. The latter file can be printed, if needed. Alternatively, you can generate a PDF file, directly from LaTeX with pdfTeX or indirectly by translating the PostScript file into PDF (for example, with Adobe's Acrobat Distiller) or by translating the DVI file into PDF (e.g., with `dvipdfm`). The PDF file can still be printed, if needed, but it is equally convenient to make it available on the Internet, since it can contain hyperlinks and is editable.

As mentioned at the beginning of this section, we can also exploit the similarities of the generic markup schemes of LaTeX and HTML (or more generally, as we explain in Chapter 6, via an instance of an XML DTD) to translate LaTeX into HTML (or an XML instance). This is labeled "L2H" ("L2X") in Figure 1.2. We can also translate between XML and HTML with an "X2H" program. Note that for rendering such files on the Web, we can make use of a style sheet language (such as CSS, DSSSL, or XSL; see Chapter 7).

We can also go in the other direction and translate XML (HTML) files into LaTeX and, therefore, profit from the powerful typographic machinery of TeX to obtain printable documents of good quality (software labeled "X2L" in Figure 1.2). We expect that XML will be used more and more as a storage format for electronic documents in the medium-term future and that LaTeX will become an interesting back-end for printing purposes.

In the following sections we give a short overview of various representations of the same LaTeX document, starting from a sample document shown as standard LaTeX output in the "normal" Figure 1.3. The text, which is taken from a physics document, contains some simple inline and displayed math formulae that will allow us to show the main characteristics of the proposed solutions. The source of the document is referenced in Appendix A.1.

---

[5] The *Virtual Reality Modeling Language* is one of the ideas that was born in informal discussion during the "Woodstock of the Web" in May 1994 at CERN. It allows for creating an animation in a three-dimensional virtual world, featuring full interactivity at the viewer level. See [↪WEB3D] and ISO/IEC standard 14772:1997ISO/IEC:14772-1 (1998).

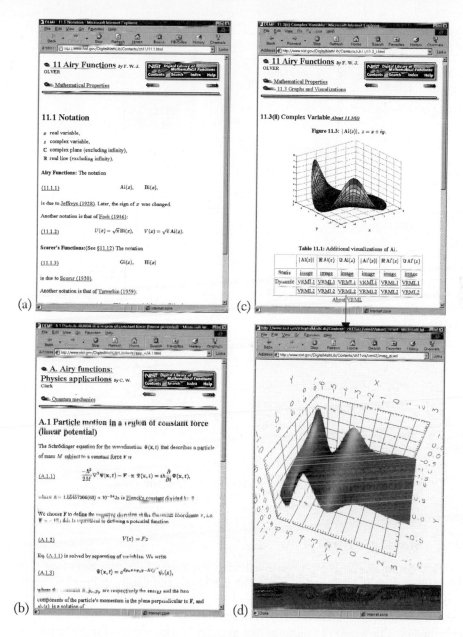

Figure 1.1: Putting a mathematics handbook on the Web

(a) the notation used for the Airy functions; (b) an example of a physics application in quantum mechanics where Airy functions are used; (c) a static visual 3D representation of an Airy function with a complex argument; (d) a VRML visualization (using a plug-in) initiated by activating the link indicated by the arrow on the HTML page shown in (c).

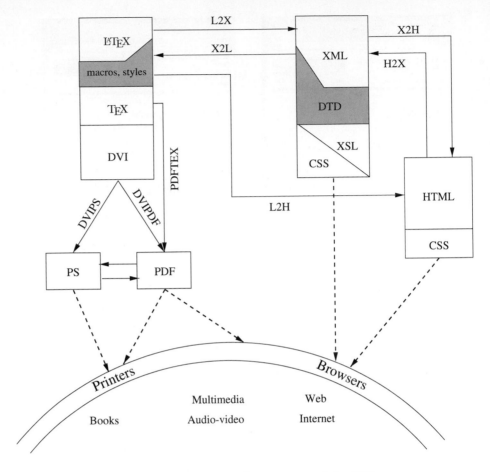

Figure 1.2: Electronic documents and the Web

1.2.2 Staying with DVI

The TeX community has been involved with hypertext for some time (see Carr et al. (1991)), and the open architecture of the \special command makes it relatively easy to embed, for instance, hypertext linking commands in DVI files. We can then extend viewers to use these link commands and to use them as simple hypertext browsers. The hyperref package (see Section 2.3) has drivers for the \special commands supported by various drivers (See Appendix B.1). Figures 1.4, 1.5, and 1.6 show three different DVI viewers (xdvi [↪XDVI] under Linux and dviwindo [↪YANDY] and dviout [↪DVIOUT] under Windows, respectively) displaying our file and highlighting the bibliographical citations in the first paragraph as links. The applications also support the loading of a Web browser when a URL link is

3 Vavilov theory

Vavilov[5] derived a more accurate straggling distribution by introducing the kinematic limit on the maximum transferable energy in a single collision, rather than using $E_{\max} = \infty$. Now we can write[2]:

$$f\left(\epsilon, \delta s\right) \quad = \quad \frac{1}{\xi} \phi_v\left(\lambda_v, \kappa, \beta^2\right)$$

where

$$\phi_v\left(\lambda_v, \kappa, \beta^2\right) \quad = \quad \frac{1}{2\pi i} \int_{c-i\infty}^{c+i\infty} \phi\left(s\right) e^{\lambda s} ds \qquad c \geq 0$$

$$\phi\left(s\right) \quad = \quad \exp\left[\kappa(1+\beta^2\gamma)\right] \; \exp\left[\psi\left(s\right)\right],$$

$$\psi\left(s\right) \quad = \quad s\ln\kappa + (s+\beta^2\kappa)\left[\ln(s/\kappa) + E_1(s/\kappa)\right] - \kappa e^{-s/\kappa},$$

and

$$F_1(z) \quad = \quad \int_z^\infty t^{-1} e^{-t} dt \qquad \text{(the exponential integral)}$$

$$\lambda_v \quad = \quad \kappa\left[\frac{\epsilon - \bar{\epsilon}}{\xi} - \gamma' - \beta^2\right]$$

The Vavilov parameters are simply related to the Landau parameter by $\lambda_L = \lambda_v/\kappa - \ln\kappa$. It can be shown that as $\kappa \to 0$, the distribution of the variable λ_L approaches that of Landau. For $\kappa \leq 0.01$ the two distributions are already practically identical. Contrary to what many textbooks report, the Vavilov distribution *does not* approximate the Landau distribution for small κ, but rather the distribution of λ_L defined above tends to the distribution of the true λ from the Landau density function. Thus the routine GVAVIV samples the variable λ_L rather than λ_v. For $\kappa \geq 10$ the Vavilov distribution tends to a Gaussian distribution (see next section).

Figure 1.3: Standard LATEX output

encountered, but it cannot be integrated within a Web browser. We will mention one DVI viewer that *does* integrate with browsers in Section 1.2.6.

1.2.3 PDF for typographic quality

Another simple approach, and one that guarantees typographic quality to the same level as that of a DVI file, is to generate a PDF file with dvipdfm or pdfTeX or with Acrobat Distiller starting from a PostScript file. In this case with the help of a PDF browser, such as Acrobat (see Figure 1.7), we can easily navigate through the document and exploit hypertext information that might be present in the LATEX source (LATEX cross-references and bibliographic citations can be automatically turned into hyperlinks). Web browsers can be configured to load Acrobat as a helper application when they meet PDF files, and they will then display your document in a browser window. Acrobat can also pass URL links to the browser to resolve, giving a seamless integration. This simple approach is explained in Chapter 2, where we also discuss page designs optimized for reading on the screen (Figure 1.8).

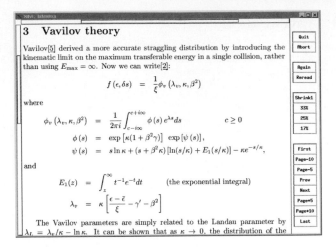

Figure 1.4: Hypertext DVI viewing with `xdvi`

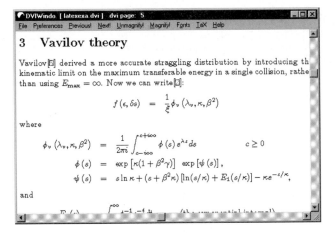

Figure 1.5: Hypertext DVI viewing with `dviwindo`

1.2.4 Down-translation to HTML

We might also decide to translate our LaTeX source document directly into HTML with tools such as LaTeX2HTML (see Chapter 3) or TeX4ht (see Chapter 4). As the current commonly used browsers have no built-in way to display mathematics properly, the translation programs transform most nonstandard characters (Greek, mathematical, and so on) into bitmap pictures. Figure 1.9 is a typical example of this approach. The information is correctly displayed, but we must be careful to tune the visual representation (font height, style, and so on) of the special characters so that

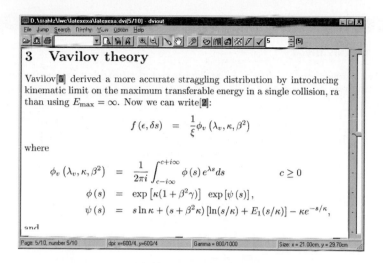

Figure 1.6: Hypertext DVI viewing with `dviout`

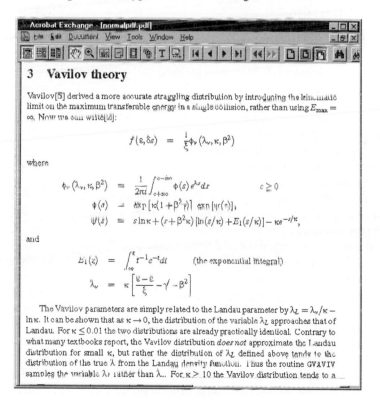

Figure 1.7: Simple PDF display (using Acrobat)

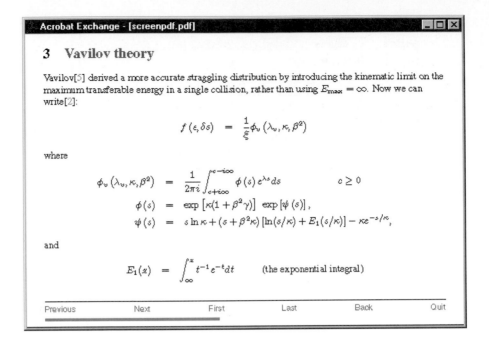

Figure 1.8: PDF display designed for the screen

their bitmap images in running text and mathematical displays match. However, since the user of a particular browser can generally change the default font and size of the normal text, it is unfortunately impossible to ensure that everyone sees the "right" result. In addition, of course, equations cannot "reflow" when the window size changes since they are fixed-size pictures.

The advantage of these systems is that with some fine tuning quite an acceptable quality can be achieved with standard browsers. Also, the cross-references, bibliographic citations, and hierarchical structure of the LaTeX source file can be translated into HTML hypertext anchor functionality, allowing for optimal navigation and integration in the Web. Far-reaching customization is possible via command options and extension files.

On the other hand, because most non-Latin symbols are translated into bitmaps, many thousands of GIF or PNG bitmap images may be created for a scientific document of more than a few pages (depending, of course, on the complexity of the mathematical content and on whether reuse of images is allowed). Because all of these small files have to be downloaded together with the HTML source of the page, the time needed to display a page in a browser can be rather long. These images also take a lot of diskspace, and often a modification in the LaTeX source necessitates rebuilding the whole set of images. Finally, the installation of a LaTeX-to-HTML translator is not always straightforward.

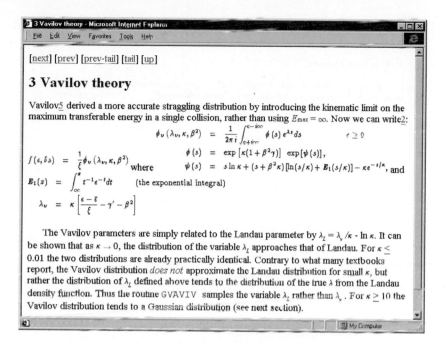

Figure 1.9: Conversion to HTML with math as pictures

An alternative, more lightweight approach is the one offered by Ian Hutchinson's TtH ([↪ TTH]; also available in a commercial version with support and more features [↪ TEX2HTML]). It exploits the presence of the Symbol font in most browsers and translates a LATEX source into HTML, displaying "special" characters with built-in fonts. Figure 1.10 shows our reference document using this technique. Note how the integral sign is composed by superimposing smaller line segments.

The big advantage of the TtH program is that it is very time efficient and can thus be used to provide an "on-the-fly" generation of HTML documents. This procedure works well for documents that contain fairly simple math (that is, using characters limited to those present in the Symbol font) and has minimal maintenance costs, since only the LATEX source is needed. Documents also continue to display properly when the user changes font or window sizes.

The drawback is that the quality is not as good as with the "picture" procedures. Above all, we cannot control the presence in the source document of characters that fall outside the font set available in the browser. Of course, this will no longer apply when Unicode support in browsers becomes universal and all the supplementary math characters discussed in Chapter 8 are included. Nevertheless, there remains the problem of the precise placement of these characters in math displays, which will be acceptable only when browsers are equipped with a typographic engine that includes a certain level of "math knowledge."

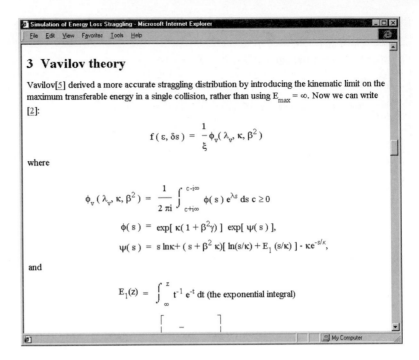

Figure 1.10: Conversion to HTML with math using Symbol fonts

A good way to generate HTML from LaTeX is to work with a modified TeX engine; this is what MicroPress' commercial VTEX has [↪TEXPIDER]. Since it writes HTML directly, all TeX macros can be handled easily, although, of course, the math is still rendered as bitmap pictures.

1.2.5   Java and browser plug-ins

The browser plug-in `techexplorer` understands a large subset of the LaTeX language and displays a LaTeX source *directly* inside a browser. The result is shown in Figure 1.11, and the software is discussed in Chapter 5. Although this technique is quite fast, a serious drawback is that the `techexplorer` plug-in must be downloaded and installed on all browsers you want to use. Moreover, a separate version is needed for each computer platform.

Finally, you can choose to translate math content into the MathML language, but in this case you must have access to a browser plug-in or some other procedure that can parse and display MathML (see Figure 1.12). An example is WebEQ [↪WEBEQ], based on Java applets, which can produce good quality display with the crucial advantage that it can adapt to resizing of the browser window size and fonts. The approach can, however, be rather slow. First you must wait for the initial

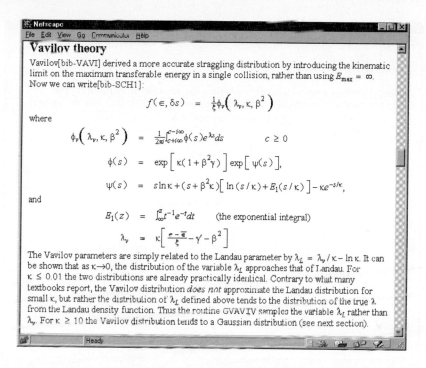

Figure 1.11: Display using `techexplorer` browser plug-in

download of the Java applets for displaying the MathML code; that can last well over half a minute. Then it takes another few seconds to render all but the most trivial equations. So all in all you will have to wait quite some time before a page is ready for viewing. Alternatively, you can install the Java code on your own machine so that it is always available; even so, you have to wait while equations are processed. Another problem with WebEQ is that it does not strictly process LATEX, but rather a variant called WebTEX.

1.2.6   Other LATEX-related approaches to the Web

Although the previous sections describe the major approaches for using TEX documents on the Web, there are some variations that might be worth investigating. However, their usage is fairly limited at this time. Several implement the TEX \special standards of the HyperTEX project, explained in more detail in Appendix B.1.

1. Ottfried Cheong's Hyperlatex [↪ HYPERLTX] is a converter from a LATEX-like language to HTML. It does not support math, but it has its own commands that extend LATEX to make it a rich language for composing advanced HTML.

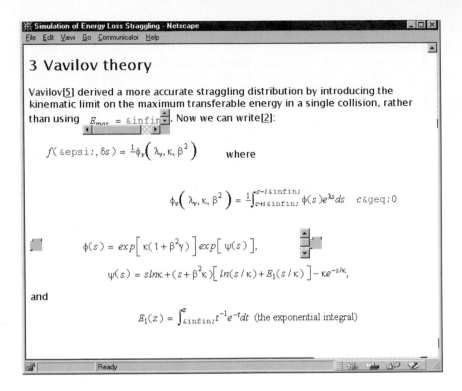

Figure 1.12: Conversion to HTML with embedded MathML rendered with plug-in

2. Garth Dickie's `idvi` is a DVI viewer (supporting the HyperTeX \special commands) written in Java. It is used as a Web browser plug-in, rendering a normal DVI file within a browser window and fetching resources like fonts over the Web as needed. Although an elegant idea, unfortunately development of this program seems to have stopped, and its performance in practice is poor.

3. Kasper Peeter's `nDVI` [↪NDVI] is a browser plug-in that renders DVI versions of an HyperTeX document directly.

4. Russell Quoung's `ltoh` is a LaTeX to HTML converter written in Perl but without any support for math.

5. Although T. V. Raman's work on Aster [↪ASTER] is not strictly related to the Web, anyone interested in rendering math other than on paper should look at it. It is a system for rendering documents that contain math marked up in TeX, using a voice synthesizer. Designed primarily for those with impaired vision, it is nevertheless a very important demonstration of how math that is well marked up can be analyzed and rendered in nontraditional ways.

1.3   Is there an optimal approach?

In deciding which of the various tools just presented is most suited in a given situation, consider the following regarding your document:

- Is it purely text, and straightforward LaTeX? Then translate it directly into HTML (for instance, with TtH), or start preparing to work in XML.

- Does it contain lots of low-level math with homegrown macros that allow you to set up your own customized notation? Then you would probably use TeX4ht or LaTeX2HTML (in the latter case, be prepared to write some Perl scripts implementing your extensions) or if you prefer a commercial solution, use Micro-Press' VTEX.

- Does it contain lots of "normal" math? Envision translating that into MathML, and use one of the browser plug-ins.

- Does it use a lot of non-Latin characters? You would probably want to use a LaTeX-to-XML converter and translate the non-Latin characters into Unicode.

- Does it have a complex layout (tables, perhaps) or typography that is essential to the document reader? Use PDF.

- Is your document fairly self-contained? Do you have little interaction with other Web material? Consider an approach based on DVI.

A real-life document probably falls into more than one of the above categories, so the choice of the optimal strategy might not be straightforward. To help you make your choice and decide which is the best approach in each case, study the material provided in the following chapters. It describes in detail the various programs at your disposal.

Do not forget when considering Web publication, to allow for readers who cannot see, or who have sight impediments like color blindness. The work of the Web Accessibility Initiative [↪WAI] is to look at ways in which Web documents can be rendered differently, and this may affect how you present your work.

A very considerable problem for the author creating new LaTeX documents is how to mark up material to take advantage of common Web "goodies" like linking, color, forms, pop-ups, and Java applets. Each package invents new syntax for these extensions. LaTeX2HTML, techexplorer, and the hyperref package all would require you to mark up your document differently, and, unfortunately, the LaTeX world has failed until now to check this unhealthy situation. We strongly recommend that you adopt the following strategy when writing LaTeX:

- Wherever possible, use "native" LaTeX syntax like \ref and \cite, which can be automatically translated.

- The `hyperref` package covers a great deal of the necessary functionality and has back-end drivers for a wide variety of TeX-based hypertext systems. It makes sense to hedge your bets by using the syntax of this package and having access to a variety of systems.

- If you want portable DVI output, follow the HyperTeX conventions (this is the default for the `hyperref` package), and ask the authors of your favorite DVI drivers to support them.

- If you need to use package-specific syntax, try to isolate it in LaTeX macros (if the system supports them), so that you can easily find them should you switch to another system.

Remember, LaTeX and the Web are still settling down together, and it is probably best to avoid committing yourself too much to any one system at this time.

1.4 Conclusion

Whereas the advent and the ready availability of the personal computer drastically reduced the production cost of electronic documents, the creation of the Web made distributing these documents worldwide a lot cheaper, easier, and faster. Taken together, these two developments have considerably changed the economic factors controlling the generation, maintenance, and dissemination of electronic documents. In addition, thanks to the development of the XML family of standards and the ubiquity of the platform-independent Java language, it is now possible to have a unified approach to the vast amount of information stored in databases and to handle their representation in various customizable forms.

We are convinced that LaTeX has an important role to play in this new and integrated worldwide cyberspace, especially in the area of mathematics, for text input and for rendering the output. In due course LaTeX may be complemented by a semantically richer MathML representation. However, LaTeX's greatest impact will remain in the area of typesetting, with TeX becoming an important intermediate format for generating high-quality printable PDF output. Studying the various tools described in this book will ensure not only that you will be ready for the XML revolution, but also that you can positively contribute to the richness and increasing wealth of the scientific hyperculture by translating your LaTeX documents into PDF, HTML, or XML using one of the proposed techniques and making them available on the Web. You do not have to choose between using LaTeX or another markup technique on the Web; you can use whichever is more appropriate in a given situation and profit from the advantages of both.

CHAPTER 2

Portable Document Format

For some applications, the methods employed to disseminate information across the World Wide Web are unacceptable. This is because they leave the rendering of the "page" to the reader's software, not to the author's software. Even if pure HTML and Cascading Style Sheets are used, the author does not know where line breaks will occur, and, of course, there is no concept of "page breaks." Graphics are often presented as low-resolution bitmaps with unreliable colors; table layout may be radically different. The author cannot even be sure which font will be seen by the reader, or whether some unsuitable symbols might be used in mathematics, for example. Finally, and perhaps most important, the current generation of Web browsers is not very sophisticated at typesetting and page makeup; the result of hitting the Print icon from a browser does not produce a high-quality result.

Who cares about these issues? On the one hand, lawyers may regard it vital that an electronic document is *exactly* the same as the traditional printed copy, down to the line breaks. On the other hand, it might simply be that an author has spent a lot of time making a beautiful page and wants it to be seen as such. In between are applications where HTML output is simply not very "nice," such as for very complex forms, tables, and mathematical material.

This chapter, set up in three parts, describes a solution—Portable Document Format (PDF). In the first part we take a general look at what PDF is, and what are the issues in creating it using TeX. In the second part, we describe a special LaTeX package (hyperref) that enables you to make enhanced PDF documents from LaTeX source, using a variety of back-end drivers and a high-level interface to hypertext commands.

The final part of the chapter describes, in some detail, a special version of TEX that generates PDF. Many readers, perhaps most, will not need to understand the new PDF primitives added to this version of TEX, since packages like `hyperref` provide a familiar LATEX interface. However, pdfTEX offers tremendous possibilities for producing advanced interactive electronic documents, and confident TEX programmers will want to understand what is going on under the hood.

2.1 What is PDF?

PDF is a descendant of Adobe Systems' PostScript language. Although Postscript has served as the preeminent typesetting page description language for nearly a decade, it suffers from age and complexity. Some crucial features (such as metadata, crudely implemented using comment conventions, and full prepress color) were added only in later revisions, and there are many small variations in implementation. More important, however, PostScript is a full-blown programming language. It is hard to write interpreters fast enough to use it for rapid screen display and hard to write displayers that can be sure each page of a text can really be shown in isolation. Display PostScript solved some of the problems, adding interaction features; and at the same time, Adobe's Illustrator program developed a functional subset of PostScript for its internal representation. Based on this experience, it seems, Adobe developed a second-generation page description language, Portable Document Format; the differences between this language and PostScript are crucial:

- There is no built-in programming language (Adobe did add JavaScript support in version 3.5 of the Acrobat Forms plug-in, but this has more to do with viewer implementation than with the PDF language).

- The format guarantees page independence, clearly separating resources from page objects.

- Hypertext and security features have been added to the language, allowing sophisticated interfaces to be built.

- Font handling allows the font itself not to be included in the file, accompanied by just enough information for applications that display PDF, like Adobe's Acrobat, to mimic the font appearance. Acrobat does this using the ingenious Multiple Master font technology.

- A great deal of effort was expended in compression features to keep the size of PDF files small.

Most of the advantages of PostScript remain: PDF guarantees page fidelity, down to the smallest glyph or piece of whitespace, while being portable across different computer platforms. PDF is used increasingly in the professional printing world as a replacement for PostScript and is now in its third revision (version 1.2 of the format). Since 1996, it has been possible to display PDF embedded in the major Web browsers, alongside HTML, using plug-in technology.

It is important to make a clear distinction between Portable Document Format, and Acrobat. PDF is an open language whose specification is published (although Adobe controls it); Acrobat is a family of commercial programs from Adobe which produces, displays, and manipulates PDF. The main components are

- Reader, which is distributed freely, for simply viewing and printing PDF files;

- Exchange, which has all the functionality of Reader, but allows for changing the file;

- Distiller, which produces PDF files from PostScript files;

- PDFWriter, which provides printer drivers for Windows and Macintosh, allowing any application to "print" to a PDF file directly;

- Catalog, which makes indexes of collections of PDF documents; and

- Capture, which produces PDF files by performing optical character recognition on bitmap-scanned pages.

Although Acrobat Reader is free and available on many (but not all) platforms, there are other viewers available as well; the best-known free ones are Ghostscript [↪ GSHOME], which can also produce PDF from PostScript, and Xpdf [↪ XPDF].

Both PDF and Acrobat are generally very well documented.[1] Besides the main PDF specification [↪ PDFSPEC] and the Acrobat documentation, there are many commercial books. Readers of this book who are accustomed to technical material will find *Web Publishing with Acrobat/PDF* (Merz, 1998) an invaluable resource for all aspects of PDF that will not be covered in this book. Topics that serious users of PDF on the Web will need to address are

- Optimizing PDF files to allow page at-a-time downloading;

- Embedding PDF in HTML pages;

- JavaScript and VBScript programming in conjunction with PDF;

- Processing forms data in Web servers; and

- Dynamic creation of PDF.

2.2   Generating PDF from TEX

TEX users discovered PDF at an early stage, and problems relating to TEX and PDF creation are now well understood. There are three broad areas to cover: how

---

[1] A notable exception is Forms, which remains an arcane area.

to create PDF, how to ensure good-quality font rendering, and how to add extra information like hypertext links and navigation buttons. We will deal with these issues in the following sections.

2.2.1   Creating and manipulating PDF

PDF documents can be created in four ways:

1. Convert existing PostScript files to PDF using a "distiller" program. The Adobe Acrobat Distiller is the most powerful and sophisticated of these, but Ghostscript also performs well, as does NikNak [↪NIKNAK]. This approach means that you can create PDF from any application that can produce PostScript (that is, almost everything).

2. Use Adobe's PDFWriter printer driver for Windows and Macintosh to produce PDF from any normal application like a word processor or spreadsheet.

3. Use Adobe's Acrobat Capture software to offer a workflow in which existing printed pages are scanned, put through an optical character recognition system, and the result saved as PDF. There is a clever feature by which words that cannot be recognized are preserved as bitmaps, resulting in a reliable-*looking* PDF file that might be a mixture of real text and small bitmaps.

4. Use an application that writes PDF directly. In the TEX world we have pdfTEX (see Section 2.4 on page 67), MicroPress' VTEX [↪MICROPRESS], and a DVI driver, Mark Wicks's dvipdfm.

The most common method by far is the first, since almost all text formatting software can write good PostScript these days. The second is not really recommended for serious work, since it gives no opportunity to add hypertext links automatically and gives no control over features like compression and sampling of art work. It is useful for quick and dirty work, however. The third method is rather specialized and is really suitable only for large-scale projects converting legacy documents with experienced staff controlling the quality. The last method is, naturally, the ideal one, but there are few examples of suitable applications. The reason is not hard to find—Acrobat Distiller is an excellent piece of software with great flexibility, and there is not much incentive to develop new back-ends for applications.

Users of Acrobat Distiller should carefully check how they set up the application. Two of the "Job Options" panels[2] are particularly important: the one that sets compression and graphics sampling (Figure 2.1), and the one that determines which fonts are embedded (Figure 2.2). We will talk more about fonts in the next

---

[2]We describe and illustrate the Windows version here, but the Macintosh version is very similar; UNIX users need to consult their documentation to see how configuration files need to be written, or how the command line options are used.

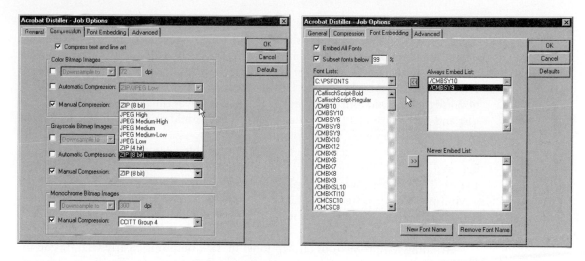

Figure 2.1: Distiller job options for graphics   Figure 2.2: Distiller job options for fonts

section, but be aware that Acrobat Distiller *is* manipulating included bitmap figures. You need to be sure that it is doing what you expect. It defaults to a behavior
that produces small files, and this may not necessarily be your priority.

Manipulating PDF files after creation is beyond the scope of this chapter. Suffice it to say that there is a large and rich selection of plug-ins for Acrobat to
perform all sorts of jobs, including prepress functions, security enhancement, and
marking-up comments. Merz (1998), pages 53–55, has a useful summary, and there
are extensive catalogs maintained by Adobe [↪ADOBE] and independent vendors
(for instance, [↪PDFZONE]).

2.2.2 Setting up fonts

One of the most confusing issues in both PostScript and PDF is the handling of
different types of fonts. A PDF-producing application can deal with a font in one of
three ways: First it can take the entire font and embed it in the file; second it can
make a subset font of just those characters used in the document and embed that
subset; or third it can simply embed some summary details about the font (such
as its name, its metrics, its encoding, its type—sans serif, symbol, for example—
and clues about its design) and rely on the display application to show something
plausible. This last strategy is preferred for documents that are to be delivered on
the Web, since it creates the smallest files. The display application can work again
in several ways. It can try to find the named fonts on the local system; it can simply
substitute system fonts as intelligently as possible; or it can use Multiple Master
fonts to mimic the appearance of the original font.

Unfortunately for TeX users, their systems have traditionally depended on the use of fixed resolution bitmap (that is, `.pk`) fonts, since TeX was established before scalable fonts were a usable reality. These are embedded in PostScript output as Type 3 fonts (see Goossens et al. (1997), Section 10.3 for a full description of PostScript's font types). Acrobat Distiller cannot deal with these fonts intelligently because there are no font descriptors available. It leaves them embedded in the PDF file, and Acrobat renders them very poorly. They would print reasonably well if the original resolution were high enough.

The contrast between three types of font display can be seen in Figures 2.3, 2.4, and 2.5. The first two figures were both set in Monotype Baskerville, but in Figure 2.4, the font was not embedded in the PDF file, so Acrobat constructed a Multiple Master instance to match Baskerville as best it could. Figure 2.5 uses TeX's Computer Modern, but because bitmap PK fonts were used, the result is almost unreadable.

Avoiding the problem of bitmap fonts in TeX output is clearly vital. If you intend to produce good-quality PDF, you need to find Type 1 (or TrueType, although this format is less well supported by most DVI drivers) versions of all the fonts that you intend to use and then inform the driver that it should use them. How this is done depends on the DVI driver; Y&Y's `dviwindo` and `dvipsone` drivers, for instance, support (except *in extremis*) *only* Type 1 scalable fonts and can access whatever is installed in Adobe Type Manager. For the widely used `dvips` driver (see Goossens et al. (1997), Section 11 for more details), it is necessary to make sure that the fonts are listed in the file `psfonts.map` or in a `map` file referenced by a configuration file. For instance, to ensure that Computer Modern is treated properly, the TeX Live [↪ TEXLIVE] distribution has a `dvips` configuration file `config.cms` that loads `cms.map`; that file contains the following lines:

```
cmb10 CMB10 <cmb10.pfb
cmbsy10 CMBSY10 <cmbsy10.pfb
cmbx10 CMBX10 <cmbx10.pfb
...
cmr10 CMR10 <cmr10.pfb
cmr12 CMR12 <cmr12.pfb
cmr17 CMR17 <cmr17.pfb
...
logo10 logo10 <logo10.pfb
logo8 logo8 <logo8.pfb
```

Usage would be something like

```
latex myfile
dvips myfile -Pcms -o myfile.ps
```

to prepare a PostScript file (`myfile.ps`) that can be fed through Acrobat Distiller to make a PDF file.

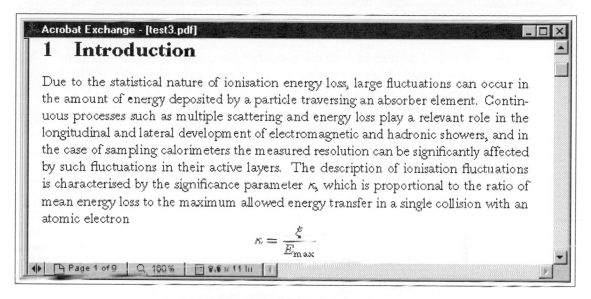

Figure 2.3: Display of PDF file using embedded fonts

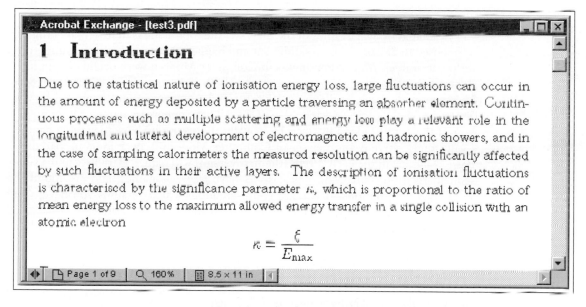

Figure 2.4: Display of PDF file using Multiple Master substitution for fonts

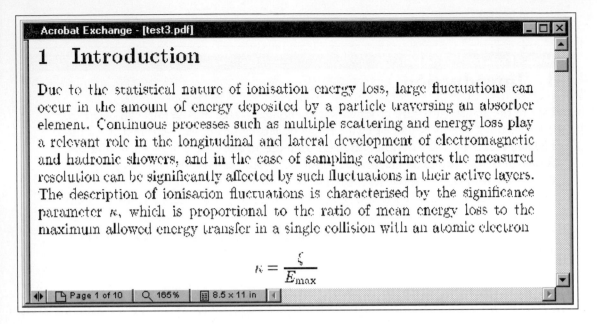

Figure 2.5: Display of PDF file using bitmap fonts

Note that in the last lines of the map file, the font name is in lowercase (`logo8`, as opposed to `CMR10`). This is significant and happens because the fonts come from different sources. Most components of Computer Modern were originally put into Type 1 format by Blue Sky Research in the 1980s, subsequently enhanced by Y&Y, and then made freely available in 1996 through an arrangement brokered by the American Mathematical Society; these fonts all have uppercase names. Other members of the family (added by Taco Hoekwater, for example) have lowercase names. Confusingly, there is another set of Computer Modern Type 1 fonts prepared by Basil Malyshev in the early 1990s (the first version was named Paradissa and a subsequent revision, BaKoMa). These fonts have *lowercase* names, and are found in some TEX distributions. If you are confused about which versions you have, you need to examine one of the `pfb` files and look at the copyright notice.

Many commonly used public domain technical fonts *have* been converted to Type 1 format; among those available in TEX archives are

- All of the Computer Modern family (including LATEX additions);
- The American Mathematical Society fonts;
- The St. Mary's Road symbol fonts;
- The RSFS script font;

- The TIPA phonetic fonts; and

- The X͟Y-pic fonts.

Type 1 and TrueType versions of the "European Computer Modern" (ec) fonts are available from MicroPress [↪MICROPRESS]. However, there are also two alternatives

1. The ae package provides virtual fonts that match the ec fonts as much as possible and draws on the original Computer Modern fonts. There are a few missing characters, like guillemets, but this package is fine for many users.

2. The commercial European Modern font set by Y&Y [↪YANDY] is a set of high-quality, fully hinted fonts that can fully replace ec.[3]

There is one final, but very important issue, to consider. If you use commercial fonts (for example, Adobe or Monotype fonts that you have purchased, Y&Y's Lucida Bright, or European Modern), you cannot embed the entire font in a PDF file and then gaily make it available on the Internet. This would clearly break your licensing conditions because other people can extract the fonts from your file. You must, at a minimum, *subset* the fonts, and possibly (for example, in the case of small vendors like Y&Y to whom font piracy presents a serious threat) pay additional license fees. Y&Y also insists that you must change Acrobat Distiller's subsetting mechanism. By default it does *not* subset the font if more than 35% of the characters are used. You should set this to 99% (see Figure ? ?) to ensure that Distiller always subsets unless *every* character is used.[4] This has, besides, the desirable quality of making the document smaller.

2.2.3   Adding value to your PDF

Creating a PDF image of your normal printed page is one thing; making an electronic document that takes advantage of all the features of PDF is another. At a minimum, cross-references need to have PDF hypertext links added. However, many people also expect the possibility of automatic bookmarks (the optional PDF "table of contents" on the left side of the display), that URLs be active links, and the possibility of adding new arbitrary links. The features can be added in four ways (in ascending order of preference):

1. By laboriously adding manual links in Acrobat Exchange. This option is error prone and has to be repeated each time the document changes.

---

[3] This book uses the European Modern sans serif and typewriter fonts.

[4] It is generally *impossible* to use 100% of most text fonts, since the encoding vector does not usually let you access all glyphs contained in a font.

2. By running an application that tries to guess linking from information in the file. It is not a very reliable method.

3. By having your application embed special PostScript code in the output that can be recognized by Acrobat Distiller and turned into links, for example.

4. By having your application generate PDF code directly. This will correspond to the cross-reference information in the source.

The third method is the most widely used and is well supported by Adobe. Acrobat Distiller recognizes a special PostScript command, `pdfmark`, and this is used as a hook to insert a vast amount of functionality into a PDF file. As an example,

```
[   /Color [1 0 0] /H /I /Border [0 0 0] /Subtype /Link
/Action << /S /GoTo /D (figure.1) >> /Rect [100 254 125 266]
/ANN pdfmark end
```

creates a hypertext link at the rectangle defined by `Rect` to a point in the document named `figure.1`, and

```
[   /Count 0 /Action << /S /GoTo /D (section.2) >> /Title
(Introduction) /OUT pdfmark end
```

creates a bookmark entry with the text `Introduction` pointing at the destination `section.2`. It is not our intention in this book to describe the `pdfmark` commands, since the majority of users will not create them directly. However, Adobe has produced good documentation [↪PDFMARKD], Thomas Merz [↪PDFMARKP] has an excellent freely available primer (a chapter of Merz (1998)), and D. P. Story's Web site [↪ACROTEX] has a detailed and well-presented tutorial on using `pdfmark` directly in TeX.

One question that arises, however, is how these `pdfmark` commands get into the PostScript file. TeX users have it rather easy, as almost all DVI to PostScript drivers allow for the insertion of raw PostScript into the output stream.[5] Using `dvips`, for instance, you can use `\special{ps:: ....}` to insert any PostScript code you like. It is, however, unlikely that you will write these commands in your LaTeX document since it is easier to do one of the following:

1. Use the HyperTeX `\special` (see Appendix B.1 on page 403) commands to insert higher-level commands, which a driver converts to the necessary `pdfmark` commands;

2. Use driver-specific `\special` commands, such as those supported by `dviwindo` or VTEX; or

---

[5]Merz (1998), Chapter 6, describes techniques for other applications like Microsoft Word and FrameMaker.

3. Better yet, operate at the level of generalized LATEX commands in a macro package, which translate to whatever mechanism is appropriate for your setup.

The last approach is that taken by `hyperref` and is described in Section 2.3. In a similar way, users of programs like Microsoft Word, FrameMaker, and Page-Maker trap their existing cross-referencing mechanisms and write `pdfmark` commands into the output PostScript file. The completely open and programmable nature of TEX makes our application particularly amenable to such an approach.

Apart from the `hyperref` package, the following packages are "PDF-aware":

- Packages that produce `\special` commands according to the HyperTEX conventions, such as Michael Mehlich's `hyper`, are PDF-aware. The resulting DVI file can be processed with the `-z` option of `dvips` to make a rich PostScript file for Acrobat Distiller.

- The ConTEXT macro package by Hans Hagen has very full support for PDF in its generalized hypertext features.

- Rich PDF from `texinfo` documents can be created with `pdftexinfo.tex`, which is a slight modification of the standard `texinfo` macros. This is part of the pdfTEX distribution and works only with that system.

- A similar modification of the `webmac`, called `pdfwebmac.tex`, allows production of hypertext PDF versions of programs written in WEB. This is also part of the pdfTEX distribution.

Finally, we must not forget what in many ways is the best solution— an application that writes PDF directly. We will look at one such solution, pdfTEX, in Section 2.4, which provides access to all features of PDF. The pdfTEX program adds a number of primitives to the TEX language that can be used directly. In practice, however, most people will find it easier to continue with the familiar LATEX syntax supported by the `hyperref` package since this has a driver that maps all the commands to the new pdfTEX primitives.

2.3 Rich PDF with LATEX: The hyperref package

The `hyperref` package by Sebastian Rahtz[6] derives from, and builds on, the work of the HyperTEX project (see Appendix B.1 on page 403 and [↪HYPERTEX]). It extends the functionality of all the LATEX cross-referencing commands (including the table of contents, bibliographies, and so on) to produce `\special` commands that a driver can turn into hypertext links; it also provides new commands to allow the user to write ad hoc hypertext links, including those to external documents and URLs.

---

[6]With considerable help over the years from many contributors, notably David Carlisle.

The package supports a variety of DVI drivers; they use either the HyperTEX \special commands or, if designed to produce *only* PDF, literal PostScript \special commands or pdfTEX-specific primitives. The commands are defined in configuration files for different drivers, selected by package options. The following drivers are supported:

hypertex For DVI processors conforming to the HyperTEX guidelines (that is, xdvi, dvips with the -z option, OzTeX, and Textures);

dvips Writes \special commands producing literal PostScript, tailored for dvips.

dvipsone Writes \special commands producing literal PostScript, tailored for dvipsone.

pdftex Writes commands for Hàn Thế Thành's TEX variant which produces PDF directly (see Section 2.4).

dvipdfm Writes \special commands for Mark Wicks's DVI to PDF driver dvipdfm.

dviwindo Writes \special commands which Y&Y's Windows previewer interprets as hypertext jumps within the previewer.

vtex Writes \special commands which MicroPress' HTML and PDF-producing TEX variants interpret as hypertext jumps.

Output from dvips or dvipsone[7] must be processed using Acrobat Distiller to obtain a PDF file. The result is generally prefererable to that produced using the hypertex driver and subsequent processing with the command dvips -z. The advantage of a DVI file written using the HyperTEX \special commands is that it can also be used with hypertext viewers like xdvi.

2.3.1   Implicit behavior of hyperref

The package can be used more or less with any normal LATEX document by requesting it in the document preamble. You must make sure it is the *last* of the loaded packages to give it a fighting chance of not being overwritten since its job is to redefine many LATEX commands. Hopefully you will find that all cross-references work correctly as hypertext, unless the implicit option is set to false, in which case only explicit hyperlink commands will be processed. Options control the appearance of links and give extra control over PDF output.

Figure 2.6 shows the result of processing our test file (see Appendix A.1), with hyperref defaults, to PDF; Figure 2.7 shows the same file displayed using xdvi.

---

[7]Both these drivers support partial font downloading; it is advisable to turn it off when preparing PostScript for Acrobat Distiller, since this has its own system of making font subsets.

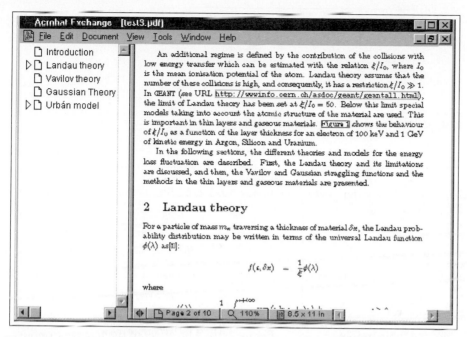

Figure 2.6: Default appearance of test document in PDF enhanced with `hyperref`

number of these collisions is high, and consequently, it has a restriction $\xi/I_0 \gg 1$. In GEANT (see URL http://wwwinfo.cern.ch/asdoc/geant/geantall.html), the limit of Landau theory has been set at $\xi/I_0 = 50$. Below this limit special models taking into account the atomic structure of the material are used. This is important in thin layers and gaseous materials. Figure 1 shows the behaviour of ξ/I_0 as a function of the layer thickness for an electron of 100 keV and 1 GeV of kinetic energy in Argon, Silicon and Uranium.

In the following sections, the different theories and models for the energy loss fluctuation are described. First, the Landau theory and its limitations are discussed, and then, the Vavilov and Gaussian straggling functions and the methods in the thin layers and gaseous materials are presented.

2   Landau theory

For a particle of mass m_x traversing a thickness of material δx, the Landau probability distribution may be written in terms of the universal Landau function $\phi(\lambda)$ as[1]:

$$f(\epsilon, \delta x) = \frac{1}{\xi}\phi(\lambda)$$

Figure 2.7: Test document displayed with `xdvi`

where $c \geq 4$. From the equations (13), (16) and (18) and from the conditions (22) and (23) the following limits can be derived:

$$\alpha_{\min} = \frac{(n_3 + c^2)(E_{\max} + I)}{n_3(E_{\max} + I) + c^2 I} \leq \alpha \leq \alpha_{\max} = \frac{(n_3 + c^2)(E_{\max} + I)}{c^2(E_{\max} + I) + n_3 I} \qquad (25)$$

This conditions gives a lower limit to number of the ionisations n_3 for which the fast sampling can be done:

$$n_3 \geq c^2 \qquad (26)$$

As in the conditions (22), (23) and (24) the value of c is as minimum 4, one gets $n_3 \geq 16$. In order to speed the simulation, the maximum value is used for α.

Figure 2.8: Test document showing use of `colorlinks` option

References

[1] L.Landau. On the Energy Loss of Fast Particles by Ionisation. Originally published in *J. Phys.*, 8:201, 1944. Rerpinted in D.ter Haar, Editor, *L.D.Landau, Collected papers*, page 417. Pergamon Press, Oxford, 1965.

[2] B.Schorr. Programs for the Landau and the Vavilov distributions and the corresponding random numbers. *Comp. Phys. Comm.*, 7:216, 1974.

[3] S.M.Seltzer and M.J.Berger. Energy loss straggling of protons and mesons. In *Studies in Penetration of Charged Particles in Matter*, Nuclear Science Series 39, Nat. Academy of Sciences, Washington DC, 1964.

[4] R.Talman. On the statistics of particle identification using ionization. *Nucl. Inst. Meth.*, 159:189, 1979.

[5] P.V.Vavilov. Ionisation losses of high energy heavy particles. *Soviet Physics JETP*, 5:749, 1957.

Figure 2.9: Normal bibliography

References

[1] L.Landau. On the Energy Loss of Fast Particles by Ionisation. Originally published in *J. Phys.*, 8:201, 1944. Rerpinted in D.ter Haar, Editor, *L.D.Landau, Collected papers*, page 417. Pergamon Press, Oxford, 1965. 2

[2] B.Schorr. Programs for the Landau and the Vavilov distributions and the corresponding random numbers. *Comp. Phys. Comm.*, 7:216, 1974. 3

[3] S.M.Seltzer and M.J.Berger. Energy loss straggling of protons and mesons. In *Studies in Penetration of Charged Particles in Matter*, Nuclear Science Series 39, Nat. Academy of Sciences, Washington DC, 1964. 4

[4] R.Talman. On the statistics of particle identification using ionization. *Nucl. Inst. Meth.*, 159:189, 1979. 2

[5] P.V.Vavilov. Ionisation losses of high energy heavy particles. *Soviet Physics JETP*, 5:749, 1957. 3

Figure 2.10: The effect of the `backref` option

Two commonly used package options are

- `colorlinks`, which colors the text of links instead of putting boxes around them (see Figure 2.8, which uses gray scales instead of color); and

- `backref`, which inserts extra "back" links into the bibliography for each entry. Figures 2.9 and 2.10 show what happens with this option set on and off. *Note:* The `backref` and `pagebackref` options can work properly only if there is a blank line after each \bibitem (as there is if it is created by BIBTEX).

2.3.2 Configuring hyperref

All user-configurable aspects of `hyperref` are set using a single "key-value" scheme (using the `keyval` package with the key `Hyp`). The options can be set either in the optional argument to the \usepackage command or with the command:

\hypersetup{*keyvalue pairs*}

Note that optional argument of the package command uses an experimental extension to LaTeX's syntax. LaTeX imposes some restrictions on the detailed content of package options and so this method may not always work; in general, options that involve only letters, digits, and punctuation will be safe.

In addition, when the package is loaded, a file `hyperref.cfg` is read if it can be found; this is a convenient place to set options on a sitewide basis. Thus the behavior of a particular file could be controlled by:

- A sitewide `hyperref.cfg` setting up the look of links, adding backreferencing, and setting a PDF display default:

  ```
  \hypersetup{backref,
      pdfpagemode=FullScreen,
      colorlinks=true}
  ```

- A global option in the file that is passed down to `hyperref`:

  ```
  \documentclass[dvips]{article}
  \usepackage{hyperref}
  ```

- File-specific options in the `\usepackage` commands that *override* the ones set in `hyperref.cfg`:

  ```
  \usepackage[pdftitle={A Perfect Day},colorlinks=false]{hyperref}
  ```

Details of all the package options are given in Section 2.3.8 on page 62. For many options you do not need to give a value because they default to the value `true` if used. These are the ones classed as Boolean. The values `true` and `false` can always be specified, however.

General options

A back-end driver can be chosen using one of the options listed in Table 2.4 on page 62. If no driver is specified, the package defaults to loading the hypertex driver. Most drivers provide the expected behavior without further ado; if you use dviwindo, however, you may need to redefine the following command:

```
\wwwbrowser
```

This command tells the dviwindo driver what program to launch; the default is `c:\netscape\netscape.exe`. Thus users of Internet Explorer might add something like the following to `hyperref.cfg`:

```
\renewcommand{\wwwbrowser}{C:\string\Program\space
    Files\string\Plus!\string\Microsoft\space
    Internet\string\iexplore.exe}
```

A number of general options, listed in Table 2.5 on page 62, apply to all drivers. The importance of the `breaklinks` option is demonstrated in Figure 2.11; this

> atom. Landau theory assumes that the number of
> these collisions is high, and consequently, it has a
> restriction $\xi/I_0 \gg 1$. In GEANT (see URL http://
> wwwinfo.cern.ch/asdoc/geant/geantall.html),
> the limit of Landau theory has been set at $\xi/I_0 =$
> 50. Below this limit special models taking into

Figure 2.11: Long link text split across lines

example was processed using pdfTEX, which has allowed the URL to break, and has made each part into separate links. The other drivers are unable to manage this trick, and the URL would have to be left protruding into the margin.

Table 2.6 on page 63 lists options that also apply to all drivers but provide extended functionality. There are various options to specify the color of text in links. All color names must be defined before use, following the normal system of the standard LATEX color package. Users must also realize that the color of colored links is part of the text; if you color URLs green and then print the page from Acrobat, for example, the text will be printed in green (that is, a gray scale on a black-and-white printer).

Using the xr package with hyperref   A collection of interacting files can be created automatically, using the xr package. However, since either dvi or pdf versions of the results may be used, the hyperref package does not necessarily know which files to refer to. Consider the following file:

```
\documentclass{article}
\usepackage{xr}
\usepackage{hyperref}
\externaldocument{other}
\begin{document}
See section \ref{facts} in the other file
\end{document}
```

The label facts is defined in the file other.tex; when the current file is processed, it reads other.aux and makes all of its labels available for \ref in the current file (this is the job of the xr package). Because we have loaded hyperref, the command \ref{facts} creates a hypertext link referring to the other file. But does it ask for other.dvi (which is what we want if we are using dviwindo, for example), or other.pdf (which Acrobat can open directly)? The hyperref package does its best to guess correctly, but on occasion you may wish to override it by specifying the file suffix with the extension option.

Options specifically for making PDF files

When the target is a PDF file, there are many options to configure the output; these are listed in Table 2.7 on page 63.

Setting link views   Setting the view for links in Acrobat can be complicated; unlike many other hypertext systems, Acrobat associates a magnification or zoom value with every link. Table 2.1 on the following page shows the possibilities, that is, a set of keys with a variable number of parameters. Unfortunately it is often rather hard for a hyperref user to work out what values to set for these parameters; they have to be expressed in the PDF default coordinate space, which is not necessarily the same as TeX is thinking in. The good news is that pdfTeX tries to work out sensible values for you, supplying default parameters for the commonly used keys, XYZ and FitBH; the bad news is that drivers using the pdfmark system do not supply defaults. So, if you say

```
\usepackage[dvips, pdfview=FitBH]{hyperref}
```

you would normally get a catastrophic result, since FitBH *must* be followed by a number. To make life a little easier in practice, hyperref supplies a value of −32768 as a parameter[8] to the view command, if none is explicitly given; this value is ignored by the pdfTeX driver.

The *default* is always XYZ followed by an appropriate value for the driver, that is, the magnification does not change when a link is followed. A typical change would be to set

```
pdfview=FitBH
```

so that links jump to a view that fills the window with something rational, the width of the text area on the current page.

Coloring links   The color of link borders in Acrobat can be specified *only* as three numbers in the range 0..1, giving an RGB color. You cannot use the colors defined in TeX. These colors do *not* form part of the text and will not show when printed.

Setting the window display   The options relating to the window display are demonstrated in Figure 2.12; this example was created with

```
\usepackage[
  pdftoolbar=false,
  pdfmenubar=false,
  pdfwindowui=false,
  pdffitwindow=true,
  pdfpagelayout=TwoColumnLeft
]{hyperref}
```

Because the toolbar and menu bar have been removed, any interaction for the user must be provided by the document itself (including basics like a Quit button); the

---

[8]This meaningless value forces Acrobat Distiller to set a usually sensible default for some keys.

Table 2.1: Possible values for PDF link view specifications

Key	Parameters	Description
XYZ	*left top zoom*	Set a coordinate for the upper left corner of the page portion to put in the window and a zoom factor. If *left*, *top*, or *zoom* is null, the current value is used. Thus values of "null null null" specify the same *top*, *left*, and *zoom* as the current page. A value of 0 is the same as null.
Fit		Fit the page to the window.
FitH	*top*	Fit the width of the page to the window; *top* specifies the *y*-coordinate of the top edge of the window.
FitV	*left*	Fit the height of the page to the window; *left* specifies the *x*-coordinate of the left edge of the window.
FitR	*left bottom right top*	Fit the rectangle specified by *left bottom right top* in the window.
FitB		Fit the page bounding box to the window.
FitBH	*top*	Fit the width of the page bounding box to the window; *top* specifies the *y*-coordinate of the top edge of the window.
FitBV	*left*	Fit the height of the page bounding box to the window; *left* specifies the *x*-coordinate of the left edge of the window.

command \Acrobatmenu (see Section 2.3.4 on page 47) comes in very useful here. The menu and toolbar can, in fact, be restored manually using Ctrl-Shift-M and Ctrl-Shift-B key sequences, respectively.

Acrobat bookmark commands

The bookmark commands need further explanation. They are stored in a file called *jobname*.out, and you can postprocess this file to remove LaTeX codes if needed. The bookmark text is *not processed* by LaTeX, so any markup is passed through literally. In addition, bookmarks must be written in Adobe's PDFDocEncoding. Figure 2.13 shows the effect of the bookmarksopen option and also the limitations of PDFDocEncoding, since math cannot be displayed. To aid any editing you need to do, the out file is not rewritten by LaTeX on the next pass if it is edited to contain

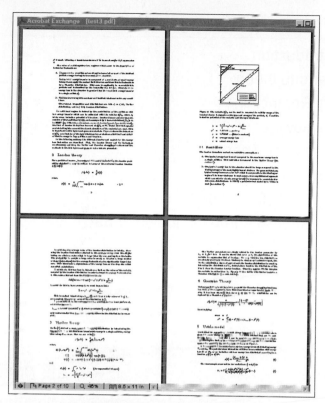

Figure 2.12: PDF document displayed with no toolbar or interface and with multiple pages visible

the line `\let\WriteBookmarks\relax`. The hyperref package does try its best to convert internal encoding for European accented characters to PDFDocEncoding.

PDF document information fields   The options listed in Table 2.8 on page 65 allow you to put text in PDF's information fields. Figure 2.14 shows the display of document information in Acrobat; the document was created with the following command in the document preamble:

```
\usepackage[
pdfauthor={Maria Physicist},
pdftitle={Simulation of Energy Loss Straggling},
pdfcreator={pdfTeX},
pdfsubject={Energy Loss},
pdfkeywords={physics,energy}
]{hyperref}
```

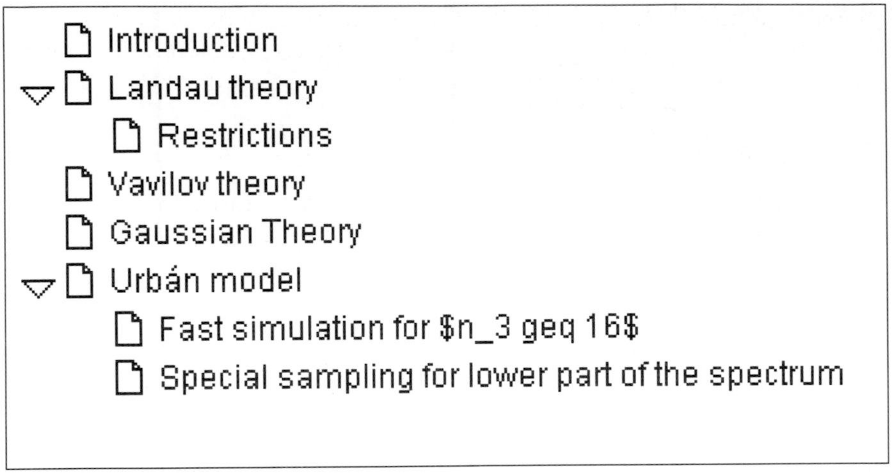

Introduction
Landau theory
Restrictions
Vavilov theory
Gaussian Theory
Urbán model
Fast simulation for $n_3 geq 16$
Special sampling for lower part of the spectrum

Figure 2.13: PDF bookmarks open

File Edit Document View Tools Window Help
Introduction
Landau theory
Restrictions
Vavilov theory
Gaussian Theory
Urbán model
Fast simulatio
Special sampl
General Info
D:\srahtz\lwc\admin\latexexa.pdf
Title: Simulation of Energy Loss Straggling
Subject: Energy Loss
Author: Maria Physicist
Keywords: physics,energy
Creator: pdfTeX
Producer: pdfTeX12.o
Created: 7/28/98 3:45:00 PM
Modified: 7/28/98 3:45:00 PM
Optimized: No
File Size (Bytes): 174793
OK
Cancel

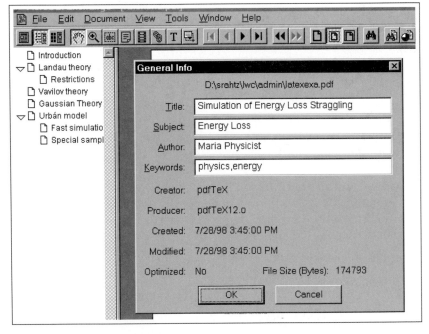

Figure 2.14: Display of PDF document information

2.3.3   Additional user macros for hyperlinks

If you need to make references to URLs or write explicit point-to-point links, the following set of user macros is provided. Note that it is possible to differentiate links and anchors by category, but the feature is not seriously exploited in hyperref.

> `\hyperbaseurl{`*url*`}`

A base *url*, prepended to other specified URLs to make it easier to write portable documents, is established.

> `\href{`*url*`}{`*text*`}`

The *text* is made into a hyperlink to the *url*; this must be a full URL (relative to the base URL, if that is defined). The special characters # and ~ do *not* need to be escaped in any way. For example,

    \href{http://www.tug.org/~rahtz/nonsense.html#fun}{Some fun}

> `\hyperimage{`*image url*`}`

The image referenced by the *image url* is inserted.

> `\hyperdef{`*category*`}{`*name*`}{`*text*`}`

A target area of the document (the *text*) is marked and given the name *category.name*.

> `\hyperref{`*url*`}{`*category*`}{`*name*`}{`*text*`}`

The *text* is made into a link to *url#category.name*.

> `\hyperref[`*label*`]{`*text*`}`

The *text* is made into a link to a point established with a normal LaTeX `\label` command with the symbolic name *label* (see the following description of `\ref*` for a use for this syntax.)

> `\hyperlink{`*name*`}{`*text*`}`
> `\hypertarget{`*name*`}{`*text*`}`

A simple internal link is created with `\hypertarget`, two parameters of an anchor *name*, and anchor *text*. The `\hyperlink` command has two arguments: the name of a hypertext object defined somewhere by `\hypertarget`, and the *text* used as the link on the page.

  In HTML parlance, the `\hyperlink` command inserts a notional # in front of each link, making it relative to the current document; `\href` expects a full URL.

> 1. The typical energy loss is small compared to the maximum energy loss in a single collision. This restriction is removed in the Vavilov theory (see section 3).
>
> 2. The typical energy loss in the absorber should be large compared to the binding energy of the most tightly bound electron. For gaseous detectors, typical energy losses are a few keV which is comparable to the binding energies of the inner electrons. In such cases a more sophisticated approach which accounts for atomic energy levels[4] is necessary to accurately simulate data distributions. In GEANT, a parameterised model by L. Urbán is used (see section 5).

Figure 2.15: The effect of `\ref` vs. `\autoref`

`\autoref{`*label*`}`

This is a replacement for the normal `\ref` command that puts a *contextual* tag in front of the reference. The difference is shown in Figure 2.15, where the first section link was made using `\autoref{...}` and the second using `\ref{...}`. The former has the word "section" as part of the link, whereas the latter has just the number. The behavior of the former is often more friendly for users than that of the latter.

The tag is worked out from the context of the original `\label` command by hyperref using the macros listed in Table 2.2. The macros can be redefined in documents using `\renewcommand`; note that some of these macros are already defined in the standard document classes. The mixture of lowercase and uppercase initial letters is deliberate and corresponds to the author's practice.

Table 2.2: Hyperref `\autoref` names

Macro	Default
`\figurename`	Figure
`\tablename`	Table
`\partname`	Part
`\appendixname`	Appendix
`\equationname`	Equation
`\Itemname`	item
`\chaptername`	chapter
`\sectionname`	section
`\subsectionname`	subsection
`\subsubsectionname`	subsubsection
`\paragraphname`	paragraph
`\Hfootnotename`	footnote
`\AMSname`	Equation
`\theoremname`	Theorem

Sometimes you might want to make a link text all by yourself and do not want `\ref` and `\pageref` to form links. For this purpose, there are two variant commands:

```
\ref*{label}
\pageref*{label}
```

A typical use would be to write

```
\hyperref[other]{that nice section (\ref*{other}) we read before}
```

where we want `\ref*{other}` to generate the right number but not to form a link. We will do this ourselves with `\hyperref`.

2.3.4 Acrobat-specific commands

If you want to access the menu options of Acrobat Reader or Acrobat Exchange, the following command is provided in the appropriate drivers:

```
\Acrobatmenu{menuoption}{text}
```

The *text* is used to create a button that activates the appropriate *menuoption*. Table 2.3[9] lists the *menuoption* names you can use. A comparison of this list with the menus in Acrobat will show what they do. Obviously some are appropriate only to Exchange.

As an example, let us add a menu bar in the footer of our document, using the fancyhdr package:

```
\usepackage{fancyhdr}
\usepackage[colorlinks]{hyperref}
\pagestyle{fancy}
\cfoot{\NavigationBar}
\newcommand{\NavigationBar}{%
  \Acrobatmenu{PrevPage}{Previous}~
  \Acrobatmenu{NextPage}{Next}~
  \Acrobatmenu{FirstPage}{First}~
  \Acrobatmenu{LastPage}{Last}~
  \Acrobatmenu{GoBack}{Back}~
  \Acrobatmenu{Quit}{Quit}%
}
```

The effect is shown in the following picture:

and

$$E_1(z) = \int_z^\infty t^{-1} e^{-t} dt \qquad \text{(the exponential integral)}$$

Previous Next First Last Back Quit

---

[9] This table was laboriously derived by Thomas Merz, who was experimenting with Acrobat Exchange, and published in Merz (1998), since the names are not listed in Adobe documentation.

Table 2.3: Acrobat menu option link names

Acrobat Menu	Available options for \Acrobatmenu
File	Open, Close, Scan, Save, SaveAs, Optimizer:SaveAsOpt, Print, PageSetup, Quit
File→Import	ImportImage, ImportNotes, AcroForm:ImportFDF
File→Export	ExportNotes, AcroForm:ExportFDF
File→DocumentInfo	GeneralInfo, OpenInfo, FontsInfo, SecurityInfo, Weblink:Base, AutoIndex:DocInfo
File→Preferences	GeneralPrefs, NotePrefs, FullScreenPrefs, Weblink:Prefs, AcroSearch:Preferences (Windows) or, AcroSearch:Prefs (Mac), Cpt:Capture
Edit	Undo, Cut, Copy, Paste, Clear, SelectAll, Ole:CopyFile, TouchUp:TextAttributes, TouchUp:FitTextToSelection, TouchUp:ShowLineMarkers, TouchUp:ShowCaptureSuspects, TouchUp:FindSuspect, Properties
Edit→Fields	AcroForm:Duplicate, AcroForm:TabOrder
Document	Cpt:CapturePages, AcroForm:Actions, CropPages, RotatePages, InsertPages, ExtractPages, ReplacePages, DeletePages, NewBookmark, SetBookmarkDest, CreateAllThumbs, DeleteAllThumbs
View	ActualSize, FitVisible, FitWidth, FitPage, ZoomTo, FullScreen, FirstPage, PrevPage, NextPage, LastPage, GoToPage, GoBack, GoForward, SinglePage, OneColumn, TwoColumns, ArticleThreads, PageOnly, ShowBookmarks, ShowThumbs
Tools	Hand, ZoomIn, ZoomOut, SelectText, SelectGraphics, Note, Link, Thread, AcroForm:Tool, Acro_Movie:MoviePlayer, TouchUp:TextTool, Find, FindAgain, FindNextNote, CreateNotesFile
Tools→Search	AcroSrch:Query, AcroSrch:Indexes, AcroSrch:Results, AcroSrch:Assist, AcroSrch:PrevDoc, AcroSrch:PrevHit, AcroSrch:NextHit, AcroSrch:NextDoc
Window	ShowHideToolBar, ShowHideMenuBar, ShowHideClipboard, Cascade, TileHorizontal, TileVertical, CloseAll
Help	HelpUserGuide, HelpTutorial, HelpExchange, HelpScan, HelpCapture, HelpPDFWriter, HelpDistiller, HelpSearch, HelpCatalog, HelpReader, Weblink:Home
Help(Windows)	About

The text can, of course, be any arbitrary LaTeX piece of typesetting. The following variation uses symbols from the ZapfDingbats font (loaded with the `pifont` package) for the same set of menu options:

```
\usepackage{pifont}
\usepackage{graphics}
\newcommand{\NavigationBar}{{\Large
  \Acrobatmenu{PrevPage}{\reflectbox{\ding{227}}}
  \Acrobatmenu{NextPage}{\ding{227}}
  \Acrobatmenu{FirstPage}{\reflectbox{\ding{224}}}
  \Acrobatmenu{LastPage}{\ding{224}}
  \Acrobatmenu{GoBack}{\reflectbox{\ding{249}}}
  \Acrobatmenu{Quit}{\ding{54}}%
}}
```

with the effect as follows:

and

$$E_1(z) \;=\; \int_z^{\infty} t^{-1} e^{-t} dt \qquad \text{(the exponential integral)}$$

Instead of a Dingbat, we could also have used a picture, with code like

```
\Acrobatmenu{Back}{\includegraphics{backpic}}
```

2.3.5   Special support for other packages

hyperref tries to cooperate with as many other package as possible, but this laudable aim is sometimes impractical. Causes of conflict are

- Packages that manipulate the bibliographical mechanisms. Peter Williams's harvard package is supported. However, the recommended package is Patrick Daly's natbib package which has specific hyperref hooks to allow reliable interaction. This package covers a very wide variety of layouts and citation styles, all of which will work with hyperref.

- Packages that typeset the contents of the \label and \ref macros, for example showkeys. The hyperref package redefines all of these commands, unless the implicit=false option is used; then these packages will not work properly.

- Packages that do anything serious with the index.

The hyperref package is distributed with variants on two useful packages designed to work especially well with it. These are xr and minitoc, which support cross-document links using LaTeX's normal \label/\ref mechanism and per-chapter tables of contents, respectively.

2.3.6   Creating PDF and HTML forms

It is fast becoming commonplace (and even necessary) to convert paper forms to an electronic equivalent. Many Web pages now use HTML forms to collect data in very complicated ways, but it is not widely realized that PDF contains all the same functionality. In this section, we look at the support in `hyperref` for creating full-fledged PDF (and HTML) forms.

Those interested in forms should keep three things in mind:

1. Fill-in forms are not the only use for form objects in PDF. D. P. Story [↪ACROTEX] and Hans Hagen [↪CONTEXT] use them for building sophisticated interactive applications and advanced navigation. Figure 2.16 shows Hans Hagen's calculator, developed in TEX (his CONTEXt package) with embedded JavaScript and graphics drawn using METAPOST and delivered as PDF.

2. The current powerful forms are a relatively recent addition to PDF; to use them, you need Acrobat 3.01 or later and the Forms 3.5 add-ons.

3. Few PDF-generating applications, apart from TEX, really support markup-based creation of PDF forms, and most documentation deals with creating them manually using Acrobat Exchange. It is also a late addition to the `hyperref` package, although the interface may need to change. *Note:* only the `pdftex`, `dvips`, and `tex4ht` drivers support forms.

The excellent book by Thomas Merz is required background reading for understanding how PDF handles forms (see Merz (1998), Chapters 7 and 10), and Story's Web site [↪ACROTEX] has both well-designed examples and a detailed tutorial on using `pdfmark` (see Section 2.2 on page 27) to create forms. You should also keep in mind that much underlying functionality requires use of JavaScript, which you will need to learn. With the Forms plug-in Adobe supplies a manual called *Acrobat Forms JavaScript Object Specification*; Netscape's *JavaScript Reference Manual* is also helpful. PDF forms have huge potential, and `hyperref` only scratches the surface of what they can do.

The form support in `hyperref` is designed to mimic that in HTML. To this end, it requires you to put all your form fields inside a `Form` environment; only one is allowed per file.

```
\begin{Form}[parameters]
... fields ...
\end{Form}
```

The *parameters* are a set of key-value pairs, as listed in Table 2.9 on page 65.

Four types of form fields are supported:

1. Text fields, that allow free entry of text;

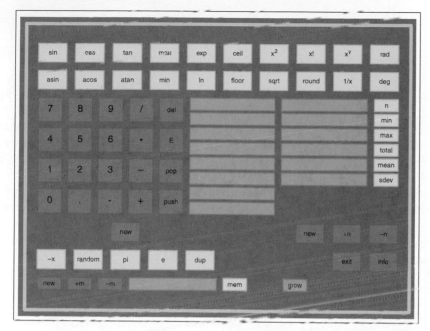

Figure 2.16. Calculator written in PDF (by Hans Hagen)

2. Checkboxes, that allow a box to be selected or deselected;

3. Choice fields, that allow the user to choose one of a range of possibilities; and

4. Push buttons, that instigate some action.

In addition, there are special Submit and Reset fields.
    The following six macros are used to prepare fields:

```
\TextField[options]{label}
\CheckBox[options]{label}
\ChoiceMenu[options]{label}{choices}
\PushButton[options]{label}
\Submit[options]{label}
\Reset[options]{label}
```

Note that at the top level there is no distinction drawn between

• simple choice menus, where all possibilities are listed;

• pop-up choice menu, where the default is shown, and the rest appear only when
   the field is selected;

- combo menus, where a list of possibilities is given, but the user can type in a new value;[10] and

- radio fields, where one of a list of possibilities can be checked.

There is a large set of options (see Table 2.10 on page 65) that affect what the form fields do.

Making a field involves supplying a textual label, possibly a list of choices, (optionally) a default, and an initial selection. The way a list of choices is presented depends on which options are used; the list is simply separated by commas. For each item, it is possible to specify a visible string separately from the value actually returned, if this choice is made, by supplying two strings separated by an = sign for the choice. The first part is what is shown; the second part is the value returned.

Each of the three main field types (text, checkbox, and choice) consists of two parts—the *label* and the *field* itself. The position of the label in relation to the field is determined by three macros that you can redefine:

```
\LayoutTextField{label}{field}
\LayoutChoiceField{label}{field}
\LayoutCheckboxField{label}{field}
```

These macros default to #1 #2, that is, the label is set to the left of the field. A typical redefinition might be

```
\renewcommand{\LayoutTextField}[2]{\makebox[2in]{#1}#2}
```

which would set all labels within a fixed-width box, 2 inches wide.

What is actually created as the typeset area for the field is determined by

```
\MakeRadioField{width}{height}
\MakeCheckField{width}{height}
\MakeTextField{width}{height}
\MakeChoiceField{width}{height}
\MakeButtonField{text}
```

These macros default to making the field a rectangle *width* wide and *height* high, with the field contents placed in the center. The *width* and *height* default to the size of the field contents but can be overridden with options (see Table 2.10 on page 65). The exception is the macro for button fields, which defaults to #1; it is used for push buttons and for the special \Submit and \Reset macros.

You might also need to redefine the following macros; these are used to work out sizes when no other information is available:

---

[10]This type does not appear to be allowed in HTML.

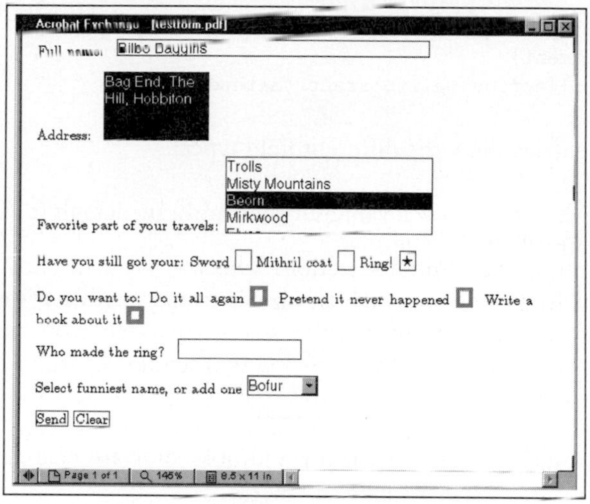

Figure 2.17: Simple Acrobat form

Macro	Default
\DefaultHeightofSubmit	12pt
\DefaultWidthofSubmit	2cm
\DefaultHeightofReset	12pt
\DefaultWidthofReset	2cm
\DefaultHeightofCheckBox	0.8\baselineskip
\DefaultWidthofCheckBox	0.8\baselineskip
\DefaultHeightofChoiceMenu	0.8\baselineskip
\DefaultWidthofChoiceMenu	0.8\baselineskip
\DefaultHeightofText	\baselineskip
\DefaultWidthofText	3cm

Note that all colors must be expressed as RGB triples in the range 0..1 (for example, color=0 0 0.5). In general, these options simply provide an interface to the relevant PDF code which is fully documented in Bienz et al (1996). Familiarity with that document is vital if you plan to go beyond the defaults and simple variations.

Now that we have all the tools described, what about a simple example? Figure 2.17 shows a typical form, demonstrating almost all of the different field types. Let us look in detail at the code that produced this form. First, in the document preamble, we load hyperref and then start a Form environment with an appropriate URL (simply mail it).

```
\documentclass{article}
\usepackage[bookmarks=false]{hyperref}
```

```
\setlength{\parindent}{0pt}\setlength{\parskip}{10pt}
\begin{document}
\begin{Form}[action=mailto:srahtz,method=post]
```

The following entries show the different field types:

1. Text field. Here we supply a value for the width; by default it would be the size of the default value:

   ```
   \TextField[width=3in,name=xname,value={Bilbo Baggins}]{Full name: }
   ```

2. Text field, multiline. The text color and box color are changed and a dashed border is drawn around the field:

   ```
   \TextField[multiline,width=1in,name=address,borderstyle=D,
       color=1 1 1,backgroundcolor=0 0 .5,
       value={Bag End, The Hill, Hobbiton}]{Address: }
   ```

3. Choice. By default, the height of the field would be enough to hold all the choices, but we limit it to showing three at a time:

   ```
   \ChoiceMenu[default=Home,menulength=3,width=2in,name=travel,default=Beorn]
       {Favorite part of your travels:}
       {Trolls,Misty Mountains,Beorn,Mirkwood,Elves,Laketown,%
       Smaug,The Battle}
   ```

4. Checkboxes. Only one box is checked at startup:

   ```
   Have you still got your:
   \CheckBox[]{Sword}
   \CheckBox[name=coat]{Mithril coat}
   \CheckBox[name=ring,checked]{\textbf{Ring!}}
   ```

5. Choice, radio style. Note here the supplying of different values shown from those returned by the checked box:

```
\ChoiceMenu[radio,default=Again,name=next,
    borderwidth=3,bordercolor=0 1 0]{Do you want to:}
    {Do it all again=Again,
     Pretend it never happened=Forget,
     Write a book about it=Write}
```

6. Text field, password style. When text is entered, it is shown as asterisks:

```
\TextField[password,name=made]{Who made the ring? }
```

7. Choice, combo style. This field type allows us either to select one of the provided options or to type in a new one:

```
\ChoiceMenu[combo,default=Bofur,name=whatdwarf]
    {Select funniest name, or add one}
    {Bofur,Thorin,Gollum,Smaug,Gandalf}
```

This shows the state when the field is not active:

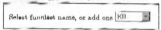

And this shows the list popping up:

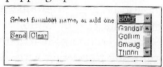

8. PushButton. This type activates some JavaScript code when the field is clicked:

```
\PushButton[name=xxx,onclick={app.beep(0)}]{Make a horrid beep}
```

9. Send & Clear fields. These submit the contents of the form, and clear all the fields, respectively:

```
\Submit{Send}        \Reset{Clear}
```

Finally, complete the Form environment and end the document.

```
\end{Form}
\end{document}
```

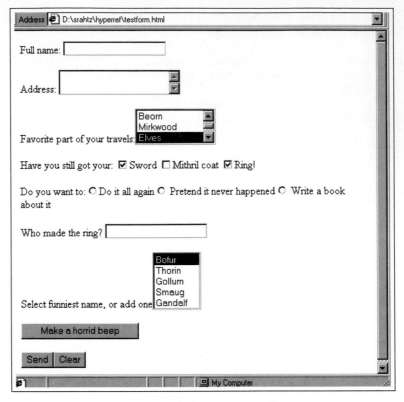

Figure 2.18: Simple form presented in HTML

The same LaTeX file can also be used to produce an almost identical HTML form (Figure 2.18) by specifying the `tex4ht` option when loading the `hyperref` package. Chapter 4 discusses how to run `tex4ht` to get the HTML file.

Now that we have a form ready to interact with, how can we get at the data? Merz (1998), Chapter 10, deals well with this issue, and in this book we can only summarize the possibilities. There are essentially two ways to process the form data:

1. If the PDF form is viewed inside a Web browser and a suitable URL is provided, clicking on the Send button will post the data to the URL.

2. There is an Acrobat menu option (File → Export → Form Data) that prompts for the name of an FDF file in which to save the data.

The FDF file format is described in detail in Bienz et al. (1996), Appendix H; and Adobe makes available a toolkit for writing programs to process it. It is a simplified form of PDF, and the following example (from our simple form) shows the straightforward data structures:

```
%FDF-1.2
1 0 obj
<<
/FDF << /Fields [
 << /V (Bag End, The Hill, Hobbiton)/T (address)>>
 << /V /Off /T (coat)>>
 << /V /next1 /T (next)>>
 << /V /Yes /T (ring)>>
 << /V /Yes /T (Sword)>>
 << /V (Mirkwood)/T (travel)>>
 << /V (Kili)/T (whatdwarf)>>
 << /V (Bilbo Baggins)/T (xname)>>
]
>>
endobj
trailer
<< /Root 1 0 R >>
%%EOF
```

2.3.6.1   Validating form fields

It is possible to write JavaScript code to perform sophisticated validation of the contents of form fields (Merz (1998), pages 141–144, shows how to check an ISBN code, for instance), but Acrobat provides a range of built-in JavaScript functions for simple checking. These can be accessed by giving the function name and arguments with the keystroke, format, validate, and calculate options. **Warning:** These functions are undocumented and unsupported by Adobe! It is possible that they may no longer be available in later versions of Acrobat.

A summary of the available JavaScript functions follows; you should enter the code exactly as it appears here, for example

```
\TextField[name=ndwarvoo,
    validate={AFRange_Validate\string\(true, 3, true, 10\string\);}]
    {How many dwarves came along:  }
```

Note the distinction between keystroke functions, which determine what the user is allowed to type, and format functions, which determine how it is displayed. Usually, both will be supplied for a given field.

Ensure field content is entered and formatted as a percentage or a number

```
AFPercent_Keystroke\string\(places, 0\string\);
AFPercent_Format\string\(value, 0\string\);
AFNumber_Keystroke\string\(places, 0, 0, 0, "", true\string\);
AFNumber_Format\string\(places, 0, 0, 0, "", true\string\);
```

where *places* is the number of decimal places.

Ensure field content is entered and formatted as a date

```
AFDate_Keystroke\string\(type\string\);
AFDate_Format\string\(type\string\);
```

where *type* is a number from the following table:

0	1/3	5	3-Jan-81	10	Jan 3, 1981
1	1/3/81	6	03-Jan-81	11	January 3, 1981
2	01/03/81	7	81-01-03	12	1/3/81 2:30pm
3	01/81	8	Jan-81	13	1/3/81 14:30
4	3-Jan	9	January-81		

Ensure field content is entered and formatted as a time

```
AFTime_Keystroke\string\(type\string\);
AFTime_Format\string\(type\string\);
```

where *type* is a number from the following table:

0	14:30
1	2.30 pm
2	14:30:15
3	2:30:15pm

Format entry in a specific way

```
AFSpecial_Format\string\(type\string\);
```

where *type* is a number from the following table:

0	Zip Code
1	Zip Code + 4
2	Phone Number
3	Social Security Number

Validate numbers to a given range

```
AFRange_Validate\string\(true, minimum, true, maximum\string\);
```

Specify that this field is derived from others

```
AFSimple_Calculate\string\("function", "list of field names"\string\);
```

The possible values for *function* are SUM, PRODUCT, AVERAGE, MINIMUM, and MAXIMUM; the *list of fields* must be separated by commas.

2.3.7   Designing PDF documents for the screen

For many people, simply having a PDF version of a printed document, with active links, is useful enough. Others, however, have started to consider the use of PDF for documents whose only existence is on the computer screen.

In Section 2.3.4 on page 47 we saw how we can access all the menu options of Acrobat from within LaTeX; this allows us to build a complete user interface using all the power of TeX.

Let us consider some of the ways in which we can design a document just for the screen. See Figures 2.19, 2.20 and 2.21.

- We set up a landscape page design, which has the same aspect ratio as the computer screen; we choose 6 in×4 in; page margins are adjusted to suit. Remember that LaTeX gives one-inch margins by default; we need to crop the page so that the margins are of minimal width. The LaTeX oneside option must be used, as there is no longer any concept of odd or even pages. When the text width is small, you should consider using the \raggedright setting;

- We set the font family to one suited for screen reading; we choose Lucida Bright;

- Since there is no reason to fill pages, we set section headings to start a new page;

- We use color; section headings are set in blue, hypertext links are colored, table rows are shaded, etc.;

- The \ref commands are replaced by \autoref (or by \hyperref if a more customized link is needed); this makes the colored links have a more visible context;

- Should you wish to disable the Acrobat menu and toolbar, a navigation and function bar can be put at the bottom of each page;

- To provide a visible pointer to the current page's location within the article, a progress gauge is placed at the bottom of each page: this works by comparing the current page number with the number of the last page, and constructing a colored bar of appropriate length.

We would also need to work out a strategy for marginal notes and footnotes, since these will look unnatural in a screen display.

Figure 2.22 shows another possible design; this one has a navigation panel on the right-hand side of every page, including a summary table of contents. C. V. Radhakrishnan's pdfscreen package (building on hyperref) implements this scheme. It has options to generate sidebar or footer menus and commands to specify logos and addresses to appear on every page.

1   Introduction

Due to the statistical nature of ionisation energy loss, large fluctuations can occur in the amount of energy deposited by a particle traversing an absorber element. Continuous processes such as multiple scattering and energy loss play a relevant role in the longitudinal and lateral development of electromagnetic and hadronic showers, and in the case of sampling calorimeters the measured resolution can be significantly affected by such fluctuations in their active layers. The description of ionisation fluctuations is characterised by the significance parameter κ, which is proportional to the ratio of mean energy loss to the maximum allowed energy transfer in a single collision with an atomic electron

$$\kappa = \frac{\xi}{E_{\max}}$$

$E_{\max}$ is the maximum transferable energy in a single collision with an atomic electron.

$$E_{\max} = \frac{2m_e\beta^2\gamma^2}{1 + 2\gamma m_e/m_x + (m_e/m_x)^2},$$

| Previous | Next | First | Last | Back | Quit |

Figure 2.19: Screen-designed PDF file I

2.1   Restrictions

The Landau formalism makes two restrictive assumptions :

1. The typical energy loss is small compared to the maximum energy loss in a single collision. This restriction is removed in the Vavilov theory (see section 3).

2. The typical energy loss in the absorber should be large compared to the binding energy of the most tightly bound electron. For gaseous detectors, typical energy losses are a few keV which is comparable to the binding energies of the inner electrons. In such cases a more sophisticated approach which accounts for atomic energy levels[4] is necessary to accurately simulate data distributions. In GEANT, a parameterised model by L. Urbán is used (see section 5).

In addition, the average value of the Landau distribution is infinite. Summing the Landau fluctuation obtained to the average energy from the dE/dx tables, we obtain a value which is larger than the one coming from the table. The probability to sample a large value is small, so it takes a large number of steps (extractions) for the average fluctuation to be significantly larger than zero. This introduces a dependence of the energy loss on the step size which can affect calculations. A solution to this has been to introduce a limit on the value of the variable sampled by the Landau distribution in order to keep the average fluctuation to 0. The value obtained from the GLANDO

| Previous | Next | First | Last | Back | Quit |

Figure 2.20: Screen-designed PDF file II

E'_{max} is the GEANT cut for δ-production, or the maximum energy transfer minus mean ionisation energy, if it is smaller than this cut-off value. The following notation is used:

r, C	parameters of the model
E_i	atomic energy levels
I	mean ionisation energy
f_i	oscillator strengths

The model has the parameters f_i, E_i, C and r ($0 \leq r \leq 1$). The oscillator strengths f_i and the atomic level energies E_i should satisfy the constraints

$$f_1 + f_2 = 1 \qquad (4)$$
$$f_1 \ln E_1 + f_2 \ln E_2 = \ln I \qquad (5)$$

The parameter C can be defined with the help of the mean energy loss dE/dx in the following way: The numbers of collisions (n_i, i = 1,2 for the excitation and 3 for the ionisation) follow the Poisson distribution with a mean number $\langle n_i \rangle$. In a step Δx the mean number of collisions is

$$\langle n_i \rangle = \Sigma_i \Delta x \qquad (6)$$

Previous   Next   First   Last   Back   Quit

Figure 2.21: Screen-designed PDF file III

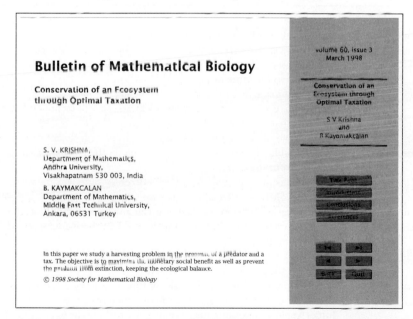

Figure 2.22: Alternate screen-designed PDF file (courtesy of River Valley Technologies and Focal Image Ltd.)

2.3.8   Catalog of package options

Table 2.4: `hyperref` options to specify drivers

Option	Value	Default	Description
draft	boolean	*false*	All hypertext options are turned off.
pdftex	boolean		Sets up `hyperref` for use with the pdfTEX program.
dvipdfm	boolean		Sets up `hyperref` for use with the dvipdfm driver.
nativepdf	boolean		An alias for `dvips`.
pdfmark	boolean		An alias for `dvips`.
dvips	boolean		Sets up `hyperref` for use with the dvips driver.
hypertex	boolean		Sets up `hyperref` for use with HyperTEX-compliant drivers.
dviwindo	boolean		Sets up `hyperref` for use with the dviwindo Windows previewer.
dvipsone	boolean		Sets up `hyperref` for use with the dvipsone driver.
vtex	boolean		Sets up `hyperref` for use with MicroPress' VTEX; the PDF and HTML back-ends are detected automatically.
latex2html	boolean		Redefines a few macros for compatibility with LaTeX2HTML.
tex4ht	boolean		Sets up `hyperref` for use with TEX4ht (see Chapter 4).

Table 2.5: Configuration options

Option	Value	Default	Description
breaklinks	boolean	*false*	Allows link text to break across lines. Since this cannot be accommodated in PDF, it is set true only by default if the `pdftex` driver is used. This makes links on multiple lines into different PDF links to the same target.
debug	boolean	*false*	Extra diagnostic messages are printed in the log file.
extension	text		Set the file extension (for example, `dvi`), which will be appended to file links that are created if you use the `xr` package.
implicit	boolean	*true*	LaTeX internals are redefined to produce hypertext links.
linktocpage	boolean	*false*	Sets the table of contents hyperlinks to be on the page number not on the text of the entry.
nesting	boolean	*false*	Allows links to be nested; no drivers currently support this since neither HTML nor PDF allows it.
pageanchor	boolean	*true*	Determines whether every page is given an implicit anchor at the top left corner. If this option is turned off, `\tableofcontents` will not contain hyperlinks.
plainpages	boolean	*true*	Forces page anchors to be named by the Arabic form of the page number, rather than by the formatted form.
raiselinks	boolean	*true*	In the `hypertex` driver, the height of links is usually calculated by the driver simply as the baseline of contained text; this option forces `\special` commands to reflect the real height of the link (which could contain a graphic).

Table 2.6: Extension options

Option	Value	Default	Description
backref	boolean	*false*	Adds backlink text to the end of each item in the bibliography as a list of section numbers.
pagebackref	boolean	*false*	Adds backlink text to the end of each item in the bibliography as a list of page numbers.
hyperindex	boolean	*false*	Makes the text of index entries into hyperlinks. This is fairly fragile, and a serious project would need to implement its own scheme.
colorlinks	boolean	*false*	Colors the text of links and anchors. The colors chosen depend on the type of link. At present the types of link distinguished are citations, page references, URLs, local file references, and other links.
linkcolor	color	*red*	Color for simple internal links.
anchorcolor	color	*black*	Color for anchor text.
citecolor	color	*green*	Color for bibligraphical citations in text.
filecolor	color	*magenta*	Color for URLs that open *local* files.
menucolor	color	*red*	Color for Acrobat menu items.
pagecolor	color	*red*	Color for links to other pages.
urlcolor	color	*cyan*	Color for linked network URLs.

Table 2.7: PDF-specific display options

Option	Value	Default	Description
a4paper	boolean	*true*	Paper size is set to 210 mm × 297 mm.
a5paper	boolean	*false*	Paper size is set to 148 mm × 210 mm.
b5paper	boolean	*false*	Paper size is set to 176 mm × 250 mm.
letterpaper	boolean	*false*	Paper size is set to 8.5 in × 11 In.
legalpaper	boolean	*false*	Paper size is set to 8.5 in × 14 in.
executivepaper	boolean	*false*	Paper size is set to 7.25 in × 10.5 in.
bookmarks	boolean	*false*	Write a set of Acrobat bookmarks, in a manner similar to the table of contents, requiring two passes of LATEX.
bookmarksopen	boolean	*false*	If Acrobat bookmarks are requested, show them with all the subtrees expanded.
bookmarksnumbered	boolean	*false*	If Acrobat bookmarks are requested, include the section numbers.
pdfpagemode	name	*None*	Determine how the file is opened in Acrobat; the possibilities are None, UseThumbs (show thumbnails), UseOutlines (show bookmarks), and FullScreen. If no mode is explicitly chosen but the bookmarks option is set, UseOutlines is used.
pdfview	name *parameters*	*XYZ*	Set the PDF view for each link.

PDF-specific display options (*cont.*)

pdfstartpage	`name`	*1*	Set the page number on which the PDF file is opened.
pdfstartview	`name`	*Fit*	Set the initial page view.
pdfhighlight	`name`	*/I*	Determine how link buttons behave when selected. `/I` is for inverse (the default); the other possibilities are `/N` (no effect), `/O` (outline), and `/P` (inset highlighting).
citebordercolor	`RGB color`	*0 1 0*	The color of the box around citations.
filebordercolor	`RGB color`	*0 .5 .5*	The color of the box around links to files.
linkbordercolor	`RGB color`	*1 0 0*	The color of the box around simple links.
menubordercolor	`RGB color`	*1 0 0*	The color of the box around Acrobat menu links.
pagebordercolor	`RGB color`	*1 1 0*	The color of the box around links to pages.
urlbordercolor	`RGB color`	*0 1 1*	The color of the box around links to URLs.
pdfpagescrop	`n n n n`		Set the default PDF crop box for pages. This should be a set of four numbers, like a PostScript BoundingBox.
pdfborder		*0 0 1*	The style of box around links. Defaults to a box with lines of 1pt thickness, but the `colorlinks` option resets it to produce no border.
pdftoolbar	`boolean`	*false*	Determine whether the viewer's toolbar is visible when the document is opened.
pdfmenubar	`boolean`	*false*	Determine whether the viewer's menu bar is visible.
pdfwindowui	`boolean`	*false*	Determine whether the user interface elements in the document's window are visible.
pdffitwindow	`boolean`	*false*	Determine whether the viewer should resize the window displaying the document to fit the size of the first displayed page of the document.
pdfcenterwindow	`boolean`	*false*	Determine whether the viewer should position the window displaying the document in the center of the computer's monitor.
pdfpagelayout	`name`	*SinglePage*	The layout for the page when the document is opened. The possibilities are listed in Table 2.11 on page 66.
pdfnewwindow	`boolean`	*false*	Determine whether links that open another PDF file should start a new window or replace the contents of the current window with the new file.[11]

---

[11] Under Windows, the new window is placed in exactly the same place on the screen as the existing window. To make them both visible at the same time, you have to use the Window→Tile... menu item; then adjust the windows by hand with the mouse, or use Ctrl-Tab.

PDF-specific display options (*cont.*)

| pdfpagetransition | name | The effect used when going to a new page; the choices are listed in Table 2.12 on page 67. |

Table 2.8: PDF information options

Option	Value	Default	Description
baseurl	URL		Sets the base URL of the PDF document.
pdftitle	text		Sets the document information Title field.
pdfauthor	text		Sets the document information Author field.
pdfsubject	text		Sets the document information Subject field.
pdfcreator	text		Sets the document information Creator field.
pdfproducer	text		Sets the document information Producer field.
pdfkeywords	text		Sets the document information Keywords field.

Table 2.9: Form environment options

Option	Value	Default	Description
action	URL		The URL that will receive the form data if a Submit button is included in the form.
encoding	name		The way the string set to the URL is encoded; the norm is FDF-encoding, and html is the only valid value here.
method	name		Values can be post or get; this is used only when generating HTML (see [↪ HTML4], Section 17.3).

Table 2.10: Forms options

Option	Value	Default	Description
accesskey	key		(As per HTML)
align	number	0	Alignment within text field; 0 is left-aligned, 1 is centered, 2 is right-aligned.
backgroundcolor	RGB color	1 1 1	Color of field box.
bordercolor	RGB color	1 0 0	Color of border.
bordersep	dimen	1pt	Gap between field content and border.
borderstyle	name	S	Style of border; the choices are S (solid), D (dashed), B (beveled), I (inset), and U (underlined). For more details see Bienz et al. (1996), Section 6.6.1.
borderwidth	number	1	Width of box border (in points).
calculate			JavaScript code to calculate the value of the field.
charsize	dimen	10pt	Font size of field text.
checked	boolean	false	Whether option selected by default.

Forms options (cont.)

color	`RGB color`	*0 0 0*	Color of text in box.
combo	`boolean`	*false*	Whether choice list is combo style.
default			Default value for field
disabled	`boolean`	*false*	Whether field is disabled.
format			JavaScript code to format the entry.
height	`dimen`		Height of field box.
hidden	`boolean`	*false*	Whether field is hidden.
keystroke			JavaScript code to control the keystrokes on entry.
maxlen	`number`	*0*	Number of characters allowed in text field (0 means unlimited).
menulength	`number`	*4*	Number of elements shown in list.
multiline	`boolean`	*false*	Whether text box is multiline.
name	`name`		Name of field (defaults to the label contents).
onblur			JavaScript code.
onchange			JavaScript code.
onclick			JavaScript code.
ondblclick			JavaScript code.
onfocus			JavaScript code.
onkeydown			JavaScript code.
onkeypress			JavaScript code.
onkeyup			JavaScript code.
onmousedown			JavaScript code.
onmousemove			JavaScript code.
onmouseout			JavaScript code.
onmouseover			JavaScript code.
onmouseup			JavaScript code.
onselect			JavaScript code.
password	`boolean`	*false*	Whether text field is password style.
popdown	`boolean`	*false*	Whether choice list is pop-down style.
radio	`boolean`	*false*	Whether choice list is radio style.
readonly	`boolean`	*false*	Whether field is read only.
tabkey			(as per HTML)
validate			JavaScript code to validate the entry.
value			Initial value for field—not the same as the default.
width	`dimen`		Width of field box.

Table 2.11: Acrobat page layout display options

Name	Description
`SinglePage`	Display a single page.
`OneColumn`	Display pages in a column.
`TwoColumnLeft`	Display the pages in two columns, with odd-numbered pages on the left.
`TwoColumnRight`	Display the pages in two columns, with odd-numbered pages on the right.

Table 2.12: Acrobat page transition options

Name	Key(s)	Description
Split	/Dm, /M	Two lines sweep across the screen to show the new page; the lines can be either horizontal or vertical and can move from the center out or from the edges in.
Blinds	/Dm	Multiple lines, evenly distributed across the screen, appear and synchronously sweep in the same direction to reveal the new page. The lines are either horizontal or vertical.
Box	/M	A box sweeps from the center out or from the edges in.
Wipe	/Di	A single line sweeps across the screen from one edge to the other, revealing the new page image.
Dissolve		The page image dissolves in a piecemeal fashion to reveal the new page.
Glitter	/Di	Similar to Dissolve, except the effect sweeps across the image in a wide band moving from one side of the screen to the other.

The *Key(s)* dictate how the effect appears, for example `pdfpagetransition={Blinds /Dm /V}`

/Di   (Direction) The direction of movement, in degrees (counterclockwise). Values are generally in 90° steps.

/Dm   (Dimension) If a choice between horizontal or vertical is allowed, value is /H (horizontal) or /V (vertical).

/M   (Motion) If an effect can be from the center out or from the edges in, value is /I (in) or /O (out).

2.4   Generating PDF directly from TeX

The purpose of Hàn Thế Thành's pdfTeX project[12] was to create an extension of TeX that can create PDF directly from TeX source files and possibly actually enhance the result of TeX typesetting with the help of PDF. The pdfTeX program contains TeX as a subset: When PDF output is not selected, pdfTeX produces normal DVI output, otherwise it produces PDF output that looks identical to the DVI output. The next stage of the project is to investigate alternative justification algorithms, possibly making use of multiple master fonts. We will not, however, discuss that aspect of the program in this book.

The pdfTeX program is based on the original TeX sources and web2c and has been successfully compiled on UNIX, Macintosh, Amiga, Win32, and DOS systems.

2.4.1   Setting up pdfTeX

The pdfTeX program [↪ PDFTEXS] is distributed with many of the free TeX packages,[13] including MikTeX and fpTeX for Windows 32, teTeX for UNIX, CMacTeX

---

[12]We are grateful to Hàn Thế Thành for considerable help with this section.

[13]At the time of writing, none of the commercial TeX vendors have adopted pdfTeX, although MicroPress (VTEX) has its own direct PDF-generating TeX engine.

for Macintosh, and the general `web2c` system on which most of these packages are based.

In addition to the normal TEX fonts and macros, a pdfTEX distribution consists of the following items:

`pdftex.pool`   pool file, needed for creating formats;

`ttf2afm`   an external program to generate AFM files from TrueType fonts, needed to create TEX font metric files;

`pdftex.cfg`   pdfTEX configuration file (see Section 2.4.1.1); and

`map`   PostScript and TrueType font maps (see Section 2.4.1.3).

When pdfTEX is running, some extra search paths beyond those normally requested by TEX itself are used:

`VFFONTS`   the path where pdfTEX looks for virtual fonts;

`T1FONTS`   the path where pdfTEX looks for Type1 fonts;

`TTFONTS`   the path where pdfTEX looks for TrueType fonts;

`PKFONTS`   the path where pdfTEX looks for PK fonts; and

`TEXPSHEADERS` the path where pdfTEX looks for its configuration file (`pdftex.cfg`), font mapping files (`map`), encoding files (`enc`), and graphics files (see Section 2.4.2.3).

2.4.1.1   The pdfTEX configuration file

When pdfTEX starts, it reads a configuration file called `pdftex.cfg`, searched for in the `TEXPSHEADERS` path. Because `web2c` systems commonly specify a private tree for pdfTEX where configuration and map files are located, this allows individual users or projects to maintain customized versions of the configuration file. It also means that individual TEX input files need not set any pdfTEX-specific macros.

The configuration file is used to set default values for the following parameters, all of which can be overridden in the TEX source file:

output_format   Integer parameter specifying the output. A value greater than zero means PDF output, otherwise DVI output.

compress_level   Integer parameter specifying the level of text compression (using `zlib`). Zero means no compression, 1 means fastest, 9 means best, 2..8 means something in between.

decimal_digits   Integer parameter specifying the precision of real numbers in PDF code. Valid values are in the range 0..5. A higher value means more precise output, but it may also mean a larger size and more time taken to display or print. In most cases the optimal value is 2.

image_resolution Integer parameter specifying the default resolution of bitmap image files that contain no resolution information.

page_width, page_height Dimension parameters specifying the page width and page height of PDF output. If not specified, then page width is calculated by taking the width of the box being shipped out and adding 2 × (horigin + \hoffset). The page height is calculated in a similar way.

horigin, vorigin Dimension parameters specifying the offset of the TEX output box from the top left corner of the "paper."

map The name of the font mapping file (similar to those used by many DVI to PostScript drivers); more than one map file can be specified, using multiple map lines. If the name of the map file is prefixed with a +, its values are appended to the existing set, otherwise they replace it. If no map files are given, a default file psfonts.map is searched for.

A typical pdftex.cfg file looks like the following. It sets up output for A4 paper size and the standard TEX offset of 1 inch, and loads two map files for fonts.

```
output_format 1
compress_level 0
decimal_digits 2
page_width 210mm
page_height 297mm
horigin 1in
vorigin 1in
map standard.map
map +cm.map
```

2.4.1.2 Setting up fonts

The pdfTEX program normally works with Type 1 and TrueType fonts; a source must be available for all fonts used in the document, except for the 14 base fonts supplied by Acrobat (the Times, Helvetica, Courier, Symbol, and Dingbats families). It is possible to use METAFONT generated fonts in pdfTEX. It is strongly recommended, however, not to do so if an equivalent is available in Type 1 or True-Type format, since the resulting Type 3 fonts render very poorly in current versions of Acrobat. Given the free availability of Type 1 versions of all the Computer Modern fonts and the ability to use standard PostScript fonts without further ado, this is not usually a problem.

2.4.1.3 Map files

The pdfTEX program reads *map files* specified in the *configuration file* (see Section 2.4.1.1), in which reencoding and partial downloading for each font are specified. Every font needed must be listed, each on a separate line, apart from PK fonts.

The syntax of each line is similiar to the `dvips` map files[14] and can contain up to six space-separated fields: *texname*, *basename*, *fontflags*, *fontfile*, *encoding*, and *special*. The only mandatory field is *texname*, and it must be the first field. The rest of the fields are optional, but if *basename* is given, it must be the second field. Similarly, if *fontflags* is given, it must be the third field (if *basename* is present) or the second field (if *basename* is left out). It is possible to vary the positions of *fontfile*, *encodingfile*, and *special*, but the first three fields must be given in fixed order.

texname: the name TEX uses, that is, the name of the TFM file. This must be present.

basename: the PostScript font name. If not given, then it will be taken from the font file. Specifying a name that does not match the name in the font file will cause pdfTEX to produce a warning, so it would be best not to use this field if the font resource is available (this is the most common case). This option is primarily intended for use of base fonts and for compatibility with `dvips` map files.

fontflags: flags specifying some characteristics of the font. The following description is taken (with some modification) from the PDF specification (Bienz et al. (1996)), Section 7.9.2 (Font descriptor flags).

The value of the Flags key in a font descriptor is a 32-bit integer that contains a collection of Boolean attributes. These attributes are true if the corresponding bit is set to 1 in the integer. The following specifies the meanings of the bits, with bit 1 being the least significant. Reserved bits must be set to zero.

Bit position	Semantics	Sample
1	Fixed-width font	`Sample Text`
2	Serif font	Sample Text
3	Symbolic font	
4	Script font	*SAMPLE TEXT*
5	Reserved	
6	Uses the Adobe Standard Roman Character Set	
7	Italic	*Sample Text*
8–16	Reserved	
17	All-cap font	SAMPLE TEXT
18	Small-cap font	SAMPLE TEXT
19	Force bold at small text sizes	
20–32	Reserved	

All characters in a fixed-width font have the same width, while characters in a proportional font have different widths. Characters in a serif font have short strokes drawn

---

[14]Most `dvips` map files can be shared with pdfTEX without problems.

at an angle on the top and bottom of character stems, while sans serif fonts do not have such strokes. A symbolic font contains symbols rather than letters and numbers. Characters in a script font resemble cursive handwriting. An all-cap font, typically used for display purposes such as titles or headlines, contains no lowercase letters. It differs from a small-cap font in that characters in the latter, while also capital letters, have been sized and their proportions adjusted so that they have the same size and stroke weight as lowercase characters in the same typeface family.

Bit 6 in the flags field indicates that the font's character set is the Adobe Standard Roman Character Set, or a subset of that, and that it uses the standard names for those characters.

Finally, bit 19 is used to determine whether bold characters are drawn with extra pixels even at very small text sizes. Typically when characters are drawn at small sizes on very low resolution devices such as display screens, features of bold characters may appear only one pixel wide. Because this is the minimum feature width on a pixel-based device, ordinary nonbold characters also appear with one-pixel-wide features and cannot be distinguished from bold characters. If bit 19 is set, features of bold characters may be thickened at small text sizes.

If no font flags are given, pdfTₑX treats the font as 3, a symbol font. If we do not know the correct value, it would be best not to provide one; specifying a wrong value of the font flags may cause Acrobat some problems.

fontfile: the name of the font source file. This must be a Type 1 or TrueType font file. The font file name can be preceded by one or two special characters that say how the font file should be handled.

- If it is preceded by a <, then the font file will be *partially downloaded*, meaning that just those glyphs (characters) used in the document are extracted and put into a new subset font, which is then embedded in the output. This is the most common use and is *strongly recommended* for any font, as it ensures portability and reduces the size of the PDF output.

- If the font file name is preceded by a double <<, the whole font file will be included—all glyphs of the font are embedded, including the ones that are not used in the document. Apart from increasing the size of the PDF file, this option may cause problems with TrueType fonts too, so it is not recommended. It is useful in cases where the font is somehow strange and cannot be subsetted properly by pdfTₑX.

- If no character precedes the font file name, the font file is read, but nothing is embedded. Only the font parameters are extracted to generate a font descriptor that is used by Acrobat to simulate the font if needed. This option is useful when we do not want to embed the font (that is, to reduce the output size) but do wish to use the font metrics and let Acrobat generate an instance that looks close to the original font, provided that resource is not installed on the system where the PDF output is viewed or printed. To use this feature, the font flags *must* be specified and have bit 6 set on, meaning that only fonts with the Adobe Standard Roman Character Set can be simulated. The only exception is the Adobe Symbol font, which is not very useful.

- If the font file name is preceded by a !, the font is not read at all and is assumed to be available on the target system. This option can be used to create PDF files that do not contain any embedded fonts. The PDF output then works only on systems where the font is available. It is not very useful for document exchange, because the file is not portable. On the other hand, it is very useful when we wish to speed up the running of pdfTeX while testing a document. This feature requires Acrobat to have access to all the installed fonts, including those that are only in the TeX support tree.

Note that the standard 14 fonts are never embedded, even if they are marked for download in map files.

encoding: name of a file containing an encoding vector to be used for the font. The file name may be preceded by a <, but the effect is the same. The format of the encoding vector is identical to that used by `dvips` (see Goossens et al. (1997), Section 11.2.4). If no encoding is specified, the font's built-in default encoding is used. It may be omitted if we are sure that the font resource has the correct built-in encoding. In general, this latter option is highly preferred and is *required* to subset TrueType fonts.

special: special instruction for font transformation as for `dvips`. Only specifications of `SlantFont` and `ExtendFont` are read; other instructions are ignored.

If pdfTeX cannot locate a font in a map file, it will look first for a source with the extension `pgc`, a PGC source (PDF Glyph Container).[15] If no PGC source is available, pdfTeX will try to use PK fonts in the same way as normal DVI drivers.

Lines containing nothing apart from *texname* indicate that a scalable Type 3 font should be used. For font types as Type 1, TrueType, and scalable Type 3, all requests for the font at any size will be provided by just one font in the PDF output. Thus if a font, for example, `csr10`, is listed in a map file, it will be treated as scalable. The font `csr10` will be downloaded only once for `csr10`, `csr10 at 12pt`, etc.

It does not hurt much if a scalable Type 3 font is not listed in a map file, except that the font source will be downloaded multiple times for different sizes, meaning the PDF output is larger. On the other hand, if a font is listed in a map file as scalable Type 3 and its PGC source is not scalable or not available (in this case pdfTeX will use PK fonts instead), the PDF output will be valid. However, some fonts may look ugly because bitmaps will be scaled.

---

[15] This is a text file containing a PDF Type 3 font, usually created using METAPOST with some utilities by Hans Hagen. In general, PGC files can contain whatever is allowed in a PDF page description to support fonts. At present PGC fonts are not very useful, since vector Type 3 fonts are not displayed very well in Acrobat. They may be more useful when Type 3 font handling gets better.

Some sample map file entries

Use a built-in font with font-specific encoding, that is, neither a downloaded font
nor an external encoding is given. SlantFont is specified in the same way as for
dvips.

```
psyr        Symbol
psyro       Symbol              ".167 SlantFont"
```

Use a built-in font with an external encoding (8r.enc). The < preceding the
encoding file name may be omitted.

```
ptmri8r     Times-Italic    <8r.enc
ptmro8r     Times-Roman     <8r.enc   ".167 SlantFont"
```

Use a partially downloaded font with an external encoding:

```
putr8r      Utopia-Regular  <8r.enc <putr8a.pfb
putro8r     Utopia-Regular  <8r.enc <putr8a.pfb      ".167 SlantFont"
```

Use the Type 1 font name taken from the downloaded font itself:

```
logo8       <logo8.pfb
```

Adjust the width but not the stroke thickness:

```
logod10          logobf10        <logobf10.pfb   ".913 ExtendFont"
```

Use entire downloaded font without reencoding:

```
pgsr8r GillSans <<pgsr8a.pfb
```

Use partially downloaded font without reencoding:

```
pgsr8r GillSans <pgsr8a.pfb
```

Do not read the font at all—the font must be available on the target system:

```
pgsr8r GillSans !pgsr8a.pfb
```

Use an entire downloaded font with reencoding:

```
pgsr8r GillSans <<pgsr8a.pfb 8r.enc
```

Use a partially downloaded font with reencoding:

```
pgsr8r GillSans <pgsr8a.pfb 8r.enc
```

Do not include the font, but extract parameters from the font file and reencode:[16]

```
pgsr8r GillSans 32 pgsr8a.pfb 8r.enc
```

Use a TrueType font in the same way as a Type 1 font:

```
verdana8r Verdana  <verdana.ttf 8r.enc
```

2.4.1.4 TrueType fonts

As we have seen, pdfTEX can work with TrueType fonts, and adding the font names to map files is straightforward. The only extra task for TrueType fonts is to create TFM font metric files. There is a program, ttf2afm, in pdfTEX distributions that can be used to extract AFM font metrics from TrueType fonts. Usage is simple:

```
ttf2afm ttf-file [encoding]
```

The name of the TrueType font file is *ttf-file*, and the optional *encoding* specifies an encoding file, which is the same as those used in map files for pdfTEX and dvips. If the encoding is not given, all the glyphs in the AFM output will be mapped to /.notdef. The ttf2afm program writes the output AFM to standard output. From this we can make a TFM from the AFM file (Goossens et al. (1997, Section 10.5)). If we need to know which glyphs are available in the font, we can run ttf2afm without encoding to get all the glyph names.

To use a new TrueType font (times.ttf), the minimal steps (assuming that test.map is included in pdftex.cfg) on a UNIX system might be

```
ttf2afm times.ttf 8r.enc >times.afm
afm2tfm times.afm -T 8r.enc
echo "times TimesNewRomanPSMT <times.ttf <8r.enc" >>test.map
```

The PostScript font name, TimesNewRomanPSMT, is reported by afm2tfm but is not strictly needed in the pdfTEX map file.

ExtendFont and SlantFont also work for TrueType fonts.

2.4.2 New primitives

The pdfTEX program adds a set of new primitives to TEX; they are described in the following sections, and allow the user access to features of the PDF format.

---

[16]This only works for fonts with Adobe Standard Encoding. The font flags say what this font is like, so Acrobat can generate a similar instance if the font resource is not available on the target system.

2.4.2.1   Document setup

```
\pdfoutput=n
```

This integer parameter specifies whether the output format should be DVI or PDF. A value greater than zero means PDF output, otherwise DVI output. This parameter cannot be specified *after* shipping out the first page. In other words, it must be set before pdfTeX ships out the first page if we want PDF output. This is the only parameter that must be set to produce PDF output; all other parameters are optional.

```
\pdfcompresslevel=n
```

This integer parameter specifies the level of text compression via zlib. Zero means no compression, 1 means fastest, 9 means best, 2..8 means something in between. A value out of this range will be adjusted to the nearest meaningful value.

```
\pdfpagewidth=dimen
```

```
\pdfpageheight=dimen
```

These dimension parameters specify the page width and page height of PDF output. If they are not given, the page dimensions will be calculated as described in Section 2.4.1.1.

```
\pdfpagesattr={tokens}
```

This token list parameter specifies optional attributes for every page of the PDF output file. These attributes can be MediaBox (rectangle specifying the natural size of the page), CropBox (rectangle specifying the region of the page being displayed and printed), and Rotate (number of degrees the page should be rotated clockwise when it is displayed or printed—must be 0 or a multiple of 90).

```
\pdfpageattr={tokens}
```

This is similiar to \pdfpagesattr, but it takes priority over it. It can be used to overwrite any attributes given by \pdfpagesattr for individual pages.

2.4.2.2   The document information and catalog

```
\pdfinfo{info keys}
```

This allows the user to add information to the document info section; if this is provided, it can be seen in Acrobat Reader with the menu option File↝ Document Info↝ General. The *info keys* parameter is a set of data pairs (a key, and a value). The key names are preceded by a /, and the values are in parentheses; all keys are optional. The possible keys are /Author, /CreationDate (defaults to current date), /ModDate, /Creator (defaults to "TeX"), /Producer (defaults to "pdfTeX"), /Title, /Subject, and /Keywords.

/CreationDate and /ModDate are expressed in the form D:YYYYMMDDhhmmss, where YYYY is the year, MM is the month, DD is the day, hh is the hour, mm is the minutes, and ss is the seconds.

Multiple uses of \pdfinfo are permitted; if a key is given more than once, the first appearance will take priority. An example of the use of \pdfinfo follows:

```
\PDFinfo{
    /Title (example.pdf)
    /Creator (TeX)
    /Producer (pdfTeX)
    /Author (Tom and Jerry)
    /CreationDate (D:19980212201000)
    /ModDate (D:19980212201000)
    /Subject (Example)
    /Keywords (cat;mouse)
}
```

> \pdfcatalog{*catalog keys*} openaction {*action*}

The document catalog is similar to the document info section, and the available keys are /URI, which provides the base URL of the document, and /PageMode, which determines how Acrobat displays the document on startup. The possibilities for the latter are:

/UseNone	Open document with neither outlines nor thumbnails visible.
/UseOutlines	Open document with outlines visible.
/UseThumbs	Open document with thumbnails visible.
/FullScreen	Open document in full-screen mode. In full-screen mode, there are no menu bar, window controls, or any other window present.

The default is /UseNone.

The *action* is the action to be taken when opening the document; it is specified in the same way as for internal links (see Section 2.4.2.6), for example goto page 3 {/Fit}.

2.4.2.3 Graphics inclusion

> \pdfimage width *width* height *height* depth *depth* {*filename*}

Insert an image, optionally changing the width, height, depth, or any combination of these attributes. The default values are zero for depth and the image's natural size for height and width. If all of them are given, the image will be resized to fit the specified values. If some of them (but not all) are given, the rest will be scaled proportionally to keep the aspect ratio the same as that of the natural size. If none of them is given, then the image will be set at its natural size. The dimension of the image can be accessed by putting the \pdfimage command into a TEX box and checking the dimensions of that box.

The image type is determined by the extension of the file name. Thus png means PNG format and pdf means it is a PDF file; otherwise, the image is treated as JPEG.

> \pdfimageresolution=*resolution*

If the image is a bitmap file and contains resolution information, then that is used; otherwise, \pdfimageresolution can be used to specify it. The default is 72 dpi.

> \pdffontprefix{*prefix string*}
> \pdfimageprefix{*prefix string*}
> \pdfformprefix{*prefix string*}

Sometimes there are problems including a PDF file as an illustration, because of conflicts in fonts, image names or PDF form objects. These three commands allow you to change the default prefixes for names. So if an included PDF file has a font resource named /F34, and you find it conflicts with an /F34 in the current file, you can use \pdffontprefix to name it, for example, /FF34. Using these commands is recommended only for experts.

2.4.2.4 XObject Forms

> \pdfform *number*

writes out the TEX box *number* as an XObject Form to the PDF file.

> \pdflastform

returns the object number of the last XObject Form written to the PDF file

> \pdfrefform *name*

puts in a reference to the XObject Form called \name.

These macros support "object reuse" in pdfTEX. The content of the XObject Form object corresponds to the content of a TEX box, which can contain text, pictures, and references to other XObject Form objects. The XObject Form can be used by simply referring to its object number. This can be useful in a large document with a lot of similar elements, since it avoids the duplication of identical objects. A common example is a document style that places an identical graphic or text in the header of every page.

2.4.2.5 Annotations

> `\pdfannot width` *width* `height` *height* `depth` *depth* `{text}`

attaches an annotation at the current point in the text. The annotation content will be raw PDF code, as specified in *text*.

> `\pdflastannot`

returns the object number of last annotation created by `\pdfannot`. These two primitives allow the user to create any annotation that cannot be created by `\pdfannotlink` (see following).

2.4.2.6 Destinations and links

> `\pdfdest ⟨ num {`*num*`} | name {`*name*`} ⟩` *appearance*

establishes a destination for links and bookmark outlines. The link must be identified by either a *number* or a symbolic *refname* and the way Acrobat is to display the page must be specified. *Appearance* must be one of the following:

fit	fit whole page in window
fith	fit whole width of page
fitv	fit whole height of page
fitb	fit whole Bounding Box page
fitbh	fit whole width of Bounding Box of page
fitbv	fit whole height of Bounding Box of page
xyz	keep current zoom factor

xyz can optionally be followed by `zoom` *factor* to provide a fixed zoom-in. The *factor* is like TeX magnification; that is, 1000 is the "normal" page view.

> `\pdfannotlink` *height* `{`*height*`}` *depth* `{`*depth*`}` *attr* `{`*attr*`}` *action*

starts a hypertext link. If the optional dimensions are not specified, they will be calculated from the box containing the link. The *attributes* (explained in great detail in Section 6.6 of the PDF manual) determine the appearance of the link. Typically they are used to specify the color and thickness of any border around the link. Thus `/C [0.9 0 0] /Border [0 0 2]` specifies a color (in RGB) of bright red and a border thickness of 2 points.

The *action* can do many things; some of the possibilities are listed in Table 2.13.

> `\pdfendlink`

ends a link; all text between `\pdfannotlink` and `\pdfendlink` will be treated as part of this link. The pdfTeX program may break the result across lines (or pages),

Table 2.13: PDF link actions

Action	Effect
page *n*	Jump to page *n*.
goto num *number*	
goto name *{refname}*	Jump to a point established as *number* or *name* with \pdfdest.
goto file *{filename}*	Open a local file; this can be used with a *refname* or *number* specification to point to a specific location on the file. For example, `goto file{foo.pdf} name{intro}`, opens `foo.pdf` at the destination *intro*.
thread num *{number}*	
thread name *{refname}*	Jump to thread identified by *number* or *refname*.
user *{spec}*	Perform user-specified action. Section 6.9 of the PDF manual explains the possibilities. A typical use of this is to specify a URL, for example, `/S /URI /URI (http://www.tug.org/)`

in which case it will make several links with the same content.

2.4.2.7   Bookmarks

```
\pdfoutline action count {count} {text}
```

creates an outline (or bookmark) entry. The first parameter specifies the action to be taken and is the same as that allowed for \pdfannotlink. The *count* specifies the number of direct subentries under this entry; it is zero if this entry has no subentries (in which case it may be omitted). If the number is negative, then all subentries will be closed, and the absolute value of this number specifies the number of subentries. The *text* is what will be shown in the outline window; note that this is limited to characters in the PDFDocEncoding vector.

2.4.2.8   Article threads

```
\pdfthread num {num} name {name}
```

starts an article thread. The corresponding \pdfendthread must be in the box in the same depth as the box containing \pdfthread. All boxes in this depth level will be treated as part of this thread. An identifier (*number* or *refname*) must be specified; threads with the same identifier will be joined together.

```
\pdfendthread
```

finishes the current thread.

> `\pdfthreadhoffset=`*dimen*

> `\pdfthreadvoffset=`*dimen*

specify thread margins.

2.4.2.9 Miscellaneous

> `\pdfliteral{`*pdf text*`}`

Like `\special` in normal TEX, this command inserts raw PDF code into the output. It allows support of color and text transformation and is used in the standard graphics package's `pdftex` driver.

> `\pdfnames{`*data*`}`

puts *data* in the names dictionary in the catalog.

> `\pdfobj` *stream* `{`*text*`}`

is similar to `\pdfliteral`, but the text is inserted as contents of an object. If the optional keyword *stream* is given, the contents will be inserted as a stream.

> `\pdflastobj`

returns the object number of the last object created by `\pdfobj`. These primitives provide a mechanism allowing insertion of a user-defined object in PDF output.

> `\pdftexversion`

returns the version of pdfTEX multiplied by 100; for example, for version `0.13b` it returns 13.

> `\pdftexrevision`

returns the revision of pdfTEX; for example, for version `0.13b` it returns `b`.

2.4.3 Graphics and color

The pdfTEX program supports inclusion of pictures in PNG, JPEG, and PDF format. The most common technique—the inclusion of Encapsulated PostScript figures—is replaced by PDF inclusion. EPS files can be converted to PDF by Ghostscript, Acrobat Distiller, or other PostScript-to-PDF convertors. The bounding box of a PDF file is taken from the `CropBox` if available, otherwise from `MediaBox`. To get the right `MediaBox`, it is necessary to transform the EPS file before conversion so that the start point is at the (0,0) coordinate and the page size is set exactly corresponding to the BoundingBox. A Perl script [↪EPSTOPDF] for this purpose has been written by Sebastian Rahtz.

Other alternatives for graphics in pdfTEX are

- LATEX picture mode   Since this is implemented simply in terms of font characters, it works in exactly the same way as usual.

- XY-pic   If the PostScript back-end is not requested, XY-pic uses its own Type 1 fonts and needs no special attention.

- tpic   The tpic \special commands (used in some macro packages) can be redefined to produce literal PDF, using macros by Hans Hagen.

- METAPOST   Although the output of METAPOST is PostScript, it is in a highly simplified form, and a METAPOST-to-PDF conversion (written by Hans Hagen and Tanmoy Bhattacharya) is implemented as a set of macros that read METAPOST output and support all of its features. The type mps is supported by the LATEX graphics package for this purpose.

The last two macro files are part of the ConTEXT macro package (supp-pdf.tex and supp-mis.tex), but they also work with LATEX and are available separately.

The inclusion of raw PostScript commands—the technique utilized by the pstricks package (Goossens et al. (1997), Chapter 4)—cannot be supported.[17] Although PDF is a direct descendant of PostScript, it lacks any programming language commands and cannot deal with arbitrary PostScript.

The standard LATEX graphics and color packages have pdftex options, which allow use of normal color, text rotation, and graphics inclusion commands. The implementation of graphics inclusion makes sure that however often a graphic is used (even if it is used at different scales or transformed in different ways), it is embedded only once.

A number of samples of pdfTEX output can be found on the TUG Web server [↪PDFTEXFX].

---

[17]This technique *can* be used with MicroPress' VTEX, which has a built-in PostScript interpreter.

CHAPTER 3

The LaTeX2HTML translator

In this chapter we take a closer look at the LaTeX2HTML translator. It uses Larry Wall's Perl language, together with other publicly available tools, to interpret LaTeX source code and translate it into hyperdocuments for viewing on the Web.

After a short historic overview and a reminder of the basic principles of generating documents for the Web, we turn our attention to the various components of the system—highlighting installation, customization, and extension mechanisms. Support for mathematics in HTML is almost absent, hence we discuss in detail three basic math modes of LaTeX2HTML and its extensions to optimize the display of mathematics on the Web. Then we go on to see how LaTeX2HTML handles non-English source documents, dealing with the translation of title and keywords, various encodings, special fonts, preprocessors, and so on. Last, but not least, we describe how you can use LaTeX2HTML as a real hypertext production tool for LaTeX sources by using extensions defined in the html package.

3.1 Introduction

LaTeX, based on the TeX typesetting system, has more extensive capabilities than most word-processing software. Its principal documentation (Lamport (1994)) presents LaTeX as a "Document Preparation System." Similarly, LaTeX2HTML is much more than a *Save As HTML* option for LaTeX; it is better described as a "Web Document Preparation System."

LaTeX2HTML is free software, distributed under the GNU Public Licence. For the examples in this chapter we used version 99.1. It runs under Linux, OS/2, Windows NT, Windows 95, and DOS, as well as most flavors of UNIX, for which it was initially developed.

By default the HTML pages produced conform to the HTML 3.2 specification. Thus the pages are readable in browsers that implement this or the more recent HTML 4.0 specification. If necessary, one can instead choose to produce pages that conform to HTML 2.0. This restriction uses images for the more complicated LaTeX environments, such as tables and alignments within mathematics. Alternatively one can choose to generate extra CLASS and ID attributes according to the HTML 4.0 specification. They allow style sheet information to be associated with particular environment types, or even with specific instances of environments, paragraphs, and snippets of text. Furthermore, a large number of European languages and dialects are supported, with LANG attributes being generated, for HTML 4.0, when several languages are used in a single document.

LaTeX2HTML is written in Larry Wall's Perl language (Wall et al. (1996)), so that in principle LaTeX2HTML runs on every system on which Perl has been installed, although some other software tools are needed before LaTeX2HTML can initiate a translation. Like LaTeX, Perl and these other software applications are publicly available. Most of them probably came with the operating system when you bought your machine, were installed by the system manager on clustered PCs, or are readily available on CD-ROM for almost all computer platforms. Missing components can be easily obtained via the Web, as explained in Section 3.2.

3.1.1   A few words on history

Initial development of LaTeX2HTML was done by Nikos Drakos. In 1995 Drakos released his program to the Internet community, via the LaTeX2HTML mailing list [↪L2HLIST]. Toward the end of 1996 a repository for use by developers was established at the University of Darmstadt in Germany. Since then many individuals have contributed code, provided optimizations for various platforms, worked on portability, and improved installation procedures. Many of these developments have been in direct response to requests received via the mailing list, to support particular LaTeX commands and packages.

Documentation, support for LaTeX packages, strategies for image generation and extensions for the latest HTML specifications, and overall coordination have been handled mainly by Ross Moore.[1]

3.1.2   Principles for Web document generation

From the earliest days of its development, the World Wide Web was recognized as a means whereby highly technical, structured information could become more

---

[1] A full list of contributors can be found in the LaTeX2HTML Users Guide.

easily accessible. TEX and LATEX are used primarily with technical fields, where the data itself has far more importance than the way in which it is presented. Thus it is a natural setting for a translation tool aimed at presenting structured data in a way that is both readable and exploits the structure for easy navigation.

The first versions of LATEX2HTML were developed by Nikos Drakos to take advantage of the newly emerging World Wide Web that could be used for computer-based learning and education. The information to be presented was always of foremost importance. Drakos also recognized the need for easy navigation through the presented information in ways that mesh with its logical structure. He listed several principles that he considered necessary for any serious software to generate Web documents [↪DRAKOSWWW]:

1. automatic creation of structure-based hypertext webs;

2. flexibility in specifying the desired node granularity;

3. automatic generation of navigation aids; and

4. inclusion of highly formatted information such as figures, tables, mathematical equations, diagrams, chemical formulae, and exotic languages.

Based on these principles, the earliest versions of LATEX2HTML were quite effective, even with just the limited capabilities of the early versions of HTML [↪HTML2SPEC]. With extensions introduced by later HTML specifications, these principles have been retained within the design of the LATEX2HTML translator; indeed, they have been firmly embraced and extended. Now all the environments that are commonly used for paper documents using LATEX are converted automatically into HTML structures and markup, giving the highest-quality results that can be reasonably achieved with a designated version of HTML.

Principle 1 is, of course, the main goal of a conversion tool like LATEX2HTML. Principle 2 is implemented using configuration variables and command-line options that are described in detail in the LATEX2HTML Users Guide (Drakos and Moore (1998)). Examples are the $MAX_SPLIT_DEPTH and $MAX_LINK_DEPTH variables and -link and -split options (see Sections 3.2.3.2 and 3.2.3.3).

A clear instance of principle 3 (and, of course, principle 1) is the example in Section 3.2.1 where we show how a LATEX source file is automatically translated by LATEX2HTML into a hyperlinked web of HTML files, with navigation aids to move around easily.

The present chapter contains many examples that illustrate how LATEX2HTML copes with principle 4, mainly for presenting mathematics, which is indeed highly structured. Many of the techniques applicable to mathematics apply in other situations as well. We will see that LATEX2HTML is more than just a translation tool. Using packages, configuration variables, and command-line options, we will see how the information in the same LATEX source can be presented as a collection of HTML pages in different ways. A specific translation can be tailored to suit considerations such as the version of HTML, capabilities of specific browsers, download times for the intended audience, and a document's relation to other Web pages.

Documents can be constructed using "conditional code," allowing the best results for both the paper version, typeset with LATEX, and the HTML version, prepared using LATEX2HTML. These capabilities justify the designation of LATEX2HTML as a genuine "Web Document Preparation System."

Another important application of principle 4 is presenting languages using exotic alphabets and scripts. Transliteration schemes are frequently used to express the languages used on the Indian subcontinent in a way that can be transmitted by computers. There are various pieces of preprocessing software that convert text coded via transliteration schemes into source suitable for typesetting using TEX and LATEX, exploiting special fonts. Several of these are supported in a fully automatic way by LATEX2HTML.

Not so much envisioned by Drakos at the beginning, but an important aspect of LATEX2HTML today, is using it as a tool for creating hypertext documents. Therefore, LATEX2HTML comes with a macro package called `html.sty`, which contains markup extensions in the form of new HTML-related commands and environments (see Section 3.5).

3.2   Required software and customization

The latest LATEX2HTML software can be obtained from several distribution sites; the main ones are in California [↪L2HSA], Germany [↪L2HSC], and the CTAN archives [↪L2HCTAN]. Development versions can be found at the developers' site [↪CVSREPOS]. Distributed versions are named `latex2html-yy_vv.tar.gz`, where yy corresponds to the year, and vv to the version. For instance, in spring 1999 the file `latex2html-99_1.tar.gz` was the latest distributed version.

The following list provides other pieces of software required for a standard LATEX2HTML installation. These are *not* provided as part of the distribution and *must* be obtained separately.

Perl   Version 5 (5.003 or later on some platforms) is required. LATEX2HTML also needs the database management module. See www.perl.com [↪PERL] for all things Perl, including how to update to the latest version.

LATEX   When HTML is not sufficient for an adequate representation of some portion of the information, an image is created. Typesetting that piece of source using LATEX is the first step in the process of producing this image.

dvips   Converts DVI output from LATEX into a set of PostScript files.

Ghostscript   Interprets the PostScript files, rendering them as images using a high-quality bitmapped format. At the least version 4.02 is required to allow LATEX2HTML to produce good-quality "anti-aliased" images. For the latest version, consult the Ghostscript Home Page [↪GSHOME].

netpbm   Suite of graphics utilities. Each performs a task in the processing of a graphic image, such as cropping, background transparency, rotation, color reduction, interlacing, and conversion to a specific output format. Get the archive from the X Windows FTP site [↪NETPBM].

Other utilities   For special purposes, such as processing transliterations of Indic scripts, LATEX2HTML has special support available for preprocessors.

The scripted nature of LATEX2HTML means that it has great flexibility. It is a basic principle in its continuing development to make use of software that already exists for specialized tasks. The tools just listed have the added advantage of being available at no cost. Other tools could be used, for instance, for graphics processing.

It is straighforward to write Perl code to make a new piece of software that performs a vital task better, faster, or simply in a different way. Incorporating other software to work with LATEX2HTML amounts to the following tasks:

1. Recognize which parts of the document source constitute information that needs to be processed using the new software.

2. Extract this information and cast it into a form suitable for input to the specialized software.

3. Prepare the correct command line to launch the software application for processing the requisite information.

4. Include its output into the HTML pages being constructed, either as tagged text or as hyperlinks to external files such as graphic images. Some postprocessing may be required.

The Perl programming language is well suited to performing these tasks. Its sophisticated pattern-matching abilities are ideal for recognizing particular forms of information contained within a larger document.

3.2.1   Running LATEX2HTML on a LATEX document

To process a document written for LATEX using LATEX2HTML, it is usually sufficient to issue a command such as the following. The extension .tex is optional.

```
latex2html <filename>[.tex]
```

Multiple files can be processed with a single command, using command-line options to specify where the resulting HTML pages are to be located and how they should be hyperlinked:

```
latex2html <options> file1 file2 file3
```

```
1   \documentclass{article}
2   \usepackage{graphicx}
3   \usepackage{francais}
4   \usepackage{makeidx}
5   \newcommand{\Lcs}[1]{\texttt{\symbol{'134}#1}}
6   \makeindex
7   \title{Exemple d'un article en fran\c{c}ais}
8   \author{Michel Goossens}
9   \begin{document}
10  \maketitle
11  \tableofcontents
12  \listoffigures
13  \listoftables
14  \section{Une figure EPS}
15  \index{section}
16  Cette section montre comment inclure une figure PostScript\cite{bib-PS}
17  dans un document \LaTeX. La figure~\ref{Fpsfig}
18  est ins\'er\'ee dans le texte \'a l'aide de la commande
19  \verb!\includegraphics{colorcir.eps}!.
20  \index{figure}
21  \index{PostScript}
22  \begin{figure}
23   \begin{center}
24    \begin{tabular}{c@{\qquad}c}
25     \includegraphics[width=3cm]{colorcir} &
26     \includegraphics[width=3cm]{tac2dim}
27    \end{tabular}
28   \end{center}
29   \caption{Deux images EPS}
30   \label{Fpsfig}
31  \end{figure}
32
33  \section{Exemple d'un tableau}
34
35  Le tableau~\ref{tab:exa} \'a la page \pageref{tab:exa}
36  montre l'utilisation de l'environnement \texttt{table}.
37
38  \begin{table}
39   \begin{center}
40    \begin{tabular}{cccccc}
41     \Lcs{primo}  & \primo & \Lcs{secundo} & \secundo & \Lcs{tertio} & \tertio \\
42     \Lcs{quatro} & \quatro& 1\Lcs{ier}    & 1\ier    & 1\Lcs{iere}  & 1\iere  \\
43     \Lcs{fprimo)}&\fprimo)& \Lcs{No} 10   & \No 10   & \Lcs{no} 15  & \no 15  \\
44     \Lcs{og} a \Lcs{fg}&\og a \fg&3\Lcs{ieme}&3\ieme & 10\Lcs{iemes}& 10\iemes
45    \end{tabular}
46   \end{center}
47   \caption{Quelques commandes de l'option \texttt{francais} de \texttt{babel}}
48   \label{tab:exa}
49   \index{tableau}
50  \end{table}
51
52  \begin{thebibliography}{99}
53  \index{r\'ef\'erences}
54  \bibitem{bib-PS}
55  Adobe Inc.
56  \emph{PostScript, manuel de r\'ef\'erence (2\ieme \'edition)}
57  Inter\'Editions (France), 1992
58  \end{thebibliography}
59  \printindex
60  \index{index}
61  \end{document}
```

Figure 3.1: Example LᴬTEX source file to be translated by LᴬTEX2HTML

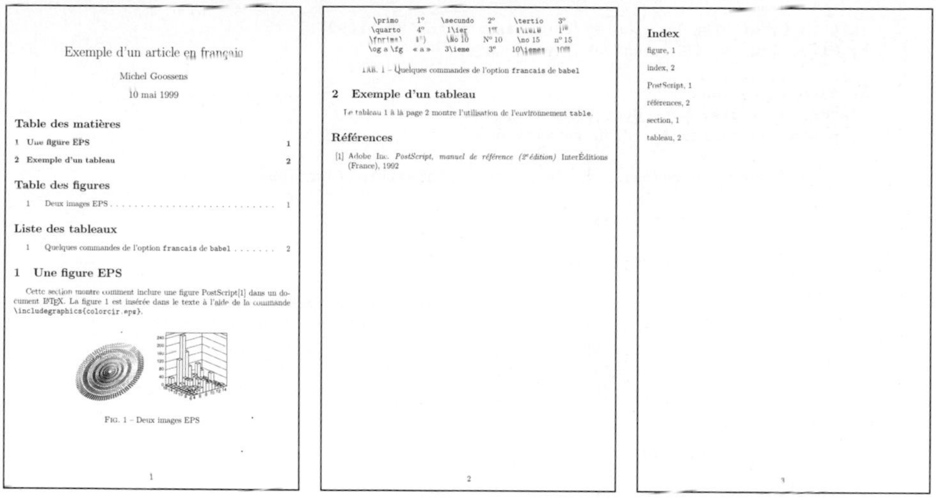

Figure 3.2: Formatted PostScript output of example file shown in Figure 3.1

To show how simple it is to run LATEX2HTML let us look at an example with a file 12hexa.tex, written in French. Figure 3.1 shows the LATEX source file. On lines 2–4 we include three packages: graphicx, francais of babel, and makeidx. We also define a new command, \Lcs, that prints a backslash followed by its argument (line 5). Then, after printing the title with \maketitle, we desire a table of contents and lists of figures and tables (lines 10–13). The body of the text consists of two sections (lines 14–31 and 33–50). It is followed by a bibliography (lines 52–58) and the index, which is generated from the various \index commands by the makeindex program and is included with the \printindex command (line 59). In the first section we have two graphics side by side (lines 25–26), while the second section shows several commands of babel's francais package in tabular form.

If we run LATEX on this source file, 12hexa.tex, then run makeindex on 12hexa.idx, and finally run LATEX a second time to resolve cross-references, and include the index file 12hexa.ind, we obtain as a result the three pages shown as PostScript files in Figure 3.2.

To generate HTML files that correspond to this LATEX source file, it is enough to type:

```
latex2html 12hexa
```

To see what is happening, LATEX2HTML prints the following information on the user's console. We are running with the standard settings of the system and will show in later sections how you can control one or more characteristics of the generated output files.

```
 1    This is LaTeX2HTML Version 99.1 release (March 30, 1999)
 2    by Nikos Drakos, CBLU, University of Leeds.
 3
 4    Revised and extended by:
 5     Marcus Hennecke, Ross Moore, Herb Swan and others
 6    ...producing markup for HTML version 3.2
 7
 8    Loading /afs/.cern.ch/asis/src/TeX/archive/latex2html/versions/html3_2.pl
 9
10     *** processing declarations ***
11
12    OPENING /afs/cern.ch/project/tex/lwc/babel/l2hexa.tex
13
14    Loading /afs/.cern.ch/asis/src/TeX/archive/latex2html/styles/texdefs.perl...
15    Loading /afs/.cern.ch/asis/src/TeX/archive/latex2html/styles/article.perl
16    Loading /afs/.cern.ch/asis/src/TeX/archive/latex2html/styles/graphicx.perl
17    Loading /afs/.cern.ch/asis/src/TeX/archive/latex2html/styles/francais.perl
18    Loading /afs/.cern.ch/asis/src/TeX/archive/latex2html/styles/makeidx.perl........
19    Reading ...
20    %,++.............
21    @@@@@@@@@@@@@@@@@@@@@@@@@
22
23    Reading /afs/cern.ch/project/tex/lwc/babel/l2hexa.aux ...
24    Processing macros ...++...........................
25    Reading /afs/cern.ch/project/tex/lwc/babel/l2hexa.lof ...
26    Processing macros ...++....
27    Reading /afs/cern.ch/project/tex/lwc/babel/l2hexa.lot ...
28    Processing macros ...++......
29    Translating ...
30    0/8:top of l2hexa: for l2hexa.html
31
32     *** translating preamble ***
33    .........
34     *** preamble done ***
35    ;;.
36
37    1/8:tableofcontents:.."Table des mati\'{e}res" for node1.html
38    ;;.
39
40    2/8:listoffigures:.."Liste des figures" for node2.html
41    ;;.
42
43    3/8:listoftables:.."Liste des tableaux" for node3.html
44    ;;.
45
46    4/8:section:..."Une figure EPS" for node4.html
47    ;,,,,,,....;........
48
49    5/8:section:.."Exemple d'un tableau" for node5.html
50    ;.,,,...................................................;....
51
52    6/8:bibliography:.."R\'{e}f\'{e}rences" for node6.html
53    ;,...........;
54
55    7/8:textohtmlindex:..."Index" for node7.html
56    ;;
57
58    8/8:sectionstar:.."\'{A} propos de ce document..." for node8.html
59    ;;.
60
61    Writing image file ...
62
63    This is TeX, Version 3.14159 (Web2C 7.2)
64    (./images.tex
65    LaTeX2e <1997/12/01> patch level 2
66    Babel <v3.6h> and hyphenation patterns for english, french, german, dumylang,
```

```
67   nohyphenation, loaded.
68
69   *** processing 2 images ***
70
71   Generating postscript images using dvips ...
72
73   images will be generated in 12h45774/
74
75   This is dvips(k) 5.78 Copyright 1998 Radical Eye Software (www.radicaleye.com)
76   ' TeX output 1998.09.07:1521' -> 12h45774/image
77   (-> 12h45774/image001) <texc.pro><special.pro><color.pro>[1<colorcir.eps>]
78   (-> 12h45774/image002) <texc.pro><special.pro><color.pro>[2<tac2dim.eps>]
79   Writing img1.gif
80   Writing img2.gif
81
82   Doing section links .....
83   Doing table of contents ..........
84   Doing the index ....
```

By default LaTeX2HTML will generate HTML files according to the HTML 3.2
specification. As much is said on line 6; the relevant Perl file is loaded on line 8.
At that point the input file is read (line 12), and parsing 12hexa.tex the necessary Perl style files are input (lines 14–18). Note in particular that for each of
the packages which we use in the source file, we have a corresponding Perl script
(lines 16–18). LaTeX2HTML then reads LaTeX's auxiliary files (lines 23, 25, and
27), and goes on to the translation step at line 29. By default, the main HTML
file will have the same name as the input source, but with the extension .html.
In our case we get 12hexa.html. Now LaTeX2HTML will generate files for each
of the subdivisions in the LaTeX source (the precise level is under user control).
Thus (lines 37–59) we obtain eight HTML files, node1.html to node8.html. Because the EPS files (lines 25–26 in Figure 3.1) cannot be handled directly by HTML
browsers, LaTeX2HTML translates these images into GIF (or PNG) bitmaps. Therefore, LaTeX2HTML copies all the necessary LaTeX code to file images.tex (line
61), which is first compiled by LaTeX (lines 63–67) and then cut into one-page EPS
files by dvips (lines 75–78). These are handled by Ghostscript and the netpbm
utilities (as explained in Section 3.2) and turned into GIF (PNG) images, with the
names img1.gif, and img2.gif (lines 79–80). Finally, LaTeX2HTML updates all
the hyperlinks between the various document components (lines 82–84).

The result of the translation is put in the subdirectory 12hexa, whose file
content follows. We first see the HTML and GIF files described earlier. The file
12hexa.css is a CSS style sheet that provides some rudimentary hooks for customizing the way the various HTML tags will be displayed (see Section 3.3.4). We
also see the file images.tex, which contains the LaTeX code used to generate the
images. (These images files can come in very handy if problems occur during image generation. In particular images.log will contain LaTeX's error messages.) The
last line shows auxiliary Perl files that relate information in the LaTeX source files
with that in the generated HTML files:

```
12hexa.css    12hexa.html
node1.html    node2.html    node3.html    node4.html
```

```
node5.html    node6.html    node7.html    node8.html
img1.gif      img2.gif
images.tex    images.aux    images.idx    images.log
images.pl     internals.pl labels.pl
```

The way the various files are interrelated is shown in Figure 3.3. The main file, l2hexa.html, is at the center. From it all other files can be reached via hyperlinks:

❶ links to the table of contents (*Tables des matières*);

❷ links to the list of figures (*Liste des figures*);

❸ links to the list of tables (*Liste des tableaux*);

❹ links to the first section (*Une figure EPS*);

❺ links to the second section (*Example d'un tableau*);

❻ links to the bibliography (*Références*);

❼ links to the index (*Index*); and

❽ links to information about the way the document was created (*À propos de ce document...*).

We also see how hyperlinks in the list of figures (❷) point to the figure in question (in ❹). The same holds for the table (in ❺) that can be reached from the list of tables (❸). More generally, the index (❼) has hyperlinks to various points in the different HTML files.

It must be emphasized that we had to do nothing special to have our source document divided into chunks of an optimal size for browsing on the Internet. All LaTeX cross-references are translated automatically into hyperlinks; complex components (pictures and graphics; mathematics, which will be treated in detail in Section 3.3; and some environments) are transformed into bitmaps. Even translations of components for non-English documents (French in our case) are taken care of.

Before going any further, we have to spend some time looking at how to install LaTeX2HTML on your system and how to get the best using the various ways of customizing the output.

3.2.2 Installation

Installation essentially consists of verifying that all the required packages are available. Exact paths to the executables are recorded, so that at runtime there is no need for time-consuming searches.

Two Perl scripts, install-test and configure-pstoimg, are supplied as part of the LaTeX2HTML distribution to perform most of the tasks required for installation. Some manual editing is required in the file latex2html.config before these can be run to get a successful installation.

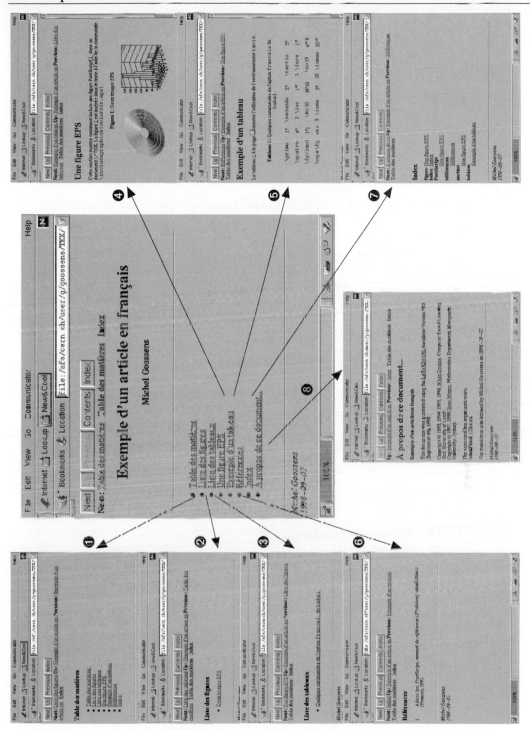

Figure 3.3: HTML structure generated by LaTeX2HTML from the LaTeX source of Figure 3.1

Following are the steps required for installation of the LaTeX2HTML software. The archive has a name like `latex2html-99.1.tar.gz` to indicate clearly which version it contains.

1. Decide where on the local file system the new software should be located.

   The most commonly chosen paths are `/usr/local/latex2html/`, `/usr/local/bin/latex2html/`, and `/usr/local/share/latex2html`, although others are possible. The archive unpacks into a directory called `latex2html`, creating it if necessary. The main `latex2html` script, together with the configuration file `latex2html.config` and the installation scripts, are all copied into the top `latex2html` directory.

2. Near the top of the `latex2html.config` script, specify the value of the variable `$LATEX2HTMLDIR` to be the complete path to the directory where these scripts are located, as chosen earlier in step 1. A complete path to the Perl program should also be given as the value of the `$PERL` variable on non-UNIX systems such as OS/2, Windows 95 and Windows NT, and DOS.

   There are several variables whose values should be customized for the local site; for example, specifying exact paths for the commands to run LaTeX and `dvips` is important on some platforms. These can be adjusted later (see Section 3.2.3 for customization options). Only `$LATEX2HTMLDIR` is needed for installation.

3. Edit the first line of `install-test` to ensure that it contains a correct path to the command that is used to run Perl on the local system. Make similar edits, if necessary, to the first lines in `latex2html`, `configure-pstoimg`, `makemap`, `texexpand`, `pstoimg`, and `pstoimg_nopipes`.

   The initial path is `#!/usr/local/bin/perl`. It is mandatory to change this to the location where the Perl executable lives.[2]

4. Run the script `install-test`.

   After verifying that the script is executable, try the commands `./install-test` or `perl install-test` if simply calling `install-test` is not sufficient.

5. The `install-test` script writes the value of `$LATEX2HTMLDIR` into appropriate places in the `latex2html` and `pstoimg` scripts and reports whether the necessary software can be found.

   For any missing pieces, it could be that the software is missing, is not the correct version, or is not on the default search paths. Explicit paths can be specified in the file `latex2html.config`. If that is sufficient to fix the problem, then rerun `install-test`.

6. The script `pstoimg-config` is run automatically to record complete paths to the utilities required for processing images; alternatively, it can be run sepa-

---

[2]If the `$PERL` variable was set in step 2, then it is not necessary to edit `texexpand`, `pstoimg`, and `pstoimg_nopipes`, if these are to be run only from LaTeX2HTML. However, `pstoimg` and `pstoimg_nopipes` are useful utility scripts in their own right, and should be configured correctly to allow this.

rately. Specify -gif for GIF or -png for PNG on the command line, or simply type g or p when prompted for an image format.

Complete paths to the various utilities are written into a file called local.pm. This file is read by pstoimg and pstoimg_nopipes when generating images. It can be edited if necessary, for example, to cope with subsequent upgrades or if pstoimg-config found a wrong version.

7. Ensure that the LaTeX packages html.sty and htmllist.sty, contained in the $LATEX2HTMLDIR/texinputs/ subdirectory, can be found by LaTeX on your system.

   For example, copy them to a subdirectory named .../texmf/tex/latex/html/ or .../texinputs/latex/html/ within the TeX hierarchy. On most TeX installations you also will have to update TeX's filename database by running a program similar to Web2C's mktexlsr. Alternatively, set the TEXINPUTS environment variable to search within $LATEX2HTMLDIR/texinputs/.

8. Copy the navigation icons (the GIF, PNG, or DOS versions, as selected in step 6) to a place where they will be accessible "on the Web." Set the $ICONSERVER variable within latex2html.config to point to the URL for this location. Get the icons from the relevant subdirectory of $LATEX2HTMLDIR.

   This step is really one of customization, so it can be delayed until later. However, the best location is usually an images/ subdirectory at the top level of the local Web site. Special administrative, or "root," privileges may be required to place the icons here. For use on DOS installations there is a special set of icons having short filenames.

9. Support for special packages (optional).
   If you are interested in Indic TeX/HTML support for traditional Indic scripts, then you should find files with the extensions .perl and .sty in the $LATEX2HTMLDIR/IndicTeX-HTML/ subdirectory. Copy them to a place where they can be found by Perl and LaTeX, respectively. Do the same with the files in the $LATEX2HTMLDIR/XyMTeX-HTML directory, if you want support for chemical structure diagrams based on X^{Υ}MTeX.

   Copy, move, or link the .perl files to the $LATEX2HTMLDIR/styles/ subdirectory and copy, move, or link the .sty files to the TeX hierarchy. Alternatively, adjust variables to search the original location.

Although the above procedure may seem rather daunting, it is actually not so difficult when one understands the purpose of each step and the options available to cope with variations on different platforms. Indeed, it is quite easy to update to a new version of LaTeX2HTML entirely by hand editing. This is because the local configuration files, latex2html.config and local.pm, rarely need to be changed. Usually just steps 3 and 4 are sufficient to upgrade an existing installation to a later version, assuming that the previous latex2html.config has been saved for reuse.

Let us see how the installation goes in practice. Suppose we have obtained the distribution from a repository and have copied the LaTeX2HTML files into a directory tree; we then move to the top of that directory tree. The directory structure should be something like the following:

```
IndicTeX-HTML
XyMTeX-HTML
cweb2html
docs/changebar    /hthtml        /psfiles
example
foilhtml
icon-dos
icons.gif
icons.png
makeseg
styles
tests
texinputs
versions
```

In the following sections we will mention the contents of most of these directories in more detail. For the moment, however, let us carry on with the installation of LaTeX2HTML and execute the Perl script `install-test`. This will write the following information to the screen (we have represented hitting just "carriage return" by <u><CR></u>):

```
 1   This is install-test for LaTeX2HTML V99.1
 2   ==========================================
 3
 4   Main script installation was... 0 1 ...successful.
 5   Testing availability of external programs...
 6   Perl version 5.004 is OK.
 7   texexpand was found.
 8   Setting up texexpand script...1 ...succeeded
 9   Checking for availability of DBM or NDBM (Unix DataBase Management)...
10   DBM was found.
11   Checking if globbing works... globbing is ok.
12   DVIPS version 5.78 is OK.
13   pstoimg was found.
14   Setting up pstoimg script...0 1 ...succeeded
15   Setting up configure-pstoimg script...1 ...succeeded
16   Looking for latex...
17   latex was found.
18   Styles directory was found.
19
20   Main set-up done.
21   You may complete this set-up by configuring pstoimg now...proceed? <u><CR></u>
22
23   This is configure-pstoimg V96.2 by Marek Rouchal
24
25   Welcome to the Configuration of pstoimg!
26
27   You will be guided in few steps through the setup of pstoimg, the part of
28   latex2html that produces bitmap images from the LaTeX source.
29   Type 'configure-pstoimg -h' for a brief usage information and a list of
30   user-definable options.
```

```
31
32  Hit return to proceed to the next configuration step. <CR>
33
34  Pstoimg can support both GIF and PNG format.
35  Please note that there are certain legal limitations on the use of the GIF
36  image format.
37
38  If you go on, pstoimg will be configured for GIF or PNG format.
39  You may reconfigure pstoimg at any time by saying configure-pstoimg.
40  Which format do you want to have supported?
41  Answer g (GIF) or p (PNG). g
42
43  Configuring for GIF format.
44  Changing $IMAGE_TYPE in latex2html.config...succeeded
45
46  Hit return to proceed to the next configuration step. <CR>
47
48  Ghostscript Configuration
49  =========================
50
51  Ghostscript is "/usr/local/bin/gs", Version 5.10
52  Pstoimg will use the ppmraw device.
53  Ghostscript library path is /usr/local/share/ghostscript/5.10
54
55  Hit return to proceed to the next configuration step. <CR>
56
57  Netpbm/Pbmplus Configuration
58  ============================
59
60  ppmtogif is /usr/local/bin/X11/ppmtogif
61      ppmtogif understands -transparent. Good!
62      ppmtogif understands -interlace. Good!
63  pnmcrop is /usr/local/bin/X11/pnmcrop
64  pnmflip is /usr/local/bin/X11/pnmflip
65  ppmquant is /usr/local/bin/X11/ppmquant
66  pnmfile is /usr/local/bin/X11/pnmfile
67  pnmcat is /usr/local/bin/X11/pnmcat
68  pbmmake is /usr/local/bin/X11/pbmmake
69
70  Hit return to proceed to the next configuration step. <CR>
71
72  Transparent/Interlaced Image Configuration
73  ==========================================
74
75  Using netpbm to make transparent GIFs.
76  Using netpbm to make interlaced GIFs.
77
78  Hit return to proceed to the next configuration step. <CR>
79
80  Setup pstoimg
81  =============
82
83  Updating local configuration file...
84
85  Well done!
86  Pstoimg is now hopefully configured to run on your system.
87  Type 'pstoimg -h' for a brief usage information.
88  Please specify the desired image format in the file latex2html.config.
```

The first part of the script (lines 1–20) locates all the tools needed by LaTeX2HTML and verifies whether the installed versions are adequate. Next bitmap generation is initiated via an implicit call to the `configure-pstoimg` script (line 32). The main choice to be made is whether you want GIF or PNG images in your HTML pages (we chose GIF by answering g in line 41). Then we proceed with the configuration of `Ghostscript` (lines 48–53), the `netpbm` utilities (lines 57–68), and the generation of interlaced and transparent images (lines 72–76). Finally the program `pstoimg` is set up (lines 80–88). All in all, very little effort was required to initiate the LaTeX2HTML system on our computer platform.

If, in the future, changes that affect the locations of utilities not supplied as part of the LaTeX2HTML distribution occur, you can simply rerun `install-test` or `configure-pstoimg` to record the new locations.

3.2.3   Customizing the local installation

There are dozens of configuration variables that affect aspects of the way the HTML pages are created by LaTeX2HTML. To preserve settings that are most appropriate for a particular site, for a particular author or group of authors, or for particular kinds of documents, LaTeX2HTML provides a hierarchy of customization mechanisms.

These mechanisms consist of reading files containing Perl code to set variables and define or redefine subroutines that will be used in the subsequent processing. In the following list, these files are named in the order in which they are processed by the main `latex2html` script. The most recently read file determines the eventual value of a variable. Thus Perl code in later-read files overrides variable settings from files loaded earlier.

3.2.3.1   The file `latex2html.config`

Site-specific customizations can be entered in the file `latex2html.config`, whose definitions apply to all users at a site. This file is located using the value of `$LATEX2HTMLDIR` which is entered in the `latex2html` script during the installation procedure described in the previous subsection.

It is important to set `$ICONSERVER` equal to a directory "visible on the Web" so that the readers of the HTML pages can access the icons; see the installation step 8 earlier. The language used for titles of automatically generated HTML pages is a good candidate for customization here. Where users are subject to quota restrictions, it is also a good idea to set `$TMP` to a directory that is "world writable." This way the most diskspace-intensive part of the processing need not take a user over quota, thereby causing the job to fail.

The Perl script `pstoimg_nopipes` is provided for platforms that do not support the use of UNIX "pipes" as a means of passing the output from one command to the input of another. This applies in particular to DOS. Set the `$PSTOIMG` variable to use `pstoimg_nopipes`. Such systems may not support "forking" either, for these also set `$NO_FORK=1;`.

At some sites it is advisable to set `$LATEX` to include a full path to the command to invoke LaTeX. Similarly, setting `$DVIPS` may be required or desired to establish a "virtual printer"[3]

---

[3] Best-quality images are obtained using PostScript fonts. File sizes are kept to a minimum when `Ghostscript` is configured to find the `.pfa` or `.pfb` files themselves, using its `Fontmap` listing or by setting the `GS_FONTPATH` environment variable. This also requires setting `$DVIPS="dvips -Pgs";` and creating a configuration file `config.gs` that refers to a file `psfonts.gs` that lists the fonts to be excluded from the output generated by `dvips`.

for Ghostscript. If PostScript fonts are not being used, there are variables that affect the automatic generation of font bitmaps using METAFONT. Read the comments present in `latex2html.config` for more information.

3.2.3.2   The file `.latex2html-init`

User-specific preferences are handled by the file `$HOME/.latex2html-init`. It normally resides in the user's home directory (hence the use of the variable `$HOME`). This file is commonly used to set a signature using the `$ADDRESS` variable or to use an alternative set of navigation icons via `$ICONSERVER`. The variable `$TEXINPUTS` can be set to allow customized input sources to be found. Similarly the `$LATEX2HTMLSTYLES` and `$LATEX2HTMLVERSIONS` variables can be adjusted to search directories containing customized Perl scripts for implementations of extra packages or extensions or as replacements for those distributed with LaTeX2HTML. Setting `$INFO=""`; suppresses the information page, which would otherwise be generated automatically. The scale factor variables `$FIGURE_SCALE_FACTOR`, `$MATH_SCALE_FACTOR`, and `$DISP_SCALE_FACTOR`, applied when creating images, may here be changed from the values set in `latex2html.config`.

You can also deposit a file `.latex2html-init` in the current directory. It allows you to set variables that will apply to all jobs run from that directory.

Apart from overriding other customizations, typically this file is used to specify the "granularity" for splitting the output into HTML pages according to sectioning levels, via `$MAX_LINK_DEPTH`. `$MAX_SPLIT_DEPTH` affects creation of navigation links between pages, while `$TOC_DEPTH` determines which section headings are hyperlinked from the Table of Contents page. The level of HTML to be produced and the type of math translation to be performed can also be specified here.

3.2.3.3   Command-line switches

Many of the variables already mentioned, plus many others, can be set for a single job via command-line switches. We will have the occasion to introduce a lot of them in examples later in this chapter.

For example, `-split 4` has the same effect as setting `$MAX_SPLIT_DEPTH=4`; for splitting the source at the level of \section commands but not at \subsection commands. Similarly, `-link 2` has the same effect as setting `$MAX_LINK_DEPTH=2`; for hyperlinks to headings deeper by two levels, on the same and other HTML pages.

More configuration files can be loaded via `-init_file <init-file>`. Command-line options are processed in order of occurrence, including reading completely any `<init-file>`s as they occur. See the LaTeX2HTML Users Guide for details on the available options, explanations of their uses, and configuration variable equivalents.

3.2.3.4   Perl packages and the file `<jobname>.perl`

When a LaTeX package using a \usepackage{<package>} command is requested, a Perl implementation is loaded from a file `<package>.perl`, if one can be found in the working directory or in any of the directories specified in the `$LATEX2HTMLSTYLES` variable. Furthermore, a file `<jobname>.perl` will be loaded if it exists for the particular job. This extension mechanism is explained next.

3.2.4 Extension mechanisms and LaTeX packages

The output from LaTeX2HTML can be controlled by three separate mechanisms for loading files containing Perl code. Analogous to those for LaTeX are the "document-class" and "package-loading" mechanisms. The former uses the main argument to the `\documentclass` command and any class options, to load particular files; the latter uses the `\usepackage` command and any options.

The extension mechanism handles translation issues that need not be of concern within the LaTeX source but that are significant for the HTML output. For example, extensions control which version of HTML to produce, what font encoding to use, and whether mathematics should be rendered as images or parsed into small pieces.

3.2.4.1 Document classes and class options

When the document source contains a line `\documentclass {<class>}` then a file `<class>.perl` will be loaded, if found in the current directory or in any of the directories specified in the `$LATEX2HTMLSTYLES` variable.

Note that a `\documentclass` or `\documentstyle` command is not strictly necessary, for LaTeX2HTML will accept *any* text file as input to convert into HTML. Any macros will be substituted, if possible, assuming the file is LaTeX source.

With class options, as in `\documentclass [<option>]{<class>}`, each class can cause a file `<option>.perl` to be loaded, if a file with this name can be found within the searched directories. Furthermore, a subroutine `do_<class>_<option>` is executed, if it has been defined in the loaded packages or initialization files.

For example, in `article.perl` there is a definition for `sub do_article_leqno` which sets a flag to indicate that equation numbers be placed at the left-hand side of displayed mathematics.

For documents prepared originally for LaTeX 2.09, LaTeX2HTML treats the `\documentstyle` command as if it were `\documentclass`. Thus support for the style and for any named packages is loaded via the mechanism explained earlier.

The standard document classes in LaTeX provide code that controls the typesetting of the source material on the output page. However, these procedures have little relevance when creating an HTML document; the only thing currently implemented in the files `article.perl`, `report.perl`, and `book.perl` is the structure for section numbering, for when section numbers are required. With `amsart.perl` and `amsbook.perl`, extra commands are defined for use on the title page; support for $\mathcal{AMS}$ mathematics packages is loaded automatically.

3.2.4.2 Packages and package options

For LaTeX instances that contain a command `\usepackage {<package>}`, a file `<package>.perl` will be loaded, if it resides in the current directory or in one specified in the variable `$LATEX2HTMLSTYLES`.

Most standard LaTeX packages are implemented in this way, as are many of the LaTeX supported packages. The `$LATEX2HTMLDIR/styles/` subdirectory, which is the default value for `$LATEX2HTMLSTYLES`, contains the corresponding `.perl` files. Alternatively, consult the LaTeX2HTML Users Guide for a listing.

For package options, as in `\usepackage [`*`<option>`*`]{`*`<package>`*`}`, a Perl subroutine named `do_`*`<package>`*`_`*`<option>`* is executed after the package support has been loaded. If no such subroutine has been defined, a warning message is printed immediately and again at the end of the job.

Of course, this subroutine may cause further `.perl` files to be loaded. For example, `do_babel_french` causes loading of `french.perl` to use French language keywords and titles. Similarly, `do_inputenc_latin2` loads support for the ISO-8859-2 encoding via a file `$LATEX2HTMLDIR/versions/latin2.pl`.

3.2.4.3   Extensions and HTML versions

The command-line switch `-html_version` takes an argument that specifies extra Perl files to be loaded for the current job. As its name suggests, this switch specifies the version of HTML that is to be produced. Further filenames appended in a comma-separated list indicate extra files to load from directories listed in the `$LATEX2HTMLVERSIONS` variable.

For example, `-html_version 4.0,math,unicode,frame` causes LaTeX2HTML to read the Perl files `html4_0.pl`, `math.pl`, and `unicode.pl`. By default these files are located in the subdirectory `$LATEX2HTMLDIR/versions/`, but this location can be changed with the `$LATEX2HTMLVERSIONS` variable. The main versions available are: `frame`, `html3_2`, `html4_0`, `lang`, `latin1` to `latin6`, `math`, and `unicode`.

3.3   Mathematics modes with LaTeX2HTML

LaTeX2HTML provides a rich set of methods for displaying mathematics within Web pages. In our examples we use a file `sampleMath.tex`, listed here:

```
 1   \documentclass[a4paper,twoside]{article}
 2   \usepackage{html}
 3   %\usepackage{amsmath}
 4
 5   \renewcommand{\d}[\partial}\providecommand{\bm}[1]{\mathbf{#1}}
 6   \providecommand{\Range}{\mathcal{R}}\providecommand{\Ker}{\mathcal{N}}
 7   \providecommand{\Quat}{\vec{\mathbf{Q}}}
 8
 9   \newcommand{\StAndrews}{\url{http://www-groups.dcs.st-and.ac.uk/~history}}%
10   \newcommand{\Pythagorians}{\htmladdnormallink
11     {Pythagorians}{\StAndrews/Mathematicians/Pythagoras.html}}
12   \newcommand{\Fermat}{\htmladdnormallink
13     {Fermat, c.1637}{\StAndrews/HistTopics/Fermat's_last_theorem.html}}
14   \newcommand{\Wiles}{\htmladdnormallink
15     {Wiles, 1995}{http://www.pbs.org:80/wgbh/nova/proof}}
16
17   \begin{document}
18   \htmlhead[center]{section}{Math examples}
```

```
19    \begin{eqnarray}
20    \phi(\lambda) & = & \frac{1} {2 \pi i}\int^{c+i\infty}_{c-i\infty}
21      \exp \left( u \ln u + \lambda u \right ) du \hspace{1cm}\mbox{for } c \geq 0 \\
22    \lambda        & = & \frac{\epsilon -\bar{\epsilon} }{\xi}
23                   - \gamma' - \beta^2 - \ln \frac{\xi} {E_{\rm max}}         \\
24    \gamma         & = & 0.577215\dots \mathrm{\hspace{5mm}(Euler's\ constant)}   \\
25    \gamma'        & = & 0.422784\dots = 1 - \gamma                          \\
26      \epsilon , \bar{\epsilon} & = & \mbox{actual/average energy loss}
27    \end{eqnarray}
28
29    Since~\ref{eqn:stress-sr} or~\ref{gdef} should hold for arbitrary $\delta\bm{c}$%
30    -vectors, it is clear that $\Ker(A) = \Range(B)$ and that when $y=B(x)$ one has...\\
31    ...the \Pythagorians{} knew infinitely many solutions in integers to $a^2+b^2=c^2$.
32    That no non-trivial integer solutions exist for $a^n+b^n=c^n$ with integers $n>2$ has long
33    been suspected (\Fermat). Only during the current decade has this been proved (\Wiles).
34
35    \begin{eqnarray}\label{eqn:stress-sr}
36    V \bm{\pi}^{sr} & = & \left< \sum_i M_i \bm{V}_i \bm{V}_i
37     + \sum_i \sum_{j>i} \bm{R}_{ij} \bm{F}_{ij}\right> \\ \nonumber
38              & = & \left< \sum_i M_i \bm{V}_i \bm{V}_i
39     + \sum_{i}\sum_{j>i}\sum_\alpha\sum_\beta \bm{r}_{i\alpha j\beta}\bm{f}_{i\alpha j\beta}
40     - \sum_i \sum_\alpha \bm{p}_{i\alpha} \bm{f}_{i\alpha}   \right>
41    \end{eqnarray}
42
43    \end{document} %%%  requires \usepackage{amsmath} to continue
44
45    \begin{subequations}\label{bgdefs}
46    \begin{align} B_{ij}^\alpha     & =
47          \left(B_{ij}^\alpha\right)_0 + \left(B_{ij}^\alpha\right)_a \label{bdef}  \\
48    \left(B_{ij}^\alpha\right)_0  & = \frac{1}{2}\left(\frac{\d N_i^\alpha}{\d X_j}
49       + \frac{\d N_j^\alpha} {\d X_i} \right)                    \label{b0def} \\
50    \left(B_{ij}^\alpha\right)_a  & = H_{ij}^{\alpha \beta} a^\beta   \label{budef} \\
51    H_{ij}^{\alpha \beta}         & =
52      \frac{1}{2}\left( \frac{\d N_k^\alpha}{\d X_i} \frac{\d N_k^\beta}{\d X_j}
53      + \frac{\d N_k^\beta}{\d X_i} \frac{\d N_k^\alpha}{\d X_j} \right)  \label{gdef}
54    \end{align}
55    \end{subequations}
56    \end{document}
```

We also use a second file `sampleAMS.tex`, identical to `sampleMath.tex` but with the `\end{document}` (line 43) commented out and with package `amsmath` (deleting the % on line 3) included.

3.3.1 An overview of LATEX2HTML's math modes

Basically, LATEX2HTML has three modes for mathematics: the "novice" mode, the "professional" mode, and the "expert" mode. Extra features are available in some modes. We will look at each mode in turn.

3.3.1.1 Novice mode

Novice mode, which is the usual default, is also known as "simple math." Expressions using just ordinary alphabetic, numeric, and arithmetic characters are presented using the browser's text font, italicized where appropriate. Superscripts and subscripts are used with HTML 3.2 and later. Any other symbol or macro causes an image to be made of the whole inline expression or logical part of an aligned environment. Exceptions are styling macros such as \mathrm, \mathbf, \mathtt, \boldmath, and \bm. Text mode macros such as \textrm, \textit, \texttt, and \rm, \bf, \it, \tt are also allowed for compatibility with older documents. This mode is suitable only when quite simple mathematical expressions occur within a document having mainly nonmathematical content. Figure 3.4 shows an example of novice mode using the command:

```
latex2html sampleMath.tex
```

In fact, the file sampleMath.tex contains too much mathematics to be suitable for novice mode. Notice how in Figure 3.4 some inline equations are set using the browser's text font, but others require images. Aligning images requires centering on the baseline whenever there is depth, as in a descender or the bottom of a parenthesis. The alignment works with some browsers, but not with others. In any case the linespacing comes out inconsistent or too wide; centering within a display also has defects. Compare the different sizes and placements of the "=" signs. Such problems can be overcome using HTML 4.0 and a CSS style sheet, as seen later in Figure 3.10.

3.3.1.2   Professional mode

Professional mode is adequate for documents with a lot of mathematics in the form of displays or inline expressions, or when mathematical symbols are used frequently. It is the default mode when one of the $\mathcal{AMS}$ packages—amsmath, amsthm, amsopn, or amstex—is loaded and with the amsart and amsbook document classes. To maintain consistent style between inline and displayed expressions, images are made of all inline mathematics, and of each equation, formula, or aligned unit within displays. Where possible, the browser's text font is used for the argument of \mbox and \text macros. Figure 3.5 shows an example of professional mode using the command:

```
latex2html sampleAMS.tex
```

In Figure 3.5 the overall effect is more balanced compared to that in Figure 3.4. Although linespacing for the inline math is consistent, it is a little too wide because on each line there is an image with depth. Even the single "=" sign in the alignments is an image that occurs seven times. The browser's text font is used for the \mbox in the last cell of equation (5). It fails to align correctly with images on the same line, as alignment between cells in a <TABLE> row is tied to the middle[4] of the text, not to its baseline. For equation (2) the words are contained in an image, otherwise the \hspace command could not be handled.

Using the -no_math option, the consistency in style afforded by professional mode is obtained without loading $\mathcal{AMS}$ packages. This means "no simple math"

---

[4] since "TOP" and "BOTTOM" would clearly be incorrect.

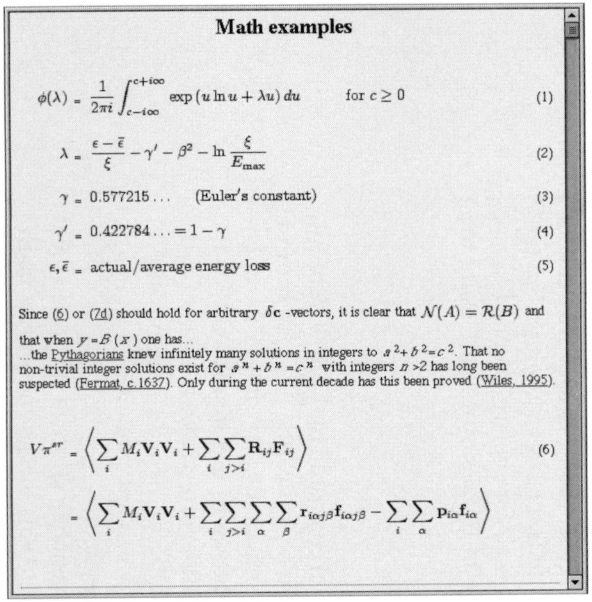

Math examples

$$\phi(\lambda) = \frac{1}{2\pi i} \int_{c-i\infty}^{c+i\infty} \exp\left(u\ln u + \lambda u\right) du \qquad \text{for } c \geq 0 \tag{1}$$

$$\lambda = \frac{\epsilon - \bar{\epsilon}}{\xi} - \gamma' - \beta^2 - \ln\frac{\xi}{E_{max}} \tag{2}$$

$$\gamma = 0.577215\ldots \qquad (\text{Euler's constant}) \tag{3}$$

$$\gamma' = 0.422784\ldots = 1 - \gamma \tag{4}$$

$$\epsilon, \bar{\epsilon} = \text{actual/average energy loss} \tag{5}$$

Since (6) or (7d) should hold for arbitrary $\delta\varepsilon$-vectors, it is clear that $\mathcal{N}(A) = \mathcal{R}(B)$ and that when $y = B(x)$ one has... the Pythagorians knew infinitely many solutions in integers to $a^2 + b^2 = c^2$. That no non-trivial integer solutions exist for $a^n + b^n = c^n$ with integers $n > 2$ has long been suspected (Fermat, c.1637). Only during the current decade has this been proved (Wiles, 1995).

$$V_{\pi^{rr}} = -\left\langle \sum_i M_i V_i + \sum_i \sum_{j>i} \mathbf{R}_{ij} \mathbf{F}_{ij} \right\rangle$$

$$= -\left\langle \sum_i M_i V_i + \sum_i \sum_{j>i} \sum_\alpha \sum_\beta \mathbf{r}_{i\alpha j\beta}\mathbf{f}_{i\alpha j\beta} - \sum_i \sum_\alpha \mathbf{p}_{i\alpha}\mathbf{f}_{i\alpha} \right\rangle \tag{6}$$

Figure 3.4: Mathematics using LaTeX2HTML with novice mode (default settings)

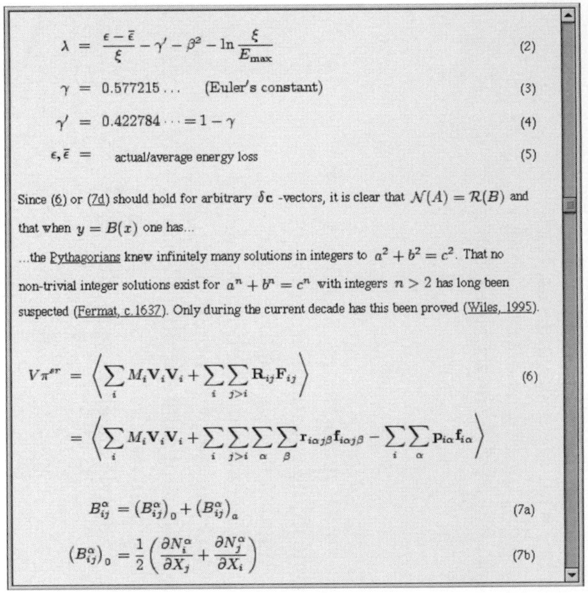

$$\lambda = \frac{\epsilon - \bar{\epsilon}}{\xi} - \gamma' - \beta^2 - \ln\frac{\xi}{E_{max}} \tag{2}$$

$$\gamma = 0.577215\ldots \qquad (\text{Euler's constant}) \tag{3}$$

$$\gamma' = 0.422784\ldots = 1 - \gamma \tag{4}$$

$$\epsilon, \bar{\epsilon} = \text{actual/average energy loss} \tag{5}$$

Since (6) or (7d) should hold for arbitrary $\delta\varepsilon$-vectors, it is clear that $\mathcal{N}(A) = \mathcal{R}(B)$ and that when $y = B(x)$ one has... the Pythagorians knew infinitely many solutions in integers to $a^2 + b^2 = c^2$. That no...

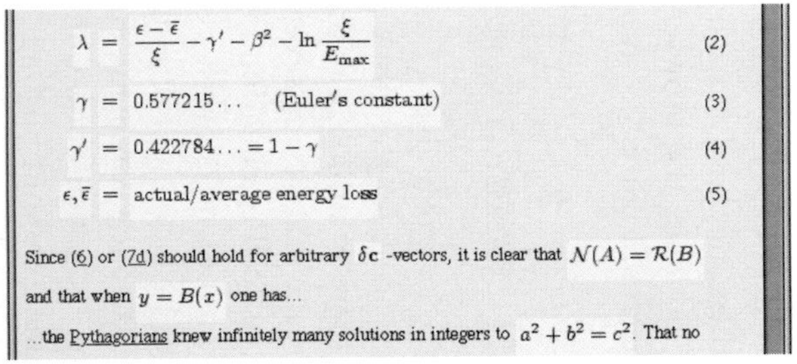

Figure 3.6: Mathematics in an HTML page using professional mode

$$\lambda = \frac{\epsilon - \bar{\epsilon}}{\xi} - \gamma' - \beta^2 - \ln\frac{\xi}{E_{max}} \tag{2}$$

$$\gamma = 0.577215\ldots \qquad (\text{Euler's constant}) \tag{3}$$

$$\gamma' = 0.422784\ldots = 1 - \gamma \tag{4}$$

$$\epsilon, \bar{\epsilon} = \text{actual/average energy loss} \tag{5}$$

Since (6) or (7d) should hold for arbitrary $\delta\varepsilon$-vectors, it is clear that $\mathcal{N}(A) = \mathcal{R}(B)$ and that when $y = B(x)$ one has...
non-trivial integer solutions exist for $a^n + b^n = c^n$ with integers $n > 2$ has long been suspected (Fermat, c.1637). Only during the current decade has this been proved (Wiles, 1995).

$$V_{\pi^{rr}} = -\left\langle \sum_i M_i V_i + \sum_i \sum_{j>i} \mathbf{R}_{ij} \mathbf{F}_{ij} \right\rangle$$

$$= -\left\langle \sum_i M_i V_i + \sum_i \sum_{j>i} \sum_\alpha \sum_\beta \mathbf{r}_{i\alpha j\beta}\mathbf{f}_{i\alpha j\beta} - \sum_i \sum_\alpha \mathbf{p}_{i\alpha}\mathbf{f}_{i\alpha} \right\rangle \tag{6}$$

$$B_{ij}^a = \left(B_{ij}^a\right)_0 + \left(B_{ij}^a\right)_a \tag{7a}$$

$$\left(B_{ij}^a\right)_0 = \frac{1}{2}\left(\frac{\partial N_i^a}{\partial X_j} + \frac{\partial N_j^a}{\partial X_i}\right) \tag{7b}$$

Figure 3.5: Mathematics using professional mode as default with $\mathcal{AMS}$ packages

$$\phi(\lambda) = \frac{1}{2\pi i} \int_{c-i\infty}^{c+i\infty} \exp\left(u\ln u + \lambda u\right) du \quad \text{for } c \geq 0 \tag{1}$$

$$\lambda = \frac{\epsilon - \bar{\epsilon}}{\xi} - \gamma' - \beta^2 - \ln\frac{\xi}{E_{max}} \tag{2}$$

$$\gamma = 0.577215\ldots \qquad (\text{Euler's constant}) \tag{3}$$

$$\gamma' = 0.422784\ldots = 1 - \gamma \tag{4}$$

$$\epsilon, \bar{\epsilon} = \text{actual/average energy loss} \tag{5}$$

Since (6) or (7d) should hold for arbitrary $\delta\varepsilon$-vectors, it is clear that $\mathcal{N}(A) = \mathcal{R}(B)$ and that when $y = B(x)$ one has... the Pythagorians knew infinitely many solutions in integers to $a^2 + b^2 = c^2$. That no

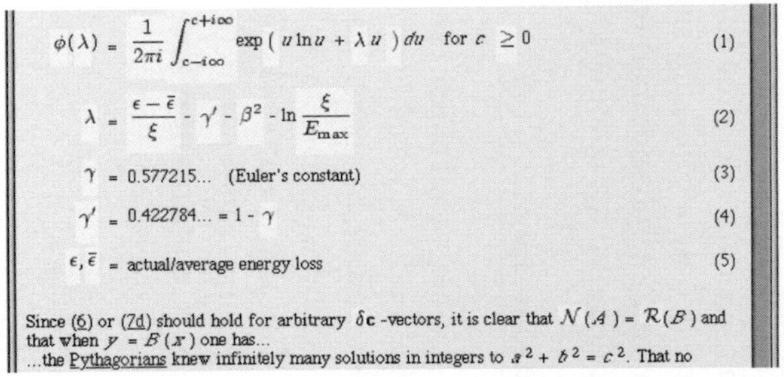

Figure 3.7: Mathematics in an HTML page using expert mode

parsing, favoring the use of images. Setting $NO_SIMPLE_MATH=1$; has the same effect. An example can be seen in Figure 3.6, for which we used the command:

```
latex2html -no_math -white -no_transparent sampleMath.tex
```

Images are shown on an opaque white background, (-no_transparent and -white options).

Summary

Professional mode offers a consistent style for all mathematical expressions, in particular, using HTML's `<TABLE>` tags for alignments and equation numbering. A drawback is that all mathematics requires the generation of an image, resulting in a potentially large number of bitmap files. This is probably not an issue when download time for images is not critical.

3.3.1.3   Expert mode

In expert mode the structure of mathematical expressions is broken into smaller pieces. It uses the browser's text font wherever possible and generates images of pieces such as fractions and symbols. The many resulting small images often require less time to download than for a smaller number of larger images. Indeed, small images can often be reused in many HTML pages so that the overall size of the Web document can be significantly reduced. With very large manuscripts, the total diskspace required for the whole document becomes appreciably less than when using professional mode.

Examples of expert mode are Figures 3.7–3.10. In the case of Figure 3.7 we typed the command:

```
latex2html -no_math -html_version 3.2,math -white \
          -no_transparent sampleMath.tex
```

3.3.2   Advanced mathematics with the math extension

To use expert mathematics mode and for detailed parsing of mathematical expressions, one should load the math extension module of Perl commands. An example is Figure 3.8, where we used the following command-line options:

```
latex2html -no_math -html_version 3.2,math sampleAMS.tex
```

and where the version of HTML must be specified also. The browser's text font is used wherever possible, resorting to images only for special symbols and structures that require vertical alignment, such as fractions, derivatives, integrals, summations, and large brackets. More details are shown in Figure 3.7, which uses an opaque background. This clearly shows which math parts are rendered as images and how alignment is achieved by equalizing depth and height.

The visual effect is generally quite good, but it does not have the complete consistency of the larger images obtained with professional mode. However, the user now has control over the size and face of the font used for the mathematics. Images do not rescale, but the size at which they are created can be altered. The variables affecting the size of images are the following (they are applicable in any mode):

$MATH_SCALE_FACTOR   magnification factor for creating images of mathematics and inline text.
Recommended value: 1.4 (corresponds to 14 pt font size in the browser).

$MATH_DISPLAY_FACTOR   extra magnification used with images of displayed mathematics; it multiplies $MATH_SCALE_FACTOR.
Recommended value: 1.2 (corresponds to 17 pt font size in the browser).

$FIGURE_SCALE_FACTOR   magnification applied when creating images of figures and whole environments. Recommended value: 1.6.

Font characters used in displayed mathematics have a <BIG> tag applied. The $MATH_DISPLAY_FACTOR ensures images are scaled similarly. There is still a slight misalignment of adjacent cells with text and images, but it is less intrusive. Failure to place superscripts directly above subscripts is an irritation. The extra gap after italicized letters, produced in some browsers, is more annoying, especially when preceding a subscript.

A major benefit of expert mode is the reduced diskspace required to store the smaller images, because much less area is rendered using bitmaps. This also means less data to be transferred, so access times are reduced. However, this is partially offset by the need for more separate connections to obtain the larger number of files for each HTML page.

For just a single page containing a fair amount of mathematics, there is not a lot to gain, but when there are many pages, the same images of symbols are reused over and over. The first few pages may be slow to load; subsequent pages are usually much faster, since most of the required images are already available locally within the browser's image cache. Indeed, image reuse can be so effective that *fewer* images may result from using expert mode. In a real-world example using professional mode, the translation of a paper in mathematical logic into 36 HTML pages totaled 1.3 Mbytes with 392 images. In expert mode it required just 800 kbytes with only 223 images.

There are other advantages of expert mode that are designed to ensure that the information contained in the original LaTeX document source is faithfully conveyed to the receiver. This is true even when there is trouble obtaining all the images required to build the intended picture in the browser window.

Images of small pieces of LaTeX source have the complete code contained in
the ALT attribute of the <IMG> tag. For example, the summations in Figure 3.8 are
marked up in the HTML as follows:

```
1   <TD ALIGN="LEFT" NOWRAP><IMG
2    WIDTH="233" HEIGHT="63" ALIGN="MIDDLE" BORDER="0"
3    SRC="img19.gif"
4    ALT="$\displaystyle \left&lt; \sum_i M_i \mathbf{V}_i \mathbf{V}_i
5    + \sum_i \sum_{j&gt;i} \mathbf{R}_{ij} \mathbf{F}_{ij}\right&gt;$"></TD>
```

This example also shows the use of entities < (line 4) and > (line 5) to
protect < and > from their special meanings in the HTML language. Most images
are smaller and shorter, as in the next example:

```
1   - <IMG
2    WIDTH="21" HEIGHT="35" ALIGN="MIDDLE" BORDER="0"
3    SRC="img10.gif"
4    ALT="$\displaystyle \beta^{2}_{}$">
```

Note on line 4 the braces and the empty subscript inserted automatically within
\beta^{2}_{}. This ensures good LaTeX style and consistent placement of the su
perscript across similar images. Hence, complete information can often be read
using a text only browser or with a browser mode where images are loaded only
upon request.

Building on this idea, when a mathematics environment is parsed into font
characters and small images, the *entire source* is included as a comment within the
HTML file. The next example shows an extract from the HTML source of Figure 3.8. These comments can be searched for occurrences of particular pieces of
mathematics. Portions can be easily extracted for reuse within other LaTeX documents. There is no need for numbered entities within comments.

```
1    <DIV ALIGN="CENTER">
2    <!-- MATH: \begin{eqnarray}
3    \phi(\lambda) & = &  \frac{1} {2 \pi i}\int^{c+i\infty}_{c-i\infty}
4     \exp \left( u\ln u +\lambda u \right) du \hspace{1cm}\mbox{for } c\geq 0\\
5    \lambda        & = &  \frac{\epsilon}  -\bar{\epsilon} }{\xi}
6     - \gamma' - \beta^2 - \ln \frac{\xi} {E_{\rm max}}          \\
7    \gamma  & = &  0.577215\dots \mathrm{\hspace{5mm}(Euler's\ constant)}   \\
8    \gamma' & = &  0.422784\dots = 1 - \gamma \\
9    \epsilon , \bar{\epsilon} & = & \mbox{actual/average energy loss}
10   \end{eqnarray} -->
11
12   <TABLE ALIGN="CENTER" CELLPADDING="0" WIDTH="100%">
13   <TR VALIGN="MIDDLE"><TD NOWRAP ALIGN="RIGHT"><IMG
14    WIDTH="35" HEIGHT="31" ALIGN="MIDDLE" BORDER="0"
15    SRC="img1.gif"
16    ALT="$\displaystyle \phi(\lambda)$"></TD>
17   <TD ALIGN="CENTER" NOWRAP><IMG
```

At the expense perhaps of longer download times, these other advantages can
be obtained along with the images of professional style, by using the following set
of command-line options:

```
latex2html -no_math_parsing -html_version 3.2,math filename
```

Summary

Expert mode with the `math` extension guarantees consistency for all the mathematics. It also includes the LATEX source as comments into the HTML files, making text searches in the math possible. This strategy results in larger images, thus requiring greater download times. It is, however, an ideal solution if the aim is to retain a maximum amount of information, combined with images of good quality.

3.3.3 Unicode fonts and named entities, in expert mode

Further reduction in the number of images is obtained by requiring the browser to use special fonts for Greek letters and for some mathematical symbols. The Unicode (or ISO-10646-1) standard (see Appendix C.2) defines codes for such characters. These are allowable within HTML pages satisfying the 3.2 or 4.0 specifications. Currently browsers support only few, if any, of these characters. Figure 3.9 shows the result when LATEX2HTML loads the `unicode` extension, as follows:

```
latex2html -no_math -html_version 3.2,math,unicode sampleAMS.tex
```

Almost all of the first aligned display in Figure 3.9 is built using font characters available to the browser. Small subscripted letters α and β are quite acceptable. The variant epsilon comes with the font used here; LATEX source code could be modified to match, using `\bar\varepsilon`. HTML character references make the `html` files difficult to read, for instance, #946 for β and #947 for γ (line 5).

```
 1  <TD ALIGN="LEFT" NOWRAP><IMG
 2   WIDTH="40" HEIGHT="47" ALIGN="MIDDLE" BORDER="0"
 3   SRC="img5.gif"
 4   ALT="$\displaystyle {\frac{\epsilon -\bar{\epsilon} }{\xi}}$">
 5   - &#947;' - &#946;<SUP>2</SUP> - ln<IMG
 6   WIDTH="44" HEIGHT="51" ALIGN="MIDDLE" BORDER="0"
 7   SRC="img6.gif"
 8   ALT="$\displaystyle {\frac{\xi}{E_{\rm max}}}$"></TD>
 9  <TD WIDTH=10 ALIGN="RIGHT">
10   (2)</TD></TR>
```

Images are still required for fractions and other constructions requiring vertical alignment. The most common perhaps are the variable-sized operators, such as integrals and summations. Superscripts and subscripts on these operators are included within the images; otherwise correct positioning cannot be obtained.

Using the -entities command-line option, numbered character references are replaced by named entity references, such as β and γ. Although these are part of the entity set valid for HTML 4.0, only the most recent browsers actually support them.

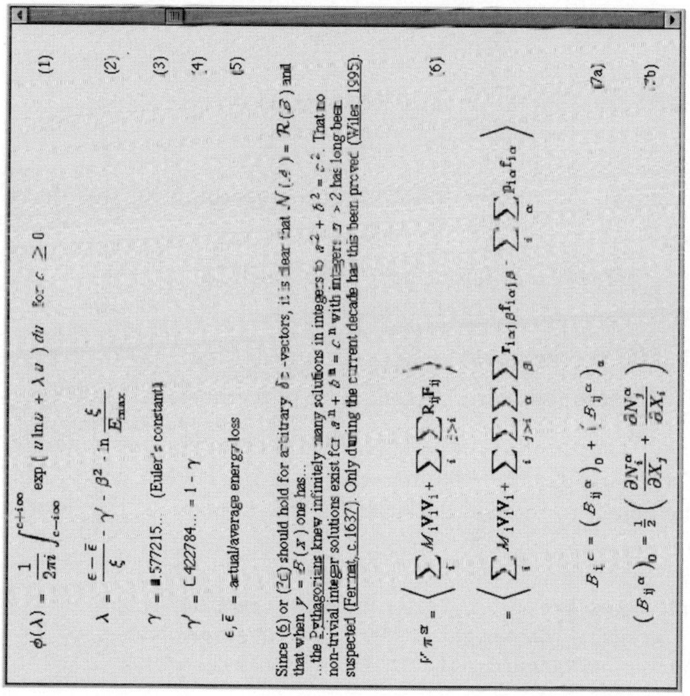

Math examples

$$\phi(\lambda) = \frac{1}{2\pi i}\int_{c-i\infty}^{c+i\infty}\exp\left(u\ln u + \lambda u\right)du \quad \text{for } c \geq 0 \tag{1}$$

$$\lambda = \frac{\epsilon - \bar\epsilon}{\xi} - \gamma - \beta^2 - \ln\frac{\xi}{E_{max}} \tag{2}$$

$$\gamma = 0.577215\ldots \quad (\text{Euler's constant}) \tag{3}$$

$$\gamma' = 0.422784\ldots = 1 - \gamma \tag{4}$$

$$\epsilon, \bar\epsilon = \text{actual/average energy loss} \tag{5}$$

Since (5) or (2a) should hold for arbitrary 6c-vectors, it is clear that $N(\mathcal{A}) = \mathcal{R}(\mathcal{B})$ and that when $\gamma = \mathcal{B}(x)$ one has... the Pythagorians knew infinitely many solutions in integers to $a^2 + b^2 = c^2$. That no non-trivial integer solutions exist for $a^n + b^n = c^n$ with integers $n > 2$ has long been suspected (Fermat, c.1637). Only during the current decade has this been proved (Wiles, 1995).

$$V^{\pi\alpha} = \left\langle \sum_i M_i V_i V_i + \sum_i \sum_{j>i} R_{ij} F_{ij} \right\rangle \tag{6}$$

$$= \left\langle \sum_i M_i V_i V_i + \sum_i \sum_{j>i} \sum_\alpha \sum_\beta r_{i\alpha|j\beta} f_{i\alpha|j\beta} - \sum_i \sum_\alpha p_{i\alpha} f_{i\alpha} \right\rangle$$

$$\mathcal{B}_{ij}{}^\alpha = (\mathcal{B}_{ij}{}^\alpha)_0 + (\mathcal{B}_{ij}{}^\alpha)_a \tag{7a}$$

$$(\mathcal{B}_{ij}{}^\alpha)_0 = \frac{1}{2}\left(\frac{\partial N_i^\alpha}{\partial X_j} + \frac{\partial N_j^\alpha}{\partial X_i}\right) \tag{7b}$$

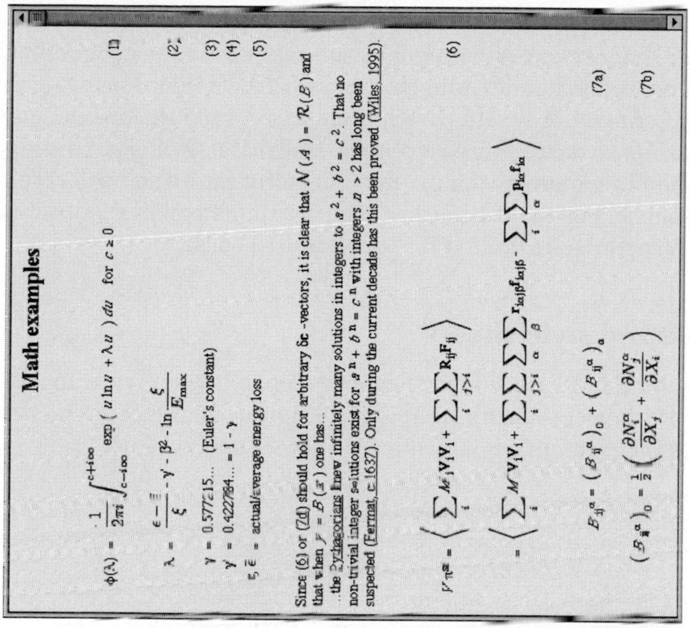

Figure 3.9: Mathematics using expert mode and Unicode font characters

Math examples

$$\phi(\lambda) = \frac{1}{2\pi i}\int_{c-i\infty}^{c+i\infty}\exp\left(u\ln u + \lambda u\right)du \quad \text{for } c \geq 0 \tag{1}$$

$$\lambda = \frac{\epsilon - \bar\epsilon}{\xi} - \gamma - \beta^2 - \ln\frac{\xi}{E_{max}} \tag{2}$$

$$\gamma = 0.577215\ldots \quad (\text{Euler's constant}) \tag{3}$$

$$\gamma' = 0.422784\ldots = 1 - \gamma \tag{4}$$

$$\epsilon, \bar\epsilon = \text{actual/average energy loss} \tag{5}$$

Since (5) or (2a) should hold for arbitrary 6c-vectors, it is clear that $N(\mathcal{A}) = \mathcal{R}(\mathcal{B})$ and that when $\gamma = \mathcal{B}(x)$ one has... the Pythagorians knew infinitely many solutions in integers to $a^2 + b^2 = c^2$. That no non-trivial integer solutions exist for $a^n + b^n = c^n$ with integers $n > 2$ has long been suspected (Fermat, c.1637). Only during the current decade has this been proved (Wiles, 1995).

$$V^{\pi\alpha} = \left\langle \sum_i M_i V_i V_i + \sum_i \sum_{j>i} R_{ij} F_{ij} \right\rangle \tag{6}$$

$$= \left\langle \sum_i M_i V_i V_i + \sum_i \sum_{j>i} \sum_\alpha \sum_\beta r_{i\alpha|j\beta} f_{i\alpha|j\beta} - \sum_i \sum_\alpha p_{i\alpha} f_{i\alpha} \right\rangle$$

$$\mathcal{B}_i{}^c = (\mathcal{B}_{ij}{}^\alpha)_0 + (\mathcal{B}_{ij}{}^\alpha)_a \tag{7a}$$

$$(\mathcal{B}_{ij}{}^\alpha)_0 = \frac{1}{2}\left(\frac{\partial N_i^\alpha}{\partial X_j} + \frac{\partial N_j^\alpha}{\partial X_i}\right) \tag{7b}$$

Figure 3.8: Mathematics using expert mode, requiring the special math extension

Summary

Expert mode using the Unicode encoding requires substantially fewer images than the techniques presented earlier, because font characters can be used for many math symbols. However, present-day browsers have limited or no support for Unicode and do not have available adequate fonts for Greek and math symbols. This approach will certainly gain in importance in the medium-term future and will result in very fast download times. For the reasons just mentioned, its practical impact is nevertheless bound to remain quite limited for some time to come.

3.3.4   HTML 4.0 and style sheets

When producing code for the HTML 4.0 specification, there is greater scope for addressing some of the visual defects mentioned earlier. All three mathematics modes are available, as well as their variants. Following are a few examples of use:

```
latex2html -html_version 4.0 sampleMath.tex
latex2html -no_math -html_version 4.0 sampleMath.tex
latex2html -no_math -html_version 4.0,math sampleMath.tex
latex2html -no_math -html_version 4.0,math,unicode sampleMath.tex
latex2html -no_math_parsing -html_version 4.0,math sampleMath.tex
```

Some simple style sheet effects are shown in Figure 3.10, for which we used the following command:

```
latex2html -no_math_parsing -html_version 4.0,math \
               -style sampleAMS.css sampleAMS.tex
```

The style sheet effects shown include the following (the line numbers correspond to the CSS style sheet below):

- a colored title with a frame of a different color (line 1);

- boldened and colored equation numbering (line 2);

- colored background for the `subequations` environment (line 3); and

- fixed line heights for paragraphs with inline images of mathematics (line 4).

When running on the file `sampleAMS.tex`, LaTeX2HTML automatically generates a "generic" CSS style sheet `sampleAMS.css`, together with the HTML pages. This style sheet can then be edited to include declarations that implement the desired effects, for example:

```
1   H2 { border : 2pt solid brown ; color : maroon ; padding : 5pt }
2   TD.eqno {color : green ; fontweight : 700 } /* equation-number cells */
3   TABLE.subequations { background-color : #E0E0E0 ; }
4   P  { line-height : 18pt ; }
```

Of course, these effects are visible only when the HTML pages are viewed using a browser that can interpret the style sheet language. Figure 3.10 was obtained with a browser that understands the CSS language.

Today, only CSS is supported as style sheet language. In the future, as other style sheet languages become commonly available, support to exploit their features will be added to LaTeX2HTML. For more information on the CSS language, see Section 7.4.

Several techniques for defining CSS style sheet entries are available to be used with HTML pages constructed by LaTeX2HTML.

1. You can edit, using any text editor, the automatically generated style sheet after running LaTeX2HTML. For each environment in the LaTeX source, an empty "stub" will have been created. This stub can then be augmented to include the desired properties and values.

2. You can link to a previously prepared style sheet, using the -style *style-file* command-line option. Alternatively, you can set the $STYLESHEET variable to have *style-file* as its string value in the form of a complete URL to the style sheet file's location or a relative URL from where the HTML pages will reside.

3. You can include style sheet information in the LaTeX source itself. This can be done for environments using an optional argument to the \begin command (the html package should be loaded to use this feature).

It is probably not a good idea to mix style information and source code too strongly, although it is sometimes useful to exert microcontrol on parts of a piece of text or a formula. Therefore let us consider in more detail the third alternative, and see how we can control the style by using the optional argument on the \begin commands of an environment. Following we describe three ways of using this feature:

\begin[*style-info*]

With this first method an attribute ID="*unid*" is included on the <DIV>, <SPAN>, or <TABLE> start tag generated for the contents of the environment. The unique identifier *unid* associates the element with the definition *style-info* in the style sheet.

\begin[*class*]

This second method associates a CLASS="*class*" attribute with the generated HTML tag. Style information associated with *class* will be inherited. A stub is written into the style sheet to add the necessary information later.

> \begin[*class* | *style-info*]

This third method is a combination of the previous two methods, with "|" separating the different types.

The contents of *style-info* can be the exact code for the style sheet entry. Alternatively, it can be a set of `key=value` pairs, using either "=" or ":" as a separator. The ";" delimits pairs, while "," can be used to separate multiple values for a single key. Names for *class* use alphanumeric characters. When there is no |, the presence of =, :, or ; indicates that the argument contains *style-info*, and not *class* names.

The following LATEX code can be used to create entries for the style effects visible in Figure 3.10 (see Section 3.5.2 for a description of the \htmlsetstyle command). The following lines 1–3 are equivalent to lines 1, 2, and 4 in the CSS style sheet on page 111, while line 3 in the style sheet is replaced with a specification directly on the start of the subequations environments (line 5).

```
1    \htmlsetstyle[H2]{}{border=2pt,solid,brown;color=maroon;padding:5pt}
2    \htmlsetstyle[TD]{eqno}{color : green ; fontweight : 700 }
3    \htmlsetstyle[P]{}{ line-height : 18pt }
4
5    \begin[background-color=\#E0E0E0]{subequations}
6      ...
7    \end{subequations}
```

Summary

HTML 4 and CSS let us apply style effects using any number of style sheets. Although many of the older generations of browsers have limited or no support for style sheets, this situation is improving rapidly. Thus a combination of HTML 4 and CSS will prove ideal in the medium term to offer full control on the presentation of information.

3.3.5   Large images and HTML 2.0

Another approach to presenting mathematics within Web pages is to use larger images, that is, images of whole environments. Visual appearance could well be the most important consideration with the amount of data and its speed of transfer irrelevant. This may be the case, for example, when browsing a CD-ROM or using a single machine or local area network. When compatibility is required for browsers capable of interpreting just HTML 2.0 markup then this is the only viable approach because <TABLE> tags are not supported.

Large images can be very attractive, as shown in Figure 3.11 which was generated with the command:

```
latex2html -no_math -html_version 2.0 sampleAMS.tex
```

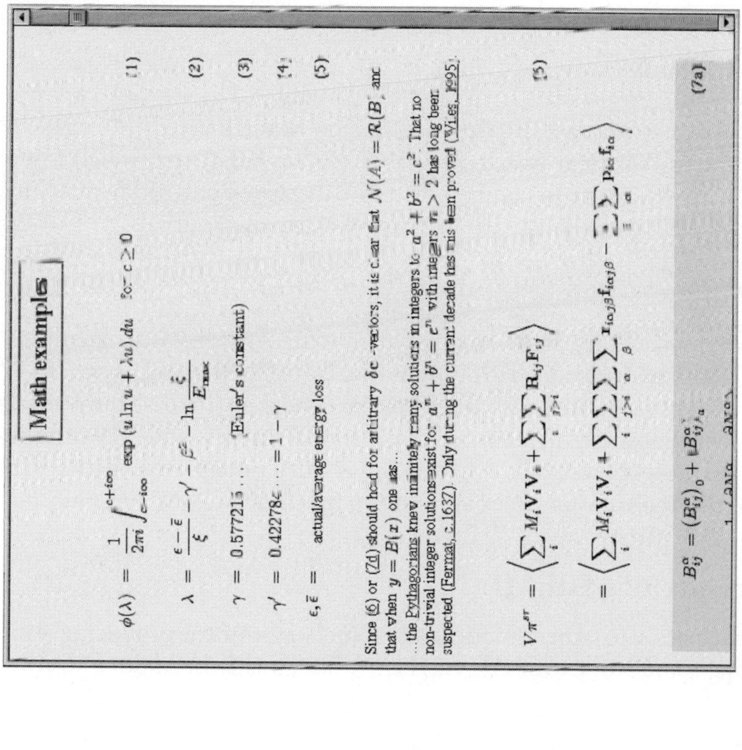

Math examples

$$\phi(\lambda) = \frac{1}{2\pi i}\int_{c-i\infty}^{c+i\infty} \exp(u\ln u + \lambda u)\, du \qquad \text{for } c \geq 0 \tag{1}$$

$$\lambda = \frac{\epsilon - \bar{\epsilon}}{\xi} - \gamma' - \beta^2 - \ln\frac{\xi}{E_{max}} \tag{2}$$

$$\gamma = 0.577215\ldots \quad (\text{Euler's constant}) \tag{3}$$

$$\gamma' = 0.422784\ldots = 1 - \gamma \tag{4}$$

$$\epsilon, \bar{\epsilon} = \text{actual/average energy loss} \tag{5}$$

Since (6) or (7d) should hold for arbitrary δc-vectors, it is clear that $\mathcal{N}(A) = \mathcal{R}(B)$ and that when $y = B(x)$ one has...

...the Pythagoreans knew infinitely many solutions in integers to $a^2 + b^2 = c^2$. That no non-trivial integer solutions exist for $a^n + b^n = c^n$ with integers $n > 2$ has long been suspected (Fermat, c.1637). Only during the current decade has this been proved (Wiles, 1995).

$$V_{\vec{\pi}}^{rr} = \left\langle \sum_i M_i V_i + \sum_i\sum_{j>i} \mathbf{R}_{ij}\mathbf{F}_{ij} \right\rangle \tag{6}$$

$$= \left\langle \sum_i M_i V_i + \sum_i\sum_{j>i}\sum_\alpha\sum_\beta \mathbf{r}_{i\alpha j\beta}\mathbf{f}_{i\alpha j\beta} - \sum_i\sum_\alpha \mathbf{p}_{i\alpha}\mathbf{f}_{i\alpha} \right\rangle$$

$$B_{ij}^a = (B_{ij}^a)_0 + (B_{ij}^a)_a \tag{7a}$$

$$(B_{ij}^a)_0 = \frac{1}{2}\left(\frac{\partial N_i^\alpha}{\partial X_j} + \frac{\partial N_j^\alpha}{\partial X_i}\right) \tag{7b}$$

$$(B_{ij}^a)_a = H_{ij}^{\alpha\beta}a^\beta \tag{7c}$$

$$H_{ij}^{\alpha\beta} = \frac{1}{2}\left(\frac{\partial N_k^\alpha}{\partial X_i}\frac{\partial N_k^\beta}{\partial X_j} + \frac{\partial N_k^\beta}{\partial X_i}\frac{\partial N_k^\alpha}{\partial X_j}\right) \tag{7d}$$

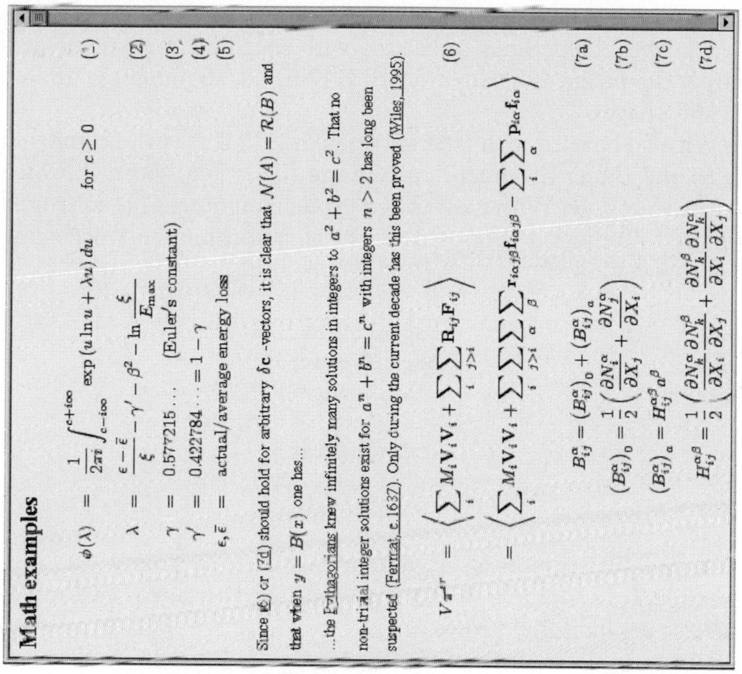

Figure 3.11: Mathematics using images of complete environments (HTML 2.0)

Figure 3.10: Mathematics using expert mode with large images, HTML 4.0, and style sheet effects

However, since equation numbering is included as part of the image, it is impossible to reuse images. Hyperlinks associated with specific equations or sub-equations must target the image as a whole. With HTML 2.0, alignment is limited to just paragraphs and images.

Large images can also be used with later versions of HTML, via the command \htmlimage (line 9) and the environment makeimage (lines 2–6), both of which are defined in the html package. With makeimage explicit alignment (flushright environment on lines 1–7) must be imposed to get equation numbers occurring flush to the edge of the window.

```
1   \begin{flushright}              8    \begin{flushright}
2     \begin{makeimage}             9    \begin{eqnarray}
3       \begin{eqnarray}            10     \htmlimage{}
4         ...                       11     ...
5       \end{eqnarray}              12   \end{eqnarray}
6     \end{makeimage}               13   \end{flushright}
7   \end{flushright}
```

The command \htmlimage requires an argument that may be empty. See Figure 3.12 for an example. It uses source from a file sampleMathImages.tex, modified from sampleAMS.tex, indicated earlier.

The full range of possible arguments to \htmlimage is listed in Section 3.5. Among them one helps alleviate some of the difficulties presented by large images by including only a smaller "thumbnail" directly on the HTML page:

```
\htmlimage{thumbnail=.4}
```

This acts as a button, hyperlinked to a full-size version of the image.

Figure 3.13 shows the result from a file sampleMathThumb.tex, which is just sampleAMS.tex with \htmlimage commands in the displayed environments. This technique has been used quite effectively with some electronic journals.

Summary

The "lowest common denominator" approach of using HTML 2.0 to guarantee math displays of good, high-quality TeX typesetting by using images has as a drawback all of the problems associated with large images. They can increase the transfer time of the document substantially, they occupy lots of diskspace, and they offer no possibility of image reuse. Nevertheless, this mode is still a valuable alternative with older browsers and when transfer times are not too much of an issue.

3.3.6   Future use of MathML

The parsed mathematics of expert mode goes some way toward producing valid MathML markup. Some work with LaTeX2HTML has already been done to drive

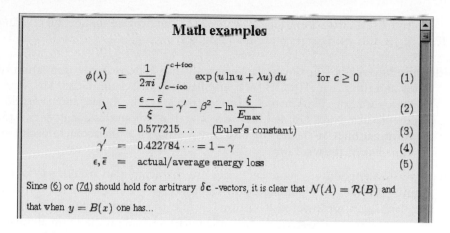

Figure 3.12: Mathematics with images of complete environments

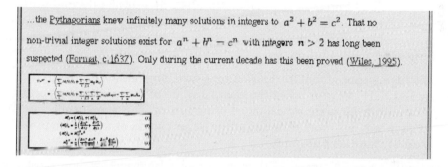

Figure 3.13: Mathematics using "thumbnails" hyperlinking to full-size images

the WebEQ wizard, producing Java applets and files of MathML markup. For these, <APPLET> tags are produced for HTML 3.2 and <OBJECT> tags for HTML 4.0. However, at present this procedure works only with a subset of LaTeX mathematics, so it is not described here further. In the future this work will be expanded to include all aspects of LaTeX math covered by MathML.

3.4   Support for different languages

Through the use of special fonts and macro packages, TeX allows typesetting in arbitrary languages. Much of this software can also be used with LaTeX2HTML. For many languages an appropriate interface already exists, as part of the LaTeX2HTML distribution. For others it is not too difficult to provide an interface by adapting an already existing one.

There are several ways in which LaTeX2HTML can provide support for creating HTML pages, using languages other than English.

Titles and keywords. For many languages all that is needed is a translation of words and titles that LaTeX2HTML automatically places on the HTML pages. Examples are titles like Chapter, Abstract, Bibliography, Index, and navigation commands like, Next, Up, and Previous. The title "About this document ..." for the Information page should also be translated as well as the actual information contained on that page.

Character-set encoding. Some languages use characters that are not part of the Latin 1 (ISO-8859-1) font encoding. Many Western European and Scandinavian languages are covered by Latin 1, while the Latin 2 (ISO-8859-2) encoding covers most Eastern European languages based on the Latin alphabet. The Latin 3 (ISO-8859-3), Latin 4 (ISO-8859-4), Latin 5 (ISO-8859-9) and Latin 6 (ISO-8859-10) encodings cover some Mediterranean, Middle Eastern, and Northern European languages. LaTeX2HTML provides the means to process correctly documents written using these encodings. Furthermore, there is limited support for the Unicode encoding and associated entity names for letters and accented characters.

Images (using special fonts). Explicit font switching macros can be recognized by LaTeX2HTML. An image can then be made of the appropriate portion of text, provided it is clearly delimited using braces. This is quite effective with single words and short phrases, but for larger chunks of text, separate images are made for each paragraph.

Preprocessing and images. With more complex languages, such as those used in India and Southeast Asian countries, various transliteration and transcription schemes allow a codified representation using the characters available on a standard Latin keyboard. Preprocessing software to convert these encodings into TeX commands to access fonts that display the traditional forms already exists. LaTeX2HTML is ideally suited for scripting such preprocessors to perform the required conversions before generating images for the traditional text. Appropriate interfaces to several preprocessors of Indic languages are included with LaTeX2HTML under the name of Indic-TeX/HTML; the preprocessing software itself must be obtained separately.

The support available for each of these strategies is discussed in more detail in the following subsections.

3.4.1 Titles and keywords

The LaTeX2HTML distribution includes Perl package interfaces for most of the languages and dialects covered by Johannes Braams's Babel system. These are named

english.perl, german.perl, usorbian.perl, and so on. They correspond to the
language definition (.ldf) files of the Babel distribution. However, for complete
language support with LaTeX2HTML, more keywords than those present within
the ldf files are required.

Typically, such a "language interface" file defines a Perl subroutine for setting the titles and keywords, for example german_titles. Moreover, two variables,
$default_language and $TITLES_LANGUAGE, are set to the language-identifier
string, for example, german. Furthermore, there may be special macros or character
sequences defined for use with the Babel package under LaTeX that differ from the
standard English/American use of LaTeX. For example, there are sequences such
as "a, "e,..., "u for typesetting umlaut accents, and other sequences for dealing
with quotation marks and hyphenation effects. The perl file contains appropriate
code to allow these character sequences to be translated correctly for the HTML
pages. When the language uses characters that are not available in the Latin 1 character set, an appropriate file to support the required encoding will be loaded (see
Section 3.4.2).

For some languages, in particular Dutch, Finnish, French, German, Spanish,
Swedish, and Turkish, all strings needed by LaTeX2HTML have been translated,
while for other languages and local variants, such as Afrikaans, Bahasa, Brazilian,
Breton, Catalan, Croatian, Czech, Danish, Esperanto, the titles and keywords are
taken from Babel's ldf files. Additions are sought to fill some gaps; improvements
and corrections are most welcome.

A "language interface" file can be loaded in various ways so that translated
words and phrases should override the English defaults.

- Copy the contents into the latex2html.config file and replace the English
  strings that are defined there. This sets the new language as a default for all
  documents processed with that installation of LaTeX2HTML.

- Create a copy of the latex2html.config file, and replace the defaults, as
  shown earlier. Now set the L2HCONFIG environment variable to load this alternative configuration file. This allows alternative language configurations to
  be used with the same LaTeX2HTML installation. One needs only to adjust the
  value of the L2HCONFIG environment variable.

- Within a .latex2html-init file include a Perl command, such as

  ```
  &do_require_package("$LATEX2HTMLSTYLES/german.perl");
  ```

- Put LaTeX like code within the document itself to use one of the package-
  loading mechanisms discussed in Section 3.2.4. Any of the following LaTeX
  commands should work:

  ```
  \usepackage{german}              \usepackage[german]{babel}
  \documentstyle[german]{style}    \documentclass[german]{class}
  ```

where, in the last example, the language name should be a valid option to the `<class>` document class. In fact, this is required only for LaTeX to process the document correctly or if images need to be generated using LaTeX. LaTeX2HTML loads the appropriate `perl` file and attempts the translation to HTML, irrespective of the document being valid for LaTeX or not.

Multilingual documents can be produced using the `babel` package. Language segments can be presented with distinctive styles, as explained in Section 3.4.3.

3.4.2 Character-set encodings

Eight-bit language encodings, even for European languages using the Latin alphabet, use different glyphs in their upper range (codepoints 128–255). Upper-range characters present in the LaTeX source are passed through to the HTML pages unchanged,[5] when they are part of ordinary text. Thus for the browser to display the correct characters, it is necessary to know which character encoding is used. The encoding is specified as an attribute of the `<META>` tag inside the `HEAD` element part of the HTML document, for example:

```
<HEAD>
<META HTTP-EQUIV="Content-Type" CONTENT="text/html"
      CHARSET="iso-8859-1">
...
</HEAD>
```

Unless otherwise specified, LaTeX2HTML uses the Latin 1 (ISO-8859-1) encoding since this is expected with HTML 3.2. Other encodings Latin 2 to Latin 5 (see Table C.4), and Unicode (UTF-8) are supported. With Unicode, named entities (for instance, for accented characters) are converted to numerical character entity references, even with HTML 4.0, since many named entities are not among those listed at the W3C site [↪HTMLENTS]. This includes many characters from the various Latin *i* encodings just mentioned.

For each supported encoding there exists a file in the `$LATEX2HTMLVERSIONS` subdirectory, with a name such as `latin1.pl,..., latin5.pl, unicode.pl`. There are various ways to load these files and change the encoding. If several files are loaded, the last determines the encoding for the HTML pages, except whenever `unicode.pl` is one of them, in which case the UTF-8 encoding is used.

Encodings can be loaded in various ways:

- Load support for a particular character set, for example:

  ```
  latex2html -html_version 3.2,math,latin2  mydocument.tex
  ```

---

[5]Except for occurrences of case-changing macros such as `\MakeUppercase`, `\MakeLowercase`, `\uppercase` and `\lowercase`.

```
latex2html -html_version 4.0,latin5,latin2,unicode  mydocument.tex
```

When more than one encoding is specified, all the corresponding files are loaded, but HTML pages will use only the last one (for instance, unicode on the second line). This can be overridden by a \selectlanguage command in the babel package in the document preamble; see Section 3.4.3.

- Load the inputenc package within the preamble of the document, specifying the appropriate encoding, for instance, \usepackage[latin2]{inputenc}.

- Load a "language interface" file, as explained in Section 3.4.1, which implicitly loads support for a particular character set.

3.4.3 Multilingual documents using babel

As mentioned earlier, special support for particular languages can be obtained by loading the babel package with options for the desired languages. Within a document the \selectlanguage command chooses which language to use for a given portion of the text. The use of LANG tags described later assumes that HTML 4.0 is being used; otherwise no such attributes are put into the HTML pages.

A \selectlanguage{*language*} command in the document preamble defines the language to be used for titles, keywords, and the navigation panels. When there is more than one \selectlanguage command, the last is used. In practice, the ISO 639 (ISO:639, 1988) identifier (see Table C.1 on page 466) for the language is used as value for the LANG attribute of the <BODY> tag. Furthermore, the document encoding is adjusted to suit this language. For example, <BODY LANG="tr"> results from \selectlanguage{turkish}, and, furthermore, the document encoding becomes Latin 5 (ISO-8859 9). A different dialect of a language can result in a customized date format on the title page; for example, \selectlanguage{american} and \selectlanguage{english} differ in this respect.

For uses of \selectlanguage {*language*} within the body of the document, the encoding is not affected. Instead, when the *language* is different from that of the document as a whole, all paragraphs within the specified portion inherit the appropriate LANG attribute. For example, \selectlanguage{austrian} will start subsequent paragraphs with <P LANG="de-AT">, until the next \selectlanguage or the current TEX grouping closes. Similarly <TABLE> tags inherit a language attribute.

```
\htmllanguagestyle{german}
```

The command \htmllanguagestyle that is defined in the html package associates a class name with subsequent paragraphs, for instance, <P LANG="de" CLASS="de">. Thus a specific style can be associated with a given language, in this case German (de).

3.4.4   Images using special fonts

Both LaTeX's \newfont and TeX's \font commands[6] receive special support in
LaTeX2HTML. These are used to define a macro for using a special-purpose font
with a small portion of text. For example, font-selecting macros can be defined as
follows, perhaps within a separate style file or document class file.

```
\font\wncyr=wncyr10      % Cyrillic Roman font
\font\wncyi=wncyi10      % Cyrillic Italiced font
\newfont{\SHa}{sinha10}  % Haralambous' Sinhala Font A
\newfont{\SHb}{sinhb10}  % Haralambous' Sinhala Font B
\newfont{\SHc}{sinhc10}  % Haralambous' Sinhala Font C
```

Such macros are normally used declaratively within braced groupings, as follows:

```
({\wncyi Russko-Singal\char126ski\char26\Slovar\char126\/}),
{\wncyr Rus\-ski ...
```

When processed by LaTeX2HTML, a single image is made of an entire grouping. This provides a way to include several languages within the same HTML
document without the need to worry about character-set encodings or whether
a browser is capable of displaying particular fonts. However, the problems with
images are similar to those encountered with inline mathematics. As well as using
Cyrillic fonts, the above lines of TeX source show code generated from a transliteration scheme for Sinhala. Such techniques are discussed next.

3.4.5   Converting transliterations using preprocessors

Languages using alphabets not based on Latin characters present a separate set of
problems for preparation of compuscripts, for example, TeX or LaTeX source documents. The usual solution is to use a "transliteration scheme"[7] whereby a collection
of Latin characters can represent a single character or syllable within the language
being represented. Documents are prepared using character strings constructed according to the transliteration scheme. Using some other piece of software, this is
then preprocessed to create TeX code for accessing the appropriate character, or
set of characters, from a specially designed font.

The example in Figure 3.14 is from a document prepared this way for the
Singhalese language script from Southern India and Sri Lanka. It first shows what
the author actually typed, with #S and #N delimiting the Sinhala portion (lines 1–
3). Then it shows the TeX code after preprocessing (lines 5–10) and finally the
resulting output as seen on the Web.

---

[6]The \newfont and \font commands are not the preferred way to define font commands in
LaTeX2ε, which uses the New Font Selection Scheme. Nevertheless, they still work, appear frequently
in older manuscripts, and are convenient for single fonts at specific sizes.

[7]Here there is no need to make a distinction between "transliteration" and "transcription." The
single term "transliteration scheme" is meant to encompass both of these related concepts.

```
1   \bibitem{belko} {\wncyr Bel\char126koviq, A.A } #Orusiyaanu"si.mhala
2   "sabdako.saya#N ({\wncyi Russko Singal\char126ski\char26\
3   Slovar\char126\/}), {\wncyr Rus\-ski\char26\ \char23zyk}, 1983.
4
5   \bibitem{belko} {\wncyr Bel\char126koviq, A.A.}
6   {\SHb\char29a\char8}{\SHb\-\char69i}{\SHb\-\char21a\char0}{\SHa\-\char213u}
7   {\SHb\-\char53i}{\SHa\char11}{\SHb\-\char77a}{\SHb\-\char37a}{\SHb\char53a}
8   {\SHa\-\char237}{\SHb\-\char163a}{\SHa\-\char5\char77a\char7}{\SHb\-\char61a}
9   {\SHb\-\char21a} ({\wncyi Russko-Singal\char126ski\char26\Slovar\char126\/}),
10  {\wncyr Rus\-ski\char26\ \char23zyk}, 1983.
```

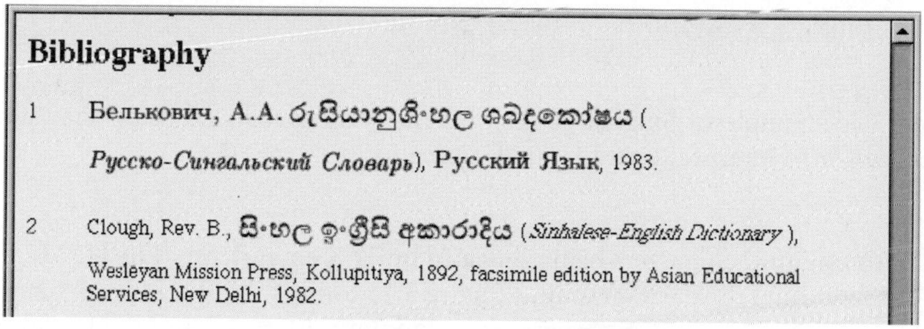

Figure 3.14: Example of preprocessing and transliteration with LaTeX2HTML

The preprocessor used with this example was Indica, which comes with Sinhala-TeX [↪SINTEX], developed by Yannis Haralambous. Indica handles twelve different Indic languages or dialects by interpreting four different transliteration or transcription schemes. It can create output for use with TeX and LaTeX using a set of three special Sinhala fonts, or it can translate directly into Unicode numeric character codes.

As well as handling the TeX source resulting from preprocessing, such as in Figure 3.14, LaTeX2HTML can also translate the original compuscript to HTML *without* the initial preprocessing step. Of course, the image-generation mechanism must be used, but now the appropriately marked segments (such as those delimited by #S and #N) are collected into a file named images.pre. It is this file that is preprocessed, using Indica, to create the usual images.tex file that will be processed by LaTeX, dvips, Ghostscript, and so on to create images for the HTML pages. Figure 3.15 presents part of the translation of a sample file that accompanies Sinhala-TeX [↪SINTEX].

When translated from the original (not preprocessed) source, each transliterated paragraph creates a separate image in order to keep image size at an acceptable level. This strategy is generally better than having an image for each letter or syllable, which can result in hundreds of images on a single page, even though they could be reused on different pages. The width of such images is determined by the $PAPERSIZE variable. In Figure 3.15 a value of $PAPERSIZE = 'b5'; was used.

Notice that, as with large images of mathematics, the original transliterated source is included as an HTML comment, preceding the image for each paragraph. When it is not too long, it is also included as the ALT attribute for the image, per-

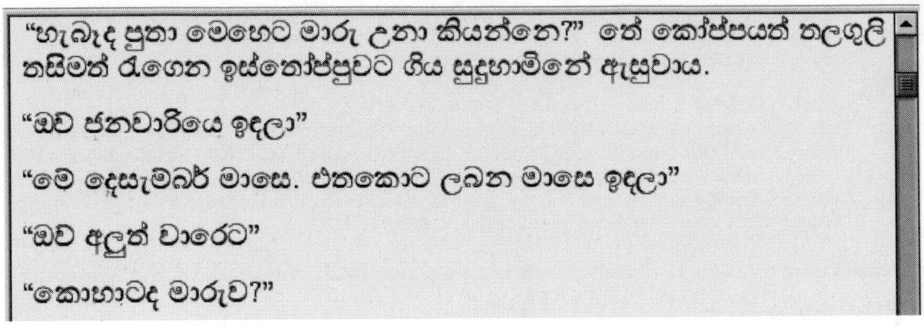

Figure 3.15: Sample of Singhalese (or Sinhala) script produced using the Indica preprocessor to interpret transliterated source

haps with awkward characters being replaced by TEX equivalents. The HTML code for the second and third paragraphs of Figure 3.15 follows. Notice in particular how the transliterated source is given, first as a comment (lines 1–3 and 9–11) and then with the ALT attribute (lines 7 and 15).

```
1   <!-- INDICA S
2   ''ov janava~riye i"ndhala~''
3   -->
4   <P><IMG
5   WIDTH="186" HEIGHT="22" ALIGN="BOTTOM" BORDER="0"
6   SRC="img2.gif"
7   ALT="\lq\lq ov janava~riye i''ndhala~''"></P>
8
9   <!-- INDICA S
10  ''me~ dhesa^mbar ma~se. ethakota labana ma~se i"ndhala~''
11  -->
12  <P><IMG
13  WIDTH="430" HEIGHT="22" ALIGN="BOTTOM" BORDER="0"
14  SRC="img3.gif"
15  ALT="\lq\lq me~ dhesa^mbar ma~se. ethakota labana ma~se i''ndhala~''"></P>
```

Whichever translation method is used, Sinhala-TEX [↪SINTEX] and Indica must be available on the local system so that they can be scripted for use. Interface files in the subdirectory $LATEX2HTMLDIR/Indic-HTML/ accompany the LATEX2HTML distribution. These are LATEX packages for the various Indic languages, together with corresponding Perl implementations. Source documents need to load an appropriate package with options corresponding to the preprocessor and transliteration scheme. For example, either of the following lines is appropriate for a document with Singhalese in the *samanala* transcription:

```
\usepackage[indica,samanala]{sinhlese}
\usepackage[sinhala,samanala]{indica}
```

Installation of Indic-TEX/HTML consists of making the language interface files available to LATEX and LATEX2HTML (file names are limited to a maximum of eight characters in the prefix so that some names look a little strange).

The files should be copied, moved, or linked into the TEX hierarchy and the `$LATEX2HTMLDIR/styles/` subdirectory, or their locations should be recorded in configuration variables, as discussed in Sections 3.2.3 and 3.2.4.

Similarly, the file `indica.perl` must be available to LATEX2HTML. Near the top of this file some Perl variables are assigned values. These may need to be adjusted for the local installation, or new values can be assigned in the `latex2html.config` or `.latex2html-init` files. Most important is `$INDICA`, which should hold the full path to the preprocessor, if specifying the command `indica` by itself is insufficient at runtime.

3.4.5.1   Supported languages and preprocessors

Other preprocessors for Indic languages are supported in a similar fashion, under the title of Indic-TEX/HTML; see TUGIndia Journal [↪TUGINDIA]. Since this article appeared, support has been added for Avinash Chopde's `itrans` [↪ITRANS] preprocessor, so that more languages and transliteration schemes can be translated using LATEX2HTML. Indic-TEX/HTML now supports the following preprocessors and fonts:

`Indica` supports the Bengali, Gujarati, Gurmukhi, Hindi, Kannada, Malayalam, Oriya, Sanskrit, Sinhala, Tamil, Telugu, and Tibetan languages, using Velthuis, CSX (ISO-646 extended), *samanala* [↪SAMANALA], and a standardized LATEX transliteration. Special fonts `sinha`, `sinhb`, and `sinhc` were designed by Yannis Haralambous. A LATEX2HTML translation [↪SINDOC] of the Sinhala-TEX [↪SINTEX] documentation is available.

`itrans` supports Bengali, Devanagari, Gujarati, Hindi, Kannada, Marathi, Punjabi (Gurmukhi), Tamil, Telugu, and Romanized Sanskrit, using a variety of fonts—for example, ItxBeng and BWTI Bengali, devnac and Xdvng, ItxGuj, kan, pun, tol, tamil, wntml, and CSUtopia.

`devnag` from the University of Washington, translates Devanagari in the Velthuis transliteration for Hindi, Marathi, Nepali, and Sanskrit. It uses the dvng font.

`tamilize` and `tmilize` translates to Tamil script using the wntml font, produced at the University of Washington.

`patc` and `mm` preprocessors used with the *Malayalam-*TEX [↪MALAYALAM] system by Jeroen Hellingman. They support Malayalam in either a traditional or reformed script, using the mm fonts and a romanized form using accents and diacritical markings. Also there is support for various transcriptions of Tamil, using the wntml font, and of Devanagari, using devnag and the dvng font.

For each of these preprocessors, interface files accompany LATEX2HTML as part of Indic-TEX/HTML. The preprocessors themselves, and whatever fonts they use, *must* be obtained separately and installed for use on the local platform.

For itrans [↪ITRANS] the file itrans.perl currently handles all of the languages supported by itrans [↪ITRANS]. In the future it should become possible to use itrans as an option to specific language packages, as with Indica, and cause other language-specific customizations to be employed. Currently, the following commands are equivalent ways to load itrans [↪ITRANS] to translate a document in Sanskrit, with the Classical Sanskrit Extended (CSX) transliteration (the appropriate command for other languages and transliterations have similar forms).

```
\usepackage[csx]{itrans}
\usepackage[csx,sanskrit]{itrans}
```

Near the beginning of the file itrans.perl some Perl variables are set. These may need to be adjusted for the local installation—for instance, by assigning new values in the latex2html.config or .latex2html-init file. The variable $ITRANSPATH ensures that the preprocessor can find all the resources it needs. Another variable $ITRANS specifies the command to run itrans [↪ITRANS] on the local installation; it should hold the full path to the preprocessor if the command itrans by itself is insufficient at runtime.

A LaTeX2HTML translation [↪ITRANS] of the itrans [↪ITRANS] documentation is available from Avinash Chopde's site. This describes the transliteration scheme used with each language. Figures 3.16 and 3.17 are extracts from these pages.

3.5 Extending LaTeX sources with hypertext commands using the html package

LaTeX2HTML comes with a LaTeX package file called html that defines macronames, commands, and environments. These allow hypertext linking and other special effects to be included in the generated HTML pages. Some commands have no effect when typesetting the compuscript with LaTeX, while other commands use different information when creating a DVI file with LaTeX or HTML files with LaTeX2HTML.

The commands defined in the html package can be grouped into several classes according to their functionality and purpose. Among these commands the variants that have an optional argument do *not* work with LaTeX 2.09; their use requires LaTeX 2$_\varepsilon$.

- Commands that create hyperlinks to external Web pages or images, that is, hyperlinks to information that is not directly part of the document nor appears when LaTeX processes the same source.

- Commands that present the same information as with LaTeX but that can incorporate extra visual effects in the HTML version.

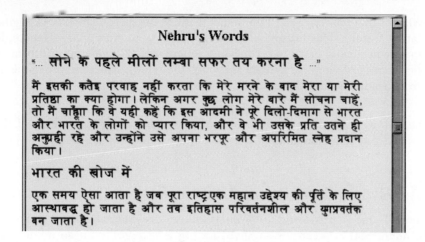

Figure 3.16: Sample of Devanagari script for the Hindi language, set with the devnag font and produced using the itrans [↪ITRANS] preprocessor

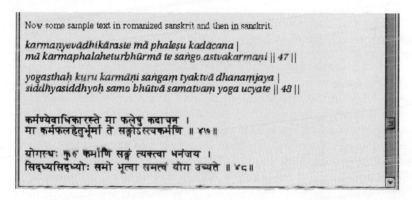

Figure 3.17: Sample of Sanskrit showing both traditional romanized forms, produced using the itrans [↪ITRANS] preprocessor

- Commands that allow alternative text to be used with active hyperlinks for citations and cross-referencing.

- Some conditional environments that allow one to use different information with the DVI and HTML versions of a document.

- Commands that customize the visual layout of the HTML pages produced by LaTeX2HTML and that have no counterpart in the DVI version.

- Special macros that help with development and debugging, for instance, to control the amount of tracing information written to the screen while the document is being processed.

- Macros that are designed to facilitate the use of the special Document Segmentation feature. This feature allows LaTeX2HTML to treat a large source document in smaller parts, nevertheless, keeping the cross-reference information between the various parts intact as though the HTML structure were generated from a single-source document.

In the following sections we discuss the commands belonging to each of these classes and give some examples of the most effective ways to use them.

3.5.1   Hyperlinks to external documents

Commands for hyperlinking to Web resources are `\htmladdnormallink` and `\htmladdnormallinkfoot`. Also `\htmladdimg` is specifically for an inline hyperlink to an image that uses the `<IMG>` tag. This displays the image on the HTML page, as if it were part of the document.

```
\htmladdnormallink[name]{link-text}{URL}
\htmladdnormallinkfoot[name]{link-text}{URL}
```

On the HTML page the *link-text* shows in the browser as an active hyperlink, usually in a different color or underlined. By clicking on the *link-text*, you will transfer to the target URL. In the LaTeX version the *link-text* is typeset normally, giving no indication that anything about the particular piece of text is special. The optional *name* allows the place on the HTML page to be marked with a meaningful name.

Generally it is poor style to have long URLs in sections of prose within a printed document; it simply looks bad, quite apart from practical problems concerning linebreaking and hyphenation. When such information must be provided explicitly, `\htmladdnormallinkfoot` is a good way to do it. This acts the same as `\htmladdnormallink` on the HTML page but includes the URL as a footnote when typeset by LaTeX.

The `\htmladdnormallink` and `\htmladdnormallinkfoot` commands can be used directly in the body of the document source, although it is recommended not to do this. Instead they are best used within expansions of macros defined in the document preamble or within input files containing many such definitions. Generally the URL will refer to a location whose address is beyond the immediate control of the document's author. If that address changes or ceases to become valid for some reason, the hyperlink needs to be changed. Collecting together all the URLs used within a document allows for easier maintenance, including such updating.

For instance, the mathematics examples in Section 3.3 refer to these commands, as seen in lines 9–15, for the definitions, and lines 31–33, for their use. How this shows up in a browser can be seen in Figure 3.4 and other figures in that section.

> `\htmlurl{`*URL*`}`

This special macro has the following property: If a macro `\url` is already defined from another package such as `url`, then `\htmlurl` binds directly to it. Similarly, if the other package is not yet loaded, but will be, then `\htmlurl` will adopt the same functionality and expansion as `\url`. Without another package, `\htmlurl` prints the URL in small typewriter style, with no provision for special characters or hyphenation, and `\url` is defined to be equivalent to `\htmlurl`.

The main use for `\htmlurl` is within expansions of other macros, especially when the same URL is to be used in several contexts. For example,

```
\newcommand{\rossURL}{\htmlurl{http://www.maths.mq.edu.au/~ross/}}
\newcommand{\thisauthor}{\htmladdnormallink{present author}{\rossURL}}
\newcommand{\RossMoore}{\htmladdnormallinkfoot{Ross Moore}{\rossURL}}
```

gives the expected hyperlinks whenever `\rossURL`, `\thisauthor`, or `\RossMoore` are used in the document. Furthermore, the correct styles, hyphenation, and treatment of special characters are applied in the LaTeX version.

> `\htmladdimg[`*attributes*`]{`*URL*`}`

This command constructs an `<IMG>` tag that sources the specified URL. Width, height, and alignment information can be given as *key=value* pairs in the optional *attributes*. Thus images can be displayed at sizes other than their natural size. You can use alignment to let text "flow" around an image— for instance, `\htmladdimage[align=left]` places the image at the left-hand side of the browser window, with text and paragraphs flowing down the right-hand side.

The following example comes from the bibliography of the LaTeX2HTML Users Guide. It shows the effect obtained in a browser.

```
\newcommand{\AWcsengURL}{http://www.awl.com/cseng}
\newcommand{\AddWes}[1]{\htmladdnormallink{Addison--Wesley}{#1}}
\newcommand{\AWtheLGC}{\AWcsengURL/titles/0-201-85469-4}
\newcommand{\LGCcover}{\AWtheLGC/coversm.gif}

\htmladdimg[ALIGN=RIGHT]{\LGCcover}
\bibitem{goossens:latexGraphics}
Michel Goossens, Sebastian Rahtz and Frank Mittelbach,
\newblock \emph{The }\LaTeX\emph{ Graphics Companion}.
\newblock ISBN 0-201-85469-4, Softcover 608 pages,
 \AddWes{\AWtheLGC/}, 1997.

\bibitem{drakos:bask}
\NikosDrakos,
\newblock Text to Hypertext conversion with \latextohtml.
...
```

3   Michel Goossens, Sebastian Rahtz and Frank Mittelbach,
        The LaTeX *Graphics Companion* .
        ISBN 0-201-85469-4, Softcover 608 pages, Addison-Wesley, 1997.

4   Nikos Drakos,
        Text to Hypertext conversion with LaTeX2HTML.
        Baskerville , December 1993, Vol.3, No.2, pp 12-15.
        May 1994, CERN, Geneva, Switzerland.
        http://cbl.leeds.ac.uk/nikos/doc/www94/www94.html

Note how both entries flow to the left of the image. Macros used here follow the principle that information that may be reused, such as publisher's data, should be defined in a single place, preferably in the document preamble.

```
\htmlrule[attributes]
\htmlrule*[attributes]
```

The `\htmlrule` command places a linebreak and a horizontal rule on an HTML page; the *-version omits the linebreak. On a printed page, `\hrule` commands should be used sparingly as separators, since some extra whitespace is usually enough. However, browsers frequently put too much whitespace, so that breaking this space with a rule has greater visual appeal. Properties, such as width, thickness, and shadow, are included as a list called *attributes*; `key=value` pairs are recognized, but if the keys can be deduced, it is sufficient to provide values only, as in the following example:

```
<BR CLEAR="LEFT">
<HR WIDTH="50%" SIZE="5" NOSHADE>              \htmlrule[50\% 5 noshade left]
```

3.5.2   Enhancements appropriate for HTML

```
\latextohtml
```

This generates the LaTeX2HTML logo, as in Example 3-5-1 in the previous section. Related logos such as TeX, LaTeX, *AMS*, and XY have special translations built into LaTeX2HTML. More are available with the `texnames` package.

```
\begin{makeimage}
```

This environment forces an image to be made of its contents, and typeset to the width determined by the `$PAPERSIZE` variable. Since the default translation of an unusual environment is to create an image, its main use is to override the usual translation. For example, sometimes a table looks better when fully typeset by LaTeX, or special formatting within paragraphed text may be desired. When using the `seminar` package, the `slide` environments are often best handled as images.

The environment's contents are scanned for any \label commands, so that cross-references can work as active hyperlinks.

Normally a figure environment is transformed as a whole into a single image. However, when it contains one or more makeimage subenvironments, the contents of the figure are normally translated into HTML as a separate <DIV> division. Images are made exclusively of the contents of each makeimage subenvironment. In particular, you can use an empty makeimage environment to prevent a figure environment from being turned into an image.

\htmlimage{*graphic effects*}

This command forces the creation of an image for an environment that would normally not be processed this way. It can also be used to include special graphic effects when an image is generated.

Environments affected by the \htmlimage command include figure and table, displaymath, equation, eqnarray, math, inline mathematics, and the aligned environments of the amsmath and amstex packages, as well as slide from the seminar package, and any environment from another package having no special support in LATEX2HTML. The \htmlimage command with its (perhaps empty) argument may appear anywhere inside the environment to force an image to be made. LATEX ignores both the command and its argument.

The *graphic effects* arguments that follow let you specify special effects to be used when creating the image.

height=*pixels*   set the HEIGHT attribute of the <IMG> tag to *pixels*.

width=*pixels*   set the WIDTH attribute of the <IMG> tag to *pixels*.

align=*option*   set the ALIGN attribute of the <IMG>.
Recognized values are TOP, BOTTOM, MIDDLE, LEFT, RIGHT, CENTER.

external   create a hyperlink to an external image file, rather than placing the image inline.

scale=*scale-factor*   scale the image by the supplied *scale-factor*.

thumbnail=*scale-factor*   combine both previous options, external and scale, and create a "thumbnail" version of the image, scaled by *scale-factor*. This thumbnail is used inline as an active button hyperlink pointing to the full-size version.

map=*URL*   make the image into a server-side image-map;
see the LATEX2HTML Users Guide for further details.

usemap=*URL*   make the image into a client-side image-map;
see the LATEX2HTML Users Guide for further details.

flip=*option*   rotate or flip the image according to a recognized *option*:
leftright, topbottom, rotate90 (or r90), rotate270 (or r270).

transparent   make the background of the image transparent when the default is to keep it opaque.

notransparent or **no_transparent**   keep the background of the image opaque when the default is to make it transparent.

antialias   request anti-aliasing of font characters within the image, irrespective of the default behavior for the image in question.

noantialias or **no_antialias**   do not use anti-aliased font characters, irrespective of the default behavior for the image in question.

\begin[*style-sheet information*]

The addition of an optional argument to LaTeX's \begin command is described with examples in Section 3.3.4. This is useful only when generating code for HTML 4.0 that supports Cascading Style Sheets (CSS). LaTeX ignores the optional argument.

The *style-sheet information* is written into the automatically generated .css style sheet file to be applied using CLASS and ID attributes. It can include names of extra CLASSes to which the subsequent environment should belong, as well as its pre-assigned default CLASS. Using an ID attribute, you can specify information to be applied exclusively to the subsequent environment.

\htmlsetstyle[*tags*]{*class*}{*style-info*}
\htmladdtostyle[*tags*]{*class*}{*style-info*}

These commands are ignored in LaTeX. Their purpose with LaTeX2HTML is to write the *style-info* into the CSS style sheet. It will be applied to tags of type *tags* and class *class*. The *tags* may be a hierarchical list of tags, such as TABLE.TR.TD or a single tag, or they may even be empty. Similarly the class may be empty. Any string may be given as the *style-info*. Currently the only checking for validity is to convert "=" into ":" and to replace any "," with a space.

\htmllanguagestyle[*class*]{*language*}

This command is to include the class *class* as an attribute for tags having *language* as the value of a LANG attribute. If *class* is not specified, a default value equal to the ISO 639 language code for *language* is used. Use a \htmlsetstyle command to apply particular style information. For example, the following code writes an entry into the CSS style sheet for setting German paragraphs with red text, using the babel package, in a document that was prepared mainly for a different language.

```
\htmllanguagestyle{german}
\htmlsetstyle[P]{de}{color:red}
```

`\htmlborder{`*attributes*`}`

This command is similar to `\htmlimage` in that it affects the environment in which
it occurs, requesting that a border be placed around the environment's contents.
It affects the `minipage`, `tabbing`, `table`, and `makeimage` environments, as well as
those mentioned earlier for `\htmlimage`. It also affects `theorem`-like environments.

The border is achieved by placing the contents inside a single `<TD>` cell of
an HTML `<TABLE>` construct. The argument *attributes* can contain any attribute
valid for HTML's `<TABLE>` tag, such as a thickness for `BORDER`, alignment, width,
`CELLSPACING`, and `CELLPADDING`.

`\begin{htmllist}[`*marker*`]`
`\htmlitemmark{`*marker*`}`

This environment is a replacement for the `description` list environment. It uses
colored balls as bullets for the listed items. In LATEX it appears as an ordinary
`description` list. This environment is defined in the `htmllist` package; it is usual
to load this and the `html` package with a single command. Colors are specified with
the *marker* argument, where *marker* can be `RedBall`, `OrangeBall`, `YellowBall`,
`GreenBall`, `BlueBall`, `PurpleBall`, `PinkBall`, or `WhiteBall`. These correspond
to icon images supplied with the navigation icons.

```
\usepackage{html,htmllist}

\begin{htmllist}[WhiteBall]
\item[Item 1:]This will have a white ball.
\item[Item 2:]
 This will also have a white ball.
\htmlitemmark{RedBall}%
\item[Item 3:]This will have a red ball.
\end{htmllist}
```

Item 1:
   This will have a white ball.
Item 2:
   This will also have a white ball.
Item 3:
   This will have a red ball.

`\strikeout{`*text*`}`

This command applies `<STRIKE>` tags to the *text*, creating the effect of a line strik-
ing out the information as no longer applicable. The *text* is simply omitted from
the LATEX typeset version.

```
\item can deal sensibly with \strikeout{at least the \emph{Common}
\LaTeX{} \emph{Commands} summarised at the back of\\}%
virtually all of the concepts and commands described in
the \LaTeX{} \htmlcite{blue book}{lamp:latex}, where there is
a meaningful interpretation appropriate to an \texttt{HTML} document.
```

- can deal sensibly with ~~at least the Common LATEX Commands summarised at the back of~~
  virtually all of the concepts and commands described in the LATEX blue book, where there is a
  meaningful interpretation appropriate to an HTML document. Also many other LATEX

3.5.3 Alternative text for hyperlinks

Page numbering has no meaning in an HTML document, since all navigation is done via active hyperlinks. Similarly numbering of sections, captions, and citations has reduced value because hyperlinks are used for cross-references as well. In addition to the LaTeX commands \ref and \cite, the commands described here offer alternative ways to handle cross-references and citations.

```
\hyperref [keyword] ...arguments...
```

This is a recommended replacement for the \ref and \pageref commands in LaTeX. The optional *keyword* specifies which form is to be used when the document is processed by LaTeX; the default is \ref.

```
\hyperref [ref] {link-text}{pre-latex}{post-latex}{label}
\hyperref {link-text}{pre-latex}{post-latex}{label}

\hyperref [page] {link-text}{pre-latex}{post-latex}{label}
\hyperref [pageref] {link-text}{pre-latex}{post-latex}{label}

\hyperref [no] {link-text}{latex-text}{label}
\hyperref [noref] {link-text}{latex-text}{label}
```

Each form in these groups of two yields identical results. The *link-text* is used only on the HTML pages, as text associated with a hyperlink that points to where the \label{label} command occurred, in the same document, or in another document produced with LaTeX2HTML. Only LaTeX uses the *pre-latex* and *post-latex* parts. These are placed on either side of the reference text (or number) associated with the *label*. With the final pair of commands, LaTeX makes no use of the *label* argument, although a hyperlink is still created for the HTML version. The example that follows clearly displays how the text of the various arguments is used differently by LaTeX (shown at the left) and by LaTeX2HTML (shown at the bottom).

...HTML pages for which there is no direct LaTeX counterpart. Most of these commands are discussed in detail in Section 4.8.

```
...\texttt{HTML} pages for which there
is no direct \LaTeX{} counterpart.
Most of these commands are discussed
in detail in \hyperref{a later section}
{Section~}{}{misceffects}.
```

The following commands implement effects on the HTML pages for which there is no direct LaTeX counterpart. Most of these commands are discussed in detail in a later section.

For processing by LaTeX there are macros corresponding to each option, namely, \hyperrefref, \hyperrefpageref, \hyperrefpage, \hyperrefno, and \hyperrefnoref. These commands process the arguments following the first optional one. The \hyperrefdef command handles the default case without any option. This allows information that is presented with the help of a particular option to be used in a different way, simply by redefining a single command rather than the whole \hyperref structure.

```
\hyperref[hyper]{URL}{category}{name}{text}
\hyperref[hyper][label]{text}
\hyperref[html]{link-text}{pre-latex}{post-latex}{label}
```

These additional variants were introduced to cope with the fact that Sebastian Rahtz's hyperref package (see Section 2.3) also uses a command called \hyperref. The first form has no symbolic *label*, and its usage is similar to \htmladdnormallink although it does allow for structure inside the hyperlink target. The second form uses an optional argument to hold the symbolic label, with the mandatory argument giving the hyperlink text. For both usages, by inserting the option [hyper] with each occurrence of \hyperref, LATEX2HTML will correctly process documents that load the hyperref package. On the other hand, a command starting with \hyperref[html] indicates that the given instance needs the version of \hyperref as implemented in the html package. Commands named \hyperrefhtml and \hyperrefhyper cater to these options for LATEX processing of the mandatory arguments.

```
\htmlref{link-text}{label}
\htmlref[ext]{link-text}[prefix]{label}
```

This is a shorter way to specify a hyperlink in the HTML version. It is equivalent to \hyperref[noref] with the *latex-text* and *link-text* being identical. For example,

With \htmlref it's easy to make links.

```
With \verb|\htmlref|
\htmlref{It's easy to make links}
{fig:example}.
```

With \htmlref it's easy to make links.

The ext option signals that the reference is made to a location inside an external document. See the \externalref and \externallabels commands that follow for an explanation of how to use this mechanism and the optional *prefix*. For alternative LATEX processing, macros \htmlrefdef and \htmlrefext can be redefined to cope with all but the first optional argument.

```
\hypercite[keyword]...arguments...
```

This is a recommended replacement for the \cite and \nocite commands in LATEX. The optional *keyword* specifies the form to be used when the document is processed by LATEX; the default is \cite.

```
\hypercite[int]{link-text}{latex-text}{opt-latex}{label}
\hypercite[cite]{link-text}{latex-text}{opt-latex}{label}
\hypercite{link-text}{latex-text}{opt-latex}{label}

\hypercite[nocite]{link-text}{latex-text}[prefix]{label}
\hypercite[no]{link-text}{latex-text}[prefix]{label}
\hypercite[ext]{link-text}{latex-text}[prefix]{label}
```

When typeset with LaTeX, all commands of the first group act the same way—
first placing the material in the *latex-text* argument, followed by issuing a command \cite[*opt-latex*]{*label*}. The second group of commands places a command
\nocite{*label*} following the material in *latex-text* to force a bibliography entry,
without any explicit reference marker on the printed page.

The *link-text* argument corresponds to a hyperlink on the HTML page, which
points to a location addressed by the symbolic *label*. The location could reside on
a bibliography page attached to the Web document being built, or it could be at
an external site. The use of symbolic labels available at external sites and the use of
prefix are explained with the \externallabels command.

For processing by LaTeX there exists a macro corresponding to each option,
namely, \hyperciteint, \hypercitecite, \hypercitenocite, \hyperciteno,
and \hyperciteext. These commands process the arguments following the first
optional one. The command \hypercitedef handles the default case without any
option. This allows information presented with a particular option to be used in
a different way, simply by redefining a single command rather than the whole
\hypercite structure.

```
\htmlcite{link-text}{label}
\htmlcite[ext]{link-text}[prefix]{label}
```

This is a shorter way to specify a hyperlinked citation on an HTML page. It is
equivalent to \hypercite[nocite] with the *latex-text* and *link-text* being identical; however, with the ext option, LaTeX omits the bibliography entry. See the
\externallabels command that follows for use of a *prefix*. For alternative LaTeX
processing, macros \htmlcitedef and \htmlciteext can be redefined to cope
with all but the first optional argument.

References can also be made to a target identified by a symbolic label. Such
labels are located in other Web documents created with LaTeX2HTML and these
documents can even reside at remote sites. In order to create hyperlinks pointing
to specific locations in remote HTML pages the following command must be given:

```
\externallabels[prefix]{URL}{local copy of labels.pl file}
```

The *URL* declares the remote location where the HTML pages are to be found.
These pages become the target for hyperlinks in the local document. One needs
first to obtain a copy of the file, usually called labels.pl, that contains infor-

mation about the symbolic *labels* used when the remote pages were created. (See page 92 where we mentioned the existence of that file when we discussed how LaTeX2HTML operates.) To avoid name clashes between labels used in the various documents, it is wise to specify the optional argument *prefix*, which will be used as a prefix whenever a *label* from this site is referenced. This copy of `labels.pl` file can be located anywhere that is convenient on the local system. Its full path and filename must be given as the last argument of the `\externallabels` command.

`\externalref` [*prefix*] {*label*}

This is analogous to `\ref` for a label defined in a remote document. When typeset by LaTeX, *label* will be ignored. In the HTML version, a hyperlink using a small icon as the visible marker is created. For a textual hyperlink, use instead `\htmlref` or `\hyperref` [`noref`]. See the `\externallabels` command, shown earlier, for the use of *prefix*.

`\externalcite` [*prefix*] {*label*}

This is the equivalent of `\nocite` for a bibliography entry residing in a remote document. When typeset by LaTeX, *label* will be ignored. In the HTML version, a hyperlink is created, using a small icon as the visible marker. For a textual hyperlink, use instead `\htmlcite` or `\hypercite` [`ext`]. See the `\externallabels` command, shown earlier, for an explanation of *prefix*. An example of how these commands are used is discussed in Section 3.5.6.

3.5.4   Conditional environments

Frequently there is material relevant only for the version of the document typeset by LaTeX or, alternatively, only for the HTML version generated by LaTeX2HTML. The expansion of a macro may need to be different in each version, perhaps for technical reasons. Special environments are provided to cope with such situations.

`\begin{htmlonly}`

The contents of the `htmlonly` environment are used only when the document is processed by LaTeX2HTML and are completely ignored by LaTeX.

`\begin{latexonly}`

The contents of the `latexonly` environment are used only when the document is processed by LaTeX and are completely ignored by LaTeX2HTML. Note that this environment has its contents contained within a TeX group and is within `\begingroup`...`\endgroup`. This environment cannot be used to set values for lengths or counters or to define macro expansions to be used only with LaTeX. Use the construction described next when you need to do this.

```
%begin{latexonly}
...
...
%end{latexonly}
```

These special comments have meaning only to LaTeX2HTML. It discards them and the portion of document source that they surround. On the other hand, because LaTeX simply sees the "%" as a comment character, it ignores those lines completely. Contents are unaffected, so any \newcommand or \newenvironment definitions and adjustments to length or counter values will take effect normally.

```
\html{text for HTML only}
\latex{text for LaTeX only}
\latexhtml{latex-text}{html-text}
```

These are shorthand forms of the earlier environments, intended for use with small pieces of text. The command and its arguments are read, and perhaps processed, before being discarded. With large portions of input source, it is better to use the environments to be sure that unwanted side effects do not occur. However, there are situations where \html works and the htmlonly environment does not, due to the way TeX reads and tokenizes the input source. This is the case, for instance, with special characters like "&" in tabular alignments.

```
\begin{imagesonly}
```

The contents of the imagesonly environment are written into the images.tex file for use with the LaTeX code to be typeset when creating images for the HTML document. For example, you can set the background and foreground color for all generated images in this way. This feature is sometimes needed to force a correct macro expansion.

```
\begin{comment}
```

The contents of the comment environment are always ignored by both LaTeX and LaTeX2HTML.

```
\begin{rawhtml}
```

The rawhtml environment is used to insert raw HTML code directly into the document at the given location, with respect to text and paragraphing, where it occurs in the source. There is no checking of the included code to see whether it is well-formed or is valid in the context of the requested version of HTML. Such considerations are left entirely to the document author. See the following \HTMLcode command for a safer way to construct HTML code.

```
\HTMLcode[attributes]{tag}
\HTMLcode[attributes]{tag}{content}
```

This command constructs an HTML tag for the given *tag* with attributes that are determined by *attributes*, provided the tag is valid for the chosen version of HTML. The *content* argument provides the content when the tag being constructed requires an end tag. Invalid attributes for a *tag* are filtered from the list, but an invalid *tag* is rejected altogether.

For the *attributes*, a list of `key=value` pairs can be given, separated by a space, a comma, or a newline character. Alternatively, it is sufficient to give just the desired values when it is possible to deduce which attributes are to accept those values. For example,

```
<HR WIDTH="50%" SIZE="3"
    NOSHADE ALIGN="center">                          \HTMLcode[50\% 3 noshade center]{HR}
```

Macro expansion occurs for each of the arguments of `\HTMLcode` (*content*, *tag*, and *attributes*). This minimizes typing when using repetitive structures. Figure 3.18 shows how this can be used in practice.

End-of-line characters in a LaTeX source are not ignored by LaTeX2HTML, as they are by LaTeX. Instead, they are retained in the resulting HTML files. Generally this does not affect the display constructed by browsers. However, it does affect the layout of the information in the `.html` files, should these be required to be read by a human. This explains why macro definitions are spread in the earlier example.

The set of tags usable with the `\HTMLcode` command can be extended. This is done in Perl by defining for each new tag a "regular expression" that will match the names of its valid attributes. For each attribute there needs to be a regular expression to match the possible values that it will accept. If you are interested to see how this is achieved, you can examine the files `versions/html3_2.pl` and `versions/html4_0.pl` that are part of the LaTeX2HTML distribution.

3.5.5   Navigation and layout of HTML pages

The commands described here are completely ignored by LaTeX.

```
\htmladdtonavigation{code}
```

This command provides an easy way to extend the navigation panel that is automatically produced by LaTeX2HTML. As the visible marker for a hyperlink, the *code* argument typically uses other commands available for showing text or an image. Each use of `\htmladdtonavigation` appends extra material, thereby allowing for quite extensive customization. Such customization applies only within a single document. You can alter the navigation panel code provided with `latex2html.config` if you want to customize all documents to be processed by LaTeX2HTML.

```
1   \newcommand{\myalign}{center}\newcommand{\mylist}{UL}
2   \newcommand{\myitem}[2]{\HTMLcode[disc]{LI}{\simpletest{#1}{#2}}}
3   \newcommand{\simpletest}[2]{%
4    \HTMLcode{#1}{ a simple test of ``#2'',} using \HTMLcode{CODE}{<#1>} .}
5   \newcommand{\tableopts}{10,border=5}
6   \newcommand{\tablelist}[4][left]{\HTMLcode[#1]{DIV}{%
7    \HTMLcode[\tableopts]{TABLE}{\HTMLcode[bottom]{CAPTION}{#3}%
8     \HTMLcode{TR}{\HTMLcode{TD}{\HTMLcode{#2}{#4}}}%
9    }}\HTMLcode[all]{BR}}
10
11  \tablelist[\myalign]{\mylist}{%
12   \textbf{A listing of the different text styles available in HTML 3.2}}{%
13    \myitem{B}{bold-face}\myitem{I}{italics}\myitem{TT}{teletype-text}
14    \myitem{U}{underlining}
15    \HTMLcode[circle]{LI}{\simpletest{STRIKE}{strikeout}}
16    \myitem{EM}{emphasis style}\myitem{STRONG}{strong style}
17    \myitem{CODE}{code style}\myitem{CITE}{citation style}
18    \myitem{DFN}{definition style}
19    \HTMLcode[square]{LI}{\simpletest{SAMP}{sample style}}
20    \HTMLcode[square]{LI}{\simpletest{KBD}{keyboard style}}
21    \myitem{VAR}{variable style}}
```

- **a simple test of ``bold-face'',** using <B> .
- *a simple test of ``italics'',* using <I> .
- a simple test of ``teletype-text'', using <TT> .
- a simple test of ``underlining'', using <U> .
- a simple test of ``strikeout'', using <STRIKE> .
- *a simple test of ``emphasis style'',* using <EM> .
- **a simple test of ``strong style'',** using <STRONG> .
- a simple test of ``code style'', using <CODE> .
- *a simple test of ``citation style'',* using <CITE> .
- a simple test of ``definition style'', using <DFN> .
- a simple test of ``sample style'', using <SAMP> .
- a simple test of ``keyboard style'', using <KBD> .
- *a simple test of ``variable style'',* using <VAR> .

A listing of the different text styles available in HTML 3.2

Figure 3.18: Using \HTMLcode commands with LaTeX2HTML

```
\htmladdtonavigation{\htmladdnormallink
{\htmladdimg[bottom]{http://bonk.ethz.ch/icon-files/find.gif}}
{http://bonk.ethz.ch/asearch.html}}
```

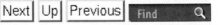

Next: Geologic Setting **Up**: Nature and cause of **Previous**: Nature and cause of

In this example by Uli Wortmann, the author has provided an easy link to a search engine to facilitate finding keywords in Web pages from his document.

```
\tableofchildlinks [option]
\tableofchildlinks* [option]
```

Long HTML pages containing subsections, subsubsections, and deeper levels of sectioning can be produced. Depending on the degree of linking being used, such pages usually start with a table of active hyperlinks to the (sub)sections contained therein. The above commands let you move this "mini-TOC" (table of contents) to where the \tableofchildlinks command occurs, or they let you omit it altogether. Allowable values for the *option* argument are

off   omit the mini-TOC on this HTML page.

none   omit the mini-TOC on this and all subsequent pages.

on   restore the mini-TOC for this HTML page.

all   restore the mini-TOC for this and all subsequent pages.

The *-version omits a break tag (<BR>) that would otherwise be inserted before the mini-TOC.

```
\htmlinfo [option]
\htmlinfo* [option]
```

This command lets you alter the location of the technical "About this document" information. By default, it is positioned at the end on a separate page. Use of \htmlinfo defines an alternative position. The *-version omits the heading, thereby allowing the automatically generated information to be included as part of the document, with extra material added afterward. Using the option off or none omits the information entirely.

These options allow the technical information to be presented in a more attractive and meaningful way. For an example of how this is used on a title page see Figure 3.19 (and [↪ MATHSYMP]).

```
\bodytext {attributes}
\htmlbody [attributes]
```

Both of these commands affect the contents of the <BODY> tag that is required on each HTML page. Most commonly, these are used to specify foreground and background colors. Colors for hyperlinks can be set this way as well. The command \bodytext is used to override the browser's defaults, and all attributes to be altered must be specified together inside the *attributes* argument. This will affect the current HTML page as well as all subsequent pages. With \htmlbody, a single attribute can be changed to have the specified *value*, retaining any other previous settings. These commands can be used several times on the same page, each use adds to (\htmlbody) or overrides (\bodytext) the effects of previous occurrences.

```
1    \htmlrule
2    \htmlhead[center]{subsubsection}{About this document.}
3    \htmladdimg[ALIGN=right]{../logos/aaslogo.gif}
4    \begin{flushleft}
5    This Web site has been constructed by \RossMoore, using the material
6    supplied by the authors and the conference organisers.
7
8    Most of this material will become available in book form, published by
9    \OzAcadSci, during 1997.
10   \end{flushleft}
11
12   \htmlrule[all,width=350]\htmlinfo*
```

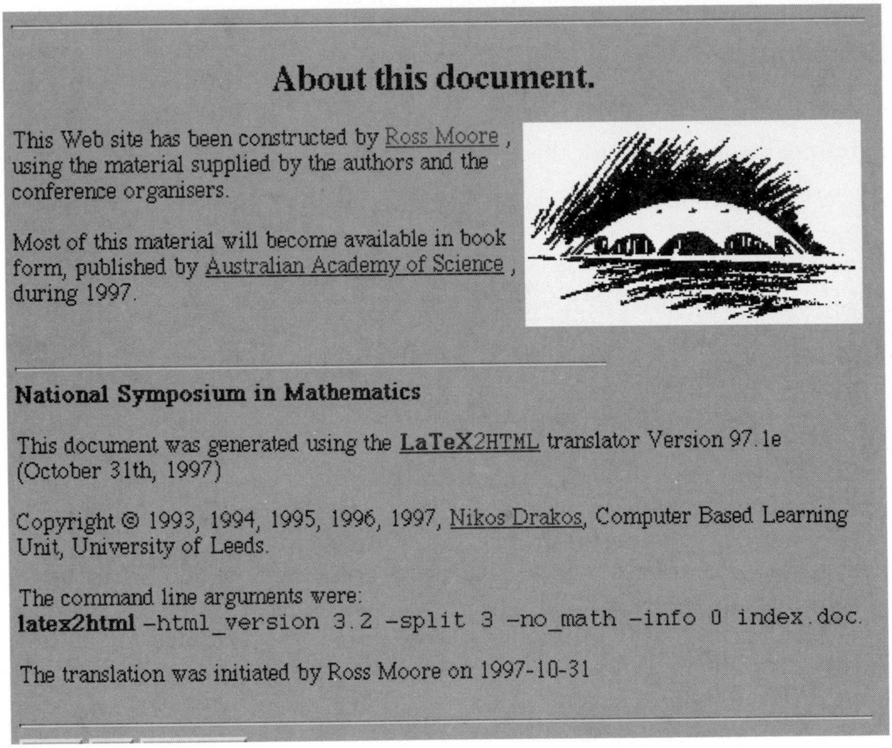

Figure 3.19: Using the \htmlinfo command with LaTeX2HTML

The foreground color for the text and the background color can also be specified using the \color and \pagecolor commands, provided that the LaTeX color package has been loaded.

\htmlbase{*URL*}

This command allows the <BASE> tag to be set to a directory different from the one where the current document resides.

3.5.6   Example of linking various external documents

In this section we show how to handle a set of composite documents, taking advantage of the hypertext extensions described in Section 3.5.

As a starting point, we take the LaTeX source document shown in Figure 3.1 and divide it, for demonstration purposes, into four subdocuments. These subdocuments, as shown in Figure 3.20, include a "master" file (ex20.tex) and three secondary files (ex21.tex, ex22.tex, and ex2bib.tex). We run all of these files through LaTeX and then *in a determined order* through LaTeX2HTML. Indeed, as we use cross-references to refer to document elements in external documents (with the commands \externalref and \externallabels introduced in Section 3.5.3), we must first treat the secondary files ex21.tex, ex22.tex, and ex2bib.tex, before tackling the master file ex20.tex.

By default, LaTeX2HTML writes the files that it creates into a subdirectory with the same name as the original file. Therefore, we end up with files in four subdirectories, as shown following (directory names are underlined):

```
ex20:    ex20.css     ex20.html     labels.pl

ex21:    ex21.css     ex21.html     labels.pl
         img1.gif     Timg1.gif
         images.idx   images.tex    images.log   images.aux   images.pl
ex22:    ex22.css     ex22.html     labels.pl    internals.pl

ex2bib:  ex2bib.css   ex2bib.html   labels.pl    internals.pl
```

The files labels.pl in the various directories contain information associating the symbolic keys of the \label commands in the original LaTeX source documents with the physical files. For instance, in lines 21–22 of the file ex20.tex we reference the key "tab-exa" that is defined on line 27 of the file ex22.tex. In fact, the labels.pl file in the ex22 directory contains the following information:

```
1   # LaTeX2HTML  99.1 (March 30, 1999)
2   # Associate labels original text with physical files.
3   $key = q/tab-exa/;
4   $external_labels{$key} = "$URL/" . q|ex22.html|;
5   $noresave{$key} = "$nosave";
6
7   $key = q/sec-tableau/;
8   $external_labels{$key} = "$URL/" . q|ex22.html|;
9   $noresave{$key} = "$nosave";
10  1;
```

Here, indeed, we find, the key (line 3) and a definition of the file where it resides (line 4).

Master file (ex20.tex)

```
1  \documentclass{article}
2  \usepackage{html}
3  %begin{latexonly}
4  \usepackage[T1]{fontenc}
5  %end{latexonly}
6  \usepackage[dvips]{graphicx}
7  \usepackage{francais}
8  \begin{document}
9  \begin{center}\Large
10   Exemple d'un document composé\\
11 \end{center}
12
13 \htmladdnormallink{Les Images}{../ex21/ex21.html}
14
15 \externallabels{../ex21}{../ex21/labels.pl}
16 Référence à une figure externe~\externalref{Fpsfig}.
17
18 \htmladdnormallink{Les tableaux}{../ex22/ex22.html}
19
20 \externallabels{../ex22}{../ex22/labels.pl}
21 Référence à un tableau externe~\externalref{tab-exa}.
22
23 \htmladdnormallink{La bibliographie}%
24                   {../ex2bib/ex2bib.html}
25 \end{document}
```

File containing images (ex21.tex)

```
1  \documentclass{article}
2  \usepackage{html}
3  %begin{latexonly}
4  \usepackage[T1]{fontenc}
5  %end{latexonly}
6  \usepackage[dvips]{graphicx}
7  \usepackage{francais}
8  \makeindex
9  \begin{document}
10 \section{Une figure EPS}
11 \label{sec-figure}
12 Cette section montre comment inclure une figure
13 \externallabels{../ex2bib}{../ex2bib/labels.pl}%
14 PostScript\externalref{bibPS} dans un document \LaTeX.
15 La \hyperref{figure}{figure }{}{Fpsfig}
16 est insérée dans le texte à l'aide de la commande
17 \verb!\includegraphics{colorcir}!.
18 \begin{figure}
19 \htmlimage{thumbnail=0.4}
20 \centering
21   \begin{tabular}{c@{\qquad}c}
22     \includegraphics[width=3cm]{colorcir} &
23     \includegraphics[width=3cm]{tac2dim}
24   \end{tabular}
25   \caption{Deux images EPS}\label{Fpsfig}
26 \end{figure}
27 \end{document}
```

File containing the table (ex22.tex)

```
1  \documentclass{article}
2  \usepackage{html}
3  %begin{latexonly}
4  \usepackage[T1]{fontenc}
5  %end{latexonly}
6  \usepackage[dvips]{graphicx}
7  \usepackage{francais}
8  \newcommand{\Lcs}[1]{\texttt{\symbol{'134}#1}}
9  \begin{document}
10 \section{Exemple d'un tableau}
11 \label{sec-tableau}
12 Le \hyperref{tableau}{tableau }{}{tab-exa} montre
13 l'utilisation de l'environnement \texttt{table}.
14 \begin{table}
15 \centering
16   \begin{tabular}{cccccc}
17   \Lcs{primo}  & \primo & \Lcs{secundo} & \secundo &
18   \Lcs{tertio} & \tertio             \\
19   \Lcs{quatro} & \quatro& 1\Lcs{ier}  & 1\ier   &
20   1\Lcs{iere}  & 1\iere               \\
21   \Lcs{fprimo})&\fprimo)& \Lcs{No} 10  & \No 10  &
22   \Lcs{no} 15  & \no 15               \\
23   \Lcs{og} a \Lcs{fg}&\og a \fg&3\Lcs{ieme}&3\ieme &
24   10\Lcs{iemes}& 10\iemes
25   \end{tabular}
26 \caption{Quelques commandes de l'option
27   \texttt{french} de \texttt{babel}}\label{tab-exa}
28 \end{table}
29 \end{document}
```

File with the bibliography (ex2bib.tex)

```
1  \documentclass{article}
2  \usepackage{html}
3  %begin{latexonly}
4  \usepackage[T1]{fontenc}
5  %end{latexonly}
6  \usepackage[dvips]{graphicx}
7  \usepackage{francais}
8  \makeindex
9  \begin{document}
10 \begin{thebibliography}{99}
11 \bibitem{bib-PS}\label{bibPS}
12 Adobe Inc.
13 \emph{PostScript, manuel de référence (2ième édition)}
14 InterÉditions (France), 1992
15 \end{thebibliography}
16 \end{document}
```

Figure 3.20: Linking external files (LaTeX files)

The other files in the directories are HTML and CSS files, in addition to GIF images generated for material that LaTeX2HTML cannot gracefully translate into HTML. Here it is the case only for the image in ex21.tex, where we generate the complete image of the table with the two EPS files (lines 21–24 in the ex21.tex, Figure 3.20). Additionally, on line 19 we indicate that we do not want to include the full image inside the HTML file, but rather a 40% reduced thumbnail image. Hence, in the directory ex21 we observe two GIF images: img1.gif, the complete image, and Timg1.gif, the corresponding thumbnail.

Additionally, lines 3–5 of all LaTeX source files in Figure 3.20 show that we *ignore* the command \usepackage[T1]{fontenc} during the LaTeX2HTML translation. This is because the font encoding is important for LaTeX only, and all Latin 1 characters, like the French diacritics present on several lines in the source documents, are handled correctly without further intervention by LaTeX2HTML. In fact, the more traditional macro-based representation of accented characters in LaTeX sources (used in Figure 3.1) and the direct use of the Latin 1 character encoding yield the same result after translation into HTML.

To guide LaTeX2HTML in translating these documents we also use a customization file, myinit.pl, containing customizations of Perl constants.

```
1   # File myinit.pl
2   $ADDRESS = "<em>Michel Goossens<BR>" .
3             "Division IT<BR>"             .
4             "T&eacute;l. 767.5028<BR>"
5             "$address_data[1]</em>",
6   $MAX_SPLIT_DEPTH = 0; # do not split document
7   $NO_NAVIGATION = 1;   # no navigation panel
8   1;        # Mandatory last line
```

Lines 2–5 define the address information displayed at the end of each HTML page, line 6 declares that we want to keep the complete document in a single piece, and line 7 eliminates the navigation panels.

Using this customization file we issue the following command to execute LaTeX2HTML on the files in Figure 3.20:

```
latex2html -init_file myinit.pl -info "External links test" filenames
```

The -init_file flag loads the customization file myinit.pl, while the -info flag changes the "About this document... (*À propos de ce document...*)" information. Finally, *filenames* stands for the list of the four LaTeX files—ex2bib.tex, ex21.tex, ex22.tex, and ex20.tex—that are treated in the correct order. The result of running this command is shown in Figure 3.21.

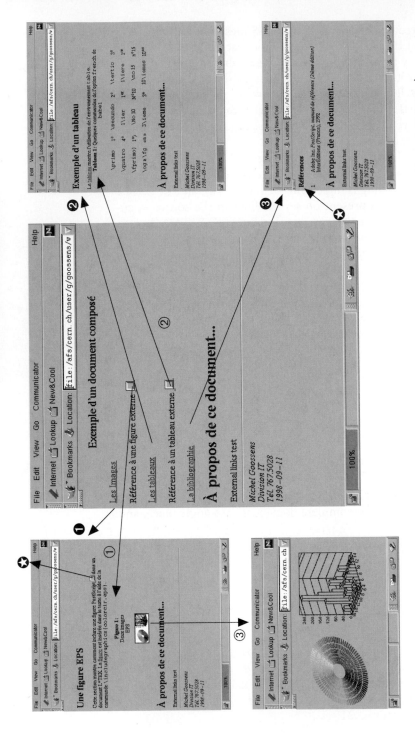

As requested in the customization file myinit.pl, there are no navigation panels, and we have a new address field. The *À propos de ce document...* information has also been customized. The arrows carrying the numbers ❶, ❷, and ❸ correspond to hyperlinks pointing to an HTML document using the \htmladdnormallink command in the LaTeX source (lines 13, 18, and 23 of ex20.tex). The arrows numbered ① and ② are cross-references that are constructed with the commands \externalref. They make use of symbolic names specified as the argument of \label commands in the target documents (lines 16 and 21 of ex20.tex, referencing labels defined on line 25 of ex21.tex and line 27 of ex22.tex, respectively). The arrow numbered ③ corresponds to a hyperlink that connects the thumbnail in the text with the real-size image available as a separate external GIF file. Finally, the start point (line 14 of ex21.tex) and the end point (line 11 of ex2bib.tex) of the bibliographic reference link are indicated by the symbol ✪.

Figure 3.21: The HTML file structure obtained from the composite document and its subdocuments (Figure 3.20) as viewed with a browser

3.5.7   Advanced features

3.5.7.1   Using a Makefile

With UNIX it is often useful to use a `Makefile` to simplify the commands that run a particular procedure, particularly when many command-line options or long filenames are required. The following `Makefile` provides a simple method for generating the example shown in Figure 3.21, just by typing <u>make ex2</u>.

```
1    # Makefile for Example 2
2    LTX = latex
3    L2H2 = latex2html -init_file myinit.pl -info "External_links_test"
4
5    ex2 :   ex21.aux ex22.aux
6              $(L2H2) ex2bib ex21 ex22 ex20
7    ex21.aux :
8              $(LTX) ex21.tex
9    ex22.aux :
10             $(LTX) ex22.tex
```

Line 6 contains the call to LaTeX2HTML; the preceding line defines a "dependency" to ensure that segment sources have been processed by LaTeX. The figure and table caption numbers are available in the `.aux` files. Each pair of lines (7–8 and 9–10) handles a call to LaTeX for one segment.

The code shown is a naive use of a `Makefile`, yet it is sufficient to indicate that much typing can be avoided. Figure 3.22 is a `Makefile` for use with another version of this example, and presented as a "segmented" document. In the next subsection we describe from the `html` package the macros that are designed specifically for this technique. The example itself is discussed in detail in Section 3.5.7.3.

3.5.7.2   Using "segmented" documents

The commands described in this section are for use mainly with the "Document Segmentation" strategy, although some can also be useful in other situations. Segmentation involves splitting the LaTeX source into segments. Each segment is contained in a different file and is processed separately by LaTeX2HTML.

Earlier versions of LaTeX2HTML could be excessively hungry for memory, particularly during the image generation phase. Recent improvements have alleviated this need, but segmentation remains a useful strategy for keeping a Web document up-to-date. Segments can be updated individually or in groups without the need to reprocess the whole document completely. The LaTeX2HTML Users Guide is maintained using this strategy; consult it for further details.

> \segment [*align*] {*file*} {*sectioning*} {*title*}

Suppose that the value of *sectioning* were `section`; then LaTeX would process the command as \section{*title*}, followed by \input *file*. First it dumps counter information into a file named *file*.ptr in the form of LaTeX commands for setting counter values. This file is included as part of the job when LaTeX2HTML processes

```
1   # Makefile for Example 3
2   L2H = $(L2HNEW)/latex2html -link 4
3   L2HTOP = $(L2HNEW)/latex2html -split 0
4   LTX = latex
5   EX = ex3
6   HTML = .html
7   TX = .tex
8   TEXES = $(EX)*$(TX)
9   TOP = ex30
10  BIB = $(EX)bib
11  TEXTOP = $(TOP)$(TX)
12  INT = internals.pl
13  BIBREF = '\#BIBLIO'
14  # Directories containing the segments
15  EX30 = ../$(TOP)/$(TOP)
16  EX31 = ../$(EX)1/$(EX)1
17  EX32 = ../$(EX)2/$(EX)2
18  EX3b = ../$(TOP)/$(TOP)$(HTML)
19  # Titles for navigation to the segments
20  EX30t = Exemple_d\'un_document_segmenté
21  EX31t = Une_figure_EPS
22  EX32t = Exemple_d\'un_tableau
23  EX3bt = Références
24
25  COMMON = -info 0 -split 1 -link 4 -no_auto_link -biblio $(EX3b) -external_file $(TOP) \
26         -up_url $(EX30)$(HTML) -up_title $(EX30t) -index $(EX3b) -index_in_navigation
27  update: $(TOP).ind
28         make $(TOP)/$(INT) $(EX)2/$(INT) $(EX)1/$(INT); make $(TOP)/$(INT)
29  fresh:
30         rm $(EX)*/$(INT) $(TOP).aux; make $(TOP).ind;
31         make $(TOP)$(HTML) $(EX)2$(HTML) $(EX)1$(HTML); make $(TOP)$(HTML)
32  $(TOP)$(HTML) :
33         $(L2HTOP) -down_url $(EX31)$(HTML) -down_title $(EX31t) -biblio $(BIBREF) $(TOP)
34  $(TOP)/$(INT) : $(TEXTOP) $(BIB)$(TX) $(EX)1/$(INT) $(EX)2/$(INT)
35         make $(TOP)$(HTML)
36  $(EX)1$(HTML) :
37         $(L2H) $(COMMON) -t $(EX31t) -prev_url $(EX30)$(HTML) -prev_title $(EX30t) \
38         -down_url $(EX32)$(HTML) -down_title $(EX32t) $(EX)1
39  $(EX)1/$(INT) : $(EX)1$(TX)
40         make $(EX)1$(HTML)
41  $(EX)2$(HTML) :
42         $(L2H) $(COMMON) -t $(EX32t) -prev_url $(EX31)$(HTML) -prev_title $(EX31t) \
43         -down_url $(EX3b)$(BIBREF) -down_title $(EX3bt) $(EX)2
44  $(EX)2/$(INT) : $(EX)2$(TX)
45         make $(EX)2$(HTML)
46
47  # handle  LaTeX/dvips/makeindex  etc.
48  $(TOP).aux: $(TEXES)
49         make dvi
50  $(TOP).dvi:
51         make dvi
52  dvi:
53         $(LTX) $(TEXTOP); $(LTX) $(TEXTOP); make $(TOP).ind
54  $(TOP).ind: $(TOP).aux
55         makeindex $(TOP).idx; $(LTX) $(TEXTOP); touch $(TOP).ind
56  ps:
57         make $(TOP).ps
58  $(TOP).ps: $(TOP).dvi
59         dvips $(TOP).dvi -o
60  clean:
61         rm *.ps *.dvi *.log *.ilg
```

Figure 3.22: Example `Makefile` for documents in Figure 3.23

the segment. The *sectioning* can be any of the recognized forms of the sectioning commands: `part`, `chapter`, `section`, `subsection`, `paragraph`, and so on.

The segment *file* should not contain its own title, unless it is shielded inside a `\begin{htmlonly}`...`\end{htmlonly}` environment because it is already provided by the *title* argument. For LaTeX2HTML, this *title* is stored using `\htmlhead` (see the following) in the `.ptr` file. This can be overridden using `\htmlnohead`, if desired.

```
\htmlhead[align]{sectioning}{title}
\htmlnohead
```

The `\htmlhead` command is normally read from a `.ptr` file (see `\segment` command earlier). In this form it becomes the first information to appear on the HTML page, following the navigation aids. However, it may be desirable to suppress this and place other information, such as an image, earlier on the page. In this case the command `\htmlnohead` should be used, followed by `\htmlhead` at an appropriate place in the source. Indeed, an alternative *title* could be used, allowing different titles for the same HTML page when it is viewed as a stand-alone document or as a section within a larger document.

Using the optional *align*, the *title* heading can be aligned to the center, the right, or the left (the default) at the top of the HTML page. Of course, LaTeX ignores both `\htmlnohead` and `\htmlhead` and its arguments.

```
\startdocument
```

For a document segment, this command acts as an artificial marker indicating where the body of the segment is presumed to begin. Material occurring before this is treated as if it were in the preamble of a complete LaTeX document and will not appear on the HTML pages. Typically such material could be `\newcommand` definitions contained within `\begin{htmlonly}`...`\end{htmlonly}`.

```
\internal[type]{prefix}
```

This command causes LaTeX2HTML to load a Perl file containing information generated within a different segment of this (or another) document. For example,

```
\internal[contents]{../segA/C}
```

This sequence causes the file `../segA/Ccontents.pl` to be read, resolving the path from the directory where the document is being processed. This file would contain information shown in the table of contents generated by `\tableofcontents`, if it were to appear within the segment being processed. Allowable values for *type* are `section`, `contents`, `figure`, `table`, `index`, `images`, and `internal`.

```
\segmentcolor [model] {color}
\segmentpagecolor [model] {color}
```

These commands should occur only inside `.ptr` files. They pass color information, defined with LaTeX's `\color` and `\pagecolor` commands, from one segment to the next or from the parent document to its segments.

```
\endsegment [sectioning]
```

This command is sometimes needed to ensure correct numbering of sections within a document that loads other segments. In LaTeX it does nothing, but with LaTeX2HTML it corrects problems with the navigation panels and table of contents for a segmented document that may otherwise become confused. It should follow the `\segment` command to ensure that hyperlinks to subsequent pages do not get mixed in with that segment or with earlier segments. The *sectioning* should match the preceding segment.

3.5.7.3 Segmentation example, with `Makefile`

Figure 3.23 shows the HTML pages that can be produced by organizing the LaTeX document sources to make use of the segmentation strategy. Comparing Figure 3.23 with Figure 3.2, we see that to enhance the usefulness of particular pages it is possible to organize the information so that it appears in a different order. In Figure 3.23 the main HTML page is longer than the depth of the screen, so it has been split into two images. They are shown superimposed vertically at the left of the figure. Of course, when you use a browser, the vertical scroll bar allows all the information to be accessed.

The source listings for the segments are given in Figure 3.24. These are similar to those in Figure 3.20 for processing pieces of LaTeX separately for HTML pages. Generally they are a little shorter because it is not necessary to process complete LaTeX documents with LaTeX2HTML. Look at the listing for the file `ex30.tex`. It contains `\segment` commands rather than `\input` or `\include` for each section. Thus when processed by LaTeX, the files `ex31.tex` and `ex32.tex` are each input, starting a new section. The resulting `.dvi` file should give a result exactly as shown in Figure 3.2, except for some entries that are in the index. Prolific use of `\htmlrule` commands helps to segregate chunks of related information on the HTML page.

Each of the files `ex31.tex` and `ex32.tex` has a `\startdocument` command in place of `\begin{document}` to indicate to LaTeX2HTML where the body begins. This is preceded by any required preamble material, mainly inside `htmlonly` conditional environments to avoid repetition when LaTeX processes the document. There are `\documentclass` and `\usepackage` commands with `ex31.tex` because these will be needed when generating an image. With `ex32.tex` there is no need

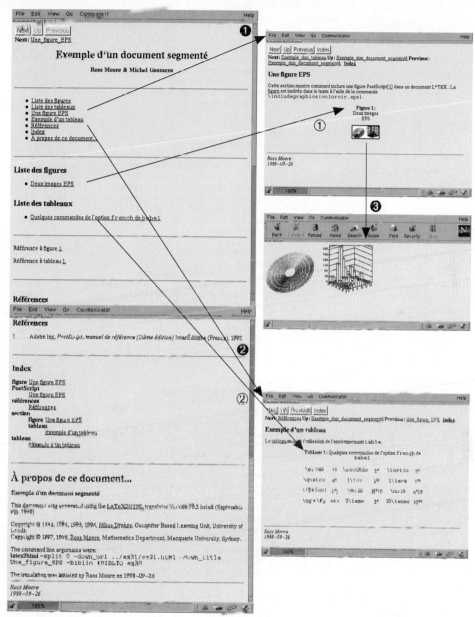

❶ and ❷ link the main document to the segments that are generated at the section level. ①
and ② are cross-reference links from the lists of figures and tables to the actual figures and
tables. ❸ links the thumbnail to the real figure.

Figure 3.23: Segmented HTML structure generated by LATEX2HTML from the
LATEX source of Figure 3.24

Master file (ex30.tex)

```
1  \documentclass{article}
2  \usepackage[dvips]{graphicx}
3  \usepackage{francais}
4  \usepackage{html}
5  \usepackage{makeidx}
6  %begin{latexonly}
7  \usepackage[T1]{fontenc}
8  %end{latexonly}
9
10 \internal{../ex31/}
11 \internal[sections]{../ex31/}
12 %\internal[contents]{../ex31/}
13 \internal[figure]{../ex31/}
14 \internal[index]{../ex31/}
15
16 \internal{../ex32/}
17 \internal[sections]{../ex32/}
18 %\internal[contents]{../ex32/}
19 \internal[table]{../ex32/}
20 \internal[index]{../ex32/}
21
22 \makeindex
23 \title{Exemple d'un document segmenté}
24 \author{Ross Moore \& Michel Goossens}
25
26 \begin{document}
27 \maketitle\htmlrule
28 \tableofchildlinks\htmlrule
29 %begin{latexonly}
30 \tableofcontents
31 %end{latexonly}
32 \listoffigures\listoftables\htmlrule
33
34 \segment{ex31}{section}{Une figure EPS}
35 \endsegment[section]
36 \html{Référence à figure~\ref{Fpsfig}.}
37
38 \segment{ex32}{section}{Exemple d'un tableau}
39 \endsegment[section]
40 \html{Référence à tableau~\ref{tab-exa}.}
41 \htmlrule \input{ex3bib}
42 \htmlrule \printindex \htmlrule
43 \end{document}
```

File with the bibliography (ex3bib.tex)

```
1  \begin{thebibliography}{99}
2  \label{BIBLIO}\index{références}
3  \bibitem{bib-PS}
4  Adobe Inc. \emph{PostScript, manuel de référence
5    (2ième édition)} InterÉditions (France), 1992
6  \end{thebibliography}
```

File containing images (ex31.tex)

```
1  \begin{htmlonly}
2  \documentclass{article}
3  \usepackage{makeidx,html}
4  \usepackage[T1]{fontenc}
5  \usepackage[dvips]{graphicx}
6  \usepackage{francais}
7  \input ex31.ptr
8  \end{htmlonly}
9  \startdocument
10 \index{section!figure}
11
12 Cette section montre comment inclure une figure
13 PostScript\cite{bib-PS} dans un document \LaTeX.
14 La \hyperref{figure}{figure }{}{Fpsfig}
15 est insérée dans le texte à l'aide de la commande
16 \verb!\includegraphics{colorcir}!.
17 \index{figure}
18 \index{PostScript}
19 \begin{figure}[h]
20 \htmlimage{thumbnail=0.4}
21 \centering
22   \begin{tabular}{c@{\qquad}c}
23     \includegraphics[width=3cm]{colorcir} &
24     \includegraphics[width=3cm]{tac2dim}
25   \end{tabular}
26   \caption{Deux images EPS}\label{Fpsfig}
27 \end{figure}
```

File containing the table (ex32.tex)

```
1  \begin{htmlonly}
2  \usepackage{makeidx,html}
3  \usepackage{francais}
4  \input ex32.ptr
5  \end{htmlonly}
6  \newcommand{\Lcs}[1]{\textttt{\symbol{'134}#1}}
7  \startdocument
8  \index{section!tableau}
9
10 Le \hyperref{tableau}{tableau }{}{tab-exa}
11 montre l'utilisation de l'environnement \textttt{table}.
12 \begin{table}[h]
13 \centering
14  \begin{tabular}{cccccc}
15  \Lcs{primo}  & \primo & \Lcs{secundo} & \secundo
16  & \Lcs{tertio} & \tertio \\
17  \Lcs{quatro} & \quatro& 1\Lcs{ier}    & 1\ier
18  & 1\Lcs{iere}  & 1\iere \\
19  \Lcs{fprimo})&\fprimo)& \Lcs{No} 10   & \No 10
20  & \Lcs{no} 15 & \no 15 \\
21  \Lcs{og} a \Lcs{fg}&\og a \fg&3\Lcs{ieme}&3\ieme
22  & 10\Lcs{iemes}& 10\iemes
23  \end{tabular}
24 \caption{Quelques commandes de l'option \textttt{french}
25      de \textttt{babel}}\label{tab-exa}
26 \index{tableau}
27 \end{table}
```

Figure 3.24: Segmentation example (LATEX files)

for a \documentclass, but the makeidx, francais, and html packages are still needed. Both segments need to \input the corresponding ptr files so that section counters are set correctly.

Notice how the \externallabels and \externalref commands that were used in Figure 3.20 are not needed. Instead the navigation is handled using LaTeX's usual \ref commands. This is possible due to the \internal commands within ex30.tex, which read the symbolic label information from the segments. Similarly one segment could resolve cross-references within another segment by including the appropriate \internal command. Information for the lists of Figures and Tables is read from the commands \internal[figure] and \internal[table], while information about the sections within each segment is obtained using the \internal[section] commands. Similar information, perhaps with slight differences, for a table of contents page could be obtained using \internal[contents]. This is not needed in this example, since the automatically generated "mini" table of contents has all that is needed. It also explains why the \tableofcontents command is being used only by LaTeX, with the position of the mini table of contents being determined by \tableofchildlinks.

Information for the index is collected through the \internal[index] commands. When the makeidx package is loaded, features such as hierarchical index listings become available. A simplified index is available when makeidx is not loaded. It is best to load makeidx in all segments; otherwise some index entries will show filenames of type html rather than section titles. For the use of \cite commands in ex31.tex, the target of the hyperlink is deduced by knowing on which html file the bibliography will appear. Such information is provided by the -biblio command-line option, when that segment is processed. Navigation between the segments is provided via the buttons at the top of each HTML page, just as in a single, unsegmented document, independent of any cross-references and sectioning commands within the LaTeX source. These hyperlinks are specified using command-line options. As a result the command line gets rather complex, and therefore it becomes essential to use a Makefile.

Look at the structure of the Makefile listing in Figure 3.22. Usually it defines variables to hold strings that are to be used often or that may reasonably be expected to change as a document is being developed. (This is similar to the use of macros in LaTeX, only more so.) Lines 2–26 contain such definitions; their values are accessed via the $(..) dereferencing notation.

As an example, in lines 25–26 the variable COMMOM is built to contain command-line options, used when processing the segments. These command-line options will be used with both segments, some of which are constructed by dereferencing other variables. The actual command lines themselves are constructed in lines 36–38 and 41–43. In those line groups, the command-line options specify the document title. The hyperlinks for the next/previous navigation buttons are also specified, as well as the actual file to be processed. Following is the resulting command line (lines 1–6), and the start of the log messages for one of the segments (lines 8–27). The command line, which is very long, has been rearranged to make it readable.

```
1    latex2html -link 4 -info 0 -split 1 -link 4 -no_auto_link -biblio ../ex30/ex30.html \
2    -external_file ex30 -up_url ../ex30/ex30.html -up_title Exemple_d'un_document_segmenté \
3    -index ../ex30/ex30.html -index_in_navigation \
4    -t Une_figure_EPS -prev_url ../ex30/ex30.html \
5    -prev_title Exemple_d'un_document_segmenté  -down_url ../ex32/ex32.html \
6    -down_title Exemple_d'un_tableau ex31
7
8    This is LaTeX2HTML Version 99.1 release (March 30, 1999)
9    Drakos, CBLU, University of Leeds.
10
11   Revised and extended by:
12    Marcus Hennecke, Ross Moore, Herb Swan and others
13   ...producing markup for HTML version 3.2
14
15   Loading /usr/local/share/latex2html/versions/html3.2.pl
16
17   *** processing declarations ***
18
19   OPENING /services/www/texdev/LWC/MICHEL/ex31.tex
20
21   Cannot create directory ex31/: File exists, reusing it.
22   Reusing directory ex31/:
23
24   Loading /usr/local/share/latex2html/styles/texdefs.perl...
25   Loading /usr/local/share/latex2html/styles/article.perl
26   Loading /usr/local/share/latex2html/styles/makeidx.perl
27   Loading /usr/local/share/latex2html/styles/html.perl
```

This `Makefile` makes it straighforward to maintain the example document. It suffices to type `make ex31.html` on the command line to execute the commands specified on lines 35–37. Alternatively, typing `make ex31/internals.pl` would cause the command to be executed only if something has changed within the LaTeX source file `ex31.tex`. Line 38 tests this "dependency," calling upon `make ex31.html` in line 39, only if necessary;[8] otherwise there is no need to reconstruct `ex31/ex31.html`. Lines 43–44 handle the similar conditional update of `ex32/ex32.html`. Updating the main page `ex30/ex30.html` is a little more complicated since it depends on changes in more than one LaTeX source file and on having up-to-date information in the `internals.pl` files from the other segments. This dependency is stated in line 33. Unlike LaTeX's aux file, which is written after each call to LaTeX on a source file, the `internals.pl` file is written *only* if the information it should contain has changed. Hence a segment can be updated for small changes without changing the date on its `internals.pl`. Such a date change would also cause the main segment to need updating.

The ability to update conditionally just those HTML pages that need it is captured in lines 26–27, whereby all the dependencies are tested as a result of the command `make update`. This includes running LaTeX to ensure that the `dvi` version is up-to-date, and the aux file has correct information.

If something goes wrong or if a change that does not cause appropriate updates to occur is made, then reprocess everything using the rule on lines 28–30 by typing

---

[8]It would be necessary only if a file named on the right-hand side of the ":" has a modification date/time later than the file named on the left-hand side.

make refresh. Typically this is necessary after altering the definition of a macro expansion within a style file.

Of course, a dependency on this style file could be added at an appropriate place within the Makefile. Lines 47–58 give rules for running LaTeX via make dvi and dvips via make ps. The former does multiple runs of LaTeX, then of makeindex, and finally of LaTeX again. Unneeded log files are removed by make clean (lines 59–60).

Be aware that the make program can vary in minor details, on different UNIX platforms, and even with a different shell on the same platform. Note the need to "escape" special characters such as # and ', using \# and \'. On the particular platform and shell used by the author, it was necessary to avoid having spaces in strings that appear on the command line; hence the use of _ in the segment titles.

3.5.7.4   Tracing and debugging

The commands in this section are intended primarily to aid LaTeX2HTML developers and to extend the program with specialized user modules.

```
\htmltracing{level}
\htmltracenv{level}
```

Both of these commands set the level of tracing to the specified *level*, which is an integer from 0 (no tracing) to 9; the default level is 1. The difference between \htmltracing and \htmltracenv depends on when the command is processed. The command \htmltracenv is processed in order with environments, whereas \htmltracing is treated as a command with a fixed static expansion. Therefore, processing can be delayed to follow environments at the same level of TeX grouping. Higher values of *level* produce more messages that concern more technical aspects of the translation process. Consult the LaTeX2HTML Users Guide for the type of information displayed with each level.

```
\htmlset{variable}{value}
\htmlset[hash]{key}{value}
\htmlsetenv{variable}{value}
\htmlsetenv[hash]{variable or key}{value}
```

These \htmlset and \htmlsetenv commands allow Perl variables to be set or changed directly during processing by LaTeX2HTML. The difference between the two forms has to do with when the command is actually processed. The command \htmlsetenv is processed in order with environments, whereas \htmlset is treated as a command with a static expansion. Therefore, processing can be delayed until after environments at the same level of TeX grouping. When the optional argument is used, the *value* is assigned to the *key* for the hash specified by *hash*.

Summary

This chapter has shown how LaTeX2HTML can be used to translate LaTeX source documents into a hyperlinked web of HTML files with source fragments that cannot be directly expressed in equivalent HTML constructs, such as mathematics, transformed into images. The default settings for the translation are often sufficient to obtain excellent results without user intervention. The user can, nevertheless, intervene directly in the translation process by setting command-line options or by editing one or more files specifically provided to facilitate user customization.

We have studied in detail how to fine-tune mathematics rendering and have looked at the facilities that are available to handle various languages. We have given examples of an implementation to support languages used on the Indian subcontinent, but the techniques shown are more general.

The final part has taught us how to profit from the rich set of extensions of the html package. This not only puts the full powers of HTML at our fingertips, but also allows us to build a real web of hyperlinked external documents.

All in all, LaTeX2HTML is a very flexible and complete tool. It can be used by a novice as a *black-box* automatic translator to make LaTeX source documents available on the Web in a simple and transparent way. However, in the hands of the devoted, LaTeX2HTML becomes a full-fledged application that lets you create, edit, and manage your hypertext documents. LaTeX2HTML thus provides a convenient bridge between the world of LaTeX and the Internet.

CHAPTER 4

Translating LaTeX to HTML using TeX4ht

TeX4ht is a system that offers a way to create configurable hypertext versions of LaTeX documents; it is an extension of TeX, in general, and of LaTeX, in particular. In this chapter we concentrate on its default setup that produces HTML output.

The system consists of two parts: style files to supplement LaTeX's existing ones with HTML features and a postprocessor for extracting HTML files from the output of the TeX program. TeX4ht leaves the major task of processing the source documents into DVI code to TeX itself. Consequently, TeX4ht has access to the full power of TeX for handling fonts, macros, variables, category codes, and other important features that are quite commonly hidden from the users but are essential for style files. Most applications need to worry about only a few major features of the system. In the case of HTML output from LaTeX sources, the user may hardly notice any intrusion from the system.

Despite being a flexible authoring system rich in capabilities, TeX4ht keeps its features transparent for most applications. Typically, compiling and viewing documents that employ TeX4ht is as simple as doing the same without using the system. The first three sections of this chapter are geared toward such applications—explaining how the system can be employed by casual users who do not need special configurations. We list the most commonly used package options, show a complete example with its input and output, and briefly describe how the process works.

The fourth section describes the new commands that are provided in the package for authors who wish to add explicit links, achieve HTML effects manually, or add information to the CSS style sheet. The fifth section explains how the system can be extensively configured to produce different effects from the same LaTeX markup.

The final part of the chapter goes into more detail of how the various parts of the TeX4ht process work and how they can be changed. This will be especially useful for system adminstrators installing TeX4ht for use by a group of authors.

TeX4ht is available from either TeX archives or its own Web page [↪ TEX4HT], where there are also many examples. Currently, TeX4ht is still a work in progress. A few of the features described here might change in time, but the changes are expected to be minor, as most features are completely stable.

4.1   Using TeX4ht

To have a source LaTeX file translated into HTML, many users will find it sufficient just to load the TeX4ht package `tex4ht.sty` (Figure 4.1).

The translation is activated with a command of the form `ht latex` *filename*, or a similar system-dependent command. The output is stored in a set of files with the root file named *filename*`.html`.

4.1.1   Package options

The outcome of the translation of the LaTeX source files into HTML can be varied using package options (for example, see Figure 4.2).

There are a number of package options available. Some are of general interest; most are not at all essential. Some options are provided as shortcut mechanisms to offer convenient ways of activating useful features without needing to learn their details.

```
<!DOCTYPE HTML PUBLIC "-//W3C//DTD
        HTML 4.0 Transitional//EN">
<HTML>
<HEAD>
<!--try.html from try.tex
   (TeX4ht, 1998-05-27 00:01:00)-->
<TITLE>try.html</TITLE>
<LINK REL="stylesheet"                      \documentclass{article}
    TYPE="text/css" HREF="try.css">         \usepackage{tex4ht}
</HEAD><BODY>                               \begin{document}
hello world                                 hello world
</BODY> </HTML>                             \end{document}
```

Figure 4.1: A simple source file and the resulting HTML code

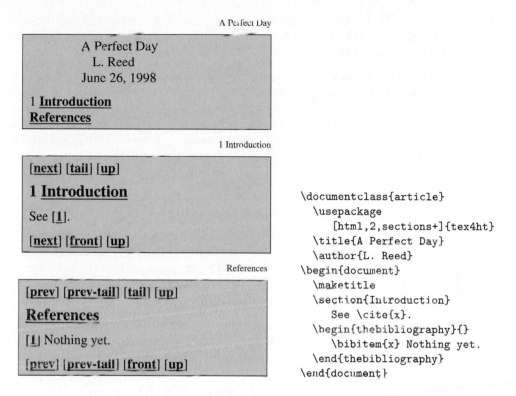

A Perfect Day

A Perfect Day
L. Reed
June 26, 1998

1 **Introduction**
References

1 Introduction

[**next**] [**tail**] [**up**]

1 Introduction

See [**1**].

[**next**] [**front**] [**up**]

References

[**prev**] [**prev-tail**] [**tail**] [**up**]

References

[**1**] Nothing yet.

[**prev**] [**prev-tail**] [**front**] [**up**]

```
\documentclass{article}
 \usepackage
    [html,2,sections+]{tex4ht}
 \title{A Perfect Day}
 \author{L. Reed}
\begin{document}
 \maketitle
 \section{Introduction}
    See \cite{x}.
 \begin{thebibliography}{}
    \bibitem{x} Nothing yet.
 \end{thebibliography}
\end{document}
```

Figure 4.2: A source document and a display of its HTML files

For instance, the options 1, 2, 3, and 4 are simply shortcuts for a single \tableofcontents and a few \CutAt and \ToCAt* commands. Users looking for a more refined outcome than that offered by these options will need to invest a little effort into studying these commands (see Section 4.5.2 on page 172 and Section 4.5.3 on page 175) and using them directly.

The first package option must be the name of a configuration file (see Section 4.5.1 on page 170) or the option html. Otherwise, the first option is ignored. The order in which the nonleading options are listed is not significant.

As its name suggests, the html option asks for HTML output. Without that option, the output should be a standard DVI file. The following are some of the other options that are available:

1, 2, 3, or 4 These options request a breakup of the documents into hierarchies of hypertext pages. The hierarchies reflect the logical organization of the content, as specified by the sectioning commands \part, \chapter, \section, and so on. The values of the option determine the desired depth of the hierarchy of hypertext pages.

`sections+` The entries in tables of contents provide hypertext links to the sections to which they refer. This option asks for extra backward hypertext links from the titles of the sections to the tables of contents.

`next` When partitioning a document into hypertext pages along sections, navigation links to establish paths between the pages are introduced. In the default setting, some paths capture previous-next relationships that reflect the logical tree-structured organization of the sections, providing connections between immediate siblings. This option asks for alternative previous-next navigation links, reflecting the linear succession of all the sections in the document.

`pic-array`, `pic-displaylines`, `pic-eqnarray`, `pic-tabbing`, `pic-tabular`
These options request pictorial representations for the named environments instead of representations employing HTML tables.

`_13`, `^13`, `no_`, `no^` TEX4ht modifies the native definitions of the special characters `_` and `^` in order to enable the inclusion of HTML tags for subscripts and superscripts in mathematical formulae. The first two options request alternative definitions (with category codes of 13 instead of 12 for the characters). The second pair of options disables that behavior.

`refcaption` References to figure and table environments inserted with the `\ref` command are assigned hypertext links pointing to the entry points of these environments. This option makes hypertext links that point to the *captions* within these environments.

`3.2` This option associates a request for HTML version 3.2 with the `html` option, instead of the default association with the Transitional 4.0 version of HTML. The latter version is considerably closer in its nature to LaTeX than 3.2 is. It differentiates issues of style from content and logical structures, and we recommend its use wherever possible.

`fonts+` The normal setting expects the browsers to use their own default fonts for the default font of the document. This option suggests a specific font for the browsers to use.

`no_style` This option turns off the loading of HTML features that are designed specifically for the specified *style file*. For instance, the option `no_amsart` asks TEX4ht not to load the code it holds for the `amsart` package and the option `no_array` makes a similar request for the code that TEX4ht has to offer especially for the package `array`. In such cases, the user might need to tailor private contributions for the packages.

`info` This option requests clues about the features of the package to be written into the log file.

`htm` This option is a variant of the `html` option in which filenames are given main names of, at most, eight characters, and the HTML filenames are given the extension of `htm`.

4.1.2   Picture representation of special content

The ultimate challenge is to get all the translated objects expressed in terms of hypertext tags capturing both the structure and the semantics of the content. When such goals cannot be met, alternative representations have to be used.

4.1.2.1   Mathematics and special characters

The inline math environments \(*formula*\) and the display math environments \[*formula*\] request pictorial representations for their content.

On the other hand, plain TEX inline math environments $*formula*$ and display math environments $$*formula*$$ produce a mixture of text output for simpler subformulae and pictures for the other parts.

In addition to mathematics, some accented characters, some other special characters, and LATEX picture environments are automatically translated into pictures in the default setup. Other entities require explicit requests to be translated to bitmap pictures.

4.1.2.2   Linking to, and making, pictures

The bitmap pictures rendered by browsers can be specified in stand-alone files referenced from the HTML code. The command

```
\Picture[alt]{filename attributes}
```

creates such a reference to an existing file and specifies attributes and alternative text representation for the pictures. The [*alt*] component is optional; when it is not provided, a default text representation is provided by the system. If attributes are given, they must be separated from the filename by a space.

For example, the command

```
\Picture[TUG logo]{http://www.tug.org/logo.gif ID="tuglogo"}
```

references a GIF file containing the logo of the TEX Users Group (TUG). This command produces the HTML code

```
<IMG SRC="http://www.tug.org/logo.gif" ALT="TUG logo" ID="tuglogo">
```

The following is a variant with a pair of commands:

```
\Picture+[alt]{filename attributes}
\EndPicture
```

This requests a bitmap picture to be *created* for what is placed between them. Here, however, a missing [*alt*] parameter is taken to be a request to produce an alternative content-related textual representation for the picture.

```
                                          \Picture+{}%
                                            \begin{tabular}{lcr}
                                            1 & 2 & 3\\
<IMG SRC="try0x.gif"                        xxx & xxx & xxx\\
ALT="1       2       3                      1 & 2 & 3
xxx    xxx   xxx                          \end{tabular}%
1      2     3">                          \EndPicture
```

The plus (+) can be replaced by a star (*). In this case the content is typeset within a vertical box. The filename is optional within the command, as is the file extension. If either is omitted, a system-created entry is provided.

The filename of the last bitmap picture created is recorded in

```
\PictureFile
```

The command

```
\NextPictureFile{filename}
```

provides a filename for the *next* bitmap picture, if no filename is provided in the \Picture command. The \NextPictureFile command can come in handy for reaching concealed \Picture commands.

```
<IMG SRC="mypic.gif" ALT="ab"> and      \NextPictureFile{mypic.gif}
<IMG SRC="mypic.gif" ALT="[Picture]">   \[\alpha^\beta\] and
use the same bitmap file.               \Picture{\PictureFile} use
                                        the same bitmap file.
```

The default setting assumes the extension gif for the names that TeX4ht assigns to the bitmap files. The extensions jpg and png can be requested as an alternative with, respectively, the package options jpg and png. On the other hand, the command

```
\ConfigurePictureFormat{extension}
```

can be used dynamically to change the setting.

4.2   A complete example

Figure 4.3 shows a display of an HTML file by a browser that is capable of handling the features of the Transitional 4.0 version of HTML. The corresponding display of the DVI output is seen in Figure 4.4, and the source LaTeX file is given in Figure 4.5.

The HTML file includes bitmap pictures—for the symbols ϕ, λ, and ∞ and for the array within the display math environment \[...\]. The quality of the pictures depends on the monitor in use and the density of the bitmap pictures. The

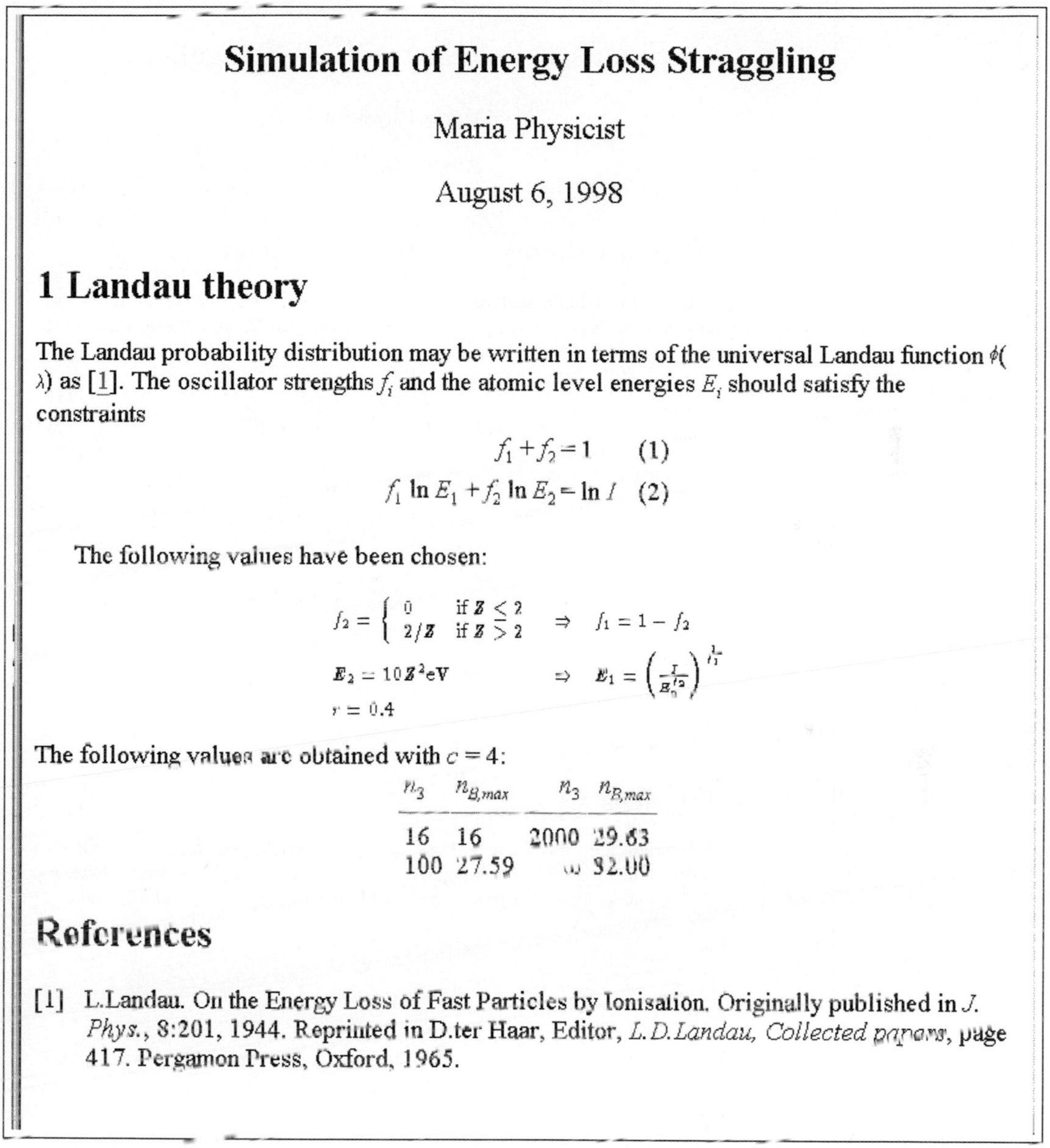

Simulation of Energy Loss Straggling

Maria Physicist

August 6, 1998

1 Landau theory

The Landau probability distribution may be written in terms of the universal Landau function $\phi($ $\lambda)$ as [1]. The oscillator strengths f_i and the atomic level energies E_i should satisfy the constraints

$$f_1 + f_2 = 1 \qquad (1)$$
$$f_1 \ln E_1 + f_2 \ln E_2 = \ln I \qquad (2)$$

The following values have been chosen:

$$f_2 = \begin{cases} 0 & \text{if } Z \leq 2 \\ 2/Z & \text{if } Z > 2 \end{cases} \quad \Rightarrow \quad f_1 = 1 - f_2$$

$$E_2 = 10 Z^2 \text{eV} \qquad \Rightarrow \quad E_1 = \left(\frac{I}{E_2^{f_2}}\right)^{\frac{1}{f_1}}$$

$$r = 0.4$$

The following values are obtained with $c = 4$:

n_3	$n_{B,max}$	n_3	$n_{B,max}$
16	16	2000	29.63
100	27.59	ω	32.00

References

[1] L.Landau. On the Energy Loss of Fast Particles by Ionisation. Originally published in *J. Phys.*, 8:201, 1944. Reprinted in D.ter Haar, Editor, *L. D. Landau, Collected papers*, page 417. Pergamon Press, Oxford, 1965.

Figure 4.3: Display of an HTML file created by TeX4ht

Simulation of Energy Loss Straggling

Maria Physicist

August 6, 1998

1   Landau theory

The Landau probability distribution may be written in terms of the universal Landau function $\phi(\lambda)$ as [1]. The oscillator strengths f_i and the atomic level energies E_i should satisfy the constraints

$$f_1 + f_2 = 1 \tag{1}$$

$$f_1 \ln E_1 + f_2 \ln E_2 = \ln I \tag{2}$$

The following values have been chosen:

$$f_2 = \begin{cases} 0 & \text{if } Z \le 2 \\ 2/Z & \text{if } Z > 2 \end{cases} \quad \Rightarrow \quad f_1 = 1 - f_2$$

$$E_2 = 10Z^2 \text{eV} \quad\quad\quad \Rightarrow \quad E_1 = \left(\frac{I}{E_2^{f_2}}\right)^{\frac{1}{f_1}}$$

$$r = 0.4$$

The following values are obtained with $c = 4$:

n_3	$n_{B,max}$	n_3	$n_{B,max}$
16	16	2000	29.63
100	27.59	∞	32.00

References

[1] L.Landau. On the Energy Loss of Fast Particles by Ionisation. Originally published in *J. Phys.*, 8:201, 1944. Reprinted in D.ter Haar, Editor, *L.D.Landau, Collected papers*, page 417. Pergamon Press, Oxford, 1965.

1

Figure 4.4: The standard LATEX output of Figure 4.3

```
\documentclass{article}
\usepackage{tex4ht}
  \title{Simulation of  Energy Loss  Straggling}
  \author{Maria Physicist}
\begin{document}
\maketitle

\section{Landau theory}
\label{sec:phys332-1}
The Landau probability distribution may be written in terms of the
universal Landau function $\phi(\lambda)$ as \cite{bib-LAND}. The
oscillator strengths $f_i$ and the atomic level energies $E_i$ should
satisfy the constraints
\begin{eqnarray}
f_1 + f_2 & = & 1  \label{eq:fisum}\\
f_1 \ln E_1 + f_2 \ln E_2 & = & \ln I \label{eq:flnsum}
\end{eqnarray}

The following values have been chosen:
\[ \begin{array}{lcl}
f_2 = \left\{ \begin{array}{ll}
            0  & \mathrm{if}\, Z \leq 2 \\
            2/Z & \mathrm{if}\, Z > 2 \\
            \end{array} \right.    &\Rightarrow & f_1 = 1 - f_2 \\
E_2 = 10 Z^2 \mathrm{eV} &\Rightarrow &E_1 = \left(\frac{I}{E_{2}^{f_2}}
                                          \right)^{\frac{1}{f_1}} \\
r  = 0.4 & & \\
\end{array} \]
The following values are obtained with $c=4$:

\begin{tabular}{llcrr}
$n_3$  & $n_{B,max}$ & & & $n_3$  & $n_{B,max}$\\ \hline
16  & 16       & & 2000  & 29.63\\
100 & 27.59    & & $\infty$ & 32.00
\end{tabular}

\begin{thebibliography}{10}
\bibitem{bib-LAND}
L.Landau.
On the Energy Loss of Fast Particles by Ionisation.
Originally published in \emph{J. Phys.}, 8:201, 1944.
Reprinted in D.ter Haar, Editor, \emph{ D.Landau, Collected
papers}, page 417.  Pergamon Press, Oxford, 1965.
\end{thebibliography}
\end{document}
```

Figure 4.5: The LaTeX source file for the document of Figure 4.3

$$f_2 = \begin{cases} 0 & \text{if } Z \leq 2 \\ 2/Z & \text{if } Z > 2 \end{cases} \quad \Rightarrow \quad f_1 = 1 - f_2$$

$$E_2 = 10Z^2\text{eV} \quad \Rightarrow \quad E_1 = \left(\frac{I}{E_2^{f_2}}\right)^{\frac{1}{f_1}}$$

$$r = 0.4$$

Figure 4.6: A bitmap with density of 144 dots per inch

bitmaps in Figure 4.4 have a density of 110 dots per inch, while Figure 4.6 shows the corresponding display of the last picture with a density of 144 dots per inch.

As contrast, Figure 4.7 is a variant of Figure 4.3. It is obtained by including the following CSS code (see Section 4.3.4) in the compilation of the source file:

```
\Css{.maketitle{ border:solid 5px; width: 100\% }}
\Css{.sectionHead, .likesectionHead {
    text-align:right;
    font-family: cursive;
    border-bottom:solid 2px; }}
\Css{.thebibliography { font-size : 70\%; }}
\Css{body { text-align: justify; }}
```

4.3   Manual creation of hypertext elements

A relatively small number of low-level commands provides the foundation on top of which the desired hypertext outcome can (usually) be tailored. These commands provide direct access to HTML tags, the means to produce hypertext pages, the support needed to establish hypertext links, and a method to request a specific appearance of the content.

4.3.1   Raw hypertext code

Many useful features can be achieved by brute force inclusion of small fragments of HTML code. The command

```
\HCode{content}
```

is handy on such occasions, because it holds the processing of its content just to macro expansion. This restricted mode of operation outputs the characters in raw

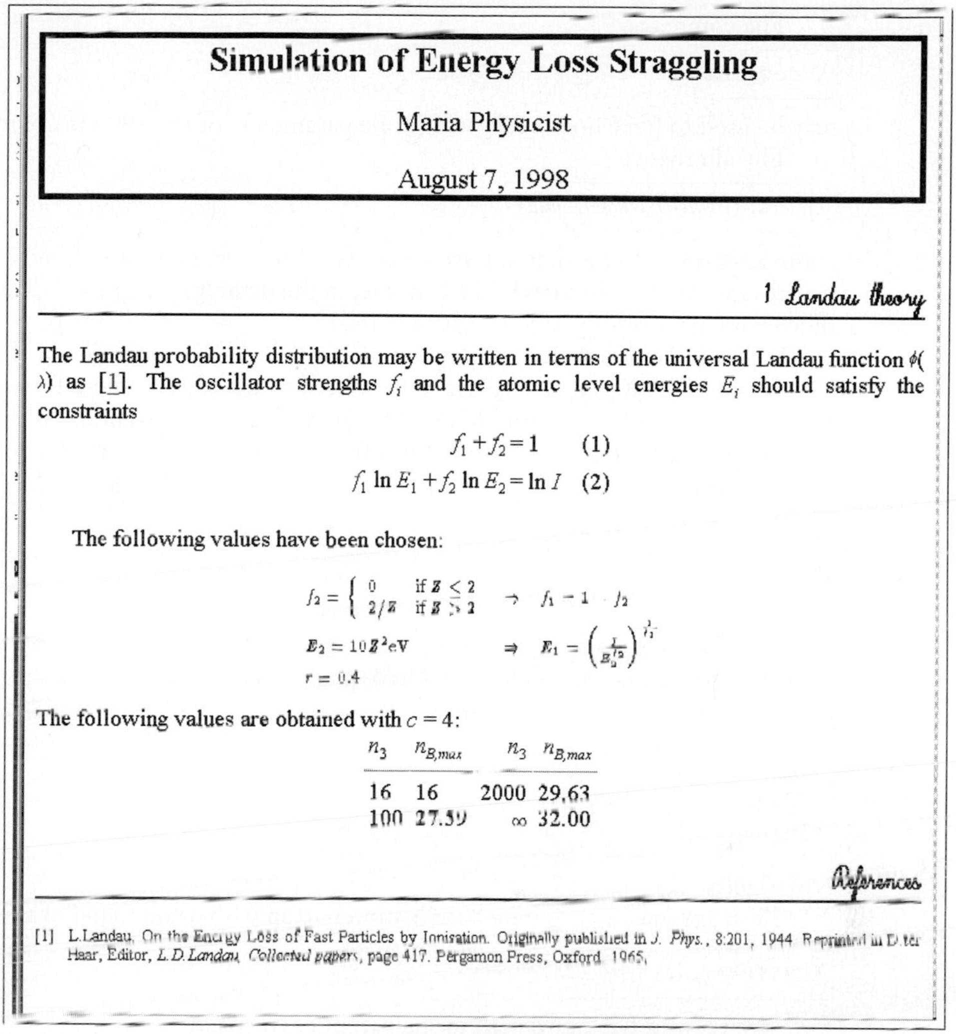

Simulation of Energy Loss Straggling

Maria Physicist

August 7, 1998

1 Landau theory

The Landau probability distribution may be written in terms of the universal Landau function $\phi($ $\lambda)$ as [1]. The oscillator strengths f_i and the atomic level energies E_i should satisfy the constraints

$$f_1 + f_2 = 1 \qquad (1)$$

$$f_1 \ln E_1 + f_2 \ln E_2 = \ln I \qquad (2)$$

The following values have been chosen:

$$f_2 = \begin{cases} 0 & \text{if } Z \le 2 \\ 2/Z & \text{if } Z > 2 \end{cases} \quad \rightarrow \quad f_1 = 1 - f_2$$

$$E_2 = 10\,Z^2 \text{eV} \qquad \Rightarrow \quad E_1 = \left(\frac{I}{E_2^{f_2}} \right)^{\frac{1}{f_1}}$$

$$r = 0.4$$

The following values are obtained with $c = 4$:

n_3	$n_{B,max}$	n_3	$n_{B,max}$
16	16	2000	29.63
100	27.59	∞	32.00

References

[1] L.Landau. On the Energy Loss of Fast Particles by Ionisation. Originally published in *J. Phys.*, 8:201, 1944. Reprinted in D. ter Haar, Editor, *L.D.Landau, Collected papers*, page 417. Pergamon Press, Oxford, 1965.

Figure 4.7: A variant of Figure 4.3

format instead of replacing them with the corresponding symbols of the current font (see Section 4.6.7 for a description of how TEX4ht works with fonts).

Make it
`<STRONG>&lt;STRONG&gt;</STRONG>`.

Make it
`\HCode{<STRONG>}\texttt {<STRONG>}\HCode{</STRONG>}`.

The command

> `\Hnewline`

may be used to force line breaks within the parameters of the `\HCode` commands.

The alternative

> `\HChar{`*html-character-code*`}`

command, on the other hand, introduces raw characters at a rate of one character per instance of the command. For example, in the default setting the LaTeX special tilde character ~ is translated to `\HChar{160}`.

It should be noted that, unlike the use of `\HCode`, a parameter of the `\verb` command of LaTeX is not necessarily translated to exactly the same format in the HTML file. All that is required is to present to the reader something that looks like the source content. The same holds for the text enclosed within a `verbatim` environment.

4.3.2   Hypertext pages

The documents are automatically partitioned into hypertext pages, based on their logical structure and the options you have chosen. For brute-force creation of hypertext pages, the pair of commands

> `\HPage{`*entry-anchor*`}`
> `\EndHPage{}`

is available.

The page may incorporate a navigation button with a command of the form

> `\ExitHPage{`*exit-anchor*`}`

for establishing a backward path to the parent of the page.

Enter the hypertext page.	`\HPage{Enter}`
enter	`and then \ExitHPage{exit}`
and then **exit**	`\EndHPage{}`
	`the hypertext page.`

If the parameter of `\ExitHPage` is empty, the navigation buttons employ the anchors supplied in the `\HPage` commands.

4.3.3   Hypertext links

HTML uses the tag `<A HREF="target-file#target-loc" NAME="cur-loc" parameters>anchor</A>` for representing hypertext links. Each tag of this kind assumes knowledge of where the target file is located and the desired entry point into the file. In addition, each of these tags provides a name for the current location and allows for other parameters.

The following command offers a similar functionality, while automatically deriving the local target files when they are not explicitly given.

`\Link`[*target-file parameters*]`{`*target-loc*`}{`*cur-loc*`}`*anchor*`\EndLink`

Specifically, when *target-file* is empty, TEX4ht assumes the target file belongs to the current document, and it takes it upon itself to find the file. A file containing a location named *target-loc* is searched for by the `\Link` command.

The component [*target-file parameters*] is optional, if both *target-file* and *parameters* are empty. When *parameters* is not empty, it must be preceded by a space.

```
An external link to
\Link[http://www.tug.org
ID="ORG"]{}{}TUG\EndLink.
```

```
An external link to TUG.
An internal link to here.
```

```
An internal \Link
{to}{}link\EndLink{} to
\Link{}{to}here\EndLink.
```

Within the parameters of the `\Link` command, the special characters ~, _, and % should be entered using the commands `\string~`, `\string_`, and `\%`, respectively.

4.3.4   Cascading Style Sheets

HTML is a language for identifying structures within hypertext documents; it resembles the way the `\section` instructions of LaTeX are employed to identify logical structures within source documents. In both cases, the entities do not deal with how the structures are to be presented to the readers, delegating such details to specifications provided elsewhere through special purpose languages.

Cascading Style Sheets (CSS) [↪CSS2] is a language for specifying presentations for HTML entities. TEX4ht collects such requests within a special file named *jobname*`.css` and issues some requests of its own.

It is beyond the scope of this chapter to describe the CSS language. However, it should be realized that the language is easy to learn and use by authors with a basic knowledge of HTML and a little familiarity with desktop publishing terminology.

The command

```
\Css{CSS code}
```

is provided for requesting presentation of document elements.

Given source code of the form

```
\section{Header} Text.
\par
More text
```

TeX4ht will produce HTML output like this:

```
<H2>1 Header</H2> <P CLASS="noindent"> Text.
<P CLASS="indent"> More text
```

and CSS code like this:

```
P.noindent { text-indent: 0em } P.indent { text-indent: 1.5em }
```

A request to color the title green can be made with a command of the form
`\Css{ H2 { color: green } }.`

A CSS file can be specifically requested with the environment

```
\CssFile[list-of-files]
content
\EndCssFile
```

CSS code can be imported from other files (*list-of-files*), as well as explicitly given within the environment.

The `\EndPreamble` command calls this environment to create a CSS file, if the user does not make an earlier request for such a file.

The CSS file should include the comment `/* css.sty */` on a separate line so that `t4ht`, the `tex4ht` postprocessor (see Section 4.6.4), can identify it as a place to put the content of the `\Css` instructions. Without such a line, that content will be ignored. The filename and the initial content of the file can be reconfigured with the `\Configure{CssFile}{filename}{content}` command.

Inline CSS code can be created using the following environment:

```
\Css content\EndCss
```

Consider the following source and configuration files:

```
% try.tex
\documentclass{article}
  \usepackage[try]{tex4ht}
\begin{document}
```

```
% try.cfg
\Preamble{html}
\begin{document}
```

```
\Css                                      \CssFile
    H2 { color : red; }                       H2 { color : blue; }
\EndCss                                       /* css.sty */
\Css{ H2 { color : green; }}              \EndCssFile
\end{document}                            \EndPreamble
```

This will create the following HTML and CSS files:

```
<!--- try.html -->                        /* try.css */
<STYLE TYPE="text/css">                   H2 { color : blue; }
  H2 { color : red; }                     H2 { color : green; }
</STYLE>
```

4.4   How TEX4ht works

It takes three phases to translate a source document into hypertext (see Section 4.6.1 on page 184): a compilation of the source by the TEX program into DVI code, a manipulation of the DVI code by the tex4ht program, and a processing of loose-end tasks required for completing the translation.

4.4.1   From LATEX to DVI

LATEX requires two compilations of a source file by TEX to establish cross-references, and TEX4ht might require a third compilation to get all the hypertext links in place. On rare occasions when a tabular environment is used, with many cells being merged, more compilations might be needed to let the system work out how the cells should look.

When LATEX loads the TEX4ht package, it loads the file tex4ht.sty and looks at just a few lines there. Then it records a request for loading the file again at a later time, when it will scan the rest of the file. The second loading takes place when the \begin{document} code is encountered, at which time the requests made by the package options are also honored.

Since TEX4ht enters into the picture only when \begin{document} is reached, some earlier user definitions might not get the full attention of TEX4ht, unless they are redefined in a configuration file. For instance, TEX4ht would have difficulties introducing HTML tags for the superscript of a macro \newcommand{\x}{a^{b}} which was defined before the start of the the document environment.

4.4.2   From DVI to HTML

DVI is a page description language that includes instructions for specifying what content should go at which location in a print-oriented medium. HTML, on the other hand, is a structure-oriented language with little regard to layout issues.

Consequently, in many respects, a translation from DVI to HTML is a backward process, having to reconstruct information that might have been lost in the translation from LaTeX to DVI. This backward process may well fail, if the DVI code results from a source document that places things outside the normal stream; `\hspace{-0.6em}` is a possible example.

During translation from DVI to HTML, font calls are processed using virtual hypertext fonts (Section 4.6.7 on page 190). If these are missing or are inappropriate, new ones can be composed by the user without too much effort.

4.4.3   Other matters

The last phase of the translation turns its attention to the production of bitmap pictures from DVI code. To that end, TeX4ht relies on tools available for the current platform and that might also offer more than one route for producing the pictures.

The creation of pictures is the bottleneck of the translation process and may take a long time to complete. Some shortcuts might be taken to speed up the process; for instance, if bitmaps from earlier compilations are already available, the system-dependent utilities may allow them to be reused.

4.5   Extended customization of TeX4ht

Most LaTeX users should require very little background information, if any, in addition to that already covered in this chapter. But TeX4ht is a large system with many facets to explore. A taste of that world is provided in the following sections, which deal with some aspects of customizing and running the system.

Most readers will probably be best served by quickly skimming over the following sections to get a general impression of the topics addressed. The details have little bearing on the flow of content in these sections, and they can be ignored until they are needed for handling specific requirements.

4.5.1   Configuration files

TeX4ht introduces intermediate interfaces of its own, located between the interfaces used by LaTeX within the source files, and those used by HTML within the output files. It does this by placing "hooks" in the LaTeX style files; these are commands that the user can redefine to get the effect they want. The intermediate interfaces separate themselves from the style concerns of LaTeX, on one hand, and offer structures similar to those of HTML, on the other. As a result, users can quite easily tailor a different outcome just by defining the different hooks to produce appropriate HTML code.

The conventional wisdom of placing definitions together in separate customization files applies also to the configuration commands of TeX4ht. However, an additional motivation for the configuration files stems from the need to direct the output to fit the structural requirements of HTML files.

Specifically an HTML file consists of a header and a body, each part expecting a different type of content. The configuration files identify these parts and provide the content for the header.

4.5.1.1   Implicit and explicit files

If the first package option is not the name of a configuration file, a default configuration is used. It looks like this:

```
\Preamble{options}
\begin{document}
\EndPreamble
```

However, if the first option *does* refer to a configuration file, then the configuration file must have the following structure:

```
early definitions
\Preamble{options}
definitions
\begin{document}
insertions into the header of the HTML file
\EndPreamble
```

Figure 4.8 shows an example of source and configuration files, as well as the HTML and CSS files they produce.

Upon reaching the \usepackage command, the file tex4ht.sty is partially loaded to scan a few definitions. Then the configuration file is read until the \Preamble command is encountered. The remainder of the style file is read and acted upon when the \begin{document} command in the source document is reached.

With the exception of a package option standing for the name of a configuration file, the distribution of the other options between the \usepackage and the \Preamble command is unimportant. Moreover, unlike the case for the first option of the \usepackage, no restriction is made on the type of the option that appears first in the \Preamble command.

4.5.1.2   Embedded configuration

The configuration file can also be embedded directly within the source document, instead of being indirectly incorporated through a \usepackage command. Such an approach might make the placement of the \begin{document} instruction in the configuration file clearer. However, to preserve the authoring style promoted by LaTeX, users are highly discouraged from employing this approach.

```
\documentclass{article}              <HTML><HEAD>
  \usepackage[try,html]{tex4ht}       <META NAME="description"
\begin{document}                         CONTENT="example">
  \begin{itemize}                      <LINK REL="stylesheet"
  \item First                             TYPE="text/css"
  \item Second                            HREF="try.css">
  \end{itemize}                       </HEAD><BODY>
\end{document}                         <UL><LI>First
                                          <LI>Second
                                       </UL></BODY></HTML>
```

(a)

```
\Preamble{}                                    (c)
  \Css{ UL{border : solid 1px;} }
\begin{document}                        UL{border : solid 1px;}
  \HCode{<META NAME="description"
            CONTENT="example">}                (d)
\EndPreamble
```

(b)

Figure 4.8: Input files: (a) `try.tex` and (b) `try.cfg`. Output files: (c) `try.html` and (d) `try.css`

The embedding can be achieved by replacing the instruction `\usepackage[`*options*`]{tex4ht}` with an `\input{tex4ht.sty}` command, and substituting the `\begin{document}` in the source document with the contents of the configuration file. In such a case, the options of the `\usepackage` command should migrate into the list of options of the `\Preamble` command.

The following source document is the source of Figure 4.8(a), with the configuration file of Figure 4.8(b) embedded in it.

```
\documentclass{article}
  \input{tex4ht.sty}
  \Preamble{html}
    \Css{UL { border : solid 1px; }}
\begin{document}
    \HCode{<META NAME="description"  CONTENT="example">}
  \EndPreamble
  \begin{itemize} \item First  \item Second  \end{itemize}
\end{document}
```

4.5.2 Tables of contents

The `\tableofcontents` command of LaTeX is enriched with new features in TEX4ht. To allow for easy control over the kind of entries it includes, the way it is presented, and the locations where it can be included, some of these features are indirectly activated by the package options 1, 2, 3, and 4 (see Section 4.1.1 on page 156).

Remember that because one LATEX file will often generate many HTML files, each output may have its own table of contents. Hence, we use the term "tables of contents" instead of the usual "table of contents."

4.5.2.1   Choice of entries

The kinds of entries to be included in the tables of contents are determined by LATEX in the usual way. As an alternative, TEX4ht adds a variant command, \tableofcontents[*units*], in which the kind of entries need to be explicitly specified. The parameter *units* is a comma-separated list of names of sectioning commands (without backslashes). Starred versions (ending in *) are replaced by names with like prefixes, and appendixes are requested by the word appendix. Thus

```
\tableofcontents[chapter,appendix,section,likesection]
```

requests a table of contents with entries pointing to the logical units created by the \chapter, \section, and \section* commands.

4.5.2.2   Local tables of contents

The command

    \TocAt{*units*}

requests a table of contents at the start of each logical unit of the specified type. The parameter *units* is a comma-separated list similar to that offered for the new variant of the \tableofcontents command; the first name in the list specifies the unit that is to have a local table of contents. The other names specify the kind of entries to be included in the table. If they are preceded with a slash, they specify *termination points* for the tables of contents. Thus

```
\TocAt[chapter,section,/likesection]
```

requests a table of contents at the start of each chapter. The entries corresponding to the \section commands that follow should be included, but the list terminates upon reaching a \section* or the next \chapter.

The tables requested by the command \TocAt{*units*} appear immediately after the titles of the section units. The variant

    \TocAt*{*units*}

produces similar tables that follow the preambles of the units instead of immediately following the titles.

```
1  A Long-expected Party
2  The Shadow of the Past
*  Three is Company

1 A Long-expected Party

2 The Shadow of the Past

Three is Company
```

```
\ConfigureToc{section}
   {\null}{~}{}{ }
\ConfigureToc{likesection}
   {}{*~}{}{ }
\tableofcontents[section,likesection]
\section{A Long-expected Party}
\section{The Shadow of the Past}
\section*{Three is Company}
```

Figure 4.9: Configuring the tables of contents

4.5.2.3   Configuring the entries

Each entry in the table of contents is derived from three fields: a mark, a title, and a page number. Typically the mark is the number of a section (or it is simply empty), and the page number is of little significance in this context.

The following command can be used to determine how the contents entries for the logical units of type *unit* are to be created. The unit names follow the same conventions as those used in the parameter of the enhanced \tableofcontents command.

> \ConfigureToc{*unit*}{*mark*}{*title*}{*page*}{*end*}

Each contents entry will be composed of the *mark* parameter followed by the mark field, the *title* parameter followed by the title, and the *page* parameter followed by the page number. Finally comes the *end* parameter. If any parameter is empty, the corresponding field is *omitted* in the table of contents. The effect is shown in Figure 4.9.

4.5.2.4   Configuring the tables

Tables of contents have hooks before their entry points, after their exit points, after their last entries, at the start of each nonindented paragraph, and at the start of each indented paragraph. The following command configures the hooks:

> \Configure{tableofcontents}{*before*}{*end*}{*after*}{*n-par*}{*i-par*}

The hook after the last entry is processed within the environments of the table of contents. The hook after the *exit point* of the table of contents is processed within the environment around the tables.

Local tables of contents can be further configured in a similar manner with the

Section 1: When I was one
I sucked my thumb.

Section 2: When I was two
I buckled my shoe.

```
\Configure{section}
  {\HCode{<HR>}} {}
  {Section \thesection: } {}

\section{When I was one}
  I sucked my thumb.
\section{When I was two}
  I buckled my shoe.
```

Figure 4.10: Configuring the section headings

commands:

```
\Configure{TocAt}{before}{after}
\Configure{TocAt*}{before}{after}
```

The new configurations must be supplied before the \TocAt and \TocAt* commands.

4.5.3   Parts, chapters, sections, and so on

Sectioning commands determine the underlying structures of documents, and they quite often guide the partitioning of hypertext documents into files. This subsection shows how such entities can be customized.

4.5.3.1   Configuring the boundary points and titles

The sectioning commands produce logical units characterized by their starting and ending points, as well as by their titles. The following command contributes content to such units; these are included at the start of the units, at the end of the units, before their titles, and after their titles, respectively.

```
\Configure{unit}{top}{bottom}{before}{after}
```

If the *top* and *bottom* parameters are both empty, that part of the configuration command is ignored and the old values remain in effect. The same applies to the parameters *before* and *after*. The effect is shown in Figure 4.10.

The unit names follow the same conventions as those provided for the parameters of the enhanced \tableofcontents command.

[When I was three] [When I was four]

[next] [tail] [up]

1 When I was three

I found a key.
[next] [front] [up]

[prev] [prev-tail] [tail] [up]

2 When I was four

I knocked on the door.
[prev] [prev-tail] [front] [up]

```
\CutAt{+section}

\section{When I was three}
I found a key.

\section{When I was four}
I knocked on the door.
```

Figure 4.11: Configuring sections to make multiple files

4.5.3.2 Partitioning into files

The package options 1, 2, 3, and 4 (see Section 4.1.1 on page 156) implicitly activate the command

```
\CutAt{units}
```

for partitioning the documents into files. The parameter *units* is a comma-separated list of unit names. The first name in the list specifies the logical units for which separate hypertext pages are requested. The hypertext pages extend until a unit whose name appears in the rest of the list is encountered. Thus

```
\CutAt{chapter,likechapter,appendix,part,likepart}
```

requests hypertext pages for the logical units defined by \chapter. Furthermore, the command says that starred chapters, appendixes, parts, and starred parts are logical units that should not be included within chapters.

Typically the \CutAt{*units*} command is used along with a table of contents whose entries provide links to the hypertext pages that are requested by the command. A possible alternative is to employ the variant command \CutAt{*+units*}, which, besides the hypertext pages, also creates links to the pages. The effect is shown in Figure 4.11.

The links to the pages are enclosed between delimiters that are configurable by the command

```
\Configure{+CutAt}{unit}{ldel}{rdel}
```

Thus

```
\Configure{+CutAt}{section}{*~}{}
```

requests left delimiters *~ and no right delimiters for the links to pages that result
from the \section command.

4.5.3.3   Setting boundary points

The \CutAt{*units*} and \CutAt{*+units*} commands work out the end points of the
sections that are placed in separate files. The end points of the other sections should
be specified using the following command:

```
\Configure{endunit}{units}
```

The *endunit* stands for a unit name prefixed by an end, and the parameter *units* is a
comma-separated list of unit names.

4.5.3.4   Customizing the navigation buttons

The hypertext pages of the sections include panels of navigation buttons both at
the top and the bottom of each page. Each of the buttons is embedded between a
left and a right delimiter. The buttons point to the next hypertext page, the front
and the tail of the previous page, the front and the tail of the current page, and
the parent page. The following command allows you to customize the buttons and
their delimiters, and the effect is shown in Figure 4.12.

```
\Configure{crosslinks}{ldel}{rdel}{next}{prev}{prev-tail}{front}{tail}{up}
```

The next command deals with the panels themselves. It specifies content to be
included before and after the front and tail panels, respectively:

```
\Configure{crosslinks+}{before-front}{after-front}{before-tail}{after-tail}
```

4.5.4   Defining sectioning commands

New sectioning commands can be introduced through instructions of the form

```
\NewSection{cmdname}{marker}
```

for the TEX4ht package to be aware of their existence and to offer its standard
services. The parameter *marker* specifies the markers to be submitted with the titles
to the tables of contents. Typically such markers either are empty or consist of the
sequence number of the current section unit. An example is shown in Figure 4.13.

```
* ⇒ * ⇑
1 When I was five
I caught a fish alive.
* ⇒ * ⇑
```

```
\Configure{crosslinks}{*~}{ }
   {$\Rightarrow$}{$\Leftarrow$}
   {}{}{}{$\Uparrow$}

\section{When I was five}
I caught a fish alive.

\section{When I was six}
I broke my sticks.
```

```
* ⇐ * ⇑
2 When I was six
I broke my sticks.
* ⇐ * ⇑
```

Figure 4.12: Configuring navigation buttons

```
1: When I was seven 2: When I was eight
1. When I was seven
I went to heaven.
2. When I was eight
I met my fate.
```

```
\NewSection{\head}{\arabic{head}}
\Configure{head}
   {\addtocounter{head}{1}}{}
   {\par\arabic{head}. }{}
\ConfigureToc{head}{ } {: }{}{}
\newcounter{head}
\tableofcontents[head]
\head{When I was seven} I went to heaven.
\head{When I was eight} I met my fate.
```

Figure 4.13: Defining a new sectioning command

4.5.5 Lists

The `list` and `trivlist` environments are basic structures of LaTeX, on top of which quite a few environments are defined. Some of these are themselves variants of listing environments, for instance, the `description`, `itemize`, `enumerate`, and `thebibliography` environments.

Other environments are display-oriented in nature, relying on empty-label, single-item lists just for their typesetting characteristics, for instance, the `center`, `flushleft`, `flushright`, `quotation`, `quote`, `verbatim`, and `verse` environments. The theoremlike environments, defined by the `\newtheorem` command, are also single-item lists, but their titles are offered as labels of `\item` commands.

The following command provides content to be included before the lists, after the lists, before the labels of the items, and after the labels of the items. The effect is shown in Figure 4.14.

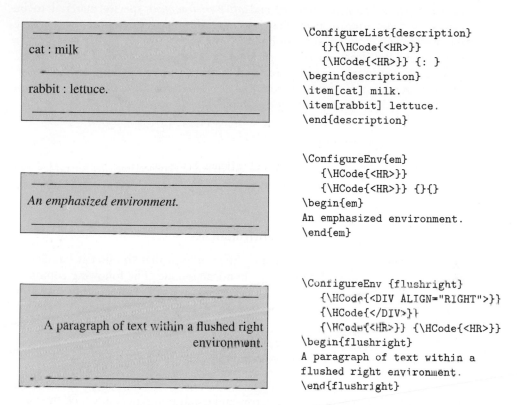

```
\ConfigureList{description}
    {}{\HCode{<HR>}}
    {\HCode{<HR>}} {: }
\begin{description}
\item[cat] milk.
\item[rabbit] lettuce.
\end{description}
```

```
\ConfigureEnv{em}
    {\HCode{<HR>}}
    {\HCode{<HR>}} {}{}
\begin{em}
An emphasized environment.
\end{em}
```

```
\ConfigureEnv {flushright}
    {\HCode{<DIV ALIGN="RIGHT">}}
    {\HCode{</DIV>}}
    {\HCode{<HR>}} {\HCode{<HR>}}
\begin{flushright}
A paragraph of text within a
flushed right environment.
\end{flushright}
```

Figure 4.14: Configuring lists and environments

\ConfigureList{*name*}{*pre-list*}{*post-list*}{*pre-label*}{*post-label*}

When list environments are defined in terms of other list environments, the contribution of \ConfigureList applies only to the lists in the top layer. Since LATEX defines the description environment in terms of the list environment, and TEX4ht configures both of them with the \ConfigureList command, the configuration given to the list environment does not show within the description lists.

4.5.6   Environments

LATEX environments constructs are customizable by commands invoked at the entry and exit points:

\ConfigureEnv{*name*}{*before-env*}{*after-env*}{*before-list*}{*after-list*}

The parameters *before-environment* and *after-environment* specify material to be placed before and after the named environment; if both parameters are empty, they are ignored. An example is show in Figure 4.14.

Similarly, if at least one of the parameters *before-list* or *after-list* is not empty, the environment is assumed to be realized in terms of a list-making environment. A call is then made to \ConfigureList{*name*}{*before-list*}{*after-list*}{}{} for configuring the underlying list-making commands.

4.5.7   Tables

TeX4ht goes a long way toward offering satisfactory representations for tables, but it does not provide a complete solution. Sometimes it fails, and special configurations or pictures might be called for.

4.5.7.1   The `array` and `tabular` environments

The `array` and `tabular` environments differ only in that the first is handled in math mode and the second is processed in normal mode. The following command customizes these environments, before the tables, after the table, before each row, after each row, before each entry, and after each entry.

```
\Configure{table}{pre-tbl}{post-tbl}
   {pre-row}{post-row}{pre-entry}{post-entry}
```

To help configure the tables, the \HRow, \HCol, and \ALIGN macros can be used. The first pair of macros produces the row and column numbers in which the commands appear; the third macro produces an encoding for the alignment information of the table, as we show here:

```
\Configure{tabular} {}{}
   {\HRow: }{\HCode{<BR>}}
   {}{(\HCol)}
\begin{tabular}{ccc}
A&B&C\\ D&E&F
\end{tabular}
```

```
1: A(1) B(2) C(3)
2: D(1) E(2) F(3)
```

For a centered column, \ALIGN gives a triplet made up of the digit 0, the column number, and the minus character -. For left-aligned, right-aligned, and paragraph columns, similar triplets are produced. The only difference is that the characters <, >, and p, respectively, are used instead of -.

Tables with \multicolumn entries need a few LaTeX compilations to stabilize; TeX4ht slowly learns about the dimension of the spanning from information provided in earlier compilations. In configuring contributions to entries of tables, the \MULTISPAN macro may be tested to determine the number of columns spanned by the entries.

Consider the following source code:

```
\Configure{tabular} {\HCode{<TABLE>}} {\HCode{</TABLE>}}
  {\HCode{<TR>}} {\HCode{</TR>}}
  {\HCode{<TD \ifnum \MULTISPAN>1 COLSPAN="\MULTISPAN"\fi>}}
  {\HCode{</TD>}}
\begin{tabular}{lr}    \multicolumn{2}{c}{merge}\\
first & second          \end{tabular}
```

The output for this is the following:

```
<TABLE><TR>   <TD COLSPAN="2">merge</TD>      </TR>
        <TR>   <TD>first</TD> <TD>second</TD> </TR></TABLE>
```

The package options `pic-array` and `pic-tabular` (Section 4.1.1 on page 156) request a picture version of all the `array` and `tabular` tables, respectively.

The \\ command is treated as a row separator. To avoid undesirable empty rows at the end of the tables, the \\ should not be inserted after the last row. On the other hand, the character ~ may be used to introduce invisible content for empty cells. This will allow for the possibility of empty and nonempty cells being treated differently by browsers.

4.5.7.2   The `eqnarray` environment and the like

The variants of the eqnarray environment are configurable by \Configure commands similar to those used for the `array` and `tabular` environments. Alternatively a picture version may be requested with the `pic-eqnarray` option.

4.5.7.3   The `tabbing` environment

The following command specifies contributions to be included before and after the rows, and before and after the entries of the `tabbing` environment. In addition, the command allows for a decimal number to specify a magnification factor for the widths of the entries.

> `\Configure{tabbing}` [*mag*] {*pre-row*}{*post-row*}{*pre-entry*}{*post-entry*}

The component [*mag*] is optional when no change in magnification is desired. The contributions offered by the parameters *pre-row*, *post-row*, *pre-entry*, and *post-entry* are ignored when all of these parameters are empty. The command \TABBING may be used to set the widths of all the entries, where entries with no bound on their width have a zero for their specified widths. The trailing entries of the rows have this feature.

Reconfiguring tables without compromising their properties is probably a task requiring more knowledge of raw TEX programming than most users possess.

However, the amount of TeX code to be written is typically quite small in size.

```
\newcount\c
\def\Width#1//{\gdef\TABBING{#1}%
   \ifnum\c>0 \HCode{ WIDTH="\the\c"}\fi}
\ConfigureEnv{tabbing}{}{}{\Configure{HtmlPar}{}{}{}{}}{}
\Configure{tabbing}
   {\HCode{<TABLE><TR>}}   {\HCode{</TR></TABLE>}}
   {\HCode{<TD}\afterassignment\Width\c\TABBING//\HCode{>}}
   {\HCode{</TD>}}
\begin{tabbing}
LaTeX: \=tabbing\\
TeX: \>settabs
\end{tabbing}
```

The above fragment of LaTeX source translates to the following HTML code.

```
<TABLE><TR><TD WIDTH="71">LaTeX:</TD>
           <TD>tabbing</TD>           </TR></TABLE>
<TABLE><TR><TD WIDTH="71">TeX:</TD>
           <TD>settabs</TD>           </TR></TABLE>
```

A picture version may be requested with the package option `pic-tabbing`. The variant `pic-tabbing'` applies only to those instances employing the `\'` directive of the `tabbing` environment. That directive is not fully supported by TeX4ht.

4.5.8   Small details

Most of the features described so far are tied to specific constructs of LaTeX, and they are of little use elsewhere. The following features, of a more general-purpose nature, deal with basic issues.

4.5.8.1   File names

HTML files may result from requests made through the package options 1, 2, 3, and 4 and from `\CutAt` and `\HPage` commands. In such cases unless the users offer names of their own, the filenames are automatically created by the system.

The `\FileName` command can be used to find out the name of the current file. On the other hand, the command

```
\NextFile{filename}
```

may be used to suggest a name for the next HTML file.

4.5.8.2   Conditional code

The command

```
\ifHtml true-part\else false-part\fi
```

enables us to choose content based on whether the `html` package option is used.

4.5.8.3   Environments for scripts

The `\HCode` command allows the user to write small fragments of raw code into the HTML file. The command

```
\ScriptEnv{name}{prefix}{suffix}
```

provides the means of defining environments for including larger fragments of raw code.

```
<STYLE TYPE="text/css">
<!--
  UL { border : solid 1px; }
  H1 { color: green }
-->
</STYLE>
```

```
\ScriptEnv{css}
  {\HCode{<STYLE TYPE="text/css">
  \Hnewline<!--}\Hnewline}
  {\HCode{-->\Hnewline</STYLE>}}
\begin{css}
  UL { border : solid 1px; }
  H1 { color: green; }
\end{css}
```

4.5.8.4   Content for paragraph breaks

The following command allows you to specify what material is to be inserted at the start of a paragraph and what is to be saved in `\EndP` at this point. There are separate parameters for when the first line of the paragraph is indented or not.

```
\Configure{HtmlPar} {noindent-P} {indent-P} {noindent-save} {indent save}
```

The task of `\EndP` is typically to deliver code from the start of a paragraph to its end.

```
<P><H2>Head </H2><P> Body
```

```
\Configure{HtmlPar}
  {\HCode{<P><H2>}}
  {\EndP \HCode{<P>}}
  {\HCode{</H2>}}  {}
\noindent Head \par Body
```

There are extra commands to enable finer local control over the contributions at the start of paragraphs. The command `\IgnorePar` ignores the contribution of content at the start of the next paragraph, and the command `\ShowPar` provides content at the start of the next paragraph. Similarly the `\NoIndent` command says that the first line of the next paragraph should not be indented, and the `\Indent` command says the first line of the next paragraph *should* be indented.

```
\newcommand{\try}{\Pre Just trying.\Post}
\NewConfigure{try}[2]{%
   \newcommand\Pre{#1}%
   \newcommand\Post{#2}}
\Configure{try}{\HCode{<H2>}}{\HCode{</H2>}}
\try
\Configure{try}{}{}
\try
```

Figure 4.15: Adding new hooks

4.5.8.5   Creating new hooks for TEX4ht

The core of TEX4ht is programmed to deal with general situations created by the underlying machinery of TEX, and in general it does a good job there. However, the underlying features typically have very little to do with *structural* properties of commands defined in private and public style files. To capture such properties, the definitions must be extended to include *hooks*. To maximize the benefit of the hooks, they should be configurable. The command

```
\NewConfigure{name}[digit]{assignments}
```

is designed for this purpose.

This command introduces a hook configurable by a \Configure command. The *digit* specifies the number of configurable fields the \Configure command will need. These fields are accessible with the \NewConfigure command through the parameter names #1, #2, and so forth. An example is shown in Figure 4.15.

TEX4ht provides hooks with initial values for the commands in the style files of LᴬTEX, the plain file of TEX, style files of AMS-LᴬTEX and AMS-TEX, and other commonly used packages.

4.6   The inner workings of TEX4ht

An insight into how the system operates can help with installation or with improving and extending its use. It can also explain the system's capabilities and limitations. Although most of these issues are typically important for only a few, more advanced users, many readers might like to skim this section quickly just to get a general impression of the topics covered.

4.6.1   The translation process

The command line

```
ht latex filename
```

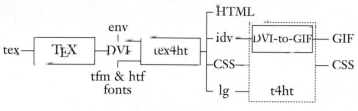

Input Files	
tex4ht.sty	Style file for LaTeX
*.4ht	Sub-style files for tex4ht.sty
*.cfg	Configurations for tex4ht.sty
*.htf	Virtual hypertext fonts
Output Files	
*.html	HTML files
*.css	Style for HTML code
*.gif	bitmap pictures
Temporary Files	
jobname.lg	A script from tex4ht for t4ht
jobname.dvi	TEX output for tex4ht
jobname.idv	DVI code for bitmap pictures
jobname.xref	Holds cross references between compilations by TEX
jobname.toc	Holds a table of contents between compilations by TEX
jobname.otc	Holds a table of contents within a compilation by TEX
tex4ht.tmp	Helper file during a compilation

Figure 4.16: The workflow and files of TEX4ht

requests a translation of the source *filename* into HTML. The script ht calls the different utilities involved in the translation process (Figure 4.16); it consists of five steps, of which the first three involve running LaTeX:

```
latex    filename
latex    filename
latex    filename
tex4ht   filename
t4ht     filename
```

4.6.2   Running LaTeX

The three compilations of the LaTeX source by TEX are needed to ensure both proper references within hypertext links and proper arrangements of cells in tables

```
1   (tex4ht.sty) (url.sty)
2   (try.cfg (tex4ht.sty
3   --- needs --- tex4ht try ---
4   (tex4ht.tmp) (try.xref)
5   --- file try.css ---
6   (tex4hta.sty)) (try.aux))  [1] [2]
7   (try.otc[3]) [4]
8   1. 19 Writing try.idv[1] (try0x.gif)
```

Figure 4.17: Runtime information in the log file from LaTeX

containing the \multicolumn command. More compilations might be needed for sources in which the \multicolumn command merges a large number of cells.

The log file of the compilation will include information similar to that shown in Figure 4.17 (without the line numbers). The third line in the example requests processing by the tex4ht program of the output file try.dvi to produce a try.html file and possibly other files as well. The fifth line tells us about the style file, named try.css, supplied for the HTML output. The eighth line mentions a bitmap file, named try0x.gif, that needs to be produced by t4ht from the first figure of the try.idv file (Section 4.6.4 on the facing page).

The first and second lines show the two times that the package file tex4ht.sty is read. The first time gets the \Preamble command and about half a dozen hooks with default configurations. The second time is activated by the \Preamble command, and it reads the portions of the style file selected by the options. The early set of hooks allows the customization of the headers before they are written during the second loading of the file. They include the hooks named HTML, HEAD, BODY, TITLE, TITLE+, and HtmlPar (use of these is discussed in Section B.2.1.4).

During a compilation, TeX4ht stores the entries for the tables of contents in a toc file; these are to be used in the next run of the source document. The entries from the previous run are moved into an otc file so that they are available during the current run. The file try.otc shown in the seventh line of the example log file shows such a file in use.

4.6.3   Running the tex4ht program

Running a source file with LaTeX outputs a standard DVI file, containing special instructions for the tex4ht package. The postprocessor program tex4ht[1] uses these instructions to determine how the DVI code should be processed. They tell tex4ht where the output files should start and end, what names should be given to the files,

---

[1]The tex4ht utility is programmed in C with system calls to a very few simple standard functions. Its hypertext fonts are system-independent files of plain text and, like fonts of TeX and its DVI output, are portable across all systems. This means that the tex4ht utility is easy to transport between different platforms, and the output independent of the platform on which the program is run.

the HTML decorations to be assigned to the symbols of the different fonts, where the code for the bitmap pictures resides, and so on.

To perform the translation into HTML, the tex4ht utility needs to know where the font metrics of TEX reside (tfm files), where the private hypertext fonts of tex4ht are stored (see htf fonts, Section 4.6.7 on page 190), and other information that relates to the environment in which the utility is working. Some of this information might be included in the executable code of tex4ht during compilation. The rest of it is specified in a control (env) file (see Section 4.6.8 on page 193).

An invocation of tex4ht, without any parameters, produces a usage message like the following:

```
tex4ht in-file[.dvi]
   [-ttfm-font-dir]
   [-ihtf-font-dir]
   [-eenv-dir]
   [-dout-dir]
   [-gbitmap-file-ext]    [-blg-divide-script]    [-slg-gif-script]
```

Usually the user will simply give the name of the dvi file. For instance, the command tex4ht try.dvi produces a main file named try.html.

The command-line option -gbitmap-file-ext determines the file extension of the bitmap files of picture symbols. The option -dout-dir specifies a directory for the output files (for instance, tex4ht try -d/tmp/ on a UNIX platform). The three options -eenv-dir, -ihtf-font-dir, and -ttfm-font-dir specify directories to be searched for the control file (see Section 4.6.8 on page 193), the virtual hypertext fonts, and the TFM files.

Figure 4.18 shows an example of messages produced during a run of tex4ht. The second line shows the TEX metric cmr10 being found, and the third line shows the corresponding virtual hypertext font being loaded. The fifth line reports the loading of the file cmr.htf instead of cmbx10.htf. The symbols of the bold font have the same HTML representations as those of the normal font. The two fonts, however, will end up with different presentations, using font information provided in the CSS file.

The tenth line requests the execution of a script (see Section 4.6.6 on page 189).

4.6.4   A look at t4ht

When tex4ht is done with processing the DVI file of TEX, it leaves behind a scaled-down DVI file with the extension name idv. This consists of all the DVI code fragments that need to be translated into pictures, with each page holding exactly one picture. The first half of the file is for pictures that are requested in the source LATEX file; the second half is for pictures requested in the fonts.

The information on how the pictures should be named is recorded in a lg file; part of that information is also shown in the log file of TEX. For instance, in the

```
1   file try.html
2   (/n/candy/tex/texmf/fonts/tfm/public/cm/cmr10.tfm)
3   (/n/soda/tex4ht.dir/cmr.htf)
4   (/n/candy/tex/texmf/fonts/tfm/public/cm/cmbx10.tfm)
5   Loading 'cmr.htf' for 'cmbx10.htf'
6   (/n/soda/tex4ht.dir/cmr.htf)
7   (/n/candy/tex/texmf/fonts/tfm/jknappen/ec/ecsl1000.tfm)
8   --- warning --- Couldn't find font 'ecsl1000.htf' (char codes: 0--255)
9   [1 file try.css ]
10  Execute script 'try.lg'
```

Figure 4.18: Messages from running `tex4ht`

```
1   Entering try.lg
2   dvips -mode ibmvga -D 110 -f try.idv -pp 1 > tmp.ps
3   convert -crop 0x0 -density 110x110 -transparent #FFFFFF tmp.ps try0x.gif
4   cmsy10-2a.gif already in
```

Figure 4.19: Messages from running `t4ht`

log of Figure 4.17, the eighth line has the statement `try.idv[1]` (`try0x.gif`). It says that the picture from the first page of `try.idv` will be stored in a file named `try0x.gif`.

The `lg` file may also contain style information for the document's `css` file, user requests for calls to system functions, and other types of entries. The `lg` file may, therefore, be regarded as a script to record the actions that must be taken after the `tex4ht` utility completes its job.

The `t4ht` script has to execute the contents of `lg` file. This may be done by using a system-dependent program for interpreting the script, or the script itself may be executed, if it is expressed in terms of a scripting language recognized by the current platform.

4.6.5   From DVI to GIF

TeX4ht does not provide tools for converting DVI code into bitmap form. It relies on external tools being available for the task.

The second and third lines of Figure 4.19 show a two-step conversion of a DVI picture into a bitmap GIF file. The first step uses the `dvips` [↪DVIPS] driver to convert the picture into an intermediate file in PostScript. The second step calls the `convert` program (part of ImageMagick, [↪IMAGEMAGICK]) to complete the task.

The fourth line in the example says that the file `cmsy10-2a.gif` already exists; therefore, it is not created again.

The dimensions of the pictures depend on the size of the source documents and, in the case of picture symbols, on the sizes of the fonts in use. However, the dimensions and quality of the pictures may also depend on the settings chosen for the external utilities in use and, of course, on the display used to view the HTML pages

4.6.6   A taste of the `lg` file

In essence, the `lg` file is just a wish list written by the `tex4ht` program. Some of the entries originate in the program itself. Other entries are requests made in the source document with `tex4ht` playing the intermediate role of passing the requests into the file.

Requests from the source document can be made with a command of the form

```
\Needs{request}
```

They will end up in the `lg` file embedded within an envelope. The envelope itself is configurable with the `\Configure{Needs}{content}` command, where the latter command should use the token #1 to refer to the parameter of `\Needs`.

Consider the following LATEX code:

```
\Needs{chmod 644 *.html}
\Configure{Needs}{#1}
\Needs{Say hello}
```

With the configuration

```
\Configure{Needs}{1. \the\inputlineno\space--- needs --- #1 ---}
```

the source code contributes the following two lines to the `lg` file:

```
1. 12 --- needs --- "chmod 644 *.html" ---
Say hello
```

The default t4ht program distributed with TEX4ht will interpret the format of the first line

```
1. integer   --- needs --- "content" ---
```

as a system call to the UNIX command `chmod 644 *.html`. On the other hand, it ignores the second line because the utility was not programmed to recognize the pattern of that line.

The `lg` file starts with all the contributions made in the source document, typically from `\Needs` commands in style files. It then lists the contributions originating in the `tex4ht` utility. The two types of contributions are separated by a distinguishing line, put there by `tex4ht`, in the `lg` file.

```
cmr 0 127                                  'ffl'       ' '           15
'G'         '1'    Gamma     0             .........................
=D=         =1=    Delta     1             'a'         ' '           97
'Q'         '1'    Theta     2             'b'         ' '           98
'/\\'       '1'    Lambda    3             .........................
'E'         '1'    Xi        4             '&#34;'     ' '           125
'TT'        '1'    Pi        5             '~'         ' '           126
.........................                  '\168\'     ' '           127
'ffi'       ' '              14            cmr 0 127
```

Figure 4.20: Portions of a virtual hypertext font file `cmr.htf`

The default patterns for the contributions of the `tex4ht` utility are determined at the time the utility is compiled for the platform in hand. These patterns can be overridden in the runtime control file.

The `lg` files generally consist of requests to create bitmap pictures, explicit contributions to the CSS file, and font information that implicitly asks for contributions to the CSS file.

4.6.7   The font control files

Text in normal LaTeX output often has many symbols coming from different fonts. These symbols are put in the source file by a character or macro pointing to a symbol in an actual font. Thus, when using the Computer Modern Roman 10pt font, character `a` in the input means "set character number 98 from font cmr10" and `\Gamma` means "set character number 1." Because TEX4ht is not in charge of rendering the symbols, it supplies content for each symbol, instead of getting the glyph from the font file (as a DVI driver would usually do). This content is specified in TEX4ht's virtual hypertext font files and is used by the Web browser to put a real character on the screen.

4.6.7.1   Using the files

For a given LaTeX font, `tex4ht` assumes a virtual hypertext font, the main filename of which is a subset of the LaTeX font name. If more than one such file is available, the one with the longest name is assumed. Accordingly, `tex4ht` searches in turn for the `cmr10.htf`, `cmr1.htf`, `cmr.htf`, `cm.htf`, and `c.htf` files when it needs a virtual hypertext font for a LaTeX font named `cmr10`.

Each virtual hypertext font file starts and ends with identical identification lines that specify the font name, the character code of the first symbol, and the character code of the last symbol (Figure 4.20).

For each character, the file has a line consisting of three fields: a text string, a class number, and a (possibly empty) comment. The first and second fields must be delimited with a single character; any delimiters can be used, but within any one line they must all be the same.

The class is a number between 0 and 255, where an empty class field is treated as 0. An entry with an even-numbered class contributes the content of the first field to the symbol. An entry with an odd-numbered class requests that a bitmap picture for the symbol be used, with the first field contributing an alternative content for character-based browsers.

From input like "a Γ", TEX4ht will request a bitmap render-ing for \Gamma in a file named cmr10-0.gif and produce the output a <IMG SRC="cmr10-0.gif" ALT="G"> in the HTML file. The cmr10 in the file-name indicates the LATEX font name; the 0 indicates the character number in the font.

The first field in the entry may refer directly to characters in a font by plac-ing the corresponding character code between backslashes. On the other hand, a backslash character \ must be represented by a pair of backslash characters \\.

The symbols <, >, and & should be represented, for instance, by the strings <, >, and &, respectively.

4.6.7.2   Configuring the fonts

The content retrieved for the symbols from the virtual hypertext font tables is writ-ten into the HTML files in a format that is governed by the following command. It provides a seven-component template for the symbols of the specified class. The delimiter must be a character that does not appear in the components.

```
\Configure{htf} {class} {delimiter}
   {parameter-1} {parameter-2} {parameter-3}
   {parameter-4} {parameter-5} {parameter-6}
   {parameter-7}
```

For example, the LATEX code \textsc{a} produces <SMALL>A</SMALL> in HTML 3.2 mode and <SPAN CLASS="small-caps">A</SPAN> in HTML 4.0 Transitional mode. The htf font provides the content A of class 4 for the character 'a' in either mode. In the first mode, the markup is due to the default configuration for symbols of class 4 set by the command

```
\Configure{htf}{4}{+}{<SMALL>}{}{}{}{}{}{</SMALL>}
```

The only difference in the second mode is in the default configuration

```
\Configure{htf}{4}{+}{<SPAN CLASS="}{}{}{} {}{small-caps"> }{</SPAN>}
```

For a symbol whose class is an even number, the first parameter is printed liter-ally. The second parameter should comply with the C language conventions, and, if it is not empty, it is used to output the font name. The third and fourth param-eters are used in a similar manner for writing the font size and its magnification, respectively. The remaining parameters are written literally, where either the fifth or the sixth parameter must be empty. The string contributed from the `htf` file is introduced just before the last parameter.

Symbols of odd classes use the parameters in a similar manner to output the font name, the alternate string from the `htf` font, a second copy of the font name, the font size, the font magnification when it differs from 100%, and the character code. The configuration for class 0 is also used to provide extra markup to symbols of the other classes.

The `\NoFonts` and `\EndNoFonts` commands suspend and resume, respectively, the contributions of the `\Configure{htf}` command.

4.6.7.3 Adding style

Contributions of `htf` fonts to the CSS file can be configured with the commands

```
\Configure{htf-css}{class}{content}
\Configure{htf-css}{fontname}{attributes}
```

The command

```
\Configure{htf-css}{4}{.small-caps {font-variant: small-caps; }}
```

contributes `.small-caps{font-variant: small-caps; }` for symbols of class 4. On the other hand, the command

```
\Configure{htf-css}{cmmi}{font-style: italic;}
```

results in contributions like `.cmmi-7{ font-size:70%; font-style: italic;}` and `.cmmi-10{ font-style: italic;}`.

4.6.7.4 Font clues

Existing virtual hypertext fonts may be redesigned by users to obtain alternative output; new ones may be produced to accommodate missing fonts. If no matching `htf` can be found, `tex4ht` will issue warning messages such as

```
---warning --- Couldn't find font 'fontname.htf'
  (char codes: first--last)
```

until the new fonts are provided.

With the package option `ShowFont`, source code like

```
\font\x=fontname\ShowFont\x
```

produces a picture showing the normal result for the different symbols in the given font.

4.6.8   The control file

The task of the runtime control file is to allow the `tex4ht` utility to adjust itself to the platform on which it runs and to the needs of its users without having to be recompiled. The file is called either `tex4ht.env` or `.tex4ht`, and it might have more than one copy in a given installation. For instance (in order of priority), one copy may reside in a directory indicated with the `-e` option of the command line (see Section 4.6.3 on page 186). A second file may reside in the working directory, and a third one may be in a directory whose location is hard coded within the program.

The file itself is made up of entries identified by the first character in each line. The following are some of the possible options:

t   Identifies a directory to be searched for the font metric (`tfm`) files of TEX.

i   Identifies a directory to be searched for the virtual hypertext fonts (`htf`) of TEX4ht.

a   Different fonts of LATEX may consist of identical sets of symbols that vary just in size or style. Such fonts would translate to identical virtual hypertext fonts, so the "a" character introduces font aliases.

g   Identifies the extension name given to bitmap files. Currently such bitmap files are used only for picture symbols in virtual hypertext fonts.

Consider the following control file (the line numbers are not part of the file):

```
1   t/n/candy/tex/texmf/fonts/tfm/!
2   i/n/soda/tex4ht.dir/
3   i/n/soda/tex4ht.dir/ht-fonts/!
4   acmbx cmr
5    acmsl cmr
6   g.jpg
```

The first line points to a directory to search for font metric files that are not available in the current directory; the exclamation mark ! indicates that the search should extend to subdirectories of all depths.

The second and third lines specify directories to locate `htf` fonts, where recursive searching into subdirectories is allowed within the directory listed in the third line.

The fourth line states that requests for `cmbx` fonts should use the `htf` file `cmr.htf`. The fifth line is ignored because it starts with a blank character; this character is not within the options available for entries of the control file.

The sixth line requests an extension name of `jpg`, instead of the default extension `gif`, for the bitmap files of the picture symbols.

Summary

This chapter has shown how TeX4ht can be used to translate LaTeX documents into a HTML files, with a very extensive set of facilities to configure the results. The strength of this system is that it uses LaTeX itself to read the file, permitting a far greater range of LaTeX constructs (such as complex macros) to be handled than most other translators.

Because much TeX4ht's work is done by hooks in a LaTeX style file, it is relatively easy to change it to generate different markup. In Appendix B.2 on page 404 we look at how to make the system generate XML, and we give some concrete examples of a LaTeX to XML translator, including MathML, in 8.2.3.2 on page 382.

CHAPTER 5

Direct display of LaTeX on the Web

In this chapter we discuss some applications that take LaTeX input and render it directly within a Web browser; these are typically browser plug-ins or Java applets. The software packages are not based on the "real" TeX source code, so they do not use METAFONT fonts or DVI files. None of the applications currently renders all LaTeX features, although you should check the product Web sites for news and updates.

The most widely used browser plug-in for rendering LaTeX input is IBM's techexplorer Hypermedia Browser. This plug-in augments Netscape Navigator and Microsoft Internet Explorer and is available for several platforms. It renders a large amount of nonmath LaTeX markup and is suitable for both showing math within an HTML document and for displaying full documents. Most of this chapter discusses how you can augment your LaTeX documents for optimal interactive rendering within techexplorer.

WebEQ is a widely used Java applet for rendering math within a browser. Since it is a Java applet, it works more or less automatically on several platforms. WebEQ offers rich functionality for displaying math, but it is limited in what it can do for text. You would use this applet most frequently within an HTML page.

When using either of these programs remember that the resolution of a typical computer monitor is significantly less that that of a printed page. This means that relative sizes of elements such as base expressions and subscripts may be different from what you are used to seeing on a page. Also, the lower resolution may cause rule widths to vary, depending on where they appear on the screen.

There are several other practical problems for using any of these products for displaying math within HTML documents. In the final section of this chapter we examine these problems and discuss how future browsers and rendering applications will improve the current situation. We also describe the ways in which these applications might communicate with other programs to provide truly interactive scientific documents.

5.1   IBM techexplorer Hypermedia Browser

IBM's techexplorer Hypermedia Browser[1] is a browser plug-in for Netscape Navigator and Microsoft Internet Explorer. IBM's techexplorer directly renders a subset of TeX and LaTeX and can be used to display mathematical expressions within an HTML page or to display full documents within the browser window. Figure 5.1 displays two sections of our test document using techexplorer (see Section A.1 on page 391) directly. In the following sections, we will see some of the ways in which we can make more active and colorful documents.

techexplorer attempts to be more than a renderer of scientific markup. The *Introductory Edition* (available for download from [↪TXPL]) displays documents but also adds features like hypertext links, GIF and JPEG images, user-defined menus, and hierarchical document navigation. The *Professional Edition* (which you have to purchase from IBM) builds on the features in the free *Introductory Edition* and adds support for printing, searching, inline video, a Java/JavaScript programming interface, and an add-in architecture for allowing techexplorer to communicate with other applications. Currently techexplorer is being enhanced by adding support for the Mathematical Markup Language (see Section 8.1 on page 368)

techexplorer works well with browser frames and thus can be used to build sophisticated sites that combine HTML pages, techexplorer documents in windows, and Java applets that dynamically update the techexplorer documents and respond to user events within their windows.

Because techexplorer is a plug-in, you need to get an appropriate version for the operating system that you are using. Versions are available for Microsoft Windows 9X and Windows NT, in addition to several UNIX flavors, including IBM AIX, Sun Solaris, SGI IRIX, and Linux. Check the Web site [↪TXPL] for updates and news about versions for other platforms. The following discussion of techexplorer is based on Version 2.0.

The full documentation for techexplorer is shipped with the product and is also available from the Web site. We will not reproduce the reference material in the documentation here because techexplorer is continuing to evolve and, in particular, the supported subset of TeX and LaTeX expands with each new release.

The Compatibility section of the online documentation describes the features that techexplorer provides from TeX and LaTeX. The Creating documents sec-

---

[1] techexplorer Hypermedia Browser is a trademark of IBM Corporation.

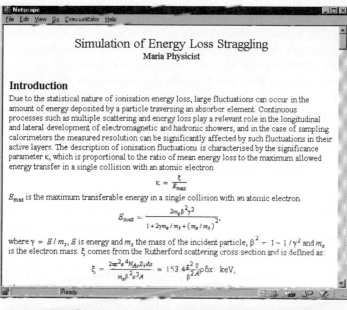

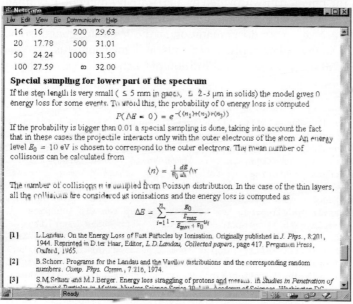

Figure 5.1: Two examples of `techexplorer` displaying text and mathematics

tion of the online documentation describes the `techexplorer`-specific features that you can use to create interactive scientific and technical documents. To facilitate your creating electronic documents that can be viewed on the screen as well as printed using LaTeX, the developers have provided a style file that implements most of the new commands that are defined by `techexplorer`. See the online documentation to get this style file and to read about what it can do.

In the following sections we describe the philosophy of `techexplorer` and discuss how you can use the `techexplorer` extensions to TeX and LaTeX to make online documents that are superior to simple electronic renditions of print documents.

5.1.1   Basic formatting issues

The `techexplorer` program *emulates* TeX and LaTeX and does not use the real TeX program. Some basic TeX features such as category codes are not supported, and the major emphasis is on providing the standard macros and environments from LaTeX. Style files are not supported, but input files and simple plain TeX `\def` macros can be used.

While `techexplorer` supports many commands from TeX and LaTeX, it sometimes accepts commands but then does nothing with them. Similarly it may support a subset of the functionality provided by a LaTeX environment. Commands or symbols that `techexplorer` does not understand at all are displayed in red within the text.[2] The `techexplorer` documentation at the Web site contains an up-to-date listing of the supported symbols, commands, and environments.

Release 2.0 of the Professional Edition of `techexplorer` supports the following commands:

```
$ $$ -- --- \! \$ \& \> \, \/ \: \; \{ \} \[ \] \( \) \^ \_ \\ \| ^ _
\acute \addtocounter \Alph \alph \arabic \arccos \arcsin \arctan \arg
\atop \author \begingroup \bf \bgroup \bibitem \big \bigl \bigm \bigr
\Bigl \Big \Bigm \Bigr \bigg \biggl \biggm \biggr \Bigg \Biggl \Biggm
\Biggr \bigskip \Bmatrix \bmatrix \bmod \bold \boxed \break \caption
\cases \cdots \centering \centerline \cfrac \chapter \choose \cite \colon
\color \colorbox \cos \cosh \cot \coth \csc \csch \date \ddot \ddots
\ddotsb \ddotsc \ddotsi \ddotsm \def \deg \det \dfrac \dim \displaylines
\displaystyle \dot \egroup \em \emph \endgroup \enskip \enspace
\ensuredisplaymath \ensuremath \eqno \erf \errmessage \exp \fbox
\fcolorbox \fnsymbol \footnotesize \frac \framebox \gcd \grave \H \hat
\hbox \hfil \hfill \hfilll \hline \hom \hphantom \hrule \hsize \hskip
\hspace \hspace* \hss \Huge \huge \idotsint \iff \ifmmode \iint \iiint
\iiiint \impliedby \implies \includegraphics \index \inf \it \kern
\joinrel \ker \label \LARGE \Large \large \LaTeX \lbrace \lbrack \lcm
\ldots \left \leftline \leqno \lg \lim \liminf \limsup \llap \ln \log
```

---

[2]Unlike HTML browsers that ignore markup they do not understand, `techexplorer` displays markup that is not understood in order to make it easier for authors to debug their documents. Thus `techexplorer` will always display all the content of a mathematical expression instead of mysteriously omitting part of it.

```
\lower \lowercase \lVert \lvert \makebox \maketitle \mathbb \mathbf
\mathbin \mathcal \mathchoice \mathclose \mathit \mathop \mathop
\mathopen \mathord \mathrel \mathsf \mathstrut \mathtt \matrix \max \mbox
\modbreak \medspace \medskip \min \mit \negmedspace \negthinspace
\newcommand \newcounter \newenvironment \newline \normalsize \not \notin
\null \operatorname \over \overbrace \overbracket \overline
\overrightarrow \overset \pagecolor \par \paragraph \parbox \part
\phantom \pmatrix \pmod \pod \Pr \prime \providecommand \qed \qedsymbol
\qquad \quad \raggedleft \quote \raise \raisebox \rbrace \rbrack
\refstepcounter \relax \renewcommand \renewenvironment \right \rightline
\rlap \rm \root \Roman \roman \rule \rVert \rvert \sb \sc
\scriptscriptsize \scriptscriptstyle \scriptsize \scriptstyle \shadowbox
\sec \sech \section \setstyle \sf \sin \sinh \sl \small \smallskip
\smallmatrix \smash \sp \space \sqrt \stackrel \stepcounter \strut
\subparagraph \subsection \subsubsection \sup \tan \tanh \TeX \text
\textbf \textcolor \textit \textrm \textsf \textsl \textstyle \texttt
\tfrac \thanks \thebibliography \thechapter \theenumi \theenumii
\theenumiii \theenumiv \theequation \thefigure \thefootnote
\thempfootnote \thepage \theparagraph \thepart \thesection
\thesubparagraph \thesubsection \thesubsubsection \thetable \thickspace
\thinspace \tilde \tiny \title \today \tt \underbar \underbrace
\underbracket \underline \underset \uppercase \value \vbox \vdots \verb
\Vmatrix \vmatrix \vphantom \vrule \vskip \vss \vtop \widehat \widetilde
\zag \zig
```

The following commands are accepted but ignored:

```
\@ \- \addcontentsline \addtocontents \addtolength \allowbreak \and
\bibliographystyle \boldmath \break \brokenpenalty \bye \cleardoublepage
\clearpage \cline \clubpenalty \DeclareMathOperator \definecolor
\displaywidowpenalty \documentclass \documentstyle \eject \end
\floatingpenalty \font \fontencoding \fontfamily \fontseries \fontshape
\fontsize \footnotemark \frenchspacing \fussy \goodbreak \hline
\hyphenation \indent \interlinepenalty \let \limits \linebreak \long
\looseness \markboth \markright \multicolumn \newblock \newif \newlength
\newpage \newtheorem \noalign \nobreak \nocite \nocorr \nofrenchspacing
\noindent \nolimits \nolinebreak \nomargins \nonumber \nopagebreak
\nopagenumbers \null \pagebreak \pagenumbering \pagestyle
\postdisplaypenalty \predisplaypenalty \protect \putat \raggedbottom
\relax \rgb \selectfont \setlength \settodepth \settoheight \settowidth
\singlespace \sloppy \special \thispagestyle \typeout \unboldmath
\usefont \usepackage \widowpenalty
```

The following environments are at least partially supported:

```
align align* abstract array Bmatrix bmatrix center description
displaymath document enumerate eqnarray eqnarray* equation figure
flushleft flushright gather gather* Huge huge itemize LARGE Large large
math matrix minipage normalsize pmatrix quotation quote slide small
smallmatrix tabbing table tabular tiny titlepage verbatim Vmatrix vmatrix
```

For simplicity, when we discuss techexplorer markup support in the following exposition, we will refer to the "LaTeX markup" rather than the longer, but more precise phrase, "TeX and LaTeX markup subset."

The LaTeX \newcommand and \newenvironment commands can be used, but the optional argument is not currently permitted. Note that macro definitions are global to the document in which they are defined, unless the \gdef or the \globalnewcommand commands are used. In this latter case, the macro definitions are available to all documents currently in memory. To reiterate: techexplorer does not allow macro definitions to be local to the groups in which they are defined. They are either global within the defining document or within all active documents. Multiple active documents might occur if you use techexplorer to display several math expressions within an HTML document or if you use browser frames and have techexplorer documents in more than one frame.

On the Microsoft Windows 95 and Windows NT platforms, techexplorer uses TrueType fonts. The Professional Edition of techexplorer provides a set of symbol fonts derived from the BlueSky and Y&Y PostScript renditions of the Computer Modern, LaTeX, and AMS Symbol fonts. Similarly on UNIX platforms techexplorer uses PostScript versions of the symbol fonts, but it does not use METAFONT fonts.

techexplorer does not process DVI files but rather reads and renders the document directly. This allows techexplorer to display LaTeX markup that is dynamically generated by a Java applet or another application.

Page layout is performed with respect to the size of the techexplorer window, rather than by using style parameters in the document. For example, paragraphs are normally flowed to the width of the window. If you change the window size, techexplorer will try to reflow your document to fit the window.[3]

Since all composition is done within your browser, techexplorer offers many ways of customizing the display environment. For example, you can set the standard fonts used and the foreground and background colors of the text. The default color for links is blue, but you can change it to another color if you prefer. Figure 5.2 shows the standard property page for setting your color choices. You access the options property pages by clicking your mouse's right button on an area of whitespace in a techexplorer document window and then choosing **Options...** from the menu displayed.

5.1.2   Your browser and techexplorer

Your Web browser can use techexplorer in one of two ways:

- to display full LaTeX documents within the full client area of the browser, and
- to display LaTeX markup in one or more windows within an HTML page.

Version 2.0 of the Professional Edition of techexplorer supports the printing of full documents but not the markup in windows within an HTML page.

---

[3] Note that in some cases the Web browser never tells techexplorer that the window has changed sizes, so the document is not recomposed. This happens most frequently when frames are involved.

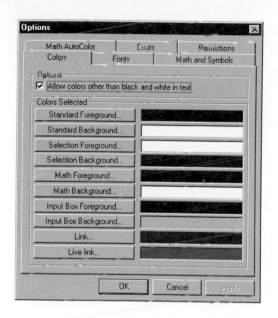

Figure 5.2: Customizing the colors used to display your documents

5.1.2.1 Displaying full documents

When your documents contain nontrivial math expressions within sentences (as opposed to between paragraphs), techexplorer will produce a better looking document than an HTML page that has math in images, plug-in, or Java applet windows. This is because techexplorer can better position and size the math expressions in relation to the surrounding text. Moreover, the formatting style and page background will be consistent across the text and the math.

Since most Web browsers and servers are preconfigured to understand that files with the extension .tex also have MIME type application/x-tex, techexplorer will automatically be invoked for your LaTeX documents if their URLs end in .tex. You can open your LaTeX documents via hypertext links in HTML or in other techexplorer documents or via the usual browser methods for specifying URLs to open.[4]

You can use techexplorer documents within browser frames in the same way that you include HTML documents. However, if you resize the browser window you will most likely have to reload the techexplorer documents to have them composed at the correct screen width (this is a shortcoming of the browser, not of techexplorer).

---

[4]At the time this section was written, opening local techexplorer files from file lists within the browser worked more reliably in Netscape Navigator than in Microsoft Internet Explorer. You may need to type explicitly in the full local file name for Internet Explorer.

5.1.2.2 Displaying math within HTML pages

You can use the HTML EMBED element to include LaTeX markup to be rendered by techexplorer within an HTML page. Figure 5.3 shows a commutative diagram sandwiched between some HTML text. The HTML source for the page is

```
<HTML>
<BODY>
This is an example of a commutative diagram
from an algebraic geometry article.
<CENTER>
<EMBED SRC="excomm.tex" TYPE="application/x-tex"
HEIGHT=110 WIDTH=400 NAME="comm-diagram">
</CENTER>
The text above and below the diagram are part of
the HTML page. The diagram itself is rendered by
<STRONG>techexplorer</STRONG> via an EMBED element.
</BODY>
</HTML>
```

There are six important attributes of the EMBED element for `techexplorer`:

SRC   the URL of the document containing your LaTeX markup.

TYPE   the MIME type of the data contained in your document.

HEIGHT   the height in pixels of the rectangle in which the markup should be rendered.

WIDTH   the width in pixels of the rectangle in which the markup should be rendered.

ALIGN   Use ALIGN=MIDDLE when you want the expression to float vertically so it looks better with respect to the baseline of the surrounding text. Simple expressions like $x - 1$ do not need this element, but more complex forms like fractions ($\frac{2}{3}$) and matrices ($\begin{bmatrix} 3 & 2 \\ 1 & 4 \end{bmatrix}$) will look better with this attribute setting.

NAME   a unique name that identifies the particular embedded `techexplorer` window. This is important if you use the `techexplorer` Scripting Interface to work with the `techexplorer` markup and the events that are generated within the window. You can omit the name if you are interested only in rendering the expression.

Since the file extension of our example embedded LaTeX document is `.tex`, the TYPE attribute is probably redundant. We recommend you use it anyway.

If you choose a height or width that is too small, your `techexplorer` window will contain vertical or horizontal scrollbars, respectively. Because users can

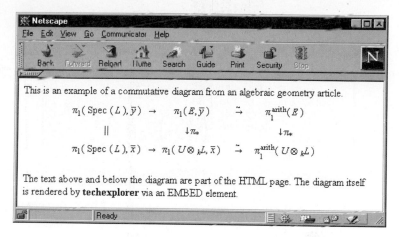

Figure 5.3: A `techexplorer` commutative diagram embedded within an HTML page

choose their own font sizes via the fonts options property page, It is impossible to know ahead of time if your window size will be sufficient for everyone. Also, techexplorer includes a narrow margin around the rendered markup, so the window you need might be slightly larger than you expect. You might try using `WIDTH="100%"` to have your expression fill the full width of the HTML page.

For browsers that are plug-in compatible with Netscape Navigator, you can include LaTeX data in the EMBED element itself rather than point to an external file. Use the `TEXDATA` attribute with the markup as value along with `TYPE="application/x-techexplorer"` to tell the browser that `techexplorer` should process the data. For example,

```
<EMBED TYPE="application/x-techexplorer"
TEXDATA="\[\pmatrix{2&3&4&5\cr 6&7&8&0\cr  1&-2&-3&-4}\]"
WIDTH=200 HEIGHT=90 ALIGN=MIDDLE>
```

displays the 3×4 matrix

$$\begin{pmatrix} 2 & 3 & 4 & 5 \\ 6 & 7 & 8 & 9 \\ -1 & -2 & -3 & -4 \end{pmatrix}$$

at the location of the EMBED element.

Here is another example (shown in Figure 5.4, using Microsoft Internet Explorer) that contains two math expressions. The first is within a sentence, and the other is in display mode.

```
<HTML>
<HEAD>
```

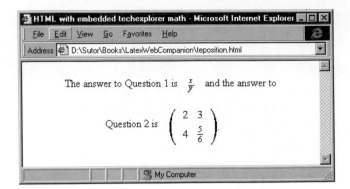

Figure 5.4: Two techexplorer expressions embedded within an HTML page

```
<TITLE>HTML with embedded techexplorer math</TITLE>
</HEAD>
<BODY>
<P ALIGN=CENTER>
The answer to Question 1 is
<EMBED TYPE="application/x-techexplorer"
       TEXDATA="\pagecolor{white}$\frac{x}{y}$"
       ALIGN=MIDDLE
       WIDTH=33 HEIGHT=45>
and the answer to<BR>Question 2 is
<EMBED TYPE="application/x-techexplorer"
       TEXDATA="\pagecolor{white}$\pmatrix{2&3\cr 4&\frac{5}{6}}$."
       ALIGN=MIDDLE
       WIDTH=114 HEIGHT=78>
</P>
</BODY>
</HTML>
```

5.1.3   Adding hypertext links

One of the primary advantages of electronic documents over paper ones is the possibility of having hypertext links. The proliferation of HTML Web sites and browsers has made hypertext a basic requirement for any application that displays documents interactively.

When running under Microsoft Windows 95, techexplorer has a maximum document length that corresponds roughly to 50 printed pages. For this reason, you will need to break longer documents into smaller ones and add hypertext links between them. These links can be placed directly in the text or in pop-up menus (see Section 5.1.6 on page 211).

The general-purpose `techexplorer` command for creating a hypertext link is `\docLink`.

```
\docLink [frameName] {url} [label] {expression}
```

The two required arguments are *url* and *expression*. The *expression* is what you see on the screen, and *url* is the address of the document to which the browser will jump when the reader clicks on *expression*. The *url* is read in a special mode so that it can contain characters such as backslashes.

Note that *text* does not have to be plain text: It can be anything that `techexplorer` can display, such as words, images, and mathematical expressions. As mentioned earlier, *text* will be displayed in blue, by default. If you want a specific hyperlink to be displayed in a given color, use `\color` within *text*. For example,

```
This \docLink{Hyperlink.tex}{\color{black}hyperlink}
might be indistinguishable from the surrounding text.
```

If the surrounding text color was black, the word "hyperlink" in the example sentence would not stand out as something special. However, the mouse cursor will still change to a hand, and the status line will display the target for the link, that is, `Hyperlink.tex`.

Unlike the default formatting in browsers, hyperlinks in `techexplorer` are not underlined; it does not make sense to underline links within mathematical expressions. Indeed, underlining in a math expression often has semantic significance.

The *url* is passed to the Web browser, even if the document is another LaTeX file for `techexplorer` to process. For such a LaTeX file, use the *label* optional argument to give a position in the document to which `techexplorer` should scroll when the document is displayed. If *label* cannot be found, the window is positioned at the top of the document.

Examples

- Use the normal URL syntax for a Web site address.

```
The \docLink{http://www.tug.org}{\TeX{} User's Group} Web site
contains much useful information about \LaTeX{}.
```

- You can refer to local file names, but remember that they are not portable across operating systems, and they may not be the same on every user's computer.

```
The \docLink{c:\classes\m101\probset1.tex}{first problem set}
contains instructions for how to submit your homework.
```

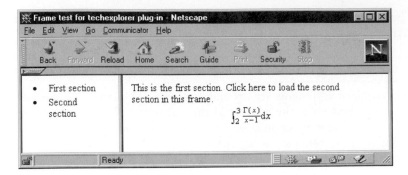

Figure 5.5: Two frames, each containing a `techexplorer` window

- You can use relative addressing to link to files in the same directory as the current file. Here we jump to the label *lecture2* in the `reading.tex` LATEX source file. This happens to be in the same directory as the document we are viewing.

```
The reading assignment before the \docLink{reading.tex}
[lecture2]{second lecture} will require about 30 hours.
```

- Links don't actually have to link to files. Here we have a `mailto` link so that the reader's mail program is invoked when the user clicks on the link.

```
If you would like, you can send mail to the techexplorer
\docLink{mailto:techexpl@watson.ibm.com}{developers}.
```

The LATEX documents that your browser displays via `techexplorer` are included in the general browser history and, in particular, can be accessed via "back" and "forward" navigation. While the browser saves information about the scroll position in the HTML documents it displays, `techexplorer` does not currently do this. Part of the problem is that `techexplorer` is usually unloaded completely and then reloaded between LATEX documents. Therefore it cannot save the current scroll state in memory. This may be remedied in a future release.

If *frameName* is specified and the current `techexplorer` document is included in an HTML frameset, the new document is displayed in the frame with the name *frameName*. If you leave out *frameName*, the new document is displayed in the current frame.

The following example illustrates two frames, each containing a `techexplorer` window. The left frame "toc" contains a table of contents and the right frame "body" contains the sections. Figure 5.5 is a screen shot of the table of contents and the first section. Following is the HTML frameset definition:

```
<HTML>
  <HEAD>
```

```
      <TITLE>
         Frame test for techexplorer plug-in
      </TITLE>
   </HEAD>
   <FRAMESET COLS="150,*">
      <FRAME MARGINWIDTH="4" SRC="toc.tex" NAME="toc">
      <FRAME MARGINWIDTH="4" SRC="first.tex" NAME="body">
   </FRAMESET>
</HTML>
```

In the LaTeX file for the table contents, the \docLinks indicate that the section file should be displayed in the "body" frame on the right.

```
% toc.tex
\begin{itemize}
\item \docLink[body]{first.tex}{First section}
\item \docLink[body]{second.tex}{Second section}
\end{itemize}
```

The first section contains a link to the second. The frame name is not required because we want to open all sections in the same frame.

```
% first.tex
This is the first section. Click here to load the
\docLink{second.tex}{second section} in this frame.

\[
\int_2^3 \, \frac{\Gamma(x)}{x - 1} \mathrm{d}x
\]
```

Similarly we don't include the frame name in the following link to the first section.

```
% second.tex
This is the second section. Click here to load the
\docLink{first.tex}{first section} in this frame.

$$
\bmatrix{
1 & 0 & 0 \cr
0 & 1 & 0 \cr
0 & 0 & 1
}
$$
```

```
\labelLink{label}{text}
```

When a hypertext link is to a target elsewhere in the same document, use \labelLink instead of \docLink.

\docLink will work, but it's overkill. You need to specify the document URL, and there might be a document maintenance problem if you decide to rename your files.

The following example will create a local hyperlink to the last section of the current document:

```
In the \labelLink{c5:final-section}{final section} we examine
these problems and discuss how future browsers and rendering
applications will improve upon the current situation.
```

For both \docLink and \labelLink the *text* argument can contain other links. The rule for executing links is that the innermost link is the one that takes precedence. Consider the following:

```
All \labelLink{label:red-phones}{red
\labelLink{label:phones}{phones}}
come with a 30 day money-back guarantee.
```

When the mouse cursor is over "phones," the label:phones link will execute when the mouse button is clicked. When the cursor is over "red," the label:red-phones link will be the one that is executed.

5.1.4   Popping up windows and footnotes

When a document is displayed by techexplorer on the screen, it is not broken into pages. It is very inconvenient to scroll to the end of long documents to see footnotes. Furthermore, footnotes in math expressions within HTML pages don't have access to the "end of the document." Therefore techexplorer supports \footnote by popping up a new window when you click on the footnote number in the text. Figure 5.6 shows a footnote in a techexplorer document.

```
\popupLink{windowText}{caption}{text}
```

A footnote is an example of a *pop-up window link*. You create pop-up window links by using \popupLink.

The *text* is displayed in the document. When you click on *text*, a pop-up window containing *windowText* is displayed. The window has *caption* displayed in its titlebar. When the mouse cursor passes over *text*, the *caption* is displayed on the browser status line.

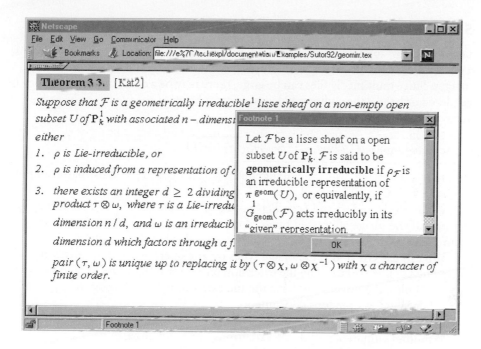

Figure 5.6: A pop-up footnote in techexplorer

Note that *caption* will be simplified so that it can be displayed using the single titlebar font. In particular, a math expression in *caption* will not be displayed in a two-dimensional format. In the following example,

```
More information about this interesting expression is available
\popupLink{Since $\alpha = 1$, the expression is simply
$(x-1)(x+1)$.}{$\frac{x^2-\alpha}{\alpha}$}[here}.
```

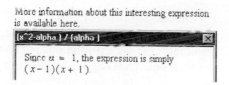

the text displayed in the titlebar and status line is (x^2-alpha)/(alpha).

The text in the pop-up window is fully formatted and can contain mathematics. Links within the window do not work yet, although they are displayed using the link color. If you include an image, sound, or video within the pop-up window text, make sure you use an absolute URL for the source location.

5.1.5   Using images, sound, and video

`techexplorer` supports multimedia via images, sounds, and video. The Microsoft Windows versions have the most support, while the UNIX editions only support images. Since multimedia files can be large, there may be a delay before the image is rendered or before the audio or video file starts playing if the file has to be retrieved across the network.

> `\includegraphics` *[lowerLeft]* *[lowerRight]* *{url}*

To include an image, use `\includegraphics`. This offers the most basic support from the LaTeX `graphics` package.

    While the *lowerLeft* and *lowerRight* optional arguments are accepted, they are ignored. If the image addressed by *url* does not exist or has not yet been retrieved from the network, a "missing image" substitute is displayed in its place.

    You can use GIF and JPEG image types on any operating system platform supported by `techexplorer`. The file extension on *url* for GIF images should be `.gif`. For JPEG files, the images can have the file extensions `.jpg`, `.jpeg`, or `.jpe`. The Microsoft Windows versions also support

- Windows bitmap files with file extensions `.bmp` and `.dib`;
- PCX images with file extension `.pcx`;
- Targa images with file extension `.tga`; and
- TIFF images with file extensions `.tif` or `.tiff`.

We recommend that you use GIF and JPEG images for maximum portability. Animated and transparent images are not supported on any platform yet; neither are Encapsulated PostScript files. When you print a `techexplorer` document, each image is scaled so that its size, relative to the text, remains the same.

> `\backgroundimage`*{url}*

Use `\backgroundimage` to tile the `techexplorer` window background with an image. You can use any image that you might use with `\includegraphics`. When you print a `techexplorer` document, the background image is ignored. If you include more than one instance of `\backgroundimage` in your document, the last one encountered is the one that is used. If the image addressed by *url* does not exist or cannot be retrieved from the network, no background image is rendered.

> `\backgroundsound`*{url}*
> `\includeaudio`*{url}*

The commands `\backgroundsound` and `\includeaudio` play audio files if your computer has the appropriate sound hardware. The sound file is played only once;

perhaps a future version will allow looping. Only WAV files with file extension `.wav` are supported, and then only on the Microsoft Windows platforms. This feature is supported only in the Professional Edition of `techexplorer`.

By default, the sound file is played as soon as it can be loaded. Figure 5.7 shows the standard property page for setting your `techexplorer` permissions. If you do not wish to have background sounds played when pages are loaded, uncheck the box labeled "Enable audio to autoplay when the document is opened".

`\audioLink{`*url*`}{`*text*`}`

To have audio played when the reader clicks the mouse button within an area on the screen, use an *audio link*. The sound file is retrieved from *url*, and *text* is displayed on the screen. Like `\backgroundsound`, only WAV files with file extension `.wav` on Microsoft Windows are supported. On other platforms, no sound is made when the link is executed.

`\videoLink{`*url*`}{`*text*`}`

Use a *video link* to play video in a pop-up window when the mouse button is clicked. The video file is retrieved from *url*, and *text* is displayed on the screen. Only AVI files with file extension `.avi` on Microsoft Windows are supported. When the video starts playing, it will continue to the end and then the pop-up window will close.

A more interesting video option where inline video can be used is available to users of the Professional Edition of `techexplorer`.

`\includevideo{`*autoPlay*`}{`*alternateText*`}{`*url*`}`

The video file is retrieved from *url*. If it cannot be found or has not yet arrived, the *alternateText* is displayed on the screen (the *alternateText* is always rendered when the document is printed). If *autoPlay* is "t", the video will start playing as soon as it is loaded. You can unilaterally prevent videos from autoplaying by unchecking the box labeled "Enable video to autoplay when the document is opened" in the permissions option property page (see Figure 5.7). To pause, stop, or replay the video, click your right mouse button on the video and select from the menu. Figure 5.8 shows an example of an inline video with the menu for controlling play.

5.1.6   Defining and using pop-up menus

A *pop-up menu*, also called a *context menu*, is a menu invoked by right clicking your mouse somewhere on the screen. `techexplorer` has a default pop-up menu that is used to access the customization options, including printing, searching, and information about the release of `techexplorer` you are using. You get the default menu by moving your mouse cursor to an empty area of the `techexplorer` window and

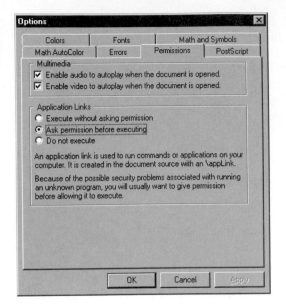

Figure 5.7: Setting permissions within techexplorer

Figure 5.8: Inline video in the Professional Edition of techexplorer

clicking the right mouse button. In the Professional Edition of techexplorer, this default menu looks like this:

You cannot alter this menu, although the availability of the "topic" items will vary according to what you have defined in your document to aid the reader in moving through the document hierarchy (see Section 5.1.8 on page 218).

You can define new menus that activate whenever you right click your mouse over a given area of text. What are the entries in such menus? They are links, rules, and other menus.

A link in a menu provides the menu item text and the action that occurs when that item is clicked. The most common types of links used in menu definitions are hypertext links and links that play sound or video.

Following is a simple three-item definition for a menu that plays songs:

```
\newmenu{SinatraSongs}{
\audioLink{http://www.sinatrafan.com/songs/young.wav}
   {You make me feel so young}
\audioLink{http://www.sinatrafan.com/songs/pennies.wav}
   {Pennies from heaven}
\audioLink{http://www.sinatrafan.com/songs/anything.wav}
   {Anything goes}
}
```

As you see, \newmenu is used to provide a named menu definition. In this case the name is *SinatraSongs*, and the definition contains three \audioLinks.

```
\newmenu{menuName}{menuDefinition}
\usemenu{menuName}{text}
```

The \usemenu command associates the menu with some text. The same menu definition can be used for as many instances of \usemenu as you wish.

For example,

```
The songs of \usemenu{SinatraSongs}{Frank Sinatra} are
loved by people of all ages.
```

When you right click your mouse on "Frank Sinatra," techexplorer displays

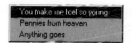

If you click on any of the menu items, the corresponding song is played.[5]

Use a rule in a menu definition to provide a separator line between entries. You can use \hrule, \vrule, or \rule since the rule is not actually drawn but is simply used as an indicator of the separator line position.

Following is a definition that includes both songs and movies starring Frank Sinatra.

```
\newmenu{SinatraSongsAndMovies}{
\audioLink{http://www.sinatrafan.com/songs/young.wav}
   {You make me feel so young}
\audioLink{http://www.sinatrafan.com/songs/pennies.wav}
   {Pennies from heaven}
\audioLink{http://www.sinatrafan.com/songs/anything.wav}
   {Anything goes}
\hrule % provides a separator line
```

---

[5]That is, if the Web site and content existed!

```
\videoLink{http://www.sinatrafan.com/movies/town.avi}
   {On the Town}
\videoLink{http://www.sinatrafan.com/movies/manchurian.avi}
   {The Manchurian Candidate}
\videoLink{http://www.sinatrafan.com/movies/eternity.avi}
   {From Here to Eternity}
}
```

This menu is used in the same way as the last one was used.

```
The songs and movies of \usemenu{SinatraSongsAndMovies}{Frank Sinatra}
are very popular.
```

Now when you right click your mouse on "Frank Sinatra," the menu displayed is

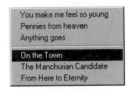

If you click on any of the menu items, the corresponding song or movie is played from our hypothetical Web site.

If you put a \usemenu inside a \newmenu definition, you will get a submenu. Let's rework the last menu so that songs and movies are separated into their own submenus. We'll keep the initial definition for *SinatraSongs* as

```
\newmenu{SinatraSongs}{
\audioLink{http://www.sinatrafan.com/songs/young.wav}
   {You make me feel so young}
\audioLink{http://www.sinatrafan.com/songs/pennies.wav}
   {Pennies from heaven}
\audioLink{http://www.sinatrafan.com/songs/anything.wav}
   {Anything goes}
}
```

and add a similar definition for *SinatraMovies*:

```
\newmenu{SinatraMovies}{
\videoLink{http://www.sinatrafan.com/movies/town.avi}
   {On the Town}
\videoLink{http://www.sinatrafan.com/movies/manchurian.avi}
   {The Manchurian Candidate}
\videoLink{http://www.sinatrafan.com/movies/eternity.avi}
   {From Here to Eternity}
}
```

Finally we'll define *SinatraSongsAndMovies2* with the two submenus, and we'll include the separator:

```
\newmenu{SinatraSongsAndMovies2}{
\usemenu{SinatraSongs}{Sinatra songs}
\hrule % provides a separator line
\usemenu{SinatraMovies}{Sinatra movies}
}
```

The final, fully opened menu can look like one of the following:

Almost any link except \altLink can be used within a menu definition. If you use a link command that takes a *url* argument but leave the argument empty (for example, \labelLink{}{Section 5}), the menu item will be disabled and will be shown in gray.

5.1.7   Using color in your documents

techexplorer supports the \color, \textcolor, \colorbox, \fcolorbox, and \pagecolor commands from the LaTeX color package. The basic colors from the color package are provided, along with several other colors that are convenient for on-screen display. In the following list of supported colors, the new techexplorer color names are set in bold: **aqua**, black, blue, cyan, **darkgray**, **fuchsia**, **gray**, green, **lightgray**, **lime**, magenta, **maroon**, **navy**, **olive**, **purple**, red, **silver**, **teal**, white, and yellow.

To change the color of rules, issue a \color command before the rule definition.

```
\bgroup
\color{red}%
\hrule height 3pt % this will be red
\egroup
\hrule height 3pt % this will probably be black
```

We enclose the color change and rule in a \bgroup/\egroup pair to preserve the default color setting.

> \backgroundcolor{*color*}

The command \backgroundcolor can be used as a synonym for \pagecolor. Both commands set the background color behind the displayed text on the screen. If you

Introduction

Figure 5.9: A gradient box in a section heading

wish to match the standard "browser gray" in an HTML window, we suggest you use \pagecolor{silver}. A restriction with the current Professional Edition of techexplorer is that the background color is ignored when printing a document.

Note that these background color commands work only for the window that displays your document. If you wish to change the background color for all techexplorer windows,

1. right click your mouse on an area of whitespace in any techexplorer document window;

2. choose **Options...** from the menu displayed;

3. click on the **Colors** tab;

4. click on the **Standard background...** button; and

5. select a color by first clicking on it and then clicking on the **OK** button.

To test your choice, click the **Apply** button. If you don't like what you see, go back to step 3 and repeat the process. Click the **OK** button to save your selection, or click **Cancel** to return to your previous background color. Figure 5.2 shows the standard property page for setting your color choices.

\rgb{*redValue*}{*greenValue*}{*blueValue*}

The \definecolor command is not currently supported, but you can use \rgb to define new colors. The values for *redValue*, *greenValue*, and *blueValue* are integers between 0 and 255, inclusive. For example,[6]

```
\def\paleYellow{\rgb{255}{255}{128}}
\pagecolor{\paleYellow}
```

sets the background color of the techexplorer document window to a light yellow.

The standard \colorbox and \fcolorbox commands allow you to place text in boxes with a given background color. techexplorer provides \gradientbox (see Figure 5.9) to let you create a box with the background color varying smoothly from one color to another.

---

[6]techexplorer does not support \newcommand fully, so we use the TeX primitive \def.

```
\gradientbox[v]{startColor}{endColor}{text}
```

By default, the gradient begins with *startColor* on the left side of the box and finishes with *endColor* on the right side. If the *v* optional argument is given,[7] the gradient is drawn vertically from top to bottom.[8]

```
\buttonbox[i]{text}
\colorbuttonbox[i]{color}{text}
```

To create boxes that look like standard Microsoft Windows buttons with a gray background, use \buttonbox. If the *i* optional argument is given (again, literally), the button is drawn in an inverted state. Such a button looks as if it has been pressed.

```
\buttonbox{This is a button box}
\buttonbox[i]{This is an inverted button box}
```

If you want a button that has a background color other than gray, use \colorbuttonbox. If the *i* optional argument is given, the button is drawn in an inverted state.

```
\colorbuttonbox{green}{This is a green button box}
\colorbuttonbox[i]{green}{This is a green inverted button box}
```

Use color carefully in your documents because too much variation can be as confusing as overusing fonts from different families. As you should with any good LaTeX document design, create macros or style files that encapsulate your design choices. You can then modify the macros or style files to achieve a global design change. Following is an example of a "Section" macro that uses a gradient box and a text color change:[9]

```
\def\Section#1{\section{%
  \gradientbox{blue}{white}{\mbox{\color{white}#1}}}}
...
\Section{Introduction}
```

Note that for techexplorer you should not skip a space after the \color command. Regular LaTeX may ignore the space, but techexplorer will not.

---

[7] Literally specify the *v*, as in \gradientbox[v]{red}{white}.

[8] The current UNIX versions of techexplorer do not draw gradients; so \gradientbox is the same as \colorbox with *startColor* as the box color.

[9] Remember that techexplorer does not support \newcommand fully.

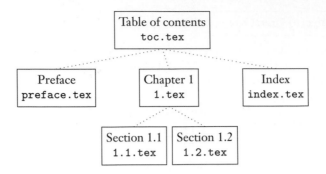

Figure 5.10: Simplified structure for a book

5.1.8   Building a document hierarchy

Most traditional documents are structured into tree-shaped hierarchies of chapters and sections. We often divide them into multiple files for convenience of editing, and the parts are included in some way into the main document when printing. Electronic versions of documents are also frequently broken into a number of files that reflect the hierarchy, but the files are usually viewed separately and are connected by hyperlinks.

For example, consider the structure in Figure 5.10, where each node shows the title of the document part and the name of the file that contains the markup for the part.

The table of contents is the root of this tree, and all top level book parts descend from this root. Some parts, like Chapter 1, have component sections themselves.

techexplorer provides a standard way to connect the pieces of the hierarchy with hyperlinks. Use \aboveTopic to give the URL of the parent document of a given part.[10]

```
\aboveTopic{url}
\nextTopic{url}
\previousTopic{url}
```

In the example in Figure 5.10, the file preface.tex should contain the command \aboveTopic{toc.tex}.

Use \nextTopic to give the URL of the next sibling document on the same level as the given part. Thus the file preface.tex should contain the command \nextTopic{1.tex}. Finally, use \previousTopic to give the URL of the previous sibling document on the same level as the given part.

The file 1.tex should contain the command \previousTopic{preface.tex}.

---

[10]The *parent document* is the next document in the tree on the direct path to the root of the tree. The root of the tree has no parent.

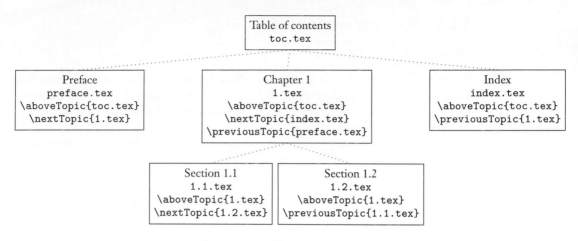

Figure 5.11: The document tree

The root document part will not have an \aboveTopic command. The first section at a given level will not have a \previousTopic command, nor will the last section at the same level have a \nextTopic command. Though it is tempting always to define the next and previous topic in some way, it will probably be more confusing for your readers unless you provide some sort of document map.

These hyperlinks are accessed by clicking the right button of your mouse in the techexplorer window. Unless you click over a user-defined pop-up menu (these are described in Section 5.1.6 on page 211), you will see a menu similar to this:

In this menu, all three topics are available. Should one of the above, next, or previous topics not be defined in the document, the corresponding menu item will be "grayed out," that is, unavailable.

Figure 5.11 summarizes this discussion with an expanded diagram of the document tree at the beginning of the section. It includes the commands to link together the direct paths in the hierarchy.

5.1.9 Running applications

> `\appLink{`*command*`}{`*text*`}`

You can use `techexplorer` as a browser-based interface for running commands on your computer. An *application link* executes a given command when you click on a given area of text on the screen. The *command* is what is executed when you click on the screen display of *text*.

The following example will display a directory listing for the root directory on your C: drive under Microsoft Windows:

```
Click \appLink{dir C:\}{here} to see the root directory of
your C drive.
```

The *command* can refer only to programs that reside on your computer, including those that are part of the operating system. Thus application links are probably not portable across platforms nor possibly even across machines running the same operating system. However, they can be quite useful for applications where `techexplorer` is utilized as part of a larger electronic publishing solution. For example, interactive books that provide all the tools needed by each student might use some application links.

There is an important security issue associated with application links or, indeed, with any Web software that can execute programs on your computer. You should know what the command does before you allow it to run, or at least you should trust the provider of the document that contains the application link.

Figure 5.7 on page 212 shows the standard property page for setting permissions within `techexplorer`. The default setting for application links is always to ask permission before they are executed. If you are a more trusting individual, you can select the option that allows application links always to run when invoked. Finally, if you want to prevent all application links from executing, choose "do not execute" from the choices.

For most users, the default choice of always asking permission is probably best. However, if you do not know what the command will do, get more information before running it.

5.1.10 Alternating between two displayed expressions

> `\altLink{`*secondText*`}{`*firstText*`}`

You can use an *alternating link* to toggle the display of an area of text between two choices. The *firstText* expression is initially displayed. When you click on that expression, `techexplorer` changes the display to *secondText*. Alternating links might seem to be a novelty, but they are useful in situations where you want the reader to think about something before you give the "answer." Consider the following problem and its solution, showing the two alternate expressions:

Problem: Solve for x in $ax^2 + bx + c = 0$.
Solution: $x = ?$

Problem: Solve for x in $ax^2 + bx + c = 0$.
Solution: $x = \dfrac{-b \pm \sqrt{b^2 - 4ac}}{2a}$

The basic expression was generated by

```
\textbf{Problem:} Solve for $x$ in $ax^2+bx+c=0$.
```

```
\textbf{Solution:} $x=\altLink{\frac{-b \pm\sqrt{b^2-4ac}}{2a}}{?}$
```

If you click again on the $\dfrac{-b \pm \sqrt{b^2 - 4ac}}{2a}$, the display will revert back to the form with the question mark.

5.1.11 Printing from techexplorer

Only the Professional Edition of techexplorer on Windows implements printing for whole documents that are displayed by the plug-in.[11] The most reliable way of printing a techexplorer document in any browser is from the default context menu. You get the default menu by moving your mouse cursor to an empty area of the techexplorer window and clicking the right mouse button. In the Professional Edition of techexplorer, this default menu looks like the following:

Select **Print...** and then proceed through the menus to select and send your output to a printer. The number of pages of the document is not known until print composition time, so print either the entire document or only specific known pages.

On some browsers (notably Netscape Navigator), you may also be able to use the **Print...** item from the **File** menu or the print button on the browser toolbar.

---

[11] Printing is not yet supported for plug-in instances embedded within an HTML page.

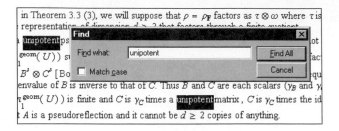

Figure 5.12: Searching for text in a document

Version 2.0 of `techexplorer` was the first version to support any form of printing. In this release, the goal was to print the LaTeX documents at a quality comparable to the HTML printed by the browser. In general, LaTeX itself will do a better job of printing, if you can use it. See the online documentation to get more information about the style file that is provided to help you develop documents that can be processed by both `techexplorer` and LaTeX.

Future editions of `techexplorer` may give you more control over the page parameters such as margins. Also, the IBM developers are working on a PostScript generation to allow printing within future UNIX editions of the Professional Edition of `techexplorer`.

5.1.12   Searching in a document

The Professional Edition of `techexplorer` includes a searching facility to allow you to locate all occurrences of a string in a document. You start the search by clicking the right mouse button within the document and choosing **Find...** from the pop-up menu. Enter your search string and press the **Find** button. Text matching your string within your document will be selected.

Figure 5.12 shows an example of looking for the word "unipotent" in the document. By way of illustration, the results of a previous search are selected behind the dialog box.

Note: You can use *only* the `techexplorer` find dialog via the document pop-up menu to locate text within a `techexplorer` document. The browser find dialog will look only within HTML pages and will not descend into embedded plug-in windows. Worse, some browsers will lock up if you invoke their find dialogs when a plug-in is in control of the whole browser window.

5.1.13   Optimizing your documents for techexplorer

This section is a cookbook for taking existing LaTeX documents and making them usable within `techexplorer`. On the way, we'll add some features to the electronic version of the documents that enhance the viewing experience.

- Determine if your document is small enough to be processed by the `techexplorer` plug-in. If not, break it into smaller documents that can be hyperlinked together.

- Even if your document is small, consider breaking it into hyperlinked components anyway. Readers like documents that arrive and render quickly.

- Use `\aboveTopic`, `\nextTopic`, and `\previousTopic` to build a document hierarchy (see Section 5.1.8 on page 218).

- `techexplorer` does not yet support cross-references such as those created by `\ref`. These should be changed into explicit hyperlinks.

- Add labels for all document sectioning commands. Use standard naming conventions for the labels so that you can use macros to simplify other markup. For example, use `chapter:2` or `section:3.4`.

- Add hyperlinks where the text refers to phrases like "Chapter 2" or "Section 3.4" (although you should remember that in hyperdocuments, phrases like "Chapter 2" make sense only for a static document). Use the labels you added earlier to create such hyperlinks. Use `\docLink` for a hypertext jump outside a given document and `\labelLink` for jumps within the document. See Section 5.1.3 on page 204 for details.

5.1.14 Scripting techexplorer from Java and JavaScript

The Professional Edition of `techexplorer` provides a programming interface for scripting via Java and JavaScript while operating within Netscape Navigator. This uses Netscape LiveConnect and, therefore, does not work within Microsoft Internet Explorer 4.0.

The programming interface allows applets and scripts to register themselves as listeners for mouse, key, and window focus events within `techexplorer` windows. The applets and scripts can also update the `techexplorer` documents within those windows.

The details of the programming interface are beyond the scope of this book, but we offer the following annotated example (Figure 5.13) of a simple LaTeX editor that is written in Java and uses `techexplorer` to display the formatted markup. The editor consists of two windows within an HTML page. The upper window is owned by `techexplorer` and contains the rendered LaTeX markup. The lower window contains the LaTeX source as it is entered by the user. You can type when the cursor is over either window, although you may have to click in one window or the other for it to respond to your key strokes. Click the **Clear input** button to delete all the markup and the rendered display. Figure 5.13 shows the editor with some sample input.

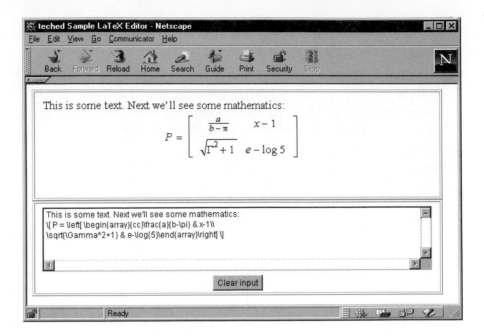

Figure 5.13: A simple LʌTEX editor built using `techexplorer`

The source code for the editor is listed in Appendix A.2. It consists of two files: The HTML source for the page is in `teched.html` (Section A.2.1 on page 399), and the Java applet source is in `teched.java` (Section A.2.2 on page 400).

5.2   WebEQ

WebEQ [↪WEBEQ] is a set of tools that includes a Java applet for displaying math.[12] It supports the Mathematical Markup Language (MathML), which we will come back to in Chapter 8, and a collection of commands it calls WebTEX.

The WebEQ package includes an editor that allows you to create a math expression and then save it as MathML source, a JPEG or PNG image, or a complete Java applet element that can be copied and pasted onto an HTML page. The editor can also open a file containing an existing MathML expression; it does not support saving your work in WebTEX form.

The editor was created using the Java programming interface WebEQ. This interface allows you to add math rendering and image generation to your own applets and allows control of the WebEQ from JavaScript. You can dynamically build new math objects and manipulate the internal structure of existing objects.

---

[12]WebEQ is a trademark of Geometry Technologies, Inc.

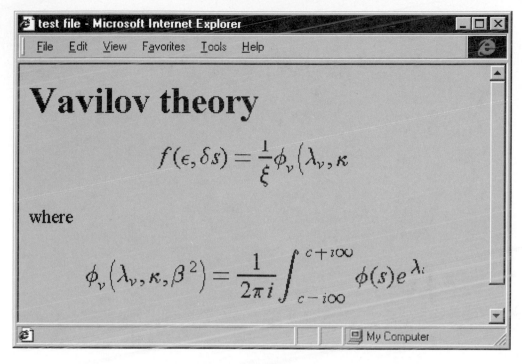

Figure 5.14: Simple example of WebEQ

To ease the insertion of math objects into Web pages, the WebEQ Wizard is provided. This application takes a source file containing HTML markup and WebTEX or MathML markup and produces a new HTML file containing images or WebEQ applet tags for the mathematical expressions. Figure 5.14 shows a slightly simplified section of our test file (refer to Figure 5.1 on page 197) processed by the WebEQ Wizard to create images. Figure 5.15 shows some WebTEX input to WebEQ's Wizard and the HTML code that results.

In the following discussion we will look in more detail at those features of WebEQ that pertain to WebTEX. We begin with a discussion of WebTEX and then show how to write the HTML APPLET tags to embed math in your document. We conclude by describing the WebEQ Wizard and look at an example of using the Wizard to insert images or APPLET tags automatically into your document.

5.2.1   An introduction to WebTEX

WebTEX is not quite TEX, and it is not quite LATEX. Usually a command is similar to something in TEX or LATEX, but it is important to check the documentation before writing new markup or converting existing markup to the WebTEX format.

Input to WebEQ Wizard:

```
1    <HTML>
2    <HEAD><TITLE>test file</TITLE></HEAD>
3    <BODY>
4    <H1>Vavilov theory</H1>
5    \[
6    f \left ( \epsilon, \delta s \right ) = \frac{1}{\xi} \phi_{v}
7    \left ( \lambda_{v}, \kappa, \beta^{2} \right )
8    \]
9    where
10   \[
11   \phi_{v} \left ( \lambda_{v}, \kappa, \beta^{2} \right ) =
12   \frac{1}{2 \pi i} \int^{c+i\infty}_{c-i\infty}\phi \left( s \right )
13   e^{\lambda s} ds   c \geq 0
14   \]
15   </body>
16   </html>
```

Output from WebEQ Wizard:

```
1      <HTML>
2    <HEAD><TITLE>test file</TITLE></HEAD>
3    <body bgcolor=#C0C0C0>
4    <H1>Vavilov theory</H1>
5    <P><CENTER>
6    <applet code="webeq.Main" width=194 height=48 align=middle>
7    <param name=eq value="\displaystyle {
8    f \left ( \epsilon, \delta s \right ) = \frac{1}{\xi} \phi_{v}
9    \left ( \lambda_{v}, \kappa, \beta^{2} \right )
10   }">
11   <param name=color value="#C0C0C0">
12   <param name=parser value="webtex">
13   <img src="xxx1.png" alt="xxx1.png" align=absmiddle>
14   </applet></CENTER><P>
15   where
16   <P><CENTER>
17   <applet code="webeq.Main" width=342 height=68 align=middle>
18   <param name=eq value="\displaystyle {
19   \phi_{v} \left ( \lambda_{v}, \kappa, \beta^{2} \right ) =
20   \frac{1}{2 \pi i} \int^{c+i\infty}_{c-i\infty}\phi \left( s \right )
21   e^{\lambda s} ds   c \geq 0
22   }">
23   <param name=color value="#C0C0C0">
24   <param name=parser value="webtex">
25   <img src="xxx2.png" alt="xxx2.png" align=absmiddle>
26   </applet></CENTER><P>
27   </body>
28   </html>
```

Figure 5.15: Simple example of WebEQ (Figure 5.14): Wizard input and output

We'll begin by looking at features that are similar to those in TEX or LaTEX. Group expressions using '{' and '}' and use _ and ^ to create subscripts and superscripts.

Use \frac to create fractions and \binom to make binomial coefficients. The \sqrt and \root commands have their familiar syntax for creating radicals. The usual loglike operators such as \cos are all supported. You can create accents using \bar, \check, \dot, \ddot, \hat, \tilde, and \vec. Use \overbrace and \underbrace to draw stretchy braces above or below an expression, respectively. The \overset and \underset commands can position an expression above or below another expression, respectively. Simple text can be inserted into an expression by using \text. The argument can include embedded math (delimited by $...$), but not much else.

The standard TEX or LaTEX symbols are supported, but the AMS symbol set is not. Unlike techexplorer, WebEQ does not require extra fonts for its symbols.[13] It contains the glyph images and format information within the applet for a fixed set of fonts and a fixed set of sizes. You can use the commands \mathrm, \mathit, \mathbf, \mathfr, \mathsf, \mathtt, \mathbb, and \mathcal to use Roman, italic, bold, fraktur, sans serif, typewriter, blackboard bold, and calligraphic font families, respectively.

You can change the font size within an expression by using \textsize, \scriptsize, or \scriptscriptsize, in order of decreasing size. The formatting style can be explicitly changed via \displaystyle or \textstyle, but commands such as \scriptstyle, \scriptscriptstyle, \large, \small, and so on are not supported.

What about the real *differences* between WebTEX and TEX/LaTEX? Macros are created using the \define command, which has a syntax similar to the LaTEX \newcommand command. Macros are passed as parameters to the WebEQ applet, via either macros or macrofile parameter. (See page 231 for information about macros.)

> \fontcolor{*color*} {*expression*}

The LaTEX color commands are not supported, but you can use \fontcolor to set the color of a particular subexpression. The first parameter to \fontcolor is the #RRGGBB color specification, and the second is the expression to be displayed in that color. For example,

    \fontcolor{#o0c0c0}{x+y}

displays $x + y$ in a light gray color.

---

[13]The Professional Edition of techexplorer does, however, provide symbol fonts in its distribution.

```
\multiscript{prescripts}{base}{scripts}
\tensor{base}{scripts}
```

WebTeX provides the `\tensor` command to allow you to specify tensors with all
their subscripts and superscripts. The `\multiscript` command is a general purpose tool for placing subscripts and superscripts before and after the base expression. For example,

```
\multiscript{_i^j}{H}{_k^l}
```

formats as

$$\prescript{j}{i}{H}^{l}_{k}$$

The usual delimiters are supported with `\left` and `\right`, but note that you
do not use a period to indicate a matching but empty delimiter. You simply omit
the delimiter. Watch this if you are converting expressions from TeX.

WebTeX provides a powerful array-formatting facility that is also quite different from that familiar to LaTeX users. The basic command is `\array`, & separates columns, and \\ separates rows. Column alignment is specified by `\colalign`
within `\arrayopts`. Compare the LaTeX expression

$$
\begin{array}{lcr}
x & y+1 & z-1 \\
y-z & x^2 & 0
\end{array}
$$

given by the markup

```
\begin{array}{lcr}
x     & y + 1 & z - 1 \\
y - z & x^2   & 0
\end{array}
```

with the corresponding WebTeX markup

```
\array{
\arrayopts{\colalign{left center right}}
x     & y + 1 & z - 1 \\
y - z & x^2   & 0
}
```

You use the `\rowalign` command `\arrayopts` to adjust the entries vertically in
each row. This allows you to push the entries in a given row down so that the each
entry is bottom aligned. You specify `top`, `bottom`, `axis`, or `baseline` for each row.

Additional array options allow you to draw a frame around the array with a
choice of line styles, have entries span more than one row or column (thus gen-
eralizing `\multicolumn`), draw lines between rows or columns, adjust the padding
between entries, and vertically adjust the whole array with respect to the baseline.

This rich choice of options provides WebEQ with the internal facilities to implement the MathML table model.

You can use \thinsp, \medsp, \thicksp, and \quad to add space within an expression. The \quad command is the same as in TEX, and the other three are the same as the familiar \thinspace, \medspace, and \thickspace. The \qquad command is not supported.

```
\space{height}{depth}{width}
```

The \space command produces an empty area with specified height, depth, and width. This differs from its standard application within NFSS.

```
\rule{height}{depth}{width}
```

The \rule command produces a solid rectangle as in LaTeX, but the arguments have a different interpretation.

It is important to note that WebEQ ignores and does not show in WebTEX any command that it does not understand. In particular, if you make a typing mistake, part of your expression will not be displayed. You should always compare the displayed result with the markup to ensure that you got what you intended.

5.2.2 Adding interactivity

```
\href{url}{expression}
```

WebTEX supports hypertext linking via the \href command. The *expression* is what you see on the screen (in blue), and *url* is the address of the document to which the browser will jump when the reader clicks *text*.

```
\statusline{message}{expression}
```

Use \statusline to change the *message* on the browser status line when the user's mouse cursor passes over an *expression*. This is very useful to explain what parts of larger expressions mean. Note that the message is displayed on the status line using plain text, so don't get too fancy with it.

```
\fghighlight{color}{expression}
\bghighlight{color}{expression}
```

To highlight an expression further, use \fghighlight or \bghighlight. The \fghighlight command changes the foreground color, that is, the text color, when the mouse cursor passes over *expression*. Similarly \bghighlight changes the background color when the mouse cursor is over *expression*. The *color* argument is of the form #RRGGBB, using the standard HTML RGB color definition format.

You can combine these features so that you can change colors and update the status line message at the same time. For example,

```
\bghilight{#c0c0c0}{
  \fghilight{#ff0000}{
    \statusline{This is y+1}{y + 1}}}
```

changes the background color to gray, changes the expression font color to red, and displays This is y+1 on the status line when the mouse cursor lies over $y + 1$ on the screen.

$\boxed{\texttt{\textbackslash toggle}\{expr1\}\{expr2\}\{message1\}\{message2\}}$

Just as techexplorer provides \altLink, WebEQ provides \toggle to alternate between two displayed expressions. The *expr1* is first displayed on the screen, and the status line displays *message1* when the mouse cursor passes over the expression. If you click on *expr1*, it will change to *expr2*, and the mouse-activated status line message will be *message2*.

5.2.3   Using the APPLET tag with WebEQ

Use the HTML APPLET element to include WebTeX markup to be rendered by WebEQ within an HTML page. For example,

```
<applet codebase="classes"
        code="webeq.Main"
        width=100 height=100 align=middle>
  <param name=eq value="\alpha^2-\frac{1}{\beta}">
  <param name=color value=#FFFFFF>
</applet>
```

There are five important attributes for using the APPLET element for WebEQ:

CODEBASE   This is the directory containing the compiled Java bytecode for WebEQ. See the product documentation for the proper value, based on the way you intend to install and use the software.

CODE   This is always webeq.Main.

HEIGHT   This is the height in pixels of the rectangle in which the markup should be rendered.

WIDTH   This is the width in pixels of the rectangle in which the markup should be rendered.

ALIGN   Use ALIGN=MIDDLE when you want the expression to float vertically so it looks better with respect to the baseline of the surrounding text.

The PARAM element is used within APPLET to give additional formatting and control information to WebEQ. The format for PARAM is

```
<param name=TheName value="TheValue">
```

where the possible values for TheName are allow_cut, color, controls, eq, linebreak, macrofile, macros, parser, size, and src.

The values corresponding to the eq and src parameter names tell WebEQ how to get the source markup for the math expression. For eq, the value is the actual WebTEX markup. For src, the value is the URL of the document containing the markup, relative to the URL of the containing HTML page.

Use parser to tell WebEQ whether the source is WebTEX or MathML. WebTEX is assumed if this parameter is not given.

The values corresponding to the macros and macrofile parameter names supply macros to apply to the WebEQ markup. Use a macros parameter to supply one or more explicit macro definitions. For example,

```
<param name=macros
       value="\define{\a}{\alpha}\define{\b}[1]{\beta_#1}">
```

provides definitions for \a and \b, where the former takes no arguments and the latter takes one. If you wish to collect several macro definitions into a file, use macrofile to tell WebEQ the URL of the file. Like the value for src, this URL is relative to the URL of the containing HTML page. If you supply both macros and macrofile, the macros are pooled before the math expression is parsed.

The size parameter value gives the initial font size in points for the math expression. WebEQ contains eight fonts at several fixed sizes. If the value you give is not one of those available, WebEQ will choose one in a nearby size. Related to size is the controls parameter. If this is true (the default), clicking the right mouse button when the cursor is over an applet will bring up a dialog box that allows you to change the font size. This will help you adjust the display of the math to the surrounding HTML text and will also allow you to correct for the differences in Java rendering across the various platforms.

Another formatting parameter is color. It allows you to set the background color for the rectangle in which WebEQ displays the math expression. The value is of the form #RRGGBB, using the standard HTML RGB color definition format. Note that HTML color names like "red" are not allowed. Use this parameter to match the background of the math expression to the background color of the HTML page. If you want to change the color of an expression rendered by WebEQ, use the \fontcolor WebTEX command within the markup itself.

For expressions that are too wide to fit in the available space, you can use the linebreak parameter with a value of true to tell WebEQ to try to break the expression into multiple lines. Figure 5.16 shows how WebEQ can break the expression $x^9 + x^8 + x^7 + x^6 + x^5 + x^4 + x^3 + x^2 + x + 1$ into two lines. You will probably

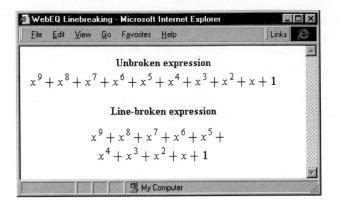

Figure 5.16: Linebreaking by WebEQ

need to increase the `HEIGHT` attribute value to allow for the increased vertical space taken up by the expression.

The final parameter is `allow_cut`. If the value of this is `true`, then subexpression selection is enabled, and it is possible to get generated MathML markup placed in a pop-up window for cut and paste.

5.2.4   Preparing HTML pages via the WebEQ Wizard

The WebEQ Wizard is an easy way to prepare HTML pages that have math in them. You start by creating an HTML source file that has WebTeX math markup contained in `$...$` for inline expressions and `\[...\]` for displayed expressions.[14] It is recommended that you use the file extension `.src` or `.wiz` for this source file to differentiate it from the final `.html` file that is generated.

Next run the WebEQ Wizard to create the HTML file for use on the Web. The Wizard will convert your math expressions into either images or Java applet tags. The tags encapsulate the math markup in WebTeX, or in MathML from the source, or MathML generated from WebTeX source. The images can be in JPEG or PNG format, although only recent Web browsers support PNG, and you need Java 1.1 or later. The applet tags will include the estimated heights and widths for the rectangles in which the math expressions are displayed.

The images may look more uniform on the screen across browser and operating system platforms and will print, although at a lower resolution than the surrounding text. The applet solution does not now allow printing, and there is a potential problem with the formatting rectangles: WebEQ truncates its display at the rectangle boundaries. The Wizard will allow a bit of padding to try to ensure that the estimated rectangle size is sufficient. You can increase this padding via an

---

[14]MathML can also be entered using `<math>` ... `<\math>`.

option (see Section 5.3.1 on page 235 for a discussion of rectangle size problems in both `techexplorer` and WebEQ).

Other Wizard formatting options allow you to set the initial font size for expressions and background color. Further options determine whether linebreaking of long math expressions should occur.

As an example of the WebEQ Wizard in action, we start with the following HTML source that has embedded mathematics:

```
<HTML>
<HEAD>
  <TITLE>Example WebEQ Wizard Page</TITLE>
</HEAD>
<BODY>
<P>
The answer to Question 1 is
<!-- the following fraction will be shown inline -->
$\frac{x}{y}$
and the answer to Question 2 is
<!-- the following matrix will be shown in display mode -->
\[\left( \array{2&3 \\ 4&\frac{5}{6}} \right).\]
</P>
</BODY>
</HTML>
```

If we choose to create Java applet tags that encapsulate the math input and use the default option settings, the following HTML source is generated:

```
<HTML>
<HEAD>
  <TITLE>Example WebEQ Wizard Page</TITLE>
</HEAD>
<body bgcolor=#C0C0C0>
<P>
The answer to Question 1 is
<!-- the following fraction will be shown inline -->

<applet code="webeq.Main" width=12 height=32 align=middle>
<param name=eq value="\frac{x}{y}">
<param name=color value="#C0C0C0">
<param name=parser value="webtex">
</applet>
and the answer to Question 2 is
<!-- the following matrix will be shown in display mode -->

<P><CENTER>
<applet code="webeq.Main" width=71 height=108 align=middle>
<param name=eq
```

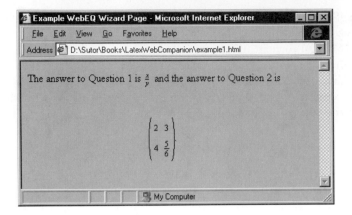

Figure 5.17: An output HTML page generated by the WebEQ Wizard

```
value="\displaystyle {\left( \array{2&3 \\ 4&\frac{5}{6}} \right).}">
<param name=color value="#C0C0C0">
<param name=parser value="webtex">
</applet></CENTER><P>

</P>
</BODY>
</HTML>
```

The final result of WebEQ in action is displayed in Figure 5.17. Note the use of the `align=middle` attribute setting so that the math objects float to roughly the correct position with respect to the text baseline.

5.3 Embedded content problems and future developments

As we mentioned in Section 5.1.2.1 on page 201, content displayed by plug-ins or Java applets embedded within an HTML page can have several rendering problems.[15] These problems all concern the math not blending in seamlessly with the surrounding HTML text. In the following sections we discuss these problems and suggest possible ways they will be solved in future browsers.

---

[15] We will refer to this form of content as *embedded content*, as opposed to that which is shown in the full-client area of the browser.

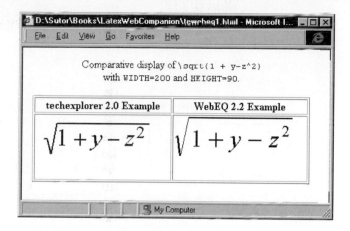

Figure 5.18: Reasonable sizes for a `techexplorer` and WebEQ expression

5.3.1 Expression size

Embedded content is displayed within a fixed-size rectangle in an HTML page. This rectangle size is explicitly given by the HEIGHT and WIDTH attributes in the EMBED element (for plug-ins) or APPLET element (for Java applets).

Let's use techexplorer and WebEQ to display $\sqrt{1 + y - z^2}$ within an HTML page. We'll use relatively large font sizes for each, along with a HEIGHT value of 90 pixels and a WIDTH value of 200 pixels. Following is the HTML markup for techexplorer:

```
<EMBED TYPE="application/x-techexplorer"
       TEXDATA="\pagecolor{white}\(\sqrt{1 + y-z^2}\)"
       WIDTH=200 HEIGHT=90>
```

This is the HTML markup for WebEQ:

```
<APPLET CODEBASE="classes" CODE="webeq.Main" WIDTH=200 HEIGHT=90>
   <PARAM NAME=color VALUE=#FFFFFF>
   <PARAM NAME=size VALUE=18>
   <PARAM NAME=eq VALUE="\sqrt{1 + y-z^2}">
</APPLET>
```

Figure 5.18 shows these expressions rendered within a table by Microsoft Internet Explorer 4.0 on Windows NT.

Figure 5.19 shows what happens when we decrease the WIDTH value to 105. Now techexplorer has inserted a horizontal scroll bar to let you move left and right to view the whole expression. This is effective, but unattractive. The displayed math expression does not blend in cleanly with the surrounding elements of the

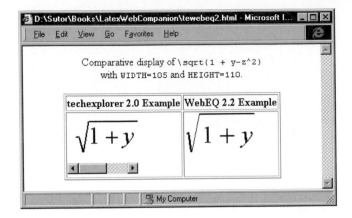

Figure 5.19: The effect of decreasing the width of the display rectangle for `techexplorer` and WebEQ

HTML page. WebEQ truncates the display of the expression on the right. Although this might look better, remember that the expression is $\sqrt{1 + y - z^2}$, not $\sqrt{1 + y}$!

The WebEQ Wizard (see Section 5.2.4 on page 232) does provide a tool for estimating the correct rectangle size for an expression, so this somewhat dangerous truncation will occur only if you manually change the width of the rectangle or change the size of the font used. A larger font might cause truncation. For both `techexplorer` and WebEQ, a smaller font will cause excessive whitespace around the expression, again making the math stand out unattractively on the HTML page.

The basic problem here is that the rectangle size is determined by the document author and not by the plug-in or applet. It is the rendering engine that knows the correct size for the rectangle. Future browsers must negotiate with the plug-in or applet to determine the optimal rectangle.

Note that there may be real constraints on the size of the rectangle, so the math rendering software may need to be flexible in how it squeezes into the allowed space. WebEQ can line break math expressions, allowing a wide expression to fit into a too narrow rectangle.

5.3.2   Ambient style

The final problem we consider concerns the formatting style of math expressions versus the surrounding HTML text. In order to have the math blend well with the text, the fonts should be the same (or at least work well together), and the font and background colors should be the same. Furthermore, if the HTML page uses a background image, the math expression rectangles should use the same image and be aligned correctly with the page background. Figure 5.20 illustrates several of these problems.

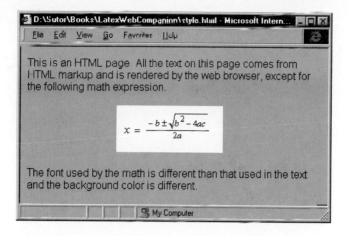

Figure 5.20: Some style matching problems

The style information for the HTML page was given by the Cascading Style Sheet:

```
P {
  font-family:   sans-serif;
}

BODY {
  background:  silver;
}
```

Note that the math expression is rendered on a white background in a Roman-style font.

Both techexplorer and WebEQ render their math opaquely on the screen. Everything in the window is overwritten, including the background. While it is possible to build plug-ins so that they write transparently over the screen, the font- and text-color problems remain. Furthermore, it is not sufficient to specify background color and font information in the markup for the mathematics, although this might look correct on the screen. This information should be obtained automatically by the plug-in or applet from the browser. Otherwise, every time you update the style for your HTML page, you need to go in and fix all the math expressions individually.

Future browsers will share ambient style information with software that renders embedded content. As we move from HTML to XML documents and develop new programming interfaces for embedded, possibly nested, content renderers, the browser formatting facilities and information will become more widely accessible to other software used to display parts of the document.

CHAPTER 6

HTML, SGML, and XML: Three markup languages

This chapter provides an insight into the relation between Standard Generalized Markup Language (SGML), the parent of all present-day nonpropriety markup languages, HyperText Markup Language (HTML), the lingua franca of the Web, and Extensible Markup Language (XML), a simplified version of SGML, that lies at the heart of a whole new family of applications optimized for use on the Web.

We first explain why we think HTML cannot be the final answer for information interchange on the Web. Then we say a few words about SGML and its history to put the recent XML proposals into perspective, before we take a close look at XML. We describe its various components, including the Document Type Definition (DTD), and review a few of the existing tools to handle XML documents.

6.1 Will HTML lead to the downfall of the Web?

The reason HTML is so popular has much to do with its intrinsic simplicity (it is easy to learn), as well as its many *nonstandard* extensions that are offered by the various browser vendors to help users make their pages look *professional* and *attractive*. However, this Tower of Babel of incompatible extensions is a real threat to the integrity of the Web, since it kills the universal availability of the information.

Most people love HTML because it is a clean little language that they can master in an afternoon. HTML is universal and runs in browsers everywhere. Moreover, many tools come with an HTML back-end. However, in the *real world* one is often confronted with broken links and a lack of portable ways to format the information. Many of us have had to (mis)use tables, frames, Java, and other scripts to get the presentation we like, because of the lack of a real tool to craft universally displayable Web pages.

It is probably worthwhile to look at the problem areas where we think HTML could be improved.

- *Invalid HTML* Many commonly used utilities produce invalid HTML, or they introduce vendor-specific extensions. Most users do not validate their HTML source code, and browsers do not object to invalid HTML; most of the time they just skip the information that does not make syntactical sense. This makes it especially difficult to get consistent results between Web browsers and across computer platforms.

- *Broken links* Whenever a Web page is deleted or moves to a different host, all URL references to that page are invalidated. There has been talk about *Uniform Resource Names* (URN, see Section 1.1.2 and [↪ URNIETF]) that would address pages by name and provide a level of indirection to cope with mapping names on physical addresses (just like name servers for Internet addresses).

- *Fixed grammar* The element and attribute set of HTML is fixed. HTML is said to have a fixed grammar, as described by a *Document Type Definition* (DTD), a formal specification that describes the syntax of an SGML application (see Sections 6.3.2 and 6.4.3). Thus one cannot adapt the language to cope with a specific set of new applications or extend its functionality to deal with new Web technology, except by extending the DTD. In the past, browser vendors have added their own extensions, resulting in Web pages optimized for a single browser, with other browsers unable to display the information fully. More recently with CSS, one can "extend" the visual presentation of HTML's fixed tag set by using the `class` attribute and the `span` and `div` element types (see Section 7.4.1.4).

- *Limited support for metadata* Only primitive support exists for metadata— information describing the contents of the document, such as keywords, author, and data. The `<meta>` tag is a step in the right direction, but there is no standard way for putting it to work; user agents can just ignore it. Therefore it remains nontrivial for search engines to extract important key information about the source document.

- *Absence of structural tags* Although HTML tags, such as `<h[1-6]>`, `<div>`, and `<p>`, could be used to structure the information, most Web applications and Web authors ignore this possibility, and use HTML tags merely for controlling the visual layout of the document. This unstructured approach makes it difficult to navigate through a tree (or network) of documents.

- *Data exchange difficulties* Because of its closed tag set aimed at presenting information on the Web, it is almost impossible to extract data according to tagged data fields. Moreover, only the Latin 1 character set, which does not even support Western European languages fully, is generally available. The use of HTML for other languages is based on extensions, preventing easy document interchange. Just think how you would view pages written in Russian or Japanese if your browser did not have Cyrillic or Kanji fonts or the right encoding.

- *Absence of modern features* As with any standard (even one coordinated by the Web Consortium, which responds relatively quickly to common practice), many *modern* ingredients are lacking. Among these are ways of refreshing information on the client side, exposing information present in dynamic entities, such as applets, and the unavailability of an object model.

Recent work has tried to address one or more of these problems. One approach was to increase the functionality of HTML, and, therefore, HTML 4 was developed. To separate form and content better, the style sheet language, *Cascading Style Sheets* (CSS), was recommended. The *Extensible Markup Language* (XML) effort deals with application specificity and better data organization. Dynamic HTML (DHTML) goes some way toward adding a dynamic representation to Web pages. The standardized cross-language, cross-product version of DHTML is called the *Document Object Model*, DOM for short. DOM is bound to play an important role by allowing programs to access HTML (XML) elements as a structured collection of object data, each having a set of properties and methods.

We look at some of these developments in this and later chapters. Bear in mind, however, that many new features are implemented only partially in the current generation of browsers. It will take some time to make even the more important browsers conform to the specifications and standards we will be describing.

6.2   HTML 4: A richer and more coherent language

On December 18, 1997, W3C issued HTML 4.0 as a *W3C Recommendation*, somewhat equivalent in status for the Web to an ISO or ANSI standard. The HTML 4 specification is a document of over 360 pages and is available as an HTML PostScript or PDF file at [↪HTML4].[1] Although HTML 4 addresses a few of the shortcomings listed in Section 6.1, it still offers only a fixed tag set and provides no generic method to tailor the markup language to a particular application. That is why HTML 4 will be the last of the existing generations of HTML standards; future work will be concentrated on building a more modular XML-based approach (see Section B.5).

---

[1] It is likely that you will find a slightly revised version of the HTML 4 specification at that URL. At the time of writing the reference number of the document was REC-html40-19980424.

6.2.1 HTML 4 goodies

Following are some of the more significant changes in HTML 4 with respect to the previous version 3.2 (released in January 1997):

- A more complete model for tables (based on the CALS[2] DTD).

- A first step toward a clearer separation between content and form with the deprecation of element and attributes that control presentation (such as color and font size) and their replacement by *Cascading Style Sheets* (see the *CSS Specification* [↪CSS2] and Chapter 7).

- Any element can be identified by a (unique) ID attribute. It can be addressed as a destination anchor of a link, as shown in the following example:

```
<H2 id="mysect">This is a uniquely identified section heading.
<P id="mypara">This is my addressable paragraph.
...
<P>As stated in a <A HREF="#mypara">paragraph</A> which
is part of a <A HREF="#mysect">section</A>...
```

- Support for internationalization, by introducing language codes (see Table C.1 on page 466) and making it possible to specify the writing direction, will make it easier to generate documents in almost any of the world's languages. Making them universally readable is, of course, a huge software problem.

- Generic objects (images, applets, and other documents) can be embedded with the OBJECT element. If a given resource is not available, then another can be defined to run instead. The following HTML code first tries to execute a Python applet featuring electrons circulating in the LEP accelerator (lines 1–2). If that is impossible, showing an MPEG movie will be attempted instead (line 3), or else a static GIF image will be shown (line 4). Finally, if all that fails, a text string will be printed (line 5).

```
1  <OBJECT title="Electrons going round and round"
2          classid="http://www.cern.xxx/CirculatingElectrons.py">
3    <OBJECT data="CirculatingElectrons.mpeg" type="application/mpeg">
4      <OBJECT data="CirculatingElectrons.gif" type="image/gif">
5        Electrons circulating in the LEP tunnel.
6      </OBJECT>
7    </OBJECT>
8  </OBJECT>
```

---

[2]CALS stands for *Continuous Acquisition and Life-Cycle Support*, a U.S. Department of Defense strategy for achieving effective creation, exchange, and use of digital data for weapons systems and equipment. CALS, adopted by at least half a dozen other countries' military institutions, has been instrumental in promoting SGML as a markup language in general. More information is available starting from the CALS home page at [↪CALS].

Note that the `OBJECT` element type replaces (and thus deprecates) elements such as `APPLET` and `IMAGE`. This allows a much cleaner and more generic approach to the handling of events, files, viewing pictures, and so on.

- Some more advanced features have also been introduced. They include *media descriptors*, which allow the use of device-sensitive style sheets, and *event attributes*, which, in conjunction with scripts, allow code to be executed when a given event occurs (for instance, when a document is loaded, or the mouse is clicked). Another innovation is the `DIV` and `SPAN` elements, which, when used with `ID` and `CLASS` attributes and style sheets, present authors with a generic mechanism for "extending" HTML by tailoring it to their needs and tastes.

Currently no browsers fully support HTML 4, although Netscape version 4 and MS Internet Explorer versions 4 and 5 go some way in the right direction. Moreover, to benefit fully from the possibilities of HTML 4, support for Cascading Style Sheets (CSS version 2) is a must, and browsers still need a lot of work here to become fully conforming.

A description and comparison of the different versions of HTML were prepared by Ian Graham using a modified version of Earl Hood's `dtd2html` and `dtddiff` programs (see Section 6.6.2). It can be found at [↪HOOD].

6.2.2 HTML 4, the end of the old road

On June 22, 1998, the W3C Consortium issued an *activity statement* that deals with the future of HTML [↪W3CFUTURE]. This issue had been debated by specialists during several workshops. It was generally felt that a completely new start should be taken by building a new generation of HTML, based on a genuine XML tag set and built in a modularized way. This would make the language more manageable and would provide a straightforward path to integrate HTML and already existing XML applications. See Section B.5.2 for more details about XHTML, a reformulation of HTML as an XML application.

6.3 Why SGML?

Since the early 1980s we have witnessed an ever-quickening transition from book publishing, exclusively on paper, to various forms of electronic media. This evolution is merely a reflection of the fact that the computer and electronics have made inroads into almost every facet of human activity. In a world in which we have to deal with ever-increasing amounts of data, we depend more and more on the computer for preparing telephone directories, dictionaries, and law texts—to mention just a few examples. However, it is not just the volume of the data that is important, but also the ease with which it can be entered, maintained, viewed, exchanged, and distributed.

Once data has been stored in electronic form, one can derive multiple "products" (or "views") from a single source document. For instance, an address list can be turned into a directory on paper, put on CD-ROM, made available as a database to allow interactive or e-mail access on the Internet, or used to print a series of labels. Similarly a set of law texts or a series of articles on history marked up in a generic language can be published as a textbook containing complete law texts, or it can be used as the basis for a historic encyclopedia. Thanks to the generic markup strategy, it is straightforward to provide regular updates or to extract a subset of articles on a given subject. From the same electronic sources one can also offer a consultation service on the Internet, via gopher or WWW, or develop a hypertext system on CD-ROM.

All of these applications suppose that the information is not saved in a format that is suited only for display or printing (for example, using a WYSIWYG-oriented system). The hierarchical structure and logical relations between the various document components should be clearly marked. This approach, which forms the basis of the LaTeX and SGML/XML-based languages, has the following strong points:

- The quality of the source document is improved by making data entry easier, increasing readability, and allowing input to be validated more fully.

- Documents can be maintained more rationally, resulting in an improved life cycle.

- Publishing costs are reduced.

- Reuse of information is easier, thus adding value to documents (they can be printed, presented as hypertext, stored, and accessed in databases).

6.3.1 Different types of markup

Today every PC comes with a text processor, mostly of the WYSIWYG (what you see is what you get) type. Therefore many users consistently confuse information and document structure with presentation by associating formatting characteristics with various textual document components.

This situation is similar to that prevailing in the 1970s with early formatting languages; specific codes were mixed with the (printable) text of the document in order to control typesetting at the micro level. For example, line and page breaks and explicit horizontal or vertical alignments or skips were specifically marked to compose the various pages. Most of the time these control characters were extremely application specific, and it was almost impossible to reuse sources marked up in one of these systems with any of the others. Nevertheless, this type of markup allows very precise control over the physical representation of a specific document and provides important advantages for fine-tuning the final layout for viewing and printing documents. An example of specific page markup is the following TeX fragment. It starts a new page and typesets a chapter title in a given hard-wired way (large and boldface font, with the word "Chapter" and the number "2" hand-coded).

```
\vfil\eject
\par\noindent
{\large\bf Chapter 2: Title of Chapter}
\par\vskip\baselineskip
```

It should be clear that modifying a document that contains such explicit markup or trying to guess the "meaning" of the commands is extremely tedious. Thus a document planned for modification and targeted for multiple use must be marked up so that its logical structure and its physical representation are clearly separated.

In *logical* or *generic* markup, the logical function of all document elements— title, sections, paragraphs, figures, tables, bibliographic references, or mathematical equations—as well as the structural relations between these elements, must be clearly defined. LaTeX is an enormous step forward in the right direction, as shown in the following code fragment, where a single line signals the beginning of a new chapter:

```
\chapter{Title of Chapter}
```

It is up to the "style" (or "class") specification to decide how a chapter gets started and how its title is typeset. At the same time, the chapter numbering and entering the chapter title into the table of contents, if desired, is under the global control of the style author. We merely have to specify the logical presence of the chapter together with its title.

A similar approach can be seen in the following HTML fragment, although it must be emphasized that HTML is now primarily used as a presentation markup language. For instance, in the example that follows, the <H1> tag is usually used only to mark the presence of a "title heading of level 1" without implying the beginning of a new document section.

```
<H1>Title of Chapter</H1>
<P>
```

Only recently has a higher level of abstraction for the relation between markup tags and visual presentation in HTML become possible via CSS style sheets. (This concept will be explained in Chapter 7; in particular see Section 7.4.)

6.3.2   Generalized logical markup

Several document instances can belong to a same document "class," since they have the same global logical structure. As an example let us consider two articles, A and B, with the explicit structure shown in Figure 6.1.

```
        Article A                    Article B
        =========                    =========
Title                        Title
Section 1                    Section 1
    Subsection 1.1               Subsection 1.1
    Subsection 1.2               Subsection 1.2
Section 2                        Subsection 1.3
Section 3                    Section 2
    Subsection 3.1               Subsection 2.1
    Subsection 3.2               Subsection 2.2
    Subsection 3.3
    Subsection 3.4
Bibliography                 Bibliography
```

Figure 6.1: Two instances of an article class

It is evident from Figure 6.1 that both articles are built according to the same logical pattern: a title, followed by one or more sections, each one subdivided into zero or more subsections, and a bibliography at the end. In LaTeX we would say that the document instances belong to the same *document class* "article."

To exploit the advantages of structured documents fully, the markup scheme must adopt a clear set of rules. When using SGML, these rules are set down in the Document Type Definition (DTD). A DTD not only defines the allowed element types (the syntax), but it also describes the structural relations between the elements. A parser then checks whether marked up documents adhere to the DTD.

This approach is somewhat similar to LaTeX, where the syntax (the document markup) is defined in Lamport's LaTeX Manual; however, the underlying TeX implementation does not in most cases verify whether the elements are nested in an "allowed" way. For instance, you can use a subsubsection without explicitly defining a section or a subsection, just like in HTML. If the DTD is built correctly, this kind of ambiguity should not be possible with SGML. Moreover, in LaTeX you can extend the language by defining new commands and environments; this also is not (practically) feasible in the case of SGML.

Therefore for our example documents of type "article" the DTD should define elements for "title," "section," "subsection," and "bibliography." It should also express the fact that the title precedes sections that can contain subsections and that articles can have a bibliography at their end. The DTD assigns a name to each structural element, often an abbreviation that conveys the function of the element in question (for example, "sec" for a section (line 3), and "stit" for a section or subsection title (lines 3 and 5)). Using the DTD as defined, you can then start marking up the document source itself (article A or article B); use the "short" names defined for each document element. For instance, with "sec" one can form a start *tag* <sec> for marking the start of a section (line 3) and an end tag </sec> to mark its end (line 8); other document components operate in a similar fashion (see Section 6.4.2 for more details).

```
1   <article>
2   <tit>SGML and XML</tit>
3   <sec><stit>Why SGML?</stit>
4        <para>  ...            </para>
5    <ssec><stit>Different types of markup</stit>
6        <para>  ...            </para>
7    </ssec>
8   </sec>
9   </article>
```

6.3.3   SGML to HTML and XML

The idea that structured documents could be exchanged and manipulated if published in a standard open format dates back to early initiatives in the 1960s. In one endeavor a committee of the Graphic Communications Association (GCA) created GenCode to develop generic typesetting codes for clients to send data to companies to be typeset using different printing devices. GenCode allowed them to maintain an integrated set of archives despite the records being set at multiple sites.

In another effort, IBM developed the Generalized Markup Language (GML) for its big internal publishing problems, including managing documents of all kinds from manuals and press releases to legal contracts and project specifications. GML was designed to be used by batch processors to produce books, reports, and electronic editions from the same source file(s).

GML provided a "simple" input format for typists, including elements of a tag syntax that we still recognize today. GML was optimized for speed of data entry. Moreover, since only a few types of documents existed, specific programs were developed to interpret the data tags for a particular document type—hardly a generic approach. Hence, with the advent of more types of documents, the Gencod and GML communities got together and started talking about standardization within the framework of ANSI, the American National Standards Institute. The ideas of DTD, markup, and syntax were formalized, and SGML was born. It was adopted as an ISO standard in 1986 (ISO·8879, 1986).

SGML is a complex standard, and its use remained limited mainly to the spheres of large companies or organizations and a few research institutes. For instance, Anders Berglund, who was for many years responsible for text processing at CERN, the European Laboratory for Particle Physics (Geneva, Switzerland), introduced a prototype version of SGML (based on IBM's GML) many years before the standard was even published. Thus it should come as no surprise that while working at CERN, Tim Berners-Lee, the inventor of the Web, was influenced by the *look and feel* of SGML while defining the syntax of HTML. His prime aim was not (at least originally) to comply to a formal DTD but to allow his early browser software to render the source material in a straightforward way.

It took some years before HTML developers like Dan Connolly and Dave Raggett recognized the need to give HTML a firmer (and more formal) basis. The first HTML DTD was developed, and HTML was turned into a conforming SGML application, making it possible to validate HTML documents formally against an HTML model represented by the DTD.

HTML, in the form of HTML 4, the present recommendation as discussed briefly in Section 6.2, still offers only a limited set of elements to mark up documents. It should also be clear that HTML, even extended, will never be able to represent all documents that people want to keep on the Web or, more generally, in electronic form.

On the other hand, because SGML has a rather large and complicated specification, it is not easy for an author to master all of its details or for a computer program to parse and manipulate complex SGML documents. Nevertheless, if we want to treat electronic documents in an optimal way, we *must* mark them up generically to indicate their logical structure, and we must choose, for that process, an agreed standard language to guarantee interchangeability. So what can we do with HTML being considered too limited and SGML too complex and without an agreed set of "standard" DTDs that are generally available?

In his seminal paper, *XML, Java, and the future of the Web* [↪BOSAKXML], Jon Bosak points out three areas where HTML has severe shortcomings: *extensibility* (being able to define new elements and attributes for a document instance), the possibility of deep *structure* (allowing arbitrary nesting), and *validation* (checking of data before use).

6.4   Extensible Markup Languages

Even though HTML 4 is without doubt a step in the right direction if one wants to support the Web in a standard way, it is still too limited and too static to cope with all of the Web's many application areas (databases, search engines, optimal presentation, professional printing, and data verification).

Consequently, in the middle of 1996 the Web Consortium set up an SGML Working Group to tackle these problems. Under the chairmanship of Jon Bosak, the group developed the Extensible Markup Language (XML), which was finalized at the end of 1997 and issued as a W3C Recommendation on February 10, 1998 (*Extensible Markup Language (XML) 1.0* [↪XMLSPEC] and errata [↪XMLERRATA]). XML is designed as a subset of SGML,[3] so that any XML document is also a conformant SGML document. Existing SGML parsers and systems in general can be used with XML. Work to allow an augmented set of hypertext possibilities (see *XML Linking Language (XLink)* [↪XLINKSPEC] and *XML Pointer Language (XPointer)* [↪XPTSPEC]) and to define an XML style language XSL (see *Extensible Stylesheet Language XSL* [↪XSL97]) is going on at present. The XSL language will be the subject of Section 7.6.

---

[3]A few extensions to the original 1986 SGML ISO standard (ISO:8879 (1986)) were necessary. These were grouped in Annex K (*Web SGML Adaptations*) and Annex L (*Additional Requirements for XML*), see [↪ISO8879TC2].

A good source of information about XML is Peter Flynn's "Frequently Asked Questions about the Extensible Markup Language" [↪ XMLFAQ]. Other interesting Web sites are Elliotte Rusty Harold's "Cafe con Leche XML News and Resources" [↪ LECHE] and "SGML and XML News" [↪ SGMLNEW], which is maintained by Robin Cover who also coordinates the "Extensible Markup Language (XML)" page [↪ XMLPAGE]. This very useful page collects a lot of information concerning XML. Pointers to a set of introductory articles on XML are available at [↪ XMLINTRO]. These articles provide interesting reading if you are starting with XML. For those who are still fond of reading books, quite a few XML books have recently been published. Bradley (1998), Goldfarb and Prescod (1998), Harold (1998), Jelliffe (1998), Leventhal et al. (1998), McGrath (1998), Megginson (1998), and St. Laurent (1997) are among the ones we have consulted.[4]

6.4.1   What is XML?

The W3C recognized the fact that SGML's scope is very broad and the language rather complex, both to learn and to implement. Therefore W3C decided to introduce a lightweight version and designed XML as a subset of SGML, doing away with its rarely used and more complex features. It is said that XML offers about 90% of SGML's functionality at some 10% of its complexity, thus making sure that the *ten commandments* of XML (its *design goals* as specified by the W3C SGML Special Interest Group when they started their activities) can be fulfilled.

6.4.1.1   XML's ten commandments

The XML Specification sets out the following goals for XML:

1. *XML shall be straightforwardly usable over the Internet.*

   XML source documents must be viewable as quickly and easily as HTML documents (when XML-capable browsers and applications are available).

2. *XML shall support a wide variety of applications.*

   XML is not only optimized for browsing but must allow for a whole realm of applications not limited just to the Web but more general. Application areas include convenient authoring, data presentation, content analysis and validation, and databases.

3. *XML shall be compatible with SGML.*

   Since XML *ab initio* was defined as a "convenient" subset of SGML by people who were historically involved with the SGML effort, we can be confident that XML and SGML will interoperate without problems.

---

[4]The number of books on XML that appeared in twelve months is far larger that the number of books published on SGML during the last twelve years—one more proof that XML is an important development.

4. *It shall be easy to write programs that process XML documents.*

   Given the expertise of the SGML community that knew which parts of SGML are difficult to implement and, therefore, could be eliminated, we can be sure that XML can be implemented in "a couple of weeks" by the average computer science student. In fact, as we will see later, more than ten XML parsers are freely available today.

5. *The number of optional features in XML is to be kept to an absolute minimum, ideally kept to zero.*

   It goes without saying that optional features are never really optional: Whenever somebody starts using them, everybody has to implement the code to interpret those features. Therefore to minimize incompatibilities and confusion, no optional features are allowed in XML, and all XML parsers in the world should be able to interpret all XML documents.

6. *XML documents should be human-legible and reasonably clear.*

   Experience has shown that it is always a big plus when you can read the contents of a document without having to put it through a dedicated program to decode it. It is so much more user-friendly to be able to display a document directly on screen or to make a small modification with your favorite editor.

7. *The XML design should be prepared quickly.*

   In the past, browser vendors kept adding incompatible extensions to their programs. W3C was trying to follow these developments by putting out more and more complex HTML specifications. Nevertheless, as we saw earlier, they were unable to solve the real problems, so it was important to come up with a solution *immediately*. The XML Working Group did a marvelous job in minimal time.

8. *The design of XML shall be formal and concise.*

   Point 4 wants XML to be easy to program. Here we state that the language itself should be easy to describe formally, thus allowing it to be analyzed by simple computer techniques and, at the same time, easy to master by the average document programmer.

9. *XML documents shall be easy to create.*

   Intelligent editors or dedicated applications should not have too hard a time generating correct XML data. Also, XML should be tractable to write authoring systems.

10. *Terseness in XML markup is of minimal importance.*

    To ease the implementation of all the previous tasks and to make XML more readable (by parsers and humans), no minimization of markup is allowed. Conciseness always comes second to clarity.

6.4.1.2   XML opens a new window on the Web

From what has been said earlier, it should be clear that XML's goal is to go beyond being a "super-HTML," by becoming a genuine "lightweight SGML for the Internet." XML opens a completely new window on the Web: It allows designers and programmers to present their data in a number of different ways by using embedding programming techniques within the standard syntax of XML. In principle they no longer need to combine various techniques and languages, such as HTML, Java, scripting, Perl, CGI, ActiveX, and other tools and plug-ins. They all can be hidden via an XML abstraction level.

As already mentioned, each element of a *valid* XML document must be declared in a DTD. This provides a formal definition for the XML language of the document class being considered. This also allows XML parsers to check the validity of document instances marked up according to that DTD, verifying, for instance, the correct nesting levels, whether all document components have been defined, and so on. Note, however, that strictly speaking the XML specification does *not require* that a DTD be present. For browsers, it could be too time-consuming for each document to download and parse a DTD and check the document against this DTD. Ideally XML applications should make sure at creation time that all documents adhere to a DTD, so that browsers can assume that they are correct. XML requires only that the document be *well-formed* (see Section 6.4.2.1).

6.4.2   The components of XML

XML is based on the concept that *documents* are composed of a series of *entities* (today it would probably be more fashionable to call them *objects*). Each entity contains one or more *elements*, and each element can be characterized by zero or more *attributes* (properties) that describe the way in which each element is to be processed. The relationships between elements and the list of their possible attributes are specified in the DTD.

The beauty of XML (SGML) is that, using this mechanism of defining a language with a DTD, each institute, group, company, organization, and so on, can define its own *language* for all the different kinds of documents they have to deal with. By being able to choose user-friendly *markup tags* adapted to a particular application domain or cultural environment, the use of these tags will be much easier to comprehend, and the markup error rate will be substantially lower than when a more generic markup scheme is used. Moreover, with the help of *intelligent editors*, which will hide the markup or guide the user by allowing only tags possible in the current context, it will be trivial to compose syntactically correct documents.

Although SGML's *reference concrete syntax* proposes certain characters to represent delimiters, and so on, these characters can nevertheless be chosen freely. Moreover, various parameters of an SGML instance can be defined at the document level. The character set (by default ASCII) can also be declared in the document instance. This complexity makes it difficult to write parsers, and, therefore, it was decided to allow only a fixed syntax for XML tags, entity references, and so on.

Elements and their attributes, if any, are entered between matched pairs of angle brackets (<...>) with attribute values *always* between a pair of single or double quotes:

```
<ename attr1="val1" attr2='val2' ...>
```

Entity references start with an ampersand and end with a semicolon:

```
&eref;
```

Element, attribute, and entity names are all *case-sensitive*; thus <HEAD>, <Head>, and <head> are tags corresponding to three different element types, while <head lev="val" Lev="val2"> shows two different attributes—lev and Lev—for the head element type. It goes without saying that one should use the possibility to exploit such subtle differences with great care, so as not to confuse the user of your tag set. A simple rule, like "all lowercase," will certainly contribute to making the use of your DTD less error-prone. As for entities, such a constraint does not necessarily exist, since, for instance, Á and á may generate Á and á, respectively (in the Latin 1 entity set).

Comments are specified between <!-- and -->.

```
<!-- Inside a comment you can write <e>&</e> -->
```

By construction XML is a subset of its parent-language SGML, and all software written to parse, validate, or otherwise handle SGML should also work with XML files.[5]

An example of correct XML syntax is the following trivial document:

```
<coolxml>XML is a cool idea!</coolxml>
```

This XML document cannot, as such, be validated since no DTD is specified. It is, however, well-formed and complete.

6.4.2.1   Valid and well-formed documents

At the end of Section 6.4.1.1, we mention that XML documents should be *well-formed* but that they can also be *valid*. Let us go into a little more detail.

To be *well-formed*, an XML document must follow a set of simple rules that enable the XML processor to parse the file correctly.

First, there must exist a *root* element that encloses the entire document instance and does not appear as contents of any other element (docu on lines 1 and 6 of the example that follows). All tags must be balanced; that is, all elements must have both start and endtags present (<el1>...</el1>), unless one is dealing with an empty element that may use the notation <.../> (a slash preceding the closing bracket, such as <empel/> on line 4, although the more verbose syntax <empe1></empe1> is also possible). Tags must be properly nested (el2 starts and ends inside el1 in the example). All attribute values, which must necessarily be of type CDATA (character data), have to be enclosed inside quotes (as on line 2), and the < and & characters must be escaped as < and &, respectively. A simple well-formed document follows:

---

[5]This is strictly true only for software that complies to the *Web SGML Adaptations*[↪ISO8879TC2].

```
1  <docu>
2  ... <el1 att="val">...
3          <el2>...</el2>
4     .. <empel/>
5     </el1>
6  </docu>
```

In Section 6.6.5 we present documents that are not well-formed to various XML parsers and study how the generated error messages can help us correct mistakes.

Valid XML documents are well-formed and must adhere to a DTD. A valid XML document must specify in the document declaration part at the beginning of the document instance which DTD has to be used and how the XML processor can access it on the local system or via the network. In the example that follows we show how the docu document type is declared by specifying an URL:

```
1  <?xml version="1.0"?>
2  <!DOCTYPE docu SYSTEM "http://www.bla.org/mydocu.dtd">
3  <docu>
4  ... <el1>...<empel/>...</el1>
5  </docu>
```

A DTD (in full or in part) can also be included inside the document declaration part of the document. If everything is present inside the document instance itself, then we can declare the document "standalone."

```
1  <?xml version="1.0" standalone="yes"?>
2  <!DOCTYPE coolxml [
3  <!ELEMENT coolxml (#PCDATA)>
4  ]>
5  <coolxml>XML is a cool idea!</coolxml>
```

Thus by adding a DTD, we have turned the well-formed trivial document introduced at the end of the previous section into a valid one.

The distinction between well-formed and valid documents makes it easier to serve XML documents over the Internet without burdening the "consumer" application (such as a browser or a database query). The client application can assume that the document has been validated on the server-side. Thus we need to check only whether the document is well-formed, that is, whether the document was not corrupted during the transfer, for example. Of course, the client is free also to validate the document. One important point is that XML-conformant applications should report a *fatal* error and stop processing data for the client when presented with a document that is not well-formed, although they can continue finding errors. This is in contrast to the behavior of many HTML applications that today mostly ignore errors in HTML documents and proceed as though nothing were wrong, thus leading to possible problems later on.

6.4.2.2 A more complex document

Let us now be a little more ambitious and define a language to compose texts for
sending invitations to our friends. We could write something like the following:

```
 1  <invitation>
 2  <to>Anna, Bernard, Didier, Johanna</to>
 3  <date>Next Friday Evening at 8 pm</date>
 4  <where>The Web Cafe</where>
 5  <why>My first XML baby</why>
 6  <par>
 7  I would like to invite you all to celebrate
 8  the birth of Invitation, my first XML document child.
 9  </par>
10  <par>
11  Please do your best to come and join me next Friday
12  evening. And, do not forget to bring your friends.
13  </par>
14  <par>
15  I really look forward to see you soon!
16  </par>
17  <signature>Michel</signature>
18  </invitation>
```

This document is clearly marked up. All elements are delimited by start and
end tags, they are properly nested, and there exists an outermost *root* element
(invitation). Thus our document is truly *well-formed*. Nevertheless, there remains
at least one shortcoming to this document; namely, its structure is hard to guess.
We have merely indicated the semantic function of a few text strings, but it is not
clear what the relation between the various document components is.

To clarify the relation between the various document elements we subdivided
our document into three parts: front, body, and back, corresponding to the introductory information, the message text itself, and the closing part, respectively. We
also emphasize a few words in the text by bracketing them with <emph>...</emph>
tags. Some comments were added as well.

```
 1  <?xml version="1.0"?>
 2  <!DOCTYPE invitation SYSTEM "invitation.dtd">
 3  <invitation>
 4  <!-- ++++ The header part of the document ++++ -->
 5  <front>
 6  <to>Anna, Bernard, Didier, Johanna</to>
 7  <date>Next Friday Evening at 8 pm</date>
 8  <where>The Web Cafe</where>
 9  <why>My first XML baby</why>
10  </front>
11  <!-- +++++ The main part of the document +++++ -->
12  <body>
13  <par>
14  I would like to invite you all to celebrate
15  the birth of <emph>Invitation</emph>, my
16  first XML document child.
17  </par>
18  <par>
19  Please do your best to come and join me next Friday
20  evening. And, do not forget to bring your friends.
21  </par>
22  <par>
```

```
23    I <emph>really</emph> look forward to see you soon!
24    </par>
25    </body>
26    <!-- +++ The closing part of the document ++++ -->
27    <back>
28    <signature>Michel</signature>
29    </back>
30    </invitation>
```

It is important to note that up to now we have said nothing about how this document should be rendered. The XML instance shown describes only the information and how its various structural elements are related. How an XML application handles this data is not specified. You can execute any action when encountering any of the tags in the document. You can render their content on an output medium, store it in a database, transform or combine it with other information, and so on. In Chapter 7, we study in detail how style languages (CSS, DSSSL, or XSL) allow us to transform XML information into a printable or viewable format.

6.4.3 Declaring document elements

In the earlier example we introduced a little language to mark up invitations in a convenient, clear, and easily processable way. If we want XML applications to validate documents written according to that scheme, we formally have to define our language. As explained earlier, this is done with the help of the Document Type Definition (DTD). The DTD formally defines the grammar of the language; in other words, it describes the structural relationship between the elements and their possible *attributes*. In the case of our `invitation` language, we could define the following DTD:

```
1     <!-- invitation DTD   -->
2     <!ELEMENT invitation (front, body, back)>
3     <!ELEMENT front      (to, date, where, why?)>
4     <!ELEMENT date       (#PCDATA)>
5     <!ELEMENT to         (#PCDATA)>
6     <!ELEMENT where      (#PCDATA)>
7     <!ELEMENT why        (#PCDATA)>
8     <!ELEMENT body       (par+)>
9     <!ELEMENT par        (#PCDATA|emph)*>
10    <!ELEMENT emph       (#PCDATA)>
11    <!ELEMENT back       (signature)>
12    <!ELEMENT signature  (#PCDATA)>
```

Although DTD syntax is expressed in a special language that is not XML based,[6] it is quite straightforward and understandable (see Section 6.5.4 for a detailed discussion). For the moment let us describe in words the meaning of the various lines. Line 2 states that a document that uses the `invitation` element *always* has three

---

[6]XML-Data [↪XMLDATA] defines a vocabulary for schemas that can be used for defining and documenting XML object classes and their relations. Based upon this work several proposals exist to describe DTD data using XML syntax: Document Content Description [↪DCD], Document Definition Markup Language [↪DDML], and Schema for Object-oriented XML [↪SOX].

parts: front, followed by body, and terminated by back. Line 3 goes on to declare that the front element is a sequence of a from, a to, a where, and, optionally, a why element (the fact that the why element is optional is signaled by the presence of the ? sign). We can force more structure on the to element by requiring that all names be separate elements. In this case, line 3 becomes

```
<!ELEMENT front (to+, date, where, why?)>
```

and we would code the `<to>` information as

```
<to>Anna</to><to>Bernard</to><to>Didier</to><to>Johanna</to>
```

We could even require the to element to have explicit subelements for dealing with names (see Section B.4.4 that describes the BIBTEX DTD). Thus, replacing line 5 in the original DTD by

```
<!ELEMENT to      (name+)>
<!ELEMENT name    (#PCDATA)>
```

we would code the `<to>` information as

```
<to><name>Anna</name><name>Bernard</name>
    <name>Didier</name><name>Johanna</name></to>
```

It is up to the DTD developer to decide which approach is more appropriate for the application in question.

Continuing our parsing of the DTD, we find line 8 tells us that the central body part of the invitation consists of one or more paragraphs (the sign + means *one or more*, while * means *zero or more*). According to line 9 each par element can itself contain *parsed character data* (#PCDATA) or emphasized text (flagged with `<emph>` tags). Finally (line 11) the back part has only a signature element. Each of the elements at the terminal nodes of the document structural tree (date on line 4, to on line 5, where on line 6, why on line 7, emph on line 10, and signature on line 12) can contain only #PCDATA. Such data is analysed (parsed) by the XML application and validated to see whether all references are known.

6.5   The detailed structure of an XML document

Now that we have a good idea of what an XML document looks like, it is time to discuss the structure of XML documents in more detail. We shall, therefore, consider the various components of a document instance and of the DTD.

A detailed commented version of the XML recommendation is Tim Bray's *Annotated XML Specification* [↪AXML]. It provides a hypertext version of the XML Specification, complemented with historical and technical annotations, as well as examples and advice. It is a *must* for those who want to learn about XML.

To be as precise as possible, we will make frequent references to the XML Specification Document that defines the XML language using 89 "productions."[7]

6.5.1   XML is truly international

From the very start, XML was designed to be international, and it can be used with all scripts in the world since it is based on the Unicode or ISO/IEC 10646 standards (see Section C.2).

Indeed, XML allows you to use any Unicode character. It subdivides the Unicode set of characters into *letters* (XMLPR[84]), *combining characters* (various kinds of diacritics that can be combined with letters, XMLPR[87]), *digits* (Roman, Arabic, Bengali, and so on, XMLPR[88]), and *extenders* (such as a middle dot, XMLPR[89]).

XML names start with a *letter*, an underscore, or a colon and can continue with a *letter*, a *digit*, a dot, a hyphen, an underscore, a colon, a *combining character*, or an *extender* (XMLPR[4-5]). Names cannot begin with the reserved character string "XML" (in upper- or lowercase).

The language in which parts of a document are written can be specified using a *language code* (XMLPR[33-38]). A special attribute xml:lang can be declared for any document element and used in the document text. Suppose that we declare an attribute for an element type p as follows (see Section 6.5.4.2 for a description of the syntax of attribute declarations in a DTD):

```
<!ATTLIST p xml:lang NMTOKEN #IMPLIED>
```

Then we could write in our document instance something like

```
<p xml:lang="en-GB">A favour, certainly!</p>
<p xml:lang="en-US">A favor, sure!</p>
<p xml:lang="fr">Une faveur, avec plaisir !</p>
<p xml:lang='de'>Eine Gunst, sicher!</p>
```

Each parsed entity of an XML document can use a different character encoding (this would be a convenient way to include Russian or Chinese text snippets inside an otherwise English-language text). To allow for this possibility, specify the encoding using the encoding keyword on the *text declaration* of document entities (XMLPR[77])—for instance,

```
<?xml encoding='UTF-8'?>        <-- one of the defaults      -->
<?xml encoding='ISO-8859-1'?>   <-- Latin 1 (Western Europe) -->
<?xml encoding="ISO-2022-JP"?>  <-- Japanese encoding        -->
```

XML processors must recognize the UTF-16 (Unicode native 16-bit codes) and UTF-8 encodings (a trick to use 7-bit ASCII as is and all other characters as a multi-

---

[7]In the following, XML production rules are identified as XMLPR[xx], where xx is the number in the XML Specification Document.

byte sequence occupying two to five bytes). All other encodings must be specified explicitly (XMLPR [80–81]).

6.5.2   XML document components

XML documents must be *well-formed*. A well-formed XML document consists of a *prolog*, one or more *elements*, and possibly some trailing information consisting of *processing instructions* and comments (XMLPR [1]).

A simple example of a valid document is the following:

```
1   <!-- ======   Start of Prolog    ===============================+ -->
2   <?xml version="1.0" standalone="yes"?> <!-- xml declaration      | -->
3   <!DOCTYPE coolxml [                    <!-- DOCTYPE declaration   | -->
4     <!ELEMENT coolxml (#PCDATA)>         <!-- ELEMENT declaration   | -->
5   ]>                              <! -- end of DOCTYPE declaration   | -->
6   <!-- ======   End   of Prolog    ===============================+ -->
7
8   <!-- ======   Start of document elements  ====================+ -->
9   <coolxml>                       <!-- start tag (root element) | -->
10  XML is a cool idea!             <!-- element content          | -->
11  </coolxml>                      <!-- end   tag (root element) | -->
12  <!-- ======   End   of document elements  ====================+ -->
```

The prolog of the document can have an *XML declaration* (XMLPR [22–27]) and an *XML document type declaration*, followed by the actual informational contents of the document (using instances of various element types and entities).

The following sections describe these various components in detail.

6.5.3   The XML declaration

The XML declaration, the very first thing that the XML parser encounters for a given document entity, declares such things as which version of XML you used to mark up your document (XMLPR [24–27]) and the encoding (XMLPR [80–81], see earlier). It declares if the document is *stand-alone* (XMLPR [32]), that is, if there are external declarations present. (Nothing is implied about external references, such as images, that can be present in a "stand-alone" document as long as they are declared internally.) The following is an example showing all three declarations:

```
<?xml  version="1.0" encoding='ISO-8859-1' standalone="yes"?>
<!DOCTYPE racine [<!ELEMENT racine (#PCDATA)>]>
<racine>Salut à vous de la racine du document !</racine>
```

Treating these three lines with an XML processor we get no errors:

```
java EventDemo racine.xml
Start document:  pubid=null, sysid=file://localhost/home/racine.xml
Resolving entity:  name=[document], pubid=null,
                   sysid=file://localhost/home/racine.xml
Doctype declaration:  name=racine, pubid=null, sysid=null
Start element:  name=racine
```

```
Data:   Salut à vous de la racine du document !
End element:  name=racine
End document:  errors=0
```

However, suppose we do not specify the encoding and present the following document to the parser:

```
<?xml  version="1.0" standalone="yes"?>
<!DOCTYPE racine [<!ELEMENT racine (#PCDATA)>]>
<racine>Salut à vous de la racine du document !</racine>
```

When no encoding is explicitly specified, depending on the first byte of the file,
UTF-8 or UTF-16 is chosen. In the present example, the XML processor will reject
the document with an error message, as follows:

```
java EventDemo racineno-enc.xml
Start document:   pubid=null,
                  sysid=file://localhost/home/racineno-enc.xml
Resolving entity:   name=[document], pubid=null,
                    sysid=file://localhost/home/racineno-enc.xml
FATAL ERROR: malformed UTF-8 sequence
  at file://localhost/home/racineno-enc.xml: line 1
java.lang.Error: malformed UTF-8 sequence
```

Since UTF-8 encoding was assumed, the accented letter "à" triggered an error condition. Its higher order bit is set, and only 7 bit ASCII characters are accepted as
pass-through, one byte sequences in the default encoding. Therefore for accented
one-byte character input (French, German, Russian, and so on), an encoding *must*
be specified or the document must be transliterated to use UTF-8 or UTF-16.

6.5.4   The document type declaration

The second part of the prolog is the XML *document type declaration* (XMLPR [28]).
It starts with the literal string <!DOCTYPE and is followed by the type of the root
element of the document. It contains further *markup declarations*, specified internally to the document (*internal subset*) or in external entities (*external subset*) or in
both. The internal subset is read first so that you can declare elements, entities, or
attributes that will be used when processing the external subset.

In the previous examples the line

```
<!DOCTYPE racine [<!ELEMENT racine (#PCDATA)>]>
```

is a document type declaration, with root element "racine" and contains only an
internal subset with a single-element declaration.

The internal and external subsets, taken together, provide the grammar for a given class of documents, known as the *document type definition*, or DTD. It can contain (XMLPR [29]) the following:

- *Element declarations* start with <!ELEMENT and contain the *type* of the element and its *content model*.

- *Attribute declarations* start with <!ATTLIST and for a given declared element contain one or more *attributes* together with their type and default values.

- *Entity declarations* start with <!ENTITY and contain the name and definition of an *entity*.

- *Notation declarations* start with <!NOTATION and contain a name and an external or public identifier associated with a special *notation* that is used with entities or attributes.

- *Processing instructions* are delimited by the character strings <? and ?> and contain nondocument data passed through to an application.

- *Comments* are delimited by the character strings <!-- and --> and can be added for documentation and clarity.

6.5.4.1 Element declarations

Each element belonging to the logical structure of a document must be declared. This declaration (XMLPR [45-46]) specifies the *type* of the element as well its *content model*. The content specification can be any of the following four possibilities:

1. The string EMPTY means that the element has *no* contents.

    ```
    <!ELEMENT linebreak EMPTY>
    ```

2. The string ANY means any other element or character data, as long as the contents remain compatible with the rules of XML.

    ```
    <!ELEMENT container ANY>
    ```

3. *Child elements* means no character data is allowed (XMLPR [47-50]). The contents are constrained to a (possibly nested) list of elements, specified between parentheses, that can be followed by the character ?, *, or +. Inside the parentheses, one can have a list of elements separated by , or |, or there can be further nesting. The meaning of these symbols is

,	elements in document instance must be used in the order indicated;
|	choice of one element in the list;
+	one or more occurrences;
*	zero or more occurrences; and
?	zero or one occurrence.

Referring to our "invitation" example in Section 6.4.3, we repeat part of its DTD here and discuss the meaning of its declarations.

```
1   <!ELEMENT invitation (front, body, back)>
2   <!ELEMENT front      (to, date, where, why?)>
3   <!ELEMENT body       (par+)>
```

Each `invitation` element (line 1) has exactly one `front`, `body`, and `back` element, and each element must be entered in that order in the document instance. The `front` element (line 2) must contain, in sequence, one `to`, `date`, `where` element, followed optionally by a `why` element. The body element (line 3) has at least one `par` element.

4. *Mixed content* (XMLPR [51]) is character data (represented by the character string #PCDATA) interspersed with child elements. Moreover, #PCDATA must come first in the content model declaration, and you can constrain only the type of child elements, not the order or their number of occurrences, since only the "choice" operator is allowed. An example from our `invitation` DTD is the content model of the `par` element, which can contain character data interspersed with zero or more `emph` elements.

```
    <!ELEMENT par        (#PCDATA|emph)*>
```

6.5.4.2   Attribute declarations

Attributes that can be specified on start tags or empty element tags associate name-value pairs with an element instance.

For validating, attributes must be explicitly declared in the DTD internal or external subsets. The DTD specifies which attributes can be used with which element types, what the type constraints are for these attributes, and what their default values are (XMLPR [52–53]). For reasons of clarity and convenience, attribute declarations often immediately follow the declaration of the element they refer to. It is, however, possible to add attributes or to redefine attribute definitions by placing them in the internal subset. As with entities, the first occurrence is taken; further definitions are ignored.

Attribute *types* come in three categories (XMLPR [54]):

1. *String types* (XMLPR [55]) can take any character string as data and are defined by the keyword CDATA.

```
    <!ATTLIST director name CDATA #REQUIRED>
```

2. *Tokenized types* (XMLPR [56]) introduce lexical and semantic constraints that fall into four basic groups:

   (a) ID is an XML name that should uniquely identify the given element type.

   (b) IDREF or IDREFS are references to elements defined with an ID attribute.

When validating a document, the XML processor must check that IDREF values match the value of some ID attribute.

(c) ENTITY and ENTITIES are references to entity names defined somewhere in the DTD.

(d) NMTOKEN and NMTOKENS refer to a set of name tokens (XMLPR [7-8]) without further constraints; for example, they do not have to correspond to some attribute or entity declaration.

To clarify this, let us consider the following attribute declarations:

```
<!ELEMENT image  EMPTY>
<!ATTLIST image
     name         ID        #REQUIRED
     size         ENTITY    #REQUIRED
     bordercolor  NMTOKEN   'red'
     title        CDATA     #IMPLIED>
```

For the element image we declare two required (name and size) and two optional (bordercolor and title) attributes. The name attribute is of type ID and will allow us to refer to images in the text of the document. For size, which is of the type ENTITY, we must use an entity definition to set its value. The attribute bordercolor, which is a name token, will, if no value is explicitly specified on an element instance, paint a "red" border. Finally, title allows us, if we wish, to associate any character data to the image.

To complement these definitions, we can define another element type, imgref, to refer to images.

```
<!ELEMENT imgref EMPTY>
<!ATTLIST imgref name IDREF #REQUIRED>
```

By thus defining the name attribute of the imgref element, we can use its value to refer to image instances elsewhere in the document source.

3. *Enumerated types* (XMLPR [57]) can take one of a list of values as specified in the declaration. There are two categories:

(a) A *notation type* (XMLPR [58]) consists of the keyword NOTATION followed by one or more names of notations that must be declared in the DTD.

```
<!ATTLIST image  type NOTATION (gif|eps|tiff) #REQUIRED>
```

Here we add an attribute type to our image element. It allows us to specify an image in three formats, namely, GIF, EPS, or TIFF. Note that each of these must have been declared with a NOTATION statement (see Section 6.5.4.4).

(b) An *enumeration* (XMLPR [59]) is an explicit list of name tokens to be associated to the given attribute value.

```
<!ATTLIST quotation type (inline|display) "inline">
```

This declares two possibilities—inline and display—for the type attribute of the quotation element. When the attribute is not specified, then the value inline is used.

To end this section on attributes we explain the format of the attribute default values, which are specified at the end of each entry (XMLPR[60]). There are four possibilites:

#REQUIRED   a value *must* be specified for the attribute whenever the element is used.

#IMPLIED   the attribute may, but need not, be assigned a value on instances of the element considered.

'defval'   the default value for the attribute in question will be used if no value is given on the start tag of the element instance.

#FIXED 'defval'   the attribute must *always* have the default value *defval* specified in the DTD.

Examples of all four cases are seen in the declaration for the attributes of the pict element following. We provided a default value for the title attribute, and *fixed* the bordercolor to take the value blue.

```
<!ATTLIST pict name        ID      #REQUIRED
               size        CDATA   #IMPLIED
               title       CDATA   'Default title'
               bordercolor NMTOKEN #FIXED 'blue'>
```

6.5.4.3   Entity declarations

Foreign material (text fragments, special characters, images, external files) can be included in an XML source with the help of entity references. XML distinguishes two types (XMLPR[70-74]):

- *General* entities
  Declarations, which can occur only in the DTD, are of the form

  ```
  <!ENTITY GEName GEDef>
  ```

  General entity *references* (XMLPR[08]) can occur both in the DTD and the document instance and consist of an ampersand (&), followed by the name of the entity, followed by a semicolon (;). They are *not* expanded in the DTD.

  ```
  &GEName;
  ```

- *Parameter* entities
  Declarations, which can occur only in the DTD, are of the form

  ```
  <!ENTITY % PEName PEDef>
  ```

  Parameter entity *references* (XMLPR[69]) can occur only in the DTD part of the document. They consist of a percent sign (%), followed by the name of the entity, followed by a semicolon (;).

  ```
  %PEName;
  ```

  The definition part `GEDef` and `PEDef` can be an *internal* entity, whose definition is given in the DTD, and for which there is no separate associated physical storage object, or an *external* entity.

Internal entities

An *internal entity* has its value specified inside the document declaration; it has no separate associated storage object. All internal entities are parsed. They are used for various purposes, details of which follow:

- Definitions of abbreviated notations to ease repetitive entry of text strings (general entities), for example,

  ```
  <!ENTITY XML "Extensible Markup Language">
  <!ENTITY MML "Mathematical Markup Language">
  ```

- Definitions of abbreviations to input special characters, accents, or symbols (general character entities). As an illustration we give the set of five predefined general entities that all XML processors must recognize.[8] They are expressed as numeric *character references* (XMLPR[66]) that represent characters in the Unicode character set in either decimal or hexadecimal representation. Character references are expanded immediately when recognized and are treated as character data.

  ```
  <!ENTITY lt     "&#60;">  <!-- "<" -->
  <!ENTITY gt     "&#62;">  <!-- ">" -->
  <!ENTITY amp    "&#38;">  <!-- "&" -->
  <!ENTITY apos   "&#39;">  <!-- "'" -->
  <!ENTITY quot   "&#34;">  <!-- '"' -->
  ```

  Several standard character entity sets have been defined for such things as national characters (the ISO 8859 series, Unicode, ISO 10646), graphical symbols,

---

[8]These five entities are, strictly speaking, available only to well-formed documents that can parse without DTD. Valid documents *must* include a definition of these entities in their DTD if they need to reference them.

mathematics, and so on. Following are a few more examples from the Unicode set, where we adopt hexadecimal notation.

```
<!ENTITY cyrya "&#x044f;"> <!-- Cyrillic small letter "ya"      -->
<!ENTITY ggg   "&#x22d9;"> <!-- Math ">>>" very much greater than -->
<!ENTITY U4E0A "&#x4e0a;"> <!-- CJK ideograph (Chinese "above")   -->
```

Usually complete, predefined sets of such entities are made available to the document instance by including them as external entity references. At present, the W3C XML mathematics working group that defined MathML is discussing with the Unicode Consortium how to include a common set of generally used mathematics characters.

- Definition of variables for use inside a DTD (parameter entities). This is very useful to modularize a DTD so that it becomes more easily maintainable. Two examples are shown:

```
<!ENTITY % inline "link | image | object | break | q">
<!ENTITY % align  "align (left|center|right|justify)  #IMPLIED">
```

The first could be used to shorten content models by allowing "inline" elements to be included globally, while the second form is a preformatted entity that can be used to declare an "align" attribute in a consistent way with various element types.

All internal entities must be declared in the internal or external DTD subsets. Entity references should follow their declaration in the source.

An entity reference triggers, at the given point in the XML file, the substitution of the entity reference by its *contents*. Entity definitions can themselves refer to other internal and already defined entities. For instance, using the definition of the entity XML at the beginning of this section, we can declare another entity XMLS as follows:

```
<!ENTITY XMLS "&XML; and other extensible languages">
```

External entities

External entities are all those that are not internal. They are used to reference data external to the given document instance. Data included via such an entity reference can be either parsed or declared with the NDATA keyword, in which case the data remains unparsed (for instance, a picture or a binary file).

External entity declarations come in three basic forms:

1. The external identifier can be preceded by the keyword "SYSTEM," and followed by a *system literal*. This is also known as the *system identifier*, which is used to retrieve the entity (XMLPR [75]). A system literal (XMLPR [11]) is an external

identifier in the form of a URI (*Universal Resource Identifier*; see Section 1.1.2) that is able to identify any resource on a given computer system.

```
<!ENTITY % subdtd SYSTEM
            "http://www.mysys.org/XML/dtds/headings-xml.dtd">
<!ENTITY chapter1 SYSTEM "chapter1.xml">
```

The first declaration defines the parameter entity `subdtd` that corresponds to part of a DTD. It can be referenced from inside the internal or external DTD subsets. The second declaration defines a general entity `chapter1` pointing to an XML source file `chapter1.xml` in the same directory as the referring master file. Such declarations can be useful for subdividing large documents into smaller chunks for easier handling. These document fragments are then included in the master document via entity references.

2. The external identifier can be preceded by the keyword "PUBLIC." It must then also contain a public identifier literal—itself followed by a system literal in the form of a URI (XMLPR[75]). A public identifier (ISO/IEC:9070, 1991) is a name that is intended to be meaningful across systems and different user environments. Formally a public identifier is composed of several fields, separated by a double solidus, "//" (see, for instance, [↪FPISYNTAX] or the standard (ISO/IEC:9070, 1991)). In short, the first part is an *owner identifier*. The entries in the example that follows have a hyphen, -. This means that the identifiers were not formally registered, while the organization that created the file was the W3C (the Web Consortium). The second part of the public identifier (following the double solidus) is called the *text identifier*. The first word indicates the *public text class* (such as DTD or ENTITIES) and is followed by the *public text description* (such as HTML, Latin1). Then optionally after another double solidus, one finds the *public text language* and a code from ISO 639 (see Table C.1), which in our case is EN, for English. Finally this can be followed by a *display version*, if needed. A server for helping you resolve public identifiers has been set up by Peter Flynn[↪FPISERVER].
    Let us look at how these public identifiers are used with entities:

```
<!ENTITY % html4-strict PUBLIC "-//W3C//DTD HTML 4.0//EN"
                        "http://www.w3.org/TR/REC-html40/strict.dtd">
<!ENTITY % ISOlat1      PUBLIC "-//W3C//ENTITIES Latin1//EN//HTML"
                        "d:\home\dtds\iso-lat1.ent">
```

In the first example we define a parameter entity `html4-strict`, known by the public identifier `-//W3C//DTD HTML 4.0//EN`. Using this public identifier, the XML application will try to construct a URI to retrieve the file (for example, using the `catalog` file proposed by the OASIS consortium; see Section 6.6.5.1). If such a URI cannot be generated, the external entity reference will be resolved by using the explicit URI specified at the end. The second example defines `ISOlat1` as a parameter entity to refer to the definition of Latin 1 characters.

In this case, the URI specified at the end is an absolute path (on a Microsoft Windows platform).

3. For handling nonparsable data (such as EPS, GIF, or JPEG images; TeX source files; or binary files), we must specify the NDATA keyword followed by the name of a notation known to the XML system (XMLPR[76]). This allows the data to be passed to and handled by an application capable of interpreting the notation in question.

```
<!ENTITY xmlfig1 SYSTEM
  "http://www.myserver.edu/book-files/figures/xmlfig1.eps" NDATA EPS>
```

Here we define an Encapsulated Postscript image that can be retrieved from a Web server. When the XML application parses the document and finds a reference to this general external entity, it must *know* how to handle such an EPS image. This is declared with a notation declaration (see Section 6.5.4.4). References to an unparsed entity can occur only in attribute values that were declared to be of types ENTITY or ENTITIES (see "*Tokenized types*" on page 261).

Note that, as with attribute declarations, the first occurrence of an entity declaration takes precedence. This allows declarations to be made in the DTD's internal subset, which is read *before* the external subset, thus overriding possible definitions for the same entity name in the external subset. To make life easier for nonvalidating parsers in the internal subset, parameter entity references cannot be used *inside* markup declarations. They can be used only at the top level where markup declarations themselves occur. As an example consider the following document:

```
1   <?xml version="1.0"?>
2   <!DOCTYPE doc [
3   <!ENTITY % a '<!ELEMENT a (#PCDATA)>'>
4   %a;
5   <!ENTITY % doc '(a|b)'>
6   <!ELEMENT doc (%doc;)+>
7   <!ELEMENT b EMPTY>
8   ]>
9   <doc><a>text</a><b/><a>more text</a></doc>
```

The parameter entity reference on line 4 at the top level is all right, whereas the one on line 6 inside an element declaration is invalid in the internal subset. However, if we transfer lines 3–7 into the file penext.dtd and we make the XML source reference that file, then we find that this limitation applies only to the internal subset. Therefore the following document is a valid one:

```
1   <?xml version="1.0"?>
2   <!DOCTYPE doc SYSTEM "penext.dtd">
3   <doc><a>text</a><b/><a>more text</a></doc>
```

6.5.4.4 Notation declarations

Notation declarations (XMLPR [82–83]) are related to how unparsed entities have to be handled. They associate a name with

- the format of an unparsed entity;
- the format of an element with a "notation" attribute; and
- the application that is going to handle the data inside a processing instruction.

A notation declaration, therefore, consists of a name for the notation, as discussed earlier, and an external or public identifier that allows the XML processor to locate a program to process data that is flagged to be in the given notation.

```
1   <!NOTATION gif SYSTEM "c:\Program Files\Internet Explorer\Ie4.dll">
2   <!NOTATION eps SYSTEM "/usr/local/bin/X11/gv">
```

On line 1 we declare, on Microsoft Windows, that GIF images should be handled by the *Explorer 4* program; on line 2 we declare how to deal with EPS files on a UNIX system.

6.5.4.5 Significant space

In order to make documents more readable and easier to maintain, it is often convenient to add blank lines or spaces. Most of the time this whitespace is not significant and is not intended for inclusion in the output instance of the document that is generated by the XML application. Sometimes, however, whitespace should be preserved as is in the output representation (e.g., for displaying computer code), and a special reserved attribute, xml:space, must be associated with the element type in question; for instance,

```
1   <!ELEMENT computercode (#PCDATA)>
2   <!ATTLIST computercode xml:space #FIXED "preserve">
```

These lines instruct the XML processor to tell the XML application to preserve all whitespace (line breaks, tabs, and so on) for material inside a computercode element. XML processors never eliminate any space characters, since they must pass on to the application all material that is not markup. Therefore it is up to the application to honor requests about whitespace handling. Note that, unless told otherwise, most applications will fold multiple whitespace into a single space, thus ruining the intended layout as coded in the source material.

6.5.4.6 Processing instructions

Processing instructions (XMLPR [16–17]) allow documents to communicate information and instructions to specific applications; processing instructions are not part of the document's character data. Their contents are passed on to the relevant application by the XML processor.

Processing instructions are enclosed inside the pair of characters <? and ?>. The opening <? is followed by a name identifying the target application (xml is a reserved name, see following); then comes the data for the application in question. A NOTATION declation (see Section 6.5.4.4) can be used to associate an application with such a name. An example of how to "talk to" a PRINT application follows:

```
<?PRINT Clear Page?>
```

A special processing instruction is the line at the beginning of an XML document, for instance,

```
<?xml version="1.0" standalone="yes"?>
```

Although this is called the *XML declaration*, it is really a processing instruction for the XML processor indicating version, encoding, and so on.

6.5.4.7   CDATA sections

CDATA sections (XMLPR[18-21]) are used to escape text where markup should not be recognized. Such sections are allowed wherever character data can be used; they start with the literal string <![CDATA[and end with the literal string]]>. Inside these delimiters any kind of markup can be used (except the closing string]]>, of course). LaTeX users will recognize similarities with the verbatim environment. In the next example the start and end tags, as well as the entity reference, are treated as character data and not as markup.

```
<![CDATA[<p>An ampersand sign looks like &amp;.</p>]]>
```

The XML processor will output the above line uninterpreted as

```
<p>An ampersand sign looks like &amp;.</p>
```

6.5.4.8   Conditional sections

Inside the external DTD subset, conditional sections (XMLPR[61-65]) can be used to include or exclude parts based on the value of a keyword. Suppose that we have the following declarations in the external subset of our DTD:

```
1   <!-- all of the following must be in the external subset -->
2   <!ENTITY % complex "IGNORE">
3   <!ENTITY % simple  "INCLUDE">
4   <![ %complex; [
5   <!ELEMENT table
6       (caption?, (col*|colgroup*), thead?, tfoot?, tbody+)>
7   ]]>
8   <![ %simple; [
9   <!ELEMENT table (caption?, tbody)>
10  ]]>
```

The parameter entity `complex` (line 2) assigns the value `IGNORE` to the keyword controlling the conditional section; hence the first (complex) definition (lines 4–7) will be ignored, and the second (simpler) declaration (lines 8–10) for the `table` element (which is "included" via the `simple` entity on line 3) is retained. However, suppose that we put the following in the internal subset of our document instance:

```
1   <!ENTITY % complex "INCLUDE">
2   <!ENTITY % simple  "IGNORE">
```

Since the first occurring entity declarations take precedence, the values of the `complex` and `simple` parameter entities in the external DTD are overridden by the values in the internal subset. As a result (line 1) the keyword `INCLUDE` gets assigned to the conditional section that controls the complex definition of the `table` element type that will thus be used in the DTD.

6.5.5   Document elements

Each XML document contains one or more *elements* (XMLPR[39]), consisting of *content* (XMLPR[43]) enclosed in a *starttag* (XMLPR[40]) and an *endtag* (XMLPR[42]), or of an *empty-element* tag (XMLPR[44]). Each element has a type, identified by a name (its "generic identifier"), and start and empty tags may have a set of attribute specifications. Each attribute specification (XMLPR[41]) has a name and a value.

For an XML document to be valid, each element and entity must have been declared in the DTD, and their contents and attributes must correspond to the content model and attribute declaration.

Let us look at part of our `invitation` document (Section 6.4.2.2) as an example:

```
1   <body>
2   <par>
3   I would like to invite you all to celebrate
4   the birth of <emph>Invitation</emph>, my
5   first XML document child.
6   </par>
7   ...
8   </body>
```

When we compare this with the `invitation` DTD (Section 6.4.3), we see that the elements are used in agreement with the relevant part of that DTD.

```
1   <!ELEMENT body      (par+)>
2   <!ELEMENT par       (#PCDATA|emph)*>
3   <!ELEMENT emph      (#PCDATA)>
```

Let us end this section on document elements with an example of the use of empty elements.

```
1   <!DOCTYPE emptyexample [
2   <!ELEMENT emptyexample (par*)>
3   <!ELEMENT par (#PCDATA|image|imref)*>
4   <!ELEMENT image EMPTY>
5   <!ATTLIST image name    ID     #IMPLIED
6                   address CDATA  #REQUIRED>
7   <!ELEMENT imref EMPTY>
8   <!ATTLIST imref name    IDREF  #REQUIRED>
9   <!ENTITY  logo-uri "http://www.ucc.ie/xml/xml.gif">
10  ]>
11  <emptyexample>
12  <par>The XML logo is seen in the image <imref name="xml-logo"/>.</par>
13  <par>The image tag shows an alternative syntax for an empty element
14  <image name="xml-logo" address="&logo-uri;"></image>.</par>
15  </emptyexample>
```

This valid XML document contains a par element type inside the root element emptyexample (line 2). The par element has a mixed content of parsed character data and image and imref elements (line 3) that are both declared empty (lines 4 and 7). At the end of the DTD internal subset, we declare a general entity logo-uri (line 9), which we shall use to specify the location of the image. The content of the first par element (line 12) shows one of the two ways to represent an empty element in XML documents. The image reference tag <imref name="xml-logo"/> in question has an attribute of type IDREF with a value of "xml-logo." For the document to be valid, there *must* exist another element with an attribute declared of type ID and a value of "xml-logo." We find such an element inside the second par element (on line 14). Here the identifier in question is defined inside the empty element image, which associates the image with a GIF file via a URI (and a reference to the entity logo-uri). Note the alternative syntax <image ...></image> for an empty element.

6.6 XML parsers and tools

Although the average user will not have to worry directly about XML parsers (just as Fortran, C, or C++ compilers for the programmer are only tools that compile computer programs into executable code), Nevertheless some information about the availability and usefulness of such parsers will help you to understand the use of these (and other) tools to generate, for example, HTML or PostScript output from your XML data.

Several XML parsers are freely available on the Internet. Most of them are written in C++ or Java, while Python, Perl, and Javascript have also been used.

New versions of browsers, such as Microsoft's Internet Explorer Version 5, Mozilla (the successor of Netscape Version 4), and other tools, such as Microsoft's Office suite, Adobe's Acrobat and FrameMaker, and symbolic algebra packages, such as Mathematica and Maple, will all include "native" support for XML.

In this section we limit ourselves to the editing and verification phases of XML documents; in the remaining chapters we will deal with ways of using the parsed data to manipulate, view, print, and exchange the information. Indeed, XML markup conveys very little about the semantic meaning of a given tag; in particular it says nothing about how a tag should be rendered. The basic principle of XML is that structure and semantics are completely decoupled, with style of rendering being addressed by XSL. This subject, together with other style-related developments, will be reviewed in Chapter 7.

We start our overview with two examples of editors for XML data and DTDs. Then we say a few words about DTD-handling tools, before looking at some of the parsers.

6.6.1   Emacs and psgml

The `emacs` editor is one of the most often used editors on UNIX (and today is also popular on Microsoft Windows). It is highly customizable via Lisp code and can easily cope with the syntax of various languages. Lennart Staflin developed the basic SGML support in the form of an `emacs` "macro mode" `psgml` [↪PSGML]. More recently, David Megginson developed an XML add-on to `psgml` [↪PSGMLXML]. For editing DTDs Tony Graham contributed his `tdtd` macros [↪TDTD].

All these modes present you with menus and commands for inserting tags, thus helping you to enter only contextually valid tags and allowing you to edit attribute values in a separate window with information about types and defaults. They also identify structural errors.

As an example, Figure 6.2 shows the "front" part of our "invitation" document. From the "SGML" pull-down menu we chose the "List valid tags" entry. The curser is positioned just following the `front` element, as shown in the top left part of the figure. Parsing the DTD, `psgml` determines that only the `to` element is valid at that point and informs us in the bottom window. In fact, `psgml` is interfaced to James Clark's `nsgmls` program, a full-blown SGML parser that will be described later.

Figure 6.3 is an example of how the `tdtd` mode is helpful in editing DTDs. Keywords, comments, entities, literal data, the content model, and delimiters are clearly identified since they are displayed in different colors. Moreover, at each point you can ask `emacs` for assistance. In particular, in the lower half of the example a list of available DTD commands can be seen. If you choose one, the program will walk you through a dialog where you can specify all relevant components for the element being dealt with.

Most users probably prefer a more "visual" (WYSIWYG) approach to editing XML documents and creating or modifying DTDs. It is expected that by the end

Figure 6.2: Emacs in psgml mode acting on the invitation example

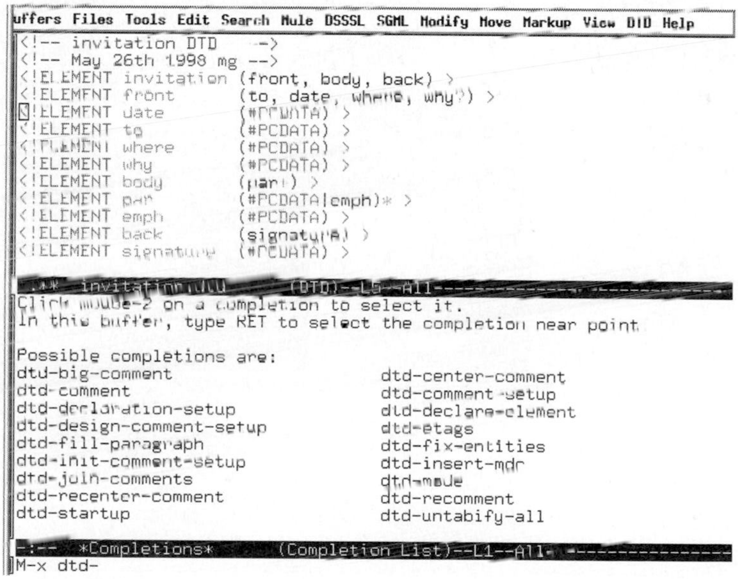

Figure 6.3: Emacs in xml and dtd mode acting on the invitation example

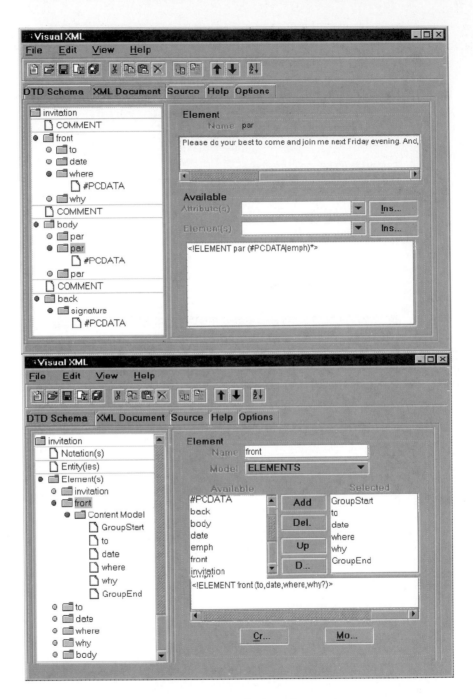

Figure 6.4: A visual editor for XML

of 1999 many visual XML editors will be available. As an early example, we show in Figure 6.4 a prototype of such a WYSIWYG editor. It was developed by Pierre Morel and allows you to edit tree based views of XML documents (see the upper part of Figure 6.4) as well as DTDs (refer to the bottom part of the same figure). It is written in Java and offers the "look and feel" of the Java Foundation Classes (see [↪VISXML] for more information and for instructions on how to download the software).

Another example is the W3C's Amaya HTML testbed editor; its description is available at [↪AMAYA]. Strictly speaking it is not yet an XML editor, but since it allows you to experiment with CSS and MathML—you can edit complex mathematical expressions via a WYSIWYG interface—it is certainly representative of the editors we will see in the near future. Figure 6.5 shows different views of the same document, a facility that eases entering and maintaining document sources.

6.6.2   The perlSGML programs

Earl Hood has developed perlSGML, a set of Perl programs and libraries for processing SGML DTDs and documents. The perlSGML distribution [↪PERLSGML] contains two Perl libraries (dtd.pl, a DTD parser, and sgml.pl, an SGML document parser), a set of Perl modules for handling SGML documents and managing entities, as well as a set of programs. They are briefly described here:

dtd2html   creates a set of HTML files to navigate and document an SGML DTD.

dtddiff   compares two DTDs and lists their differences.

dtdtree   outputs the hierarchical relations between the elements of a DTD as a tree structure.

dtdview   allows you to query a DTD interactively.

stripsgml   strips a file of its SGML markup and replaces entity references by standard ASCII characters.

Let us have a closer look at the dtdtree program

```
1   dtdtree -dtd invitation.dtd
2   =--------------------------
3                INVITATION
4   --------------------------------
5   INVITATION
6   |_(front,
7   |   |_(to,
8   |   |   |_(#PCDATA)
9   |   |
10  |   |__date,
11  |   |   |_(#PCDATA)
12  |   |
13  |   |__where,
14  |   |   |_(#PCDATA)
15  |   |
16  |   |__why?)
17  |        |_(#PCDATA)
18  |
19  |
20  |__body,
21  |   |_(par+)
22  |       |_(#PCDATA |
23  |       |__emph)*
24  |            |_(#PCDATA)
25  |
26  |
27  |
28  |__back)
29      |_(signature)
30          |_(#PCDATA)
```

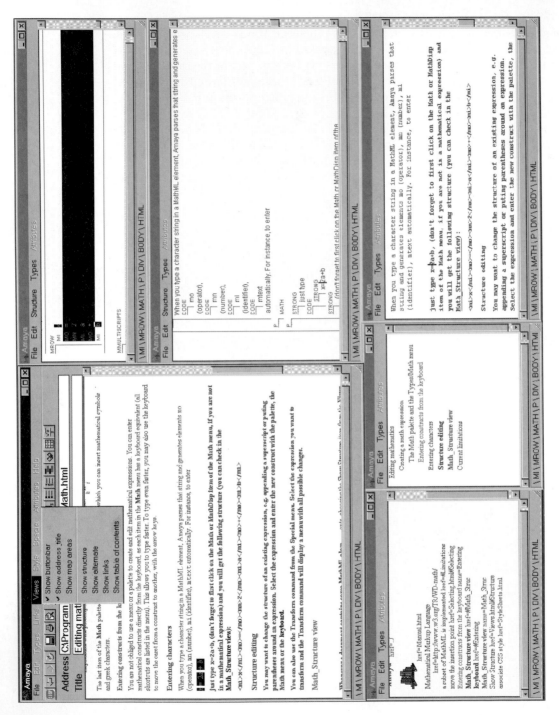

Figure 6.5: The Amaya visual editor

As seen in the previous example, which is the tree representation generated by `dtdtree` for our invitation DTD, the `dtdtree` program provides a convenient visual representation of the hierarchical relations that exist between the various elements of a DTD. The command we typed is shown on line 1. The structure of the various content models is clearly displayed. Take, for instance, the `par` element (line 21): It is at once evident that its parent is `body` (line 20) and its children are `#PCDATA` and `emph` elements (lines 22 and 23).

6.6.3   The DTDParse tool

Norman Walsh has written another tool for documenting DTDs with the help of HTML files. His tool is part of the `DTDParse` suite of programs, available from [↪DTDPARSE]. Once more Perl is the implementation language. Walsh takes a two-step approach: The DTD is first parsed and then entered into a database, which is easier to search for later access. Following we show the `dtdparse` utility generating the database for our invitation DTD:

```
 1   dtdparse -v 2 invitation.dtd          16   Expanding date
 2   Loading catalog: ./CATALOG           17   Expanding body
 3   Loading catalog: /usr/local/sgml/CATALOG   18   Finding parents...
 4   Loading catalog: ~/sgml/CATALOG      19   Finding parents of back
 5   Expanding entities...                20   Finding parents of signature
 6   Finding children...                  21   Finding parents of par
 7   Expanding back                       22   Finding parents of to
 8   Expanding signature                  23   Finding parents of invitation
 9   Expanding par                        24   Finding parents of why
10   Expanding to                         25   Finding parents of front
11   Expanding invitation                 26   Finding parents of emph
12   Expanding why                        27   Finding parents of where
13   Expanding front                      28   Finding parents of date
14   Expanding emph                       29   Finding parents of body
15   Expanding where                      30   Storing elements...
```

Once the elements are stored in the database, we can transform that information into a set of HTML or UNIX man pages by using Norman Walsh's `dtd2html` (this program is *different* from Earl Hood's program, mentioned in Section 6.6.2) or `dtd2man` program, respectively. An interesting example of the use of this tool is the documentation of the DocBook DTD, which can be viewed at [↪DBVIEW] (this DTD, which is frequently used for marking up technical documentation, will be discussed briefly in Section B.4.1).

6.6.4   The Language Technology Group XML toolbox

The Language Technology Group of Edinburgh University has been developing SGML tools for many years. They recently released version 1 of their LTXML library. It consists of a developer's toolkit, based on a C-based API for handling XML documents, as well as a set of stand-alone programs built using that API. The

Language Technology Group has a lot of experience dealing with large *corpora*—collections of text files consisting of several tens of millions of characters. To handle such large documents they had to develop extremely efficient batch-processing tools that are able to deal with the huge data streams. In the following we will look at a few of those tools. A more detailed description can be found at [↪LTXML].

6.6.4.1   XML transformations and regular expression searches

The `sgmltrans` program translates XML files into some other format, such as HTML or LaTeX. It is based on the paradigm that specific actions take place for given start or end tags, depending also on the context. The program allows you to print only some text onto the output stream.

`sggrep` is similar to `grep` on UNIX. It allows searching a file for regular expressions, taking into account the tree structure of XML files.

```
sggrep [-h] [-u base-url]   [-d doctype] [-v] [-n] [-r]
       [-m mark-query] [-a element-name] [-q query]
       [-s sub-query] [-t regexp] [--] [inputs...]
```

The more important arguments are

-u *base-url*   base URL used when resolving relative URLs.

-n   print no newline between output matches (the default is to print a newline).

-q *query*   pattern of the items to select, a path of terms separated by "/" where each term is an SGML element.

-r   attribute values in queries are regular expressions;

-s *sub-query*   selects subelements of query-selected item for *regexp* to match.

-t *regexp*   regular expression to match against text directly contained in query-selected item (if no subquery) or in any subquery selected subelement of query-selected item. An empty string ("") matches anything, including empty elements; indeed, this is the only way to specify empty elements if they are needed.

Next we look at a few examples using the `invitation.xml` file on page 254. The query string consists in specifying a "path" to reach the selected elements.

```
1   sggrep -q "invitation/body/par" invitation.xml
2   <?xml version='1.0' encoding='UTF-8'?>
3   <!DOCTYPE invitation SYSTEM "invitation.dtd">
4   <par>
5   I would like to invite you all to celebrate
6   the birth of <emph>Invitation</emph>, my
7   first XML document child.
8   </par>
9   <par>
10  Please do your best to come and join me next Friday
```

```
11   evening. And, do not forget to bring your friends.
12   </par>
13   <par>
14   I <emph>really</emph> look forward to see you soon!
15   </par>
16
17   sggrep -q ".*/emph"  invitation.xml
18   <?xml version='1.0' encoding='UTF-8'?>
19   <!DOCTYPE invitation SYSTEM "invitation.dtd">
20   <emph>Invitation</emph>
21   <emph>really</emph>
22
23   sggrep -q "invitation/body/par[0]/emph"  invitation.xml
24   <?xml version='1.0' encoding='UTF-8'?>
25   <!DOCTYPE invitation SYSTEM "invitation.dtd">
26   <emph>Invitation</emph>
27
28   sggrep -q "././.[2]/." invitation.xml
29   <?xml version='1.0' encoding='UTF-8'?>
30   <!DOCTYPE invitation SYSTEM "invitation.dtd">
31   <emph>really</emph>
32
33   sggrep -q "./.[0]/.[2]" invitation.xml
34   <?xml version='1.0' encoding='UTF-8'?>
35   <!DOCTYPE invitation SYSTEM "invitation.dtd">
36   <where>The Web Cafe</where>
```

The first command (line 1) queries all the par elements inside a body, inside an invitation element. We see the three paragraphs and their content (lines 4–15). The second command (line 17) uses a wildcard syntax for showing all emph elements (lines 20 and 21); while the third command (line 23) goes to the emph element in the first (counting starts from zero) par inside a body, inside an invitation element. We can also use a different kind of wildcard syntax, as in the fourth command (line 28), where we want to see *any* element inside a third element, inside any element, inside the top element; while the last command (line 33) shows us the second element inside the first element, inside the top element.

A more complex tool is sgrpg, which allows XML queries and general transformations. You can select a set of XML elements and, if needed, transform them into a different format. This program allows quite complex (nested) queries. It is rather more general than sggrep. LTXML tools are very useful for simple ad hoc queries. However, general-purpose applications that have to locate information in XML files based on their hierarchical structure will probably use the XSL or DSSSL languages since they are better suited for complex searches.

6.6.4.2 Other tools

The LTXML system comes with a few more interesting little tools for handling XML files. We consider a couple of them:

sgcount counts elements in an XML file.

```
sgcount [-o nb] [-t] [inputs...]
```

-t   counts only top-level elements.

-o *nb*   an integer defined as follows:

> 0   default printout format; this is a table, showing for each document element, its type, its frequency, and its frequency accompanied by an attribute of type ID.
>
> 1   shows only tag names and counts.
>
> 2   shows only total number of tags.

```
 1  sgcount invitation.xml
 2  invitation     1       0
 3  front          1       0
 4  to             1       0
 5  date           1       0
 6  where          1       0
 7  why            1       0
 8  body           1       0
 9  par            3       0
10  emph           2       0
11  back           1       0
12  signature      1       0
13  *Total*        14      0
14
15  sgcount emptyexample.xml
16  emptyexample   1       0
17  par            2       0
18  imref          1       0
19  image          1       1
20  *Total*        5       1
21
22  sgcount -o 1 emptyexample.xml
23  emptyexample   1
24  par            2
25  imref          1
26  image          1
27  *Total*        5
28
29  sgcount -o 2 emptyexample.xml
30  5
31
32  sggrep -q "invitation/body/par" invitation.xml | sgcount -o 1
33  par     3
34  emph    2
35  *Total* 5
```

These examples show the number and type of elements in the invitation (lines 1–13) and emptyexample (lines 15–20) XML files, as well as the effect of the -o option (lines 22–30). Of particular interest is the last command (line 32); here we have added the sggrep command to select the section of the invitation.xml file inside par elements, and we have counted the included elements (lines 33–35).

The utility textonly strips all XML markup from a file.

```
textonly [-h] [-u base-url] [-t tag] [-s c] [-x] filename
```

The more relevant options are

-u *base-url*   base URL.

-t *tag*   outputs only text present inside the element *tag*.

-s *string* outputs a separator between successive text units. Special values are ' ' for a space, '\n' for a newline (this can be useful if you want one word per line), and '' for the empty string.

```
1   textonly -t par invitation.xml
2   I would like to invite you  all to celebrate
3   the birth of Invitation, my first XML document
4   child.
5
6   Please do your best to come and join me next Friday
7   evening. And, do not forget to bring your friends.
8
9   I really look forward to see you soon!
10  textonly -t signature invitation.xml
11  Michel
12  textonly -t front -s '\n' invitation.xml
13  Anna, Bernard, Didier, Johanna
14  Next Friday Evening at 8 pm
15  The Web Cafe
16  My first XML baby
```

We will use once more our invitation.xml example. The first textonly command (line 1) gets all data of par elements (lines 2–9); the second command (line 10) gets the data inside the signature element (line 11); while the third command (line 12) gets all data in the front part of the document, adding a newline between the various text strings to separate them (lines 13–16).

You can easily build many more tools using the LTXML API. For instance, the toolkit also contains an ESIS generator (see Section 6.6.5.2), which provides output similar to the parsers described in the next section.

6.6.5   Validating documents with XML parsers

It is often important and, in any case, useful to be able to check an XML file for being well-formed or valid. Sometimes we might want to analyze a document and decompose it into its constituent parts for further manipulation, possibly needing to get access to the DTD. In all such cases XML parsers come in handy. A complete and up-to-date list of XML tools, including parsers, can be found at [↪XMLPARS] and [↪XMLRES]. In the following sections we look at a few representative examples. As already mentioned, it is to be expected that the upcoming versions of the browsers and office tools that will be available mid-1999 will come with a built-in XML parser.

6.6.5.1   Interoperability of XML documents

An XML document must know where to find the data corresponding to external entity references. To make it possible to move documents between computers, a mechanism that would allow such transparent entity management had to be agreed upon by the SGML/XML community.

Therefore the OASIS Consortium (Organization for the Advancement of Structured Information Standards, until 1997 known as SGML-Open) proposed a set of conventions to map external entity identifiers to filenames, URIs, or other storage objects. Moreover, they define a catalog file that contains public identifiers associated with each of the files to be interchanged. The details are at [↪OASIS].

In order to get an idea of what a `catalog` file looks like, consider the following small file:

```
1   OVERRIDE YES

2

3   SGMLDECL "/afs/cern.ch/user/g/goossens/sgml/dtds/xml.decl"

4

5   PUBLIC "ISO 8879-1986//ENTITIES Added Latin 1//EN" "iso-lat1.gml"
6   PUBLIC "-//LWC//DTD Invitation//EN"

7                            "http://lwc.org/dtds/invitation.dtd"

8

9   ENTITY    "mylogo" "graphicsfiles/mylogo.eps"
10  NOTATION  "gif"    "/usr/local/bin/xv"
11  BASE      "http://wwwinfo.cern.ch/~goossens/sgml/dtds/"
```

When the `OVERRIDE` is `YES` (line 1), the `PUBLIC`, `ENTITY`, `DOCTYPE`, or `NOTATION` entries in the catalog will take precedence over an explicit system identifier that might have been specified for a given external identifier. `SGMLDECL` (line 3) specifies the location of the SGML declaration that defines the syntax of the SGML document. (For HTML or XML this declaration is fixed, but it should be specified for a general SGML parser like `nsgmls`; see Section 6.5.3.) Lines 5–7 associate a URI with a public identifier.

A `catalog` file can also define entities and notations (lines 9 and 10). The `BASE` keyword allows system identifiers to be specified relative to the given absolute system path (line 11)

Efforts are underway to cast catalogs into an XML syntax [↪XCATALOG].

6.6.5.2 The Element Structure Information Set

Several parsers analyse XML documents and output a simple text representation of its Element Structure Information Set (ESIS) (see [↪ESIS] for a detailed description). ESIS was probably the first proposal for a standard output format for parsed SGML data. It is very convenient for transmitting data between a parser and an application, for example, one that will format or otherwise transform the input instance. Hence it comes as no surprise that many XML parsers provide an ESIS output stream making it easy to compare their behavior. Therefore we will show an example of ESIS output obtained by an XML processor. Note that most XML processors will also provide more modern interfaces in the form of event-based Application Programmer Interfaces (APIs), such as SAX (see Section B.6), or tree-based APIs, such as DOM [↪DOMGEN].

6.6.5.3   The nsgmls parser

Many providers of SGML software have adapted their products to treat XML. As an example, let us begin with one of the longest standing and most general tools, the SGML suite of James Clark and, in particular, his nsgmls parser. This parser can be used to validate XML documents against a DTD; it generates ESIS output (see Section 6.6.5.2), which is also available with other parsers.

nsgmls can be downloaded from James Clark's home page at [↪ SP]. The program is part of the SP suite of programs and is implemented in the C++ language. A binary executable version is available for various platforms, but you can also download the source to compile the program yourself in the rare case that the programs are not directly available as executables for your platform. The command-line options that follow are explained in detail in the documentation that comes with the program. (It can also be found at [↪ SPDOC].)

```
nsgmls [-vCegBdlprsu] [-b bctf] [-f error_file] [-c catalog_file]
       [-D dir] [-a link_type] [-A arch] [-E max_errors] [-i entity]
       [-w warning_type] [-m catalog_sysid] [-o output_option]
       [-t rast_file] input_file(s)
```

Usually only the -c switch to indicate the location of catalog file(s), -s (run *silently*) to show only error messages, and -w to set the *warning level*, together with the name(s) of the XML input file(s) need concern the average user. By default ESIS output for the input document is generated (unless -s is specified). Before starting to parse the document, nsgmls looks for a "catalog" file that describes where commonly used SGML files, entity sets, and SGML declarations are located on the system (see the following section).

6.6.5.4   Example of ESIS output

As explained in Section 6.6.5.2, SGML and XML parsers often provide ESIS output to represent the structure of the document. Following we show sample output generated by nsgmls. For clarity, we first explain the meaning of the most common elements of the ESIS output format.

\\   a \.

\n   a *record end*.

\nnn   character whose octal code is nnn.

(*gi*   start of element whose generic identifier is *gi*; attributes for this element are specified with A commands.

)*gi*   end of element whose generic identifier is *gi*.

-data   data.

&*name*   reference to external data entity *name*.

Aname key   next element has an attribute *name* with keyword *key* (as described in Section 6.5.4.2).

?pi   processing instruction with data *pi*.

Nnname   notation *nname* (preceded by p or s command to specify public or system identifier, respectively).

ssysid   system identifier *sysid* associated with some other commands (which it precedes).

ppubid   public *pubid* identifier associated with some other commands (which it precedes).

C   signals that the document was a conforming document (it will then be the last line in the output).

We obtain the following ESIS output by running the file `emptyexample.xml` (see page 271) through `nsgmls`. The meaning of the various keywords printed at the beginning of the lines should be clear from the earlier list.

```
1   (emptyexample
2   (par
3   -The XML logo is shown in the image
4   Aname TOKEN xml-logo
5   (imref
6   )imref
7   -.
8   )par
9   (par
10  -The image shows an alternative syntax for an empty element \n\012
11  Aname TOKEN xml-logo
12  Aaddress CDATA http://www.ucc.ie/xml/xml.gif
13  (image
14  )image
15  )par
16  )emptyexample
17  C
```

Similarly the ESIS output obtained after parsing the file `invitation.xml` (see page 254) follows:

```
1   ?xml version="1.0"
2   (invitation
3   (front
4   (to
5   -Anna, Bernard, Didier, Johanna
6   )to
7   (date
8   -Next Friday Evening at 8 pm
9   )date
10  (where
11  -The Web Cafe
12  )where
13  (why
14  -My first XML baby
15  )why
16  )front
```

```
17   (body
18   (par
19   -\n\012I would like to invite you all to celebrate\n\012the birth of
20   (emph
21   -Invitation
22   )emph
23   -, my\n\012first XML document child.\n\012
24   )par
25   (par
26   -\n\012Please do your best to come and join me next Friday\n\012
27   evening. And, do not forget to bring your friends.\n\012
28   )par
29   (par
30   -\n\012I
31   (emph
32   -really
33   )emph
34   - look forward to see you soon!\n\012
35   )par
36   )body
37   (back
38   (signature
39   -Michel
40   )signature
41   )back
42   )invitation
43   C
```

6.6.5.5 Handling incorrect documents gracefully

In order to show how parsers handle source files containing errors, let us consider
the following (invalid) document—we will call it wrong.xml for convenience.

```
1    <?xml version="1.0"?>
2    <!DOCTYPE wrong [
3    <!ELEMENT wrong (par*)>
4    <!ELEMENT par   (#PCDATA|emph)*>
5    <!ELEMENT emph (#PCDATA)*>
6    ]>
7    <wrong>
8    <par>This part has wrong entity syntax &lt;par&gt.</par>
9    <emph>Emph text outside scope.</emph>
10   <par>Here comes another error <par>a second level
11   paragraph</par>.</par>
12   <par>A wrongly nested <emph>construct</par></emph>.
13   Some more text outside valid scope.
14   <par>Reserved characters "&" "<" ">" ";" .</par>
15   </wrong>
```

We obtain the following error messages from running nsgmls in XML mode on the
file above (we had to break some lines that were too long):

```
nsgmls -s -wxml wrong.xml
wrong.xml:8.47:E: general entity "gt." not defined and no default entity
wrong.xml:8:50:W: reference not terminated by refc delimiter
wrong.xml:9:5:E: document type does not allow element "emph" here;
                             assuming missing "par" start-tag
wrong.xml:10:4:E: document type does not allow element "par" here
wrong.xml:10:34:E: document type does not allow element "par" here
wrong.xml:12:4:E: document type does not allow element "par" here
```

```
wrong.xml:12:43:E: end tag for "emph" omitted, but OMITTAG NO was specified
wrong.xml:12:23: start tag was here
wrong.xml:12:50:E: end tag for element "emph" which is not open
wrong.xml:14:4:E: document type does not allow element "par" here
wrong.xml:14:26:W: character "&" is the first character of a delimiter
                                but occurred as data
wrong.xml:14:30:W: character "<" is the first character of a delimiter
                                but occurred as data
wrong.xml:15:7:E: end tag for "par" omitted, but OMITTAG NO was specified
wrong.xml:9:0: start tag was here
```

It is important to realize that `nsgmls` continues parsing (and signaling errors) until the end of the file. Several of the parsers stop at the first *fatal* error and thus do not signal all problems present in the file.[9] In our example the first message tells us about the absence of the entity reference end character (the semicolon ;) for `gt` on source line 8. On source line 9 the presence of the `<emph>...</emph>` tags out of context (outside of a `par` element) is signaled. The parser tries to be clever and inserts a `<par>` start tag on line 9, but this means that the `<par>` start tags on line 10 are (rightly) detected as invalid (`par` elements cannot be nested according to the DTD). On line 12 the absence of the end tag `</emph>` is detected at the close of the `par` element (since no tags can be omitted in XML, the parser displays a `No Omittag` message). Then the close element tag for the `emph` element is found at the end of the line and declared invalid. Once more, on line 14 the `<par>` start tag is rejected, since the (implicitly inserted) `<par>` start tag on line 9 is still active. The out-of-context line 13 is not signaled, and the "reserved" characters "&" and "<" are flagged. Then there are some complaints about unbalanced `par` tags. One can conclude that most errors have been caught, but information out of context is not always detected. One should try to correct the errors starting at the top of the file and work down until all error messages (and warnings) have disappeared. To see a few other parsers at work, we present them with the same file `wrong.xml` and show the error message they generate.

6.6.5.6   XML for Java

XML for Java is a validating XML parser written in Java. It was developed by Kent Tamura and Hiroshi Maruyama of the Tokyo Research Laboratory, IBM Japan, and can be downloaded from [↪XML4J]. It has support for the DOM and namespaces and offers a prototype for XPointers [↪XPTSPEC].

When we run the file "`wrong.xml`" through this parser, we get the messages that follow (we must set the `classpath` variable to inform the Java interpreter where the classes reside). Note that this application uses standard Java so that it

---

[9]Although this strategy appears not to be very useful if one wants to locate all errors in a minimum of time, it is compatible with XML's principle of "Draconian" error-handling. Indeed, in Section *Terminology* of the XML Specification [↪XMLSPEC] under the heading *fatal error* it is stated that a conforming XML processor must "not continue normal processing" once it detects a fatal error (although it *may* continue processing the data, it does not have to).

can be run on any computer platform where the Java environment is installed (the output that follows was obtained on Windows NT).

```
set classpath=d:\xml4j\xml4j.jar,d:\jdk1.1.6\src
java trlx wrong.xml
wrong.xml: 8, 51: Reference must end with ';'.
wrong.xml: 8, 51: Undefined entity reference, "&gt.;".
wrong.xml: 11, 22: Element "<par>" is not valid because it does not follow the rule, "(#PCDATA|emph)*".
wrong.xml: 12, 42: "</emph>" expected.
wrong.xml: 12, 43: Element name expected.
wrong.xml: 14, 28: Reference must end with ';'.
wrong.xml: 14, 28: Invalid character, '"', in reference.
wrong.xml: 14, 31: Element name expected.
wrong.xml: 15, 7: "</par>" expected.
wrong.xml: 15, 8: Element "<par>" is not valid because it does not follow the rule, "(#PCDATA|emph)*".
```

Again, the out-of-context line 9 is not detected, and the second-level <par> start tag on line 10 is not flagged. On the other hand, at the end of line 11 an invalid content is signaled. The incorrectly nested par and emph elements on line 12 are correctly found, and, moreover, the "." at the end of line 12 is flagged as out of context (nothing is said about line 13). The reserved characters "&" and "<" are detected, but the associated error messages are somewhat indirect. Similarly the complaints referring to line 15 are not particularly useful since they refer to an expected /par and an invalid par element.

6.6.5.7 Event handling and the Ælfred parser

Ælfred is a parser written by David Megginson. It is a nonvalidating Java parser, optimized for maximal speed and minimal size. It is portable and works with most Java implementations. An important point is that Ælfred supports Unicode to the fullest extent possible in Java. It correctly handles XML documents encoded using UTF-8, UTF-16, Unicode, ISO-10646, and ISO-8859-1, so Ælfred can handle all major languages.

The parser and its documentation are available from the Ælfred home page at [↪AELFRED]. The class library comes with a few example classes that demonstrate how an application sees XML "parse events." It means that each time the parser detects an element, an attribute, an entity, character data, and so on, it does a callback to a class where the consumer application can then take the necessary action (e.g., write ESIS output or write some informative text or prepare output in an output language, such as TₑX). The eventdemo.class, which comes with the Ælfred distribution, writes information about each "event" to the output stream. Following we show the generated output for the emptyexample.xml file:

```
1   java -classpath "$CLASSPATH:java/aelfred" EventDemo emptyexample.xml
2   Start document
3   Resolving entity:  [document], pubid=null, sysid=file:emptyexample.xml
4   Starting external entity:  file:emptyexample.xml
5   Doctype declaration:  emptyexample, pubid=null, sysid=null
6   Start element:  name=emptyexample
7   Ignorable whitespace:  "\n"
```

```
8   Start element:  name=par
9   Character data:  "The XML logo is shown in the image "
10  Attribute:  name=name, value=xml-logo (specified)
11  Start element:  name=imref
12  End element:  imref
13  Character data:  "."
14  End element:  par
15  Ignorable whitespace:  "\n"
16  Start element:  name=par
17  Character data:
18    "The image shows an alternative syntax for an empty element \n"
19
20  Attribute:  name=name, value=xml-logo (specified)
21  Attribute:  name=address, value=http://www.ucc.ie/xml/xml.gif (specified)
22  Start element:  name=image
23  End element:  image
24  End element:  par
25  Ignorable whitespace:  "\n"
26  End element:  emptyexample
27  Ending external entity:  file:emptyexample.xml
28  End document:  errors=0
```

To make it easier to write code that can handle events coming from various parsers, David Megginson and Tim Bray (in collaboration with others) decided that it would be appropriate to define a standard event-based API for XML parsers that they called SAX (for *Simple API for XML*, see [↪SAX]). We will discuss this important topic in Section B.6.

Summary

In this chapter, we have looked at the two decades that preceded the advent of XML. We noted the first occurrence of specific markup, followed by the realization that a more generic approach had many benefits. This culminated after many years in the publication of the SGML standard in 1986. Then came the Web and the HTML earthquake. Finally it was realized that better formal foundations were needed if the Web was going to live up to its promise and provide a truly global environment for information exchange, storage, and handling: XML was born.

We have discussed in some detail the various componentes of XML. We have shown how to construct XML applications optimized for a given task by defining a dedicated language whose syntax is described with a document type definition (DTD). Various tools to help us develop, analyze, and debug DTDs have been discussed. In the final section we showed how XML parsers can be used to analyze the structure of an XML document. In Chapter 7 we will use this information to display the contents of an XML document in various output formats using style sheet languages.

CSS, DSSSL, and XSL: Doing it with style

In this chapter we first give a short historical overview of the main style sheet languages. Then we explain how you can use programming tools to associate formatting commands with XML documents. The remaining sections discuss the CSS, DSSSL, and XSL style sheet languages in some detail and show how they associate style with XML elements. In particular, we will show how to generate HTML and LaTeX output from XML source files.

7.1   Style sheet languages: A short history

As we explained in Section 6.3.1, when the first computer typesetting languages appeared, formatting commands and text were interspersed in the source documents; there was no direct way to express the structural relation between the various document components. Once the drawbacks of this situation were recognized, several authors developed higher-level markup systems, such as GML, LaTeX, and Scribe. The structural commands of these systems became macros that were expressed in function of commands written in a lower-level typesetting language (Script, TeX, and so on). This approach tried to separate content and presentation and contributed to making document sharing and reuse a lot easier.

Previously we discussed the markup languages SGML, XML, and HTML; we stressed that these languages, in principle, do not specify how the various document element types are to be represented visually (on paper or screen), aurally (e.g., for the visually impaired), and so on.

This statement is, of course, not completely true for HTML, since it started life as a simple communication language for disseminating information only on the Web, so structure and presentation were fully mixed. We have to only think about such elements as FONT, B, or attributes like ALIGN, COLOR, or WIDTH that have nothing to do with structural relations between document elements per se. The flaw in the approach of mixing presentation and structuring elements was soon realized, and one of the first standards to be developed by the W3C was CSS1, which became a recommendation in December 1996 ([↪CSS1], Lie and Bos (1997)). Since then the language has been substantially extended, and in May 1998, CSS2 [↪CSS2] was issued as a recommendation, replacing CSS1. CSS is a declarative language using a specialized ad hoc notation that is not user-extensible. It is targeted at HTML, but it can also be used with XML, provided that the XML document has a reasonably simple and linear structure that can be displayed without extensive manipulation.

On the other hand, the SGML community had been working on ways to associate presentation with SGML tags. An important landmark was the publication in 1990 of the Formatting Output Specification Instance (FOSI) specification [↪FOSI]. This American military standard, developed in the framework of the CALS initiative, proposes a way to render documents marked up in SGML. Each SGML document has to be delivered with a FOSI that also uses SGML syntax. A FOSI contains values for characteristics for every tag used in the SGML DTD, in particular for every context in which the tag has a unique formatting requirement. It also specifies characteristics for attributes that affect formatting.

For many years within the framework of ISO, research had gone on to develop a standard to describe general transformations between SGML documents and their formatting. This work culminated in the publication of the Document Style Semantics and Specification Language (DSSSL) standard (ISO/IEC:10179, 1996). However, the DSSSL Specification was considered too complex for use with Internet documents, and in 1996 a subset, DSSSL-online [↪DSSSLONL], also known as XS, was proposed for use with XML. Yet, as discussed in Section 7.5.2, DSSSL's (and hence XS's) expression language is based on Scheme, a dialect of the programming language Lisp. The syntax of Scheme looks rather unfamiliar to most end users of the Internet; therefore in August 1997, several major players in the XML world submitted a proposal for an *Extensible Stylesheet Language*, XSL for short, which adopted an XML-based syntax [↪XSL97]. It included most of the functionality of DSSSL-online and CSS1, but many desirable features for a style language for complex XML documents (as opposed to linear, one-pass HTML documents, the target of CSS), were still lacking.

After a lot of discussion, particularly on various XML-related Internet discussion lists, such as the XSL [↪XSLMAIL] and DSSSL [↪DSSSLLIST] mailing lists, an *XSL Requirements Summary* [↪XSLREQ] was published in May 1998. Soon thereafter, the W3C XSL Working Group started work on defining a first core version for XSL, which addresses part of the main issues raised in the Requirements document. A first working draft was released in mid-August 1998 [↪ XSLWD]. Some changes will surely still be made before the final specification is published in the second half of 1999. However, as we are convinced that the basic syntax of XSL will not change drastically, in Section 7.6 we will take a closer look at XSL, as it is defined in the current draft.

If you want to remain informed about the latest developments in the area of W3C style sheet activities, in particular CSS and XSL, consult the W3C Style Web Page [↪ W3CSTYLE].

It is evident that CSS and XSL are likely to coexist because they address somewhat different needs. CSS will remain the style sheet language for Web documents, especially for dynamic formatting of online documents for multiple media. On the other hand, XSL will allow you to handle complex documents, such as those using multiple columns, interleaved column sets with multiple text flows, footnote zones, synchronized marginalia, math formatting, and mixed vertical and horizontal writing directions. In other words XSL is the tool you need to work with genuinely internationalized automated print publishing.

The formatting parts of XSL and CSS are expected to become quite similar. In particular, the XSL Working Group will ensure that all CSS-based properties and values in XSL have the same meaning as in CSS. Conversely, additional formatting functionality that is included in XSL will be exposed and described in such a way that it can be used from CSS. The important point is that all formatting functionality described in W3C recommendations should use the same underlying model and the same terminology. Therefore a W3C Working Group has been set up to define a common *W3C Formatting Model*. It will underpin the specifications of all W3C specifications that expose formatting functionality, including HTML, MathML, CSS, XSL, SMIL (Synchronized Multimedia Integration Language), and SVG (Scalable Vector Graphics).

Detailed information about style sheets, especially CSS, as well as the old syntax of XSL, and some pages on DSSSL-online, can be found in Boumphrey (1998).

7.2   Programming or style sheets, which is better?

Users of SGML systems have, since the very beginning, been faced with the problem of printing or viewing their documents; many solutions have been developed over the years. A quite detailed overview of SGML filters for transforming SGML source documents into an output format can be found in Smith (1998), while Flynn (1998) provides you with a practical guide to the many (commercial and free) SGML and XML tools available. Most of these tools come with their own particular syntax for describing how SGML element types are to be rendered in the target language. The book reviews commercial systems that offer full-blown SGML environments, such as *Balise* [↪BALISE], *Omnimark* [↪OMNIMARK], *SGMLC* [↪SGMLC], as well as freely available tools based on Perl, `awk`, `nsgmls`, and so on. It should also be mentioned that several text processing and document handling tools, such as Adobe's *FrameMaker* [↪FRM] and its PDF language and Microsoft's *Office Suite*, plan to use XML internally to save the structural information about the source document. This is supposed to make the exchange of electronic documents between applications of different vendors a lot easier.

Most of the filters available to transform XML documents into a format to be viewed, printed, or otherwise made available on the Internet involve programming. Therefore we will start our overview by presenting a simple Perl-based system, where we ourselves will program what we want to output for each of the element types in the XML source document. In Section B.6 we will consider a more general approach based on Java.

In our first programming examples we target LaTeX and HTML directly, because it is easier for you to follow what we try to achieve. However, as we explain later, a more generic approach, based on the notion of *formatting objects*, is almost always a better investment because starting from a single style sheet several output formats can be generated merely by exchanging back-ends. Thus the choices between a programming language or a style sheet approach and between using flow objects or targeting a formatting language directly are questions you should consider before embarking on a project. By showing you several possibilities, we hope we will be able to give you a feeling for what is best in a given situation.

7.3   Formatting with Perl

In Section 6.6.5.2 we explained how XML parsers generate ESIS output to represent the structure of a document instance. David Megginson has developed SGMLSpm [↪SGMLSPM], an extensible Perl5 class library for processing the output from the `sgmls` and `nsgmls` parsers. The distribution comes with a simple sample application `sgmlspl`, that shows how to use the class library.

The application `sgmlspl` can be used to convert SGML documents to other formats by providing a *specification file*, where you specify in detail how each element, external data entity, `CDATA` string, and so on should be handled. Two example SGML files—`sgmlspm.sgml`, describing the class library, and `sgmlspl.sgml`, describing the application `sgmlspl` itself—come with the distribution. These files are marked up according to the DocBook DTD. There are also two Perl *specification files*, `tolatex.pl` and `tohtml.pl`, that provide code to transform the DocBook markup used in the two SGML files into LaTeX and HTML markup, respectively.

To show how the procedure operates we will use the `sgmlspl` application to prepare LaTeX and HTML formats for the `invitation` example that was introduced in Section 6.4.2.2 and used on several occasions in Chapter 6.

7.3.1   Principles of operation

The application sgmlspl uses an *event* model for treating the ESIS representation of a document. That is, each time the XML parser writes an ESIS "event" corresponding to a certain configuration in the XML source file, sgmlspl will "perform" an action, expressed as a set of Perl instructions defined in the *specification* file. In this file, which imports the SGMLSpm Perl5 class module, you can define Perl packages and routines, read files, and create variables. However, most of the time you can limit yourself to adding simple Perl code. Moreover, in the interest of maintainability and orthogonality, it is good practice to put all low-level formatting commands in language-specific output files (such as LaTeX packages or CSS style files).

The distribution comes with a skeleton file skel.pl that will generate a specification file containing stubs for all elements in the source XML document. The Perl module works with any parser that generates ESIS output. For our example we have chosen James Clark's nsgmls to run the following command sequence:

```
nsgmls invitation.xml | perl sgmlspl.pl skel.pl > invitation.pl
```

The first part of the command generates an ESIS output stream that is piped into the sgmlspl.pl Perl application. This itself is controlled by the file skel.pl. The output of this chain of programs is written in the output file invitation.pl. The exact contents of this customized skeleton file depend on the document instance because a new procedure reference is written to the file for each distinct "SGML" event in the source. Let us look at what we find inside that file.

```
 1    ###########################################################
 2    # SGMLSPL script produced automatically by the script sgmlspl.pl
 3    #
 4    # Document Type: invitation
 5    # Edited by:
 6    ###########################################################
 7
 8    use SGMLS;                      # Use the SGMLS package.
 9    use SGMLS::Output;              # Use stack-based output.
10
11    #
12    # Document Handlers.
13    #
14    sgml('start', sub {});
15    sgml('end', sub {});
16
17    #
18    # Element Handlers.
19    #
20
21    # Element: invitation
22    sgml('<invitation>', "");
23    sgml('</invitation>', "");
24
25    # Element: front
26    sgml('<front>', "");
27    sgml('</front>', "");
28
29      [ ... ]
```

The file contains a line calling the `sgml` procedure for each of the start tags (lines 22 and 26) and end tags (lines 23 and 27) of the elements in the XML source document. At the end of the file default handlers are provided for other events that can occur when parsing an XML document, such as character data, entities, and processing instructions.

7.3.2   Generating a LaTeX instance

Let us first concentrate on LaTeX and generate a version of the skeleton file for translating the XML file into a LaTeX file that can be printed. We want to put as little low-level LaTeX code at the Perl level as possible, so we will merely store necessary information in a set of variables and let the LaTeX package file `invitation.sty` deal with the formatting details. Following is the LaTeX incarnation `inv2lat.pl` of the skeleton file `invitation.pl`:

```
1   ########################################################################
2   # SGMLSPL script produced automatically by the script sgmlspl.pl
3   #
4   # Document Type: invitation --> customization for LaTeX
5   # Edited by: mg (August 14th 1998)
6   ########################################################################
7
8   use SGMLS;                        # Use the SGMLS package.
9   use SGMLS::Output;                # Use stack-based output.
10
11  #
12  # Document Handlers.
13  #
14  sgml('start', sub {});
15  sgml('end', sub {});
16
17  #
18  # Element Handlers.
19  #
20
21  # Element: invitation
22  sgml('<invitation>', "\\documentclass[]{article}\n" .
23                       "\\usepackage{invitation}\n" .
24                       "\\begin{document}\n");
25  sgml('</invitation>', "\\end{document}\n");
26
27  # Element: front
28  sgml('<front>', "\\begin{Front}\n");
29  sgml('</front>', "\\end{Front}\n");
30
31  # Element: to
32  sgml('<to>', "\\To{");
33  sgml('</to>', "}\n");
34
35  # Element: date
36  sgml('<date>', "\\Date{");
37  sgml('</date>', "}\n");
38
39  # Element: where
40  sgml('<where>', "\\Where{");
41  sgml('</where>', "}\n");
42
43  # Element: why
```

```
44    sgml('<why>', "\\Why{");
45    sgml('</why>', "}\n");
46
47    # Element: body
48    sgml('<body>', "\\begin{Body}\n");
49    sgml('</body>', "\\end{Body}\n");
50
51    # Element: par
52    sgml('<par>', "\\par ");
53    sgml('</par>', "\n");
54
55    # Element: emph
56    sgml('<emph>', "\\emph{");
57    sgml('</emph>', "}");
58
59    # Element: back
60    sgml('<back>', "\\begin{Back}\n");
61    sgml('</back>', "\\end{Back}\n");
62
63    # Element: signature
64    sgml('<signature>', "\\Signature{");
65    sgml('</signature>', "}\n");
66    #
67    # Default handlers
68    #
69    sgml('start_element',sub { die "Unknown element: " . $_[0]->name; });
70    sgml('cdata',sub { output $_[0]; });
71    sgml('re'," ");
72    sgml('pi',sub { die "Unknown processing instruction: " . $_[0]; });
73    sgml('entity',sub { die "Unknown external entity: " . $_[0]->name; });
74    sgml('conforming','');
75
76    1;
```

You can clearly see how the outer document element invitation has been made to correspond to the LaTeX document initialization, where we load the package invitation (lines 22–24). The front, body, and back elements become Front, Body, and Back environments (lines 28–29, 48–49, and 60–61, respectively). Most other elements are transformed into high-level LaTeX commands with the same name (lines 33–45, and 64–65). Only for the par and emph XML elements do we use the explicit basic LaTeX equivalents \par (line 52) and \emph (lines 56–57).

Now that we have prepared our Perl script we can run the command

```
nsgmls invitation.xml | perl sgmlspl.pl inv2lat.pl > invitation.tex
```

and obtain the following LaTeX file:

```
1    \documentclass[]{article}
2    \usepackage{invitation}
3    \begin{document}
4    \begin{Front}
5    \To{Anna, Bernard, Didier, Johanna}
6    \Date{Next Friday Evening at 8 pm}
7    \Where{The Web Cafe}
8    \Why{My first XML baby}
9    \end{Front}
10   \begin{Body}
11   \par I would like to invite you all to celebrate
12   the birth of \emph{Invitation}, my
```

```
13   first XML document child.
14   \par Please do your best to come and join me next Friday
15   evening. And, do not forget to bring your friends.
16   \par I \emph{really} look forward to see you soon!
17   \end{Body}
18   \begin{Back}
19   \Signature{Michel}
20   \end{Back}
21   \end{document}
```

Before formatting this file with LaTeX, we must also look at the LaTeX package file `invitation.sty`. In principle, thanks to the fact that we used high-level commands, we are free to format the above LaTeX markup in many ways. In the instance that follows we choose one possible implementation, and it is perhaps interesting to clarify a few points about it. We use a `tabular` environment to typeset the `front` material (lines 10–16). Moreover, at the end (lines 25–29) we store the content of the components of the `front` material, as well as of the signature in *global* variables (\gdef),[1] so that their value can be used inside the table (lines 12–15) and the boxed `signature` at the end (line 22). It is clear that it is straightforward to change the code shown. *Without having to modify* the XML source or Perl script upstream, you can command almost any presentation you want.

```
1    % invitation.sty
2    % Package to format invitation.xml
3    \setlength{\parskip}{1ex}
4    \setlength{\parindent}{0pt}
5    \pagestyle{empty}%% Turn off page numbering
6    \RequirePackage{array}
7    \newenvironment{Front}%
8      {\begin{center}\huge \sffamily Memorandum\end{center}
9       \begin{flushleft}
10      \begin{tabular}{@{}>{\bfseries}p{.2\linewidth}@{}p{.8\linewidth}@{}}\hline
11     }
12     {To whom:  & \@To      \\
13      Occasion: & \@Why     \\
14      Venue:    & \@Where   \\
15      When:     & \@Date    \\\hline
16      \end{tabular}
17      \end{flushleft}
18     }
19   \newenvironment{Body}{\vspace*{\parskip}}{\vspace*{\parskip}}
20   \newenvironment{Back}
21     {\begin{flushleft}}
22     {\hspace*{.5\linewidth}\fbox{\emph{\@Sig}}
23      \end{flushleft}
24     }
25   \newcommand{\To}[1]{\gdef\@To{#1}}
26   \newcommand{\Date}[1]{\gdef\@Date{#1}}
27   \newcommand{\Where}[1]{\gdef\@Where{#1}}
28   \newcommand{\Why}[1]{\gdef\@Why{#1}}
29   \newcommand{\Signature}[1]{\gdef\@Sig{#1}}
```

---

[1] Here the \gdef TeX commands define in a global way the command sequence given immediately following the value of its argument. For convenience, inside LaTeX package and class files, the @ character is used as a letter to define internal command names that are associated with user-callable commands (see Goossens et al. (1994), pages 15–16).

Memorandum

To whom:	Anna, Bernard, Didier, Johanna
Occasion.	My first XML baby
Venue:	The Web Cafe
When:	Next Friday Evening at 8 pm

I would like to invite you all to celebrate the birth of *Invitation*, my first XML document child.

Please do your best to come and join me next Friday evening. And, do not forget to bring your friends.

I *really* look forward to see you soon!

Michel

Figure 7.1: XML file formatted with LaTeX using the `sgmlspl` procedure

After compiling the LaTeX file with TeX using the given package instance, we obtain the result shown in Figure 7.1. The frame is not part of the source but was added for clarity.

7.4 Cascading Style Sheets

The second version of the Cascading Style Sheets specification (CSS2, [↪CSS2]), published in May 1998, is a style sheet language that associates style (rendering information) with structured documents (primarily HTML, but also XML). It is important to realize that the CSS model allows both producers and consumers of a document to intervene in the process of controlling presentation. On the one hand, authors or publishers often prefer to define a set of style characteristics that give a distinctive and recognizable look to their publications. On the other hand, readers may have different expectations and be guided by their personal tastes, limitations in their software or hardware, or other physical constraints (color blindness, impaired sight, and so on).

Therefore conflicts between different style sheets must be resolved. That is where the *cascading* in CSS comes into play. CSS has the possibility to assign an implicit or explicit priority to each style element. The style that has the highest priority wins. By default, the author's style sheet overrides declarations in the user's style sheet. However, the author and user can associate `!important` keywords with certain rules, and for those the user specifications take precedence.

In the following, we review those aspects of the CSS2 specification that we need to address the simple rendering of XML documents. For a complete treatment, the full specification or one of the many books on CSS should be consulted.

7.4.1   The basic structure of a CSS style sheet

A CSS style sheet consists of a list of *statements*. These statements can be of two forms: *at-rules* and *rule sets*.

At-rules start with an @ sign followed immediately by an identifier (e.g., @import, @charset, @media) and terminate with a semicolon. CSS-aware software must ignore at-rules that it does not recognize. Especially interesting is the @import rule that allows style rules to be imported from other style sheets. All @import rules must precede all rule sets in the style sheet and must refer to the URI of the style sheet to be included. For instance,

```
@import "mystyle.css";
```

will import the CSS style sheet mystyle.css.

A rule set consists of a *selector* followed by a *declaration block*. A declaration block starts with a left curly brace {, follows a set of semicolon-separated *declarations*, and terminates with a right curly brace }. A selector, whose syntax will be detailed following, is everything preceding the open curly brace of the declaration block. If the CSS application cannot parse a selector, it must ignore the complete rule set, that is, all declarations in the declaration block.

```
selector {declaration 1; declaration 2, ...}
```

A declaration consists of a *property*, followed by a colon (:), followed by a *value*.

```
selector {property 1: value 1; property 2: value: 2}
```

A property is an identifier. The syntax of value depends on the property in question. CSS applications must ignore declarations with an invalid property name or invalid value syntax.

7.4.1.1   Selectors in more detail

A selector is a pattern to select elements in the document tree to which a given style rule should be applied. If a certain element fulfills all the conditions of the pattern, then the selector is said to *match* the element.

A selector is a chain of one or more *simple selectors* separated by combinators (whitespace, >, or +).

A *simple selector* is either an element-type selector or a *universal selector* followed immediately by zero or more *attribute selectors*, id selectors, or *pseudoclasses*, in any order.

Selections are made more specific by prepending a supplementary simple selector or combinator to an existing selector. The last simple selector can also have one pseudoelement appended.

Several declarations for a same selector can be grouped, for instance,

```
front {font-size: 12pt}
front {font-style: bold}
front {text-indent: 0pt}
```

is equivalent to

```
front {font-size: 12pt; font-style: bold; text-indent: 0pt}
```

Similarly, identical declarations for multiple selectors can also be grouped. Thus the four statements:

```
date    {text-align: left}
to      {text-align: left}
where   {text-align: left}
why     {text-align: left}
```

can be collapsed into the following single rule:

```
date, to, where, why {text-align: left}
```

The *universal* selector (*) matches the name of *any* single element in the document tree. A *type* selector matches the name of, at most, *one* element type in the document tree.

Ancestor relationships can be conveniently expressed by enumeration. As an example, "A D" states that element type D can be any descendant of its ancestor A.

```
front emph {font-style: italic}
body  emph {font-style: italic; color: blue}
```

The first rules specify that emph elements with a front ancestor are represented in an italic font style, whereas emph elements with a body ancestor will be in an italic font and painted in blue.

Direct *parent-child* relations are expressed with the > notation. For instance,

```
body > par > emph {font-style: italic; color: red}
```

specifies that emph elements that have a par parent and a body grandparent are in red italic type.

Adjacent siblings can be selected with the + notation. For instance, the text associated with a why element that is immediately preceded by a where in the document tree will be painted in yellow by the following declaration:

```
where + why {background-color: yellow}
```

7.4.1.2 Handling attributes

You can also associate a rule with an element for which an attribute has a certain value. The syntax allows several ways to select elements. The more important are shown in the following example:

```
1   invitation[to] {font-size: 14pt}
2   invitation[signature="Peter"] {text-align: right}
3   invitation[why~="birthday"][date~="Friday"] {background-color: green}
```

Line 1 chooses all invitation elements with an attribute to, independent of the value specified for that attribute. Line 2 chooses invitation elements whose signature attribute is *exactly* Peter. Finally, line 3 chooses invitation elements with a why attribute containing the string "birthday" and a date attribute containing the string "Friday."

To differentiate between default and explicitly specified attribute values, one can specify a general rule for an element and then specialize it by associating it with an attribute.

```
1   invitation {text-align: left}
2   invitation[why] {text-align: center}
```

The general rule (line 1) specifies that invitation elements should be set left justified, whereas invitation elements with a why attribute specified should be center aligned (line 2).

One can select specific elements in the document tree with an id selector and can associate specific styling information with them. In this case the DTD must declare id attributes for the elements in question. In particular, the HTML 4 DTD declares id attributes for all its elements. Hence, it is straightforward to associate a specific style with an element by using its id attribute. The syntax that is used in the style sheet is to precede the corresponding definition with a hash sign (#), for instance,

```
1   *[color~='myblue'] {color="blue"}
2   sect1#specialblue  {color="navyblue"}
```

Line 1 defines the characteristics of *all* elements (we use the universal selector *) in the document with a color attribute equal to myblue. Line 2 selects among the sect1 element types the one that has an id attribute equal to specialblue.

7.4.1.3   Pseudoclasses and pseudoelements

The CSS2 Specification allows for a more fine-grained selection of information present in the document by using *pseudoelements* (e.g., the first letter of a paragraph) and *pseudoclasses* (choosing elements by characteristics that cannot usually be deduced from the element's name, its attribute, or its content). A few examples follow:

```
1   body > par:first-child          {text-indent: 0pt}
2   body * emph                      {color: black}
3   section > par:first-child emph   {color: red}
```

Line 1 assigns a text indentation of zero points to a par element that is the first child of a body element. Line 2 says that all emph elements that have a body element as an ancestor should be shown in black. Finally, line 3 specifies that all emph elements inside a "first-child" par element inside a section element should be in red.

Some other pseudoclasses follow:

:link   unvisited link;

:visited visited link;

:active   element activated by the user; and

:focus   element in focus (accepting events).

See Section 5.11 of the CSS2 Specification for more details.

Similarly, pseudoelements allow one to single out the first line or the first letter of a document element or to generate text. See Section 5.12 of the CSS2 Specification.

7.4.1.4   HTML's span and div elements and class attribute

Today, few browsers support the XML document model, so most documents must still be converted to HTML for viewing. As the HTML tag set is fixed, the HTML community came up with a convenient way to "extend" the language with the introduction of the span and div element types and the class attribute. We will use this combination in the CSS-based formatting examples in the following sections, so we want to explain its basis.

CSS HTML *classes*[2] allow you to create grouping schemes among styled HTML element types by specializing the style definition of a particular class with respect to the generic definition for the same element types that do not belong to that class. In CSS1 style sheets, a class name is preceded by a period (.), while CSS2 deprecates that format and replaces it with the attribute notation [class~=value] to identify class-specific commands.

---

[2]This technique can also be used with XML by declaring a class attribute for each element in the DTD, as is the case in the HTML 4 DTD.

For instance, in a style sheet you could specify the following:

```
1  par {font-family: serif; font-size: 10pt}
2  to  {font-family: sans-serif; font-weight: bold}
3  [class="red"]    {color: red}   /* generic class specification    */
4  to[class="green"] {color: green} /* class specification to element */
5  .blue {color: blue}  /* Deprecated syntax, HTML only, DO NOT USE!  */
```

These specifications are used as follows (remember an XML DTD must declare a class element for each element for this to work):

```
1  <par>Serif 10pt font.</par>
2  <par class="blue">Serif 10pt but in blue.</par>
3  <to class="red">Sans-serif, bold and in red.</to>
4  <to class="green">Sans-serif, bold and in green.</to>
```

With HTML 4, the span element allows you to control the style of an inline text fragment, for instance,

```
1  <p>Usual style with a <span class="spec">bit of text rendered using
2  the ''spec'' style rule.</span> Back to the previous style.</p>
```

On the other hand, the HTML 4 div element lets you apply a style to a whole block of text, which can include other HTML elements, as follows:

```
1  <div class="mydiv">
2  <p>The style ''mydiv'' controls this whole text block,
3  including <q>this quote</q> and <cite>this citation</cite>.</p>
4  <p>It even extends over several paragraphs, since here also
5  the same ''mydiv'' style rules.</p>
6  </div>
```

In HTML the class, id, and style attributes can be used with the <span> and <div> tags. This allows for an implicit extension mechanism for HTML, by allowing you to define logical containers and apply a customized style to their contents.

7.4.2   Associating style sheets with a document

In HTML, <LINK> or <STYLE> *tags* inside the document's HEAD element are available to associate a style sheet with the document instance. Moreover, locally you can use STYLE *attributes* to customize presentation for a single element. This latter practice is, however, discouraged, since it mixes form and content in a document. It is much better to use the id attribute to associate style information with one or more elements.

On the document level, a W3C Note [↪XMLSTYLE] by James Clark proposes to use an XML processing instruction with a target xml-stylesheet to provide the same functionality as the HTML <LINK> tag. For instance, the semantics of the following HTML 4 <LINK> tag:

```
<LINK href="mystyle.css" rel="stylesheet" type="text/css">
```

would correspond to the following XML processing instruction:

```
<?xml-stylesheet href="mystyle.css" type="text/css"?>
```

Multiple processing instructions are allowed by using the `alternate` attribute on the processing instruction `xml-stylesheet`. The `title` attribute in the example is optional.

```
1  <?xml-stylesheet alternate="yes"    title="alt1"
2                   href="special1.css" type="text/css"?>
3  <?xml-stylesheet alternate="yes"    title="alt2"
4                   href="special2.css" type="text/css"?>
5  <?xml-stylesheet href="generic.css"  type="text/css"?>
```

7.4.3   A quick look at CSS properties

CSS2 has over one hundred properties (see Appendix F of the CSS2 Specification for a tabular overview). This section takes a quick look at the more frequently used properties—those with which most LaTeX users will be familiar and those which we will use in our examples.

7.4.3.1   Setting background/foreground colors and images

The `color` property controls the foreground color of an element, while the `background-color` property controls the background color or image of an element.

Colors are specified by a predefined name or a triplet value in rgb (red-green-blue) color space, for example, the box element can have its text and background given in the following (equivalent) ways:

```
1  box {color: red; background-color: yellow}
2  box {color: #FF0000; background-color: #FFFF00}
3  box {color: rgb(255,0,0); background-color: rgb(255,255,0)}
4  box {color: rgb(100%,0,0); background-color: rgb(100%,100%,0)}
```

Line 1 uses one of the sixteen predefined color names in HTML and CSS. Lines 2–4 express colors in function of the rgb color model, lines 2–3 as a number between zero (no such color component) and 255 (full quota of the given color component). In particular, line 2 uses a compact hexadecimal notation, while on line 3 a decimal representation is chosen. Line 4 expresses the same colors as percentages of the primary components.

7.4.3.2 Fonts

font-family	Name of the typeface or font family. It can be a specific name, such as Baskerville or Helvetica, or one of the following generic names: serif, sans-serif, monospace, cursive, or fantasy.
font-style	Style of the typeface: normal, italic, or oblique.
font-variant	Variation of typeface: normal or small-caps.
font-stretch	Amount of condensing or expanding.
font-weight	Weight (boldness) of the typeface. It can be a keyword (bold, lighter,...) or a number from the series 100, 200,..., 900 (higher numbers are darker).
font-size	Size of the typeface. It can be specified in absolute (12pt, x-small) or relative units (larger, 120%,...).

Examples of definitions for different kinds of paragraphs follow. You can see that font weight, stretch, and size can all be expressed absolutely or relative to the value of the same characteristic of the parent element.

```
 1  P[class="normal"]
 2    {font-family: serif}
 3  P[class="italic"]
 4    {font-family: serif; font-style: italic}
 5  P[class="bold"]
 6    {font-family: serif; font-weight: bold}
 7  P[class="explight"]
 8    {font-family: serif; font-weight: lighter; font-stretch: expanded}
 9  P[class="ttsc14"]
10    {font-family: monospace; font-variant: small-caps; font-size: 14pt}
11  P[class="ssolarger"]
12    {font-family: sans-serif; font-style: oblique; font-size: larger}
```

There also exists a shorthand notation "font," which sets font-style, font-variant, font-weight, font-size, line-height, and font-family in one go, a usual practice in traditional typography. All properties that are not explicitly specified are set to their default values. Let us consider the following example:

```
P {font: normal small-caps bigger/120% Helvetica}
```

This sets the font-variant to "small-caps," the font-size one step "bigger" than that of the parent element, the line-height to "120%" of that font size (using the conventional typographer's notation *font-size/line-height*), and the font-family to "Helvetica." The keyword "normal" applies to the two remaining properties, font-style and font-weight.

7.4.3.3 Text and visual formatting

`line-height`	Minimal height of each generated inline box. This is also used to specify the normal spacing between lines of text.
`text-indent`	Indentation of first line in a block of text.
`text-align`	Alignment of inline content of a block (`left`, `right`, `center`, or `justify`).
`text-decoration`	Decorations (`underline`, `overline`, `blink`, `line-through`).
`letter-spacing`	Spacing between text characters.
`word-spacing`	Spacing between words.
`text-transform`	Capitalization control (`capitalize`, `uppercase`, `lowercase`, `none`).
`vertical-align`	Vertical alignment of inline boxes (`baseline`, `top`, `middle`, `bottom`, and so on).

An example for a title heading follows:

```
title {text-decoration: underline; text-transform: uppercase;
    letter-spacing: .1em; word-spacing: .5em}
```

The text of the `title` element will be uppercase and underlined. The spacing between each letter will be *increased* by .1 em with respect to the normal spacing of the font, while .5 em will be *added* to the default space between words.

7.4.3.4 Boxes

CSS's formatting model is based on rectangular boxes that are generated from elements in the document tree. Each box has a content area and is surrounded optionally by margin, border, or padding areas. Box properties control the dimensions and characteristics of these rectangles and determine how the content of the element is formatted to fit into the provided space.

The following properties:

`margin-top`, `margin-bottom`, `margin-left`, `margin-right`, `margin`
    control the size of the top, bottom, left, right, and all margins.

`padding-top`, `padding-bottom`, `padding-left`, `padding-right`, `padding`
    set padding on the top, bottom, left, right, and all sides of the element.

`border-top`, `border-bottom`, `border-left`, `border-right`, `border`
    specify width, style, and color of the border on the top, bottom, left, right, or all sides of the element.

There are more specific `border-width`, `border-style`, and `border-color` box properties to set each of these characteristics separately.

The content width and height of a box are specified with the width and height properties (e.g., for scaling images). One can also make box material shift with respect of the current line using the float property, which can have as values left, right, or none, meaning no float.

An example is the following itemize list element and its item child, for which we allow two variants: with and without a border.

```
1   itemize {margin: 1em 1em 1em 1em; padding: .3em}
2   item    {margin: .5; padding: .2em 0em .2em .2em}
3   item[class=border]
4           {border-style: dotted; border-width: thin; border-color: red}
```

Line 1 specifies that all margins of the itemize element are one quad (1 em) wide, with a padding equal to .3 em at all sides.[3] Line 2 specifies a margin of half a quad for the item element inside the itemize element, with a padding equal to .2 em at all sides except the right, where the text flows up to the margin. Finally, lines 3–4 specify that for an item element of class border, on top of the characteristics of line 2, a border consisting of a thin, red sequence of dots will be drawn.

7.4.3.5 Displays

The display property specifies how a certain block-level element has to be shown (displayed). This property can have many values, in particular, inline, block, run-in, and compact. A special value is none, which results in the element and its descendants generating *no* boxes in the output (formatting) tree and thus having no effect whatsoever on the layout. This does not imply that the material in question is invisible, since visibility itself is controlled by the visibility property, whose values are visible, hidden, and collapse.

7.4.4 CSS style sheets for formatting XML documents

With the information of the previous section we can now write a CSS style sheet for formatting an XML document. Once more, let us take our invitation document and transform it into HTML, the only language most present-day browsers display succesfully.

We use the same procedure as in Section 7.3, this time with the following Perl script inv1html.pl:

```
1   ######################################################################
2   # SGMLSPL script produced automatically by the script sgmlspl.pl
3   #
4   # Document Type: inv1html.pl (for HTML/CSS formatting)
```

---

[3]When only one value is specified, it applies to all four sides; with two values the top and bottom are set to the first value, the left and right to the second value; with three values, the top is set to the first, the left and right to the second, and the bottom to the third value; four values are assigned in the order top, right, bottom, left.

```
5    # Edited by: mg (24 Aug 98)
6    ##############################################################
7
8    use SGMLS;                    # Use the SGMLS package.
9    use SGMLS::Output;            # Use stack-based output.
10
11   #
12   # Document Handlers.
13   #
14   sgml('start', "<HTML>\n<HEAD>\n" .
15                   "<TITLE> Invitation (sgmlpl/CSS formatting) </TITLE>\n" .
16                   "<LINK href=\"invit.css\" rel=\"style-sheet\" type=\"text/css\">\n" .
17                   "<!-- 24 August 1998 mg -->\n" .
18                   "</HEAD>\n");
19   sgml('end', "</HTML>");
20
21   #
22   # Element Handlers.
23   #
24
25   sgml('<invitation>', "<BODY>\n<H1>INVITATION</H1>\n");
26   sgml('</invitation>', "</BODY>\n");
27
28   sgml('<front>', "<P><TABLE>\n<TBODY>\n");
29   sgml('</front>', "</TBODY>\n</TABLE>\n");
30
31   sgml('<to>', "<TR><TD class=\"front\">To: </TD>\n<TD>");
32   sgml('</to>', "</TD></TR>\n");
33
34   sgml('<date>', "<TR><TD class=\"front\">When: </TD>\n<TD>");
35   sgml('</date>', "</TD></TR>\n");
36
37   sgml('<where>', "<TR><TD class=\"front\">Venue: </TD>\n<TD>");
38   sgml('</where>', "</TD></TR>\n");
39
40   sgml('<why>', "<TR><TD class=\"front\">Occasion: </TD>\n<TD>");
41   sgml('</why>', "</TD></TR>\n");
42
43   sgml('<body>', "");
44   sgml('</body>', "");
45
46   sgml('<par>', "<P>");
47   sgml('</par>', "</P>\n");
48
49   sgml('<emph>', "<EM>");
50   sgml('</emph>', "</EM>");
51
52   sgml('<back>', "");
53   sgml('</back>', "");
54
55   sgml('<signature>', "<P CLASS=\"signature\">");
56   sgml('</signature>', "</P>\n");
57
58   sgml('start_element',sub { die "Unknown element: "  @_[0]->name; });
59   sgml('cdata',sub { output $_[0]; });
60
61   1;
```

On lines 14-18 we initialize the HTML document and define its header. On line 16 in particular, we associate the style sheet invit.css with the HTML file. On line 25 we start the body of the document with an H1 element, which will be typeset in a particular way. We decide to use a TABLE (line 28) for formatting the front material and exploit the HTML/CSS class mechanism to control the formatting of the left-most cells in the table (lines 31, 34, 37, and 40). The paragraphs (lines 46–47) and emphatic text (lines 49–50) elements are translated into their HTML equivalents. The signature is translated into a special `signature` class P element (line 55). The character data of the input file is transferred to the HTML file with the output statement on line 59.

When we run the command:

```
nsgmls invitation.xml | perl sgmlspl.pl inv1html.pl > invcss.html
```

we obtain the HTML file shown here:

```
1    <HTML>
2    <HEAD>
3    <TITLE> Invitation (sgmlpl/CSS formatting) </TITLE>
4    <LINK href="invit.css" rel="style-sheet" type="text/css">
5    <!-- 24 August 1998 mg -->
6    </HEAD>
7    <BODY>
8    <H1>INVITATION</H1>
9    <P><TABLE>
10   <TBODY>
11   <TR><TD class="front">To: </TD>
12   <TD>Anna, Bernard, Didier, Johanna</TD></TR>
13   <TR><TD class="front">When: </TD>
14   <TD>Next Friday Evening at 8 pm</TD></TR>
15   <TR><TD class="front">Venue: </TD>
16   <TD>The Web Cafe</TD></TR>
17   <TR><TD class="front">Occasion: </TD>
18   <TD>My first XML baby</TD></TR>
19   </TBODY>
20   </TABLE>
21   <P>I would like to invite you all to celebrate
22   the birth of <EM>Invitation</EM>, my
23   first XML document child.</P>
24   <P>Please do your best to come and join me next Friday
25   evening. And, do not forget to bring your friends.</P>
26   <P>I <EM>really</EM> look forward to see you soon!</P>
27   <P CLASS="signature">Michel</P>
28   </BODY>
29   </HTML>
```

Finally, we have a look at the style sheet file `invit.css`, which serves as a link between the input XML source and the way the HTML output file will be displayed.

```
1    /* invit.css: CSS style-sheet for invitation1 in HTML */
2    BODY {margin-top: 1em;     /* global page parameters */
3          margin-bottom: 1em;
4          margin-left: 1em;
5          margin-right: 1em;
6          font-family: serif;
7          line-height: 1.1;
8          color: black;
9    }
10   H1   {text-align: center;  /* for global title   */
11         font-size: x-large;
12   }
13   P    {text-align: justify; /* paragraphs in body */
```

```
14          margin-top: 1em;
15     }
16     TD[class="front"] {        /* table data in front matter */
17          text-align: left;
18          font-weight: bold,
19     }
20     EM    {font-style: italic;   /* emphasis in body    */
21     }
22     P[class="signature"] {      /* signature           */
23          text-align: right;
24          font-weight: bold;
25          margin-top: 1em;
26     }
```

Lines 2–8 set some global characteristics for the whole HTML document. We use the H1 (lines 10–11) element for making a large centered title. The treatment of paragraphs (lines 13–14) and emphatic text (line 20) is straightforward. Table data elements TD of class "front" (lines 16–18) have their text in bold and left-aligned, while paragraphs P of class "signature" have bold text, but right-aligned. However, current versions of both Netscape and Microsoft Internet Explorer do not yet implement the complete CSS2 Specification. Therefore for using the CSS style sheet shown earlier for viewing the HTML file with those browsers, we had to use old CSS1 syntax when specifying class-specific declarations: TD.front (on line 16) and P.signature (on line 22).

The result of viewing the HTML file invcss.html with a browser that applies the CSS style sheet invit.css is shown in Figure 7.2.

7.4.5 The invitation example revisited

The invitation XML document and its DTD, first introduced in Section 6.4.2.2, contain only elements and do not use attributes. Let us introduce a variant of the invitation DTD, where most of the elements have been replaced by attributes. It is equivalent informationwise to the original version.[4] The new DTD, invitation2.dtd, follows:

```
1    <!-- invitation2 DTD -->
2    <!ELEMENT invitation (par+)>
3    <!ATTLIST invitation date      CDATA #REQUIRED
4                         signature CDATA #REQUIRED
5                         to        CDATA #REQUIRED
6                         where     CDATA #REQUIRED
7                         why CDATA #IMPLIED >
8    <!ELEMENT par   (#PCDATA|emph)*>
9    <!ELEMENT emph (#PCDATA)>
```

We are now reduced to three elements: invitation (line 2), par (line 8), and emph (line 9). All supplementary information is specified as attributes of the invitation

---

[4]See also Sections B.4.4.2 and B.4.4.3 in the Appendix where we develop two alternate DTDs for BIBTEX using a similar strategy.

Figure 7.2: XML file formatted with HTML using the `sgmlspl` procedure

element (lines 3–7). The XML document `invitation2.xml` itself is marked up relative to this DTD as follows:

```
1    <?xml version="1.0"?>
2    <!DOCTYPE invitation SYSTEM "invitation2.dtd">
3    <invitation to="Anna, Bernard, Didier, Johanna"
4              date="Next Friday Evening at 8 pm"
5              where="The Web Cafe"
6              why="My first XML baby"
7              signature="Michel"
8    >
9    <par>
10   I would like to invite you all to celebrate
11   the birth of <emph>Invitation</emph>, my
12   first XML document child.
13   </par>
14   <par>
15   Please do your best to come and join me next Friday
16   evening. And, do not forget to bring your friends.
17   </par>
18   <par>
19   I <emph>really</emph> look forward to see you soon!
20   </par>
21   </invitation>
```

One could argue that the structure of the document is a little less clear and that the attributes do not add anything, but it will serve as an example to show how attributes are handled. We emphasize once more that the information content is completely identical to that of the document on page 254.

7.4.6   Generating HTML with another document instance

To show that the principle of reusing style sheets also works for CSS, let us consider the alternate form `invitation2.xml` of the invitation example as introduced in the previous section. Once more we use David Megginson's SGMLSpm Perl module but with a different user script `inv2html.pl`, as follows:

```
1    ##########################################################################
2    # SGMLSPL script produced automatically by the script sgmlspl.pl
3    #
4    # Document Type: inv2html.pl (for HTML/CSS formatting)
5    # Edited by: mg (25 Aug 1998)
6    ##########################################################################
7
8    use SGMLS;                       # Use the SGMLS package.
9    use SGMLS::Output;               # Use stack-based output.
10
11   #
12   # Document Handlers.
13   #
14   sgml('start', sub [
15       output "<HTML>\n<HEAD>\n";
16       output "<TITLE> Invitation (sgmlpl/CSS formatting) </TITLE>\n";
17       output "<LINK href=\"invit.css\" rel=\"style sheet\" type=\"text/css\">\n";
18       output "<!-- 24 August 1998 mg  >\n";
19       output "</HEAD>\n";
20   });
21   sgml('end', "</HTML>");
22
23   #
24   # Element Handlers.
25   #
26
27   # Element: invitation
28   sgml('<invitation>', sub {
29       my ($element,$event) = @_;
30       # First save the information for further use
31       # local variables
32       my $date  = $element->attribute('date')->value;
33       my $to    = $element->attribute('to')->value;
34       my $where = $element->attribute('where')->value;
35       my $why   = $element->attribute('why')->value;
36       # Global variable (saved for end of document)
37       $main::GLoig  = $element->attribute('signature')->value;
38       # Output the HTML commands needed for the front matter
39       output "<BODY>\n<H1>INVITATION</H1>\n";
40       output "<P><TABLE>\n<TBODY>\n";
41       output "<TR><TD class=\"front\"> To: </TD>\n<TD>$to</TD></TR>\n";
42       output "<TR><TD class=\"front\">When: </TD>\n<TD>$date</TD></TR>\n";
43       output "<TR><TD class=\"front\">Venue: </TD>\n<TD>$where</TD></TR>\n";
44       output "<TR><TD class=\"front\">Occasion: </TD>\n<TD>$why</TD></TR>\n";
45       output "</TBODY>\n</TABLE>\n";
46   });
47
```

```
48    sgml('</invitation>', sub{ # signature and end of document
49          output "<P CLASS=\"signature\">$main::GLsig</P>\n";
50          output "</BODY>\n";
51    });
52
53    # Elements: par and emph
54    sgml('<par>', "<P>");
55    sgml('</par>', "</P>\n");
56
57    sgml('<emph>', "<EM>");
58    sgml('</emph>', "</EM>");
59
60    sgml('cdata',sub { output $_[0]; });
61    1;
```

As with the script inv1html.pl shown in Section 7.4.4, we also need to handle attribute values here. As the attributes are specified on the <invitation>
tag (lines 3–7 of the invitation2.xml source document on page 310), we
have to extract these attributes when the invitation start element event occurs
(lines 28–46). First, the element handle is extracted on line 29 into the variable
$element. The value of the attributes is accessed using the value method of the
SGMLS_Attribute class. The class is obtained by applying the attribute method
of the SGMLS_Element class (lines 32–35 for the local variables—those preceded
with the my specifier—and line 37 for the global variable $main::GLsig, whose
value we store until we encounter the end of the invitation element, where we
use it to output the signature on line 49). Thus we generate essentially the same
HTML code as in Section 7.4.4. In particular we reference (line 17) the same CSS
style sheet (invit.css) as before. When we treat the XML source with the earlier
Perl script, we obtain a file inv2css.html as follows:

```
nsgmls invitation2.xml | perl sgmlspl.pl inv2html.pl > inv2css.html
```

Viewing this HTML file with a browser, we observe a layout identical to the one
shown in Figure 7.2. This clearly shows that CSS styles are very convenient to
manage the display characteristics of documents in a global way.

7.5   Document Style Semantics and Specification Language

Document Style Semantics and Specification Language (DSSSL) ISO/IEC:10179
(1996) is an international ISO/IEC standard to specify the formatting and transformation of SGML (and hence XML) documents. As we explained before, an SGML
document should completely ignore the rendering and other processing aspects
of its data. DSSSL's two basic aims are to format SGML documents for paper or
electronic media presentation and to transform SGML documents between markup
schemes defined by different DTDs. DSSSL offers a standardized framework and

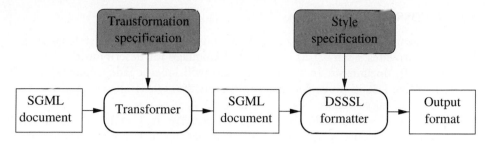

Figure 7.3: The DSSSL process

methods for associating processing information with SGML element instances or
general classes of element types.

This section contains an introduction to DSSSL that should allow you to
develop a simple DSSSL style sheet for your XML document. More in-depth
tutorial-like introductions to DSSSL have been written by Daniel M. Germán
[↪DSSSLTUTB] and Paul Prescod [↪DSSSLTUTA]. A lot of DSSSL-related information is also available from James Clark's DSSSL Web page [↪DSSSLCLARK].

7.5.1   The components of DSSSL

DSSSL provides four distinct areas of standardization (clauses that follow refer to
the DSSSL specification (ISO/IEC:10179, 1996)):

1. A language and processing model for transforming SGML documents into
    other SGML documents. Here we use a transformation language and a trans-
    formation specification, which is a list of associations (Clause 11).

2. A language for specifying how to apply formatting characteristics to an SGML
    document. The formatting process is controlled by a style specification, which
    contains a list of construction rules. DSSSL standardizes only the form and
    semantics of the style language, *not* the formatting process itself (Clause 12).

3. A Standard Document Query Language (SDQL) for identifying portions of
    an SGML document. SDQL allows for easy navigation through the hierarchi-
    cal SGML structure and lets one identify pieces of a document for processing.
    DSSSL also defines a subset called the *core query language* (Clause 10).

4. An expression language used in the previous languages to create and manipulate
    objects. DSSSL also defines a subset called the *core expression language*. DSSSL's
    expression language uses a side-effect-free subset of the Scheme Programming
    Language (Clause 8).

Figure 7.3 shows the complete DSSSL process schematically.

7.5.1.1   DSSSL's style language

In the following discussion we shall be mainly interested in DSSSL's style language because it provides a standardized, powerful language for describing the formatting of SGML documents. In Section 7.5.3 we will look at Jade, a powerful and freely available DSSSL processor that implements the style language. It will be the workhorse for our examples.

Central to the style language is the *flow object tree*. It is an abstract representation of how the source document and the formatting specifications are merged. At the nodes of this tree we find *flow objects* that provide a standard framework for describing document layout with constructs, such as page sequences, paragraphs, tables, and artwork. Each flow object has a set of characteristics, such as page margins, paragraph indentation, a table border, and a picture's height and width (these are similar to the CSS properties of Section 7.4.3).

The result of formatting a flow object is a sequence of *areas*. An area is a rectangular box with a fixed width and height. It comes in two types: display and inline.

Display areas are not directly parts of lines; they have an inherent absolute orientation, and their positioning is specified by *area containers*. These containers have their own coordinate system with a filling direction that defines their starting edge. They can have a fixed size or be allowed to grow. Various writing modes are possible inside such a container.

Inline areas are parts of lines. An inline area has reference points on its edges so that subsequent inline areas can be positioned to form lines. Kerning can influence this positioning.

Flow objects that are formatted to produce a sequence of inline areas are said to be *inlined*, while flow objects formatted to produce a sequence of display areas are said to be *displayed*. The fact that a flow object class instance can be only inlined, only displayed, or both inlined and displayed depends on the characteristics of the flow object or on the flow object attached to it.

7.5.1.2   DSSSL's other components

The *transformation language* is a standard language for transforming the SGML markup, according to a given DTD, into a markup following another DTD. For instance, translating a DocBook document into "equivalent" TEI markup or, more probably, generating an HTML instance, because today most browsers support only that language. Formally the transformation language, especially in its expression part that is based on Scheme, has a lot in common with the style language.

DSSSL specifications operate on trees of nodes to create new trees, such as the "flow object tree" that represents the formatted document instance or a new SGML document, obtained by a transformation. The nodes are organized into a specialized data structure, a "grove," a kind of tree of trees, or more technically, a possibly cyclic directed graph of nodes. Each node can have a set of "properties," that can have "atomic" values (such as strings, booleans, or integers), or be lists of nodes or references to nodes. This document model with groves as a parse tree data structure in the form of a graph of nodes with properties was developed for the specific needs of DSSSL and HyTime [↪HYTIME]. These two standards share the same fundamental abstract data view of SGML documents (for more information on groves, see [↪GROVES]).

The Query Language is for selecting and returning document components in the form of nodes of the DSSSL/HyTime document model described earlier. Because we do not need this component of DSSSL we will not discuss it any further.

7.5.2   Creating style sheets with DSSSL

At first sight DSSSL's syntax looks somewhat unusual, as it is based on Scheme, a member of the Lisp family of languages. However, as you will see in the examples that follow, once you "get used to the parentheses," DSSSL becomes quite straightforward.

7.5.2.1   Construction rules

As with other style languages, a DSSSL style sheet consists of a series of statements, called *construction rules*, that "construct" a formatted document from an SGML source document. Let us first look at the line that follows. It instructs the DSSSL application that all par elements in the SGML source should produce a paragraph flow object in the output formatted flow object tree.

```
(element par (make paragraph quadding: 'justify ))
```

As we explained earlier, a flow object corresponds to a formatting object. The detailed description of DSSSL flow object classes, together with their characteristics, is given in Section 12.6 of ISO/IEC:10179 (1996).[5] For easy reference, we list all flow object classes available in DSSSL, together with their identification number in that section (for instance, entry 5 corresponds to Subsection 12.6.5 in the DSSSL Specification). Entries marked with [†] were not in the DSSSL-online subset, which was originally proposed as a style sheet language for XML.

1 sequence
2 display-group
3 simple-page-sequence
4 page-sequence[†]
5 column-set-sequence[†]
6 paragraph
7 paragraph-break

---

[5] An online PDF version of the DSSSL Specification for personal use is at [↪DSSSLPDF].

 8 `line-field`

 9 `sideline`

10 `anchor`[†]

11 `character`

12 `leader`

13 `embedded-text`[†]

14 `rule`

15 `external-graphic`

16 `included-container-area`[†]

17 `score`

18 `box`

19 `side-by-side`[†]

20 `side-by-side-item`[†]

21 `glyph-annotation`[†]

22 `alignment-point`

23 `aligned-column`

24 `multi-line-inline-note`[†]

25 `emphasizing-mark`[†]

26 flow object classes for mathematical formulae[†]
     (1) `math-sequence`, (2) `unmath`, (3) `subscript`, (4) `superscript`, (5) `script`,
     (6) `mark`, (7) `fence`, (8) `fraction`, (9) `radical`, (10) `math-operator`,
     (11) `grid`, (12) `grid-cell`

27 flow object classes for tables
     (1) `table`, (2) `table-part`, (3) `table-column`, (5) `table-row`,
     (6) `table-cell`, (7) `table-border`

28 flow object classes for online display
     (1) `scroll`, (2) `multi-mode`, (3) `link flow`, (4) `marginalia`

A list of the characteristics of all flow class objects, together with other useful tables, are available from Harvey Bingham's DSSSL syntax summary Web page [↪DSSSLSUM].

For instance, if you want to find all the characteristics of the `paragraph` flow object that we used in the earlier example, then you should, according to the above list, consult Section 12.6.6. There you will find more than eight pages of characteristics. In particular, for `quadding` it states that it controls "the alignment of lines other than the last line in the paragraph...." The relevant text also lists all the other values that `quadding` can take.

Implementors can add their own flow objects. Jade (see Section 7.5.3) uses this possibility to generate SGML output; therefore you can use Jade to transform an

XML document into HTML, for instance. Instead of writing Perl or Java code, as we have done in previous sections, you can, if you know a little about DSSSL, use Jade to transform XML documents into HTML, LaTeX, and so on.

For example, we can take the same par element type as earlier and instruct Jade to translate it into an HTML <P> tag, as follows (here we make use of Jade's SGML extension):

```
(element par (make element gi: "P")) ;creates an HTML paragraph
```

7.5.2.2   A simple DSSSL specification

DSSSL specifications are genuine SGML documents and are contructed according to a DTD. With the Jade distribution comes a file style-sheet.dtd, which has its own public identifier.

```
-//James Clark//DTD DSSSL Style Sheet//EN
```

In fact, writing a DSSSL style sheet is not so difficult, and in most cases only a few flow objects have to be mastered.

As an example, we will take our invitation example and generate simple HTML output (as we did with CSS in the previous section) but without writing the HTML code ourselves. Instead we use DSSSL's flow objects and let Jade handle the translation.

```
1   <!-- invitation.dsl -->                              27   (make paragraph
2   <!DOCTYPE style-sheet PUBLIC                          28     (literal "Venue: ")
3   "-//James Clark//DTD DSSSL Style Sheet//EN"           29     (process-children)))
4   >                                                     30   (element (front why)
5   <style-sheet>                                         31   (make paragraph
6   <style-specification>                                 32     (literal "Occasion: ")
7   <style-specification-body>                            33     (process-children)))
8   (define *FontSize* 12pt)                              34   (element (body par)
9   (root                                                 35   (make paragraph
10    (make simple-page-sequence                          36     quadding: 'justify
11      left-margin:   5mm                                37     font-size: *FontSize*
12      page-width:    100mm                              38     space-before: *FontSize*
13      right-margin:  5mm                                39     (process-children)))
14      (make scroll                                      40   (element emph
15        font-size: *FontSize*                           41   (make sequence
16        line-spacing: *FontSize*                        42     font-posture:  'italic
17        (process-children))))                           43     (process-children)))
18   (element (front date)                                44   (element (back signature)
19    (make paragraph                                     45   (make paragraph
20      (literal "When: ")                                46     quadding: 'end
21      (process-children)))                              47     space-before: *FontSize*
22   (element (front to)                                  48     (literal "From: ")
23    (make paragraph                                     49     (process-children)))
24      (literal "To: ")                                  50   </style-specification-body>
25      (process-children)))                              51   </style-specification>
26   (element (front where)                               52   </style-sheet>
```

Let us look at the DSSSL style sheet invitation.dsl above. Line 8 shows how we define a constant (*Fontsize*). By convention, we put stars at both ends of the constants so that they are easily recognizable in the code. Then we compose the output representation by assembling flow objects. We define a root object and create a `simple-page-sequence` (line 10), setting some of its characteristics (lines 11–13). Inside the `simple-page-sequence` we create a `scroll` (line 14) that accepts flow objects for online display that do not have to be divided into pages. Apart from defining characteristics, inside a `make` expression and after the keyword argument list, we can specify a "content expression" that instructs the DSSSL processor what to put inside the current flow object. For instance, on line 17 we call the procedure `process-children`, which processes the child nodes of the current element that is the `root` element (the complete document) in the present case. If no content expression is specified, DSSSL will include a (`process-children`) line automatically. However, if the current flow object cannot have children, it is called an "atomic flow object," for example, a character flow object. For clarity, though, it is good practice always to specify a content expression, if one can be present. In particular, you have to provide the content expression if you want to suppress some child nodes or otherwise selectively process children. Otherwise you have to introduce some flow objects that do not correspond directly to elements in the source document.

The next part of the style sheet deals with the creation of flow objects for each of the possible elements in the source XML document. For instance, lines 18–21 apply to `date` elements inside `front` elements (this is similar to the selector syntax `front > element` for CSS rules as explained in Section 7.4). On line 19 we create a `paragraph` flow object that builds line elements for inline areas. The `paragraph` element is always displayed. In the present case, it consists of the literal "`When:` " followed by whatever is the result of processing the child nodes of the current `date` element node. Similar `paragraph` flow objects are built for the other elements of the `front` matter. In lines 34–39 we encounter the code to deal with `par` elements inside a `body` element that is also turned into a `paragraph` flow object, but in this case we specify explicitly a few of its characteristics. In particular, we want to leave a space equal to the value of the variable `*FontSize*`, defined at the beginning of the file, in front of each new paragraph. Lines 40–43 declare how to handle `emph` elements, and here we introduce the `sequence` flow object that produces a concatenation of the areas produced by each of its children. In the present case we use it to set the font posture to italic. Finally for the `back` element and its `signature` (lines 44–49), we build another `paragraph` flow object with the literal "`From:` " and the content of the element.

This DSSSL style sheet and our XML source file can now be interpreted by a DSSSL processor to obtain formatted output. We will use Jade for our examples.

7.5.3   Introducing Jade

James Clark was the first to release a DSSSL processor. His Jade (James' Awesome DSSSL Engine) is a fast C++ based processor that is available for Win32 and UNIX platforms [↪JADE]. Jade implements a large subset of DSSSL's style language, but it has (almost) no support for the transformation language. Jade can generate the following output formats: Microsoft's RTF (*Rich Text Format*), TEX (with JadeTEX), XML, HTML (using a nonstandard DSSSL extension), a nonstandard "FOT" (Flow Object Tree in the form of flow objects as XML elements), and MIF (Adobe's *Maker Interchange Format* for FrameMaker).

Binary distributions are available for some platforms, including Microsoft Windows, which makes installation a simple matter of unpacking the distribution. On other platforms, Jade might have to be built from sources.

Once Jade has been set up correctly, as described in the documentation, it is straightforward to run it. Jade uses an environment similar to that of `nsgmls` (see Section 6.6.5.1). In particular, you should set the `SGML_CATALOG_FILES` environment variable to inform Jade where the `catalog` file is located. Jade shares many of its command-line options with `nsgmls`. The others are explained on the Jade home page [↪JADE].

```
jade [-vCegG2] [-b encoding] [-f error_file] [-c catalog_sysid]
     [-D dir] [-a link_type] [-A arch] [-E max_errors]
     [-i entity] [-w warning_type] [-d dsssl_spec] [-V variable]
     [-t (fot|rtf|html|tex|mif|sgml|xml)] [-o output_file] input_file(s)
```

For our purposes the more important new switches are -d, which allows you to specify the name of the DSSSL style sheet; -t, which lets you define the type of output (the possibilities are listed above); -G, which initiates debugging and will show the evaluation stack when something goes wrong; and -o, which lets you specify the output file name.

7.5.3.1   Running Jade

Before we do some real work with Jade, let us mention an interesting feature that allows us to obtain the full textual content of a document. When an empty style sheet (empty.dsl, see below) is specified, the system executes a process-children instruction recursively for the root element down to the deepest level children.

```
1   <!-- empty.dsl -->
2   <!DOCTYPE style-sheet PUBLIC "-//James Clark//DTD DSSSL Style Sheet//EN">
3   <style-sheet>
4     <style-specification>
5       <style-specification-body>
6       </style-specification-body>
7     </style-specification>
8   </style-sheet>
```

The `catalog` file that is needed to associate the DSSSL public identifiers with system resources should contain the following:

```
1   PUBLIC "-//James Clark//DTD DSSSL Flow Object Tree//EN" "fot.dtd"
2   PUBLIC "-//James Clark//DTD DSSSL Style Sheet//EN" "style-sheet.dtd"
3   PUBLIC "ISO/IEC 10179:1996//DTD DSSSL Architecture//EN" "dsssl.dtd"
```

With these files and the XML document `invitation.xml`, we now run Jade.

```
jade -t xml -d empty.dsl d:\jade\xml.dcl invitation.xml
```

The XML declaration file `xml.dcl` must be loaded in front of `invitation.xml` because by default Jade accepts only standard "SGML" syntax and will reject XML-specific features, such as empty-element syntax.

The output is shown here. We see that we get the character data content of all elements in the XML source file `invitation.xml`.

```
Anna, Bernard, Didier, JohannaNext Friday Evening at 8 pmThe Web
CafeMy first XML babyI would like to invite you all to celebrate the
birth of Invitation, my first XML document child.Please do your best
to come and join me next Friday evening. And, do not forget to bring
your friends.I really look forward to see you soon!Michel
```

Let us return to our DSSSL style sheet `invitation.dsl` that we introduced in Section 7.5.2.2 and run it through Jade with the XML source file `invitation.xml` to obtain various output formats. If we do not explicitly specify an output format (with the `-t` option), Jade produces an XML presentation of the flow object tree.

```
jade -dinvitation.dsl d:\jade\xml.dcl invitation.xml
```

The generated file `invitation.fot` follows. It displays clearly how the output is built according to the instructions for each element of the source tree described in the `invitation.dsl` style sheet. The order of the flow objects corresponds to the order with which the elements are constructed from parsing the source document `invitation.xml` (see page 254).

```
1   <?xml version="1.0"?>                        <!-- invitation.fot -->
2   <fot>
3   <simple-page-sequence left-margin="14.17pt" page-width="283.46pt" right-margin="14.17pt">
4   <scroll font-size="12pt" line-spacing="12pt">
5   <paragraph>
6   <a name="0"/>
7   <a name="1"/>
8   <a name="2"/>
9   <text>To: </text>
10  <text>Anna, Bernard, Didier, Johanna</text>
11  </paragraph>
12  <paragraph>
13  <a name="3"/>
14  <text>When: </text>
15  <text>Next Friday Evening at 8 pm</text>
16  </paragraph>
17  <paragraph>
18  <a name="4"/>
19  <text>Venue: </text>
20  <text>The Web Cafe</text>
21  </paragraph>
22  <paragraph>
23  <a name="5"/>
24  <text>Occasion: </text>
```

```
25   <simple-page-sequence font-size="12pt">
26   <scroll>
27   <paragraph space-before="12pt" quadding="justify" font-size="12pt">
28   <a name="6"/>
29   <a name="7"/>
30   <text>
31   I would like to invite you all to celebrate
32   the birth of </text>
33   <sequence font-posture="italic">
34   <a name="8"/>
35   <text>Invitation</text>
36   </sequence>
37   <text>, my
38   first XML document child.
39   </text>
40   </paragraph>
41   <paragraph space-before="12pt" quadding="justify" font-size="12pt">
42   <a name="9"/>
43   <text>
44   Please do your best to come and join me next Friday
45   evening. And, do not forget to bring your friends.
46   </text>
47   </paragraph>
48   <paragraph space-before="12pt" quadding="justify" font-size="12pt">
49   <a name="10"/>
50   <text>
51   I </text>
52   <sequence font-posture="italic">
53   <a name="11"/>
54   <text>really</text>
55   </sequence>
56   <text> look forward to see you soon!
57   </text>
58   </paragraph>
59   <paragraph space-before="12pt" quadding="end">
60   <a name="12"/>
61   <a name="13"/>
62   <text>From: </text>
63   <text>Michel</text>
64   </paragraph>
65   </scroll>
66   </simple-page-sequence>
67   </fot>
```

With the same input files we now ask Jade to generate an RTF file by entering the following command:

```
jade -dinvitation.dsl -t rtf d:\jade\xml.dcl invitation.xml
```

This generates a file invitation.rtf that we can view with Microsoft Word (Figure 7.4). Similarly by specifying -t tex (rather than -t rtf), Jade will transform our flow object specifications into TEX code that can be interpreted by the TEX back-end JadeTEX (see Section 7.5.4). In Figure 7.5 we obtain an output file that is almost identical to Figure 7.4.

7.5.3.2   Making tables in DSSSL

Let us now get a little more ambitious and put the front material inside a DSSSL table construct to align the material better.

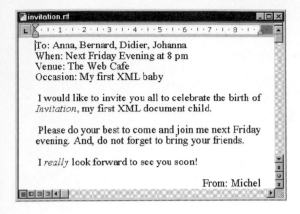

To: Anna, Bernard, Didier, Johanna
When: Next Friday Evening at 8 pm
Venue: The Web Cafe
Occasion: My first XML baby

I would like to invite you all to celebrate the birth of
Invitation, my first XML document child.

Please do your best to come and join me next Friday
evening. And, do not forget to bring your friends.

I *really* look forward to see you soon!

                                                    From: Michel

Figure 7.4: Simple DSSSL style with RTF   Figure 7.5: Simple DSSSL style with TEX

```
 1   <!DOCTYPE style-sheet PUBLIC          43   (make table-row
 2   "-//James Clark//DTD DSSSL Style Sheet//EN"  44     (make table-cell
 3   >                                      45       (make paragraph quadding: 'start
 4   <style-sheet>                          46         (literal "To:")))
 5   <style-specification>                  47     (make table-cell
 6   <style-specification-body>             48       (process-children))))
 7                                          49   (element (front where)
 8   (define FontSize 12pt)                 50     (make table-row
 9                                          51       (make table-cell
10   (root                                  52         (make paragraph quadding: 'start
11     (make simple-page-sequence           53           (literal "Venue:")))
12       left-margin:  2cm                  54       (make table-cell
13       page-width:   15cm                 55         (process-children))))
14       right-margin: 2cm                  56   (element (front why)
15       (make scroll                       57     (make table-row
16         font-size: FontSize              58       (make table-cell
17         (process-children))))            59         (make paragraph quadding: 'start
18                                          60           (literal "Occasion:")))
19   (element front                         61       (make table-cell
20     (make sequence                       62         (process-children))))
21       (make paragraph                    63
22         quadding:    'center             64   (element (body par)
23         space-before:  20pt              65     (make paragraph
24         font-weight: 'bold               66       quadding: 'justify
25         font-size:   24pt                67       font-size: FontSize
26         (literal "INVITATION"))          68       space-before: FontSize
27       (make table                        69       (process-children)))
28         table-border:   #f  ; no border  70   (element emph
29         display-alignment: 'start        71     (make sequence
30         space-before:   20pt             72       font-posture: 'italic
31         (make table-part                 73       (process-children)))
32           (make table-column width: 25mm) 74
33           (make table-column width: 10cm) 75   (element (back signature)
34           (process-children)))))         76     (make paragraph
35   (element (front date)                  77       quadding: 'end
36     (make table-row                      78       space-before: FontSize
37       (make table-cell                   79       (literal "From: ")
38         (make paragraph quadding: 'start 80       (process-children)))
39           (literal "When:")))            81
40       (make table-cell                   82   </style-specification-body>
41         (process-children))))            83   </style-specification>
42   (element (front to)                    84   </style-sheet>
```

Our approach is quite similar to the one we had with LaTeX, but, of course, we have to specify the table in somewhat more detail. If we refer to the list of DSSSL flow object classes starting on page 315, we see that the table components (heading 27) are described in Section 12.6.27 of the DSSSL specification, to which you should refer if you want to get more details about the way we construct the table.

Lines 27–34 define a few general characteristics of the table (no border, column width, alignment, and distance from previous material) and instruct DSSSL to handle the children of the front element. These children are each handled in term: date (lines 35–41), to (lines 42–48), where (lines 49–55), and why (lines 56–62). In each case we construct the left-hand cell by specifying some literal text (lines 39, 46, 53, and 60). Then in the right-hand cell, we deposit the contents of the front element's child being considered. Lines 64–69 take care of starting a new paragraph by creating a paragraph flow object, while lines 70–73 translate XML's emph element into an italic text sequence flow object. Finally lines 75–80 put the contents of the signature element right-justified (line 77), preceded by the literal From: (line 79).

The main advantage of this approach is that invtab1.dsl, our DSSSL style sheet, can be used with Jade to obtain formatted output in various forms. In particular, we can generate RTF (for viewing or editing with Microsoft tools; Figure 7.6 shows the RTF output viewed with Microsoft Word97):

```
jade -dinvtab1.dsl -t rtf d:\jade\xml.dcl invitation.xml
```

We can also generate TeX output. For this we use the flag -t tex, and post-process the TeX file with JadeTeX, discussed in more detail in Section 7.5.4. An output file is shown in Figure 7.7.

```
jade -dinvtab1.dsl -t tex d:\jade\xml.dcl invitation.xml
jadetex invitation
```

It should be stressed that only the option specified with the -t flag was different between the two runs of Jade.

7.5.3.3   Handling attributes

We can also write a style sheet for handling the invitation2.xml source file. Here we need to get access to the value of the attributes of the elements to format the document. Such a style sheet invtab2.dsl follows:

```
1   <!DOCTYPE style-sheet PUBLIC "-//James Clark//DTD DSSSL Style Sheet//EN">
2   <style-sheet>
3   <style-specification>
4   <style-specification-body>
5   (define FontSize 12pt)
6   (root
7     (make simple-page-sequence
8       left-margin:   1cm
9       page-width:    10cm
```

Figure 7.6: Word97 view of RTF output

INVITATION

To: Anna, Bernard, Didier, Johanna
When: Next Friday Evening at 8 pm
Venue: The Web Cafe
Occasion: My first XML baby

I would like to invite you all to celebrate the birth of *Invitation*, my first XML document child.

Please do your best to come and join me next Friday evening. And, do not forget to bring your friends.

I *really* look forward to see you soon!

From: Michel

Figure 7.7: PostScript view of TₑX output

```
10        right-margin: 1cm
11      (make scroll
12        font-size: FontSize
13        (process-children))))
14    (element invitation
15      (make sequence
16        (make paragraph
17          quadding:     'center
18          space-before:   20pt
19          font-weight: 'bold
20          font-size:    24pt
21          (literal "INVITATION"))
22        (make table
23          table-border:   #f  ; no border
24          display-alignment: 'start
25          space-before:   20pt
26          (make table-part
27            (make table-column width: 25mm)
28            (make table-column width: 10cm)
29            (make table-row
30              (make table-cell
31                (make paragraph quadding: 'start
32                  (literal "When:")))
33              (make table-cell
34                (make paragraph quadding: 'start
35                  (literal (attribute-string "date")))))
36            (make table-row
37              (make table-cell
38                (make paragraph quadding: 'start
39                  (literal "To:")))
40              (make table-cell
41                (make paragraph quadding: 'start
42                  (literal (attribute-string "to")))))
43            (make table-row
44              (make table-cell
45                (make paragraph quadding: 'start
46                  (literal "Venue:")))
```

```
47            (make table-cell
48              (make paragraph quadding: 'start
49                (literal (attribute-string "where")))))
50          (make table-row
51            (make table-cell
52              (make paragraph quadding: 'start
53                (literal "Occasion:")))
54            (make table-cell
55              (make paragraph quadding: 'start
56                (literal (attribute-string "why")))))))
57       (process-children)
58       (make paragraph
59         quadding: 'end
60         space-before: FontSize
61         (literal "From: "
62           (attribute-string "signature")))))
63  (element par
64    (make paragraph
65      quadding: 'justify
66      font-size: FontSize
67      space-before: FontSize
68      (process-children-trim)))
69  (element emph
70    (make sequence
71      font-posture: 'italic
72      (process-children-trim)))
73  </style-specification-body>
74  </style-specification>
75  </style-sheet>
```

We use the same strategy to build the table here as we did in Section 7.5.3.2. However, instead of the process-children rule we extract the information with the procedure attribute-string, for which we specify the name of the attribute as a character string (see lines 35, 42, 49, 56, and 62). We also reduce the margins and page width somewhat (compare lines 8–10 in the two versions).

We execute the same jade command as earlier, changing the DSSSL style sheet to invtab2.dsl and the XML input file to invitation2.xml. Then we run the obtained TEX file through jadetex and finally get the EPS file shown in Figure 7.8, which should be compared to Figure 7.7.

7.5.4   The TEX back-end for Jade and the JadeTEX macros

As we mentioned earlier, Jade also has a TEX back-end. This offers several advantages:

1. TEX is free, well-understood, and available for all machines

2. TEX is designed for rule-based batch typesetting.

3. TEX is, generally speaking, good at page makeup and very good at paragraph makeup.

4. TEX understands the full range of typesetting minutiae (hyphenation, fonts, math, and so on).

INVITATION

When: Next Friday Evening at 8 pm
To: Anna, Bernard, Didier, Johanna
Venue: The Web Cafe
Occasion: My first XML baby

I would like to invite you all to celebrate the birth of *Invitation*, my first XML document child.

Please do your best to come and join me next Friday evening. And, do not forget to bring your friends.

I *really* look forward to see you soon!

From: Michel

Figure 7.8: PostScript view of TeX output (alternate DSSSL formatting)

We also have the perspective of using Unicode directly in TeX, with the Omega variant [↪OMEGA]. This gives us a means to move onto the more complicated scripts, writing directions, and language conventions with which TeX itself has difficulties.

Thus with Jade style sheets we have a chance to write device-independent specifications and to use TeX's power to instantiate them.

Jade's TeX back-end was originally written by David Megginson and later modified by Sebastian Rahtz and Kathleen Marszalek. It has a very simple model: It emits a TeX command for the start and end of every flow object, defining any changed characteristics at the start of the command. This abstract TeX markup can then be fleshed out by writing definitions for each of the flow object commands, and this is what the JadeTeX macro package provides.

JadeTeX is implemented on top of the widely used LaTeX macro package primarily because LaTeX provides standardized font support (the New Font Selection System) that resembles that of DSSSL. The multilingual, color, graphics inclusion, hypertext, and tabular packages are also conveniently in place. This means that JadeTeX provides a good shortcut to an implementation and allows us to see whether TeX can, in fact, meet the demands of DSSSL. For better performance, it would be possible to rewrite the font handling inside the Jade back-end and to optimize the handling of labels and references to minimize memory requirements for cross-references.

It is important for regular LaTeX users to realize that this back-end cannot use LaTeX's high-level constructs and their favorite style class files. Indeed, DSSSL expresses everything in terms of flow elements and has no notion of such familiar concepts as sections, lists, cross-references, or bibliographies. Thus TeX's only responsibilities are page and line breaks; all the rest is specified by the DSSSL code.

It would be possible to consider a system that translated the DSSSL style specification itself into a LaTeX class file and to transform the document instance into a LaTeX file using high-level constructs, but this has not, to our knowledge, been attempted.

7.5.4.1   Installation and usage

After downloading the JadeTeX macros from the CTAN archives [↪JADETEX], you should make them available to TeX. It is most convenient to build a new TeX format file. The sequence of commands you have to type would look like the following (if you are working with a modern TeX system based on Web2c 7.2 or later):

```
tex jadetex.ins
pdftex -ini "&pdflatex" -progname=pdfjadetex pdfjadetex.ini
tex -ini "&hugelatex" -progname=hugetex jadetex.ini
```

This produces two format files pdfjadetex.fmt and jadetex.fmt that can be moved to a directory where TeX can find them. The "huge" version of LaTeX (hugelatex on the third line) needs to be set up, if it does not exist, since JadeTeX is extremely hungry for memory. Users of Web2c 7.2 (or a later version) can do this by adding the following lines to the file texmf.cnf:

```
main_memory.hugetex = 1100000
hash_extra.hugetex = 15000
pool_size.hugetex = 500000
string_vacancies.hugetex = 45000
max_strings.hugetex = 55000
pool_free.hugetex = 47500
nest_size.hugetex = 500
param_size.hugetex = 1500
save_size.hugetex = 5000
stack_size.hugetex = 1500
```

and running

```
tex -ini -fmt=hugelatex -progname=hugetex latex.ltx
```

which generates hugelatex.fmt. Other TeX implementations have their own methods for generating format files with extra memory, and you should consult their documentation.

Assuming everything was successful, you are then ready to generate a TeX file and run it through JadeTeX:

```
jade -dinvtab1.dsl -t tex xml.dcl invitation.xml
jadetex invitation    or    pdfjadetex invitation
dvips -E invitation -oinvitation
```

The first line generates a TeX file containing commands reflecting the DSSSL flow object structure. These commands are interpreted by the JadeTeX macros and pdfTeX or LaTeX (line 2), generating directly a PDF or a DVI file, which can be transformed into an EPS file. This procedure was used to generate Figure 7.7.

7.5.4.2   JadeTeX, a closer look

To clarify how JadeTeX handles the DSSSL information with the characteristics of flow objects, let us consider the following:

```
1   (root (make simple-page-sequence              \SpS{%
2           center-footer: (page-number-sosofo)
3           font-family-name: body-font-family     \def\fFamName{iso-serif}
4           page-n-columns: 2                       \def\PageNColumns{2}
5           page-column-sep: 16pt                   \def\PageColumnSep{16\p@}
6           header-margin: .5in                     \def\HeaderMargin{36\p@}
7           footer-margin: .5in                     \def\FooterMargin{36\p@}
8           left-margin: 1in                        \def\LeftMargin{72\p@}
9           right-margin: 1in                       \def\RightMargin{72\p@}
10          top-margin: 1in                         \def\TopMargin{72\p@}
11          bottom-margin: 1in                      \def\BottomMargin{72\p@}
12          page-width: 211mm                       \def\PageWidth{598.11\p@}
13          page-height: 297mm))                    \def\PageHeight{841.89\p@}}
```

At the left-hand side we show a DSSSL specification that specifies parameters for a simple page sequence. At the right-hand side you see how Jade's TeX back-end translates this into an intermediate form that can be readily digested by the JadeTeX macros ([↪JADETEXB] gives a detailed description of these parameters and the translation process).

Look at the body of a document with the simple XML markup:

```
some <it>go italic</it> others not...
```

Look, too, at the following DSSSL declaration:

```
1   (element it
2     (make sequence
3       font-posture: 'italic
4       (process-children-trim)))
```

Jade's TeX back-end will generate the following:

```
1   some \Node{\def\Element{11}}%
2   \Seq{\def\fPosture{italic}}%
3   go italic
```

```
4   \endSeq{}\endNode{}  others
5   not...\endSeq{}\endNode{}
```

Notice how the contents of the "italic" element type it has been processed as a DSSSL sequence that translates to TeX macros \Seq...\endSeq. The required changes in the font-posture characteristic are expressed with a TeX macro definition as a parameter to \Seq. Almost every object that comes out of Jade has an "Element" identifier (line 1) that can be used for cross-reference purposes.

7.5.4.3   JadeTeX and mathematics

What about mathematics? This is TeX's traditional strength and something that few typesetting systems handle well. Let us consider the following example; the XML markup and displayed result should be fairly clear.

```
<fd><fr><nu>X</nu><de>Y</de></fr></fd>
```

$$\frac{X}{Y}$$

We could write a DSSSL specification like this:

```
1   ; displayed equation           11     (make fraction
2   (element fd                     12       (process-children-trim))))
3    (make display-group            13   (element nu
4     (make math-sequence           14     (make math-sequence
5       math-display-mode: 'display 15       label: 'numerator
6       min-leading: 2pt            16     (process-children-trim)))
7       font-posture: 'math         17   (element de
8       (process-children-trim))))  18     (make math-sequence
9    ; fraction                     19       label: 'denominator
10   (element fr                    20     (process-children-trim)))
```

This uses the slightly difficult DSSSL concept of "ports" (the label characteristic) that allows the numerator and denominator to feed material to the relevant portions of the fraction flow object. Jade's TeX back-end would transform this into something like.

```
1   \DisplayGroup{}
2    \MathSeq{\def\MathDisplayMode{display}
3            \def\MinLeading{2\p@}
4            \def\MinLeadingFactor{0}
5            \def\fPosture{math}}
6     \FractionSerial{}
7      \insertFractionBar{}
8      \FractionNumerator{}
9       \MathSeq{}X\endMathSeq{}
10      \endFractionNumerator{}
11      \FractionDenominator{}
12       \MathSeq{}Y\endMathSeq{}
13      \endFractionDenominator{}
14     \endFractionSerial{}
15    \endMathSeq{}
16   \endDisplayGroup{}
```

We clearly see how the structure of the original formula has been conserved. Thanks to the TeX commands, which are called at each level, you could easily customize the presentation of the various math elements. The default implementation (simplified) of these macros is as follows:

```
1  \def\FractionSerial#1{#1\bgroup}
2  \def\endFractionSerial{\egroup}
3  \def\FractionDenominator{}
4  \def\endFractionDenominator{}
5  \def\FractionNumerator{}
6  \def\endFractionNumerator{\over }
7  \def\insertFractionBar{}
```

An interesting initiative is David Carlisle's work on a DSSSL style sheet for mathematics expressed using the MathML DTD[↪DSSSLMML]; we discuss this in more detail in Section 8.2.4.

7.5.4.4 Is JadeTEX usable in practice?

It is not hard to process simple texts with Jade and to see more or less identical output from the RTF and the TEX back-ends (Figures 7.6 and 7.7). For conventional scientific publication, however, the simple page model that Jade implements is insufficient. The TEX back-end, therefore, implements a number of extensions[6] which can be activated with the following DSSSL code:

```
1  (declare-flow-object-class page-float
2       "UNREGISTERED::Sebastian Rahtz//Flow Object Class::page-float")
3  (declare-flow-object-class page-footnote
4       "UNREGISTERED::Sebastian Rahtz//Flow Object Class::page-footnote")
5  (declare-characteristic page-n-columns
6       "UNREGISTERED::James Clark//Characteristic::page-n-columns" 1)
7  (declare-characteristic page-column-sep
8       "UNREGISTERED::James Clark//Characteristic::page-column-sep" 4pt)
```

These declarations allow you to specify a two-column page layout with specifications like the following:

```
1  (make simple-page-sequence
2           page-n-columns: 2
3           page-column-sep: 16pt
4           ..... )
```

and to create a new footnote flow object (`page-footnote`) or float new flow object (`page-float`). The result is demonstrated in Figure 7.9; it shows that a DSSSL specification, Jade, and JadeTEX can produce plausible output for scientific texts. On the other hand, we found that mathematics support in RTF is too poor to provide acceptable output, so for math (at the moment) the only realistic way from XML to formatted output for print seems to be to go via TEX and JadeTEX.

The potential power of SGML/XML, DSSSL, and TEX working together really holds a lot of promise. Although there are some problems, the Jade DSSSL implementation already supports a huge amount of useful transformation and specification code, and TEX is close to being a DSSSL-capable formatter.

---

[6]Support for multiple columns is also provided in the RTF back-end.

Test file for math, multicolumns, and footnotes

Sebastian Rahtz

Abstract: Altera C. Caesaris, qui illos publicatis bonis per municipia Italiae distribueudos ac vinculis sempiternis tenendos existimabat. Cum acautem plures senatores ad C. Caesaris quam ad D. Silani sententiam inclinare viderentur, M. Cicero ea, quae infra legitur, oratione Silani sententiam commendare studuit.

1. Maths tests

0. Simple fraction

$$\frac{X}{Y}$$

1. display equation with radical 123 and fraction

$$\frac{(x+y)+\sqrt{123}}{2}$$

2. Display equation with super and subscripts

$$1I/I_0 = (1-\Theta)^{\Sigma}\lg.$$

3. Matrix with braces

$$\{\ a\quad b\quad c\quad d\quad e\quad f\quad\}a=0b=2$$

4. Line with | (after matrix)

$$\{\ a\quad b\quad c\quad d\quad e\quad f\quad\}|a=0b=2$$

5. Line with | (before matrix)

$$|\{\ a\quad b\quad c\quad d\quad e\quad f\quad\}a=0b=2$$

6. Nested matrix with braces

$$(X\{\ a\quad b\quad c\quad d\quad e\quad f\quad\}a=0b=2)$$

7. Nested fraction

$$\frac{(x+y)+\frac{X}{Y}}{2}\qquad \frac{(x+y)^2-4a}{2}$$

8. Fence

$$(\{\ aaa\quad b\quad c\quad d\quad e\quad f\quad\}|_{\sin\alpha}^{b\times 5-\sqrt{49202}}a=0b=2$$

9. Boxing $\boxed{A+B}$

10. Some operators: summation, product, and integral. First, display math:

$$\sum_a^b \prod_c^d \int_e^f \overset{h}{\underset{g}{=}}\sin\alpha \sum_{1111^{bbb}_{aaa}}^{2222^{3333}_{5555}}$$

Now inline math: $\sum_a^b$ $\prod_c^d$ $\int_e^f$ $\overset{h}{\underset{y}{=}}\sin\alpha$ $\sum_{-1111^{bbb}_{aaa}}^{-2222^{3333}}$

11. A radical with a radix

$$\sqrt[3]{123}$$

1.1. Second-level header

2. Footnotes

13. A footnote, number 63[63] A footnote, number 65[65] A footnote, number 64[64]

3. Special character entities

AElig	Æ
And	∧
Cap	⋒
Colon	::
Cup	⋓
Dagger	‡
Delta	Δ
ETH	Ð
Gamma	Γ
Gt	≫
Lambda	Λ
Larr	⇐
Lt	≪
OElig	Œ
Omega	Ω
Or	∨
Oslash	Ø

[63] Never leave home without rope, Sam could have told you
[65] It always pays to be polite to trees that walk and talk
[64] Little can beat stewed rabbit in the heather.

Figure 7.9: Mathematics generated with SGML, DSSSL, and TeX

7.5.5 The Jade SGML transformation interface

Jade does not implement the DSSSL Transformation Language. However, it provides some simple, nonstandardized extensions to the DSSSL Style Language that allow it to be used for SGML transformations.

These Jade extensions are available with the `-t sgml` and `-t xml` options; the latter of which uses XML syntax for empty elements and processing instructions.

Following we give a list of the major SGML flow object classes that Jade defines to complement the standard ones of DSSSL. The extensions consist of a collection of flow object classes and their noninherited characteristics. They are used instead of the standard DSSSL-defined flow object classes.

element A compound flow object that can have child flow objects so that both start and end tags are generated for `element`.

empty-element An atomic flow object without child flow objects so that only a start is generated for `empty-element`. It is mostly for handling elements with a declared content of EMPTY.

Both `element` and `empty-element` have two characteristics:

gi String specifying the element's generic identifier (default: the gi of the current node).

attributes The element's attributes as a list of lists, each consisting of exactly two strings—the first specifying the attribute name and the second the attribute value (default: empty list).

processing-instruction An atomic flow object resulting in a processing instruction. Its characteristic is

data String specifing the content of the processing instruction (default: empty string).

document-type An atomic flow object generating a DOCTYPE declaration. Possible characteristics are

name *Required* string giving the name of the document type that must be identical to the name of the document element type.

system-id String specifying the system identifier of the document type (default: empty string).

public-id String specifying the public identifier of the document type (default: empty string).

entity A compound flow object storing its content in a separate entity. A possible characteristic is

system-id System identifier of the entity. It must be a filename.

This flow object emits no entity reference or declaration.

entity-ref An atomic flow object creating an entity reference. It supports one characteristic:

name The entity name.

formatting-instruction An atomic flow object that inserts characters into the output without change. It has a single characteristic:

data String to be inserted. The &, <, and > characters do not need to be escaped.

In any DSSSL specification that makes use of these flow object classes you must declare them with `declare-flow-object-class` as follows:

```
1   (declare-flow-object-class element
2     "UNREGISTERED::James Clark//Flow Object Class::element")
3   (declare-flow-object-class empty-element
4     "UNREGISTERED::James Clark//Flow Object Class::empty-element")
5   (declare-flow-object-class document-type
6     "UNREGISTERED::James Clark//Flow Object Class::document-type")
7   (declare-flow-object-class processing-instruction
8     "UNREGISTERED::James Clark//Flow Object Class::processing-instruction")
9   (declare-flow-object-class entity
10    "UNREGISTERED::James Clark//Flow Object Class::entity")
11  (declare-flow-object-class entity-ref
12    "UNREGISTERED::James Clark//Flow Object Class::entity-ref")
13  (declare-flow-object-class formatting-instruction
14    "UNREGISTERED::James Clark//Flow Object Class::formatting-instruction")
```

Following we show a style sheet that transforms the `invitation.xml` XML source file into an HTML file using Jade's transformation interface:

```
1   <!DOCTYPE style-sheet PUBLIC "-//James Clark//DTD DSSSL Style Sheet//EN">
2   <style-sheet>
3   <style-specification>
4   <style-specification-body>
5   (declare-flow-object-class element
6     "UNREGISTERED::James Clark//Flow Object Class::element")
7   (declare-flow-object-class empty-element
8     "UNREGISTERED::James Clark//Flow Object Class::empty-element")
9   (declare-flow-object-class document-type
10    "UNREGISTERED::James Clark//Flow Object Class::document-type")
11
12  (define FontSize 12pt)
13  (root
14    (make simple-page-sequence
15      left-margin:  25mm
16      page-width:   205mm
17      right-margin: 25mm
18      (make sequence
19        font-size: FontSize
20        line-spacing: FontSize
21        (make document-type
22          name: "HTML"
23          public-id: "-//W3C//DTD HTML 3.2//EN")
24        (make element gi: "HEAD"
25          (make element gi: "TITLE"
26            (literal "Invitation (XML to HTML transformation)"))
27          (make empty-element gi: "LINK"
28                        attributes: (list (list "href" "invit.css")
29                                          (list "rel" "stylesheet")
30                                          (list "type" "text/css"))))
31        (make element gi: "BODY"
32          (make sequence
33            (make element gi: "H1"
34              (literal "INVITATION"))
35            (process-children))))))
36
37  (element (front)
38    (make element gi: "TABLE"
39                attributes: (list (list "border" "5")
40                                  (list "frame" "hsides")
41                                  (list "rules" "none")
42                                  (list "width" "100%"))
43      (process-children)))
```

```
44   (element (front date)
45     (make element gi: "TR"
46       (make sequence
47         (make element gi: "TD"
48                     attributes: (list (list "class" "front"))
49           (literal "When: "))
50         (make element gi: "TD"
51           (process-children)))))
52   (element (front to)
53     (make element gi: "TR"
54       (make sequence
55         (make element gi: "TD"
56                     attributes: (list (list "class" "front"))
57           (literal "To: "))
58         (make element gi: "TD"
59           (process-children)))))
60   (element (front where)
61     (make element gi: "TR"
62       (make sequence
63         (make element gi: "TD"
64                     attributes: (list (list "class" "front"))
65           (literal "Venue: "))
66         (make element gi: "TD"
67           (process-children)))))
68   (element (front why)
69     (make element gi: "TR"
70       (make sequence
71         (make element gi: "TD"
72                     attributes: (list (list "class" "front"))
73           (literal "Occasion: "))
74         (make element gi: "TD"
75           (process-children)))))
76   (element (body par)
77     (make element gi: "P"
78       (process-children)))
79   (element emph
80     (make element gi: "EM"
81       (process-children)))
82   (element (back signature)
83     (make element gi: "P"
84                 attributes: (list (list "class" "signature"))
85       (make sequence
86         (literal "From: ")
87         (process-children))))
88   </style-specification-body>
89   </style-specification>
90   </style-sheet>
```

Now that we have looked at quite a few examples of DSSSL code, this DSSSL style sheet should be straightforward and easy to understand. Notice the "SGML" flow objects on lines 21 (document-type), 24, 25, 31, 33,...(element), and 27 (empty-element); these special flow objects were declared on lines 5–10. Referring to the characteristics of these flow elements discussed earlier, we find on lines 22 and 23 the name and public-id associated with the document type. For the elements (empty or not) we must specify the generic identifier (element type in XML terminology) gi, and we can specify attributes, if applicable. On lines 28–30 we see that attributes are specified as a list of lists, each consisting of a pair of strings: the first is the name of the attribute, and the second is its value. For instance, the LINK element specification on lines 27–30 results in line 4 shown in the HTML file.

Similarly note the way we specify the attributes for the TABLE element type (lines 39–42), which result in line 8 in the HTML file.

The resulting HTML file invitation.html, following, is obtained typing the command:

```
jade -dinvhtml.dsl -t xml -oinvitation.hmtl xml.dcl invitation.xml
```

```
1   <!DOCTYPE HTML PUBLIC "-//W3C//DTD HTML 3.2//EN">
2   <HEAD>
3   <TITLE>Invitation (XML to HTML transformation)</TITLE>
4   <LINK href="invit.css" rel="stylesheet" type="text/css">
5   </HEAD>
6   <BODY>
7   <H1>INVITATION</H1>
8   <TABLE border="5" frame="hsides" rules="none" width="100%">
9   <TR><TD class="front">To: </TD>
10      <TD>Anna, Bernard, Didier, Johanna</TD></TR>
11  <TR><TD class="front">When: </TD>
12      <TD>Next Friday Evening at 8 pm</TD></TR>
13  <TR><TD class="front">Venue: </TD>
14      <TD>The Web Cafe</TD></TR>
15  <TR><TD class="front">Occasion: </TD>
16      <TD>My first XML baby</TD></TR>
17  </TABLE>
18  <P>I would like to invite you all to celebrate the
19  birth of <EM>Invitation</EM>, my first XML document child.</P>
20  <P>Please do your best to come and join me next Friday
21  evening. And, do not forget to bring your friends.</P>
22  <P>I <EM>really</EM> look forward to see you soon!</P>
23  <P class="signature">From: Michel</P>
24  </BODY>
```

Figure 7.10 shows the result of viewing the HTML file with an HTML browser that also uses our CSS style sheet invit.css to customize the formatting of the various HTML elements. Pay attention to the way the attributes of the TABLE elements, as specified in the XSL style sheet, generate horizontal lines over the full width of the screen above and below the table material.

7.5.6   Formatting real-life documents with DSSSL

Of course, the simple examples in this section give only a very limited idea of the possibilities of the DSSSL system. Therefore let us show you a more complex case before saying something about real-life solutions based on DSSSL.

Suppose we are working in a multilingual environment, and, as with the babel package of LaTeX, we would like certain strings to come out correctly in each of the languages we are interested in. Let us consider the following code fragment:

```
1   (define (FIGNAME)
2     (case (inherited-attribute-string "xml:lang")
3       (("de") "Abbildung ")
4       (("nl") "Figuur ")
5       (else "Figure ")))
6   (define (TABNAME)
7     (case (inherited-attribute-string "xml:lang")
8       (("de") "Tabelle ")
```

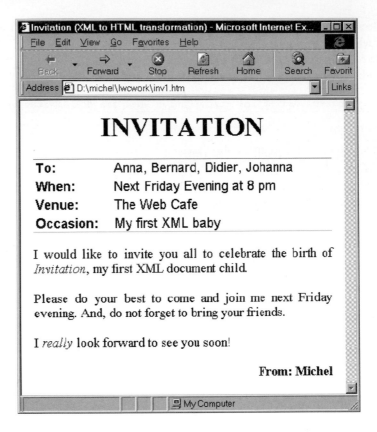

Figure 7.10: XML to HTML transformation with DSSSL

```
 9        (("nl") "Tabel ")
10        (else "Table ")))
11     (element (caption)
12      (make paragraph
13       space-before: 6pt
14       space-after: 10pt
15       (make sequence
16        font-weight: 'bold
17        (literal (if (have-ancestor? "figure") (FIGNAME) (TABNAME)))
18        (literal (format-number
19         (if (have-ancestor? "figure")
20            (element-number (ancestor "figure"))
21            (element-number (ancestor "table")))
22         "1"))
23        (literal ". "))
24       (process-children-trim)))
```

In Section 6.5.1 we introduced the attribute xml:lang, which specifies the language of the content of a given element type. This attribute value is inherited by all children elements. So, if we have part of a document for which this attribute is set to a given value, the case statements on lines 2 and 7 will activate one of the lines in the range 3–5 and another line in the range 8–10, depending on the result of the evaluation of the procedure "(inherited-attribute-string "xml:lang")". For instance, with a value of xml:lang equal to "de," for German, FIGNAME would get the value "Abbildung" (line 3), and TABNAME would get the value "Tabelle" (line 8). With these constant definitions we can construct the caption element using the appropriate character strings for the language considered. On line 17 the if state-ment verifies whether the ancestor of the caption element is figure, in which case the literal string FIGNAME will be placed into the paragraph flow object at that point, otherwise TABNAME. Similarly, lines 18–24 take care of putting the right fig-ure or table number following the text string chosen earlier. In fact, to get the num-ber, DSSSL counts the number of figure or table elements (the "if" test and its branches on lines 19–21). This number is then formatted using the format-number procedure (line 18) and represented as a "decimal" number (hence the "1" on line 23 specifies the format to be used for the number),[7] followed by a dot (line 24).

This example shows clearly the kind of manipulations that are possible with DSSSL using the many procedures and flow objects defined in the DSSSL standard. Another useful feature is the use of "modes," which allows certain elements to be processed (and output) more than once in different modes. For instance, heading titles or figure and table captions, can be output once when one is composing the main text, and a second time when contructing the table of contents and lists of tables and figures.

If you want to find out how DSSSL is used in real-life applications dealing with large documents, you should take a look at Norman Walsh's modular DocBook style sheets [↪ DBDSSSL] for formatting SGML documents marked up using the DocBook DTD. Walsh provides two style sheets: a generic one for printing Doc-Book documents using RTF, TeX, or MIF, and another one for transforming them into HTML. Several hooks are provided to allow the user to customize the output. Apart from their practical usefulness, these complex style sheets are also a good place to learn about DSSSL.

7.6   Extensible Stylesheet Language

Work on the "Extensible Stylesheet Language" (XSL) is ongoing, and the syntax that we will present in this section is based on the specification available at the time of writing. It is thus possible that the final recommendation, which is expected by summer 1999, will differ in some details from what we describe here. Nevertheless, the basic principles of the XSL language, and the way it can be used with XML documents, will remain mostly unchanged.

---

[7] Section 8 of the DSSSL Standard describes the expression language. It is here that you will find an explanation of the various procedures we have used in this and other examples. In particular, Section 8.5.7.24 details the format-number procedure.

XSL is a language for expressing style sheets that describe rules for the presentation of XML elements. It proposes a syntax for describing two subprocesses:

1. a *transformation* of the source tree of the XML document into a result tree; and

2. an interpretation of the result tree to produce *formatting objects* for output on various media, such as a computer screen, paper, or audio.

An XSL style sheet consists of a set of template rules, with each rule having two parts: a *pattern* that is matched against elements in the source tree, and a *template*, which is instantiated to create part of the result tree.

Source and result trees are separate objects, which can have quite different structures, since when constructing the result tree, information from the XML source can be reordered, or filtered or arbitrary branches can be added by the XSL application. XSL can be used for general XML transformations, for instance, to tranform XML into "well-formed" HTML.

One of the main aims of XSL is to be able to use the result tree to format the XML information using the vocabulary defined in the XSL specification. The objects of this formatting vocabulary and their characteristics are very much influenced by the CSS and DSSSL languages, since one of XSL's design aims is to provide a formatting functionality of *at least* CSS and DSSSL.

7.6.1 The general structure of an XSL style sheet

An XSL style sheet uses XML syntax. It contains one `xsl:stylesheet` document element, which contains zero or more `xsl:template` elements specifying template rules.

The following is an example of a simple XSL style sheet that constructs a result tree for a sequence of `par` elements containing `emph` elements using XSL's formatting object vocabulary:

```
1   <?xml version='1.0'?>
2   <xsl:stylesheet xmlns:xsl="http://www.w3.org/TR/WD-xsl"
3                   xmlns:fo="http://www.w3.org/TR/WD-xsl/FO"
4                   result-ns="fo">
5     <xsl:template match="/">
6       <fo:basic-page-sequence font-family="Helvetica" font-size="10pt" >
7         <xsl:apply-templates/>
8       </fo:basic-page-sequence>
9     </xsl:template>
10    <xsl:template match="par">
11      <fo:block indent-start="10pt" space-before="12pt">
12        <xsl:apply-templates/>
13      </fo:block>
14    </xsl:template>
15    <xsl:template match="emph">
16      <fo:inline-sequence font-style="italic">
17        <xsl:apply-templates/>
18      </fo:inline-sequence>
19    </xsl:template>
20  </xsl:stylesheet>
```

Lines 2 and 3 define the `xsl` and `fo` (flow object) namespaces (see Section B.3 for details). The string following `xmlns:` declares a shorthand for a namespace to allow the parser to interpret the elements in the document instance, a URI-like string indicating where those elements are defined. Thus line 2, which must always be present in the case of an XSL style sheet, specifies in which document the XSL syntax is defined, while line 3 defines the formatting object syntax. In fact, we target the XSL formatting objects namespace, whose elements are defined in a subsection of the XSL document, as can be seen from the URI. However, we could also use CSS formatting objects, and a proposal exists as a W3C note [↪XSLCSS]. In that case we would replace line 3 with the following namespace definition:

```
xmlns:css="http://www.w3.org/TR/NOTE-XSL-and-CSS"
```

Line 4 (`result-ns`) specifies the namespace for the result tree. In our example it is "`fo`," indicating that we express the output in terms of the formatting object vocabulary, defined on line 3. If we planned to use CSS flow objects instead, line 4 would be replaced by:

```
result-ns="css"
```

Then we write three template rules. The first rule (lines 5–9) is for the root node, and it specifies that the document as a whole should be formatted as a "page sequence" formatting object, set in a 10 pt Helvetica typeface. The second rule (lines 10–14) declares that each par element should result in a "block" formatting object, which is separated from the previous block by twelve points and whose first text line is indented by ten points. Finally the third rule (lines 15–19) declares that an emph element corresponds to a sequence formatting object, and that its contents are typeset in an italic typeface.

A general XSL style sheet can contain zero or more instances of each of the nine elements (six are empty, lines 3–8, and three can have a content, lines 9–11) following. The ellipses (. . .) indicate where additional content is possible.

```
1   <?xml version="1.0"?>
2   <xsl:stylesheet xmlns:xsl="http://www.w3.org/TR/WD-xsl">
3     <xsl:import href="..."/>
4     <xsl:include href="..."/>
5     <xsl:id attribute="..."/>
6     <xsl:strip-space element="..."/>
7     <xsl:preserve-space element="..."/>
8     <xsl:macro name="..."> ... </xsl:macro>
9     <xsl:attribute-set name="..."> ... </xsl:attribute-set>
10    <xsl:constant name="..." value="..."/>
11    <xsl:template match="..."> ... </xsl:template>
12  </xsl:stylesheet>
```

Line 2 declares the xsl namespace. On line 11 we recognize the template rule element xsl:template, the workhorse of XSL style specifications. The order in which the nine possible children elements of the xsl:stylesheet element occur is not significant, except that xsl:import elements *must* always be specified first, at the beginning of the style sheet. In the following sections we explain the use of these elements in more detail as we need them.

7.6.2   Building the source tree

XSL operates on an XML document as a source tree. Documents with the same source tree will be processed identically by XSL. The XML tree data model allows for six kinds of nodes:

Root node   The root of the tree. It cannot occur anywhere else in the tree. It has a single child, namely the document element node.

Element nodes   Such a node exists for every element of the source document. Its children are the element nodes and characters of its content. All entity references are expanded, and character references are resolved. An order can be assigned to the nodes. In particular, the *document* order is identical to the order of the element start tags in the source document. It is possible to associate an identifier to an element by using a unique identifier that is an attribute declared as type ID in the DTD. Moreover, in the absence of a DTD you can specify in the XSL style sheet, using an <xsl:id .../> tag, which attribute should be treated as the identifier of type ID

Attribute nodes   Each element node has an associated set of attribute nodes. Defaulted attributes are treated the same as specified attributes, while unspecified attributes declared as #IMPLIED in the DTD do not get an attribute node.

Namespace   Each element has an associated set of namespace nodes, one for each namespace prefix that is in scope for the element and one for the default namespace.

Processing instruction nodes   There exists such a node for each processing instruction in the source. The name of the processing instruction is its target.

Comment nodes   Every comment in the source generates a corresponding comment node.

Before handing the tree to XSL for further handling, some whitespace is stripped, both from the source document and from the style sheet. The xml:space elements can be used to control this process, since they are retained in the source tree. Inside a style sheet, the xsl:text element preserves space. Moreover, the xsl:strip-space and xsl:preserve-space elements allow you also to control the way whitespace is stripped from source elements.

7.6.3 Template rules

The basic XSL building block is the template rule that describes how a given XML source element node is transformed into an XSL element node for further treatment. Templates are specified with the xsl:template element, which has two basic parts:

- a match attribute, identifying the XML source node(s) to which the rule applies; and

- the *content* of the xsl:template element, which provides the template to generate the formatting object. An action or formatting, styling, and processing part details the transformation and styling of the resulting node.

Let us reproduce here lines 15–19 of the first example in Section 7.6.1:

```
1    <xsl:template match="emph">                 <!-- match pattern     -->
2      <fo:inline-sequence font-style="italic"> <!-- action template + -->
3        <xsl:apply-templates/>                 <!--                  | -->
4      </fo:sequence>                           <!-- action template + -->
5    </xsl:template>
```

This template will match all elements of type *emph* (line 1). For each occurrence of an emph element in the source tree, a fo:inline-sequence formatting object (lines 2–4) should be added to the result tree. The xsl:apply-templates element (line 3) will recursively process the children of the source element in question.

Only one template rule can apply for each node in the source tree. To guarantee this, a detailed conflict-resolving mechanism exists, which is described in Section 7.6.5.6.

When no successful pattern matches exist for a rule in the style sheet, a *default* built-in template rule is implicitly applied for the root and all element nodes. It corresponds to the following definition:

```
1    <xsl:template match="*|/">
2      <xsl:apply-templates/>
3    </xsl:template>
```

This default rule stipulates that processing should continue with the child elements (xsl:apply-templates element on line 2). Although this template (line 1) matches the root and any other element, it has a smaller priority than any other template rule in a style sheet. This mechanism provides you with a convenient way to specify your own default rule by substituting your XSL commands for those on line 2. In this way your rule will override the default built-in behavior.

Similarly there exists a built-in template rule that copies text nodes through to the output tree. It has the form:

```
1    <xsl:template match="text()">
2      <xsl:value-of select="."/>
3    </xsl:template>
```

This rule does not apply to processing instructions and comments. They have to be matched by an explicit rule, otherwise nothing is created.

As an example, consider the following minimal "empty" (and trivial) style sheet, which declares only the xsl namespace.

```
1   <xsl:stylesheet xmlns:xsl="http://www.w3.org/TR/WD-xsl">
2   </xsl:stylesheet>
```

This style sheet, which we call empty.xsl, will (implicitly) apply the built-in default template rule and process all elements of the document. This is similar to the DSSSL file empty.dsl that we introduced in Section 7.5.3.1.

7.6.4   XSL processors

Today, not many processors that can handle XSL style files exist. To run our examples we have chosen James Clark's xt processor [↪XTPROC], a Java implementation of the tree construction part of XSL. Yet, for the sake of completeness, at the end of this section we will look briefly at other possible choices.

7.6.4.1   Introducing the xt processor

The xt program uses Clark's xp XML parser [↪XPPARS], which is also written in Java. It is thus sufficient, if you have Java installed on your machine, to download the xp and xt zip archives from Clark's Web site. They contain the Java archives sax.jar, xp.jar, and xt.jar. Add them to your Java class path, and off you go. On Windows the commands could be something like (depending on which version of Java you have available) the following:

```
1   set classpath=d:\xml\xt.jar;d:\xml\xp.jar;d:\xml\sax.jar;d:\jdk1.1.6\src;
2   %JAVA_HOME%\bin\java com.jclark.xsl.sax.Driver %1 %2 %3
```

where the JAVA_HOME environment variable (line 2) is the directory where your Java installation lives. Similarly on UNIX (Bourne shell), you could write the following:

```
1   DIR=/afs/cern.ch/asis/src/archive/java
2   CLASSPATH=$DIR/xt.jar:$DIR/xp.jar:$DIR/sax.jar:$CLASSPATH
3   export CLASSPATH
4   java com.jclark.xsl.sax.Driver $1 $2 $3
```

The variable DIR (line 1) is the directory where you keep your Java archives, while line 4 assumes that the java program is in your search path for executables.

If you save these lines in a command script xt.bat (Windows) or xt (UNIX), you can execute xt by typing:

```
xt XML-source-file XSL-style-sheet Output-file
```

If the third argument is not specified, the output is written to the "standard output" (e.g., the computer screen). We can use the style sheet empty.xsl and the XML example invitation2.xml of Section 7.4 5 with xt by entering the command:

```
xt invitation2.xml empty.xsl
```

We get the following output:

```
1   I would like to invite you all to celebrate
2   the birth of Invitation, my
3   first XML document child.
4
5   Please do your best to come and join me next Friday
6   evening. And, do not forget to bring your friends.
7
8   I really look forward to see you soon!
```

As expected, we see the contents of the text nodes for all elements of the document. The attribute values (of the invitation element) are not copied to the output. The copying-through feature of text nodes can assist you in developing an XSL style sheet step-by-step. Indeed, for a complex document this allows you to construct and fine tune the rules gradually, since the content of all nonspecified elements are copied to the output. It thus provides a convenient context for development and debugging.

7.6.4.2 Other XSL applications

We would like to mention two other XSL tools: the Koala XSL engine for Java [↪ KOALAXSL] and fop [↪ FOP], a program that converts XSL formatting objects to PDF.

7.6.4.3 The Koala XSL engine

The Koala XSL engine is a processor written in Java, using the SAX and DOM models. The package also contains xslSlideMaker, a postprocessor that handles slides prepared with XML and XSL and produces HTML output.

The (UNIX) setup script koalaxsl takes the form:

```
1   D=/afs/cern.ch/asis/oic/archive/java/Xsl
2   CLASSPATH=$D/domcore.jar:$D/sax.jar:$D/parser.zip:$D/xsl.jar:$CLASSPATH
3   export CLASSPATH
4   java    fr.dyade.koala.xml.xsl.Main $*
```

On line 2 we see the presence of four Java archives that are distributed with the package. To run the script, you can type:

```
koalaxsl -r xsl-style-sheet xml-source-file
```

where `koalaxsl` is the name we gave to the script shown earlier. The result, which corresponds to the rules specified in the style sheet following the -r switch, is written to standard output. The `xslSlideMaker` postprocessor is based on this parser. See the Koala Web page for more details [↪ KOALAXSL].

7.6.4.4 Formatting objects to PDF

The `fop` system consists of a set of Java classes that, via SAX, reads an XML document representing formatting objects and turns it into PDF. The author James Tauber is working actively to let his tool cover most of the characteristics of XSL's formatting objects. We discuss this tool in Section 7.6.10.

7.6.5 Patterns

A pattern is a string that selects a set of nodes (zero or more) in a source document. The selection is *relative to the current node*. The simplest pattern is the name of an element type; it selects all child elements of the current node with the given name. For example, the pattern `par` selects all the par(agraph) child elements of the current node.

7.6.5.1 Element patterns

A node is said to *match* a pattern if the node can be selected by the pattern. For instance, the pattern `par` matches any `par` element because if the current node was the parent of the `par` element, the `par` element would be one of the nodes selected by the pattern in question (even with `par` as document element, since the root is the parent of the document element).

The *union* operator "|" allows you to propose alternatives; for example, a|b|c matches a, b, and c elements individually.

Parent-child relations are expressed with the help of the "path" notation using the "/" operator. As an example, the pattern `par/emph` first selects `par` child elements of the current node, and then for each such element it selects its `emph` children.

The path operator / has a higher precedence than the union operator |, so that a/c|b/c matches c elements that have either an a or a b element as parent. For reasons of readability you can leave whitespace around operators inside patterns so that the above pattern can also be expressed as a/c | b/c, making its meaning somewhat clearer.

More general ancestor-descendant relationships are expressed with the // operator that allows zero or more generations between the element at the left and right side of the operator. Hence body//emph selects all `emph` descendants of the body children of the current node.

The "wildcard" character "*" can be used to represent any single element type, so that the pattern * selects all children of the current node, and */emph selects all emph grandchildren of the current node. On the other hand, the pattern par/* matches any element with a par element as parent.

The pattern "." selects the current node. This can be used, for instance, to represent the current node explicitly in ancestor-descendant relations, as in par//., a pattern that selects all par ancestors of the current node, or .//emph that selects all its emph descendants. In a similar way, the pattern ".." selects the parent of the current node, so that ../par selects par sibling elements of the current node.

7.6.5.2   Patterns for other types

The other node types are treated in a way similar to elements.

In particular, attributes of an element are handled as child elements, but syntactically their name is prefixed with the "@" character. For instance, @to selects the to attribute of the current element, whereas student/@name selects the name attribute of each student child element of the current node. The wildcard pattern @* selects all attributes of the current node.

Similarly, the pattern comment() matches any comment node; text() matches any text node. Processing instructions use the pattern pi() where the argument allows you to specify the target, as in pi("latex"), which matches any processing instruction with latex as target.

7.6.5.3   Tests in patterns

To qualify further the set of nodes selected by a pattern, you can use a test following the pattern by using square brackets as delimiters []. Each node in the node set will be tested in turn, and the result node set will include only nodes that satisfy the test condition. Following we list what can be used inside tests:

Patterns   The test will be true if one or more nodes starting from the current node match the test pattern. For instance, par[emph] selects par children elements of the current node that have at least one emph child element, while student[@middle-name] selects student elements with a middle-name attribute.

String   You can compare a pattern or subpattern to a string. For instance, student[@middle-name="Paul"] will match student child nodes of the current node that have an attribute middle-name equal to the string "Paul", while student[origin="BE"] selects student children with an origin child containing the text string "BE".
Another example relevant to the file invitation.xml is

```
<xsl:template match='par[emph="Invitation"]'>
```

This selects a par element with an *emph* child whose contents is the string "Invitation", that is, the first par in our XML source file.

Position   You can impose positional constraints on a node relative to its siblings. In the following, the test at the left is successful if the node being tested fulfills the condition at the right:

`first-of-any()`   node is first element child.

`last-of-any()`   node is last element child.

`first-of-type()`   node is first element child of its element type.

`last-of-type()`   node is last element child of its element type.

Booleans   You can use the `not()` Boolean function or the `and` and `or` Boolean operators. An example is the pattern `student[not(@middle-name)]` that selects `student` child elements without `middle-name` attribute. Similarly the pattern `p/emph[first-of-type() and last-of-type()]` matches an `emph` element when it is the only `emph` child of a `p` parent.

The `[]` operator has a higher precedence than the union operator `|`, so that `a|b[@x]` matches either `a` elements or `b` elements with an `x` attribute. For implementation reasons inside a `[]`, match pattern, `/`, `//`, and `[]` are not allowed.

7.6.5.4   Root and ancestor nodes

When a pattern starts with the path separator `/`, it represents the *root* node, which is interpreted in a special way. Thus a pattern that is just `/` matches the root node. The pattern `/invitation` matches the document element (if it corresponds to an `invitation` element), while `/*` *always* matches the document element, whatever it is called. More generally, the symbol `//` allows one to select descendants of the root node in a straightforward way. For instance, `//par` selects *any* `par` descendants of the root node, meaning, in fact, that any `par` element will match that pattern. For patterns starting with `/` or `//` the current node is irrelevant.

The first ancestor of the current node that matches a pattern can be selected using the syntax `ancestor(...)`, where the argument contains a match pattern. selected. For instance, `ancestor(article)/author` selects all `author` children of the first ancestor of the current node that is an `article`. More generally,

```
<xsl:template match="footnote[ancestor(footnote)]">
```

matches `footnote` elements with a `footnote` ancestor, that is, we are dealing with nested `footnotes` elements. As this is forbidden, for instance, in LaTeX, you can use such a pattern to warn about the presence of constructs that are otherwise allowed by the DTD (see Section B.4.5.1 for a discussion of this point).

7.6.5.5   Selection by identifier

To select individual nodes by identifier, the function `id`, whose argument can contain a blank-separated list of the identifier strings to be used in the match, is provided. As an example, id('michelg') will select the element with ID michelg, while id('michelg sebastianr') would select elements with an ID equal to michelg or sebastianr. When no element is found, the empty set is returned. The argument can also be a pattern rather than a literal string. In that case for each node selected by the pattern, the value of the node is treated as a whitespace-separated list of ID references. For example, if the current node is an element with an IDREF or IDREFS attribute (see page 261) named myref, then the pattern id(@myref) will effectively dereference the myref attribute, get its value, and select the element(s) that it references.

7.6.5.6 Resolving match conflicts

When several template rules apply to the same source tree element, the following strategy is applied:

- First, all matching template rules that are less *important* than the most important matching template rule or rules are eliminated from consideration. In particular, the default template (see Section 7.6.3) is less important than explicitly specified ones. Also rules and definitions in the importing style sheet are more important than those in imported style sheets, although rules and definitions in any given imported style sheet are considered more important than those present in previously imported style sheets.

- You can also specify an explicit priority attribute on rules (a positive or negative real number) to distinguish among various matching rules. In this case the matching rule with the highest priority is selected.

When at the end still more than one matching template rule is selected, an error condition results. In that case the XSL processor signals the error, or it must use the matching template rule that occurs last in the style sheet.

In practice such ambiguities should, of course, be minimized to ease the understanding, documentation, and maintainability of style sheets.

7.6.5.7 A first complete example

Let us consider the following XML document sectionexa.xml, consisting of an article with a title, two authors, an abstract, two sections, each with a section title, and a few paragraphs:

```
1    <article>
2      <title>This is the article's title</title>
3      <author>Michel Goossens</author>
4      <author>Sebastian Rahtz</author>
5      <abstract>A <emph>short</emph> description of the contents</abstract>
6      <section sectid="S1">
7        <stitle>First section title</stitle>
8        <par ident="first">The first paragraph for this section.</par>
9        <par ident="normal">A normal paragraph with <emph>emphasised</emph> text.</par>
10       <par>Here we have <emph>no</emph> attribute.</par>
```

```
11      <par ident="last">This is the end of the section.</par>
12    </section>
13    <section sectid="S2">
14      <stitle>Second section title</stitle>
15      <par ident="first">The first paragraph for this section.</par>
16      <par>Here we <emph>also</emph> have <emph>no</emph> attribute.</par>
17      <par ident="normal" id="special">A normal paragraph with
18          <emph>emphasised</emph> text.</par>
19      <par>Another attribute-less paragraph.</par>
20      <par ident="last">This is the end of the section.</par>
21    </section>
22  </article>
```

We want to address (match) the various elements of this document using
the patterns introduced in this section. Therefore we construct a style sheet
`sectionexa.xsl`. It contains an ad hoc set of templates, showing a few of the pattern rules in action. Note in particular how we must assign a `priority` value to
some of the templates to ensure that only a single rule fires for each element in the
XML source file.

```
1   <?xml version='1.0'?>
2   <xsl:stylesheet xmlns:xsl="http://www.w3.org/TR/WD-xsl" result-ns="">
3   <xsl:template match="/">
4     <xsl:text>(*root*)</xsl:text>
5     <xsl:apply-templates/>
6     <xsl:text>(/*root*)</xsl:text>
7   </xsl:template>
8   <xsl:template match="*" priority="-1">
9     <xsl:text>(*)</xsl:text>
10     <xsl:apply-templates/>
11     <xsl:text>(/*)</xsl:text>
12   </xsl:template>
13   <xsl:template match="par">
14     <xsl:text>(T1)</xsl:text>
15     <xsl:apply-templates/>
16     <xsl:text>(/T1)</xsl:text>
17   </xsl:template>
18   <xsl:template match="par[@ident]" priority="1">
19     <xsl:text>(T2)</xsl:text>
20     <xsl:apply-templates/>
21     <xsl:text>(/T2)</xsl:text>
22   </xsl:template>
23   <xsl:template match="par[@ident='first']" priority="2">
24     <xsl:text>(T3)</xsl:text>
25     <xsl:apply-templates/>
26     <xsl:text>(/T3)</xsl:text>
27   </xsl:template>
28   <xsl:template match="section[@sectid='S2']
29                /par[@ident='normal' and @id='special']">
30     <xsl:text>(T4)</xsl:text>
31     <xsl:apply-templates/>
32     <xsl:text>(/T4)</xsl:text>
33   </xsl:template>
34   <xsl:template match="section[last-of-type()]">
35     <xsl:text>(P1)</xsl:text>
36     <xsl:apply-templates/>
37     <xsl:text>(/P1)</xsl:text>
38   </xsl:template>
39   <xsl:template match="section[not(first-of-type())]/par[first-of-type()]">
40     <xsl:text>(P2)</xsl:text>
41     <xsl:apply-templates/>
42     <xsl:text>(/P2)</xsl:text>
```

```
43    </xsl:template>
44    <xsl:template match="author">
45      <xsl:text>(A1)</xsl:text>
46      <xsl:apply-templates/>
47      <xsl:text>(/A1)</xsl:text>
48    </xsl:template>
49    <xsl:template match="author[last-of-type()]" priority="1">
50      <xsl:text>(A2)</xsl:text>
51      <xsl:apply-templates/>
52      <xsl:text>(/A2)</xsl:text>
53    </xsl:template>
54    <xsl:template match="*[first-of-type() and last-of-type()]">
55      <xsl:text>(WD)</xsl:text>
56      <xsl:apply-templates/>
57      <xsl:text>(/WD)</xsl:text>
58    </xsl:template>
59    <xsl:template match="emph[first-of-type() and last-of-type()]" priority="1">
60      <xsl:text>(E1)</xsl:text>
61      <xsl:apply-templates/>
62      <xsl:text>(/E1)</xsl:text>
63    </xsl:template>
64    <xsl:template match="emph[not (first-of-type() and last-of-type())]">
65      <xsl:text>(E2)</xsl:text>
66      <xsl:apply-templates/>
67      <xsl:text>(/E2)</xsl:text>
68    </xsl:template>
69    </xsl:stylesheet>
```

The XML source `sectionexa.xml` and the XSL style sheet `sectionexa.xsl`
are processed with the `xt` program by typing the following command:

    xt sectionexa.xml sectionexa.xsl

This generates the following output:

```
1    (*root*)(WD)
2      (WD)This is the article's title(/WD)
3      (A1)Michel Goossens(/A1)
4      (A2)Sebastian Rahtz(/A2)
5      (WD)A (E1)short(/E1) description of the contents(/WD)
6      (*)
7        (WD)First section title(/WD)
8        (T3)The first paragraph for this section.(/T3)
9        (T2)A normal paragraph with (E1)emphasised(/E1) text.(/T2)
10       (T1)Here we have (E1)an(/E1) attribute.(/T1)
11       (T2)This is the end of the section.(/T2)
12     (/*)
13     (P1)
14       (WD)Second section title(/WD)
15       (T3)The first paragraph for this section.(/T3)
16       (T1)Here we (E2)also(/E2) have (E2)no(/E2) attribute.(/T1)
17       (T2)A normal paragraph with
18           (E1)emphasised(/E1) text.(/T2)
19       (T1)Another attribute-less paragraph.(/T1)
20       (T2)This is the end of the section.(/T2)
21     (/P1)
22   (/WD)(/*root*)
```

Let us review these lines and see how they relate to the way the style sheet
matches the lines in the XML source file. To clearly indicate which rule is applied,
we added tags in front of and following each match pattern by using `xsl:text`

elements. This makes it easy to find out which rule matches various parts of the XML file.

Lines 3–7 of the style sheet define the template for the root element. We observe, indeed, that it encloses the entire document, inclusive of the document element `article`. The default pattern for element nodes (lines 8–12 in the XSL file) applies to those nodes that are not matched by any other rules in the style sheet. This is the case only for the `section` element on line 6 of the XML file. Now we consider lines 13 to 33 in the XSL style sheet. The four match patterns use elements, children, or attribute qualifiers. All `par` elements (lines 8–11 and 15–20 in the XML source) match line 13 (T1), while the refinement of line 18 (T2) matches `par` elements that also have an `ident` attribute (lines 8, 9, 11, 15, 17, and 20 in the XML source). On line 23 we add one more constraint (T3) that matches `par` elements with their `ident` attribute equal to "`first`" (lines 8 and 15 in the XML source). The more complex pattern on lines 28–29 in the XSL style sheet (T4) matches a `par` element whose `ident` attribute has the value "normal," its `id` attribute has the value "special," and whose parent is a `section` element that has an attribute `sectid` equal to "S2" (only line 17 in the XML source matches all of these conditions). To disambiguate the `par` rules that would match more than one element, we had to add a `priority` attribute on pattern lines 18 and 23.

The other patterns use positional qualifiers. An interesting case is the match pattern on line 54 (WD), where we combine a wildcard with the positional operators `first-of-type` and `last-of-type`. Because we combine them with the `and` Boolean operator, we, in fact, match elements that occur only once (since they are both first and last instances of their type) and that are not matched by a pattern with a higher priority (as on line 59, see next paragraph). Referring to the XML source, we see this is the case for the `article` element on line 1, the `title` element on line 2, and the `abstract` element on line 5, as well as for the `stitle` elements on lines 7 and 14, since they are unique inside their respective `section` elements.

The remaining patterns in the XSL style sheet are straightforward and easy to understand. We merely comment on the match patterns on lines 59 (E1) and 64 (E2). The first pattern (E1) looks for an `emph` element without siblings of the same type (to disambiguate with respect to the more general rule on line 54, we need the `priority` attribute) as on lines 9, 10, and 17–18 of the XML source, which contain only one `emph` element inside the `par` element. The second pattern (E2) looks for `emph` elements that have at least one sibling of the same type, as on line 16 of the XML source, which has two `emph` elements inside the `par` element.

This example should have made it clear that XSL is a quite complete pattern language to select element nodes in an XML document tree.

7.6.6   Templates

Once a rule fires for a given element, the rule's template is instantiated. A template can add literal result elements, character data (text), and instructions for creating fragments of the result tree (copying, sorting, numbering, or executing macros).

A template can output a set of formatting objects. Alternatively, as we shall show later, you can write HTML or even LaTeX code directly.

It is not our intention to describe them in any detail. We merely give a list of the instructions and then present an overview of the formatting objects in the next section. This should be enough to understand the examples later in this chapter. It should also be clear that some of the instruction names can still change in the final recommendation.

Possible constructs that can occur inside templates as defined in the XSL style sheet DTD follow:

xsl:apply-templates   Processes child nodes, including text nodes. A select attribute lets you choose which nodes to process (see Section 7.6.5 for an overview of patterns that can be used).

xsl:attribute   Adds an attribute node specified by the name attribute to the containing result element node. The value of the created attribute is given by the content of the xsl:attribute element.

xsl:attribute-sets   Assigns a name to a set of attributes that can be referenced in an xsl:use element.

xsl:choose   Allows selection of a node among several alternatives. It consists of a series of xsl:when elements and zero or one xsl:otherwise element. Each xsl:when element has a test attribute specifying a select pattern. The content of the first (only!) xsl:when element whose test is true will be instantiated. If none of the xsl:when elements selects a node, then the template of the xsl:otherwise element, if present, is instantiated, or else in the absence of an xsl:otherwise element, nothing is created.

xsl:comment   Creates a comment node in the result tree. The value of the comment is the content of the xsl:comment element.

xsl:constant   Creates a global string constant. The name attribute allows you to assign a name to identify the constant, while its value is specified with the value attribute.

xsl:copy   Copies the current node. The xsl:copy element will be replaced by a copy of the current node, including its namespace nodes, but the children and attribute nodes are not automatically copied.

xsl:contents   Used in macro processing to include the result tree fragment selected by the match pattern.

xsl:element   Creates an element with a computed name that is set equal to the value of the name attribute. Attributes and children of the created element are specified as the contents of the xsl:element element.

xsl:for-each   When the result document is known to have a regular structure, you can specify directly the template for selected elements by using the xsl:for-each element. It has a select attribute whose pattern selects element nodes for which the specified template will be instantiated.

`xsl:if` Provides a simple if-then functionality. The attribute `test` specifies a select pattern. If one or more nodes are selected, then the content of the `xsl:if` element is instantiated, otherwise nothing is created.

`xsl:import` Style sheets can be imported. Rules and definitions in the importing style sheet are considered more *important* than rules and definitions in any imported style sheets, while rules and definitions in an imported style sheet *override*, that is, are more important than those in previously imported style sheets. The `href` attribute tells the XSL processor where the style sheet resides by specifying its URI. The `xsl:import` elements must be grouped at the beginning of a style sheet.

`xsl:include` Style sheets can be combined textually by including other style sheets. The `href` attribute tells the XSL processor where the style sheet resides by specifying its URI. If an included style sheet contains an `xsl:import` element, then the latter will be moved up to the beginning of the including style sheet to just after any existing `xsl:import` elements.

`xsl:invoke` Used to invoke the processing of a macro defined with an `xsl:macro` element inside a template. The name of the macro is specified with the help of the `macro` attribute. If the macro had arguments, then `xsl:arg` elements with `name` and `value` attributes can be specified if the defaults value set in the `xsl:macro` element is not appropriate.

`xsl:macro` Defines a macro containing multiple result fragments that can be referenced conveniently as a unit by using `xsl:invoke`. The macro is identified by assigning it a name with the `name` attribute. One or more macro arguments can be specified by including `xsl:macro-arg` elements with `name` and `default` attributes inside an `xsl:macro` element.

`xsl:number` Allows numbering in the source and result trees and provides control over the presentation format of the counters. See the XSL specification for details.

`xsl:pi` Creates a processing instruction node with a name specified by the `name` attribute and a value given by content of the `xsl:pi` element.

`xsl:sort` Sorts nodes inside `xsl:apply-templates` and `xsl:for-each` elements. The `xsl:sort` has a `select` attribute that specifies a pattern evaluated for the node in question. The value of the first selected node is used as a sort key for that node. Further attributes are:

`order`	can be `ascending` or `descending`;
`lang`	specifies language of sort keys;
`data-type`	can be `text` or `number`; and
`case-order`	can be `upper-first` or `lower-first`.

`xsl:text` Places text in the result tree.

`xsl:value-of` Computes generated text by extracting text from the source tree or by inserting a value of a text string with the help of the `select` attribute.

7.6.7 Formatting objects and their properties

Formatting objects are applied to the result tree node by being contained in the pattern part of the element. The general syntax is the following:

```
<xsl:template match="pattern">
  <fo:formatting-object (style property="value")*>
    [processing instructions]*
  </fo:formatting-object>
</xsl:template>
```

We have already seen an example of this syntax at the beginning of Section 7.6.1.

The XSL specification tries, as far as possible, to define a formatting model that is compatible with both CSS and DSSSL in the names for objects, definitions, and property names.

The draft XSL specification available in December 1998 defines only formatting objects for basic word processor support. Following is a short overview of the available formatting objects.

7.6.7.1 Layout formatting objects

The following objects describe layouts for a series of pages (per chapter or for front, body, or back matter)

basic-page-sequence Object describing the general layout of a (series of) "pages" (online, print, audio). It holds a set of simple-page-master or queue children. It is convenient as a means to define style rules that can be inherited by all "pages" of a document.

simple-page-master Object to describe the general layout of a simple page by dividing it into five areas: header, body, footer, start-side, and end-side. In addition, one can specify a title that may be used, for instance, in the title bar of a Web browser. The characteristics of these areas and title can be defined with queue elements (see following).

7.6.7.2 Content flow objects

block Represents paragraphs, titles, headlines, captions, and so on. Blocks usually correspond to a rectangular area with a width equal to that of the containing area and a height determined by the material the block contains. A block can be separated from preceding and subsequent block-level objects.

character Atomic unit to the formatter. This can be used to override one or more characters with specific glyph representations.

display-graphic, inline-graphic Holds an image or vector graphic that is placed as a separate block or inline.

`display-link, inline-link`   Creates a (block level or inline) area that can be selected by the user to request traversal to another resource. A `link` contains
`link-end-locator` flow objects.

`display-rule, inline-rule`   Draws a block-level or inline rule (line-segment).

`display-sequence, inline-sequence`   Groups content and allows the assign-
ment of shared inherited properties. An example is choosing a local font
change. They can be block level (like HTML's `DIV` element) or inline (like
HTML's `SPAN` element).

`link-end-locator`   Target (destination) for a `link`.

`list-block`   A block-level object that acts as a container for the following flow
objects: `list-item`, `list-item-label`, and `list-item-body`.

> `list-item`   Groups the `list-item-label` and `list-item-body` for each
> item in the list.
>
> `list-item-label`   Contains the number or label of a list item.
>
> `list-item-body`   Contains main content of a list item. Multiparagraph
> list items are formatted properly. If lists are nested, the second list
> must be contained as a child of a `list-item-body` flow object.

`page-number`   Instructs formatter to construct and present a page number.

`queue`   Collects a sequence or tree of formatting objects to be presented in an
area whose name corresponds to one of the queue names defined inside a
`simple-page-master` element.

Section 3 of the XSL Specification gives a detailed description of all of these
formatting objects, enumerating all the possible attributes.

7.6.7.3   Missing flow objects

The current draft does not yet have support for the following:

- multicolumn and more sophisticated page layouts;
- layout-driven formatting, such as side-by-side material, floats, and extracted
  content (index, table of contents, endnotes, and so on);
- full internationalization (mixed scripts, locale-dependent formatting);
- more formatter-generated text, such as auto-leaders, cross-references, citations, layout-derived numbering;
- mathematics and tables; and
- interactivity and multimedia.

7.6.8   Proposed extensibility mechanism

The current draft does not allow for scripting or for otherwise escaping to an (external) program or procedure to perform an action or (more or less) simple calculation that could influence the result tree. To gain some experience with such a functionality, which seems to be desired by many users of XSL, James Clark included in his xt program an experimental extensibility mechanism that is based on the idea of filtering fragments of the result tree through an object.

7.6.8.1   A filtering mechanism

Clark lets you use the element type `xsl:invoke` to specify a "filter." With its `classid` attribute you can specify an external object (much like the HTML4 `OBJECT` tag). The content of the `xsl:invoke` element contains the result tree fragment to be filtered. The `xsl:invoke` element can start with one or more `xsl:arg` elements to present parameters to the object. The result of the `xsl:invoke` element is a "filtered result tree fragment." Thus the proposed extension mechanism affects only the result tree and does not act on the input source tree. The `xsl:invoke` elements can be nested, as seen in the second example that follows.

In principle, the filters could use various interfaces, for example the DOM. However, in the current xt test implementation the Java object must implement an extension of the SAX `DocumentHandler` interface (see Section B.6.1), as follows:

```
1   package com.jclark.xsl.sax;
2
3   public interface Filter extends org.xml.sax.DocumentHandler {
4     void setDocumentHandler(org.xml.sax.DocumentHandler handler);
5     void setParameter(String name, String value) throws SAXException;
6   }
```

Direct scripting is possible by allowing something as shown following, where the script would be defined by the contents of the value argument of the `xsl:arg` element (line 4). The script is later referenced by the `select` attribute of a `xsl:for-each` construct (line 5).

```
1   <xsl:template match="mytemplate">
2     <xsl:invoke classid="java:JSFilter">
3       <xsl:arg name="script"
4         value=' ... your JavaScript code ... '/>
5       <xsl:for-each select="value">
6         <xsl:apply-templates/>
7         ...
8       </xsl:for-each>
9     </xsl:invoke>
10  </xsl:template>
```

7.6.8.2   Examples of using filters

In order to get a feeling of what is possible in the current test implementation, we present two variants of demonstration programs that come with the xt distribution.

The XSL style sheet `writefile.xsl`, shown here, writes a file whose name is defined by the `filename` attribute of the `file` tag (see line 4) in the XML source;

the java call `TextFileOutputFilter` (line 3) is part of xt's class library and actually instantiates the file.

```
1    <xsl:stylesheet xmlns:xsl="http://www.w3.org/TR/WD-xsl" default-space="strip">
2      <xsl:template match="file">
3        <xsl:invoke classid="java:com.jclark.xsl.sax.TextFileOutputFilter">
4          <xsl:arg name="file" value="{@filename}"/>
5          <xsl:apply-templates/>
6        </xsl:invoke>
7      </xsl:template>
8    </xsl:stylesheet>
```

Now we run the file `writefiles.xml`, shown here, together with the style sheet `writefile.xsl` through the xt XSL processor.

```
1    <outputfiles>
2    <file filename="filea.out">10 &lt; 20
3    </file>
4    <file filename="fileb.out">43 &gt; 34
5    An ampersand character: &amp;.
6    </file>
7    </outputfiles>
```

This generates a file `filea.out` (see line 2 above), containing one line:

```
10 < 20
```

and a file `fileb.out` (lines 4–5 above), containing two lines:

```
43 > 34
An ampersand character: &.
```

See how the `filename` attribute of the `file` element defines the name of the output file, and how the entities are translated into the characters they represent.

A second example sums a set of numerical strings. We use the XSL style sheet `makesum.xsl` as shown here:

```
1    <xsl:stylesheet xmlns:xsl="http://www.w3.org/TR/WD-xsl" default-space="strip">
2      <xsl:template match="makesum">
3        <xsl:invoke classid="java:com.jclark.xsl.sax.TextFileOutputFilter">
4          <xsl:arg name="file" value="sum.out"/>
5          <xsl:invoke classid="java:com.jclark.xsl.sax.TotalFilter">
6            <xsl:apply-templates/>
7          </xsl:invoke>
8        </xsl:invoke>
9      </xsl:template>
10     <xsl:template match="real">
11       <number><xsl:apply-templates/></number>
12     </xsl:template>
13   </xsl:stylesheet>
```

The style sheet uses two templates. The first one (lines 2–9) matches a `makesum` element in the XML input file. It defines the output file name `sum.out` with the help of the `arg` element of the first `xsl:invoke` element that uses the class TextFileOutputFilter (lines 3–4, as in the previous example). A second xsl:invoke element (lines 5–7), nested inside the first, applies a class TotalFilter on the children of the makesum element. This Java class is also part of the xt distribution and sums at set of character strings. The second template (lines 10–12) matches real elements and puts them between number tags in the result tree, where they will be summed by the TotalFilter class.

Suppose we present the following XML file makesum.xml together with the style sheet makesum.xsl to the xt processor.

```
1    <makesum>
2    <real>3.0</real>
3    <real>0.14159</real>
4    <real>.0000026536</real>
5    </makesum>
```

Now the output file sum.out contains 3.1415926536, which is indeed the sum of the three numbers in the input file.

7.6.8.3   Simple string evaluation

Often we do not need the full complexity of the approach outlined earlier, since our need for extensibility can be limited to string-to-string manipulations. For instance, converting between units, formatting of counters, simple arithmetic, or stripping whitespace can be handled as a transformation on strings. For this, one could define a special case of xsl:invoke that would build a string starting from the text content of the result tree fragment being filtered, apply a script to that string, and replace the result tree fragment by a single text node containing the result of evaluating the script. As an example, suppose we want to add five to the string at the present result node fragment, we could then write something like

```
<xsl:transform string script="Number(this)+5">
  <xsl:number format="a"/>
</xsl:transform-string>
```

where the xsl:number element would generate a lowercase alphabetic representation of the number at the present result node after applying the script.

We want to stress once more that the extension mechanism discussed in this section is a proposal and presents only one possible approach to the problem. The form finally adopted for the XSL language might end up being very different from what is described here.

7.6.9   Using XSL to generate HTML or LaTeX

To show some of the possibilities of XSL in the area of formatting an XML document, once more we are going to use the two versions of the invitation XML files. First we will generate LaTeX, in much the same way as we did with Perl, and use the same class file. We have to define templates for all the XML elements that we want to treat, as shown in the following XSL style file `invlat1.xsl`:

```
1   <?xml version='1.0'?>
2
3   <xsl:stylesheet xmlns:xsl="http://www.w3.org/TR/WD-xsl"
4                   default-space="strip"
5                   result-ns="">
6
7   <xsl:template match="invitation">
8   <xsl:text>\documentclass[]{article}
9   \usepackage{invitation}
10  \begin{document}
11  </xsl:text>
12  <xsl:apply-templates/>
13  <xsl:text>\end{document}
14  </xsl:text>
15  </xsl:template>
16
17  <xsl:template match="invitation/front">
18  <xsl:text>\begin{Front}
19  \To{</xsl:text>
20  <xsl:value-of select="to"/>
21  <xsl:text>}
22  \Date{</xsl:text>
23  <xsl:value-of select="date"/>
24  <xsl:text>}
25  \Where{</xsl:text>
26  <xsl:value-of select="where"/>
27  <xsl:text>}
28  \Why{</xsl:text>
29  <xsl:value-of select="why"/>
30  <xsl:text>}
31  \end{Front}
32  </xsl:text>
33  </xsl:template>
34
35  <xsl:template match="invitation/body">
36  <xsl:text>\begin{Body}
37  </xsl:text>
38    <xsl:apply-templates/>
39  <xsl:text>\end{Body}
40  </xsl:text>
41  </xsl:template>
42
43  <xsl:template match="invitation/body/par">
44  <xsl:text>\par</xsl:text>
45  <xsl:apply-templates/>
46  </xsl:template>
47
48  <xsl:template match="invitation/body/par/emph">
49  <xsl:text>\emph{</xsl:text>
50  <xsl:apply-templates/>
51  <xsl:text>}</xsl:text>
52  </xsl:template>
53
54  <xsl:template match="invitation/back">
55  <xsl:text>\begin{Back}
56  \Signature{</xsl:text>
57  <xsl:value-of select="signature"/>
58  <xsl:text>}
59  \end{Back}
60  </xsl:text>
61  </xsl:template>
62  </xsl:stylesheet>
```

After defining the usual namespace (xsl) on line 3, the next line (4) indicates that we want all "default" space to be collapsed. This means that only whitespace, which we enter ourselves, will be retained. This is useful because XML and XSL by default leave whitespace untouched, which can lead to strange effects with LaTeX.

The first template (lines 7–15) treats the invitation element. It initializes LaTeX (lines 8–9), starts the document (line 10), and then lets XSL process all its child elements (line 12) before finalizing the document (line 13). The LaTeX commands are entered literally in the output stream by the xsl:text elements. Inside this element, space and newline characters are significant and are faithfully written to the output.

The second template (lines 17–33) deals with the front element and its children. First we open the Front environment (line 18), write the \To command, and then tell XSL to go and fetch the content of the to element (line 20) with the help of the xsl:value command. Similarly we get the information for the \Date (lines 22–24), \Where (lines 25–27), and \Why (lines 28–30) commands. Lines 30–32 take care of closing the Front environment.

We now arrive at the body element of the XML file, which is handled with lines 35–41. The action consists of starting the Body environment (lines 36–37), telling XSL to handle the children of the XML body element (line 38), and closing the Body environment (lines 39–40).

The par children of the body element are handled with the pattern on lines 43–46; a LaTeX \par command is issued for each such element (line 44) before continuing to treat children elements of par itself (line 45).

The character content of the emph elements inside par, inside body, and inside invitation (line 48 is a good example of explicit ancestor match selection) gets transferred into the argument of the LaTeX \emph command (lines 49–51).

Finally we arrive at the back element, which is handled on lines 54–61. Line 55 starts a LaTeX Back environment, while lines 56–58 take care of copying the content of the signature element into the argument of LaTeX's \Signature command. Line 59 ends the Back environment.

We use the XML file invitation.xml defined on page 254 and the earlier XSL style sheet with the xt XSL processor, as follows:

```
xt invitation.xml invlat1.xsl invlat1.tex
```

The LaTeX file invlat1.tex that we obtain follows. It is completely identical to the TeX file we showed on page 295.

```
1   \documentclass[]{article}
2   \usepackage{invitation}
3   \begin{document}
4   \begin{Front}
5   \To{Anna, Bernard, Didier, Johanna}
6   \Date{Next Friday Evening at 8 pm}
7   \Where{The Web Cafe}
8   \Why{My first XML baby}
9   \end{Front}
10  \begin{Body}
```

```
11   \par
12   I would like to invite you all to celebrate
13   the birth of \emph{Invitation}, my
14   first XML document child.
15   \par
16   Please do your best to come and join me next Friday
17   evening. And, do not forget to bring your friends.
18   \par
19   I \emph{really} look forward to see you soon!
20   \end{Body}
21   \begin{Back}
22   \Signature{Michel}
23   \end{Back}
24   \end{document}
```

Our next example will show how to generate an HTML file for the XML file `invitation2.xml` described in Section 7.4.5. We take advantage of a feature of the XSL xt processor that allows you to specify which is the default namespace for the elements inside the XSL style sheet. Thus in the file `invhtml2.xsl`, on line 4, we specify that element types with unspecified namespace in the style sheet refer to the HTML4 specification. This makes it very convenient to mix XSL and HTML commands in the body of the templates.

```
1    <?xml version='1.0'?>
2    <xsl:stylesheet
3     xmlns:xsl="http://www.w3.org/TR/WD-xsl"
4     xmlns="http://www.w3.org/TR/REC-html40"
5     result-ns="">
6
7    <xsl:template match="/">
8    <html>
9    <head>
10   <title> Invitation (XSL/CSS formatting) </title>
11   <link href="invit.css" rel="stylesheet" type="text/css"/>
12   <!-- 4 January 1998 mg -->
13   </head>
14   <body>
15   <h1>INVITATION</h1>
16   <table>
17   <tbody>
18   <tr><td class="front">To: </td>
19   <td><xsl:value-of select="@to"/></td></tr>
20   <tr><td class="front">When: </td>
21   <td><xsl:value-of select="@date"/></td></tr>
22   <tr><td class="front">Venue: </td>
23   <td><xsl:value-of select="@where"/></td></tr>
24   <tr><td class="front">Occasion: </td>
25   <td><xsl:value-of select="@why"/></td></tr>
26   </tbody>
27   </table>
28   <xsl:apply-templates/>
29   <p class="signature"><xsl:value-of select="@signature"/></p>
30   </body>
31   </html>
32   </xsl:template>
33   <xsl:template match="invitation/par">
34   <p><xsl:apply-templates/></p>
35   </xsl:template>
36   <xsl:template match="invitation/par/emph">
37   <em><xsl:apply-templates/></em>
38   </xsl:template>
39   </xsl:stylesheet>
```

In this style sheet, lines 7–32 take care of the root element. In particular, the HTML file is initialized (lines 8–14) with the link to the CSS style sheet `invit.css` on line 11. A level 1 heading is defined (line 15), and a table is started on line 16. This is to represent nicely the various attributes of the `invitation` element. For instance, on line 19 you can see how to get access to the attribute of an XML element by using XSL's `xsl:value-of` element and the attribute @ specifier on its `select` attribute. In this case, we are after the value of the `to` attribute, which is put in the right-hand cell of the first row of the table that contains the string "To: " in the left-hand cell (line 18). The following pairs of lines 20 to 25 build rows for the other attributes of the `invitation` element. On lines 26–27 we end the table before instructing XSL first to process the children of `invitation` (line 28) and then to write an HTML p element of class `signature` with as content the value of the `signature` attribute of the `<invitation>` start tag (line 29). Lines 30–31 end the HTML document gracefully.

The remaining tasks are to handle the `par` and `emph` elements. These are dealt with in lines 33–35 and 36–38, respectively. Compare the procedure to the one described in Section 7.4.6.

The style sheet `invhtml2.xsl` and XML file `invitation2.xml` are presented to the `xt` processor.

```
xt invitation2.xml invhtml2.xsl invhtml2.html
```

We obtain the HTML file `invhtml2.html`, listed here. It is equivalent to the HTML file shown on page 308.

```
1    <!DOCTYPE html PUBLIC "-//W3C//DTD HTML 4.0 Transitional//EN">
2    <html>
3    <head>
4    <title> Invitation (sgmlpl/CSS formatting) </title>
5    <link href="invit.css" rel="stylesheet" type="text/css">
6    </head>
7    <body>
8    <h1>INVITATION</h1>
9    <table>
10   <tbody>
11   <tr><td class="front">To: </td>
12   <td>Anna, Bernard, Didier, Johanna</td></tr>
13   <tr><td class="front">When: </td>
14   <td>Next Friday Evening at 8 pm</td></tr>
15   <tr><td class="front">Venue: </td>
16   <td>The Web Cafe</td></tr>
17   <tr><td class="front">Occasion: </td>
18   <td>My first XML baby</td></tr>
19   </tbody>
20   </table>
21   <p>I would like to invite you all to celebrate
22   the birth of <em>Invitation</em>, my
23   first XML document child.</p>
24   <p>Please do your best to come and join me next Friday
25   evening. And, do not forget to bring your friends.</p>
26   <p>I <em>really</em> look forward to see you soon!</p>
27   <p class="signature">Michel</p>
28   </body>
29   </html>
```

7.6.10   Using XSL to generate formatting objects

As we have already explained several times, the best approach for setting up a style sheet for a given class of documents is to express it in terms of generic formatting objects. This way your style sheet can be translated into various output formats. We have shown that this works well in the case of DSSSL, where we used Jade as a processing engine (see Section 7.5.3). Similarly we can write an XSL style sheet using only XSL's formatting objects and translate those into various output representations. However, at present, because the XSL standard is not yet finalized, no general-purpose tool, such as Jade, is available. Nevertheless, we can use James Tauber's `fop` Java processor, which transforms (a subset of) XSL formatting objects into PDF.

Let us first look at the XSL style sheet `invfo1.xsl` that we have prepared for use with the `invitation` XML source file.

```
1    <?xml version='1.0'?>
2    <xsl:stylesheet xmlns:xsl="http://www.w3.org/TR/WD-xsl"
3                    xmlns:fo="http://www.w3.org/TR/WD-xsl/FO"
4                    result-ns="fo"
5                    default-space="">
6    <xsl:constant name="Fontsize" value="12pt"/>
7    <xsl:macro name="listitem">
8      <xsl:macro-arg name="itemid"/>
9      <xsl:macro-arg name="itemtext"/>
10     <fo:list-item id="{arg(itemid)}">
11       <fo:list-item-label font-style="italic">
12         <xsl:value-of select='arg(itemtext)'/><xsl:text>:</xsl:text>
13       </fo:list-item-label>
14       <fo:list-item-body>
15         <xsl:contents/>
16       </fo:list-item-body>
17     </fo:list-item>
18   </xsl:macro>
19
20   <xsl:template match='/'>
21    <fo:basic-page-sequence font-family="serif" font-size="{constant(Fontsize)}"
22                            margin-top="15mm"   margin-bottom="15mm"
23                            margin-left="15mm"  margin-right="15mm"
24                            page-width="120mm"  id="pageseq">
25      <xsl:apply-templates/>
26    </fo:basic-page-sequence>
27   </xsl:template>
28
29   <xsl:template match="invitation/front">
30     <fo:display-sequence>
31       <fo:block font-family="sans-serif"  font-size="24pt"
32                 font-weight="bold"        text-align="center">
33         <xsl:text>INVITATION</xsl:text>
34       </fo:block>
35       <fo:list-block label-width="2cm">
36         <xsl:invoke macro="listitem">
37           <xsl:arg name="itemtext" value="To"/>
38           <xsl:arg name="itemid" value="listto"/>
39           <xsl:value-of select="to"/>
40         </xsl:invoke>
41         <xsl:invoke macro="listitem">
42           <xsl:arg name="itemtext" value="When"/>
43           <xsl:arg name="itemid" value="listdate"/>
44           <xsl:value-of select="date"/>
45         </xsl:invoke>
```

```
46          <xsl:invoke macro="listitem">
47            <xsl:arg name="itemtext" value="Venue"/>
48            <xsl:arg name="itemid" value="listwhere"/>
49            <xsl:value-of select="where"/>
50          </xsl:invoke>
51          <xsl:invoke macro="listitem">
52            <xsl:arg name="itemtext" value="Occasion"/>
53            <xsl:arg name="itemid" value="listwhy"/>
54            <xsl:value-of select="why"/>
55          </xsl:invoke>
56        </fo:list-block>
57      </fo:display-sequence>
58    </xsl:template>
59
60    <xsl:template match="invitation/body/par">
61      <fo:block space-before="{constant(Fontsize)}">
62        <xsl:apply-templates/>
63      </fo:block>
64    </xsl:template>
65
66    <xsl:template match="invitation/body/par/emph">
67      <fo:inline-sequence font-style="italic">
68        <xsl:apply-templates/>
69      </fo:inline-sequence>
70    </xsl:template>
71
72    <xsl:template match="invitation/back">
73    <fo:block space-before="{constant(Fontsize)}"
74            font-weight="bold" text-align="right">
75      <xsl:text>From: </xsl:text>
76      <xsl:value-of select="signature"/>
77    </fo:block>
78    </xsl:template>
79    </xsl:stylesheet>
```

In this style sheet we take an approach quite similar to what we did in the case of DSSSL (see Section 7.5.2.2). We declare a constant Fontsize (line 6) that controls the default size of the document font. To show how macros are handled in XSL, we define a macro named listitem on lines 7–18. The macro has two arguments: itemid (line 8), which corresponds to an identifier of the list item (line 10), and itemtext (line 9), which is used for generating text for the item label (line 12). Notice how the syntax arg(...) is used to access the actual value of the arguments. On line 15 the <xsl:contents/> element is a placeholder for the actual contents of the macro when it is invoked (see following).

The page dimensions are defined (lines 21–26) inside the root template (lines 20–27), where we also set the default size of the document font (line 21), using the constant Fontsize declared earlier.

We then select the front part of the document (lines 29–58) and start by writing the text "INVITATION" in a sans serif 24 pt font centered on the output medium as a block object (lines 31–34). The rest of the front matter is displayed in a list (lines 35–56). The list has a label width of 2 cm to write the fixed texts (line 35). For each of the four elements inside the front element, we invoke the listitem macro, defined previously. Let us review in detail one of the invocations. On lines 36–40 we deal with the to element. First we set the itemtext argument to the string "To" and the itemid argument to "listto" identifier. The contents of the to element in the XML source document is retrieved with the `<xsl:value of select="to"/>` syntax. It is then consumed as body of the macro by the `<xsl:contents/>` element in the macro definition (line 15). All this gives the result shown on lines 12–15 following. Lines 41–55 handle the `date`, `where`, and `why` elements in a similar way.

We then go to the body part of the document, where for each paragraph (`par` element type) we generate a block object (lines 61–63), skipping a space equal to the font size (line 61). The `emph` elements (lines 66–70) are transformed into a sequence using an italic font (lines 67–69).

Finally, for the back matter (lines 72–78) we create a block object (lines 73–77), where, after setting the space before, we require a bold font and right-justified text (line 74). We output the string "From: " followed by the contents of the `signature` element type.

This style sheet `invfo1.xsl` and the XML source file `invitation.xml` can be compiled by James Clark's `xt` tool, as follows:

```
xt invitation.xml invfo1.xsl invfo1.fop
```

The file `invfo1.fop` contains the formatting objects. It has the following form (the correspondence between style sheet and generated code is easily identified):

```
1   <fo:basic-page-sequence xmlns:fo="http://www.w3.org/TR/WD-xsl/FO"
2       font-family="serif" font-size="12pt" margin-top="15mm" margin-bottom="15mm"
3       margin-left="15mm" margin-right="15mm" page-width="120mm" id="pageseq">
4   <fo:display-sequence>
5       <fo:block font-family="sans-serif" font-size="24pt"
6               font-weight="bold" text-align="center">
7       INVITATION
8       </fo:block>
9       <fo:list-block label-width="2cm">
10        <fo:list-item id="listto">
11          <fo:list-item-label font-style="italic">To:</fo:list-item-label>
12          <fo:list-item-body>Anna, Bernard, Didier, Johanna</fo:list-item-body>
13        </fo:list-item>
14        <fo:list-item id="listdate">
15          <fo:list-item-label font-style="italic">When:</fo:list-item-label>
16          <fo:list-item-body>Next Friday Evening at 8 pm</fo:list-item-body>
17        </fo:list-item>
18        <fo:list-item id="listwhere">
19          <fo:list-item-label font-style="italic">Venue:</fo:list-item-label>
20          <fo:list-item-body>The Web Cafe</fo:list-item-body>
21        </fo:list-item>
22        <fo:list-item id="listwhy">
23          <fo:list-item-label font-style="italic">Occasion:</fo:list-item-label>
24          <fo:list-item-body>My first XML baby</fo:list-item-body>
25        </fo:list-item>
26      </fo:list-block>
27   </fo:display-sequence>
28   <fo:block space-before-optimum="12pt">
29   I would like to invite you all to celebrate the birth of
30   <fo:inline-sequence
31   font-style="italic">Invitation</fo:inline-sequence>,
32   my first XML document child.
33   </fo:block>
34   <fo:block space-before-optimum="12pt">
35   Please do your best to come and join me next Friday
36   evening. And, do not forget to bring your friends.
```

INVITATION

To: Anna, Bernard, Didier, Johanna
When: Next Friday Evening at 8 pm
Venue: The Web Cafe
Occasion: My first XML baby

I would like to invite you all to celebrate the birth of *Invitation*, my first XML document child.

Please do your best to come and join me next Friday evening. And, do not forget to bring your friends.

I *really* look forward to see you soon!

From: Michel

Figure 7.11: PDF generated from flow objects with `fop`

```
37   </fo:block>
38   <fo:block space-before-optimum="12pt">
39   <fo:inline-sequence font-style="italic">really</fo:inline-sequence>
40   look forward to see you soon!
41   </fo:block>
42   <fo:block space-before-optimum="12pt" font-weight="bold" text-align="right">
43   From: Michel
44   </fo:block>
45   </fo:basic-page-sequence>
```

This file can now be input into James Tauber's `fop` program, as follows:

```
java com.jtauber.fop.FOP invfo1.fob invfo1.pdf
James Tauber's FOP 0.5.0
successfully read and parsed temp.fob
successfully wrote invfo1.pdf
```

This program generates the PDF file `invfo1.pdf` shown in Figure 7.11. Although we used a completely different style sheet language and data model, we obtain a result that is quite similar to the one in Figure 7.8. This shows that XSL is certainly a promising technology. Once the specification is finalized, XSL will allow us to use XML-based syntax and tools for all stages of our document handling.

Summary

It should be clear from the discussion in this chapter that currently there are various interesting approaches to handling XML-tagged files. Most of the methods presented rely on interpreting the output from an XML parser (directly or indirectly) and applying "action" rules to the various XML input elements. Interpreters, such as Perl, Java, or Python, are available to drive the process of generating LaTeX or HTML output. However, we stress once again that it is important to program the translation at a high level of abstraction, via the use of a LaTeX class or CSS style sheet that can be reused by various document instances, even those constructed according to a different DTD.

We have looked in detail into three style sheet languages: CSS, DSSSL, and XSL. *Cascading Style Sheets* are linked strongly with the Web and are thus particularly well-suited for separating form and content for screen display. More recently the second edition of the CSS specification has added capabilities in the area of multimedia and printing.

Today the most complete formatting model is offered by the *Document Style Semantics and Specification Language*. It is an ISO standard and can handle complex page layouts, tables, and mathematics. It is the only possible choice if one needs high-quality typography of nontrivial documents.

The latest arrival on the style sheet market is the *Extensible Style Language*. It is supposed to offer, in due course, at least the functionality of both CSS and DSSSL, but with a syntax that is well integrated with the "X (extensible)" family of tools. Efforts are underway to ensure that the formatting models of all W3C activities, including CSS, XSL, and SVG, will converge. However, XSL is at present far from finalized, and it certainly is not easy to decide whether XSL will live up to its promises of offering a complete solution for handling all XML documents with style.

In the few pages dedicated to each of these style sheet languages, we could only scratch the surface of each. Nevertheless, we have given you an idea of their basic functionality and general syntax. This should allow you to read and understand files written in any of these languages, modify them according to your needs, or even write your own.

The information and examples presented in this chapter should give you enough insight to decide which of the various possibilities (CSS, DSSSL, and XSL) is most useful for solving your problem today. Moreover, thanks to the references in the text, you can choose to follow the evolution of these tools. It is to be expected that XSL and CSS will develop into full-blown style sheet languages, the former as a viable replacement for DSSSL for complex offline documents, the latter for multimedia applications on the Web.

CHAPTER 8

MathML, intelligent math markup

This chapter is directed at people who are currently using LaTeX as their main markup format, but who also want to consider moving onto SGML-like systems. It is obvious that HTML is not rich enough to be considered a permanent storage medium, and from what we have seen in Chapters 6 and 7, it is clear that XML is the best way to go. However, many people are worried about how to deal with their legacy documents, particularly those containing math (often the reason they chose TeX in the first place). We will look at an answer to the math problem—the Mathematical Markup Language—and consider how to convert existing LaTeX documents to XML.

This chapter is divided into three parts. First we provide a summary of the new language; second we look at the first generation of software that supports the language; and third we go back to cover in more detail a practical LaTeX-to-XML (including MathML) translation system using TeX4ht.

We must stress that the use of MathML is in its infancy, as is the development of reliable LaTeX-to-XML converters. In this chapter, we will be looking at early versions of software and suggesting some approaches to take, but you should not consider these as definitive. We will be obliged to be much vaguer and less precise about details, than elsewhere in this book.

8.1   Introduction to MathML

After being virtually ignored for some years, mathematics on the Web is making a comeback. Several small scale studies and experiments on how to deal with math in SGML and with browsers took place. Only recently, however, did the big players in the math business (computer algebra vendors like Maple, Mathcad, Mathematica; large scientific publishers like Elsevier and the American Mathematical Society; and software companies like Adobe, as well as the W3C) get together to define a language to describe the structure and content of mathematical expressions. The first outcome of their efforts is a specification for MathML (Mathematical Markup Language). The full details are available on the Web [↪MMLSPEC], as are extensive lists of MathML resources at [↪MMLRES] and [↪MMLGUID].

MathML is a markup language for math to be used with XML. Its design goals, as specified by the W3C Mathematics Working Group, state that MathML should

- encode mathematical material for teaching and scientific communication at all levels;

- encode both mathematical notation and its meaning;

- be well-suited to template and other math editing techniques;

- facilitate conversion to and from other math formats, both presentational and semantic. Output formats should include graphical displays, speech synthesizers, computer algebra systems' input, other math layout languages such as TeX, plain text displays, and print media, including Braille. It is recognized that conversion to and from other notations may lose information in the process;

- allow the passing of information intended for specific renderers;

- support efficient browsing for lengthy expressions; and

- provide for extensibility (in as yet undefined ways).

The original aim that MathML be easy to learn and to edit *by hand* for basic math notation was effectively dropped when the working group decided to use XML rather than full SGML (the project started before XML).

MathML contains two "views" of mathematics: *presentation markup* and *semantic markup*. Presentation markup describes math notation, with expressions being built up using layout schemata, and specifying how to arrange subexpressions, such as fractions, and super- and subscripts. Semantic markup describes mathematical objects and functions, where an expression tree is constructed with each node representing a particular schema, and branches representing its subexpressions.

To illustrate the two approaches, let us look at the following simple formula that we will mark up according to the two schemes.

$$x^2 - 6x + 9 = 0$$

The LaTeX code for this would be

```
\[ x^{2} - 6x + 9 = 0\]
```

The first way of using MathML is to use *presentation tags* to describe the *visual layout* of a mathematical formula.

```
1   <mrow>
2     <mrow>
3       <msup>
4         <mi>x</mi>
5         <mn>2</mn>
6       </msup>
7       <mo>-</mo>
8       <mrow>
9         <mn>6</mn>
10        <mo>&InvisibleTimes;</mo>
11        <mi>x</mi>
12      </mrow>
13      <mo>+</mo>
14      <mn>9</mn>
15    </mrow>
16    <mo>=</mo>
17    <mn>0</mn>
18  </mrow>
```

You see here two kinds of MathML tags. First there are those that contain data, such as <mi> for identifiers (lines 4 and 11), <mn> for numbers (lines 5, 9, 14, and 17), and <mo> for operators (lines 7, 10, 13, and 16). Second there are those that contain only other nested MathML elements, such as <msup> (lines 3–6) and <mrow> (lines 1–8, 2–15, and 8–12). The nested mrow elements denote terms—in this case the left-hand side of the equation functioning as an operand of the equal sign. By specifying the type of the data and marking terms, we greatly facilitate things like spacing for visual rendering, voice rendering, linebreaking, as well as automatic processing by external applications. Notice that, in contrast to LaTeX, the <msup> element has two parts: the superscript itself and the material to which it is attached—<msup><mi>x</mi><mn>2</mn></msup>. Compare this with LaTeX's x^{2}, where there is no markup *before* the x.

The second way to use MathML is to express the *semantic content* of the same expression as follows:

```
1   <reln>
2     <eq/>
3     <apply>
4       <plus/>
5       <apply>
6         <minus/>
7         <apply>
8           <power/>
9           <ci>x</ci>
10          <cn>2</cn>
11        </apply>
12        <apply>
13          <times/>
14          <cn>6</cn>
```

```
15            <ci>x</ci>
16          </apply>
17        </apply>
18        <cn>9</cn>
19      </apply>
20      <cn>0</cn>
21    </reln>
```

MathML content tags are typically contained within an `<apply>` tag that denotes a semantically meaningful expression (lines 3–19, 5–17, 7–11, and 12–16) and acts like a pair of parentheses. Prefix notation is used to build up the expression (the `<plus/>`, `<times/>`, and `<minus/>` tags). Token elements are used to indicate numbers (`<cn>`) and symbols (`<ci>`).

Can MathML succeed in its aims? Some practicing mathematicians think that MathML presentation markup can be made to work, despite its extreme verbosity when compared to TeX. The biggest change in working methods and software that will be needed is to support a distinction between authoring convenience, archival markup, and rendering markup. LaTeX users are accustomed to writing something like

```
\newcommand{\Wotsit}{\ensuremath{E_{\beta}^{\infty}}}
\Wotsit{} means whatever you like
```

This combines the establishment of a higher level of abstract markup than standard LaTeX, a typing shortcut, and the details of an actual rendition. In the XML world you would do this in two stages—first adding a new element `<Wotsit>` to your Document Type Definition and second adding a rule to your style sheet that mapped the element onto

```
<math>
  <msubsup>
    <mi>E</mi>
    <mi>&beta;</mi>
    <mo>&infty;</mo>
  </msubsup>
</math>
```

While this seems highly inconvenient compared to current LaTeX, it has many advantages, such as better syntax checking, context-sensitive editing, searching, and the possibility of using different rendering engines. It could replace TeX markup for authoring in some systems. Naturally we can continue to use the TeX typesetting engine, Computer Modern fonts, and so on, for producing printed pages. An alternative scenario is that a "Next Generation" LaTeX could adopt a syntax much closer to that of MathML and share many of the same advantages.

Semantic math markup is another matter; for parts of math it can be established as a communication medium quite easily. Some classify its coverage as everything up to university level; others more unkindly classify it as everything before the 20th century! For research-level math, it is not clear whether the constraints of MathML will prove too much. When doing semantic math, we cannot adopt the system of ad hoc high-level "little languages" for a particular domain of math that would then expand to the fixed MathML semantic markup, since the point of content markup is to allow interchange between computer programs. Exchange of content must be at the highest level of meaning.

8.1.1 MathML, Unicode, and XML entities

MathML is an application of XML, so symbols must come entirely from the Unicode (see Appendix C.2) character set. There are two problems with this system:

1. Unicode (version 2) does not contain the myriad special symbols mathematicians have developed over the years.

2. When reading MathML (let alone writing it by hand), most authors will not (in the short term) be using fully Unicode-aware software or may be using the UTF-8 encoding (Appendix C.2.3). They may not, therefore, see the math symbols but would instead see some unintelligible encoding.

The first problem should be solved by a project set up in 1997 by a group of scientific publishers and software suppliers (STIPUB). They made a comprehensive collection of all the characters used in modern scientific publishing and computer software. Those that were not present in the current Unicode were proposed, at the end of 1998, to the Unicode consortium for inclusion in the next revision of the Unicode character set. Until the proposed additions to Unicode are accepted, practical use of MathML has to include the Unicode private zone (see the following). Even when the characters *are* in Unicode, the problem of no immediately available fonts to cover the whole set remains. To remedy this, the same group of publishers and software vendors plans to commission a completely new set of math fonts and make them freely available.

The second problem can be solved by the use of entity references in the DTD that is, using *symbolic names* for the characters instead of the Unicode character itself. Thus a ϕ is written and read as φ. There are, however, some problems here too. First, entities declared in an XML *must* resolve eventually to characters in the Unicode scheme. If the character is not in the current version of Unicode, we must pick on an arbitrary position in Unicode's "private zone," and all MathML software must agree on the convention. There is an obvious danger that some other application may use the same positions in the private zone, and be unable to co-exist with MathML. Second, XML software does not *have* to read a DTD when it processes MathML documents, and so entities may have to be defined in the *document* rather than in the DTD (which is highly inconvenient) or the documents have to be preprocessed in some way to remove the entity references.

The situation is confused by the fact that some MathML software (notably techexplorer and WebEQ) does not process documents using a normal XML parser but rather recognizes a predefined set of entity names and renders them directly.

The practical solution adopted in the MathML Recommendation is to publish a list of proposed entity names. This gives a corresponding Unicode position, if known; if not, a position in the private zone is proposed. The entity lists are extensions of the standard ISO 9573 lists and fall into the following groups:

Math symbols	
ISOAMSA	Math Symbols: Arrows
ISOAMSB	Math Symbols: Binary Operators
ISOAMSC	Math Symbols: Delimiters
ISOAMSN	Math Symbols: Negated Relations
ISOAMSO	Math Symbols: Ordinary
ISOAMSR	Math Symbols: Relations
MMALIAS	MathML Aliases
MMEXTRA	MathML Additions
General technical symbols	
ISOTECH	General Technical
ISOPUB	Publishing
ISODIA	Diacritical Marks
ISONUM	Numeric and Special Graphic
ISOBOX	Box and Line Drawing
Scripts	
ISOGRK3	Greek Symbols
ISOMSCR	Math Script Font
ISOMOPF	Math Open Face Font
ISOMFRK	Math Fraktur Font
ISOGRK1	Greek Letters
ISOGRK2	Monotoniko Greek
ISOGRK4	Alternative Greek Symbols
ISOCYR1	Russian Cyrillic
ISOCYR2	Non-Russian Cyrillic

Solving the problem of the special math characters and developing widely available fonts to display them are a crucial task for the nascent MathML community, and rapid progress can be expected.

8.2   MathML software

Several vendors and organizations have announced plans to develop implementations of the MathML Recommendation. Currently several of the tools described in this book can interpret, render, or produce MathML markup from LaTeX input. Similarly some level of support is finding its way into the popular browsers.

We can divide MathML software into five categories:

1. symbolic math manipulation packages;

2. equation editors that will either export MathML or use it as their main storage format;

3. Web browsers, and their plug-ins and helper programs;

4. free-standing conversion programs from formats like LaTeX; and

5. typesetting systems that can process XML documents containing MathML.

It is beyond the scope of this book to look in any detail at the first category; Mathematica [↪MATHEMATICA] and Maple [↪MAPLE] are planning to export and import MathML for exchange with other software. It is probable they will start to work with the *semantic* part of the language. While this is clearly a very important use of MathML, implementations are not yet available.

The remaining four categories of software are examined in the following sections.

8.2.1   Equation editors

Currently the best example of an interactive equation editor that works with MathML is the commercial MathType (version 4 onwards; see [↪MATHTYPE]), the full version of the equation editor used in Microsoft Word. In the short term, export to MathML is in *presentation* form, until experience is gained with interfaces for writing semantic math.

MathType is designed to be used as an assistant to other Windows or Macintosh programs (such as Word), so it does not have a native file type. Instead it puts a compact representation of the editable form of the math as a comment in one of its various output formats. You can also choose one of a variety of translators that determines what format will be placed on the Windows or Mac clipboard when you do a "copy." These formats include MathML and various flavors of TeX (that is, plain TeX, LaTeX, and $\mathcal{AMS}$-LaTeX); the translators that manage this are configurable and easily editable. For example, the rule file for LaTeX includes

```
paren  = "\left( #1 \right)";                      // parentheses (both)
brack  = "\left[ #1 \right]";                      // brackets (both)
brace  = "\left\{ #1 \right\}";                     // braces (both)
abrack = "\left\langle #1 \right\rangle ";         // angle brackets (both)
bar    = "\left| #1 \right|",                       // bars (both)
dbar   = "\left\| #1 \right\|";                     // double bars (both)
floor  = "\left\lfloor #1 \right\rfloor ";          // floor
```

showing how MathType internal constructs (like brack) map quite neatly to TeX.

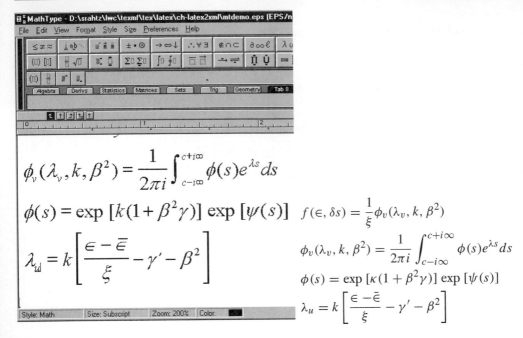

Figure 8.1: MathType equation editor   Figure 8.2: Example equations typeset by TEX

The editor screen is shown in action in Figure 8.1, where a few of the equations from the example text used in Chapter 1 have been entered. When translation to *AMS*-LATEX is requested, the output looks like the following in TEX source. The result of typesetting this with TEX is shown in Figure 8.2.

```
\[
\begin{gathered}
\phi _{v} (\lambda _{v} ,k,\beta ^{2} ) =
 \frac{1}{{2\pi i}}\int_{{c - i\infty }}^{{c + i\infty }}
 {\phi (s)e^{{\lambda s}} ds}  \hfill \\
\phi (s) = \text{exp }[\kappa(1 + \beta ^{2} \gamma )]
 \text{ exp }[\psi (s)] \hfill \\
\lambda _{u}  = k\left[ {\frac{{ \in  - \bar  \in }}
 {\xi } - \gamma ’ - \beta ^{2} } \right] \hfill \\
\end{gathered}
\]
```

The reason why the right and left brackets in the first line do not extend to cover the β^2 is that simple "(" and ")" characters were used rather than the MathType "bracketed object" construct.

When we request a translation to MathML, we get the following (the third equation is omitted, to save space):

```
<math displaystyle='true'>
 <semantics>
  <mtable columnalign='left'>
   <mtr>
   <mtd>
    <msub>
     <mi>&phi;</mi>
     <mi>v</mi>
    </msub>
    <mo stretchy='false'>(</mo><msub>
     <mi>&lambda;</mi>
     <mi>v</mi>
    </msub>
    <mo>,</mo><mi>k</mi><mo>,</mo><msup>
     <mi>&beta;</mi>
     <mn>2</mn>
    </msup>
    <mo stretchy='false'>)</mo><mo>=</mo><mfrac>
     <mn>1</mn>
     <mrow>
      <mn>2</mn><mi>&pi;</mi><mi>i</mi>
     </mrow>
    </mfrac>
    <msubsup>
     <mo>&int;</mo>
     <mrow>
      <mi>c</mi><mo>-</mo><mi>i</mi><mo>&infin;</mo>
     </mrow>
     <mrow>
      <mi>c</mi><mo>+</mo><mi>i</mi><mo>&infin;</mo>
     </mrow>
    </msubsup>
    <mrow>
     <mi>&phi;</mi><mo stretchy='false'>(</mo>
     <mi>s</mi><mo stretchy='false'>)</mo>
     <msup>
      <mi>e</mi>
      <mrow>
      <mi>&lambda;</mi><mi>s</mi>
      </mrow>
     </msup>
     <mi>d</mi><mi>s</mi>
    </mrow>
   </mtd>
```

```
    </mtr>
    <mtr>
    <mtd>
     <mi>&phi;</mi><mo stretchy='false'>(</mo>
     <mi>s</mi><mo stretchy='false'>)</mo>
     <mo>=</mo><mtext>exp </mtext>
     <mo stretchy='false'>[</mo><mi>k</mi>
     <mo stretchy='false'>(</mo><mn>1</mn><mo>+</mo><msup>
      <mi>&beta;</mi>
      <mn>2</mn>
     </msup>
     <mi>&gamma;</mi>
     <mo stretchy='false'>)</mo>
     <mo stretchy='false'>]</mo><mtext> exp </mtext>
     <mo stretchy='false'>[</mo><mi>&psi;</mi>
     <mo stretchy='false'>(</mo><mi>s</mi>
     <mo stretchy='false'>)</mo><mo stretchy='false'>]</mo>
    </mtd>
    </mtr>
   </mtable>
  </semantics>
 </math>
```

It is interesting to compare the translation rules with those for LaTeX; if we take the same constructs as before, the MathML rules look like the following:

```
paren = "<mrow><mo>(</mo>$+$n#1$-$n<mo>)</mo></mrow>$n";
brack = "<mrow><mo>[</mo> #1 <mo>]</mo></mrow>";
brace = "<mrow><mo>{</mo> #1 <mo>}</mo></mrow>";
abrack = "<mrow><mo>&langle;</mo> #1 <mo>&rangle;</mo></mrow>";
bar = "<mrow><mo>|</mo> #1 <mo>|</mo></mrow>";
floor = "<mrow><mo>&lfloor;</mo> #1 <mo>&rfloor;</mo></mrow>";
```

W3C's experimental Web browser Amaya can also be used to create MathML. Although this is not intended to be a serious production tool, it shows that simple authoring, editing, and display are not too hard to set up.

8.2.2   Web browser support for MathML

The Amaya browser can be used to display MathML markup, simply by embedding <math> elements (and their children) in plain HTML. This is shown in Figure 8.3 (and in Figure 6.5 on page 276). The support for MathML is incomplete, not the least problem being the lack of suitable symbol fonts (see Section 8.1.1), but, nonetheless, it remains a useful technology preview.

The techexplorer browser plug-in and the WebEQ Java helper (described in Chapter 5) also display MathML embedded in HTML. The markup required

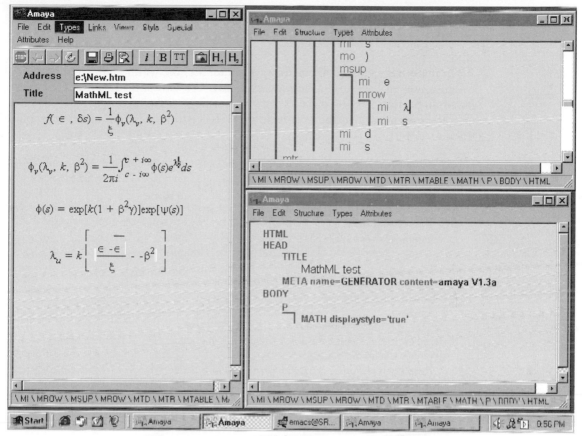

Figure 8.3: Amaya Web browser showing MathML

is slightly different, as the former uses the `<embed>` tag and the latter uses the `<applet>` tag. Thus if we take a fragment of LaTeX from our test file

```
The Vavilov parameters are simply related to the Landau parameter by
$\lambda_L = \lambda_v/\kappa - \ln\kappa $. It can be shown that as
$\kappa \rightarrow 0$, the distribution of the variable $\lambda_L$
approaches that of Landau.
```

and convert it to a mixture of HTML and MathML for rendering by techexplorer, the HTML looks like this:

```
The Vavilov parameters are simply related to the Landau parameter by
<embed src="htmlmathml71.mml" width="215" height="46" align="middle">.
It can be shown that as
<embed src="htmlmathml72.mml" width="89" height="37" align="middle">,
the distribution of the variable
```

```
<embed src="htmlmathml73.mml" width="50" height="42" align="middle">
approaches that of Landau.
```

Each math fragment is contained in a separate file, the width and height of which when rendered have to be specified explicitly. We have already considered these issues in Section 5.3.1 on page 235.

If we want to load the Java code of WebEQ to process the math, we would instead write:

```
The Vavilov parameters are simply related to the Landau parameter by
<applet code="webeq.Main" width="215" height="46" align="middle">
 <param name="eq" value="
  <math><msub><mi>&lambda;</mi><mrow><mi>L</mi></mrow></msub> <mo>=</mo>
   <msub><mi>&lambda;</mi><mrow><mi>v</mi></mrow></msub>
   <mo>/</mo><mi>&kappa;</mi>
   <mo>-</mo> <mi>l</mi><mi>n</mi> <mi>&kappa;</mi>
   </math>">
 <param name="color" value="#C0C0C0">
 <param name="parser" value="mathml">
</applet>.
It can be shown that as
<applet code="webeq.Main" width="89" height="37" align="middle">
 <param name="eq" value="
  <math><mi>&kappa;</mi><mo>&rarr;</mo> <mn>0</mn>
   </math>">
 <param name="color" value="#C0C0C0">
 <param name="parser" value="mathml">
</applet>, the distribution of the variable
<applet code="webeq.Main" width="50" height="42" align="middle">
 <param name="eq" value="
  <math><msub><mi>&lambda;</mi><mrow><mi>L</mi></mrow></msub>
   </math> ">
 <param name="color" value="#C0C0C0">
 <param name="parser" value="mathml">
</applet>
approaches that of Landau.
```

We embed the MathML code in the HTML inside an `<applet>` element but again we have to supply the width and height. This is an annoyance for translation systems,[1] and we must hope that future systems will incorporate size negotiation between browsers and special purpose helpers or plug-ins.

It looks unlikely that the current generation of mainstream Web browsers (Netscape, Internet Explorer, and so on) will have direct support for MathML before the year 2000 at the earliest. Until then, we will have to work with plug-in applications.

---

[1] These translations were created using experimental configuration files for TEX4ht.

One possible way in which future browsers might support MathML is via transformation to a standardized vector graphics markup language (the equivalent of PostScript) for the Web. More details on developments of this language can be found at [↪W3CGR].

8.2.3   Converting LaTeX to MathML

Conversions from LaTeX are likely to be to *presentational* form in the short- and medium-term future, simply because LaTeX and plain TeX are not designed to express math semantics. Even managing presentation markup is not straightforward.

LaTeX to XML converters in general can be based on a number of philosophies (see Rahtz (1995) for more discussion):

1. Free-standing programs are written in a conventional language like C, Perl, or Java, which attempt to parse TeX markup. We have already seen examples of these in Chapter 1 (TtH) and Chapter 3 (LaTeX2HTML).

2. Systems based on TeX macros add to the DVI file information that a later program can extract. We have seen an extensive exposition of such an approach in Chapter 4 (TeX4ht).

3. Systems are based on an extension of TeX, where the innards of the program are replaced so that it emits XML.

The majority of TeX math is fairly easy to translate, since most constructs map to MathML presentation markup easily. Thus a fraction in LaTeX, with a simple non-Latin character, translates from

```
\frac{\xi}{E_{x}}
```

to:

```
<mfrac>
 <mrow><mi>&xi;</mi></mrow>
 <mrow>
   <msub>
     <mi>E</mi>
     <mrow><mi>x</mi></mrow>
   </msub>
 </mrow>
</mfrac>
```

Unfortunately we have two problems to overcome, both of which are best solved by different methods. The first is the obvious one that LaTeX authors writing non-trivial math very often make extensive use of macros to set up private markup schemes, something like

```
\newcommand{\htheta}{\hat\theta}
```

This is fairly easy for programs like TtH and LaTeX2HTML to follow. However, consider a plain TeX delimited macro with conditionals in the expansion, such as

```
\def\Fraction:#1/#2:{\ifmmode\frac{#1}{#2}\else #1 divided by #2\fi}
```

Used with something like `\Fraction:36/72:` this will almost certainly break most converters, unless they use the TeX parser. Of course, most LaTeX users will not write this sort of macro; the LaTeX `\newcommand` does not support it, but the full power of TeX does get called up by advanced users.

The second problem is that we have to deal with LaTeX like the following:

```
\[ (a+b)^{2} \]
```

This should translate to the MathML code

```
<mrow>
 <msup>
  <mrow><mo>(</mo><mi>a</mi><mo>+</mo><mi>b</mi><mo>)</mo></mrow>
  <mrow><mn>2</mn></mrow>
 </msup>
</mrow>
```

As we already noted, superscripted expressions in MathML need to be marked explicitly. In LaTeX, approaches based on simple redefinition of macros run into difficulties, since the macro programmer does not have straightforward access to the start of (a+b). The programmer in C or Perl can backtrack quite easily and find the most plausible expression to include inside the MathML `<msup>`. While there are not many constructs like this to deal with, they arise very often, and a translator has to have a reliable solution. One answer is for LaTeX users to adopt an extended input syntax so that there is no ambiguity; thus the previous example could be marked up as

```
\[ \Sup{(a+b)}{2} \]
```

making translation to MathML trivial. This approach is used by WebEQ (see the following). Another answer is to rewrite the entire math-handling part of LaTeX at a low level and identify the necessary subexpressions directly. There are currently no implementations of this idea.

At the time of writing there are three preliminary implementations of LaTeX to XML/MathML converters (described later), while `techexplorer` is likely to add the facility at some point. It should be clear from the following sections that we

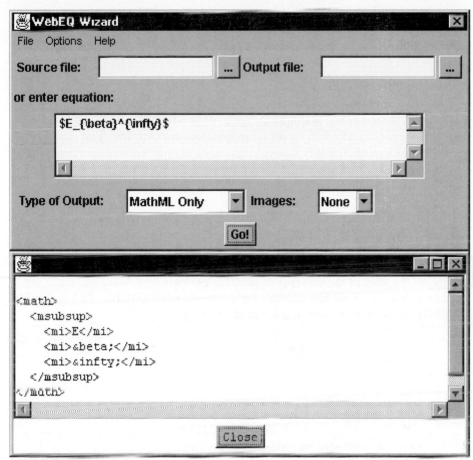

Figure 8.4: WebEQ "wizard" in action translating LaTeX to MathML

have the necessary technology to translate LaTeX to MathML, but we can not yet recommend a reliable, tested setup that can process arbitrary LaTeX documents.

8.2.3.1   LaTeX to MathML with WebEQ

The first converter was written as part of the WebEQ software. This "wizard" is shown in action in Figure 8.4; it provides an interactive mode in which TeX code can be typed in one window, and the MathML equivalent is shown in another.

Unfortunately, the translator does *only* TeX math (not a complete LaTeX article) and cannot follow the more complex macros we described earlier. A system based on LaTeX2HTML by Ross Moore [↪L2HMML] does provide a translation for an entire LaTeX document. It uses the existing LaTeX2HTML system to translate normal text to HTML. It then passes bits it identifies as math to WebEQ for conversion to MathML, which are then embedded in the HTML.

The disadvantage is that the WebEQ Wizard does not fully support LaTeX markup; it supports only a variant called WebTeX. This means that documents need extra preparation. There is more discussion of WebEQ in Section 5.2.

8.2.3.2   Using TeX4ht to convert LaTeX to XML/MathML

In Chapter 4 we looked at how TeX4ht can be extensively configured when writing HTML. Since HTML is simply an application of SGML, it should be obvious that TeX4ht can equally well be set up to generate an XML file. The tags that are generated for a particular LaTeX command can be changed in configuration files to whatever you like. In Appendix B.2 we provide the full details of how to strip the TeX4ht conversion back to basics and then build up a new system based on simple XML tags.

A full translation to MathML can, therefore, be configured using TeX4ht. This program solves the problem of "back-tracking" in superscripts and subscripts by using a two-stage process. Clues are embedded in the DVI file as TeX \special commands, and then the postprocessor analyzes the entire math expression to try and locate the start of the subscripted part, for example.

Let us look at a complete example and generate a full XML file. The source file, as follows, is a subset of the example file given in Appendix A.1:

```
\documentclass{article}
  \usepackage[x2ldemo]{tex4ht}
  \title{Simulation of  Energy Loss  Straggling}
  \author{Maria Physicist}
\begin{document}
\maketitle
\section{Landau theory}\label{sec:phys332-1}
The Landau probability distribution may be written in
terms of the universal Landau function \cite{bib-LAND}.
\subsection{Restrictions}
The Landau formalism makes two restrictive assumptions:
\begin{enumerate}
\item The typical energy loss is small.
\item The typical energy loss in the absorber should be
  large (see section \ref{urban}).
\end{enumerate}
\section{Urb\'an model}\label{urban}
The following values are obtained:

\begin{tabular}{llcrr}
16   & 16      & & 2000  & 29.63\\
100  & 27.59   & &  100  & 32.00
\end{tabular}

\begin{thebibliography}{10}
\bibitem{bib-LAND} L.Landau. On the Energy Loss of Fast Particles by
Ionisation. Originally published in \emph{J. Phys.}, 8:201, 1944.
\end{thebibliography}
\end{document}
```

The configuration file is as follows:

```
1   \Configure{html}{xml}
2   \Preamble{html,0.0,ref-,fonts}
```

```
 3    \Configure{HTML} {\IgnorePar\Tg<?xml version="1.0"?>
 4       \Tg<document>}
 5       {\Tg</document>}
 6    \Configure{section}
 7       {\EndP \IgnorePar\par  \GetLabel \Tg<section  \PutLabel>}
 8       {\EndP \IgnorePar \Tg</section>}
 9       {\Tg<stitle>}{\Tg</stitle>}
10    \Configure{subsection}
11       {\EndP \IgnorePar\par  \GetLabel \Tg<subsection \PutLabel>}
12       {\EndP \IgnorePar \Tg</subsection>}
13       {\Tg<stitle>}{\Tg</stitle>}
14    \Configure{likesection}
15       {\EndP  \IgnorePar\par\GetLabel \Tg<section \PutLabel class="star">}
16       {\EndP \Tg</section>}
17       {\Tg<stitle>}{\Tg</stitle>}
18    \ConfigureList{thebibliography}
19       {\EndP  \GetLabel \Tg<bibliography \PutLabel>
20         \def\EndItem{\def\EndItem{\EndP \Tg</bibitem>}}}
21       {\EndItem \Tg</bibliography>}
22       {\EndItem \DeleteMark}
23       {\Tg<bibitem id="\AnchorLabel">\par}
24    \ConfigureList{enumerate}
25       {\EndP  \GetLabel \Tg<lalist \PutLabel class="enumerate">
26         \def\EndItem{\def\EndItem{\EndP\Tg</item>}}} {\EndItem \Tg</lalist>}
27       {\EndItem \DeleteMark}              {\Tg<item>\par}
28    \Configure{tabular}
29       {\Tg<tabular preamble="\Clr">}   {\Tg</tabular>}
30       {\Tg<row>}{\Tg</row>}  {\Tg<cell \Hnewline>}{\Tg</cell>}
31    \Configure{maketitle}  {}{} {\Tg<title>}{\Tg</title>}
32    \Configure{thanks author date and}
33       {}{} {\Tg<author>}{\Tg</author>} {\Tg<date>}{\Tg</date>} {} {}
34    \Configure{emph}{\Tg<emph>}{\Tg</emph>}
35    \Configure{label}{id="#1"}{\Tg<pagelabel id="#1"/>}
36    \Configure{pageref}{\Tg<pageref refid="#1"/>}
37    \Configure{ref}{\Tg<ref refid="#1"/>}
38    \Configure{cite}{\Tg<cite refid="#1"/>}
39    \begin{document}
40    \EndPreamble
41    \Configure{HtmlPar}  {\EndP\Tg<P>} {\EndP\Tg<P>}  {\Tg</P>} {\Tg</P>}
```

The first line of the configuration file requests an extension name xml, instead of html, for the output file.

The package option fonts, in line 2 of the configuration file, requests hooks for the font commands of LaTeX. On the other hand, the package option ref- asks the cross-reference commands of LaTeX to keep their labels, instead of exchanging them for section and page numbers, and to use these labels within attributes of hypertext tags. In addition, this option adds a pair of commands

```
\GetLabel
\PutLabel
```

for extracting the label of the next \label command and for inserting that label into the output file, respectively.

The arguments id="#1" and \Tg{pagelabel id="#1"/} of the "label" hook in line 35 show how \PutLabel and \label, respectively, should set their labels.

The \Clr command in line 29 produces the argument of the tabular environment that is preserved in the XML output.

The \ConfigureList commands in lines 18 and 24 employ the following command at the end of their third argument:

> \DeleteMark

It removes the native marks created at the start of the items by the corresponding list environments.

> \AnchorLabel

This command (used on line 23) then inserts these marks back into the output.

When all this is run through TEX4ht, it produces the XML output as follows:

```
<?xml version="1.0"?>
<document>
<title>Simulation of Energy Loss Straggling</title>
<author>Maria Physicist</author>
<date>November 9, 1998</date>
<section id="sec:phys332-1">
<stitle>Landau theory</stitle>
<p>   The Landau probability distribution may be written in
terms of the universal Landau function <cite refid="bib-LAND"/> .
</p>
<subsection>
<stitle>Restrictions</stitle>
<p>The Landau formalism makes two restrictive assumptions:</p>
<lalist class="enumerate">
     <item><p>The typical energy loss is small.</p></item>
     <item><p>The typical energy loss in the absorber should be
     large (see section <ref refid="urban"/> ).</p></item>
</lalist>
</subsection>
</section>
<section id="urban">
<stitle>Urb&aacute;n model</stitle>
<p>   The following values are obtained:
</p><p>   <tabular preamble="llcrr"><row>
<cell>16</cell><cell>16</cell><cell></cell><cell>2000</cell>
<cell>29.63</cell></row><row><cell>100</cell>
<cell>27.59</cell><cell></cell><cell>100</cell><cell>32.00</cell>
   </row></tabular></p>
</section>
<section class="star">
<stitle>References</stitle>
<bibliography >
<bibitem id="bib-LAND">
 <p>L.Landau. On the Energy Loss of Fast Particles by Ionisation.
 Originally published in <emph>J. Phys.</emph>, 8:201, 1944.</p>
</bibitem>
</bibliography>
</section>
</document>
```

By its nature MathML deals with low-level structural properties that are not always handled by LATEX macros but rather are hardwired into TEX itself. This means that MathML is a natural candidate for exploiting the features of TEX4ht as described in the previous section and in Appendix B.2.

A few lines of simple LaTeX is sufficiently structured to serve as an example for illustrating many of the features of a LaTeX to MathML conversion:

```
\begin{eqnarray}
\bar u &=& \int_{I}^E g(x)dx  \nonumber \\
E &=& \frac{I}{1-\mathrm{max}}\label{xx}
\end{eqnarray}
```

When typeset, this comes out as:

$$\bar{u} = \int_I^E g(x)dx$$

$$E = \frac{I}{1 - \max} \tag{1}$$

Now we need to construct a new TeX4ht configuration file to deal with the math and to generate the right MathML:

```
1   \Preamble{html,0.0,ref-,fonts,math}
2   \Configure{$$}{\DviMath}{\EndDviMath}{}
3   \Configure{eqnarray}
4     {\GetLabel \Tg<eqnarray \PutLabel>}
5     {\GetLabel \Tg</eqnarray>}
6     {\GetLabel \Tg<subeqn \PutLabel>\Tg<math>}
7     {\Tg</math>\Tg</subeqn>}
8     {\ifnum \Col=4 \Tg<mtext>\PauseMathClass \fi}
9     {\ifnum \Col=4 \EndPauseMathClass\Tg</mtext>\fi}
10  \Configure{label}{id="#1"}{\Tg<pagelabel id="#1"/>}
11  \Configure{SUBSUP}
12    {\Send{BACK}{<msubsup>]\Tg<mrow>}
13    {\Tg</mrow>\Tg<mrow>}
14    {\Tg</mrow>\TG</msubsup>}
15  \Configure{frac}
16    {\Tg<mfrac>\Tg<mrow>} {\Tg</mrow>\HCode{<!--}}
17    {\HCode{-->}\Tg<mrow>}{\Tg</mrow>\Tg</mfrac>}
18  \Configure{mathrm}{\Tg<mi>\PauseMathClass}
19    {\EndPauseMathClass\Tg</mi>}
20  \Configure{accent}\=\bar{{}{}}
21    {}{\Tg<mover accent="true">#2\Tg<mo>\HCode{&OverBar;}\Tg</mo>\Tg</mover>}
22  \Configure{MathClass}{0}{*}{<mi>}{</mi>}{}
23  \Configure{MathClass}{1}{*}{<mo>}{</mo>}{}
24  \Configure{MathClass}{2}{*}{<mo>}{</mo>}{}
25  \Configure{MathClass}{3}{*}{<mo>}{</mo>}{}
26  \Configure{MathClass}{4}{*}{<mrow><mo>}{</mo>}{}
27  \Configure{MathClass}{5}{*}{<mo>}{</mo></mrow>}{}
28  \Configure{MathClass}{6}{*}{<mo>}{</mo>}{}
29  \Configure{MathClass}{7}{*}{<mn>}{</mn>}{0123456789}
30  \begin{document}
31  \EndPreamble
```

With the exceptions of <eqnarray>, </eqnarray>, <subeqn>, and </subeqn>, all the tags in the configuration file are related to MathML.

LaTeX invokes the math environment $$*formula*$$ as part of the eqnarray environment. Line 2 in the configuration file has the task of setting the conditions for processing this material.

Whenever TEX4ht processes a table, it holds in its "variables" \Row and \Col the row and column numbers of the current cell. \Col is used, in lines 8 and 9 of the configuration file, to allow for the equation numbers.

```
<eqnarray>
<subeqn><math>
    <mover accent="true">
        <mi>u</mi>
        <mo>&OverBar;</mo>
    </mover>
    <mo>=</mo>
    <msubsup>
        <mo>&int;</mo>
        <mrow><mi>I</mi></mrow>
        <mrow><mi>E</mi></mrow>
    </msubsup>
    <mi>g</mi><mrow><mo>(</mo><mi>x</mi><mo>)</mo></mrow>
    <mi>d</mi><mi>x</mi>
    <mtext></mtext>
</math></subeqn><subeqn><math>
</math></subeqn><subeqn id="xx"><math>
    <mi>E</mi> <mo>=</mo>
    <mfrac>
        <mrow><mi>I</mi></mrow>
        <mrow><mn>1</mn> <mo>-</mo> <mi> max </mi> </mrow>
    </mfrac>
    <mtext>(1)</mtext>
</math></subeqn><subeqn><math>
</math></subeqn>
</eqnarray>
```

8.2.3.3 LATEX to MathML with Omega

A robust approach is that taken by the third converter, using an extension of the TEX program called Omega by John Plaice and Yannis Haralambous [↪OMEGA]. Omega's main extensions to TEX are that it uses Unicode internally and a set of "translation processes" that are applied at input and output. To support MathML, Omega also outputs XML directly during the TEX run, under control of user macros. Thus the LATEX \frac command is redefined with

```
\renewcommand{\frac}[2]{%
\SGMLstarttag{mfrac}{#1}{#2}\SGMLendtag{mfrac}}
```

making use of some new Omega primitives:[2]

```
\SGMLstarttag{tag name}
\SGMLendtag{tag name}
\SGMLentity{entity name}
```

There is a new primitive to start generation of XML output instead of DVI.

---

[2] These names may change in time; there are also new primitives to specify attributes and to generate some special characters. The Omega documentation gives current details.

The considerable advantage of this approach is that the knowledge that TEX has about the inner workings of math mode can be harnessed; the program *does* have some ideas about where, for example, superscripted expressions start, but does not make it available to macros. By changing the TEX engine itself, we can get at the details we need, and also be quite sure that there are no problems with user macros. The downside is that TEX does not in fact have quite as much knowledge as MathML demands (see Knuth (1986, p.129) for a discussion of what superscripts are attached to). It may be more sensible to simply have TEX place all the information it *does* have in the DVI file in some form, and then use a scheme like TEX4ht's for post-processing the DVI and writing XML.

Like TEX4ht, Omega supports editable font encoding files that map characters in TEX math fonts to MathML entities and distinguish types of math operators.

8.2.4   Typesetting MathML

When we move away from the Web and the problems of how to *generate* MathML, and we want simply to *print* our new math documents, we are on more familiar territory. TEX is too heavyweight and monolithic to use in a dynamic environment like a browser, but as a batch formatting engine, it is excellent. We should easily be able to convert our XML markup to TEX and get the usual results.

There are basically three approaches to using TEX as a formatting engine for XML, as we have already seen in Chapter 7:

1. We can write a special-purpose program, using something like the SAX or DOM models, and convert `<mfrac>` elements directly to LATEX `\frac`, for example.

2. We can use the XSL or DSSSL style languages to map MathML elements onto math formatting objects and then use TEX as a back-end for the style engine.

3. We can write a TEX macro package to interpret and typeset XML directly.

The first approach has the advantage of giving to the programmer good control over what comes out; there is no need to specify layout very precisely, since we can take advantage of existing LATEX packages (like $\mathcal{AMS}$-LATEX) to do the hard work. The downside is that it requires a new program for each XML DTD, and the translation is specific to TEX; translation to another math formatter like that in FrameMaker would require an entirely separate XML to MIF converter.

The second approach, going via the abstract style sheet, is potentially far superior. It removes the dependence on a particular formatting engine and leaves the hard work of mapping math flow objects to TEX to be done just once, in a style sheet language implementation's back-end. Unfortunately there are also some important problems:

*   The current version of XSL does not yet include any math formatting objects, and those in DSSSL have not been tested enough that we can sure they are up to the task.

$$f(\in, \delta s) = \tfrac{1}{\xi}\phi_v(\lambda_v, k, \beta^2)$$
$$\phi_v(\lambda_v, k, \beta^2) = \tfrac{1}{2\pi i}\int_{c-i\infty}^{c+i\infty}\phi(s)e^{\lambda s}ds$$
$$\phi(s) = \exp[k(1 + \beta^2 y)]\exp[\psi(s)]$$
$$\lambda_u = k[\tfrac{\in - \in}{\xi} - y' - \beta^2]$$

Figure 8.5: MathML sample processed by the Jade DSSSL engine and TeX

- If the results are not perfect, it is almost impossible to tweak the machine-generated, low-level TeX code.

- We may get different results with different style engines, if they have errors in their back-end modules.

- All the work has to be done in the style sheet; we can no longer rely on the crutch of mature packages like $\mathcal{AMS}$-LaTeX.

The fairly mature support for math in DSSSL is implemented in James Clark's Jade and supported by the `jadetex` macros [↪JADETEX]. David Carlisle has written a DSSSL style sheet that deals with practically all presentational and semantic MathML[↪DSSSLMML]. Most of the mapping is fairly easy to implement as that for fractions shows:

```
(element mfrac
  (make fraction
    (let ((nl (children(current-node))))
    (sosofo-append
      (make math-sequence
        label: 'numerator
          (process-node-list (node-list-first nl)))
      (make math-sequence
        label: 'denominator
          (process-node-list (node-list-rest nl)))))))
```

The result of processing our earlier example through Jade and then `jadetex` is shown in Figure 8.5. There remain, however, some areas of MathML that are not dealt with properly (such as full support of stretch operators) due to limitations in DSSSL's math flow objects.

An interesting, intermediate, working method is TeXML, proposed and implemented by IBM's Doug Lovell (see [↪TEXML]). This is an XML representation of TeX syntax, and the typesetting of a document works in two stages:

1. The transformation facilities of a language like XSL are used to convert the source XML document to a simpler XML representation using only TeXML elements.

2. The TeXML document is transformed to TeX using a simple program, and TeX is run on the result.

The advantage of this approach is that any XML-to-XML transformation system (of which there are many) can be used without any need to worry about TeX backslashes and braces and special output. The user does, however, have access to more or less any TeX facility, like macros; and the translation to real TeX is straightforward.

Summary

After a brief explanation of why we think that MathML is an important development to exchange, store, and transform mathematics information on the Web, we discussed the problems of special characters and presented an overview of MathML-aware software packages. We looked at tools that generate MathML from LaTeX with some detailed examples of how TeX4ht can turn LaTeX source files into XML and MathML. Finally we explained how LaTeX can be used as a printing back-end for MathML.

It is evident that a long road remains to be traveled before the full expressive power of LaTeX will be browsable on the Web in the form of MathML. Yet there is hope that in the medium-term future, users will be able to transform their LaTeX source files into MathML for input into algebraic manipulation programs for viewing on the Web or for inclusion into one of the many document processing systems. At the same time it will be possible to profit from the typographic excellence of the TeX engine for rendering Web documents that contain a lot of math. The next millennium will probably see a perfect symbiosis between LaTeX and XML/MathML, by allowing users to switch easily between the presentation most suited to their needs at any given moment. Thus you will not have to choose between MathML and LaTeX for marking up your scientific texts or data; you will use the format you are most comfortable with and still profit from the benefit of both at no extra cost.

Example files

A.1 An example LaTeX file and its translation to XML

We have tried throughout this book to give as many examples as we can from the same document (a simple physics paper from CERN) so that readers can make sensible comparisons. In this section we give a partial listing of the LaTeX source and a translation into XML, prepared using TeX4ht (see Section 8.2.3.2 and Appendix B.2) with its corresponding DTD.

The full version of the files can be found on CTAN (Comprehensive TeX Archive Network) in the directory info/lwc.

A.1.1 The LaTeX source

```
1   \documentclass{article}
2   \usepackage{graphicx}
3   \usepackage{url}
4   \title{Simulation of  Energy Loss  Straggling}
5   \author{Maria Physicist}
6   \newcommand{\Emax}{\ensuremath{E_{\mathrm{max}}}}
7   \newcommand{\GEANT}{\texttt{GEANT}}
8   \begin{document}
9   \maketitle
10
11  \section{Introduction}
12
13  Due to the statistical nature of ionisation energy loss, large
14  fluctuations can occur in the amount of energy deposited by a particle
15  traversing an absorber element.  Continuous processes such as multiple
16  scattering and energy loss play a relevant role in the longitudinal
17  and lateral development of electromagnetic and hadronic
18  showers, and in the case of sampling calorimeters the
19  measured resolution can be significantly affected by such fluctuations
```

```
20  in their active layers.  The description of ionisation fluctuations is
21  characterised by the significance parameter $\kappa$, which is
22  proportional to the ratio of mean energy loss to the maximum allowed
23  energy transfer in a single collision with an atomic electron
24  \[
25  \kappa =\frac{\xi}{\Emax}
26  \]
27  \Emax{}
28  is the maximum transferable energy in a single collision with
29  an atomic electron.
30
31  .......
32
33  \section{Vavilov theory}
34  \label{vavref}
35
36  Vavilov\cite{bib-VAVI} derived a more accurate straggling distribution
37  by introducing the kinematic limit on the maximum transferable energy
38  in a single collision, rather than using $ \Emax = \infty $.
39  Now we can write\cite{bib-SCH1}:
40  \begin{eqnarray*}
41  f \left ( \epsilon, \delta s \right ) & = & \frac{1}{\xi} \phi_{v}
42  \left ( \lambda_{v}, \kappa, \beta^{2} \right )
43  \end{eqnarray*}
44  where
45  \begin{eqnarray*}
46  \phi_{v} \left ( \lambda_{v}, \kappa, \beta^{2} \right ) & = &
47  \frac{1}{2 \pi i} \int^{c+i\infty}_{c-i\infty}\phi \left( s \right )
48  e^{\lambda s} ds \hspace{2cm} c \geq 0 \\
49  \phi \left ( s \right ) & = &
50  \exp \left [ \kappa ( 1 + \beta^{2}\gamma ) \right ]
51  ~ \exp \left [ \psi \left ( s \right ) \right ], \\
52  \psi \left ( s \right )  & = & s \ln \kappa + ( s + \beta^{2} \kappa )
53  \left [ \ln (s/\kappa) + E_{1} (s/\kappa) \right ] - \kappa e^{-s/\kappa},
54  \end{eqnarray*}
55  and
56  \begin{eqnarray*}
57  E_{1}(z) & = & \int^{\infty}_{z} t^{-1} e^{-t} dt
58  \mbox{\hspace{1cm} (the exponential integral)} \\
59  \lambda_v & = & \kappa \left [ \frac{\epsilon - \bar{\epsilon}}{\xi}
60  - \gamma' - \beta^2 \right]
61  \end{eqnarray*}
62
63  The Vavilov parameters are simply related to the Landau parameter by
64  $\lambda_L = \lambda_v/\kappa - \ln\kappa $. It can be shown that as
65  $\kappa \rightarrow 0$, the distribution of the variable $\lambda_L$
66  approaches that of Landau. For $\kappa \leq 0.01$ the two
67  distributions are already practically identical. Contrary to what many
68  textbooks report, the Vavilov distribution \emph{does not} approximate
69  the Landau distribution for small $\kappa$, but rather the
70  distribution of $\lambda_L$ defined above tends to the distribution of
71  the true $\lambda$ from the Landau density function.  Thus the routine
72  \texttt{GVAVIV} samples the variable $\lambda_L$ rather than
73  $\lambda_v$.  For $\kappa \geq 10$ the Vavilov distribution tends to a
74  Gaussian distribution (see next section).
75  ....
76
77  \begin{thebibliography}{10}
78  \bibitem{bib-LAND}
79  L.Landau.
80  \newblock On the Energy Loss of Fast Particles by Ionisation.
81  \newblock Originally published in \emph{J. Phys.}, 8:201, 1944.
82  \newblock Reprinted in D.ter Haar, Editor, \emph{L.D.Landau, Collected
83    papers}, page 417.  Pergamon Press, Oxford, 1965.
84
```

```
85   \bibitem{bib-SCH1}
86   B.Schorr.
87   \newblock Programs for the Landau and the Vavilov distributions and the
88     corresponding random numbers.
89   \newblock \emph{Comp. Phys. Comm.}, 7:216, 1974.
90
91   \bibitem{bib-SELT}
92   S.M.Seltzer and M.J.Berger.
93   \newblock Energy loss straggling of protons and mesons.
94   \newblock In \emph{Studies in Penetration of Charged Particles in
95     Matter}, Nuclear Science Series~39, Nat. Academy of Sciences,
96     Washington DC, 1964.
97
98   \bibitem{bib-TALM}
99   R.Talman.
100  \newblock On the statistics of particle identification using ionization.
101  \newblock \emph{Nucl. Inst. Meth.}, 159:189, 1979.
102
103  \bibitem{bib-VAVI}
104  P.V.Vavilov.
105  \newblock Ionisation losses of high energy heavy particles.
106  \newblock \emph{Soviet Physics JETP}, 5:749, 1957.
107  \end{thebibliography}
108
109  \end{document}
```

A.1.2   LaTeX converted to XML

```
1    <?xml version="1.0"?>
2    <!DOCTYPE document SYSTEM "latexexa.dtd" []>
3    <document>
4    <frontmatter>
5     <title>Simulation of Energy Loss Straggling</title>
6     <author>Maria Physicist</author>
7     <date>January 14, 1999</date>
8    </frontmatter>
9    <bodymatter>
10   <section id="intro"> <stitle>Introduction</stitle>
11   <par>Due to the statistical nature of ionisation energy loss, large
12   fluctuations can occur in the amount of energy deposited by a particle
13   traversing an absorber element. Continuous processes such as multiple
14   scattering and energy loss play a relevant role in the longitudinal
15   and lateral development of electromagnetic and hadronic showers, and
16   in the case of sampling calorimeters the measured resolution can be
17   significantly affected by such fluctuations in their active
18   layers. The description of ionisation fluctuations is characterised by
19   the significance parameter <inlinemath>
20   <math><mi>&kappa;</mi></math></inlinemath>, which is proportional to
21   the ratio of mean energy loss to the maximum allowed energy transfer
22   in a single collision with an atomic electron
23
24   <displaymath><math><mrow>
25   <mi>&kappa;</mi><mo>=</mo> <mfrac> <mrow>
26   <mi>&xi;</mi></mrow></mrow><msub><mi>E</mi><mrow><mi>max </mi> </mrow>
27   </msub> </mrow> </mfrac> </mrow></math></displaymath>
28
29   <inlinemath><math><msub><mi>E</mi><mrow><mi>max </mi> </mrow> </msub>
30   </math></inlinemath> is the maximum transferable energy in a single
31   collision with an atomic electron.
32
33   ....
34
35   </section>
```

```
36   <section id="vavref"><stitle>Vavilov theory</stitle>
37   <par>Vavilov<cite refid="bib-VAVI"/> derived a more accurate
38   straggling distribution by introducing the kinematic limit on the
39   maximum transferable energy in a single collision, rather than using
40   <inlinemath> <math><msub><mi>E</mi><mrow><mi>max </mi> </mrow> </msub>
41   <mo>=</mo><mi>&infin;</mi></math></inlinemath>. Now we can write<cite
42   refid="bib-SCH1"/>: <eqnarray><subeqn><math><mi>f</mi> <mfenced
43   open='('
44   close=')'><mi>&epsi;</mi><mo>,</mo><mi>&delta;</mi><mi>s</mi></mfenced>
45   <mo>=</mo>
46   <mfrac><mrow><mn>1</mn></mrow><mrow><mi>&xi;</mi></mrow></mfrac>
47   <msub><mi>&phi;</mi><mrow><mi>v</mi></mrow>
48   </msub> <mfenced open='('
49   close=')'><msub><mi>&lambda;</mi><mrow><mi>v</mi></mrow> </msub>
50   <mo>,</mo><mi>&kappa;</mi><mo>,</mo><msup><mi>&beta;</mi><mrow><mn>2</mn>
51   </mrow> </msup> </mfenced> <mtext></mtext> </math></subeqn></eqnarray>
52   where
53   <eqnarray><subeqn><math><msub><mi>&phi;</mi><mrow><mi>v</mi></mrow>
54   </msub> <mfenced open='('
55   close=')'><msub><mi>&lambda;</mi><mrow><mi>v</mi></mrow> </msub>
56   <mo>,</mo><mi>&kappa;</mi><mo>,</mo><msup><mi>&beta;</mi><mrow><mn>2</mn>
57   </mrow> </msup> </mfenced> <mo>=</mo>
58   <mfrac><mrow><mn>1</mn></mrow><mrow><mn>2</mn><mi>&pi;</mi><mi>i</mi></mrow>
59   </mfrac><msubsup><mo>&int;</mo>
60   <mrow><mi>c</mi><mo>+</mo><mi>i</mi><mi>&infin;</mi></mrow>
61   <mrow><mi>c</mi><mo>-</mo><mi>i</mi><mi>&infin;</mi>
62   </mrow></msubsup><mi>&phi;</mi><mfenced
63   open='('
64   close=')'><mi>s</mi></mfenced><msup><mi>e</mi><mrow><mi>&lambda;</mi><mi>s</mi>
65   </mrow> </msup> <mi>d</mi><mi>s</mi><mspace
66   width='2cm'/><mi>c</mi><mo>&geq;</mo><mn>0</mn> <mtext></mtext>
67   </math></subeqn><subeqn><math> </math></subeqn><subeqn
68   ><math><mi>&phi;</mi><mfenced open='(' close=')'><mi>s</mi></mfenced>
69   <mo>=</mo> <mo>exp</mo><mfenced open='['
70   close=']'><mi>&kappa;</mi><mrow><mo>(</mo><mn>1</mn><mo>+</mo>
71   <msup><mi>&beta;</mi><mrow><mn>2</mn>
72   </mrow> </msup>
73   <mi>&gamma;</mi><mo>)</mo></mrow></mfenced><mo>exp</mo><mfenced
74   open='[' close=']'><mi>&psi;</mi> <mfenced open='('
75   close=')'><mi>s</mi></mfenced></mfenced><mo>,</mo> <mtext></mtext>
76   </math></subeqn><subeqn><math> </math></subeqn><subeqn
77   ><math><mi>&psi;</mi> <mfenced open='(' close=')'><mi>s</mi></mfenced>
78   <mo>=</mo> <mi>s</mi><mo>ln</mo>
79   <mi>&kappa;</mi><mo>+</mo><mrow><mo>(</mo><mi>s</mi><mo>+</mo><msup>
80   <mi>&beta;</mi><mrow><mn>2</mn>
81   </mrow> </msup> <mi>&kappa;</mi><mo>)</mo></mrow><mfenced open='['
82   close=']'><mo>ln</mo>
83   <mrow><mo>(</mo><mi>s</mi><mo>/</mo><mi>&kappa;</mi><mo>)</mo></mrow>
84   <mo>+</mo><msub><mi>E</mi><mrow>
85   <mn>1</mn> </mrow> </msub>
86   <mrow><mo>(</mo><mi>s</mi><mo>/</mo><mi>&kappa;</mi><mo>)</mo>
87   </mrow></mfenced><mo>-</mo><mi>&kappa;</mi><msup><mi>e</mi><mrow>
88   <mo>-</mo><mi>s</mi><mo>/</mo><mi>&kappa;</mi>
89   </mrow> </msup> <mo>,</mo> <mtext></mtext> </math></subeqn></eqnarray>
90   and <eqnarray><subeqn><math><msub><mi>E</mi><mrow><mn>1</mn> </mrow>
91   </msub> <mrow><mo>(</mo><mi>z</mi><mo>)</mo></mrow>
92   <mo>=</mo><msubsup> <mo>&int;</mo>
93   <mrow><mi>&infin;</mi></mrow><mrow><mi>z</mi></mrow></msubsup>
94   <msup><mi>t</mi><mrow><mo>-</mo><mn>1</mn>
95   </mrow> </msup> <msup><mi>e</mi><mrow><mo>-</mo><mi>t</mi> </mrow>
96   </msup> <mi>d</mi><mi>t</mi><mspace width='1cm'/><mtext>(the
97   exponential integral)</mtext> <mtext></mtext> </math></subeqn><subeqn
98   ><math> </math></subeqn><subeqn
99   ><math><msub><mi>&lambda;</mi><mrow><mi>v</mi></mrow> </msub>
100  <mo>=</mo> <mi>&kappa;</mi><mfenced open='['
```

```
101  close=']'><mfrac><mrow><mi>&epsi;,</mi><mo>-</mo><munderover
102  accent='true'><mi>&epsi;</mi><mrow></mrow><mo>&barwed;</mo></munderover>
103  </mrow> <mrow><mi>&xi;</mi></mrow></mfrac>
104  <mo>-</mo><mi>&gamma;</mi><mi>&prime;</mi>
105  <mo>-</mo><msup><mi>&beta;</mi><mrow><mn>2</mn> </mrow> </msup>
106  </mfenced> <mtext></mtext> </math></subeqn></eqnarray>
107  </par>
108  <par>The Vavilov parameters are simply related to the Landau parameter
109  by <inlinemath><math><msub><mi>&lambda;</mi><mrow><mi>L</mi> </mrow>
110  </msub> <mo>=</mo><msub><mi>&lambda;</mi><mrow><mi>v</mi></mrow>
111  </msub> <mo>/</mo><mi>&kappa;</mi><mo>-</mo><mo>ln</mo>
112  <mi>&kappa;</mi></math></inlinemath>. It can be shown that as
113  <inlinemath> <math>
114  <mi>&kappa;</mi><mo>&rarr;</mo><mn>0</mn></math></inlinemath>, the
115  distribution of the variable <inlinemath> <math>
116  <msub><mi>&lambda;</mi><mrow><mi>L</mi> </mrow> </msub>
117  </math></inlinemath> approaches that of Landau. For <inlinemath>
118  <math>
119  <mi>&kappa;</mi><mo>&leq;</mo><mn>0</mn><mo>.</mo><mn>0</mn><mn>1</mn>
120  </math></inlinemath>
121  the two distributions are already practically identical. Contrary to
122  what many textbooks report, the Vavilov distribution <emph> does
123  not</emph> approximate the Landau distribution for small
124  <inlinemath><math><mi>&kappa;</mi></math></inlinemath>, but rather the
125  distribution of <inlinemath> <math>
126  <msub><mi>&lambda;</mi><mrow><mi>L</mi> </mrow> </msub>
127  </math></inlinemath> defined above tends to the distribution of the
128  true <inlinemath><math><mi>&lambda;</mi></math></inlinemath> from the
129  Landau density function. Thus the routine <texttt> GVAVIV</texttt>
130  samples the variable <inlinemath>
131  <math><msub><mi>&lambda;</mi><mrow><mi>L</mi> </mrow> </msub>
132  </math></inlinemath> rather than <inlinemath> <math>
133  <msub><mi>&lambda;</mi><mrow><mi>v</mi></mrow> </msub>
134  </math></inlinemath>. For <inlinemath> <math>
135  <mi>&kappa;</mi><mo>&geq;</mo><mn>1</mn><mn>0</mn></math></inlinemath>
136  the Vavilov distribution tends to a Gaussian distribution (see next
137  section). </par>
138  </section>
139  .....
140  </section>
141  <section class="star"><stitle>References</stitle>
142  <bibliography>
143  <bibitem id="bib-LAND">
144  <par>L.Landau. On the Energy Loss of Fast Particles by
145  Ionisation. Originally published in <emph>J. Phys.</emph>, 8:201,
146  1944. Reprinted in D.ter Haar, Editor, <emph>L.D.Landau, Collected
147  papers</emph>, page 417. Pergamon Press, Oxford, 1965. </par>
148  </bibitem>
149  <bibitem id="bib-SCH1">
150  <par>B.Schorr. Programs for the Landau and the Vavilov distributions
151  and the corresponding random numbers. <emph>Comp. Phys. Comm.</emph>,
152  7:216, 1974. </par>
153  </bibitem>
154  <bibitem id="bib-SELT">
155  <par>S.M.Seltzer and M.J.Berger. Energy loss straggling of protons and
156  mesons. In <emph>Studies in Penetration of Charged Particles in
157  Matter</emph>, Nuclear Science Series 39, Nat. Academy of Sciences,
158  Washington DC, 1964. </par>
159  </bibitem>
160  <bibitem id="bib-TALM">
161  <par>R.Talman. On the statistics of particle identification using
162  ionization. <emph>Nucl. Inst. Meth.</emph>, 159:189, 1979. </par>
163  </bibitem>
164  <bibitem id="bib-VAVI">
165  <par>P.V.Vavilov. Ionisation losses of high energy heavy
```

```
166    particles. <emph>Soviet Physics JETP</emph>, 5:749, 1957.</par>
167    </bibitem>
168    </bibliography>
169    </section>
170    </bodymatter>
171    </document>
```

A.1.3   Document Type Definition for XML version

```
1     <!-- latex.dtd: XML version of LaTeX + MathML -->
2
3     <!ENTITY % fontchange  "emph|textit|textbf|textsf|textsl|texttt" >
4     <!ENTITY % misc "url|quad|hspace|vspace|includegraphics|footnote|tag|ent">
5     <!ENTITY % xref "ref|cite|pageref">
6     <!ENTITY % chunk "lalist|par|tabular|figure|table|align|bibliography">
7     <!ENTITY % mathobj   "displaymath|inlinemath|equation|eqnarray" >
8     <!ENTITY % inline "#PCDATA|%fontchange;|%chunk;|%misc;|%xref;|%mathobj;">
9
10    <!ELEMENT document (frontmatter?,bodymatter)>
11    <!ATTLIST document class CDATA "article">
12
13    <!ELEMENT frontmatter (title,author,date?,abstract?,keywords?)>
14    <!ELEMENT bodymatter  ((par|section)*,appendix*)>
15
16    <!-- front matter -->
17    <!ELEMENT title (%inline;)*>
18    <!ELEMENT author (%inline;)*>
19    <!ELEMENT date (#PCDATA)>
20
21    <!-- structuring -->
22    <!ELEMENT section (stitle,(%chunk;|subsection)*)>
23    <!ATTLIST section
24     class CDATA #IMPLIED
25     id ID #IMPLIED>
26    <!ELEMENT subsection (stitle,(%chunk;|paragraph)*)>
27    <!ATTLIST subsection
28     class CDATA #IMPLIED
29     id ID #IMPLIED>
30    <!ELEMENT paragraph (stitle,(%chunk;|subparagraph)*)>
31    <!ATTLIST paragraph
32     class CDATA #IMPLIED
33     id ID #IMPLIED>
34    <!ELEMENT subparagraph (stitle,(%chunk;)*)>
35    <!ATTLIST subparagraph
36     class CDATA #IMPLIED
37     id ID #IMPLIED>
38    <!ELEMENT stitle (%inline;)*>
39
40    <!-- font changes -->
41    <!ELEMENT emph    (%inline;)*>
42    <!ELEMENT textit (%inline;)*>
43    <!ELEMENT textbf (%inline;)*>
44    <!ELEMENT textsf (%inline;)*>
45    <!ELEMENT textsl (%inline;)*>
46    <!ELEMENT texttt (%inline;)*>
47
48    <!-- lists -->
49    <!ELEMENT lalist (item)*>
50    <!ATTLIST lalist
51     id ID #IMPLIED
52     class (enumerate|itemize|description) #REQUIRED>
53    <!ELEMENT item (%inline;)*>
54
```

```
55    <!-- bibliography -->
56    <!ELEMENT bibliography (bibitem)*>
57    <!ELEMENT bibitem (%inline;)*>
58    <!ATTLIST bibitem
59     id ID #REQUIRED>
60
61    <!-- floats -->
62    <!ELEMENT table (%chunk;|caption|includegraphics)*>
63    <!ELEMENT figure (%chunk;|caption|includegraphics)*>
64    <!ELEMENT caption (%inline;)*>
65    <!ATTLIST caption
66     id ID #IMPLIED>
67    <!ELEMENT includegraphics EMPTY>
68    <!ATTLIST includegraphics
69        width CDATA #IMPLIED
70        height CDATA #IMPLIED
71        scale CDATA #IMPLIED
72        file CDATA #IMPLIED>
73
74    <!-- tables -->
75    <!ELEMENT tabular (hline|row)*>
76    <!ATTLIST tabular
77        preamble CDATA #REQUIRED>
78    <!ELEMENT row (cell)*>
79    <!ELEMENT hline EMPTY>
80    <!ELEMENT cell (%inline;)*>
81    <!ELEMENT newline EMPTY>
82    <!ATTLIST newline
83     id ID #IMPLIED>
84
85    <!-- low-level bits and pieces -->
86    <!ELEMENT align (%inline;)*>
87    <!ATTLIST align
88        style CDATA #REQUIRED>
89    <!ELEMENT url EMPTY>
90    <!ATTLIST url
91     name CDATA #REQUIRED>
92    <!ELEMENT par (%inline;)*>
93    <!ELEMENT quad EMPTY>
94    <!ELEMENT hspace EMPTY>
95    <!ATTLIST hspace
96        dim CDATA #REQUIRED>
97    <!ELEMENT vspace EMPTY>
98    <!ATTLIST vspace
99        dim CDATA #REQUIRED>
100   <!ELEMENT tag (#PCDATA)>
101   <!ELEMENT ent EMPTY>
102   <!ATTLIST ent
103       value CDATA #REQUIRED
104       name CDATA #REQUIRED>
105
106   <!-- cross-refs - >
107   <!ELEMENT cite EMPTY>
108   <!ATTLIST cite
109       refid IDREF #REQUIRED>
110   <!ELEMENT ref EMPTY>
111   <!ATTLIST ref
112    refid IDREF #REQUIRED>
113
114   <!-- maths. must reduce to <math> elements  for MathML -->
115   <!ELEMENT equation (math)*>
116   <!ATTLIST equation
117    id ID #IMPLIED>
118   <!ELEMENT displaymath (math)*>
119   <!ELEMENT inlinemath  (math)*>
```

```
120    <!ELEMENT subeqn (math)*>
121    <!ATTLIST subeqn
122     id ID #IMPLIED>
123    <!ELEMENT eqnarray (subeqn)*>
124    <!ATTLIST eqnarray
125     number (yes|no) "yes"
126     id ID #IMPLIED>
127
128    <!-- sub DTDs and entities -->
129    <!--Added Math Symbols: Arrows-->
130    <!ENTITY % isoamsae.dtd SYSTEM "isoamsae.dtd">
131
132    <!--Added Math Symbols: Binary Operators-->
133    <!ENTITY % isoamsbe.dtd SYSTEM "isoamsbe.dtd">
134
135    <!--Added Math Symbols: Delimiters-->
136    <!ENTITY % isoamsce.dtd SYSTEM "isoamsce.dtd">
137
138    <!--Added Math Symbols: Negated Relations-->
139    <!ENTITY % isoamsne.dtd SYSTEM "isoamsne.dtd">
140
141    <!--Added Math Symbols: Ordinary-->
142    <!ENTITY % isoamsoe.dtd SYSTEM "isoamsoe.dtd">
143
144    <!--Added Math Symbols: Relations-->
145    <!ENTITY % isoamsre.dtd SYSTEM "isoamsre.dtd">
146
147    <!--General Technical-->
148    <!ENTITY % isoteche.dtd SYSTEM "isoteche.dtd">
149
150    <!--Numbers and Currency symbols-->
151    <!ENTITY % isonume.dtd SYSTEM "isonume.dtd">
152
153    <!--MathML Aliases (From ISO PUB,DIA,NUM)-->
154    <!ENTITY % mmaliase.dtd SYSTEM "mmaliase.dtd">
155
156    <!--Greek Symbols-->
157    <!ENTITY % isogrk3e.dtd SYSTEM "isogrk3e.dtd">
158
159    <!--Math Script Font-->
160    <!ENTITY % isomscre.dtd SYSTEM "isomscre.dtd">
161
162    <!--Math Open Face Font-->
163    <!ENTITY % isomopfe.dtd SYSTEM "isomopfe.dtd">
164
165    <!--MathML Entities-->
166    <!ENTITY % mmlent.dtd SYSTEM "mmlent.dtd">
167
168    <!--Main MathML DTD -->
169    <!ENTITY % mathml.dtd     SYSTEM "mathml.dtd">
170
171    %mathml.dtd;
172    %isoamsae.dtd;
173    %isoamsbe.dtd;
174    %isoamsce.dtd;
175    %isoamsne.dtd;
176    %isoamsoe.dtd;
177    %isoamsre.dtd;
178    %isoteche.dtd;
179    %isonume.dtd;
180    %mmaliase.dtd;
181    %isogrk3e.dtd;
182    %isomscre.dtd;
183    %isomopfe.dtd;
184    %mmlent.dtd;
```

```
185     <!ENTITY aacute "&#x00E1;">
186     <!ENTITY OverBar "[UverBar]">
187     <!ENTITY negationslash "/">
188
189
190     <!-- end of latex.dtd -->
```

A.2   Scripting examples for techexplorer

A.2.1   teched.html

```
1     <HTML>
2     <!-- teched.html -->
3     <!-- (C) Copyright 1998 by Robert S. Sutor. All rights reserved. -->
4     <HEAD>
5         <META HTTP-EQUIV="Content-Type"
6               CONTENT="text/html; charset=iso-8859-1">
7         <META NAME="GENERATOR"
8               CONTENT="Mozilla/4.01 [en] (Win95; I) [Netscape]">
9         <TITLE>teched Sample LaTeX Editor</TITLE>
10    </HEAD>
11
12    <!-- This is a very simple LaTeX editor built using the      -->
13    <!-- IBM techexplorer Hypermedia Browser and a Java applet. - >
14
15    <BODY>
16    <CENTER>
17
18    <!-- The upper window is controlled by techexplorer. We   -->
19    <!-- give the name 'teInput' to this window. We are        -->
20    <!-- using a table to put a frame around the window.       -->
21
22    <TABLE BORDER=1>
23        <TR>
24            <TD>
25                <EMBED TYPE="application/x-techexplorer"
26                TEXDATA="\(\)"
27                NAME="teInput" WIDTH=600 HEIGHT=150>
28            </TD>
29        </TR>
30    </TABLE>
31
32    <!-- The lower window is handled by the 'teched' Java      -->
33    <!-- applet. Like the techexplorer window, it is 600       -->
34    <!-- pixels wide.                                          -->
35
36    <TABLE BORDER=1>
37        <TR>
38            <TD>
39                <APPLET CODE="teched.class"
40                NAME="teched" ALIGN=CENTER
41                WIDTH=600 HEIGHT=130 MAYSCRIPT></APPLET>
42            </TD>
43        </TR>
44    </TABLE>
45    </CENTER>
46    </BODY>
47    </HTML>
```

A.2.2   teched.java

```
1    // teched.java
2    // (C) Copyright 1998 by Robert S. Sutor. All rights reserved.
3
4    // We first import the classes we need from the standard Java
5    // distribution. This will work with Java 1.0 or higher.
6
7    import java.awt.*;
8    import java.awt.event.*;
9    import java.lang.*;
10   import java.applet.Applet;
11
12   // The following brings in the Netscape LiveConnect classes
13   // that we will use.
14
15   import netscape.javascript.JSObject;
16
17   // These are the classes that we use that are exposed by
18   // techexplorer. The first is the basic interface to the
19   // plug-in. The others are the event and listener classes.
20
21   import ibm.techexplorer.plugin.techexplorerPlugin;
22   import ibm.techexplorer.awt.AWTEvent;
23   import ibm.techexplorer.awt.event.KeyListener;
24   import ibm.techexplorer.awt.event.KeyEvent;
25
26   public class teched
27       extends java.applet.Applet
28       implements KeyListener
29   {
30       // The JavaScript window object
31       JSObject          Window           = null;
32       // The JavaScript document object
33       JSObject          Document         = null;
34
35       // The techexplorer plug-in instance
36       techexplorerPlugin tePlugin        = null;
37       // The editable text area for the markup source
38       TextArea          markupInputArea  = null;
39       // The 'Clear input' button
40       Button            clearInputButton = null;
41
42       // A utility buffer for holding the markup.
43       StringBuffer      markupString     = new StringBuffer("");
44
45       public boolean action(Event evt, Object arg) {
46           // We only handle the 'Clear input' action.
47
48           boolean result = false;
49
50           if ( evt.target == clearInputButton ) {
51               // Empty the markup edit area.
52               markupInputArea.setText( "" );
53
54               // Reinitialize the techexplorer document. This
55               // needs to be a non-empty string to actually
56               // updated the document, so we give it some
57               // non-visible input.
58
59               tePlugin.reloadFromTeXString( "\\(\\)" );
60
61               result = true;
62           }
63
```

```
64          return result;
65     }
66
67     public void init() {
68          // Initialize the components we are displaying
69          // with this Java applet.
70
71          clearInputButton  = new Button("Clear input");
72          markupInputArea   = new TextArea( 5, 80 );
73
74          this.setLayout( new FlowLayout() );
75          this.add( markupInputArea );
76          this.add( clearInputButton );
77     }
78
79     public void keyPressed( ibm.techexplorer.awt.event.KeyEvent e ) {
80          // We don't do anything with this event given us by
81          // techexplorer. But see 'keyTyped'.
82     }
83
84     public void keyTyped( ibm.techexplorer.awt.event.KeyEvent e ) {
85          // This is a naive (but effective!) way of dealing with
86          // keys coming to us from techexplorer. We grab the key
87          // that was pressed and put it on the end of our markup.
88          // Then we update the techexplorer window.
89
90          if ( e.getSource() == tePlugin ) {
91              markupInputArea.appendText(
92                  ( new Character( e.getKeyChar() )).toString() );
93
94              // This replaces the document within the techexplorer
95              // window with that gotten by parsing the string
96              // passed to it.
97
98              tePlugin.reloadFromTeXString( markupInputArea.getText() );
99          }
100    }
101
102    public void keyReleased( ibm.techexplorer.awt.event.KeyEvent e ) {
103         // This is where we deal with key release events coming to
104         // us from the techexplorer window.
105
106         switch ( e.getKeyCode() ) {
107           case KeyEvent.VK_DELETE:
108             // When we see a 'delete' key, we remove the last character
109             // in the markup.
110
111             if ( e.getSource() == tePlugin ) {
112                 markupString = new StringBuffer( markupInputArea.getText() );
113                 int length = markupString.length();
114                 if ( length > 0 )
115                     --length;
116                 markupString.setLength( length );
117                 markupInputArea.setText( markupString.toString() );
118                 tePlugin.reloadFromTeXString( markupInputArea.getText() );
119             }
120             break;
121
122           case KeyEvent.VK_ENTER:
123             // When we see that the 'enter' key has been pressed, we
124             // insert a newline in the markup. This improves readability.
125
126             if ( e.getSource() == tePlugin ) {
127                 markupInputArea.appendText( "\n" );
128                 tePlugin.reloadFromTeXString( markupInputArea.getText() );
```

```
129                }
130                break;
131
132             default:
133                break;
134          }
135       }
136
137       public boolean keyUp( Event evt, int key )
138       {
139          // This key is one from the markup input area.
140          // When a key is released, update the techexplorer
141          // document with the current markup.
142
143          boolean result = false;
144
145          if ( evt.target == markupInputArea ) {
146             if ( evt.id == Event.KEY_RELEASE ) {
147                int length = markupInputArea.getText().length();
148                if ( length > 0 )
149                   tePlugin.reloadFromTeXString(
150                      markupInputArea.getText() );
151                else
152                   tePlugin.reloadFromTeXString( "\\(\\)" );
153             }
154
155             result = true;
156          }
157
158          return result;
159       }
160
161       public void start() {
162          // Initialize the Netscape JavaScript objects.
163
164          Window   = (JSObject) JSObject.getWindow(this);
165          Document = (JSObject) Window.getMember("document");
166
167          // Try to get the techexplorer plug-in object.
168          tePlugin = (techexplorerPlugin) Document.getMember("teInput");
169
170          if ( tePlugin == null )
171             // If we didn't get it, print a debug message.
172             System.out.println("teched: start(): null teched");
173          else
174             // Otherwise add the listener for techexplorer keys.
175             tePlugin.addKeyListener( (KeyListener) this );
176       }
177
178       public void stop() {
179          if ( tePlugin == null )
180             // If we don't have the techexplorer plug-in object,
181             // print a debug message.
182             System.out.println("teched: stop(): null teched");
183          else
184             // Otherwise remove the listener for techexplorer keys.
185             tePlugin.removeKeyListener( (KeyListener) this );
186       }
187    }
```

B

Technical appendixes

B.1   The HyperTEX standard

An important standardization effort for TEX and hypertext is the HyperTEX project
[↪HYPERTEX]. It was set up by Tanmoy Bhattacharya and Mark Doyle for the E-
Print archive [↪EPRINT] at the Los Alamos National Laboratory in the United
States under the leadership of Paul Ginsparg. The HyperTEX specification says that
conformant viewers and translators must recognize the following set of \special
constructs:

```
href    html:<a href = "href_string">
name    html:<a name = "name_string">
end     html:</a>
image   html:<img src = "href_string">
base    html:<base href = "href_string">
```

The href, name, and end commands are used to do the basic hypertext operations of establishing links between sections of documents. The image command is
intended (as with HTML browsers) to place an image of arbitrary graphical format
on the page at the current location. The base command is used to communicate
to the DVI viewer the full (URL) location of the current document so that files
specified by relative URLs may be retrieved correctly.

The href and name commands must be paired with an end command later
in the TEX file—the TEX commands between the two ends of a pair form an *anchor* in the document. In the case of an href command, the *anchor* is to be highlighted in the DVI viewer. When it is clicked on, it will cause the scene to shift

to the destination specified by *href_string*. The *anchor* associated with a name command represents a possible location to which other hypertext links may refer, either as local references (of the form href="#*name_string*" with the attribute *name_string* identical to the one in the name command) or as part of a URL (of the form *URL#name_string*). Here *href_string* is a valid URL or local identifier, while *name_string* could be any string at all: The only caveat is that " characters should be escaped with a backslash (\); if it looks like a URL name, it might cause problems.

The HyperTEX \special commands are implemented by (at least) the following DVI drivers: xdvi under UNIX, dviout and dviwindo under Windows, and OzTeX and Textures on the Macintosh. The dvips program also supports the commands, and can translate them into a form suitable for conversion to PDF.

B.2   Configuring TEX4ht to produce XML

The basic idea of LATEX is interfaces for identifying structural entities in documents and for associating presentations with such entities. SGML and its descendants aim at a generalization of such an idea in which the interfaces are provided in formats suitable for further processing. The ultimate objective of TEX4ht is to offer a tool that recognizes TEX-based interfaces in general, and of LATEX in particular, and that provides the means to translate these interfaces into arbitrary SGML-based representations.

With this in mind, as we saw in Chapter 4, TEX4ht delegates to the native TEX compiler the task of processing the source files, relieving itself from dealing with many painful details that have little to do with structural issues in documents. To identify the structure of a document, TEX4ht seeds the style files with hooks at strategic locations within the definitions of macros and then offers the means to configure the hooks to produce any sort of output you want. This means that you can create translations to different SGML-based representations.

Section 4.5 on page 170 showed how the hooks can be configured. We now go on to describe a friendly interface for identifying and configuring hooks and then wander more deeply into low-level features associated with the TEX compiler.

The reader is encouraged to get a live demonstration of the interface discussed in the next two sections, by actually running the different stages of the example.

B.2.1   Starting from scratch

The fast evolution of HTML between different versions in recent years and the emergence of the XML language highlight the importance of allowing for large-scale modifications to the output of TEX4ht, to meeting the challenges that arise from new requirements. Let us look at how to strip TEX4ht back to basics and then build up a new converter.

B.2.1.1   Loading empty configurations

The package option 0.0 requests empty configurations for the hooks, implying an output consisting of text with no hypertext tags. For example, the following source document outputs just the text 1 Demo With A List without any tags:

```
\documentclass{article}
  \usepackage[html,0.0]{tex4ht}
\begin{document}
\section{Demo}
With
  \begin{description}
    \item[A] List
  \end{description}
\end{document}
```

We will keep this simple example in mind for the next few sections in order to demonstrate the outcome of the features discussed.

B.2.1.2   Looking for hooks

A major problem in reconfiguring the TₑX4ht hooks is to find out where they are and what they can do. The option hooks gives us a good start by requesting *pseudohypertext tags* for hooks that have no other configuration. A *pseudohypertext tag* shows the name of a hook, the index of an argument within the hook, and, when it is not obvious, the number of arguments for the hook.

Compiling the example source document with the html,0.0,hooks package options will produce output that looks like this in a browser:

In this display, the tag <HTML1:2> comes from the first argument of the "HTML" hook. That hook is configured with the command

\Configure{HTML} *{first-argument}* *{second-argument}*.

The `<Env(description)2>` tag comes from the second argument of the description environmental hook, configured by the command

> \ConfigureEnv{description} *{first-argument} {second-argument} {third-argument} {fourth-argument}*

The `<List(description)4>` tag comes from the fourth argument of the description list hook, configured by the command

> \ConfigureList{description} *{first-argument} {second-argument} {third-argument} {fourth-argument}*

B.2.1.3   Viewing the hooks

While current browsers are likely to display the output resulting from the hooks option, the file itself is missing a proper HTML code at the start and the end of the file. That code can be quite easily introduced by configuring the "HTML" hook. We can also give the tags special characteristics within the display to attract the attention of the reader to their presence. The appearance may be modified within the CSS file, as well as by changing the following default configuration:

```
\Configure{hooks}
  {\HCode{<STRONG CLASS="hooks">&lt;}} {\HCode{&gt;</STRONG>}} {}{}
```

By introducing a configuration file `try.cfg` as follows and loading it with the option list `try,html,0.0,hooks`, the HTML file will become legal, and the tags will shown in green.

```
\Configure{HTML}{\StartHtml}{\EndHtml}
\newcommand\StartHtml{\IgnorePar\HCode{<!DOCTYPE HTML PUBLIC
            "-//W3C//DTD HTML 4.0 Transitional//EN">\Hnewline
               <HTML><HEAD><LINK REL="stylesheet"
            TYPE="text/css" HREF="\jobname.css">\Hnewline
          <TITLE>\jobname</TITLE></HEAD>\Hnewline <BODY>}
         \Css{.hooks{color:green;}}}
\newcommand\EndHtml{\HCode{</BODY></HTML>}}
\Preamble{}
\begin{document}
\EndPreamble
```

B.2.1.4   Reconfiguring the hooks

Starting from output consisting of *pseudohypertext* tags, you can gradually configure the different hooks to get the output you want. Along the way, distracting tags of no interest can be removed by assigning invisible nonempty code to their corresponding parameters.

By configuring the hooks "BODY", "HEAD", "TITLE+", "TITLE", "TocAt*", "TocAt", and "toc" to add the \empty to their parameters, the example reduces to the following:

1 Demo_{<section3:4>} With
  <List(description)1> <List(description)2> A
  <List(description)3> List <List(description)4> <Env(description)2>
  <section2:4>

With straightforward configurations supplied to the remaining hooks, you obtain a view like this:

```
[DOC] [SECTION][NUM]1[/NUM] [TITLE]Demo[/TITLE] With [DLIST]
[MARK] A [/MARK]List [/DLIST] [/SECTION][/DOC]
```

A configuration file which produces output like this is as follows:

```
\Configure{HEAD}{\empty}{\empty}
\Configure{HTML}
  {\IgnorePar\HCode{<HTML><HEAD> <TITLE></TITLE></HEAD><BODY>}[DOC]}
  {[/DOC]\HCode{</BODY></HTML>}}
\Preamble{}
  \Configure{BODY}{\empty}{\empty}
  \Configure{TITLE}{\empty}{\empty}
  \Configure{TITLE+}{\empty}
  \Configure{TocAt}{\empty}{\empty}
  \Configure{TocAt*}{\empty}{\empty}
  \Configure{toc}{\empty}
  \ConfigureEnv{description} {[DLIST]}{[/DLIST]}{}{}
  \ConfigureList{description}{}{}{[MARK]}{[/MARK]}
  \Configure{section}    {[SECTION]}{[/SECTION]}
      {[NUM]\arabic{section}[/NUM][TITLE]}{[/TITLE]}
\begin{document}
\EndPreamble
\Configure{HtmlPar}{}{\empty}{}{}
```

B.2.1.5   Cleaning up

Having completed configuring the hooks of interest, we can remove the code we introduced just for getting an improved view of the output, and we can take out the hooks option in the \usepackage command.

B.2.2   Adding XML tags

The XML language is good for exhibiting how TEX4ht can be reconfigured, so we will now look at adding some XML tags to our output. As long as the newly assigned configurations to the hooks do not contain HTML tags, the browsers should have no problem displaying the outcome of these assignments.

TEX4ht provides the three commands:

```
\Tg<name>
\Tg</name>
\Tg<name/>
```

for producing start, end, and empty XML tags, respectively. The edit package option makes these new commands produce visible forms of the tags by introducing code for *displaying* the tags instead of actually *creating* them.

For example, replacing the [*name*] with commands of the form \Tg<*name*> in the configuration file of our example, we get a view like this in HTML browsers:

```
<DOC> <SECTION> <NUM> 1</NUM><TITLE>Demo</TITLE>
With <DLIST> <MARK> A </MARK>List </DLIST> </SECTION> </DOC>
```

using the following version of the configuration file:

```
\Configure{HTML} {\Tg<DOC>}{\Tg</DOC>}
\Preamble{}
  \ConfigureEnv{description} {\Tg<DLIST>}{\Tg</DLIST>}{}{}
  \ConfigureList{description}{}{}{\Tg<MARK>}{\Tg</MARK>}
  \Configure{section}    {\Tg<SECTION>}{\Tg</SECTION>}
      {\Tg<NUM>\arabic{section}\Tg</NUM>\Tg<TITLE>}{\Tg</TITLE>}
\begin{document}
\EndPreamble
```

The default look of the visible "tags" is set by the command

```
\Configure{edit}{\HCode{<STRONG>&lt;}}{\HCode{&gt;</STRONG>}}
```

Removing the edit option would make a proper XML document.

B.2.2.1 Typesetting the abstract tags

The job of the XML tags is to identify logical units within the document. During the editing phase in which the tags are introduced, it can be very useful to highlight the nature of the different tags and the structural relationships they maintain.

To meet this objective, the \Tg tags can be enhanced with the commands

```
\Configure<name>{before}{after}
\Configure</name>{before}{after}
\Configure<name/>{before}{after}
```

for producing whatever sort of display you find useful.

The addition of commands like

```
\Configure<NUM>{\HCode{<DIV ALIGN="CENTER">}}{}
\Configure</TITLE>{}{\HCode{</DIV>}}
\Configure<DLIST>{\HCode{<BR>}}{}
\Configure</DLIST>{}{\HCode{<BR>}}
```

to the configuration file results in a layout like the following within the browser:

```
<DOC> <SECTION>
      <NUM>1</NUM><TITLE>Demo</TITLE>
With
<DLIST> <MARK> A </MARK>List </DLIST>
</SECTION></DOC>
```

When the first argument is a hyphen character –, the configuration commands produce just the second argument without showing the tag itself. In this case, the configuration commands define a virtual browser for the new tags.

Consider the following variants of the configuration commands:

```
\Configure<NUM>-{\HCode{<DIV ALIGN="CENTER">}}
\Configure</NUM>-{ }
\Configure<TITLE>-{}
\Configure</TITLE>-{\HCode{</DIV>}}
```

These commands will produce a browser display like this:

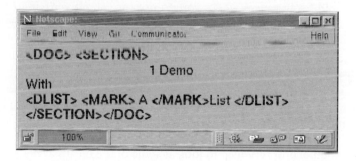

B.2.2.2   Checking containment relationships

The `verify` option requests warning messages for unknown parent-child containment relationships among the tags defined by the \Tg command. Containment relationships can be specified by listing pairs of parent and child names with the string --> between the commands

```
\Verify
\EndVerify
```

Different pairs within the listing should be separated by a comma. Thus if

```
\Verify --> DOC, DOC --> SECTION \EndVerify
```

is placed before the \begin{document} of the configuration file try.cfg, and the package option verify is used, you will get warning messages like these:

```
4. --- warning --- SECTION --> NUM ?
4. --- warning --- SECTION --> TITLE ?
4. --- warning --- SECTION --> DLIST ?
4. --- warning --- DLIST --> MARK ?
```

All we have specified is that the SECTION tag is expected within a DOC tag. The system reports that it has found a MARK within a DLIST.

The package option verify+ is an extension of the verify option in which the containment relations found by the system are detailed in the log file.

Similarly the hooks+ package option is an extension of the hooks option. Besides requesting a display of how parameters of hooks are used, this option also asks for a listing in the log file of how hooks are configured. This is useful when looking at example configurations which may provide useful guidelines on how to define new configurations. Typically such examples are spread around different files and might be buried within other unrelated code.

A \Tg<argument> command is a special case of a \HCode{<argument>} command that allows us, during an editing phase, to show the tags and to check that they satisfy proper containment relationships. A weaker \TG version of the command is offered for instances where you do not care about verifying containment relationships. On the other hand, a \tg variant of the \TG command which corresponds to an <argument>, instead of to \HCode{<argument>}, is available.

B.2.3   Getting deeper for extra configurations

Our attention so far has been on structural features that apply mainly to large items such as chapters, lists, and tables. These entities are typically defined within style files; they do not really rely on the low-level features that are provided in the TeX typesetting engine. Now we need to look at some of the means available in TeX4ht for dealing with these low-level commands.

B.2.3.1   Math mode

Mathematical formulae are rich in low-level TeX features. The default settings of TeX4ht provide graphic versions of mathematical formulae that are likely to have complex structures. The package option math requests an alternative setup in which the formulae are seeded by hooks that can be configured to specify new output representations.

The mathematical environments \(*formula*\), \[*formula*\], $*formula*$, and $$*formula*$$ can be configured with the following commands:

```
\Configure{()}{before$at-start}{at-end$after}
\Configure{[]}{before$$at-start}{at-end$$after}
\Configure{$}{before}{after}{at-start}
\Configure{$$}{before}{after}{at-start}
```

The configuration of the latter pair of environments applies also to the math and displaymath environments, respectively.

[equation]a + b[/equation]

```
\Configure{()}{[equation]$}{$[/equation]}
\(a+b\)
```

Some of the features we will look at require TEX4ht to be in a special mode of operation. The commands

```
\DviMath
\EndDviMath
```

may be used to set this up.

B.2.3.2   Math classes for symbols

At the lowest level of math reside the primitive tokens representing numbers, variables, operators, parentheses, and so forth. Inspired by the classification of mathematical symbols within TEX, a similar (but independent) classification is applied to symbols in TEX4ht.

Specifically the symbols might be assigned a class number between 0 and 9, where an initial classification puts large operators in class 1, binary operators in class 2, relational operators in class 3, opening delimiters in class 4, closing delimiters in class 5, punctuation symbols in class 6, and the rest of the symbols in class 0.

The following command may be used to associate output tags with the symbols of a particular class and to add symbols into the class:

```
\Configure{MathClass}{class-number}{string}{before}{after}{symbols}
```

If the *string* argument is not empty, it must be a single character not appearing in the arguments *before* and *after*. In this case, those arguments specify a content to be inserted before and after the symbols of the *class*.

The argument *symbols* should be a sequence of symbols. When it is not empty, the symbols specified in the argument are assigned to the specified class.

```
\Configure{()}{\DviMath$}{$\EndDviMath}
\Configure{MathClass}{0}{*}
    {[ordinary]}{[/ordinary]}{}
\Configure{MathClass}{2}{*}
    {[operator]}{[/operator]}{}
\Configure{MathClass}{7}{*}
    {[digit]}{[/digit]}{0123456789}
\(a+1\)
```

[ordinary]a[/ordinary] [operator]+[/operator] [digit]1[/digit]

As when the arguments of \HCode are processed, the *before* and *after* are processed just for macro expansions and not for fonts, definitions, and computations.

The commands

```
\PauseMathClass
\EndPauseMathClass
```

can be used temporarily to suppress the contributions of the different classes.

B.2.3.3   Math classes for delimiters and words

Open and close delimiter symbols, which group tokens for the \Send{BACK} instructions (Section B.2.3.4), should be assigned their math classes with the command:

```
\Configure{MathDelimiters}{open}{close}
```

When the package option math is used, the default setting invokes the command \Configure{MathDelimiters}{(}{)} to assign the parentheses symbols "(" and ")" to the math classes 4 and 5, respectively, and to inform TEX4ht about the pairing of these delimiters.

TEX4ht provides the commands \mathord, \mathop, \mathbin, \mathrel, \mathopen, \mathclose, and \mathpunc for associating, respectively, classes 0 through 6 to subformulae. The following instruction configures these commands, while indirectly referring to the commands through their class numbers:

```
\Configure{FormulaClass}{class-number}{string}{before}{after}
```

If the argument *string* is not empty, it should be a character not appearing in the arguments *before* and *after*. If *string is* empty, we specify the configuration to be used for the characters of the specified *class-number*.

```
\Configure{()}{\DviMath$}{$\EndDviMath}
\Configure{FormulaClass}{4}{*}{}{[}
\Configure{FormulaClass}{5}{*}{]}{}
\(\mathopen{open}a+1\mathclose{close}\)
```

open[a + 1]close

B.2.3.4   DVI-based groups

The output of TEX is the low-level page-description language DVI, which relies heavily on a hierarchical grouping mechanism. That hierarchy reflects the structure specified explicitly and implicitly in the source document. You sometimes need access to this information when writing translators.

```
\Trace{GROUP}
\EndTrace{GROUP}
\Configure{GROUP}{string}{open-1}{open-2}{close-1}{close-2}
```

The first two commands delimit the region in which the groups are to be shown. The third command controls the manner in which the groups are shown.

The arguments *open-1* and *open-2* specify what is to be inserted at the start of groups, and, if the first of these arguments is not empty, the level of nesting and the group number are also included. The arguments *close-1* and *close-2* specify in a similar manner the content to be inserted at the end of groups.

```
\Configure{GROUP}{*}{[}{]}{[/}{]}
```

```
\noindent \Trace{GROUP}
\(A \stackrel{\string~}{=} B\)
\EndTrace{GROUP}
```

A[3 480][4 481] =[/4 481] [4 482] [/4 482][/3 480] B

The next two commands enable us to submit content to the start and end points of the current group. The groups are identified by their level of nesting, relative to where the command appears. Level 0 refers to the group that immediately includes the \Send command. The higher levels refer to groups that follow the command.

```
\Send{GROUP}{level}{content}
\Send{EndGROUP}{level}{content}
```

```
\Configure[()]{\DviMath
    \Send{GROUP}{1}{[1]}
    \Send{EndGROUP}{1}{[/1]}
    \Send{GROUP}{2}{[2]}
    \Send{EndGROUP}{2}{[/2]}
  $}{$\EndDviMath}
\(A \stackrel{\string~}{=} B\)
```

A[1][2] =[/2] [/1] B

The command

```
\Send{BACK}{content}
```

may be used to send content backwards over the most recent symbol, group, or region enclosed between delimiters that have been declared a pair with the \Configure{MathDelimiters}{open}{close} command.

B.2.3.5 Subscripts and superscripts

There are several alternative ways to configure subscripts and superscripts. They can all make use of the \Send{BACK}{*content*} instructions, when the bases of the subscripts and superscripts also need to be configured.

```
\Configure{SUB}{before}{after}
\Configure{SUP}{before}{after}
\Configure{SUBSUP}{before}{between}{after}
\Configure{SUPSUB}{before}{between}{after}
\Configure{SUB/SUP}{before-1}{between-1}{after-1}
                   {before-2}{between-2}{after-2}
```

The first pair of commands are for cases where the subscripts and superscripts appear in isolation.

The third command applies to adjacent subscripts and superscripts, but only if subscripts are always to appear before the superscript in the output, regardless of their order in the source code. The fourth command is a variant of the third command, where subscripts always are to appear after the superscripts. The fifth command is another variant, requesting the output to preserve the order of the subscripts and superscripts in the source.

The arguments *before-1*, *between-1*, and *after-1* apply when the subscript precedes the superscript and the arguments *before-2*, *between-2*, and *after-2*, when the superscript comes first.

```
\Configure{()}{\DviMath$}{$\EndDviMath}
\Configure{SUBSUP}
  {\Send{BACK}{[base]}[/base][sb]}
  {[/sb][sp]}
  {[/sp]}
\(a^b_c\)
```

[base]a[/base][sb]c[/sb][sp]b[/sp]

B.2.3.6 Accents

TeX4ht deals with accents by looking up a table constructed by use of the following command:

```
\Configure{accent}\textcmd\mathcmd
{{in-1}{out-1}{in-2}{out-2}...{}{out-last}}
{do-found} {do-not-found}
```

The pairs {*in-1*}{*out-1*}, {*in-2*}{*out-2*}, ... set up series data records for the accent. The first field of the last pair of data fields must be empty.

The table is assigned to a text-based accent command \textcmd and a corresponding math-based accent command \mathcmd.

When an accent command is encountered in the source document, its table is searched for a record where the first field matches the argument of the command. If a match is found, the parameter *do-found* is activated. In this case, the second field of the pair is available as the macro parameter #1.

If no match is found, the *do-not-found* is activated. In this case, the parameter #1 represents the accent command under its original meaning in LaTeX, and the parameter #2 represents the argument of the command.

```
\Configure{accent}\^\hat{a{a}{}{}}
    {[hat]#1[/hat]}
    {[HAT]#2[/HAT]}
\Configure{accent}\vec\vec{{}{}}
    {} {[vec]#2[/vec]}
$\vec a=(\hat a,\hat b)$
```

```
[vec]a[/vec] = ([hat]a[/hat] , [HAT]b[/HAT]
)
```

If the second argument is empty, the previous table for the accent commands is used. Similarly, if both *do-found* and *do-not-found* are empty, the previous fragments of code are used.

B.3   XML namespaces

An XML document may contain elements and attributes that refer to multiple software modules, each with its own vocabulary. Thus it is possible that the same names are used by one or more of these modules with different purposes; this then results in name collisions. Therefore a mechanism for *name scoping*, that is, indicating to which namespace a given element type or attribute refers, is highly desirable.

The W3C tackled this problem in the "Namespaces in XML" recommendation [↪XMLNS]. That document defines an *XML namespace* as a collection of names, identified by a URI, that are used in XML documents as element types and attribute names.

Names from XML namespaces consist of a *namespace prefix*, which is mapped to a URI to select the namespace,[1] followed by a single colon, and then a *local part*. As URIs can contain characters that are not allowed in names, one uses a proxy that associates the namespace prefix with the given URI. Such an abbreviation is prefixed with the string xmlns. An example is the XSL style sheet that we discussed in Section 7.6.1, and where we have the following two declarations:

```
1    <xsl:stylesheet xmlns:xsl="http://www.w3.org/TR/WD-xsl"
2                     xmlns:fo="http://www.w3.org/TR/WD-xsl/FO"
```

---

[1] In fact this "URI" is, strictly speaking, only a string that uniquely identifies a namespace. It does not require corresponding to a real document on the Internet, although it is good practice to specify a genuine URI if it exists.

We see the `xmlns` prefix, followed by the name of the namespace shorthand that will be used in the document to scope the different element types and attributes. For instance, in the same document we find constructs like:

```
1    <xsl:template match="par">
2      <fo:block indent-start="10pt" space-before="12pt">
3        <xsl:apply-templates/>
4      </fo:block>
5    </xsl:template>
```

Lines 1 and 5 refer to the `xsl` namespace defined by the first of the two declaration of the `xsl:stylesheet` element type above. Lines 2 and 4 refer to the formatting objects part of the XSL document, as defined by the second declaration of the `xsl:stylesheet` element (for `fo` namespace). The part of the name following the colon is called the *local* part of the name. It should have a meaning in the framework of the namespace defined by the URI. The prefix, defined in the document instance (e.g., the `xsl` and `fo` prefixes above), has no meaning outside of the document where it is declared, since it is merely a placeholder for a URI. It is thus important always to export the prefix declarations together with elements that use them.

One should note that the prefix `xml` (any combination of upper- and lowercase) is reserved for use by XML-related specifications.

A special case is when one declares the *default* namespace by omitting the colon and namespace prefix. Thus element types without a namespace specifier refer to that default namespace. For instance, line 2 below declares the default namespace of the document to be HTML4, as defined in the HTML4 specification found at the given URI.

```
1    <xsl:stylesheet xmlns:xsl="http://www.w3.org/TR/WD-xsl"
2                    xmlns="http://www.w3.org/TR/REC-html40">
```

In the style sheet instance one then can directly write:

```
1    <xsl:template match="invitation/par/emph">
2    <em><xsl:process-children/></em>
3    </xsl:template>
```

where the `<em>` tags on line 2 are pure HTML.

The default namespace, once declared, may be overridden.

```
1    <?xml version='1.0'?>
2    ...
3    <particles>
4      <!-- Default namespace is set to HTML -->
5      <table xmlns='http://www.w3.org/TR/REC-html40'>
6        <tr><td>Particle</td><td>Mass</td><td>Details</td></tr>
7        <tr>
8          <td><em>neutron</em></td>
```

```
 9          <td>939.56 MeV</td>
10          <td>
11            <pdg xmlns="mypdgnamespace">
12            <!-- HTML namespace is no longer used -->
13            <quarks>udd</quarks><lifetime>886.7 s</lifetime>
14            <decay>p,e,anue</decay>
15            </pdg>
16          </td>
17        </tr>
18      </table>
19    </particles>
20    ...
```

Starting with the `table` element (line 5), we use the HTML4 namespace as default until we get to the data in the third column (line 10). Here the default namespace for the `pdg` element and its children is no longer HTML, but it is set to `mypdgnamespace` (line 12). Once we leave the `pdg` element (line 15), the namespace will automatically become HTML again.

Namespace scoping is not limited to element types; it can also be used for attributes and in DTD declarations.

B.4 Examples of important DTDs

In order to get a better idea of what DTDs for more complex documents look like, we will briefly look at a few representative examples in this section. We start by saying a few words about the DocBook, ISO-12083, TEI, and HTML DTDs. Then we discuss in much greater detail how to construct DTDs for BIBTEX and LATEX documents.

B.4.1 The DocBook DTD

The DocBook DTD was developed specifically for computer software documentation, such as user manuals and programming references. DocBook was originally maintained by the Davenport Group [↪DAVENPORT], a discussion forum sponsored by individuals representing large-scale producers and consumers of software documentation. Since July 1998, the maintenance has been handled by the DocBook Technical Committee under the umbrella of OASIS. Recently DocBook was adopted for the Linuxdoc-SGML initiative, which uses the SGML-Tools package [↪SGMLTOOLS]. Previously, Linuxdoc-SGML was based on the `qwertz` DTD, mentioned in Section B.4.5.

The DocBook DTD is available from [↪DOCBOOK]. It is a complete SGML DTD that has been used by many documentation providers to mark up their documents. More recently Norman Walsh has completely restructured the DTD to make it XML-compliant [↪DBXML].

The DocBook DTD uses a "book" model for the documents. A book is composed of book elements such as prefaces, chapters, appendixes, and glossaries. Five section levels are available, and these may contain paragraphs, lists, index entries, cross-references, and links.

```
book
  meta information
  chapter
    sect1
       sect2
    sect1
  chapter
    sect1
  appendix
    sect1
  appendix
    sect1
    ...
  glossary
```

The DTD leaves room for localizations. The user of the DTD is free to provide variant content models for appendixes, chapters, equations, indexes, and so on.

```
1   <!ENTITY % local.appendix.class "">
2   <!ENTITY % appendix.class "appendix %local.appendix.class;">
3
4   <!ENTITY % local.chapter.class "">
5   <!ENTITY % chapter.class  "chapter %local.chapter.class;">
6
7   <!ENTITY % local.index.class "">
8   <!ENTITY % index.class     "index|setindex %local.index.class;">
9
10  <!ELEMENT book ((%div.title.content;)?, bookinfo?, dedication?,
11                 toc?, lot*, (glossary|bibliography|preface)*,
12                 (((%chapter.class;)+, reference*) | part+
13                 | reference+ ),
14                 (%appendix.class;)*, (glossary|bibliography)*,
15                 (%index.class;)*, lot*, toc?)>
```

The book element type (lines 10–14) is quite a complex combination of different element types, but in a few cases (appendix, chapter, and index, see lines 1–8) the content model explicitly defines parameter entities that can be used for convenient customization by the user. Indeed, since the first definition of an entity takes precedence, all such parameter entities (starting with local.) can be defined before the complete DTD is read. In Sections B.4.4 and B.4.5 we show how this technique is applied in practice.

Similarly in the case of the attributes for the book element type, the parameter entity local.book.attrib (defined on line 1 and referenced on line 8 below) provides a means to complement the attributes applied by the DTD.

```
1   <!ENTITY % local.book.attrib "">
2   <!ENTITY % book.role.attrib "%role.attrib;">
3
4   <!ATTLIST book  %label.attrib;
```

```
5                       %status.attrib;
6                       %common.attrib;
7                       %book.role.attrib;
8                       %local.book.attrib;
9       >
```

In fact, Norman Walsh's distribution contains a file dbgenent.ent, which has empty definitions for the user-definable entities discussed earlier. Thus it is sufficient to edit this file to declare your own supplementary general entities, notations, and parameter entities.

B.4.2   The AAP effort and ISO 12083

Since the publication of the SGML Standard in 1985 the American Association of Publishers (AAP) has been working on promoting SGML as an electronic standard for manuscript preparation. Over several years they developed a document, the AAP Standard that was later promoted by the Electronic Publishing Special Interest Group (EPSIG) and the AAP as the Electronic Manuscript Standard. This AAP Standard achieved two major goals. First, it established an agreed way to identify and tag parts of an electronic manuscript by proposing an SGML tagset, thus allowing computers to recognize these parts. Second, it provided a logical way to represent special characters, symbols, and tabular material, using only the ASCII character set.

Based on the work mentioned earlier, the AAP and the European Physical Society (EPS) agreed upon a standard method for marking up scientific documents. This was later formalized as the International Standard ISO 12083, considered the successor to the AAP/EPSIG Standard, and four DTDs have been distributed by EPSIG as the "ISO" DTDs [↪EPSIG].

This DTD has a basic book structure consisting of chapters, sections, and subsections down to six levels. What is interesting is that it includes a DTD for math, which is quite similar, although not identical, to the visual presentation model of MathML, as discussed in Section 8.1. For instance, the AAP math visual markup tags provide for the following element categories:

character transformations   <bold>, <italic>, <sansser>, <typewrit>, <smallcap>, <roman>;

fractions   <fraction>, <num>, <den>;

superiors, inferiors   <sup>, <inf>;

embellishments   <top>, <middle>, <bottom>;

fences, boxes, overlines, and underlines   <mark>, <fence>, <post>, <box>, <overline>, <undrline>;

roots   <radical>, <radix>, <radicand>;

arrays   `<array>, <arrayrow>, <arraycol>, <arraycel>;`

spacing   `<hspace>, <vspace>, <break>, <markref>;`

formulae   `<formula>, <dformula>, <dformgrp>.`

Emphasis is on creating fences at the right places inside a formula. A simple markup example is the following:

```
1   <formula>
2     S = &sum;<inf>n=1</inf><sup>10</sup>
3         <fraction>
4           <num>1</num>
5           <den>
6             <radical>3<radix>n</radical>
7           </den>
8         </fraction>
9   </formula>
```

B.4.3   Text Encoding Initiative

The Text Encoding Initiative (TEI, see [↪TEIHOME]) emphasizes the interchange of textual information, although other forms of information, such as images and sound, are also considered. The basic aim is to make certain features of a text explicit in such a way as to aid the processing of that text by computer programs that run on a variety of computer platforms. The document is encoded by the introduction of markup in the sources.

A set of guidelines for marking up documents was agreed. Those interested in these guidelines should see [↪TEIGUIDE]. Since the TEI is supposed to be used throughout the world across many disciplines, certain principles should be obeyed. They are briefly listed:

- The common core of textual features should be easily shared.
- Additional specialist features should be easy to add to (or remove from) a text.
- Multiple parallel encodings of the same feature should be possible.
- The richness of markup should be user-defined, with a very small minimal requirement.
- Adequate documentation of the text and its encoding should be provided.

A full set of guidelines has been prepared, but often only a manageable "starter set," *TEI-Lite* [↪TEILITE], is actually used in practice. It should, therefore, come as no surprise that work for adapting the TEI DTD to XML has started with *TEI-Lite*. Patrice Bonhomme has made an XML version of *TEI-Lite*, as well as a prerelease of the full TEI P3 DTD. He has also translated a few of the TEI reference documents into XML [↪TEIXML].

B.4.4   A DTD for BIBTEX

As practice is the best way of assimilating ideas, it is an interesting problem to see how we can apply the XML techniques we have introduced in Chapter 6 to an area where most LaTeX users have already some experience, that is LaTeX itself, and BIBTEX databases. Therefore in this section we construct two variants of a DTD for a BIBTEX database, explaining which are important points to consider. In the next section we build a DTD for a subset of LaTeX.

B.4.4.1   Fine points for developing a DTD

Consider the following important points when you decide to write a DTD: What is the application area of its use, what kind of information do we want to model, is it important that humans can understand the markup, or are documents going to be marked up and maintained automatically? Similarly the DTD architecture should be easy to maintain. It should be relatively easy to find and correct bugs and to extend the DTD, even for somebody who was not involved in its original design and without relying on the help of the original author, who might no longer be available.

DTD design is probably more an art than a science, and only a lot of practice will allow you to write good DTDs. Eve Maler and Jeanne El Andaloussi (Maler and Andaloussi (1996)) examine in detail a lot of the SGML issues involved in how to model data, implement DTDs, and maintain them. David Megginson's recent book (Megginson (1998)) is more directly applicable to XML in that it discusses the differences between XML and SGML. He also dedicates a chapter to the various DTD we mentioned in Sections B.4.1 to B.4.3.

One of the main decisions when building a model is what should be "content" and what should be "characteristics," in other words, which components of our document model should correspond to *elements*, and which ones to *attributes*. Various schools of thought exist, and many pages have been written about this subject; the conclusion is that there is almost never one unique answer (see [↪ ELEMATTR] for an overview).

Oversimplifying, we can say that complex information, which contains markup, is almost always better enclosed inside elements, whereas attributes are convenient when there is a choice only between various keywords (e.g., a color if one of "red," "blue," or "green"), or when there is a set of characteristics of an element that can be specified simply (e.g., the height, the width, the name of a month, a country, or a language).

Nevertheless, since XML has rather fewer constructs than SGML (see Norman Walsh's discussion of how to convert SGML to XML DTDs [↪ SGML2XML] and Megginson (1998)), we are more constrained in the choice of plausible document models than in the case of full-blown SGML. For instance, it is extremely tedious in XML to express in a content model that a set of element types can be entered in any order in a document instance. Similarly there is no way to specify inclusion or exclusion of certain element types with respect to model groups (see Eve Maler's article on handling exceptions in SGML and XML [↪MALEREX]). Therefore constructing XML DTDs that provide maximum flexibility is no trivial task and often compromises and simplifications have to be made with respect to SGML.

In the following two sections we present two quite different DTDs that model a BIBTEX database. The first is based almost exclusively on elements for containing the information, while the second tries to specify as much information as feasible using attributes.

B.4.4.2 A first version of the BIBTEX DTD

As a design decision, elements and attributes will carry the same names as the corresponding entries and fields described by Leslie Lamport in *Appendix B* of Lamport (1994). However, the link between entries in the database and citation keys in the document is made via an XML ID type attribute. We call this attribute `id` (line 5), thus allowing each entry to be cross-referenced with the `crossref` attribute of type IDREF (line 6). Each entry gets these two attributes assigned via the parameter entity `atype` (defined on lines 5–6 and referenced on lines 19, 24, and so on).

Appendix B does not prescribe an order for specifying the fields ("required" or "optional") for the various entry types. However, since XML does not have an easy way to express the fact that certain entries must be present, but can be specified in any order (XML lacks SGML's & operator inside model groups), we *impose* an order that we take to be the one in which the fields are enumerated by Lamport. Moreover, at the end of each entry we allow a set of optional fields with the help of the `info` parameter entity (line 14).

Names are handled with `names` elements, which consist of one or more sets of `first` and `last` element pairs, separated by an empty `and` element (lines 99–102). Most of the simple fields are just declared as #PCDATA, while fields that can have a more complex content (mostly those that we cannot assign to attributes in the alternative version of the DTD, and which we will discuss in Section B.4.4.3) can also include emphatic elements (line 88).

The complete text of the DTD `biblioxml1.dtd` follows (the line numbers in the previous paragraphs refer to those shown here):

```
1    <!-- biblioxml1.dtd: XML DTD for BibTeX markup: version 1 -->
2
3    <!-- Every biblio entry _must_ have an identifier and
4                        _can_ have a cross-reference to an existing entry -->
5    <!ENTITY % atype "id       ID    #REQUIRED
6                     crossref IDREF #IMPLIED">
7
8    <!-- Possible types of biblio entries -->
9    <!ELEMENT biblio (#PCDATA | article| book| booklet| inbook| incollection|
10                        inproceedings| manual| mastersthesis| misc|
11                        phdthesis| proceedings| techreport| unpublished)*>
12
13    <!-- Optional annotation, note, ISBN, or key (the latter for sorting) -->
14    <!ENTITY % info "(annote|note|ISBN|key)*">
15
```

```
16   <!-- An article from a journal or magazine -->
17   <!ELEMENT article (author, title, journal, year,
18                      volume?, number?, pages?, month?, %info;)>
19   <!ATTLIST article %atype;>
20
21   <!-- A book with an explicit publisher -->
22   <!ELEMENT book ((author|editor), title, publisher, year,
23                   (volume|number)?, series?, address?, edition?, month?, %info;)>
24   <!ATTLIST book %atype;>
25
26   <!-- A work that is printed or bound, but without a named -->
27   <!--   publisher or sponsoring institution                -->
28   <!ELEMENT booklet (title ,
29                      author, howpublished?, address?, month?, year?, %info;)>
30   <!ATTLIST booklet %atype;>
31
32   <!-- A part of a book, usually untitled;                   -->
33   <!--   (a chapter, a sectional unit, or just a range of pages) -->
34   <!ELEMENT inbook ((author|editor), title, (chapter|pages)*, publisher, year,
35                     (volume|number)?, series?, type?, address?, edition?, month?, %info;)>
36   <!ATTLIST inbook %atype;>
37
38   <!-- A part of a book with its own title -->
39   <!ELEMENT incollection (author, title, booktitle, publisher, year,
40                           editor?, (volume|number)?, series?, type?, chapter?,
41                           pages?, address?, edition?, month?, %info;)>
42   <!ATTLIST incollection %atype;>
43
44   <!-- An article in a conference proceedings -->
45   <!ELEMENT inproceedings (author, title, booktitle, year,
46                            editor?, (volume|number)?, series?, pages?, address?,
47                            month?, organization?, publisher?, %info;)>
48   <!ATTLIST inproceedings %atype;>
49
50   <!-- Technical documentation -->
51   <!ELEMENT manual (title,
52                     author?, organization?, address?, edition?, month?, year?, %info,)>
53   <!ATTLIST manual %atype,>
54
55   <!-- A master's thesis -->
56   <!ELEMENT mastersthesis (author, title, school, year,
57                            type?, address?, month?, %info;)>
58   <!ATTLIST mastersthesis %atype;>
59
60   <!-- Miscellaneous; use this type if nothing else fits -->
61   <!ELEMENT misc (author?, title?, howpublished?, month?, year?,%info;)>
62   <!ATTLIST misc %atype;>
63
64   <!-- A Ph. D. thesis -->
65   <!ELEMENT phdthesis (author, title, school, year,
66                        type?, address?, month?, %info;)>
67   <!ATTLIST phdthesis %atype;>
68
69   <!-- The porceedings of a conference -->
70   <!ELEMENT proceedings (title , year ,
71                          editor?, (volume|number)?, series?, address?,
72                          month?, organization?, publisher?, %info;)>
73   <!ATTLIST proceedings %atype;>
74
75   <!-- A report published by a school or other institution -->
76   <!--   usually numbered within a series                   -->
77   <!ELEMENT techreport (author, title, institution, year,
78                         type?, number?, address?, month?, %info;)>
79   <!ATTLIST techreport %atype;>
80
```

```
81   <!-- A document with author and title, but not formally published -->
82   <!ELEMENT unpublished (author, title, note,
83                          month? , key?)>
84   <!ATTLIST unpublished %atype;>
85
86   <!-- For adding typographic emphasis to the information -->
87   <!ELEMENT emph (#PCDATA)>
88   <!ATTLIST emph style (textbf|emph|textsf|textsl|texttt|quote) "emph">
89
90   <!ENTITY % inline "(#PCDATA|emph)*">
91   <!-- The basic fields (Lamport (1994), pages 162-164) -->
92
93                   <!-- Usually the address of publisher or institution -->
94   <!ELEMENT address      (#PCDATA|emph)*>
95                   <!-- Annotation (not used by standard styles)        -->
96   <!ELEMENT annote       (#PCDATA|emph)*>
97                   <!-- Author(s) in format described on pp. 157-158    -->
98   <!ELEMENT author       (names)>
99   <!ELEMENT names        ((first,last),(and,first,last)*)>
100  <!ELEMENT last         (#PCDATA|emph)*>
101  <!ELEMENT first        (#PCDATA|emph)*>
102  <!ELEMENT and          EMPTY>
103      <!-- Title of a book, used in incollection and inproceedings -->
104  <!ELEMENT booktitle    (#PCDATA|emph)*>
105                  <!-- Chapter (or sectional unit) number             -->
106  <!ELEMENT chapter      (#PCDATA|emph)*>
107                  <!-- Edition of a book (e.g., "third")               -->
108  <!ELEMENT edition      (#PCDATA|emph)*>
109                  <!-- Names of editor(s)                              -->
110  <!ELEMENT editor       (names)>
111                  <!-- Describe how something strange is published     -->
112  <!ELEMENT howpublished (#PCDATA|emph)*>
113                  <!-- Sponsoring institution of a technical report    -->
114  <!ELEMENT institution  (#PCDATA|emph)*>
115                  <!-- The ISBN number (non-standard, but useful       -->
116  <!ELEMENT ISBN         (#PCDATA)>
117                  <!-- A journal's name                                -->
118  <!ELEMENT journal      (#PCDATA|emph)*>
119                  <!-- Used for ordering the biblio entries            -->
120  <!ELEMENT key          (#PCDATA)>
121              <!-- Month of publication (or writing, if not published) -->
122  <!ELEMENT month        (#PCDATA)>
123              <!-- Additional information to help the user             -->
124  <!ELEMENT note         (#PCDATA|emph)*>
125              <!-- Number of a journal, magazine, report, etc.         -->
126  <!ELEMENT number       (#PCDATA)>
127              <!-- Sponsor of conference or publisher of manual        -->
128  <!ELEMENT organization (#PCDATA|emph)*>
129              <!-- page, or page range                                 -->
130  <!ELEMENT pages        (#PCDATA)>
131              <!-- Publisher's name                                    -->
132  <!ELEMENT publisher    (#PCDATA|emph)*>
133              <!-- Name of the school where thesis was written         -->
134  <!ELEMENT school       (#PCDATA|emph)*>
135              <!-- Name of the series or set of books                  -->
136  <!ELEMENT series       (#PCDATA|emph)*>
137              <!-- A work's title                                      -->
138  <!ELEMENT title        (#PCDATA|emph)*>
139              <!-- Type of a technical report, e.g., "Research Note"   -->
140  <!ELEMENT type         (#PCDATA|emph)*>
141              <!-- Volume number of a journal or multi-volume book     -->
142  <!ELEMENT volume       (#PCDATA)>
143              <!-- Year of publication (or writing, if not published)  -->
144  <!ELEMENT year         (#PCDATA)>
```

Now we can use this DTD with an example document, and we choose the
BIBTEX source shown in Figure 13.4 of *The LATEX Companion* (Goossens et al.
(1994)) as basis. Following you see how we mark up the document relative to our
DTD. At the start of the file (lines 2–10) we define some entities that were handled by the `bibnames.sty` file or defined in the original file. Note how we use
entities for the abbreviations of the names of the months (lines 12–23), which are
predefined in BIBTEX. For reasons of convenience and typographic consistency,
throughout the file we have used these entity references for recurring text strings.
Of course, if we were to target a text processing system different from LATEX, we
would have to define some of the entities differently (in particular lines 4–11, which
are LATEX-specific).

Citation references would use the values defined with the `id` attribute with
each entry. Note how the cross-reference on line 85 also exploits XML's ID/IDREF
system. However, since the identifiers in an XML document instance share a global
namespace, one should try to use a transparent and consistent naming scheme for
document element identifiers.

```
 1   <!DOCTYPE biblio SYSTEM "biblioxml1.dtd" [
 2   <!ENTITY AW "Addison-Wesley">
 3   <!ENTITY AW:adr "Reading, Massachusetts">
 4   <!ENTITY emdash "---">
 5   <!ENTITY endash "--">
 6   <!ENTITY ouml '\"o'>
 7   <!ENTITY j-TUGboat "TUGboat">
 8   <!ENTITY LaTeX "\LaTeX{}">
 9   <!ENTITY TeX "\TeX{}">
10   <!ENTITY WEB "\textsc{web}">
11   <!-- abbreviations for the months -->
12   <!ENTITY jan "Jan.">
13   <!ENTITY feb "Feb.">
14   <!ENTITY mar "Mar.">
15   <!ENTITY apr "Apr.">
16   <!ENTITY may "May">
17   <!ENTITY jun "Jun.">
18   <!ENTITY jul "Jul.">
19   <!ENTITY aug "Aug.">
20   <!ENTITY sep "Sep.">
21   <!ENTITY oct "Oct.">
22   <!ENTITY nov "Nov.">
23   <!ENTITY dec "Dec.">
24   ]>
25   <biblio>
26   <manual id="Dynatext">
27     <title>Dynatext, Electronic Book Indexer/Browser</title>
28     <organization>Electronic Book Technology Inc.</organization>
29     <address>Providence, Rhode Island</address>
30     <year>1991</year>
31   </manual>
32     <book id="Eijkhout:1991">
33     <author><names><first>Victor</first><last>Eijkhout</last></names></author>
34     <title>&TeX; by Topic, a &TeX;nicians Reference</title>
35     <publisher>&AW;</publisher>
36     <year>1991</year>
37     <address>&AW:adr;</address>
38   </book>,
39   <techreport id="EVH:Office">
40     <author><names><first>Eric</first><last>van Herwijnen</last></names></author>
```

```
41        <title>Future Office Systems Requirements</title>
42        <institution>CERN DD Internal Note</institution>
43        <year>1988</year>
44        <month>&nov;</month>
45     </techreport>
46     <article id="Felici:1991">
47        <author><names><first>James</first><last>Felici</last></names></author>
48        <title>PostScript versus TrueType</title>
49        <journal>Macworld</journal>
50        <year>1991</year>
51        <volume>8</volume>
52        <pages>195&endash;201</pages>
53        <month>&sep;</month>
54     </article>
55     <techreport id="Knuth:WEB">
56        <author><names><first>Donald E.</first><last>Knuth</last></names></author>
57        <title>The &WEB; System of Structured Documentation</title>
58        <institution>Department of Computer Science, Stanford University</institution>
59        <year>1983</year>
60        <number>STAN-CS-83-980</number>
61        <address>Stanford, CA 94305</address>
62        <month>&sep;</month>
63     </techreport>
64     <phdthesis id="Liang:1983">
65        <author><names><first>Franklin Mark</first><last>Liang</last></names></author>
66        <title>Word Hy-phen-a-tion by Com-pu-ter</title>
67        <school>Stanford University</school>
68        <year>1983</year>
69        <address>Stanford, CA 94305</address>
70        <month>&jun;</month>
71        <note>Also available as Stanford University, Department of
72           Computer Science Report No. STAN-CS-83-977</note>
73     </phdthesis>
74     <article id="Mittelbach-Schoepf:1990">
75        <author><names><first>Frank</first><last>Mittelbach</last><and/>
76               <first>Rainer</first><last>Sch&ouml;pf</last></names></author>
77        <title>The New Font Selection &emdash; User Interface to
78           Standard &LaTeX;</title>
79        <journal>&j-TUGboat;</journal>
80        <year>1990</year>
81        <volume>11</volume>
82        <number>2</number>
83        <pages>297&endash;305</pages>
84     </article>
85     <incollection id="Wood:color" crossref="Roth:postscript">
86        <author><names><first>Pat</first><last>Wood</last></names></author>
87        <title>PostScript Color Separation</title>
88        <booktitle>Real World PostScript</booktitle>
89        <publisher>&AW;</publisher>
90        <year>1988</year>
91        <pages>201&endash;225</pages>
92     </incollection>
93     <book id="Roth:postscript">
94        <editor><names><first>Stephen E.</first><last>Roth</last></names></editor>
95        <title>Real World PostScript</title>
96        <publisher>&AW;</publisher>
97        <year>1988</year>
98        <address>&AW:adr;</address>
99        <ISBN>0-201-06663-7</ISBN>
100    </book>
101    <inproceedings id="Yannis:1991">
102       <author><names><first>Yannis</first><last>Haralambous</last></names></author>
103       <title>&TeX; and those other languages</title>
104       <booktitle>1991 Annual Meeting Proceedings, Part 2, &TeX; Users Group,
105               Twelfth Annual Meeting, Dedham, Massachusetts, July 15--18, 1991
```

```
106        </booktitle>
107        <year>1991</year>
108        <editor><names><first>Hope</first><last>Hamilton</last></names></editor>
109        <volume>12</volume>
110        <series>&j-TUGboat;</series>
111        <pages>539&endash;548</pages>
112        <address>Providence, Rhode Island</address>
113        <month>&dec;</month>
114        <organization>&TeX; Users Group</organization>
115     </inproceedings>
116     </biblio>
```

B.4.4.3   A second version of the BIBTEX DTD

In developing an alternative version of a BIBTEX DTD we want to experiment with
specifying as much information as possible with attributes. We already know that
it would be very difficult to use attributes for complex fields, such as (book)title,
author, and editor, which consist of names, note, and annote, which can contain
free text notes. These are thus defined as elements (lines 179–194 at the end of the
DTD), while all other fields are given as attributes following the definition of the
various entries (lines 24–30, 34–43, and so on).

In this version we provide the possibility of extending the DTD by introducing
a parameter entity local.info (defined as the empty string on line 4) and putting a
reference to it in the definition of the info parameter entity (line 7). The user of the
DTD can thus define new elements by entering them in the variable local.info, as
shown in the following example. In this way, new fields can easily be made available.
Similarly by defining the parameter entity local.biblio, the user can add new
entry types (we added a reference to local.biblio at the end of the definition
of the content model for the root element biblio, see line 20). Line 6 declares
local.keys, which provides a global way to add attributes to all entries.

Below we show the alternative version of the BIBTEX DTD biblioxml2.dtd:

```
1    <!-- biblioxml2.dtd: XML DTD for BibTeX markup: version 2 -->
2
3    <!-- Supplementary entry types, optional fields and attributes       -->
4    <!ENTITY % local.info "">
5    <!ENTITY % local.biblio "">
6    <!ENTITY % local.keys "">
7    <!ENTITY % info  "note %local.info;">
8
9    <!-- All base elements must have ID and can have cross-reference to   -->
10   <!-- an existing ID and include a  key to sort, if needed            -->
11   <!ENTITY % keys   "id      ID    #REQUIRED
12                      crossref IDREF #IMPLIED
13                      key     IDREF #IMPLIED
14                      %local.keys;">
15   <!ENTITY % month  'month (jan|feb|mar|apr|may|jun|jul|aug|sep|oct|nov|dec) #IMPLIED'>
16   <!-- Possible types of biblio entries -->
17   <!ELEMENT biblio (#PCDATA | article| book| booklet| inbook| incollection|
18                              inproceedings| manual| mastersthesis| misc|
19                              phdthesis| proceedings| techreport| unpublished
20                              %local.biblio;)*>
21
22   <!-- An article from a journal or magazine -->
23   <!ELEMENT article (author,title,(%info;)*)>
```

```
24   <!ATTLIST article %keys;
25                      journal  CDATA  #REQUIRED
26                      year     CDATA  #REQUIRED
27                      %month;
28                      number   CDATA  #IMPLIED
29                      pages    CDATA  #IMPLIED
30                      volume   CDATA  #IMPLIED>
31
32   <!-- A book with an explicit publisher -->
33   <!ELEMENT book      ((author|editor),title,(%info;)*)>
34   <!ATTLIST book      %keys;
35                      publisher CDATA  #REQUIRED
36                      year      CDATA  #REQUIRED
37                      address   CDATA  #IMPLIED
38                      edition   CDATA  #IMPLIED
39                      %month;
40                      number    CDATA  #IMPLIED
41                      series    CDATA  #IMPLIED
42                      volume    CDATA  #IMPLIED
43                      ISBN      CDATA  #IMPLIED>
44
45   <!-- A work that is printed or bound, but without a named -->
46   <!--    publisher or sponsoring institution                -->
47   <!ELEMENT booklet (title,author?,(%info;)*)>
48   <!ATTLIST booklet %keys;
49                      address      CDATA  #IMPLIED
50                      howpublished CDATA  #IMPLIED
51                      %month;
52                      year         CDATA  #IMPLIED
53                      ISBN         CDATA  #IMPLIED>
54
55   <!-- A part of a book, usually untitled;                    -->
56   <!--    (a chapter, a sectional unit, or just a range of pages) -->
57   <!ELEMENT inbook  ((author|editor),title,(%info;)*)>
58   <!ATTLIST inbook  %keys;
59                      pages     CDATA  #REQUIRED
60                      publisher CDATA  #REQUIRED
61                      year      CDATA  #REQUIRED
62                      address   CDATA  #IMPLIED
63                      chapter   CDATA  #IMPLIED
64                      edition   CDATA  #IMPLIED
65                      %month;
66                      number    CDATA  #IMPLIED
67                      series    CDATA  #IMPLIED
68                      type      CDATA  #IMPLIED
69                      volume    CDATA  #IMPLIED
70                      ISBN      CDATA  #IMPLIED>
71
72   <!-- A part of a book with its own title -->
73   <!ELEMENT incollection  (author,title,booktitle,editor?,(%info;)*)>
74   <!ATTLIST incollection  %keys;
75                      publisher CDATA  #REQUIRED
76                      year      CDATA  #REQUIRED
77                      address   CDATA  #IMPLIED
78                      chapter   CDATA  #IMPLIED
79                      edition   CDATA  #IMPLIED
80                      %month;
81                      number    CDATA  #IMPLIED
82                      pages     CDATA  #IMPLIED
83                      series    CDATA  #IMPLIED
84                      type      CDATA  #IMPLIED
85                      volume    CDATA  #IMPLIED
86                      ISBN      CDATA  #IMPLIED>
87
88   <!-- An article in a conference proceedings -->
```

```
 89   <!ELEMENT inproceedings (author,title,booktitle,editor?,(%info;)*)>
 90   <!ATTLIST inproceedings %keys;
 91                           year         CDATA  #REQUIRED
 92                           address      CDATA  #IMPLIED
 93                           %month;
 94                           number       CDATA  #IMPLIED
 95                           organization CDATA  #IMPLIED
 96                           pages        CDATA  #IMPLIED
 97                           publisher    CDATA  #IMPLIED
 98                           series       CDATA  #IMPLIED
 99                           volume       CDATA  #IMPLIED
100                           ISBN         CDATA  #IMPLIED>
101
102   <!-- Technical documentation -->
103   <!ELEMENT manual (title,author?,(%info;)*)>
104   <!ATTLIST manual  %keys;
105                     address      CDATA  #IMPLIED
106                     edition      CDATA  #IMPLIED
107                     organization CDATA  #IMPLIED
108                     %month;
109                     year         CDATA  #IMPLIED
110                     ISBN         CDATA  #IMPLIED>
111
112   <!-- A master's thesis -->
113   <!ELEMENT mastersthesis (author,title,(%info;)*)>
114   <!ATTLIST mastersthesis %keys;
115                           school  CDATA  #REQUIRED
116                           year    CDATA  #REQUIRED
117                           address CDATA  #IMPLIED
118                           %month;
119                           type    CDATA  #IMPLIED
120                           ISBN    CDATA  #IMPLIED>
121
122   <!-- Miscellaneous: use this type if nothing else fits -->
123   <!ELEMENT misc  (((author,title)|(title,author))?,(%info;)*)>
124   <!ATTLIST misc  %keys;
125                   howpublished CDATA  #IMPLIED
126                   %month;
127                   year         CDATA  #IMPLIED>
128
129   <!-- A Ph. D. thesis -->
130   <!ELEMENT phdthesis (author,title,(%info;)*)>
131   <!ATTLIST phdthesis %keys;
132                       school  CDATA  #REQUIRED
133                       year    CDATA  #REQUIRED
134                       address CDATA  #IMPLIED
135                       %month;
136                       type    CDATA  #IMPLIED
137                       ISBN    CDATA  #IMPLIED>
138
139   <!-- The proceedings of a conference -->
140   <!ATTLIST proceedings %keys;
141                         year         CDATA  #REQUIRED
142                         address      CDATA  #IMPLIED
143                         %month;
144                         number       CDATA  #IMPLIED
145                         organization CDATA  #IMPLIED
146                         publisher    CDATA  #IMPLIED
147                         series       CDATA  #IMPLIED
148                         volume       CDATA  #IMPLIED
149                         ISBN         CDATA  #IMPLIED>
150
151   <!-- A report published by a school or other institution -->
152   <!--    usually numbered within a series                 -->
153   <!ELEMENT techreport (author,title,(%info;)*)>
```

```
154   <!ATTLIST techreport    %keys;
155                           institution  CDATA   #REQUIRED
156                           year         CDATA   #REQUIRED
157                           address      CDATA   #IMPLIED
158                           %month;
159                           number       CDATA   #IMPLIED
160                           type         CDATA   #IMPLIED
161                           ISBN         CDATA   #IMPLIED>
162
163   <!-- A document with author and title, but not formally published -->
164   <!ELEMENT unpublished   (author,title,(%info;)*)>
165   <!ATTLIST unpublished   %keys;
166                           address      CDATA   #IMPLIED
167                           %month;
168                           number       CDATA   #IMPLIED
169                           type         CDATA   #IMPLIED>
170
171   <!-- For adding typographic emphasis to the information -->
172   <!ELEMENT emph (#PCDATA)>
173   <!ATTLIST emph style (bf|em|it|sf|sl|tt|qu) "em">
174
175   <!-- The basic fields (pages 162-164) -->
176   <!-- Only fields with names (author, editor) and titles are left as -->
177   <!-- basic elements -->
178                   <!-- Author(s) in format described on pp. 157-158 -->
179   <!ELEMENT author     (name,(and,name)*)>
180   <!ELEMENT name       (first,last)>
181   <!ELEMENT last       (#PCDATA)>
182   <!ELEMENT first      (#PCDATA)>
183   <!ELEMENT and        EMPTY>
184                   <!-- The names of the editor(s)                    -->
185   <!ELEMENT editor     (name,(and,name)*)>
186                   <!-- The work's title                              -->
187   <!ELEMENT title      (#PCDATA|emph)*>
188       <!-- Title of a book, used in incollection and inproceedings -->
189   <!ELEMENT booktitle  (#PCDATA|emph)*>
190   <!-- Optional notes at end of entries -->
191                   <!-- Annotation (not used by standard styles)      -->
192   <!ELEMENT annote     (#PCDATA|emph)*>
193                   <!-- Additional information to help the user        -->
194   <!ELEMENT note       (#PCDATA|emph)*>
```

We can use this new version of the BIBTEX DTD by referring to it in a little DTD mybiblio.dtd, which follows. Line 2 defines the parameter entity biblio.dtd, which will allow us to include the DTD biblioxml2.dtd on line 17. Lines 4–12 define the same general entities as lines 2–10 in the document instance of Section B.4.4.2.

```
1   <!-- mybiblio.dtd (refers to "biblioxml2.dtd" -->
2   <!ENTITY % biblio.dtd SYSTEM "biblioxml2.dtd">
3
4   <!ENTITY AW "Addison-Wesley">
5   <!ENTITY AW:adr "Reading, Massachusetts">
6   <!ENTITY emdash "---">
7   <!ENTITY endash "--">
8   <!ENTITY ouml '\"o'>
9   <!ENTITY j-TUGboat "TUGboat">
10  <!ENTITY LaTeX "\LaTeX{}">
11  <!ENTITY TeX "\TeX{}">
12  <!ENTITY WEB "\textsc{web}">
13  <!ENTITY % local.info "| url |annote">
14  <!ELEMENT url (#PCDATA)>
15  <!ENTITY % local.biblio "| webdocument">
```

```
16
17    %biblio.dtd;
18
19    <!-- Document published on the Web -->
20    <!ELEMENT webdocument (title,author?,(%info;)*)>
21    <!ATTLIST webdocument    %keys;
22                             organization CDATA  #IMPLIED
23                             %month;
24                             year         CDATA  #IMPLIED>
```

Because we cannot reference parameter entities before they are defined, we must be careful with the order in which we specify the various entries in the DTD. Therefore we now define the entity `local.info` (line 13), where we add a new field `url` plus include the `annote` field, which is defined in the DTD (line 192), but is not included in any of the content models. Line 14 defines the content of the `url` element as #PCDATA. Of course, we could have preferred to specify URLs as an attribute, in which case we would have to replace lines 13–14 with the following:

```
<!ENTITY % local.info "|annote">
<!ENTITY % local.key "url CDATA IMPLIED">
```

However, in the example that follows, we will use the element definition.

Finally, because we want to define a new entry type, `webdocument`, we include it in the `local.biblio` parameter entity (line 15). We include the orignal DTD via the entity reference `biblio.dtd` (line 17). The DTD will consume the values of all the "`local`" parameter entities, and the element definitions will be adapted accordingly.

Only now (in lines 20–24) can we place the definition of the new entry type `webdocument` since it refers to various parameter entities (`info`, `keys`, and `month`) that are defined in the DTD. For the same reason, we cannot define this element and its attributes in the internal subset of the document instance. The latter is read before the external subset, when these same parameters are not yet defined.

With the `mybiblio.dtd` DTD we mark up the same BIBTEX database as in Section B.4.4.2. One recognizes how the information is now spread over elements and attributes. The fields that can be specified with attributes can be entered in any order, making data entry somewhat easier. Note how the names of the months have become name tokens of an attribute list (as defined on line 15 of the DTD `biblioxml2.dtd`) and are no longer specified with general entity references (lines 20, 29, and so on). As a novelty, at the end (lines 102–113) we add a supplementary entry that is not present in the original example. It is of type `xmldocument` as defined in the DTD `mybiblio.dtd` shown earlier in lines 20–24.

```
1    <!DOCTYPE biblio SYSTEM "mybiblio.dtd">
2    <biblio>
3    <manual id         ="Dynatext"
4         organization="Electronic Book Technology Inc."
5         address     ="Providence, Rhode Island"
6         year        ="1991">
7      <title>Dynatext, Electronic Book Indexer/Browser</title>
8    </manual>
```

```
 9   <book id        ="Eijkhout:1991"
10       publisher="&AW;"
11       year      ="1991"
12       address  ="&AW:adr;">
13     <author>
14       <name><first>Victor</first><last>Eijkhout</last></name>
15     </author>
16     <title>&TeX; by Topic, a &TeX;nicians Reference</title>
17   </book>
18   <techreport id        ="EVH:Office"
19               institution="CERN DD Internal Note"
20               month      ="nov"
21               year      ="1988">
22     <author>
23       <name><first>Eric</first><last>van Herwijnen</last></name>
24     </author>
25     <title>Future Office Systems Requirements</title>
26   </techreport>
27   <article id      ="Felici:1991"
28           journal="Macworld"
29           month  ="sep"
30           year    ="1991"
31           volume ="8"
32           pages  ="195&endash;201">
33     <author><name><first>James</first><last>Felici</last></name></author>
34     <title>PostScript versus TrueType</title>
35   </article>
36   <techreport id        ="Knuth:WEB"
37               institution="Department of Computer Science, Stanford University"
38               address    ="Stanford, CA 94305"
39               month      ="sep"
40               year        ="1983"
41               number      ="STAN-CS-83-980">
42     <author><name><first>Donald E.</first><last>Knuth</last></name></author>
43     <title>The &WEB; System of Structured Documentation</title>
44   </techreport>
45   <phdthesis id      ="Liang:1983"
46             school="Stanford University"
47             address="Stanford, CA 94305"
48             month  ="jun"
49             year    ="1983">
50     <author><name><first>Franklin Mark</first><last>Liang</last></name></author>
51     <title>Word Hy-phen-a-tion by Com-pu-ter</title>
52     <note>Also available as Stanford University, Department of
53       Computer Science Report No. STAN-CS-83-977
54     </note>
55   </phdthesis>
56   <article id="Mittelbach-Schoepf:1990"
57           journal="&j-TUGboat;"
58           year="1990"
59           volume="11"
60           number="2"
61           pages="297&endash;305">
62     <author><name><first>Frank</first><last>Mittelbach</last></name>
63             <and/>
64             <name><first>Rainer</first><last>Sch&ouml;pf</last></name>
65     </author>
66     <title>
67       The New Font Selection &emdash; User Interface to Standard &LaTeX;"
68     </title>
69   </article>
70   <incollection id        ="Wood:color"
71                 crossref ="Roth:postscript"
72                 publisher="&AW;"
73                 year      ="1988"
```

```
74                     pages   ="201&endash;225">
75        <author><name><first>Pat</first><last>Wood</last></name></author>
76        <title>PostScript Color Separation</title>
77        <booktitle>Real World PostScript</booktitle>
78    </incollection>
79    <book id        ="Roth:postscript"
80         publisher="&AW;"
81         year     ="1988"
82         address  ="&AW:adr;"
83         ISBN     ="0-201-06663-7">
84        <editor><name><first>Stephen E.</first><last>Roth</last></name></editor>
85        <title>Real World PostScript</title>
86    </book>
87    <inproceedings id        ="Yannis:1991"
88                   series    ="&j-TUGboat;"
89                   volume    ="12"
90                   pages     ="539&endash;548"
91                   organization="&TeX; Users Group"
92                   address   ="Providence, Rhode Island"
93                   month     ="dec"
94                   year      ="1991">
95        <author><name><first>Yannis</first><last>Haralambous</last></name></author>
96        <title>&TeX; and those other languages</title>
97        <booktitle>1991 Annual Meeting Proceedings, Part 2, &TeX; Users Group,
98                Twelfth Annual Meeting, Dedham, Massachusetts, July 15--18, 1991
99        </booktitle>
100       <editor><name><first>Hope</first><last>Hamilton</last></name></editor>
101   </inproceedings>
102   <webdocument id="xml-latest-news"
103                organization="OASIS">
104       <title>SGML and XML News</title>
105       <author><name><first>Robin</first><last>Cover</last></name></author>
106       <url>http://www.oasis-open.org/cover/sgmlnew.html</url>
107       <note>
108          Information about what is (relatively) new in the 'SGML/XML Web Page'
109       </note>
110       <annote>This page keeps you informed about the latest developments
111          in the area of SGML, XML, and related areas.
112       </annote>
113   </webdocument>
114   </biblio>
```

B.4.4.4   Summary for BIBTEX DTDs

Based on the discussion in Sections B.4.4.2 and B.4.4.3, where we describe two
versions of the BIBTEX DTD, it should be clear that the same data can be marked
up in several equivalent ways without loss of information. This shows the flexibility
of the XML approach, which also allows the designer of the DTD to provide hooks
to extend and customize the data model and functionality of the original DTD. It,
of course, depends very much on the application and, more important, the targeted
user community to decide which form of specifying the information (that is, which
kind of data schema or DTD) is more useful.

B.4.5   LATEX-like markup, from DTD to printed document

Several attempts have been made to develop an SGML application for LATEX. The
most successful is probably the qwertz Project by Tom Gordon of the German

National Research Center for Computer Science [↪ QWERTZ]. The latest version of the system converts HTML documents into LaTeX with the help of a built-in Java SGML parser or James Clark's `nsgmls` parser. The main advantage is having one source to generate both printed and Web documents, but, since the DTD is static, you cannot add your own macros, and math and pictures are treated specially. The main user of this system was, until recently, the Linux Documentation Project. However, this project now has adopted the `SGMLtools` package, which is based on the DocBook DTD [↪ SGMLTOOLS].

In this section we first build a mini-DTD for LaTeX, which implements the structural elements of the LaTeX language. This leaves aside a lot of the typographic elements, as well as the details of mathematics, which were discussed in Chapter 8 in the framework of a more complete implementation. We then use the markup scheme defined by that DTD to write a multilingual sample document, that we will print with an XSL style sheet by translating the XML into LaTeX.

B.4.5.1   The LaTeX-based DTD

For our DTD model (`minilatex.dtd`), whose complete source text follows, we do not try to follow LaTeX too closely, since in some cases LaTeX confuses structural and presentation elements (so does HTML in *most* cases). For instance, sectioning elements become real containers, with a title, followed by paragraph-like material and floats (line 139) and lower-level sectioning elements (lines 142–155). Thus sectioning commands are structural only and indicate the subdivisions of the document, while their title must be specified separately.

It is sometimes difficult to decide where to include a given LaTeX element in the DTD. LaTeX has some elements that can occur almost anywhere, yet at the same time they have the constraint that they cannot be nested (for instance, footnotes and marginpars). We have chosen to ignore these elements and leave them under full user control. Such elements, if needed, can be inserted explicitly by extending the DTD, and it is left up to the user to exploit them wisely. Our sample file, presented in Section B.4.5.3, will show you how you can achieve this extension mechanism.

Copying good practice introduced in the HTML4 DTDs, we let most elements carry an `id` attribute of type ID so that they can be the target of cross-references (following), as well as `style` and `class` attributes (lines 3–5). The latter two come in handy when you want to visualize XML document elements as we explained in Chapter 7. We also provide an attribute `xml:lang` (line 7), which lets you specify the language in which a given part of the text is written. This is useful for spell checking, hyphenation algorithms, typographic rendering, and so on.

The cross-reference system is fully based on XML's identifier mechanism (the ID and IDREF token types for attributes, see Section 6.5.4.2). As explained earlier, we allow an `id` attribute on most elements, and, as seen in lines 43–50, the `cite`, `pageref`, and `ref` elements all have an `idref` attribute. Taken together, we can reference almost any document element in a straightforward way.

In writing the DTD, we have tried to keep the DTD somewhat modular by defining parameter entities to structure the information (fontchange, xref, and so on, on lines 10–27). To make it easy to extend the DTD, each of these parameter entities has a companion ending in .new (fontchange.new, xref.new, and so on). These are defined as empty strings, but the user can redefine them in the internal subset of the document instance or in another DTD. Thus new elements can be conveniently added at various points of the document hierarchy.

Most of the entries in the source listing that follows should be simple to understand. The handling of mathematics (lines 162–172) refers to two further DTD fragments that are discussed separately in Section B.4.5.2.

```
1   <!-- minilatex.dtd: XML version of a subset of LaTeX -->
2   <!-- Most elements have the following attributes  -->
3   <!ENTITY % all    "id    ID #IMPLIED
4                      class CDATA #IMPLIED
5                      style CDATA #IMPLIED">
6   <!-- Most non-empty elements have this language attribute -->
7   <!ENTITY % i18n   "xml:lang NMTOKEN #IMPLIED">
8   <!ENTITY % basic  "%all; %i18n;">
9   <!-- Declaration of parameter entities for structuring the DTD -->
10  <!ENTITY % fontchange.new "">
11  <!ENTITY % fontchange "emph|textbf|textsc|textsf|textsl|texttt %fontchange.new;">
12  <!ENTITY % misc.new "">
13  <!ENTITY % misc "url|quad|hspace|vspace|includegraphics|tag|ent %misc.new;">
14  <!ENTITY % xref.new  "">
15  <!ENTITY % xref "cite|pageref|ref %xref.new;">
16  <!ENTITY % mathobj.new "">
17  <!ENTITY % mathobj "displaymath|inlinemath|equation|eqnarray" >
18  <!ENTITY % inline.new "">
19  <!ENTITY % inline "%fontchange;|quote|tabular|%misc;|%xref;|%mathobj; %inline.new;">
20  <!ENTITY % list.new "">
21  <!ENTITY % list     "lalist|description|enumerate|itemize|bibliography %list.new;">
22  <!ENTITY % preformat.new "">
23  <!ENTITY % preformat "verbatim|verse %preformat.new;">
24  <!ENTITY % likepara.new "">
25  <!ENTITY % likepara "%list;|quotation|align|%preformat; %likepara.new;">
26  <!ENTITY % floats.new "">
27  <!ENTITY % floats "figure|table %floats.new,">
28
29  <!-- The top level document declarations                    -->
30  <!ELEMENT document (frontmatter?,bodymatter,backmatter?)>
31  <!ATTLIST document %i18n;
32                     class CDATA "article">
33  <!ELEMENT frontmatter (title,author?,date?,abstract?,keywords?)>
34  <!ELEMENT bodymatter  ((par|%likepara;|%floats;|part|chapter|section)*,appendix*)>
35  <!ELEMENT backmatter  (index|glossary)*>
36  <!-- fontchanges -->
37  <!ELEMENT emph    (#PCDATA|%inline;)*>
38  <!ELEMENT textbf  (#PCDATA|%inline;)*>
39  <!ELEMENT textsc  (#PCDATA|%inline;)*>
40  <!ELEMENT textsf  (#PCDATA|%inline;)*>
41  <!ELEMENT textsl  (#PCDATA|%inline;)*>
42  <!ELEMENT texttt  (#PCDATA|%inline;)*>
43  <!-- cross-references -->
44  <!ENTITY % idref  "refid IDREF #REQUIRED">
45  <!ELEMENT cite    EMPTY>
46  <!ATTLIST cite    %idref;>
47  <!ELEMENT pageref EMPTY>
48  <!ATTLIST pageref %idref;>
49  <!ELEMENT ref     EMPTY>
50  <!ATTLIST ref     %idref;>
```

```
51  <!-- quoted material inline and displayed -->
52  <!ELEMENT quote         (#PCDATA|%inline;|par)*>
53  <!ATTLIST quote         %basic;>
54  <!ELEMENT quotation     (#PCDATA|%inline;|par)*>
55  <!ATTLIST quotation     %basic;>
56  <!-- lists -->
57  <!ELEMENT description   ((term*,item*)+)>
58  <!ELEMENT enumerate     ((term*,item*)+)>
59  <!ATTLIST enumerate     %basic;>
60  <!ELEMENT itemize       ((term*,item*)+)>
61  <!ATTLIST itemize       %basic;>
62  <!ELEMENT lalist        ((term*,item*)+)>
63  <!ATTLIST lalist        %basic;>
64  <!ELEMENT term          (#PCDATA|%inline;)*>
65  <!ATTLIST term          %basic;>
66  <!ELEMENT item          (#PCDATA|%inline;|par|%likepara;)*>
67  <!ATTLIST item          %basic;>
68  <!ELEMENT bibliography (bibitem)*>
69  <!ATTLIST bibliography %basic;>
70  <!ELEMENT bibitem       (#PCDATA|%inline;|par|%likepara;)*>
71  <!ATTLIST bibitem       %basic;>
72  <!-- low-level bits and pieces -->
73  <!ELEMENT url     EMPTY>
74  <!ATTLIST url     name CDATA #REQUIRED>
75  <!ELEMENT quad    EMPTY>
76  <!ELEMENT hspace EMPTY>
77  <!ATTLIST hspace dim CDATA #REQUIRED>
78  <!ELEMENT vspace EMPTY>
79  <!ATTLIST vspace dim CDATA #REQUIRED>
80  <!ELEMENT tag     (#PCDATA)>
81  <!ELEMENT ent     EMPTY>
82  <!ATTLIST ent     value CDATA #REQUIRED
83                    name  CDATA #REQUIRED>
84  <!-- everything that can go into a paragraph -->
85  <!ELEMENT par           (#PCDATA|%inline;|%likepara;)*>
86  <!ATTLIST par           %basic;>
87  <!-- "floats" and their contents -->
88  <!ELEMENT figure   (#PCDATA|par|%inline;|%likepara;|includegraphics|caption)*>
89  <!ATTLIST figure   %basic;>
90  <!ELEMENT table    (#PCDATA|par|%inline;|%likepara;|tabular|caption)*>
91  <!ATTLIST table    %basic;>
92  <!ELEMENT includegraphics EMPTY>
93  <!ATTLIST includegraphics %basic;
94                            file    CDATA #REQUIRED
95                            width   CDATA #IMPLIED
96                            height  CDATA #IMPLIED
97                            bb      CDATA #IMPLIED
98                            scale   CDATA ".5"
99                            angle   CDATA #IMPLIED>
100 <!ELEMENT caption (#PCDATA|par|%inline;)*>
101 <!ATTLIST caption %basic;>
102 <!-- tabular material -->
103 <!ELEMENT tabular (hline|row)*>
104 <!ATTLIST tabular %basic;
105                   preamble CDATA  #REQUIRED
106                   width    CDATA  #IMPLIED
107                   border   CDATA  #IMPLIED>
108 <!ELEMENT row     (cell)*>
109 <!ATTLIST row     %basic;>
110 <!ELEMENT hline   EMPTY>
111 <!ELEMENT cell    (#PCDATA|%inline;)*>
112 <!ATTLIST cell    %basic;
113                   rowspan CDATA "1"
114                   colspan CDATA "1"
115                   align   (left|center|right) "center">
```

```
116   <!-- verbatim material    >
117   <!ELEMENT verbatim (#PCDATA)>
118   <!ATTLIST verbatim %basic;
119                      xml:space (default|preserve) 'preserve'>
120   <!ELEMENT verse     (#PCDATA|%inline;)*>
121   <!ATTLIST verse     %basic;
122                      xml:space (default|preserve) 'preserve'>
123   <!-- things that go in the frontmatter -->
124   <!ELEMENT newline   EMPTY>
125   <!ELEMENT title     (#PCDATA|%inline;|thanks|newline)*>
126   <!ATTLIST title     %basic;>
127   <!ELEMENT author    (#PCDATA|%inline;|name|thanks|inst)*>
128   <!ELEMENT name      (#PCDATA|%inline;)*>
129   <!ATTLIST name      %basic;>
130   <!ELEMENT thanks    (#PCDATA|%inline;|newline)*>
131   <!ATTLIST thanks    %basic;>
132   <!ELEMENT inst      (#PCDATA|%inline;|newline)*>
133   <!ATTLIST inst      %basic;>
134   <!ELEMENT date      (#PCDATA)>
135   <!ATTLIST date      %basic;>
136   <!ELEMENT abstract (par+)>
137   <!ATTLIST abstract %basic;>
138   <!-- structuring -->
139   <!ENTITY % sect        "stitle, (par|%likepara;|%floats;)* ">
140   <!ELEMENT stitle        (#PCDATA|%inline;)*>
141   <!ATTLIST stitle         %basic;>
142   <!ELEMENT part          (%sect;, (chapter|section|subsection|subsubsection)*)>
143   <!ATTLIST part           %basic;>
144   <!ELEMENT chapter       (%sect;, section*)>
145   <!ATTLIST chapter        %basic;>
146   <!ELEMENT section       (%sect;, subsection*)>
147   <!ATTLIST section        %basic;>
148   <!ELEMENT subsection    (%sect;, subsubsection*)>
149   <!ATTLIST subsection     %basic;>
150   <!ELEMENT subsubsection (%sect;, paragraph*)>
151   <!ATTLIST subsubsection  %basic;>
152   <!ELEMENT paragraph     (%sect;, subparagraph*)>
153   <!ATTLIST paragraph      %basic;>
154   <!ELEMENT subparagraph  (%sect;)>
155   <!ATTLIST subparagraph   %basic;>
156   <!ELEMENT appendix      EMPTY>
157   <!-- backmatter: index and glossary -->
158   <!ELEMENT index (par|%likepara;)*>
159   <!ATTLIST index %basic;>
160   <!ELEMENT glossary (par|%likepara;)*>
161   <!ATTLIST glossary %basic;>
162   <!-- LaTeX math constructs -->
163   <!ENTITY % LaTeXmath  "INCLUDE">
164   <!ENTITY % latexmath.dtd SYSTEM "latexmath.dtd">
165   <![ %LaTeXmath; |
166   %latexmath.dtd;
167   ]]>
168   <!ENTITY % MathML.      "IGNORE">
169   <!ENTITY % latexmml.dtd SYSTEM "latexmml.dtd">
170   <![ %MathML; [
171   %latexmml.dtd,
172   ]]>
173   <!-- Basic XML entities -->
174   <!ENTITY lt     "&#60;"> <!-- "<" -->
175   <!ENTITY gt     "&#62;"> <!-- ">" -->
176   <!ENTITY amp    "&#38;"> <!-- "&" -->
177   <!ENTITY apos   "&#39;"> <!-- "'" -->
178   <!ENTITY quot   "&#34;"> <!-- '"' -->
```

B.4.5.2 LᴬTₑX math and our DTD

As we mentioned in the previous section, we have not really addressed the subject of the mathematical markup in the main DTD file `minilatex.dtd`.

Generally speaking, either we can use TₑX markup for describing math (as we do in our sample document in the next section), or we can decide to use MathML, in which case we must include the full DTD for that language. In fact, as already mentioned, we have provided hooks for handling these two cases in our `minilatex.dtd` file (lines 163–172). Indeed, two entities, "LaTeXmath" and "MathML," control which of the two math models (LᴬTₑX or MathML markup) is to be used. By default we use LᴬTₑX markup (the value of `LaTeXmath` is INCLUDE (line 163), whereas that of `MathML` is set to IGNORE (line 168)).

Let us see what happens in each case. First we consider the simpler situation, where we decide to use LᴬTₑX-based markup (this is the default for our DTD). Then line 166 is active, and we include the file `latexmath.dtd` into the master DTD. This file follows:

```
1   <!-- latexmath.dtd +++ inline and display math -->
2   <!ELEMENT  inlinemath  (#PCDATA)>
3   <!ATTLIST  inlinemath  %all;>
4   <!ELEMENT  displaymath (#PCDATA)>
5   <!ATTLIST  displaymath %all;>
6   <!ELEMENT  equation    (#PCDATA)>
7   <!ATTLIST  equation    %all;>
8   <!ELEMENT  eqnarray    (#PCDATA)>
9   <!ATTLIST  eqnarray    %all;>
10  <!ELEMENT  align       (#PCDATA)>
11  <!ATTLIST  align       %all;>
```

This file `latexmath.dtd` contains the usual LᴬTₑX math containers, and we declare their contents as #PCDATA, so that we do not impose any constraints on their internal structure. Inside XML files the characters <, >, and & have to be escaped; therefore it is more practical to put the data inside the math elements inside a CDATA section, where one can use all LᴬTₑX characters without needing to use special precautions (in particular, see lines 51–53 of the sample XML file in Section B.4.5.3).

If, on the other hand, we decide to use MathML markup by setting the value of the entity `MathML` to INCLUDE (and that of `LaTeXmath` to IGNORE), we include the file `latexmml.dtd`, shown here:

```
1   <!-- latexmml.dtd -->
2   <!ELEMENT equation (math)*>
3   <!ATTLIST equation %all;>
4   <!ELEMENT displaymath (math)*>
5   <!ELEMENT inlinemath  (math)*>
6   <!ELEMENT subeqn (math)*>
7   <!ATTLIST subeqn %all;>
8   <!ELEMENT eqnarray (subeqn)*>
9   <!ATTLIST eqnarray %all;
10                    number (yes|no) "yes">
11  <!ELEMENT align (%inline;)*>
12  <!ATTLIST align %all; >
13
14  <!-- ISO and MathML DTDs and entities -->
```

```
15  <!--Added Math Symbols: Arrows  >
16  <!ENTITY % isoamsae.dtd SYSTEM "isoamsae.dtd">
17  <!--Added Math Symbols: Binary Operators-->
18  <!ENTITY % isoamsbe.dtd SYSTEM "isoamsbe.dtd">
19  <!--Added Math Symbols: Delimiters-->
20  <!ENTITY % isoamsce.dtd SYSTEM "isoamsce.dtd">
21  <!--Added Math Symbols: Negated Relations-->
22  <!ENTITY % isoamsne.dtd SYSTEM "isoamsne.dtd">
23  <!--Added Math Symbols: Ordinary-->
24  <!ENTITY % isoamsoe.dtd SYSTEM "isoamsoe.dtd">
25  <!--Added Math Symbols: Relations-->
26  <!ENTITY % isoamsre.dtd SYSTEM "isoamsre.dtd">
27  <!--General Technical-->
28  <!ENTITY % isoteche.dtd SYSTEM "isoteche.dtd">
29  <!--Numbers and Currency symbols-->
30  <!ENTITY % isonume.dtd SYSTEM "isonume.dtd">
31  <!--MathML Aliases (From ISO PUB,DIA,NUM)-->
32  <!ENTITY % mmaliase.dtd SYSTEM "mmaliase.dtd">
33  <!--Greek Symbols-->
34  <!ENTITY % isogrk3e.dtd SYSTEM "isogrk3e.dtd">
35  <!--Math Script Font-->
36  <!ENTITY % isomscre.dtd SYSTEM "isomscre.dtd">
37  <!--Math Open Face Font-->
38  <!ENTITY % isomopfe.dtd SYSTEM "isomopfe.dtd">
39  <!--MathML Entities-->
40  <!ENTITY % mmlent.dtd SYSTEM "mmlent.dtd">
41  <!--Main MathML DTD -->
42  <!ENTITY % mathml.dtd    SYSTEM "mathml.dtd">
43
44  %mathml.dtd;
45  %isoamsae.dtd;
46  %isoamsbe.dtd;
47  %isoamsce.dtd;
48  %isoamsne.dtd;
49  %isoamsoe.dtd;
50  %isoamsre.dtd;
51  %isoteche.dtd;
52  %isonume.dtd;
53  %mmaliase.dtd;
54  %isogrk3e.dtd;
55  %isomscre.dtd;
56  %isomopfe.dtd;
57  %mmlent.dtd;
```

Since the MathML DTD uses the math element as global container, in the file latexmml.dtd we must declare the LaTeX containers as consisting of math elements (lines 2 and 4–6). The rest of the above DTD file contains a set of entity definitions (lines 14–40), as well as a reference to the MathML DTD itself (line 42). The files defined by these entities are all included at the end (lines 44–57).

The minilatex.dtd and latexmml.dtd DTD files can be used with the XML file derived from the LaTeX test file used throughout this book and shown in Appendix A.1. Following is the start of that file:

```
1  <?xml version="1.0"?>
2  <!DOCTYPE document SYSTEM "minilatex.dtd"[
3  <!ENTITY % MathML     "INCLUDE">
4  <!ENTITY % LaTeXmath  "IGNORE">
5  <!ENTITY % inline.new  "|math">
6  <!ENTITY aacute "&#x00E1;">
7  <!ENTITY OverBar "[OverBar]">
```

```
8   <!ENTITY negationslash "/">
9   ]>
10  <document>
11  <frontmatter>
12  <title>Simulation of Energy Loss Straggling</title>
13  <author>Maria Physicist</author>
14  <date> January 14, 1999</date>
15  </frontmatter>
16  <bodymatter> ...
```

The beginning of the file defines the DTD to be used and sets the values of the entities `MathML` and `LaTeXmath` appropriately. We also define the `math` element needed as a container with MathML markup by introducing it in the `inline.new` entity parameter, so that it will be included in the `inline` elements in the `minilatex.dtd` (line 19). The remaining lines (6–8) define entities that are referenced in the test document but are not defined in the already loaded entity reference sets.

B.4.5.3 A sample document

Let us now show how we can use the `minilatex` DTD, which we introduced in Section B.4.5.1. In the present section we look at a sample XML file, marked up according to that DTD. The contents of the document are partly based on the text of Figures 9.2 and 9.3 in the Babel chapter of *The LaTeX Companion* (Goossens et al. (1994)).

On line 1 you notice the `<?xml` processing instruction that declares the use of the Latin 1 (ISO-8859-1) encoding in the document (used by the German text on lines 60–99 and 128–131 and the French text on lines 100–126 and 132–135). We also define (lines 3–8) a few entities that occur in the document text and are not defined in the external DTD subset. They are customized for translation into LaTeX. For translation into HTML or another format, these entities should be defined appropriately. The same holds for certain sections of the text, whose context we put inside `CDATA` sections, since we know we will be using LaTeX as back-end (for example lines 40 and 41, as well as the math segments on lines 51–53). In fact, we do not need to use a `CDATA` section to prepare output directly for LaTeX, since we can use XML entities to represent special characters, as shown on lines 42–43. It is only a matter of convenience as to which approach you want to take. Note, however, that we preceded the & character with a \ (lines 40, 42, and 43), since we know that ampersands must be escaped for use as a literal in LaTeX.

At the end of the internal subset we define a `footnote` element that is to be included in the `inline` parameter entity (line 19 of the `minilatex` DTD), so that it will become available for use in the document instance that follows. Therefore we enter it into the `inline.new` parameter entity (line 9) and declare its contents as `#PCDATA` and `par` elements (line 10). However, `par` elements, according to line 85 of the file `minilatex.dtd`, refer to the `inline` entity. Thus since our `footnote` element will also become part of `inline`, it is our responsibility to make sure that we do not inadvertently nest `footnote` elements (the DTD does not disallow this, but LaTeX forbids it; see Section 7.6.5.4 for a way to deal with this in XSL).

The two main parts of the document, its `frontmatter` (lines 13–19) and its `bodymatter` (lines 20–137), are clearly discernible. Similarly thanks to the sectioning tags (`<section>`, `<subsection>`, and so on) and their nesting, the hierarchical structure of the sectioning element tree can be easily reconstructed and checked for consistency.

Various languages inside the same document are easily supported. The present document starts with a section in English (this is the default language for the document as declared on line 12 of the document instance), is followed by a section in German (starting on line 60 of the document instance), and then one in French (starting on line 100). In addition the two bibliographic `bibitem` elements have different language attributes (lines 128–131 are in German, while lines 132–135 are in French; the surrounding `thebibliography` element is in English—the default).

The `includegraphics` command and its attributes are defined on lines 93–99 in the `minilatex` DTD. It is used on line 74 of the example, where we want to include an Encapsulated PostScript image inside a `figure` element (lines 73–76).

The rest of the markup should be quite straightforward, and we will not comment on the remaining parts of the sample file.

Nevertheless, we want to draw your attention to an inportant point. As we mentioned at the beginning of this section, on lines 51–53 we directly use LaTeX's math notation inside the `inlinemath` elements (this corresponds to the default setting in the `minilatex` DTD). Although we use CDATA sections to escape the need to use entity references for certain characters, XML or XSL processors, which can output only valid XML files, will represent all <, >, and & symbols by their XML equivalents `&lt;`, `&gt;`, and `&amp;`. Thus a postprocessor will have to transform these characters into their LaTeX equivalents, as shown at the end of the next section.

```
1    <?xml version="1.0" encoding="ISO-8859-1"?>
2    <!DOCTYPE document SYSTEM "minilatex.dtd"[
3    <!ENTITY LaTeX   "\LaTeX{}">
4    <!ENTITY TeX     "\TeX{}">
5    <!ENTITY dots    "\dots">
6    <!ENTITY endash  "--">
7    <!ENTITY emdash  "---">
8    <!ENTITY nbsp    "~">
9    <!ENTITY % inline.new "|footnote">
10   <!ELEMENT footnote (#PCDATA|par)*>
11   ]>
12   <document class="article" xml:lang="en">
13   <frontmatter>
14   <title>The &LaTeX; DTD and multiple languages</title>
15   <author><name>Michel Goossens</name>
16   <thanks>Partly from an example in <emph>The &LaTeX; Companion</emph>
17   </thanks></author>
18   <date>August 4th, 1998</date>
19   </frontmatter>
20   <bodymatter>
21   <section id="sec-en">
22   <stitle>The basic principles</stitle>
23   <par>
24   This is an example input file. We start in English to show the
25   principle. You should especially pay attention that we have used
```

```
26   slightly different notation for some of the common &LaTeX; constructs,
27   such as the dashes, which come in three sizes: an intra-word dash, a
28   medium dash for number ranges like 1&endash;2, and a punctuation
29   dash&emdash;like this.  Text can be emphasized as <emph>shown
30   here</emph>. An ellipsis is made with &dots; Footnotes<footnote>This
31   is a simple footnote.<par>It can also contain <texttt>par</texttt>
32   elements.</par></footnote> are tricky constructs, since one must be
33   careful not to nest them.
34   </par>
35   <subsection>
36   <stitle>Dealing with special characters</stitle>
37   <par>
38   XML has a different set of reserved characters than &LaTeX;, in
39   particular, when you want to use any of the three characters
40   <texttt><![CDATA[\&]]></texttt>, <texttt><![CDATA[<]]></texttt>,
41   and <texttt><![CDATA[>]]></texttt>, you should enter them as
42   <texttt>\&amp;amp;</texttt>, <texttt>\&amp;lt;</texttt>, and
43   <texttt>\&amp;gt;</texttt>, respectively.
44   </par>
45   </subsection>
46   <subsection id="sec-math">
47   <stitle>&LaTeX; and mathematical formulae</stitle>
48   <par>
49   &LaTeX; and <emph>a fortiori</emph> &TeX; are very good at typesetting
50   mathematical formulae, like
51   <inlinemath><![CDATA[x- 3 y + z < 7]]></inlinemath> or
52   <inlinemath><![CDATA[a_{1} > x^{2n} + y^{2n} > x']]></inlinemath> or
53   <inlinemath><![CDATA[(A, B) = \sum_{i} a_{i} b_{i}]]></inlinemath>.
54   Do not forget that for reasons of consistency, if you want to refer to
55   a variable in one of the formulae, such as the symbol
56   <inlinemath>x</inlinemath>, you must also use math mode in the text.
57   </par>
58   </subsection>
59   </section>
60   <section xml:lang="de">
61   <stitle>Beispiel eines Textes in deutscher Sprache</stitle>
62   <subsection>
63   <stitle>Eine EPS Abbildung</stitle>
64   <par>
65   Dieser Abschnitt zeigt, wie man eine PostScript-Abbildung
66   <cite refid="bib-PS"/> in ein Dokument einbinden kann.
67   Abbildung <ref refid="fig-psfig"/> wurde mit dem Befehl
68   <verbatim>
69   <![CDATA[\includegraphics[width="3cm"]{file="colorcir.eps}]]>
70   </verbatim>
71   in den Text aufgenommen.
72   </par>
73   <figure id="fig-psfig">
74   <includegraphics width="3cm" file="colorcir.eps"/>
75   <caption xml:lang="de">Ein EPS Bild</caption>
76   </figure>
77   </subsection>
78   <subsection>
79   <stitle>Beispiel einer Tabelle</stitle>
80   <par>Die Tabelle <ref refid="tab-exag"/> auf Seite <pageref
81   refid="tab-exag"/> zeigt eine Tabelle.
82   </par>
83   <table id="tab-exag">
84   <caption xml:lang="de">
85   Eingabe der deutschen Zusatzzeichen in &LaTeX;</caption>
86   <tabular preamble="ccccccc">
87   <row>
88   <cell><texttt>&#34;a</texttt> ä</cell>
89   <cell><texttt>&#34;A</texttt> Ä</cell>
90   <cell><texttt>&#34;o</texttt> ö</cell>
```

```
91   <cell><texttt>&#34;O</texttt> Ö</cell>
92   <cell><texttt>&#34;u</texttt> ü</cell>
93   <cell><texttt>&#34;U</texttt> Ü</cell>
94   <cell><texttt>&#34;s</texttt> &#223;</cell>
95   </row>
96   </tabular>
97   </table>
98   </subsection>
99   </section>
100  <section xml:lang="fr">
101  <stitle>Continuation du texte en français</stitle>
102  <subsection id="sec-list">
103  <stitle>Traiter les listes</stitle>
104  <par>
105  Les listes sont utilisées fréquemment pour structurer ou mettre
106  en évidence certains éléments d'un document (voir <cite refid="bib-Liste"/>).
107  </par>
108  <itemize>
109    <item>Ceci est le premier élément d'une liste non-ordonnée. Chaque élément
110      de ce type de liste est précédé d'un signe distinctif, comme une
111      puce, un tiret, etc.
112    </item>
113    <item>Ce second élément de la même liste contient une liste de
114      <emph>description</emph> imbriquée.
115      <description>
116        <term>XML</term>
117        <item>Meta langage pour définir des classes de documents</item>
118        <term>XLL</term>
119        <item>Langage pour définir des hyperliens entre différentes
120        parties de documents XML</item>
121      </description>
122      Nous continuons notre texte à l'intérieur de la première liste.
123    </item>
124  </itemize>
125  </subsection>
126  </section>
127  <bibliography>
128  <bibitem id="bib-PS" xml:lang="de">
129  Adobe Inc. <emph>PostScript Handbuch (2. Auflage)</emph>
130          Addison-Wesley (Deutschland) GmbH, Bonn, 1991.
131  </bibitem>
132  <bibitem id="bib-Liste" xml:lang="fr">
133  Michel Goossens. Personnaliser les listes &LaTeX;
134          <emph>Cahiers GUTenberg</emph>, 17:32&endash;48, mai 1994.
135  </bibitem>
136  </bibliography>
137  </bodymatter>
138  </document>
```

B.4.5.4   Preparing a printed version

We can validate the sample file `minilatexexa.xml`, presented in the previous section, with any of the many available XML parsers against the DTD `minilatex.dtd`. As an example we can run it through the `xml4j` parser, discussed in Section 6.6.5.6.

```
xml4j.oh minilatexexa.xml
minilatex.dtd: 18, 25: Warning: Entity name, "inline.new", already
defined. This declaration will be ignored.
```

This validating parser shows that our sample document is indeed valid relative to the `minilatex` DTD. Moreover, the parser warns us that the definition of the entity `inline.new` in the DTD is ignored. This is precisely what we want since, as explained in Section 6.5.4, the internal DTD subset is read first so that definitions in the internal subset are honored and override those in the external DTD (this is true only for entity and attribute definitions, *not* for elements, which thus cannot be redefined with respect to the external DTD).

Another interesting application is to generate a printable version of our file. We can use an XSL style sheet `minilatex.xsl`, which we show below. Its purpose is to translate the XML instance `minilatexexa.xml` into a LaTeX file.

```
1   <?xml version='1.0'?>
2   <!-- minilatex.xsl -->
3   <xsl:stylesheet xmlns:xsl="http://www.w3.org/TR/WD-xsl"
4                   xmlns="http://www.tug.org/latex"
5                   default-space="strip"
6                   result-ns="">
7
8   <xsl:macro name="label">
9     <xsl:if test="../@id"><xsl:text>\label{</xsl:text>
10    <xsl:value-of select="../@id"/><xsl:text>}</xsl:text></xsl:if>
11  <xsl:text>}
12  </xsl:text>
13  </xsl:macro>
14
15  <xsl:template match="document">
16  <xsl:text>\documentclass[]{</xsl:text>
17  <xsl:value-of select="@class"/>
18  <xsl:text>}
19  \usepackage[dvips]{graphicx}
20  \usepackage[T1]{fontenc}
21  \begin{document}
22  </xsl:text>
23  <xsl:apply-templates/>
24  <xsl:text>\end{document}
25  </xsl:text>
26  </xsl:template>
27
28  <!--   =============== Frontmatter element ======================= -->
29  <xsl:template match="frontmatter">
30    <xsl:apply-templates/>
31  <xsl:text>
32  \maketitle
33  </xsl:text>
34  </xsl:template>
35  <xsl:template match="frontmatter/title">
36  <xsl:text>
37  \title{</xsl:text>
38    <xsl:apply-templates/>
39  <xsl:text>}</xsl:text>
40  </xsl:template>
41  <xsl:template match="frontmatter/author">
42  <xsl:text>
43  \author{</xsl:text>
44    <xsl:apply-templates/>
45  <xsl:text>}
46  </xsl:text>
47  </xsl:template>
48  <xsl:template match="frontmatter/author/name">
49    <xsl:apply-templates/>
```

```
50  </xsl:template>
51  <xsl:template match="frontmatter/author/thanks">
52  <xsl:text>
53  \thanks{</xsl:text>
54    <xsl:apply-templates/>
55  <xsl:text>}</xsl:text>
56  </xsl:template>
57  <xsl:template match="frontmatter/author/inst">
58  <xsl:text>
59  \thanks{</xsl:text>
60    <xsl:apply-templates/>
61  <xsl:text>}</xsl:text>
62  </xsl:template>
63  <xsl:template match="frontmatter/date">
64  <xsl:text>
65  \date{</xsl:text>
66    <xsl:apply-templates/>
67  <xsl:text>}
68  </xsl:text>
69  </xsl:template>
70  <xsl:template match="frontmatter/abstract">
71  <xsl:text>
72  \begin{abstract}
73  </xsl:text>
74    <xsl:apply-templates/>
75  <xsl:text>
76  \end{abstract}
77  </xsl:text>
78  </xsl:template>
79  <xsl:template match="frontmatter/keywords">
80  <xsl:text>\keywords{</xsl:text>
81    <xsl:apply-templates/>
82  <xsl:text>}</xsl:text>
83  </xsl:template>
84
85  <!--  ======================= Bodymatter element ==================== -->
86  <xsl:template match="bodymatter|part|chapter|section|subsection|
87                       subsubsection|paragraph|subparagraph">
88    <xsl:apply-templates/>
89  </xsl:template>
90  <!--  =================== Section headings ===================== -->
91  <xsl:template match="part/stitle">
92    <xsl:text>\part{</xsl:text><xsl:apply-templates/>
93    <xsl:invoke macro="label"></xsl:invoke>
94  </xsl:template>
95  <xsl:template match="chapter/stitle">
96    <xsl:text>\chapter{</xsl:text><xsl:apply-templates/>
97    <xsl:invoke macro="label"></xsl:invoke>
98  </xsl:template>
99  <xsl:template match="section/stitle">
100   <xsl:text>\section{</xsl:text><xsl:apply-templates/>
101   <xsl:invoke macro="label"></xsl:invoke>
102 </xsl:template>
103 <xsl:template match="subsection/stitle">
104   <xsl:text>\subsection{</xsl:text><xsl:apply-templates/>
105   <xsl:invoke macro="label"></xsl:invoke>
106 </xsl:template>
107 <xsl:template match="subsubsection/stitle">
108   <xsl:text>\subsubsection{</xsl:text><xsl:apply-templates/>
109   <xsl:invoke macro="label"></xsl:invoke>
110 </xsl:template>
111 <xsl:template match="paragraph/stitle">
112   <xsl:text>\paragraph{</xsl:text><xsl:apply-templates/>
113   <xsl:invoke macro="label"></xsl:invoke>
114 </xsl:template>
```

```
115  <xsl:template match="subparagraph/stitle">
116    <xsl:text>\subparagraph{</xsl:text><xsl:apply-templates/>
117    <xsl:invoke macro="label"></xsl:invoke>
118  </xsl:template>
119  <!--   ====================== Font changes ========================= -->
120  <xsl:template match="emph">
121  <xsl:text>\emph{</xsl:text>
122    <xsl:apply-templates/>
123  <xsl:text>}</xsl:text>
124  </xsl:template>
125  <xsl:template match="textbf">
126  <xsl:text>\textbf{</xsl:text>
127    <xsl:apply-templates/>
128  <xsl:text>}</xsl:text>
129  </xsl:template>
130  <xsl:template match="textsc">
131  <xsl:text>\textsc{</xsl:text>
132    <xsl:apply-templates/>
133  <xsl:text>}</xsl:text>
134  </xsl:template>
135  <xsl:template match="textsf">
136  <xsl:text>\textsf{</xsl:text>
137    <xsl:apply-templates/>
138  <xsl:text>}</xsl:text>
139  </xsl:template>
140  <xsl:template match="textsl">
141  <xsl:text>\textsl{</xsl:text>
142    <xsl:apply-templates/>
143  <xsl:text>}</xsl:text>
144  </xsl:template>
145  <xsl:template match="texttt">
146  <xsl:text>\texttt{</xsl:text>
147    <xsl:apply-templates/>
148  <xsl:text>}</xsl:text>
149  </xsl:template>
150  <!--   =================== Cross-references ======================= -->
151  <xsl:template match="cite">
152    <xsl:text>\cite{</xsl:text>
153    <xsl:value-of select="@refid"/>
154    <xsl:text>}</xsl:text>
155  </xsl:template>
156  <xsl:template match="pageref">
157    <xsl:text>\pageref{</xsl:text>
158    <xsl:value-of select="@refid"/>
159    <xsl:text>}</xsl:text>
160  </xsl:template>
161  <xsl:template match="ref">
162    <xsl:text>\ref{</xsl:text>
163    <xsl:value-of select="@refid"/>
164    <xsl:text>}</xsl:text>
165  </xsl:template>
166  <!--   =============== quotes, footnotes, verbatim =============== -->
167  <xsl:template match="footnote">
168  <xsl:text>\footnote{</xsl:text>
169    <xsl:apply-templates/>
170  <xsl:text>}</xsl:text>
171  </xsl:template>
172  <xsl:template match="quote">
173  <xsl:text>
174  \begin{quote}</xsl:text>
175    <xsl:apply-templates/>
176  <xsl:text>\end{quote}</xsl:text>
177  </xsl:template>
178  <xsl:template match="quotation">
179  <xsl:text>
```

```
180    \begin{quotation}</xsl:text>
181      <xsl:apply-templates/>
182    <xsl:text>\end{quotation}</xsl:text>
183    </xsl:template>
184    <xsl:template match="verbatim">
185    <xsl:text>
186    \begin{verbatim}</xsl:text>
187      <xsl:apply-templates/>
188    <xsl:text>\end{verbatim}</xsl:text>
189    </xsl:template>
190    <!-- ========================= Lists =========================== -->
191    <xsl:template match="description">
192    <xsl:text>
193    \begin{description}
194    </xsl:text>
195      <xsl:apply-templates/>
196    <xsl:text>
197    \end{description}
198    </xsl:text>
199    </xsl:template>
200    <xsl:template match="description/term">
201    <xsl:text>
202    \item[</xsl:text>
203      <xsl:apply-templates/>
204    <xsl:text>]</xsl:text>
205    </xsl:template>
206    <xsl:template match="description/item">
207      <xsl:apply-templates/>
208    </xsl:template>
209    <xsl:template match="enumerate">
210    <xsl:text>
211    \begin{enumerate}
212    </xsl:text>
213      <xsl:apply-templates/>
214    <xsl:text>\end{enumerate}
215    </xsl:text>
216    </xsl:template>
217    <xsl:template match="itemize">
218    <xsl:text>
219    \begin{itemize}
220    </xsl:text>
221      <xsl:apply-templates/>
222    <xsl:text>\end{itemize}
223    </xsl:text>
224    </xsl:template>
225    <xsl:template match="enumerate|itemize/item">
226    <xsl:text>
227    \item </xsl:text>
228      <xsl:apply-templates/>
229    </xsl:template>
230    <xsl:template match="bibliography">
231    <xsl:text>
232    \begin{thebibliography}{99}
233    </xsl:text>
234      <xsl:apply-templates/>
235    <xsl:text>
236    \end{thebibliography}
237    </xsl:text>
238    </xsl:template>
239    <xsl:template match="bibliography/bibitem">
240    <xsl:text>\bibitem{</xsl:text>
241    <xsl:value-of select="@id"/>
242    <xsl:text>}</xsl:text>
243    <xsl:apply-templates/>
244    </xsl:template>
```

```
245    <!-- ===================== Mathematics ======================= -->
246    <xsl:template match="inlinemath">
247    <xsl:text>$</xsl:text>
248      <xsl:apply-templates/>
249    <xsl:text>$</xsl:text>
250    </xsl:template>
251    <xsl:template match="displaymath">
252    <xsl:text>
253    \begin{displaymath}
254    </xsl:text>
255      <xsl:apply-templates/>
256    <xsl:text>
257    \end{displaymath}
258    </xsl:text>
259    </xsl:template>
260    <xsl:template match="equation">
261    <xsl:text>
262    \begin{equation}
263    </xsl:text>
264      <xsl:apply-templates/>
265    <xsl:text>
266    \end{equation}
267    </xsl:text>
268    </xsl:template>
269    <xsl:template match="eqnarray">
270    <xsl:text>
271    \begin{eqnarray}
272    </xsl:text>
273      <xsl:apply-templates/>
274    <xsl:text>
275    \end{eqnarray}
276    </xsl:text>
277    </xsl:template>
278    <!-- ===================== A paragraph ======================= -->
279    <xsl:template match="par">
280    <xsl:text>
281    \par
282    </xsl:text>
283      <xsl:apply-templates/>
284    </xsl:template>
285    <!-- ======================= Tabular ======================= -->
286    <xsl:template match="tabular">
287    <xsl:text>
288    \begin{tabular}{</xsl:text>
289      <xsl:value-of select="@preamble"/><xsl:text>}
290    </xsl:text>
291      <xsl:apply-templates/>
292    <xsl:text>
293    \end{tabular}
294    </xsl:text>
295    </xsl:template>
296    <xsl:template match="tabular/row">
297    <xsl:apply-templates/>
298    <xsl:text>\\
299    </xsl:text>
300    </xsl:template>
301    <xsl:template match="tabular/row/cell[not(last-of-type())]">
302    <xsl:apply-templates/><xsl:text>&amp;</xsl:text>
303    </xsl:template>
304    <xsl:template match="tabular/row/cell[last-of-type()]">
305    <xsl:apply-templates/>
306    </xsl:template>
307    <!-- ================== "floats" and their contents ============= -->
308    <xsl:template match="figure">
309    <xsl:text>
```

```
310  \begin{figure}\centering
311  </xsl:text>
312    <xsl:apply-templates/>
313  <xsl:text>\end{figure}
314  </xsl:text>
315  </xsl:template>
316  <xsl:template match="table">
317  <xsl:text>
318  \begin{table}\centering
319  </xsl:text>
320    <xsl:apply-templates/>
321  <xsl:text>\end{table}
322  </xsl:text>
323  </xsl:template>
324  <xsl:template match="figure/caption | table/caption">
325    <xsl:text>\caption{</xsl:text><xsl:apply-templates/>
326    <xsl:invoke macro="label"></xsl:invoke>
327  </xsl:template>
328  <!--  ==================== Includegraphics ====================  -->
329  <xsl:template match="includegraphics">
330  <xsl:text>
331  \includegraphics[</xsl:text>
332  <xsl:if test="@width"><xsl:text>width=</xsl:text>
333      <xsl:value-of select="@width"/><xsl:text>, </xsl:text></xsl:if>
334  <xsl:if test="@height"><xsl:text>height=</xsl:text>
335      <xsl:value-of select="@height"/><xsl:text>, </xsl:text></xsl:if>
336  <xsl:if test="@bb"><xsl:text>bb=</xsl:text>
337      <xsl:value-of select="@bb"/><xsl:text>, </xsl:text></xsl:if>
338  <xsl:if test="@angle"><xsl:text>angle=</xsl:text>
339      <xsl:value-of select="@angle"/><xsl:text>, </xsl:text></xsl:if>
340  <xsl:if test="@scale"><xsl:text>scale=</xsl:text>
341      <xsl:value-of select="@scale"/><xsl:text></xsl:text></xsl:if>
342  <xsl:text>]{</xsl:text><xsl:value-of select="@file"/><xsl:text>}
343  </xsl:text>
344  </xsl:template>
345
346  </xsl:stylesheet>
```

Most of the above code should be more or less trivial to understand after reading Section 7.6, where we explained how XSL style sheets are written and how they can generate HTML or LaTeX output. In fact, for each element in the document instance we have to provide a unique rule so that the XSL parser knows how to translate it into the target language. In our case, most XML elements map one-to-one onto their LaTeX equivalents (the template rules for the font-changing elements on lines 120–149 are a clear example).

Therefore it should be enough to look in more detail at three areas, namely cross-references, tabular material, and the handling of optional attributes, such as those of the includegraphics element.

As noted in Section B.4.5.1, cross-referencing is based on XML's id and idref attributes. Therefore we define a macro "label" (lines 8–13), which puts a LaTeX \label command inside elements for which it makes sense in LaTeX. For a given parent we look whether an id attribute is present (xsl:if construct on lines 9 and 10). If it exists, we insert a \label command with the key extracted from the id attribute of the XML parent element (line 10). We end the macro by providing the closing brace for the enclosing element (lines 11–12).

In the present version of the XSL file we reference this macro for all `stitle` elements of the sectioning commands (lines 93, 97, 101, 105, 109, 113, and 117) and the `caption` command (line 326). The `bibitem` command (lines 239–244) uses its own item identifier as key (line 241).

References to these keys are made with the `cite` (line 151–155), `pageref` (line 156–160), and `ref` (lines 161–165) elements. In each case we simply get the value of the `refid` attribute and enter it as an argument in the relevant LaTeX command.

Tabular material (lines 286–293) specified with the `tabular` element is to be transformed into a format compatible with LaTeX's `tabular` environment. We first get the preamble (line 289) and then handle the rows (lines 296–300) by ending each row with a \\ (line 298). Cells are a little trickier since we must be careful with the & column separators. Indeed, we must distinguish between nonterminal columns (lines 301–303), where we add a & separator following the contents (line 302) and the last column of a row (which we choose with XSL's `last-of-type` specifier; see lines 304–306), where we put only the contents (line 305).

Finally at the end of the XSL file we treat the `includegraphics` command (lines 329–344). The only minor difficulty in this case is that we must be careful to verify which optional attributes have been specified. Each of these attributes has its own `xsl:if` construct to test for its presence (lines 332–341). For each attribute that was specified, we get its value and enter it following the relevant selection string for LaTeX (e.g., `width=` on line 332). At the end the mandatory filename (specified in the XML file with the `file` attribute) is output between curly braces (line 342).

When we run the sample file `minilatexexa.xml` together with the above XSL style sheet `minilatex.xsl` through the `xt` processor and then postprocess the result to obtain LaTeX compatible output for XML reserved characters, we obtain a LaTeX source file `minilatexexa.tex`.[2]

```
xt minilatexexa.xml ../minilatex.xsl | \
sed -e 's/&gt;/>/g' -e 's/&lt;/</g' -e 's/\&amp;/\&/g' \
 > minilatexexa.tex
```

After running the file `minilatexexa.tex` through the LaTeX processor, we generated the PostScript file shown in Figure B.1.

B.5   Transforming HTML into XML

HTML's popularity has grown exponentially in recent years because of the increased importance of distributing documents on the Web. HTML is used by ever more applications, for which new tags are constantly being introduced, so that HTML has grown into a compatibility nightmare. Cross-platform portability is increasingly

---

[2]Because `xt` generates UTF-8 output for non-ASCII characters, we had to transform the UTF-8 characters to Latin 1, which we did with the help of the `Yudit` program (see Section C.3.2). Future XSL programs will probably make it possible to choose the output encoding directly.

The LaTeX DTD and multiple languages

Michel Goossens *

August 4th, 1998

1   The basic principles

This is an example input file. We start in English to show the principle. You should especially pay attention that we have used slightly different notation for some of the common LaTeX constructs, such as the dashes, which come in three sizes: an intra-word dash, a medium dash for number ranges like 1–2, and a punctuation dash—like this. Text can be emphasized as *shown here*. An ellipsis is made with … Footnotes[1] are tricky constructs, since one must be careful not to nest them.

1.1   Dealing with special characters

XML has a different set of reserved characters than LaTeX, in particular, when you want to use any of the three characters &, <, and >, you should enter them as &, <, and >, respectively.

1.2   LaTeX and mathematical formulae

LaTeX and *a fortiori* TeX are very good at typesetting mathematical formulae, like $x - 3y + z < 7$ or $a_1 > x^{2n} + y^{2n} > x'$ or $(A, B) = \sum_i a_i b_i$. Do not forget that for reasons of consistency, if you want to refer to a variable in one of the formulae, such as the symbol x, you must also use math mode in the text.

2   Beispiel eines Textes in deutscher Sprache

2.1   Eine EPS Abbildung

Dieser Abschnitt zeigt, wie man eine PostScript-Abbildung [1] in ein Dokument einbinden kann. Abbildung 1 wurde mit dem Befehl

```
\includegraphics[width="3cm"]{file="colorcir.eps}
```

in den Text aufgenommen

___
*Partly from an example in *The LaTeX Companion*
[1] This is a simple footnote.
It can also contain par elements.

1

Figure 1: Ein EPS Bild

Table 1: Eingabe der deutschen Zusatzzeichen in LaTeX

"a ä	"A Ä	"o ö	"O Ö	"u ü	"U Ü	"s SS

2.2   Beispiel einer Tabelle

Die Tabelle 1 auf Seite 2 zeigt eine Tabelle.

3   Continuation du texte en français

3.1   Traiter les listes

Les listes sont utilisées fréquemment pour structurer ou mettre en évidence certains éléments d'un document (voir [2]).

- Ceci est le premier élément d'une liste non-ordonnée. Chaque élément de ce type de liste est précédé d'un signe distinctif, comme une puce, un tiret, etc.

- Ce second élément de la même liste contient une liste de *description* imbriquée.

  XML Meta langage pour définir des classes de documents

  XLL Langage pour définir des hyperliens entre différentes parties de documents XML.

  Nous continuons notre texte à l'intérieur de la première liste.

References

[1] Adobe Inc. *PostScript Handbuch (2. Auflage)* Addison-Wesley (Deutschland) GmbH, Bonn, 1991.

[2] Michel Goossens. Personnaliser les listes LaTeX. *Cahiers GUTenberg*, 17-32-48, mai 1994.

2

Figure B.1: PostScript rendering of our LaTeX based XML document

---

difficult to guarantee, and this has now become the largest obstacle for HTML to keep up with the Internet's rapid evolution.

Therefore to find solutions for distributed document handling on an ever-growing set of different computer and communication environments, a successor to HTML is urgently needed. At a *Future of HTML* workshop held in May 1998, it was agreed that the way forward was to make a fresh start with a new generation of HTML, which would be defined as a suite of XML tag sets.

This new HTML includes a *core tag set*, used to mark up headings, paragraphs, lists, hypertext links, images, and other basic documents idioms. On the other hand, the markup for forms, tables, multimedia, graphics, and so on is each defined by its own separate tag sets. These tag sets adopt XML syntax, and you will be able to use them in any combination. This will allow you to mark up a much wider range of documents than with a monolithic markup scheme.

A clear separation of content and form is more strictly imposed, so that style sheets become increasingly important to associate such characteristics like color, font, and document layout with structural elements. Style sheets also help in describing how markup can be adapted or transformed to optimize its rendering on different kinds of devices.

In order to describe which HTML tags a given type of device supports and which style sheet features it implements, *conformance profiles* are used. The principle is that two different devices must render markup in the same way if they belong to the same conformance profile, and the document uses only features of that profile.

A conformance profile not only specifies which HTML tags sets and which style sheet functionality are supported, but also contains information about semantic constraints, data format, scripting support, and so on. A device can send its profile to a Web server where transformational software can repurpose the markup in a simple and reliable fashion and return a document customized for the device in question. Document and device profiles will encode the information in Resource Description Framework (RDF, [↪RDF]), and in function of a set of DTDs.

B.5.1   HTML in XML

To formalize the points discussed in the previous section, W3C recently released a working draft [↪HTMLINXML] that reformulates HTML4.0 as an XML application and defines the corresponding namespaces. It introduces document profiles as a basis for interoperability between different sets of HTML in heterogeneous environments.

B.5.1.1   HTML modularization

HTML has been split into modules, each corresponding to a well-defined set of HTML tags that can be mixed and matched at will. For instance, a "table module" would contain the elements and attributes necessary to support tables, and a "forms module" would contain elements and attributes needed for forms.

This modularization is important to ease the support necessary to maintain and deliver content on an ever-increasing number of diverse platforms—not only computer screens, but also mobile devices (handheld computers, portable phones), television devices (digital televisions, TV-based Web browsers), and appliances (with a fixed function). They all have their own requirements and constraints.

By dividing HTML into different modules, it becomes possible to specify for a given device which tag set it can deal with. These modules can be used as standard building blocks to support the device in question.

B.5.1.2   Document profiles

The syntax and semantics of documents are specified by a *document profile*. Interoperability is guaranteed by enforcing conformance to a document profile that describes such things as which data formats (e.g., for images) can be used, levels of scripting, and style sheet support (see central bottom part of Figure B.2). The document profile is expressed in RDF.

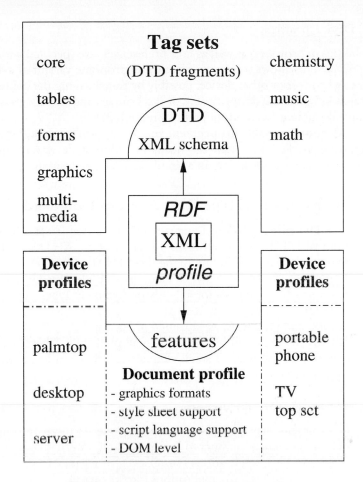

Figure B.2: XHTML tag sets and profiles

A DTD (or other schema system) specifies the syntax of documents that conform to a document profile in terms of which HTML modules are used, as well as
which additional modules for other XML tag sets are available (chemical formulae, mathematics, musical notation, and vector graphics; see also the upper part of
Figure B.2).

A document profile that defines the minimal support expected of user agents
consists of assertions written in RDF. It provides the basis for interoperability guarantees and can be used by servers to establish whether the server has a version of
a document suitable for delivery to a user agent with a given device profile. This
concept is explained in the next section.

B.5.1.3 Device profiles

The capabilities of browsers, as well as user preferences, are specified with the help of *device profiles*. This allows servers to select the appropriate variant of a document to deliver to a browser or other device, possibly by transforming the content, based on the match between the device profile of the browser and the document profile of the source document (see bottom part of Figure B.2).

The descriptions available in document and device profiles should greatly simplify optimizing markup to match the needs of different devices by tuning the markup to the given class of devices in a simple and reliable fashion.

B.5.2   The Extensible HyperText Markup Language

The Extensible HyperText Markup Language (XHTML; see [↪ HTMLINXML]) is a reformulation of HTML 4.0 as an XML 1.0 application. XHTML 1.0 specifies three XML namespaces, corresponding to the three HTML 4.0 DTDs: Strict, Transitional, and Frameset. Each of these three namespaces is identified by its own URI.

XHTML 1.0 provides the basis for a family of document types that will extend and subset XHTML. This will allow XHTML to support a wide range of new devices, applications, and platforms, as explained in Section B.5.1. It is clear that not all of the XHTML elements will be required on all platforms. Therefore XHTML will be broken up into modules of small element sets that can be recombined to meet the needs of different communities.

B.5.2.1   Writing XHTML documents

An XHTML document may be transmitted using one of three Internet Media Types. This allows document authors to create portable Internet content that can be served to generic XML applications (`text/xml`), to legacy HTML user agents (`text/html`), and to new XHTML applications (`text/xhtml`).

An example of a simple XHTML document follows:

```
1   <!DOCTYPE html PUBLIC "-//W3C//DTD XHTML 1.0 Strict//EN" "xhtml1-strict.dtd">
2   <html xmlns="http://www.w3.org/Profiles/xhtml1-strict.dtd">
3     <head>
4       <title>An XHTML document</title>
5     </head>
6     <body>
7       <p>The <a href="http://www.w3.org/">W3C Home Page</a>.</p>
8     </body>
9   </html>
```

Because XHTML is an XML application, certain practices that were perfectly legal in SGML-based HTML must be changed. A series of guidelines for delivering XHTML documents follow:

- *XHTML documents must be well-formed XML.* In practice this means that all elements must either have closing tags and that all the elements must nest correctly. When documents that are not well-formed are presented to an XML parser, a fatal error will occur, and the parser would usually stop processing at the first occurrence of such an error. This is rather unexpected to HTML users, since browsers usually ignore incorrect markup and continue processing.

- *Use the xmlns attribute to designate the document profile.* The xmlns attribute on the html element must be used to designate the document profile. When XHTML documents are delivered as text/html, the presence of the xmlns attribute implies that the contents of the html element are written in well-formed XML and *must* be processed according to the XML 1.0 specification.

- *Tag and attributes names must be entered in lowercase.* Names of element types and attributes are case-sensitive in XML (and hence XHTML). Since the XHTML DTDs define them in lowercase all tags and attributes should be entered in lowercase in the document instance.

- *Closing tags are always required.* All elements must have a closing tag. In particular, empty tags must end with />, for example
 (the space before the / is to allow the tag to be handled by current HTML browsers).

- *Attribute minimization is disallowed.* Attributes must be specified as name-value pairs, with the value between quotes. Thus a compact description list (dl) will have the form:

```
1    <dl compact="compact">
2      <dt>France</dt><dd>Paris</dd>
3      <dt>Spain</dt><dd>Madrid</dd>
4    </dl>
```

Note that XHTML strips leading and trailing whitespace in attribute values, and maps sequences of one or more whitespace characters (including line-breaks) to a single interword space.

- *Be careful with script and style elements.* In XHTML, the script and style elements are declared as having #PCDATA content, so that entities, such as < and &, will be expanded by the XML processor to < and &, respectively. If this is not desired, then you should wrap your script statements inside a CDATA marked section, that is,

```
1    <script>
2      <![CDATA[
3        ... unescaped script content ...
4      ]]>
5    </script>
```

B.5.2.2   XHTML namespaces

XML namespaces for three profiles are defined.

```
http://www.w3.org/Profiles/xhtml1-strict.dtd
```

For documents converted from HTML 4.0 strict and conforming to the XHTML xhtml1-strict DTD.

http://www.w3.org/Profiles/xhtml1-transitional.dtd

For documents converted from HTML 4.0 transitional (or loose), which includes a number of presentational elements and attributes. They must conform to the XHTML xhtml1-transitional DTD.

http://www.w3.org/Profiles/xhtml1-frameset.dtd

For documents converted from HTML 4.0 frameset and acting as frame sets. They must conform to the XHTML xhtml1-frameset DTD.

B.5.2.3 Converting existing content to XHTML

Dave Raggett's HTML Tidy [↪HTMLTIDY] program allows you to tidy up existing HTML source files and transform them to XHTML. Tidy is able to correct a wide range of HTML problems. It will signal things that it cannot handle by itself, so that you can take the necessary action yourself.

Tidy corrects the markup in a way that matches, where possible, the observed rendering in existing browsers, such as Netscape and Microsoft Internet Explorer. Following is a list of the main problems that Tidy can detect and handle:

- detects and corrects missing or mismatched closing tags;
- corrects incorrect nesting;
- adds missing "/" in closing tags;
- completes lists by putting in "missing" tags;
- includes quotes around attribute values, when needed;
- reports unknown and proprietary attributes and element types (with respect to the HTML 4.0 DTDs); and
- signals tags that lack a terminating ">".

B.5.2.4 Running Tidy

Tidy uses terminal input (stdin) and screen output (stdout) as default input/output streams, if no filename is specified. Errors are written to stderr by default. The general form of the command sequence is as follows:

tidy [[*options*] *filename*]*

Possible values for *options* are:

-indent or -i   indent element content;

-omit or -o   omit optional endtags;

-wrap 72   wrap text at column 72 (default is 68);

-upper or -u   force tags to uppercase;

-clean or -c	replace font, nobr, and center tags by CSS;
-raw	do not output entities for chars 128 to 255;
-ascii	use ASCII for output, Latin 1 for input;
-latin1	use Latin 1 for both input and output;
-utf8	use UTF-8 for both input and output;
-iso2022	use ISO2022 for both input and output;
-numeric or -n	output numeric rather than named entities;
-modify or -m	to modify original files;
-errors or -e	show only error messages;
-f *file*	write errors to *file*;
-xml	use this when input is in XML;
-asxml	to convert HTML to XML;
-slides	to burst into slides on h1 elements;
-help	list command line options.

For instance, the command line:

```
tidy -f errs.txt -m myfile.html
```

runs Tidy on the file index.html, updating it in place and writing error messages to the file errs.txt. Single-letter options apart from -f can be combined, for example,

```
tidy -f errs.txt -imu myfile.html
```

Let us take as an explicit example the HTML output we prepared on page 308. We reduce that file to a minimum number of tags, especially getting rid of all closing tags that are implied. The tidytest.html file we end up with is the following.

```
 1   <TITLE> Invitation (sgmlpl/CSS formatting) </TITLE>
 2   <LINK href="invit.css" rel="style sheet" type="text/css">
 3   <H1>INVITATION</H1>
 4   <P><TABLE>
 5   <TR><TD class="front">To:
 6   <TD>Anna, Bernard, Didier, Johanna
 7   <TR><TD class="front">When:
 8   <TD>Next Friday Evening at 8 pm
 9   <TR><TD class="front">Venue:
10   <TD>The Web Cafe
11   <TR><TD class="front">Occasion:
12   <TD>My first XML baby
13   </TABLE>
14   <P>I would like to invite you all to celebrate
15   the birth of <EM>Invitation</EM>, my
16   first XML document child.
17   <P>Please do your best to come and join me next Friday
18   evening. And, do not forget to bring your friends.
```

```
19    <P>I <EM>really</EM> look forward to see you soon!
20    <P CLASS="signature">Michel
```

We run Tidy on the `tidytest.html` file with the following instruction:

```
tidy -im tidytest.html
Parsing "tidytest.html"
line 4 column 3 - Warning: <TABLE> lacks "summary" attribute
line 4 column 3 - Warning: trimming empty <P>
```

We see that the <P> tag in line 4 of the HTML source file is redundant and that we should specify a `summary` attribute on the `table` tag. Let us look at the following generated XML output:

```
1     <?xml version="1.0"?>
2     <!DOCTYPE html PUBLIC "-//W3C//DTD HTML 4.0//EN">
3     <html>
4       <head>
5         <title>
6           Invitation (sgmlpl/CSS formatting)
7         </title>
8         <link href="invit.css" rel="style sheet" type="text/css" />
9       </head>
10      <body>
11        <h1>
12          INVITATION
13        </h1>
14        <table>
15          <tr>
16            <td class="front">
17              To:
18            </td>
19            <td>
20              Anna, Bernard, Didier, Johanna
21            </td>
22          </tr>
23          <tr>
24            <td class="front">
25              When:
26            </td>
27            <td>
28              Next Friday Evening at 8 pm
29            </td>
30          </tr>
31          <tr>
32            <td class="front">
33              Venue:
34            </td>
35            <td>
36              The Web Cafe
37            </td>
38          </tr>
39          <tr>
40            <td class="front">
41              Occasion:
42            </td>
43            <td>
44              My first XML baby
45            </td>
46          </tr>
```

```
47        </table>
48        <p>
49          I would like to invite you all to celebrate the birth of <em>
50          Invitation</em>, my first XML document child.
51        </p>
52        <p>
53          Please do your best to come and join me next Friday evening.
54          And, do not forget to bring your friends.
55        </p>
56        <p>
57          I <em>really</em> look forward to see you soon!
58        </p>
59        <p class="signature">
60          Michel
61        </p>
62      </body>
63    </html>
```

You see how all tags have become lowercase, closing tags have been output written for all elements, and html, head, and body elements have been introduced. Tidy is thus a very convenient tool for transforming HTML files into correct XML files that conform to the XHTML DTD.

B.6   Java event-based interface

With so many XML parsers available, it is no light task for application writers to support all corresponding Application Programmer's Interfaces (APIs). Therefore at the end of 1997, Peter Murray-Rust, the author of Jumbo, one of the first XML parsers written in Java [↪JUMBO], proposed on the XML-DEV XML developers list [↪XMLDEV] that parser writers should support a common Java event-based API. This idea was taken up by Tim Bray, one of the editors of the XML Specification and by David Megginson, the author of Ælfred (see Section 6.6.5.7) and the SGMLSpm system, described in Section 7.3. The design was a collaborative effort with a lot of contributors participating in the discussion on the XML-DEV list. It resulted in a single, standard, event-based API for XML parsers SAX ("A Simple API for XML," see [↪SAX]), which was released in May 1998. Implementations are currently available in Java and Python.

In the next section, we will first briefly review the classes present in the SAX Java distribution. Then we will use a few of these classes to reimplement the translation of a variant of our invitation example to get it translated into LaTeX.

B.6.1   The SAX Java classes

The SAX Java distribution of David Megginson [↪SAXJAVA] contains eleven core classes and interfaces together with three optional helper classes, although, as we shall see, a simple XML application needs only one or two of these.

The SAX classes and interfaces can be subdivided into four groups:

Interfaces for Parser Writers (`org.xml.sax package`)

`Parser` Main interface to a SAX parser. It registers handlers for callbacks, sets the language environment for error reporting, and starts parsing the XML document.

`AttributeList` Simple interface to iterate through an attribute list.

`Locator` Simple interface to locate the current point in the XML source document.

Interfaces for Application Writers (`org.xml.sax package`)

`DocumentHandler` Interface normally used to implement an application. It provides access to basic document-related events, such as the start and end of elements.

`ErrorHandler` Interface for implementation of special error handling.

`DTDHandler` Interface that handles notations and unparsed (binary) entities (`NOTATION` and `ENTITY` declarations in the DTD).

`EntityResolver` Interface providing customized handling for resolving external entities.

Standard SAX Classes (`org.xml.sax package`)

`InputSource` Class containing information for a single input source.

`SAXException` General SAX exception class.

`SAXParseException` SAX exception class tied to a specific point in an XML document.

`HandlerBase` Default implementations for `DTDHandler`, `ErrorHandler`, `DocumentHandler`, and `EntityResolver`. In our example we extend `Handlerbase` to implement a handler.

Java-Specific Helper Classes (`org.xml.sax.helpers package`)
Classes not part of the core SAX distribution but provided as a convenience for Java programmers.

`ParserFactory` The static methods in this class allow the application to load SAX parsers dynamically at runtime, based on the class name.

`AttributeListImpl` Makes a persistent copy of an `AttributeList` or supplies a default implementation of `AttributeList` to the application.

LocatorImpl Makes a persistent snapshot of the value of a Locator at any point during a document parse.

B.6.2   Running a SAX application

To run a SAX application, you need a parser with a SAX interface, as well as the SAX libraries themselves. For our examples we use components written by David Megginson, namely his Ælfred parser and his Java implementation of SAX.

To generate a LaTeX or HTML format of an XML document, we need to write an event handler to receive information from the parser. As explained in Section B.6.1, a convenient interface is DocumentHandler, which receives events for the start and end of elements, character data, and other basic XML structures. However, as we are not interested in implementing the entire interface, we can limit ourselves to the creation of a class that extends HandlerBase, where we define only the methods we need.

The list of methods available with the HandlerBase class follows:

characters(char[], int, int)   Receive notification of character data inside an element.

endDocument()   Receive notification of the end of the document.

endElement(String)   Receive notification of the end of an element.

error(SAXParseException)   Receive notification of a recoverable parser error.

fatalError(SAXParseException)   Report a fatal XML parsing error.

ignorableWhitespace(char[], int, int)   Receive notification of ignorable whitespace in element content.

notationDecl(String, String, String)   Receive notification of a notation declaration.

processingInstruction(String, String)   Receive notification of a processing instruction.

resolveEntity(String, String)   Resolve an external entity.

setDocumentLocator(Locator)   Receive a Locator object for document events.

startDocument()   Receive notification of the beginning of the document.

startElement(String, AttributeList)   Receive notification of the start of an element.

unparsedEntityDecl(String, String, String, String)   Receive notification of an unparsed entity declaration.

warning(SAXParseException)   Receive notification of a parser warning.

We also need the methods of the `AttributeList` interface:

`getLength()`   Return the number of attributes in this list.

`getName(int)`   Return the name of an attribute in this list (by position).

`getType(int)`, `getType(String)`   Return the type of an attribute in the list (by position or name).

`getValue(int)`, `getValue(String)`   Return the value of an attribute in the list (by position or name).

Now we are ready to write our Java class `InvitationSAX.java`, which extends the `HandlerBase` class and uses the `AttributeList` interface. We will develop an application for formatting the XML document `invitation2.xml` described in Section 7.4.5, which is, information-wise, equivalent to the `invitation.xml` document that we handled with the Perl interface in Section 7.3.

Following is the listing of `InvitationSAX.java`:

```
1   import org.xml.sax.HandlerBase;
2   import org.xml.sax.AttributeList;
3
4   public class InvitationSAX extends HandlerBase {
5
6     public void startElement (String Ename, AttributeList atts)
7     { if (Ename.equals("invitation"))
8        {System.out.print("\\documentclass[]{article}\n"
9                         + "\\usepackage{invitation}\n"
10                        + "\\begin{document}\n"
11                        + "\\begin{Front}\n");
12        for (int i = 0; i < atts.getLength(); i++) {
13          String Aname = atts.getName(i);
14          String type = atts.getType(i);
15          String value = atts.getValue(i);
16          if (Aname.equals("date"))
17            System.out.print("\\Date{" + value + "}\n");
18          else if (Aname.equals("signature"))
19            System.out.print("\\Signature{" + value + "}\n");
20          else if (Aname.equals("to"))
21            System.out.print("\\To{" + value + "}\n");
22          else if (Aname.equals("where"))
23            System.out.print("\\Where{" + value + "}\n");
24          else if (Aname.equals("why"))
25            System.out.print("\\Why{" + value + "}\n");
26          else System.out.print("INVALID ATTRIBUTE!!! " + value + "\n");
27        } // end attributes of invitation
28        System.out.println("\\end{Front}");
29        System.out.println("\\begin{Body}");
30        } // end element invitation
31      if (Ename.equals("par"))
32        System.out.print("\\par ");
33      if (Ename.equals("emph"))
34        System.out.print("\\emph{");
35    } // End of startElement
36
37    public void endElement (String Ename)
38    { if (Ename.equals("invitation"))
39        System.out.print("\\end{Body}\n"
40                        + "\\begin{Back}\n"
41                        + "\\end{Back}\n");
```

```
42                        + "\\end{document}\n");
43        if (Ename.equals("emph"))
44           System.out.print("}");
45   //   if (Ename.equals("par"))  ---> do nothing
46        } // End of endElement
47
48     public void characters(char ch[],int start,int length)
49     { for (int i=start; i<start+length; i++)
50         {System.out.print(ch[i]);}
51     } // End of characters
52
53     } // end of InvitationSAX
```

We see some of the methods of the `HandlerBase` class at work: `startElement`
(lines 6–35) for the beginning of elements, `endElement` (lines 37–47) for the end
of elements, and `characters` (lines 49–53) for handling character data. In the first
two methods we define an action that depends on the element being handled. In
particular, at the start of the `invitation` element, we initialize the LaTeX document
(lines 9–12). We write to standard output by using the method `System.out.print`
(lines 9, 18, 20, and so on), and its variant the `System.out.println` (lines 28
and 29) method. We loop over the various attributes and use the methods of the
`AttributeList` interface. The number of attributes is given by `getLength` (line
13), which controls the number of iterations of the `for` loop (lines 13–27). Inside
the loop `getName` (line 14) returns the name of the attribute, `getType` (line 15)
its type, and `getValue` (line 16) its value. Using the attribute name `if` statements
(lines 17–26) take care of setting LaTeX variables to their required value.

Similarly, the beginning of a `par` element generates a `\par` command (lines
31–32), and for the `emph` start tag a LaTeX `\emph` command is started (lines 33–34).

Regarding the end of the elements (lines 37–47), we do nothing for `par` (line 46
is a Java comment), and we close the curly brace for the `emph` end tag (lines 44–45).
When we reach `</invitation>`, we end the LaTeX document (lines 39–43).

The character data of the XML source document is transferred from the character array `ch`, the first argument of the `characters` method (line 49), to the output
stream by a loop (lines 31–32) whose range is given in the argument of the method.

Our only remaining task is to write a main driver class `MySAXApp.java` that
uses our handler `InvitationSAX`. This is shown following.

```
1    // MySAXApp.java -- Main driver class
2    //   --> calls InvitationSAX which has customized code
3    import org.xml.sax.Parser;
4    import org.xml.sax.DocumentHandler;
5    import org.xml.sax.helpers.ParserFactory;
6
7    public class MySAXApp {
8       static final String parserClass = "com.microstar.xml.SAXDriver";
9       public static void main (String args[])
10         throws Exception
11      { Parser parser = ParserFactory.makeParser(parserClass);
12        DocumentHandler handler = new InvitationSAX();
13        parser.setDocumentHandler(handler);
14        for (int i = 0; i < args.length; i++) {parser.parse(args[i]);}
15      }
16    }
```

Our application first creates a `Parser` object by supplying a class name to the `ParserFactory` (defined on line 8 and used on line 11). Then our handler class `InvitationSAX` is instantiated (line 12) and registered with the parser (line 13). Finally all XML documents that are specified as arguments on the command line are parsed (the `for` loop on lines 14). The current implementation requires that the documents are specified as absolute URLs.

We now are ready to compile our application and handler for the document `invitation2.xml` and run it (the example is on Windows/NT).

```
set classpath=.;d:\aelfred;d:\SAX;d:\jdk1.1.6\src
d:\javac InvitationSAX.java
d:\javac MySAXApp.java
d:\java MySAXApp file:d:/invitation2.xml > inv2.tex
```

The first line declares where the Java class libraries are located; the next two lines compile our two Java classes with the Java compiler `javac`. The last line runs the application `MySAXApp`, which loads the other classes automatically on the file `invitation2.xml` (given as an absolute URL) and writes the resulting LaTeX file `inv2.tex`. That file is shown here:

```
 1   \documentclass[]{article}
 2   \usepackage{invitation}
 3   \begin{document}
 4   \begin{Front}
 5   \To{Anna, Bernard, Didier, Johanna}
 6   \Date{Next Friday Evening at 8 pm}
 7   \Where{The Web Cafe}
 8   \Why{My first XML baby}
 9   \Signature{Michel}
10   \end{Front}
11   \begin{Body}
12   \par
13   I would like to invite you all to celebrate
14   the birth of \emph{Invitation}, my
15   first XML document child.
16   \par
17   Please do your best to come and join me next Friday
18   evening. And, do not forget to bring your friends.
19   \par
20   I \emph{really} look forward to see you soon!
21   \end{Body}
22   \begin{Back}
23   \end{Back}
24   \end{document}
```

The LaTeX code is a little different from the one on page 295. We, nevertheless, can use (line 3) the same package `invitation.sty` as defined on page 296, since it is written in such a way that high-level commands guide the formatting process. Hence, different LaTeX source files will produce identical results after typesetting (see Figure 7.1). This shows once more the advantage of writing high-level LaTeX code on the application level and handling low-level typesetting or rendering commands in a style sheet.

Internationalization issues

C.1 Codes for languages, countries, and scripts

Table C.1 shows codes for the representation of names of languages as defined in ISO Standard 639. The first column is the current three-letter code (ISO:639-2, 1998). The second column contains, where it is available, the older two-letter code (ISO:639, 1988). The third column contains the name of the language (or its variant). Although the two-letter code can only cope with the most common languages it is still used in many computer applications; in particular HTML and XML usually use only two-letter codes to identify languages.

Table C.2 shows codes for the representation of names of countries as defined in ISO Standard 3166 (ISO:3166, 1997). The first column is the two-letter code that is used in HTML/XML for specifying the country; the second column provides a more mnemonic three-letter extension. The third column specifies the country name.

Table C.3 shows codes for the representation of names of scripts as proposed in the draft for ISO Standard 15924 (ISO:15924, 1999). The first column is the two-letter code, and the second column provides a more mnemonic three-letter extension. The third column specifies the name of the script.

Table C.4 gives an overview of the various ISO 8859 coding standards (see ISO/IEC:8839-1 (1998) and following). In particular, Latin 9 (ISO/IEC:8859-15), which was approved recently, is essentially equal to the Latin 1 layout for Western European languages. However, in Latin 9, there are a few less-used characters replaced by œ, Œ, and ÿ (for French), š, Š, ž, and Ž (for Finnish), and € (the Euro currency symbol). Of course, all these ISO/IEC 8859 tables should ideally be replaced by Unicode as soon as possible (see Section C.2).

Table C.1: Language codes and names (ISO 639)

aar	aa	Afar	abk	ab	Abkhazian
ace		Achinese	ach		Acoli
ada		Adangme	afa		Afro-Asiatic (other)
afh		Afrihili	afr	af	Afrikaans
ajm		Aljamia	aka		Akan
akk		Akkadian	ale		Aleut
alg		Algonquian languages	amh	am	Amharic
ang		English, Old (ca. 450–1100)	apa		Apache languages
ara	ar	Arabic	arc		Aramaic
arn		Araucanian	arp		Arapaho
art		Artificial (other)	arw		Arawak
asm	as	Assamese	ath		Athapascan languages
aus		Australian languages	ava		Avaric
ave		Avestan	awa		Awadhi
aym	ay	Aymara	aze	az	Azerbaijani
bad		Banda	bai		Bamileke languages
bak	ba	Bashkir	bal		Baluchi
bam		Bambara	ban		Balinese
bas		Basa	bat		Baltic (other)
bej		Beja	bel	be	Belarussian
bem		Bemba	ben	bn	Bengali
ber		Berber (other)	bho		Bhojpuri
bih	bh	Bihari	bik		Bikol
bin		Bini	bis	bi	Bislama
bla		Siksika	bnt		Bantu (other)
bod	bo	Tibetan	bra		Braj
bre	br	Breton	btk		Batak (Indonesia)
bua		Buriat	bug		Buginese
bul	bg	Bulgarian	cad		Caddo
cai		Central American Indian (other)	car		Carib
cat	ca	Catalan	cau		Caucasian (other)
ceb		Cebuano	cel		Celtic (other)
ces	cs	Czech	cha		Chamorro
chb		Chibcha	che		Chechen
chg		Chagatai	chk		Chuukese
chm		Mari	chn		Chinook jargon
cho		Choctaw	chp		Chipewyan
chr		Cherokee	chu		Church Slavic
chv		Chuvash	chy		Cheyenne
cmc		Chamic languages	cop		Coptic
cor	kw	Cornish	cos	co	Corsican

Language codes and names (*cont.*)

cpe	Creoles and pidgins, English-based (other)	cpf	Creoles and pidgins, French-based (other)
cpp	Creoles and pidgins, Portuguese-based (other)	cre	Cree
crp	Creoles and pidgins (other)	cus	Cushitic (other)
cym cy	Welsh	dak	Dakota
dan da	Danish	day	Dayak
del	Delaware	den	Slave (Athapascan)
deu de	German	dgr	Dogrib
din	Dinka	div	Divehi
doi	Dogri	dra	Dravidian (other)
dua	Duala	dum	Dutch, Middle (ca. 1050–1350)
dyu	Dyula	dzo dz	Dzongkha
efi	Efik	egy	Egyptian (Ancient)
eka	Ekajuk	ell el	Greek, Modern (post-1453)
elx	Elamite	eng en	English
enm	English, Middle (1100–1500)	epo eo	Esperanto
est et	Estonian	eth	Ethiopic
eus eu	Basque	ewe	Ewe
ewo	Ewondo	fan	Fang
fao fo	Faroese	fas fa	Persian
fat	Fanti	fij fj	Fijian
fin fi	Finnish	fiu	Finno-Ugrian (other)
fon	Fon	fra fr	French
frm	French, Middle (ca. 1400–1600)	fro	French, Old (ca. 842–1400)
fry fy	Frisian	ful	Fulah
fur	Friulian	gaa	Ga
gai ga	Irish	gay	Gayo
gba	Gbaya	gdh gd	Gaelic (Scots)
gem	Germanic (other)	gez	Geez
gil	Gilbertese	glg gl	Gallegan
gmh	German, Middle High (ca. 1050–1500)	goh	German, Old High (ca. 750–1050)
gon	Gondi	gor	Gorontalo
got	Gothic	grb	Grebo
grc	Greek, Ancient (to 1453)	grn gn	Guarani
guj gu	Gujarati	gwi	Gwich'in
hai	Haida	hau ha	Hausa
haw	Hawaiian	heb he/iw	Hebrew
her	Herero	hil	Hiligaynon
him	Himachali	hin hi	Hindi
hit	Hittite	hmn	Hmong
hmo	Hiri Motu	hrv hr	Croatian
hun hu	Hungarian	hup	Hupa

Language codes and names (*cont.*)

hye	hy	Armenian	iba		Iban
ibo		Igbo	ijo		Ijo
iku	iu	Inuktitut	ile	ie	Interlingue
ilo		Iloko	ina	ia	Interlingua (International Auxiliary Language Association)
inc		Indic (other)	ind	id/in	Indonesian
ine		Indo-European (other)	ipk	ik	Inupiak
ira		Iranian (other)	iro		Iroquoian languages
isl	is	Icelandic	ita	it	Italian
jaw	jw	Javanese	jpn	ja	Japanese
jpr		Judeo-Persian	jrb		Judeo-Arabic
kaa		Kara-Kalpak	kab		Kabyle
kac		Kachin	kal	kl	Kalaallisut
kam		Kamba	kan	kn	Kannada
kar		Karen	kas	ks	Kashmiri
kat	ka	Georgian	kau		Kanuri
kaw		Kawi	kaz	kk	Kazakh
kha		Khasi	khi		Khoisan (other)
khm	km	Khmer	kho		Khotanese
kik		Kikuyu	kin	rw	Kinyarwanda
kir	ky	Kirghiz	kmb		Kimbundu
kok		Konkani	kom		Komi
kon		Kongo	kor	ko	Korean
kos		Kosraean	kpe		Kpelle
kro		Kru	kru		Kurukh
kua		Kuanyama	kum		Kumyk
kur	ku	Kurdish	kut		Kutenai
lad		Ladino	lah		Lahnda
lam		Lamba	lao	lo	Lao
lat	la	Latin	lav	lv	Latvian
lez		Lezghian	lin	ln	Lingala
lit	lt	Lithuanian	lol		Mongo
loz		Lozi	ltz	lb	Lëtzeburgesch
lua		Luba-Lulua	lub		Luba-Katanga
lug		Ganda	lui		Luiseno
lun		Lunda	luo		Luo (Kenya and Tanzania)
lus		Lushai	mad		Madurese
mag		Magahi	mah		Marshall
mai		Maithili	mak		Makasar
mal	ml	Malayalam	man		Mandingo
map		Austronesian (other)	mar	mr	Marathi
mas		Masai	max		Manx
mdr		Mandar	men		Mende
mga		Irish, Middle (900–1200)	mic		Micmac
min		Minangkabau	mis		Miscellaneous languages
mkd	mk	Macedonian	mkh		Mon-Khmer (other)

Language codes and names (*cont.*)

mlg	mg	Malagasy	mlt	mt	Maltese
mni		Manipuri	mno		Manobo languages
moh		Mohawk	mol	mo	Moldavian
mon	mn	Mongolian	mos		Mossi
mri	mi	Maori	msa	ms	Malay
mul		Multiple languages	mun		Munda languages
mus		Creek	mwr		Marwari
mya	my	Burmese	myn		Mayan languages
nah		Aztec	nai		North American Indian (other)
nau	na	Nauru	nav		Navajo
nbl		Ndebele, South	nde		Ndebele, North
ndo		Ndonga	nep	ne	Nepali
new		Newari	nia		Nias
nic		Niger-Kordofanian (other)	niu		Niuean
nld	nl	Dutch	non		Norse, Old
nor	no	Norwegian	nso		Sohto, Northern
nub		Nubian languages	nya		Nyanja
nym		Nyamwezi	nyn		Nyankole
nyo		Nyoro	nzi		Nzima
oci	oc	Occitan (post-1500)	oji		Ojibwa
ori		Oriya	orm	om	Oromo
osa		Osage	oss		Ossetic
ota		Turkish, Ottoman (1500–1928)	oto		Otomian languages
paa		Papuan (other)	pag		Pangasinan
pal		Palilavi	pam		Pampanga
pan	pa	Panjabi	pap		Papiamento
pau		Palauan	peo		Persian, Old (ca. 600–400 B.C.)
phi		Philippine (other)	phn		Phoenician
pli		Pali	pol	pl	Polish
pon		Polimpeian	por	pt	Portuguese
pra		Prakrit languages	pro		Provençal, Old (to 1500)
pus	ps	Pushto	que	qu	Quechua
raj		Rajasthani	rap		Rapanui
rar		Rarotongan	roa		Romance (other)
roh	rm	Rhaeto-Romance	rom		Romany
ron	ro	Romanian	run	rn	Rundi
rus	ru	Russian	sad		Sandawe
sag	sg	Sango	sai		South American Indian (other)
sal		Salishan languages	sam		Samaritan Aramaic
san	sa	Sanskrit	sas		Sasak
sat		Santali	sco		Scots
sel		Selkup	sem		Semitic (other)
sga		Irish, Old (to 900)	shn		Shan
sid		Sidamo	sin	si	Sinhalese
sio		Siouan languages	sit		Sino-Tibetan (other)

Language codes and names (*cont.*)

sla		Slavic (other)	slk	sk	Slovak
slv	sl	Slovenian	smi	se	Sámi languages
smo	sm	Samoan	sna	sn	Shona
snd	sd	Sindhi	snk		Soninke
sog		Sogdian	som	so	Somali
son		Songhai	sot	st	Sotho, Southern
spa	es	Spanish	sqi	sq	Albanian
srd		Sardinian	srp	sr	Serbian
srr		Serer	ssa		Nilo-Saharan (other)
ssw	ss	Swati	suk		Sukuma
sun	su	Sundanese	sus		Susu
sux		Sumerian	swa	sw	Swahili
swe	sv	Swedish	syr		Syriac
tah		Tahitian	tai		Tai (other)
tam	ta	Tamil	tat	tt	Tatar
tel	te	Telugu	tem		Timne
ter		Tereno	tet		Tetum
tgk	tg	Tajik	tgl	tl	Tagalog
tha	th	Thai	tig		Tigre
tir		Tigrinya	tiv		Tiv
tkl		Tokelau	tli		Tlingit
tmh		Tamashek	tog		Tonga (Nyasa)
ton		Tonga (Tonga Islands)	tpi		Tok Pisin
tsi		Tsimshian	tsn	ts	Tswana
tso		Tsonga	tuk	tk	Türkmen
tum		Tumbuka	tur		Turkish
tut		Altaic (other)	tvl		Tuvalu
twi	tw	Twi	tyv		Tuvinian
uga		Ugaritic	uig	ug	Uighur
ukr	uk	Ukrainian	umb		Umbundu
und		Undetermined	urd	ur	Urdu
uzb	uz	Uzbek	vai		Vai
ven		Venda	vie	vi	Vietnamese
vol	vo	Volapük	vot		Votic
wak		Wakashan languages	wal		Walamo
war		Waray	was		Washo
wen		Sorbian languages	wol	wo	Wolof
xho	xh	Xhosa	yao		Yao
yap		Yapese	yid	yi/ji	Yiddish
yor		Yoruba	ypk		Yupik languages
zap		Zapotec	zen		Zenaga
zha	za	Zhuang	zho	zh	Chinese
znd		Zande	zul	zu	Zulu
zun		Zuñi			

Table C.2: Country codes and names (ISO 3166)

AF	AFG	Afghanistan	AL	ALB	Albania
DZ	DZA	Algeria	AS	ASM	American Samoa
AD	AND	Andorra	AO	AGO	Angola
AI	AIA	Anguilla	AQ	ATA	Antarctica
AG	ATG	Antigua and Barbuda	AR	ARG	Argentina
AM	ARM	Armenia	AW	ABW	Aruba
AU	AUS	Australia	AT	AUT	Austria
AZ	AZE	Azerbaijan	BS	BHS	Bahamas
BH	BHR	Bahrain	BD	BGD	Bangladesh
BB	BRB	Barbados	BY	BLR	Belarus
BE	BEL	Belgium	BZ	BLZ	Belize
BJ	BEN	Benin	BM	BMU	Bermuda
BT	BTN	Bhutan	BO	BOL	Bolivia
BA	BIH	Bosnia and Herzegovina	BW	BWA	Botswana
BV	BVT	Bouvet Island	BR	BRA	Brazil
IO	IOT	British Indian Ocean Territory	BN	BRN	Brunei Darussalam
BG	BGR	Bulgaria	BF	BFA	Burkina Faso
BI	BDI	Burundi	KH	KHM	Cambodia
CM	CMR	Cameroon	CA	CAN	Canada
CV	CPV	Cape Verde	KY	CYM	Cayman Islands
CF	CAF	Central African Republic	TD	TCD	Chad
CL	CHL	Chile	CN	CHN	China
CX	CXR	Christmas Island	CC	CCK	Cocos (Keeling) Islands
CO	COL	Colombia	KM	COM	Comoros
CG	COG	Congo	CD	COD	Congo, Democratic Republic
CK	COK	Cook Islands	CR	CRI	Costa Rica
CI	CIV	Côte d'Ivoire	HR	HRV	Croatia
CU	CUB	Cuba	CY	CYP	Cyprus
CZ	CZE	Czech Republic	DK	DNK	Denmark
DJ	DJI	Djibouti	DM	DMA	Dominica
DO	DOM	Dominican Republic	TP	TMP	East Timor (provisional)
EC	ECU	Ecuador	EG	EGY	Egypt
SV	SLV	El Salvador	GQ	GNQ	Equatorial Guinea
ER	ERI	Eritrea	EE	EST	Estonia
ET	ETH	Ethiopia	FK	FLK	Falkland Islands (Malvinas)
FO	FRO	Faroe Islands	FJ	FJI	Fiji
FI	FIN	Finland	FR	FRA	France
FX	FXX	France, Metropolitan	GF	GUF	French Guiana
PF	PYF	French Polynesia	TF	ATF	French Southern Territories
GA	GAB	Gabon	GM	GMB	Gambia
GE	GEO	Georgia	DE	DEU	Germany
GH	GHA	Ghana	GI	GIB	Gibraltar
GR	GRC	Greece	GL	GRL	Greenland
GD	GRD	Grenada	GP	GLP	Guadaloupe
GU	GUM	Guam	GT	GTM	Guatemala

Country codes and names (*cont.*)

GN	GIN	Guinea	GW	GNB	Guinea-Bissau
GY	GUY	Guyana	HT	HTI	Haiti
HM	HMD	Heard Island and McDonald Islands	HN	HND	Honduras
HK	HKG	Hong Kong	HU	HUN	Hungary
IS	ISL	Iceland	IN	IND	India
ID	IDN	Indonesia	IR	IRN	Iran
IQ	IRQ	Iraq	IE	IRL	Ireland
IL	ISR	Israel	IT	ITA	Italy
JM	JAM	Jamaica	JP	JPN	Japan
JO	JOR	Jordan	KZ	KAZ	Kazakhstan
KE	KEN	Kenya	KI	KIR	Kiribati
KP	PRK	Korea, North	KR	KOR	Korea, South
KW	KWT	Kuwait	KG	KGZ	Kyrgyzstan
LA	LAO	Laos	LV	LVA	Latvia
LB	LBN	Lebanon	LS	LSO	Lesotho
LR	LBR	Liberia	LY	LBY	Libya
LI	LIE	Liechtenstein	LT	LTU	Lithuania
LU	LUX	Luxembourg	MO	MAC	Macau
MK	MKD	Macedonia	MG	MDG	Madagascar
MW	MWI	Malawi	MY	MYS	Malaysia
MV	MDV	Maldives	ML	MLI	Mali
MT	MLT	Malta	MH	MHL	Marshall Islands
MQ	MTQ	Martinique	MR	MRT	Mauritania
MU	MUS	Mauritius	YT	MYT	Mayotte
MX	MEX	Mexico	FM	FSM	Micronesia
MD	MDA	Moldova	MC	MCO	Monaco
MN	MNG	Mongolia	MS	MSR	Montserrat
MA	MAR	Morocco	MZ	MOZ	Mozambique
MM	MMR	Myanmar	NA	NAM	Namibia
NR	NRU	Nauru	NP	NPL	Nepal
NL	NLD	Netherlands	AN	ANT	Netherlands Antilles
NC	NCL	New Caledonia	NZ	NZL	New Zealand
NI	NIC	Nicaragua	NE	NER	Niger
NG	NGA	Nigeria	NU	NIU	Niue
NF	NFK	Norfolk Island	MP	MNP	Northern Mariana Islands
NO	NOR	Norway	OM	OMN	Oman
PK	PAK	Pakistan	PW	PLW	Palau
PA	PAN	Panama	PG	PNG	Papua New Guinea
PY	PRY	Paraguay	PE	PER	Peru
PH	PHL	Philippines	PN	PCN	Pitcairn
PL	POL	Poland	PT	PRT	Portugal
PR	PRI	Puerto Rico	QA	QAT	Qatar
RE	REU	Réunion	RO	ROM	Romania
RU	RUS	Russian Federation	RW	RWA	Rwanda
SH	SHN	Saint Helena	KN	KNA	Saint Kitts and Nevis

Country codes and names (*cont.*)

LC	LCA	Saint Lucia	PM	SPM	Saint Pierre and Miquelon
VC	VCT	Saint Vincent and the Grenadines	WS	WSM	Samoa
SM	SMR	San Marino	ST	STP	São Tomé and Príncipe
SA	SAU	Saudi Arabia	SN	SEN	Senegal
SC	SYC	Seychelles	SL	SLE	Sierra Leone
SG	SGP	Singapore	SK	SVK	Slovakia
SI	SVN	Slovenia	SB	SLB	Solomon Islands
SO	SOM	Somalia	ZA	ZAF	South Africa
GS	SGS	South Georgia and the South Sandwich Islands	ES	ESP	Spain
LK	LKA	Sri Lanka	SD	SDN	Sudan
SR	SUR	Suriname	SJ	SJM	Svalbard and Jan Mayen
SZ	SWZ	Swaziland	SE	SWE	Sweden
CH	CHE	Switzerland	SY	SYR	Syria
TW	TWN	Taiwan	TJ	TJK	Tajikistan
TZ	TZA	Tanzania	TH	THA	Thailand
TG	TGO	Togo	TK	TKL	Tokelau
TO	TON	Tonga	TT	TTO	Trinidad and Tobago
TN	TUN	Tunisia	TR	TUR	Turkey
TM	TKM	Turkmenistan	TC	TCA	Turks and Caicos Islands
TV	TUV	Tuvalu	UG	UGA	Uganda
UA	UKR	Ukraine	AE	ARE	United Arab Emirates
GB	GBR	United Kingdom	US	USA	United States
UM	UMI	United States Minor Outlying Islands	UY	URY	Uruguay
UZ	UZB	Uzbekistan	VU	VUT	Vanuatu
VA	VAT	Vatican City State (Holy See)	VE	VEN	Venezuela
VN	VNM	Vietnam	VG	VGB	Virgin Islands, British
VI	VIR	Virgin Islands, U.S.	WF	WLF	Wallis and Fortuna Islands
EH	ESH	Western Sahara (provisional)	YE	YEM	Yemen
YU	YUG	Yugoslavia	ZM	ZMB	Zambia
ZW	ZWE	Zimbabwe			

Table C.3: Script codes and names (ISO 15924)

Am	Ama	Aramaic ②	Ar	Ara	Arabic ②
Av	Ave	Avestan ②	Bn	Ben	Bengali ④
Bh	Bhm	Brahmi (Ashoka) ④	Bi	Bid	Buhid ④
Bo	Bod	Tibetan ④	Bp	Bpm	Bopomofo ③
Br	Brl	Braille ⑥	Bt	Btk	Batak ④
Bu	Bug	Buginese (Makassar) ④	By	Bys	Blissymbols ⑥
Ca	Cam	Cham ④	Ch	Chu	Old Church Slavonic ③
Ci	Cir	Cirth ③	Cm	Cmn	Cypro Minoan ⑤

① Hieroglyphic and cuneiform, ② Right-to-left alphabetic, ③ Left-to-right alphabetic,
④ Brahmi-derived, ⑤ Syllabic, ⑥ Ideographic, ⑦ Undeciphered.

Script codes and names (*cont.*)

Co	Cop	Coptic ③	Cp	Cpr	Cypriote syllabary ⑤
Cy	Cyr	Cyrillic ③	Ds	Dsr	Deseret (Mormon) ③
Dv	Dvn	Devanagari (Nagari) ④	Ed	Egd	Egyptian demotic ①
Eh	Egh	Egyptian hieratic ①	Eg	Egy	Egyptian hieroglyphs ①
El	Ell	Greek ③	Eo	Eos	Etruscan and Oscan ③
Et	Eth	Ethiopic ⑤	Gl	Glg	Glagolitic ③
Gm	Gmu	Gurmukhi ④	Gt	Gth	Gothic ③
Gu	Guj	Gujarati ④	Ha	Han	Han ideographs ⑥
He	Heb	Hebrew ②	Hg	Hgl	Hangul ⑤
Hm	Hmo	Pahawh Hmong ⑤	Ho	Hoo	Hanunóo ④
Hr	Hrg	Hiragana ⑤	Hu	Hun	Old Hungarian runic ②
Hv	Hvn	Kök Turki runic ②	Hy	Hye	Armenian ③
Iv	Ivl	Indus Valley ⑦	Ja	Jap	Han + Hiragana + Katakana
Jl	Jlg	Cherokee syllabary ⑤	Jw	Jwi	Javanese ④
Ka	Kam	Georgian (Mxedruli) ③	Kn	Kan	Kannada ④
Kx	Kax	Georgian (Xucuri) ③	Km	Khm	Khmer ④
Kh	Khn	Hangul + Han	Kk	Kkn	Katakana ⑤
Kr	Krn	Karenni (Kayah Li) ④	Ks	Kst	Kharoshthi ④
Lf	Laf	Latin (Fraktur variant) ③	Lg	Lag	Latin (Gaelic variant) ③
Lo	Lao	Lao ④	La	Lat	Latin ③
Lp	Lpc	Lepcha (Róng) ④	Mh	May	Mayan hieroglyphs ①
Md	Mda	Mandaean ②	Me	Mer	Meroitic ②
Ml	Mlm	Malayalam ④	Mn	Mon	Mongolian ②
My	Mya	Burmese ④	Na	Naa	Linear A ⑤
Nb	Nbb	Linear B ⑤	Og	Ogm	Ogham ③
Or	Ory	Oriya ④	Os	Osm	Osmanya ③
Ph	Pah	Pahlavi ②	Ph	Phx	Phoenician ②
Pl	Pld	Pollard Phonetic ③	Pq	Pqd	Klingon pIQaD ③
Pr	Prm	Old Permic ③	Ps	Pst	Phaistos Disk ⑦
Rn	Rnr	Runic (Germanic) ③	Rr	Rro	Rongo ⑦
Sa	Sar	South Arabian ②	Si	Sin	Sinhala ④
Sl	Slb	Canadian Aboriginal Syllabics ⑤	Sw	Sww	Shavian (Shaw) ③
Sj	Syj	Syriac (Jacobite variant) ②	Sn	Syn	Syriac (Nestorian variant) ②
Sy	Syr	Syriac (Estrangelo) ②	Tg	Tag	Tagalog ④
Ta	Tam	Tamil ④	Tb	Tbw	Tagbanwa ④
Te	Tel	Telugu ④	Tf	Tfn	Tifinagh ②
Th	Tha	Thai ④	Tn	Tna	Thaana ②
Tw	Twr	Tengwar ③	Va	Vai	Vai ⑤
Vs	Vsp	Visible Speech ③	Xa	Xas	Cuneiform, Sumero Akkadian ①
Xf	Xfa	Cuneiform, Old Persian ②	Xk	Xkn	Hiragana + Katakana ⑤
Xu	Xug	Cuneiform, Ugaritic ②	Yi	Yii	Yi ⑤
Zx	Zxx	Code for unwritten languages	Zy	Zyy	Code for undetermined
Zz	Zzz	Code for uncoded			

① Hieroglyphic and cuneiform, ② Right-to-left alphabetic, ③ Left-to-right alphabetic, ④ Brahmi-derived, ⑤ Syllabic, ⑥ Ideographic, ⑦ Undeciphered.

Table C.4: The ISO/IEC 8859 standards and the language families covered

8859-1	Western Europe, Latin America (Latin 1)
8859-2	Eastern European languages (Latin 2)
8859-3	Other Latin script languages (Latin 3)
8859-4	North European languages (Latin 4)
8859-5	Latin/Cyrillic
8859-6	Latin/Arabic
8859-7	Latin/Greek
8859-8	Latin/Hebrew
8859-9	Variant of Latin 1 for Turkey (Latin 5)
8859-10	Lappish/Nordic/Eskimo languages (Latin 6)
8859-11	Latin/Thai
8859-12	(unassigned)
8859-13	Baltic Rim (Latin 7)
8859-14	Celtic (Latin 8)
8859-15	Variant of Latin 1 for French, Finnish, and Euro symbol (Latin 9)

C.2   The Unicode standard

The Unicode standard (Unicode Consortium (1996)) is a universal character encoding standard used for representing multilingual texts on electronic media. It is supposed to make the international exchange of computer text files more straightforward. It not only contains most commonly used text characters of all major languages of the world but encodes various technical and mathematical symbols so that scientists and engineers might also gainfully adopt this standard.

Unicode was developed mainly by industry and is supported by all major computer manufacturers. It is fully compatible with ISO/IEC standard 10646-1 (ISO/IEC:10646-1:1993, 1993). Presently, working closely with academic and research groups, the Unicode Consortium, which oversees the coordination of the Unicode standard [↪ UNICODE], is busy filling the remaining slots of the approximately 65,000 positions with an agreed set of mathematical symbols and technical characters.

Unicode is basically a 16-bit extension of the 7-bit ASCII standard and the 8-bit Latin 1 (see Table C.4) character code. However, even when 65,000 characters seem sufficient for encoding thousands of commonly used characters of all major world languages, more codepoints are needed for some applications. Therefore Unicode provides an extension mechanism, UTF-16, that maps onto further 16-bit planes of ISO/IEC 10646-1, allowing for the encoding of about 1,000,000 characters. This is more than sufficient to deal with all characters known to mankind, including all historic scripts of the world.

Figure C.1 shows the layout of the Unicode plane: 256 rows numbered 00 to FF in hexadecimal of 256 characters. This row number, shown at the left-hand side of the figure, corresponds to the most significant byte of the 16-bit character code. By

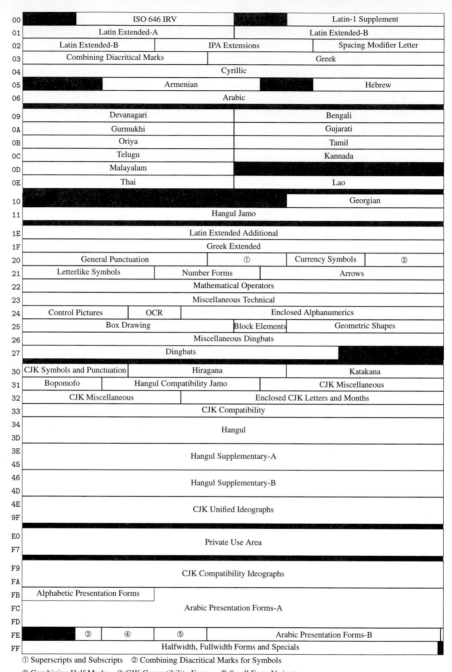

Figure C.1: Character layout of Unicode (ISO/IEC 10646 BMP)

construction Unicode is identical to the base plane of the 32-bit ISO/IEC 10646-1 standard. The figure shows a few of the scripts covered by Unicode, namely Latin, Greek, Cyrillic, Armenian, Hebrew, Arabic, Devanagari, Bengali, Gurmukhi, Gujarati, Oriya, Tamil, Telugu, Kannada, Malayalam, Thai, Lao, Georgian, Tibetan, Japanese Kana, the complete set of modern Korean Hangul, and a unified set of Chinese/Japanese/Korean (CJK) ideographs. More scripts and characters, such as Ethiopic, Canadian Syllabics, Cherokee, Sinhala, Syriac, Burmese, Khmer, and Braille are in the process of being added.

The central part (rows 20–27) of Figure C.1 shows that Unicode also includes punctuation marks, currency symbols, diacritics, mathematical symbols, technical symbols, arrows, dingbats, and so on.

Rows 4E–9F contain ideographs for East-Asian languages. To avoid duplicate encoding, characters were *unified* within scripts across languages. This means that equivalent characters in form were mapped to a single code. In particular, Chinese/Japanese/Korean (CJK) consolidation is achieved by assigning a single code for each ideograph that is common to more than one of these languages. This set of characters is known under the name "Unified Han." This unification of the character codes does not mean, however, that the characters in question cannot be rendered by appropiate customized fonts to make them appear "natural" to native readers.

C.2.1   Character codes and glyphs

It is important to realize that Unicode encodes only the code ("semantic meaning") of a character, not its rendering on an output medium (paper, screen, audio). For instance, "LATIN CAPITAL LETTER A" (codepoint U-0041), "GREEK CAPITAL LETTER ALPHA" (U-0391), and "CYRILLIC CAPITAL LETTER A" (U-0410) have a different semantic meaning, although they have the same visual representation, the *glyph* "A."

Unicode defines only how characters are interpreted, not how glyphs are rendered as images. Unicode has nothing to say about size, weight, shape, writing direction, and so on of characters on the output screen. That is the responsibility of the glyph-rendering software in the viewer or printing engine.

C.2.2   Unicode and ISO/IEC 10646-1

Unicode is closely aligned with the international standard ISO/IEC 10646-1, also known as UCS (*Universal Character Set*). In fact, by construction, Unicode is identical to ISO/IEC 10646-1 and its amendments.

The ISO/IEC 10646-1 standard, however, has a much greater application area, since it is basically a 32-bit code; thus it can encode over two billion characters. The canonical form of ISO/IEC 10646-1 uses a four-dimensional coding space consisting of 256 three-dimensional *groups*. Each group consists of 256 two-dimensional *planes*

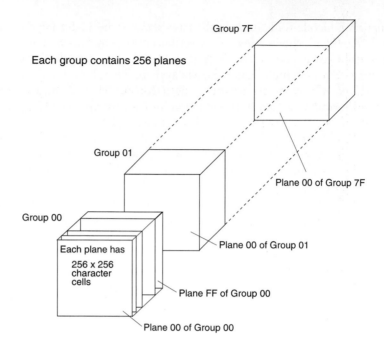

Figure C.2: Entire 4-octet coding space of ISO/IEC 10646-1

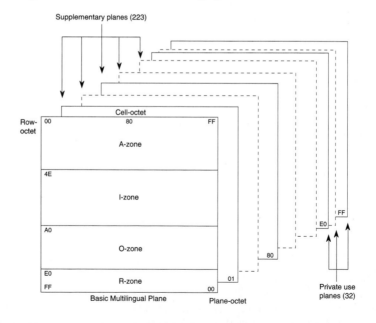

Figure C.3: Structure of Group 00 of ISO/IEC 10646-1

with each plane containing 256 one-dimensional *rows*, each having 256 *cells* (see Figure C.2). Thus character codes consist of up to four octets, which, ordered from least to most significant, correspond to the cell (C-octet), row (R-octet), plane (P-octet), and group (G-octet) numbers.

The first plane (Plane 00) of Group 00 is called the *Basic Multilingual Plane* (BMP). It is, by construction, identical to the Unicode layout.

The subsequent 223 planes (01 to DF) of Group 00 (see Figure C.3), as well as planes 00 to FF in Groups 01 to 5F are reserved for further standardization (for instance to cope with rarely used Han characters, old historic scripts). The last 32 planes (E0 to FF) of Group 00, as well as all code positions of 32 groups (60 to 7F) are reserved for private use, and are not specified in ISO/IEC 10646-1.

C.2.3   UTF-8 and UTF-16 encodings

The ISO/IEC 10646-1 standard defines two transformation formats UTF-8 and UTF-16, which were also adopted by Unicode (Appendix A of Unicode Consortium (1996)). The UTF-16 transformation assumes 16-bit characters, just like Unicode itself, but it allows for a certain range of characters to be used as an extension mechanism to access an additional million characters using 16-bit character pairs.

Perhaps more useful in the near future is the UTF-8 transformation format that transforms all Unicode characters into a *variable length* encoding of up to four bytes. The first 128 characters (the ASCII subset) have the same bit sequences in UTF-8 and in ASCII, making it easy to handle documents using only that subset. This means that a lot of existing software can be used with Unicode (and UTF-8) without a major software rewrite.

UTF-8 can be described as a method to transform Unicode or ISO 10646-1 streams into 8-bit streams, leaving ASCII as it is and expanding the other characters to up to six bytes. In fact, three bytes suffice for the 16-bit Unicode range; four bytes are enough for encoding about a million characters. The latter approach is similar to UTF-16 that reserves 2048 codepoints in Unicode (D000-DFFF) to index one million additional characters. These one million codepoints should be enough for all the rare Chinese ideograms and historical scripts that do not fit into the Basic Multilingual Plane of ISO 10646.

Following we show how the 31 bits of the ISO 10646 code are distributed over up to six UTF-8 bytes. It must be stressed that for Unicode, never more than three bytes are needed.

```
ISO 10646 range covered          UTF-8 representation
-----------------------          --------------------
Bits  Hex Min   Hex Max          Byte Sequence in Binary
   7  00000000  0000007F         0vvvvvvv
  11  00000080  000007FF         110vvvvv 10vvvvvv
  16  00000800  0000FFFF         1110vvvv 10vvvvvv 10vvvvvv

  21  00010000  001FFFFF         11110vvv 10vvvvvv 10vvvvvv 10vvvvvv
  26  00200000  03FFFFFF         111110vv 10vvvvvv 10vvvvvv 10vvvvvv 10vvvvvv
  31  04000000  7FFFFFFF         1111110v 10vvvvvv 10vvvvvv 10vvvvvv 10vvvvvv 10vvvvvv
```

It is seen that any UTF-8 octet that starts with binary 0 is a sequence of one (pure ASCII). Any octet starting with 10 is a trailing octet of a multioctet sequence. Any other octet is the start of a multioctet UTF-8 sequence, with the number of binary 1 digits indicating the number of octets of the multioctet encoding sequence. This makes it efficient to find the start of a character starting from an arbitrary location in an octet stream.

To allow coding for a million characters with UTF-16, the range 0000D800 to 0000DFFF is excluded from this conversion process. The following table shows in hexadecimal form the various ranges of the UTF-16 and UTF-8 sequences corresponding to the complete UCS-4 encoding. A semicolon shows the separation between the basic information unit in each case.

```
UCS-4            UTF-16          UTF-8

0000 0001;       0001;           01;
0000 007F;       007F;           7F;
0000 0080;       0080;           C2; 80;
0000 07FF;       07FF;           DF; BF;
0000 0800;       0800;           E0; A0; 80;
0000 FFFF;       FFFF;           EF; BF; BF;

0001 0000;       D800; DC00;     F0; 90; 80; 80;
0010 FFFF;       DBFF; DFFF;     F4; 8F; BF; BF;
001F FFFF;                       F7; BF; BF; BF;
0020 0000;                       F8; 88; 80; 80; 80;
03FF FFFF;                       FB; BF; BF; BF; BF;
0400 0000;                       FC; 84; 80; 80; 80; 80;
7FFF FFFF;                       FD; BF; BF; BF; BF; BF;
```

C.3 Foreign languages in XML

How do XML and XSL deal with non-ASCII sources? We explained in Section 6.5.1 that XSL is based on Unicode. Thus it should not be very difficult to deal with most common world languages. Therefore let us look at two examples that illustrate how to deal with such situations.

C.3.1 Latin-based encodings

In the first case we use an 8-bit ASCII extension, called Latin 1 (ISO-8859-1; see Table C.4), to represent a French text. The source file `invitationfr.xml` follows:

```
1   <?xml version="1.0" encoding="ISO-8859-1"?>
2   <!DOCTYPE invitation SYSTEM "invitationfr.dtd">
3   <invitation>
4   <!-- ++++ Partie entête ++++ -->
5   <entête>
6   <à>Anna, Bernard, Didier, Johanna</à>
7   <date>Vendredi prochain à 20 heures</date>
8   <où>Le Café du Web</où>
9   <pourquoi>Mon premier bébé XML</pourquoi>
10  </entête>
11  <!-- ++++ Partie corps  ++++ -->
```

```
12   <corps>
13   <par>
14   J'ai le plaisir de vous inviter à la célébration
15   de la naissance d'<emph>Invitation</emph>, mon
16   premier enfant document XML.
17   </par>
18   <par>
19   S'il vous plaît, faites tout votre possible pour me rejoindre
20   vendredi prochain. Et n'oubliez pas d'emmener vos amis.
21   </par>
22   <par>
23   Je me réjouis <emph>vraiment</emph> d'avance de votre présence.
24   </par>
25   </corps>
26   <!-- ++++ Partie finale  ++++ -->
27   <fin>
28   <signature>Michel</signature>
29   </fin>
30   </invitation>
```

Accented characters were used in the text as well as for some of the element types, as seen in the DTD invitationfr.dtd, which follows:

```
1    <?xml version='1.0' encoding="ISO-8859-1"?>
2    <!-- DTD invitation (version française) -->
3    <!-- 11 novembre 1998 mg -->
4    <!ELEMENT invitation (entête, corps, fin) >
5    <!ELEMENT entête    (à, date, où, pourquoi?) >
6    <!ELEMENT date      (#PCDATA) >
7    <!ELEMENT à         (#PCDATA) >
8    <!ELEMENT où        (#PCDATA) >
9    <!ELEMENT pourquoi  (#PCDATA) >
10   <!ELEMENT corps     (par+) >
11   <!ELEMENT par       (#PCDATA|emph)* >
12   <!ELEMENT emph      (#PCDATA) >
13   <!ELEMENT fin       (signature) >
14   <!ELEMENT signature (#PCDATA) >
```

We can use the xt or koalaxsl tool for transforming this XML file into, for instance, LaTeX. We chose to use the Koala tool (see Section 7.6.4.3) with the following XSL style sheet invlatlfr.xsl:

```
1    <?xml version='1.0' encoding="ISO-8859-1"?>
2    <xsl:stylesheet xmlns:xsl="http://www.w3.org/TR/WD-xsl"
3                    default-space="strip"
4                    indent-result="no"
5                    result-ns="">
6
7    <xsl:template match="/">
8    <xsl:text>\documentclass[francais]{article}
9    \usepackage{invitation}
10   \usepackage[T1]{fontenc}
11   \begin{document}
12   </xsl:text>
13   <xsl:apply-templates/>
14   <xsl:text>\end{document}
15   </xsl:text>
16   </xsl:template>
17
18   <xsl:template match="invitation/entête">
19   <xsl:text>\begin{Front}
```

```
20    \To{</xsl:text>
21    <xsl:value-of select="à"/>
22    <xsl:text>}
23    \Date{</xsl:text>
24    <xsl:value-of select="date"/>
25    <xsl:text>}
26    \Where{</xsl:text>
27    <xsl:value-of select="où"/>
28    <xsl:text>}
29    \Why{</xsl:text>
30    <xsl:value-of select="pourquoi"/>
31    <xsl:text>}
32    \end{Front}
33    </xsl:text>
34    </xsl:template>
35
36    <xsl:template match="invitation/corps">
37    <xsl:text>\begin{Body}
38    </xsl:text>
39      <xsl:apply-templates/>
40    <xsl:text>\end{Body}
41    </xsl:text>
42    </xsl:template>
43
44    <xsl:template match="invitation/corps/par">
45    <xsl:text>\par</xsl:text>
46    <xsl:apply-templates/>
47    </xsl:template>
48
49    <xsl:template match="invitation/corps/par/emph">
50    <xsl:text>\emph{</xsl:text>
51    <xsl:apply-templates/>
52    <xsl:text>}</xsl:text>
53    </xsl:template>
54
55    <xsl:template match="invitation/fin">
56    <xsl:text>\begin{Back}
57    \Signature{</xsl:text>
58    <xsl:value-of select="signature"/>
59    <xsl:text>}
60    \end{Back}
61    </xsl:text>
62    </xsl:template>
63
64    </xsl:stylesheet>
```

On the first line we note, as in all the other XML files in this section, the presence of the encoding attribute with a value equal to ISO-8859-1. We *must* specify the encoding, as explained in section 6.5.3, since only UTF-8 and Unicode are recognized by default. Furthermore (lines 8–11), we are specifying a few more LaTeX commands than when we were dealing with English-only texts (see Section 7.3.2 on page 295). In addition, we augmented the package file invitation.sty somewhat to deal with the French header.

```
1    % invitation.sty
2    % Package to format invitation.xml
3    \setlength{\textwidth}{22pc}
4    \setlength{\parskip}{1ex}
5    \setlength{\parindent}{0pt}
6    \pagestyle{empty}%% Turn off page numbering
7    \RequirePackage{array,calc}
```

```
 8  \newcommand{\ToTitle}{To whom}
 9  \newcommand{\WhyTitle}{Occasion}
10  \newcommand{\WhereTitle}{Venue}
11  \newcommand{\DateTitle}{When}
12  \newcommand{\SignatureTitle}{From}
13  \DeclareOption{francais}{%  French text for fixed texts
14    \renewcommand{\ToTitle}{À}
15    \renewcommand{\WhyTitle}{À l'occasion de}
16    \renewcommand{\WhereTitle}{Où}
17    \renewcommand{\DateTitle}{Quand}
18    \renewcommand{\SignatureTitle}{De la part de}}
19  \newenvironment{Front}%
20    {\begin{center}
21       \Huge\sffamily INVITATION
22     \end{center}
23    }
24    {\begin{flushleft}
25     \rule{\linewidth}{1pt}\\[2mm]
26     \begin{tabular}{@{}>{\bfseries}ll@{}}
27      \ToTitle:    & \@To      \\
28      \WhyTitle:   & \@Why     \\
29      \WhereTitle: & \@Where   \\
30      \DateTitle:  & \@Date
31     \end{tabular}\\[2mm]
32     \rule{\linewidth}{1pt}
33     \end{flushleft}
34    }
35  \newenvironment{Body}{\vspace*{\parskip}}{\vspace*{\parskip}}
36  \newenvironment{Back}
37    {\begin{flushleft}}
38    {\hspace*{.5\linewidth}\fbox{\SignatureTitle: \emph{\@Sig}}
39     \end{flushleft}
40    }
41  \newcommand{\To}[1]{\gdef\@To{#1}}
42  \newcommand{\Date}[1]{\gdef\@Date{#1}}
43  \newcommand{\Where}[1]{\gdef\@Where{#1}}
44  \newcommand{\Why}[1]{\gdef\@Why{#1}}
45  \newcommand{\Signature}[1]{\gdef\@Sig{#1}}
46  \ProcessOptions
```

As can be seen, we parameterized the "fixed texts" that are used in the heading and the signature. We also check for the presence of the option francais to redefine the "fixed text" as needed. This more complex version should be compared to the previous one on page 296; the result is shown in Figure C.4.

C.3.2   Handling non-Latin encodings with UTF-8

Since XML can handle Unicode in a native way, we expect it should not be too involved to code languages that use non-Latin alphabets, such as Russian, Greek, Chinese, Japanese, Arabic, and so on. In this section we show how you can handle Russian, Greek, and a little math in a single file without problems; the same applies to more complex situations, however.

We have used the Yudit [↪YUDIT] Unicode editor, which supports input in several languages and allows you to read and write in many encodings. It was originally written by Gaspar Sinai and features a relatively simple and intuitive graphical user interface.

INVITATION

À:	Anna, Bernard, Didier, Johanna
À l'occasion de:	Mon premier bébé XML
Où:	Le Café du Web
Quand:	Vendredi prochain à 20 heures

J'ai le plaisir de vous inviter à la célébration de la naissance d'*Invitation*, mon premier enfant document XML.

S'il vous plaît, faites tout votre possible pour me rejoindre vendredi prochain. Et n'oubliez pas d'emmener vos amis.

Je me réjouis *vraiment* d'avance de votre présence.

De la part de: *Michel*

Figure C.4: A French invitation (LaTeX version)

Figure C.5 shows an XML-coded file. Its first part shows three ways you can input Russian text. We reproduce (part) of these lines here for closer scrutiny:

```
1   <?xml version="1.0"?>
2   <!DOCTYPE mydoc [
3   <!ELEMENT mydoc (#PCDATA)>
4   <!ENTITY % ISOcyr1 SYSTEM "ISOcyr1.pen">
5   %ISOcyr1;
6   ]>
7   <mydoc>
8   <par>The word Russian (ÐāÑČÑĄÑĄÐŽÐÿÐź) in Cyrillic: <br/>
9   Using ISO Cyrillic set:
10  &Rcy;&ucy;&scy;&scy;&kcy;&icy;&jcy;   <br/>
11  Using XML Unicode entities:
12  &#x0420;&#x0443;&#x0441;&#x0441;&#x043a;&#x0438;&#x0439;
13  </par>
```

Lines 4–5 define an external entity set ISOcyr1, which will be read on the local system in the file ISOcyr1.pen. It contains definitions for Cyrillic letters, such as:

```
<!ENTITY rcy    "&#x440;"> <!--small er, Cyrillic -->
<!ENTITY Rcy    "&#x420;"> <!--capital ER, Cyrillic -->
<!ENTITY scy    "&#x441;"> <!--small es, Cyrillic -->
<!ENTITY Scy    "&#x421;"> <!--capital ES, Cyrillic -->
```

Figure C.5: A UTF-8 encoded XML file with Russian, Greek, and math

The above excerpt defines the small and capital Cyrillic letters "r" and "s" in function of their Unicode number. That is how we get Cyrillic letters by symbolic name on line 10 in our source file. Of course, as on line 12, we can also directly enter the Unicode character references ourselves (compare the entity references "Р" on line 10 and "Р" on line 12; decide which is more readable and maintainable). On the other hand, on line 8 we have entered Russian directly by using Yudit, which saved it as UTF-8, that is, two bytes for alphabetic non-ASCII characters. These byte-codes print in a funny way in the T1 encoding used in this book, but if you look at the T1 character table (see, for instance, Table 9.1 on page 261 of Goossens et al. (1994)) you easily see that they represent the byte sequence

```
D0A0D183D181D181D0BAD0B8D0B9
```

which, as explained in Section C.2.3, is the UTF-8 equivalent of the Unicode sequence on line 12.

Going back to Figure C.5, we see several line pairs, where the first line shows which is the letter or letter combination to be entered on an English "qwerty" keyboard, and the second shows the result in Yudit. For instance, following the line "Russian-English correspondence," we selected "Russian" in the "Input" menu, and following the line "Greek-English correspondence," we selected "Greek" in the "Input" menu. Depending on the selected language "Input" menu, Yudit will show the correct character on screen and save it in an encoding you can select in the "Encoding" menu. So we had to switch input language English to Russian to English again, to input the lines in the Russian part of the text. Similarly we switched from English to Greek and back in the Greek part. You see how we put the text in the three languages inside elements with tag names that correspond to the language's name in its native alphabet. Thus, as in Section C.3.1, where we used Latin 1 XML element names, XML can define element names that make sense to the native writers of documents in every part of the world (see also Section 6.5.1), a big step forward from HTML where the tag set was fixed and tag names had a real meaning only in English.

The final part of the XML file is the following:

```
1    <head>Math characters</head>
2    <par>And here is one of Maxwell's equations:
3    &#x2207;&#x00B7;&#x0042;&#x003d;&#x0030;</par>
4    </mydoc>
```

Line 3 shows Unicode character references to write a small mathematics formula.

Our next task is to transform this file onto something we can browse or print. The style sheet utf8.xsl that follows transforms the earlier XML file utf8.xml into HTML.

```
1    <?xml version='1.0'?>
2    <xsl:stylesheet
3      xmlns:xsl="http://www.w3.org/TR/WD-xsl"
4      xmlns="http://www.w3.org/TR/REC-html40"
5      result-ns="">
6    <xsl:template match="/">
7      <html  xmlns="http://www.w3.org/Profiles/xhtml1-transitional.dtd">
8      <head>
9      <title>UTF8 files</title>
10     <meta http-equiv="Content-Type" content="text/html;charset=UTF-8" />
11     </head>
12     <body>
13     <h1>Handling UTF-8 files</h1>
14     <xsl:apply-templates/>
15     </body>
16     </html>
```

```
17   </xsl:template>
18   <xsl:template match="br">
19     <br />
20   </xsl:template>
21   <xsl:template match="par">
22     <p><xsl:apply-templates/></p>
23   </xsl:template>
24   <xsl:template match="head">
25     <h2><xsl:apply-templates/></h2>
26   </xsl:template>
27   <!-- eliminate English keyboard input -->
28   <xsl:template match="eng">
29   </xsl:template>
30   <!-- transmit Russian keyboard input -->
31   <xsl:template match="&#x0440;&#x0443;&#x0441;">
32   <p>&#x25c6;&#x00a0;<xsl:apply-templates/></p>
33   </xsl:template>
34   <!-- transmit Greek keyboard input -->
35   <xsl:template match="ΑΙΑ·ΑΙΑ·ΑΙΑ·">
36   <p>ΑαŮŘ&#x00a0;<xsl:apply-templates/></p>
37   </xsl:template>
38   </xsl:stylesheet>
```

```
<xsl:template match="ελλ">
<p>●&#x00a0;<xsl:apply-templates/></p>
```

The most interesting part of the style sheet is its beginning. Line 4 defines the output namespace as HTML (see Section 7.6.9). This allows us to output straight HTML tags. Lines 6–17 enclose the whole file inside a correct HTML structure where we indicate that we deal with XHTML-based HTML-compatible XML code (line 7). Line 10 is very important because it tells the browser that the character set is UTF-8. The meaning of the remaining lines should be straightforward. In particular, lines 28–29 eliminate the English input lines from the output. Because XSL style sheets are genuine XML files, we can use the full set of alphabetic and ideographic Unicode characters; in particular we can refer to the non-Latin element names of our XML document (again they show up strangely on lines 35 and 36). In fact, we can mix native as well as character reference codes in the XSL file to refer to Unicode characters. On line 31 we use character references to match the Cyrillic string "рус" and to put the Unicode character "25c6" (black diamond) at the beginning of each paragraph. For the Greek part (lines 34–35) we use the Unicode characters natively (we show the relevant part of the style sheet to the right of the lines in question). In both cases we add a nonbreaking space ( ) between the diamond or bullet and the subsequent text.

As a final comment, it is worthwhile to pay attention to the extra blank between the element name and the closing "/>" for empty elements (see lines 9 and 18 in the style sheet). This allows current HTML browsers that do not yet understand XML syntax to interpret these lines correctly (in fact they will ignore the final "/", see also Section B.5.2.1).

We can run these two files through an XSL parser, such as xt, and output the HTML file utf8.html:

```
xt utf8.xml utf8.xsl utf8.html
tidy -utf8 -m utf8.html
```

Figure C.6: HTML rendering of UTF-8 file with Netscape

Finally we run the output of xt through Tidy (see Section B.5.2.3) to translate everything into UTF-8 because xt translates some characters (such as Greek)
into entity references, and we want a clean UTF-8 file. The result as viewed with
Netscape is shown in Figure C.6.

Glossary

AIML Astronomical Instrument Markup Language [↪AIML].

Instrument description language that encompasses instrument characteristics, control commands, data stream descriptions (including image and housekeeping data), message formats, communication mechanisms, and pipeline algorithm descriptions.

Amaya W3C test-bed browser/authoring system [↪AMAYA].

Versatile and extensible tool provided by the W3C to demonstrate and test new developments in Web protocols and data formats. Among other things Amaya lets you edit complex mathematical expressions within HTML pages through a WYSIWYG interface.

AML Astronomical Markup Language [↪AML].

Metadata exchange markup language for astronomy that supports a set of astronomical objects, such as article, table, image, person.

Attribute see Section 6.5.4.2.

Lets you specify named characteristics about an element type in an SGML/XML DTD.

BIOML BIOpolymer Markup Language [↪BIOML].

Allows the specification of experimental information about molecular entities composed of biopolymers, such as proteins and genes.

BMP Basic Multilingual Plane (see Section C.2).

Subset of the 31-bit ISO/IEC10646-1 UCS encoding (plane 0, group 0). By construction its contents are identical to Unicode.

BSML   Bioinformatic Sequence Markup Language [↪BSML].

Standard for the encoding and display of DNA, RNA and protein sequence information.

CALS   Continuous Acquisition and Life-Cycle Support [↪CALS].

United States Department of Defense initiative to improve weapon system acquisition and life-cycle support processes through accelerated creation and application of digital product data and technical information.

CDATA   Character Data (see Section 6.5.4.7).

Information in an XML document that should not be parsed at all. This allows the use of the markup characters &, <, and > within the text, even though no elements or entities may appear in the section. CDATA declarations may appear in XML attributes (Section 6.5.4.2), and CDATA sections may appear in documents.

CML   Chemical Markup Language [↪CML].

Allows you to manage chemical information with XML. CML and associated tools provide a platform- and convention-independent specification for information interchange in the molecular sciences. It comes with a browser (Jumbo) for visualizing the data.

CSS   Cascading Style Sheets [↪STYLECSS] (see Section 7.4).

A simple declarative language that allows authors and users to apply stylistic information (for fonts, spacing, color, and so on) to structured documents written in HTML or XML. Two levels of CSS style sheets, CSS1 [↪CSS1] and CSS2 [↪CSS2], are available; work is continuing on CSS3.

DCD   Document Content Description [↪DCD].

A structural schema facility for specifying rules covering the structure and content of XML documents. DCD is an RDF vocabulary and is intended to define document constraints in an XML syntax, including providing basic datatypes.

DDML   Document Definition Markup Language [↪DDML].

A simple schema language for XML to encode the logical content of a DTD as an XML document. This allows schema information to be explored and used with widely available XML tools.

DOM   Document Object Model [↪DOMGEN].

A platform- and language-neutral interface that allows programs and scripts to access and update the content, structure, and style of documents dynamically. The document can be further processed and the results of that processing can be incorporated back into the presented page. A first level has been accepted as a recommendation [↪DOML1], while work continues on a level 2 specification [↪DOML2] that will add interfaces for a CSS object model, an event model, and queries.

DSSSL   Document Style Semantics and Specification Language (see Section 7.5).

International Standard ISO 10179 ISO/IEC:10179 (1996) was adopted at the beginning of 1995. It presents a framework to express the concepts and actions necessary for transforming a structurally marked up document into its final physical form. Although this standard is primarily targeted at document handling, it can also define other layouts, such as those needed for use with databases. More on DSSSL by James Clark is available at [↪DSSSLCLARK].

DTD   Document Type Definition (see Section 6.5.4).

A set of rules describing which elements types are allowed in an XML document and what their content model is. A DTD also specifies the possible attributes of each element type and declares the entities referenced in the document, as well as the notations that can be used.

EAD   Encoded Archival Description [↪EAD].

A nonproprietary encoding standard for machine-readable finding aids such as inventories, registers, indexes, and other documents created by archives, libraries, museums, and manuscript repositories to support the use of their holdings.

GIF   Graphics Interchange Format [Murray and vanRyper (1996)].

A format originally developed by Compuserve to facilitate image transfers between various platforms by storing multiple bitmap images in the same file. GIF files used the patented LZW compression method. If licencing issues could be a problem, it is wise to envisage using the PNG format instead.

HL7 Kona Proposal   [↪KONA].

A method in which electronic healthcare records (EHR) can be created, exchanged, and processed using SGML/XML.

HTML   Hypertext Markup language (see Section 1.1.3).

The most important SGML-based markup language used on the Web.

HTTP   Hypertext Transport Protocol (see Section 1.1.1).

Method that allows WWW servers to communicate with each other.

ICE   Information and Content Exchange [↪ICE].

The ICE protocol defines the roles and responsibilities of syndicators and subscribers and defines the format and method of content exchange. It provides support for management and control of syndication relationships, so that ICE will be useful in automating content exchange and reuse.

Java   Object-oriented programming language developed by Sun [↪JAVADOC].

Java was designed from the ground up to allow for secure execution of code across a network, even when the source code is untrusted and possibly malicious. Java offers cross-platform portability not only in source form, but also in compiled binary form. To make this possible, Java is compiled to an intermediate byte-code which is interpreted on the fly by the Java interpreter. Thus only the interpreter and a few native code libraries need to be ported on different platforms; Java programs themselves run unchanged everywhere. Since Java is quite a small language, with strong typing and no unsafe constructs, it is easy to read and write and, above all, relatively easy to debug. See [↪JAVAFAQ] for a lot of useful information.

Javascript   Scripting language [↪JAVASC].

Netscape's cross-platform, object-based scripting language for client and server applications. Javascript is not Java! It lets you create applications that run over the Internet. Client applications run in a browser, while server applications run on the server side. JavaScript allows you to create dynamic HTML pages that process user input and maintain persistent data using special objects, files, and relational databases. Javascript was first introduced by Netscape in their browser Netscape Navigator 2.0, but today a "standard" version exists under the name of Ecmascript [↪ECMASC].

JPEG   Joint Photographic Experts Group [↪JPEG].

An ISO standard describing image compression mechanisms for either full-color or gray-scale images of natural, real-world scenes. It works well on photographs, naturalistic artwork, and similar material. For a good description see Murray and vanRyper (1996).

JSML   Java Speech Markup Language [↪JSML].

A language used by applications to annotate text input to Java Speech API speech synthesizers. The JSML elements provide a speech synthesizer with detailed information on how to say the text. JSML includes elements that describe the structure of a document, provide pronunciations of words and phrases, and place markers in the text. JSML also provides prosodic elements that control phrasing, emphasis, pitch, speaking rate, and other important characteristics. Appropriate markup of text improves the quality and naturalness of the synthesized voice. JSML uses the Unicode character set, so JSML can be used to mark up text in most languages of the world.

LinuxML   Linux Markup Language [↪LINUXML].

Project devoted to changing the UNIX de facto standard for interprocess communication and storage from line-based ASCII records to XML. The idea is that UNIX commands will produce XML output. This would allow downstream programs, like `sort` or `xterm`, to understand the semantic content of the incoming data and hence do more useful things with it.

MathML   Mathematical Markup Language [↪W2CMATH] (see Section 8.1).

MathML deals with the (re-)use of mathematical and scientific content on the Web and with other applications such as computer algebra systems, print typesetting, and voice synthesis.

MIME   Multipurpose Internet Mail Extensions [↪RFC2045].

MIME is a set of specifications that support the structuring of the message body in terms of body parts. Body parts can be of various types, such as text, image, audio, or complete encapsulated messages. It also provides for the encoding of messages in character sets other than 7-bit ASCII.

MPEG   Motion Picture Experts Group [↪MPEG].

An ISO Standard that specifies how to encode data streams for compressing audio and video information. See ISO/IEC:11172 (1993); Murray and vanRyper (1996).

OASIS Organization for the Advancement of Structured Information Standards [↪OASIS].

A nonprofit, international consortium, composed of users and suppliers of products and services, and dedicated solely to product-independent document and data interchange. Founded in 1993 as SGML Open, OASIS has expanded to embrace the complete spectrum of structured information processing standards including XML, SGML, and HTML.

OFE Open Financial Exchange [↪OFX].

OFE standardizes the electronic exchange of financial data between financial institutions, business, and consumers via the Internet. Originally set up at the beginning of 1997, it now supports a wide range of financial activities including consumer and small business banking; consumer and small business bill payment; bill presentment and investments, including stocks, bonds, and mutual funds. Other financial services, including financial planning and insurance, will be added in the future and will be incorporated into the specification. Markup is likely to be generated and interpreted by programs, with no human intervention.

OSD Open Software Format Description.

Software distribution and update via the network, including "push" updates of software and hands-free installation. Markup is likely to be generated by a software packaging program and used to install the software without ever being read by a human.

Parser see Section 6.6.

A program that converts a serial stream of markup (an XML or SGML file, for example) into an output structure accessible by another higher level program. XML parsers may perform validation or check to see if a markup is well-formed as they process it. Section 6.6 presents a few XML parsers.

PDF Portable Document Format (see Chapter 7)

A descendant of Adobe Systems' PostScript language, optimized for improving navigation and delivery on the Internet. In particular PDF introduces page independence, adds hypertext and security features, allows font subsitution, and incorporates performant compression features to minimize file size.

Perl [↪PERL]

A high-level programming language written initially by Larry Wall. It inherits a lot of features from the C programming language but also includes good ideas of many other UNIX tools. Perl's process, file, and text manipulation facilities make it particularly well suited for tasks involving quick prototyping, system utilities, software tools, system management tasks, database access, graphical programming, networking, and WWW programming.

PGML Precision Graphics Markup Language [↪PGML].

An XML instance implementing the PDF/PostScript imaging model.

PNG   Portable Network Graphics [↪PNG].

An extensible file format for the lossless, portable, well-compressed storage of raster images. It is a patent-free replacement for GIF and can also replace many common uses of TIFF. Indexed-color, grayscale, and truecolor images are supported, as is an optional alpha channel. PNG works well in online viewing applications (like WWW) since it is fully streamable with a progressive display option. It is robust, providing both full file integrity checking and simple detection of common transmission errors. PNG can store gamma and chromaticity data for improved color matching on heterogeneous platforms.

PostScript   Page description language [↪ADOBEPS].

A computer language that describes the appearance of a page, including elements such as text, graphics, and scanned images, to a printer or other output device. It was introduced by Adobe [↪ADOBE] in 1985. It has become the language of choice in high quality printing on a wide range of output devices, including black-and-white and color printers, imagesetters, platesetters, screen displays, and direct digital presses.

RDF   Resource Description Format [↪RDF].

Describes the contents of Web resources in order to enable automatic processing. May be used to describe the contents of a Web site, to provide additional information for search engines or intelligent agents, to declare property rights, and so on.

SAX   Standard API for event-based XML parsing [↪SAX].

Section B.6 shows how SAX can be applied to handle XML documents.

SDML   Signed Document Markup Language [↪SDML].

Language designed to allow the creation of digitally signed electronic documents. There is provision for tagging individual text items making up a document and grouping them into parts that can have business meaning and can be signed individually or together. Document parts can be added and deleted without invalidating previous signatures; signing, cosigning, endorsing, coendorsing, and witnessing operations can be performed on whole documents or on parts.

SGML   Standard Generalized Markup Language (see Chapter 6).

An International Standard (ISO 8879:1986) that describes a generalized markup scheme for representing the logical structure of documents in a system-independent and platform-independent manner.

SMIL   Synchronized Multimedia Integration Language [↪SMIL].

An XML application that allows you to integrate a set of independent multimedia objects into a synchronized multimedia presentation. The functionality of SMIL includes describing the temporal behavior of a presentation, describing its layout on a screen, and associating hyperlinks with media objects.

SOX   Schema for Object-oriented XML [↪SOX].

A schema facility for defining the structure, content, and semantics of XML documents to enable XML validation and higher levels of automated content checking. It provides basic intrinsic datatypes, an extensible datatyping mechanism, content model and attribute interface inheritance, a powerful namespace mechanism, and embedded documentation.

SpeechML   SpeechML Markup Language [↪SPEECHML].

A language for building network-based conversational applications that interact with the user through spoken input and output. SpeechML could be used to enable conversational access from a car, a telephone, a PDA, a desktop PC, and so on to information sources and applications anywhere on the Internet.

SVG   Scalable Vector Graphics [↪SVGSPEC].

A proposed open vector graphics format that works across platforms, for various output resolutions, in several kinds of color spaces, and on a range of available bandwidths. The aim of SVG is to make Web documents smaller, faster, more interactive, and displayable on a wider range of device resolutions from small mobile devices to office computer monitors to high resolution printers.

TEI   Text Encoding Initiative [↪TEIHOME] (see Section B.4.3).

A scholarly international project to promote the interchange and preparation of electronic texts. Structural features of a text are marked up in the source using a standardized scheme to ease exchange and processing by computer.

TeXML   [↪TEXML] see Section 8.2.4.

Allows you to typeset XML documents with the TEX formatter.

TIFF   Tag Image File Format [↪TIFF6].

Originally a method for storing black-and-white scanned images, although later treatment of color was added, so that TIFF has become the standard file format for most paint, imaging, and desktop publishing tools.

UCS   Universal Character Set

ISO/IEC10646-1 international standard for the encoding of all writing systems and character encodings in the world. It uses a 31-bit encoding with Unicode as a pure 16-bit subset corresponding to the Basic Multilingual Plane (see Section C.2).

Unicode   see Section C.2 [↪UNICODE].

A standard for international character encoding. Unicode supports characters that are two bytes wide rather than the 8-bit codes currently supported by most systems. This makes it possible to encode 65,536 characters rather than only 256 with one byte on codings.

URI   Universal Resource Identifier (see Section 1.1.2).

Universal addressing scheme to locate information on the Internet.

URL   Universal Resource Locator (see Section 1.1.2).

A special form of a URI, originally used when the Web was invented.

Valid   see Section 6.4.2.1.

A valid document is a well-formed document that adheres to its DTD.

VML   Vector Markup Language [↪VML].

An XML application that defines a format for the encoding of vector information together with additional markup to describe how that information may be displayed and edited.

VRML   Virtual Reality Modeling Language [↪WEB3D]

File format standard for 3D multimedia and shared virtual worlds on the Internet. VRML adds interaction, structured graphics, and extra dimensions (z and time) to HTML's graphical interface. Applications areas of VRML include business manufacturing, scientific, and educational graphics, with more recently 3D shared virtual worlds and communities.

WAP   Wireless Application Protocol.

An XML markup language to exchange information over narrow-band devices.

WebDAV   World Wide Web Distributed Authoring and Versioning [↪WEBDAV].

Extensions to the HTTP protocol to provide better support for distributed authoring.

Well-Formed   see Section 6.4.2.1.

A well-formed document may or may not have a DTD. Well-formed documents must begin with an XML declaration and contain properly nested and marked-up elements.

WIDL   Web Interface Definition Language [↪WIDL].

An XML application that defines a metalanguage that implements a service-based architecture over the document-based WWW resources. WIDL allows interactions with Web servers to be defined as functional interfaces that can be accessed by remote systems over standard Web protocols and provides the structure necessary for generating client code in languages such as Java, C/C++, COBOL, and Visual Basic.

W3C   World Wide Web Consortium [↪W3C].

This international industry consortium was founded in October 1994 to lead the World Wide Web to its full potential by developing common protocols that promote its evolution and ensure its interoperability. W3C is jointly hosted by the Massachusetts Institute of Technology Laboratory for Computer Science in the United States; the Institut National de Recherche en Informatique et en Automatique [INRIA] in Europe; and the Keio University Shonan Fujisawa Campus in Japan. Services provided by the Consortium include a repository of information about the World Wide Web for developers and users, reference code implementations to embody and promote standards, and various prototype and sample applications to demonstrate use of new technology.

XCatalog   Proposal to adopt XML syntax for catalog [↪XCATALOG].

Proposed specification based the OASIS document [↪ENTIMAN] for managing entities by mapping XML public identifiers to XML system identifiers using URIs.

XHTML Extensible HyperText Markup Language [↪HTMLINXML] (see Section B.5.2).

A specification that reformulates HTML 4.0 as an XML 1.0 application. XHTML specifies three document profiles as XML namespaces, each with its own URI. The semantics of the elements and their attributes are defined in the W3C Recommendation for HTML 4.0, and they will provide the foundation for future extensibility of XHTML.

Xlink XML Linking Language [↪XLINKSPEC].

Specifies constructs that may be inserted into XML resources to describe links between objects. A link (in the Xlink context) is an explicit relationship between two or more data objects or portions of data objects. XLink uses XML syntax to create structures that can describe the simple unidirectional hyperlinks of today's HTML as well as more sophisticated multiended and typed links.

XMI XML Metadata Interchange Format [↪XML].

Enables easy interchange of metadata between modeling tools based on the Object Management Group's Unified Modeling Language OMG (UML) and between tools and metadata repositories using the OMG Meta Object Facility (MOF). This architecture allows tools to share metadata programmatically using CORBA interfaces specified in the MOF and UML standards or by using XML-based stream (or file) containing MOF and UML compliant modeling specifications (see [↪OMGTECH] for specifications of the OMG standards mentioned).

XML Extensible Markup Language [↪XMLSPEC].

A subset of SGML whose goal is to enable generic SGML to be served, received, and processed on the Web in the way that is possible with HTML. XML is designed for ease of implementation and for interoperability with both SGML and HTML. XML in general is discussed in Chapter 6, while the translation of LaTeX (with and without math) to XML is dealt with in Chapter 8.

XML-Data [↪XMLDATA].

XML vocabulary for schemas to define and document object classes.

XML/EDI Electronic Data Interchange [↪XMLEDI].

A standard framework to exchange different types of data—for instance, an invoice, a healthcare claim, project status—so that the information in a transaction, exchanged via an Application Program Interface (API), Web automation, database portal, catalog, or workflow document or message can be searched, decoded, manipulated, and displayed consistently and correctly by first implementing EDI dictionaries and extending the vocabulary via online repositories to include our business language, rules, and objects.

Xpointer XML Pointer Language [↪XPTSPEC].

A language that supports addressing into the internal structures of XML documents. In particular, it provides for specific reference to elements, character strings, and other parts of XML documents, whether or not they bear an explicit ID attribute.

XSL   Extensible Stylesheet Language [↪XSLWD] (see Section 7.6).

A language for expressing style sheets. It consists of a transformation language and a formatting objects vocabulary.

XUL   Extensible User Interface Language [↪XUL].

Describes the contents of windows and dialogs. XUL has constructs for typical dialog controls and for widgets such as toolbars, trees, progress bars, and menus.

URL catalog

ACROTEX: PDF-based math tutorials making extensive use of Acrobat forms.
   `http://www.math.uakron.edu/~dpstory/acrotex.html`

ADOBE: Adobe's home page.
   `http://www.adobe.com/`

ADOBEPS: PostScript information at Adobe.
   `http://www.adobe.com/prodindex/postscript/main.html`

AELFRED: David Megginson's Ælfred XML parser.
   `http://www.microstar.com/aelfred.html`

AIML: Astronomical Instrument Markup Language.
   `http://pioneer.gsfc.nasa.gov/public/aiml/`

AMAYA: Experimental browser/authoring system.
   `http://www.w3.org/Amaya/`

AML: Astronomical Markup Language.
   `http://www.infm.ulst.ac.uk/%7Edamien/these/`

ASTER: T. V. Raman's system for spoken mathematics reading TEX source.
   `http://www.cs.cornell.edu/Info/People/raman/aster/demo.html`

AXML: The XML standard, annotated by Tim Bray.
   `http://www.xml.com/axml/axml.html`

BALISE: SGML programming environment for structured documents.
   `http://www.balise.com`

BIOML: XML language for annotating biopolymer sequence information.
   `http://www.proteometrics.com/BIOML/`

BOSAKXML: *XML, Java, and the Future of the Web* by Jon Bosak.
`http://metalab.unc.edu/pub/sun-info/standards/xml/why/xmlapps.html`

BSML: Bioinformatic Sequence Markup Language for graphic genomic displays.
`http://visualgenomics.com/sbir/rfc.htm`

CALS: Continuous Acquisition and Life-Cycle Support.
`http://navysgml.dt.navy.mil/cals.html`

CERN: The European Laboratory for Particle Physics.
`http://www.cern.ch/Public/`

CML: Chemical Markup Language resources.
`http://xml-cml.org`

CONTEXT: The CONTEXt macro package by Hans Hagen.
`http://www.ntg.nl/context/`

CSS1:   Cascading Style Sheets, version 1, W3C recommendation (December 1996).
`http://www.w3.org/TR/REC-CSS1`

CSS2:   Cascading Style Sheets, version 2, W3C recommendation (May 1998).
`http://www.w3.org/TR/REC-CSS2/Overview.html`

CVSREPOS: LaTeX2HTML CVS repository.
`http://saftsack.fs.uni-bayreuth.de/~latex2ht/`

DARPA: Defense Advanced Research Projects Agency.
`http://www.arpa.mil/`

DAVENPORT: Davenport Group, developers of the Docbook DTD.
`http://www.oasis-open.org/docbook/`

DBDSSSL: The Modular DocBook Stylesheets.
`http://nwalsh.com/docbook/dsssl/index.html`

DBVIEW: DocBook 3.0: User Element Index.
`http://www.ora.com/homepages/dtdparse/docbook/3.0/elements.htm`

DBXML: The Docbook DTD translated XML.
`http://nwalsh.com/docbook/xml/index.html`

DCD: Document Content Description for XML.
`http://www.w3.org/TR/NOTE-dcd`

DDML: Document Definition Markup Language Specification, Version 1.0.
`http://www.w3.org/TR/NOTE-ddml`

DOCBOOK: DocBook Homepage at OASIS.
`http://www.oasis-open.org/docbook/`

DOMGEN: OASIS page on the W3C Document Object Model (DOM).
`http://www.oasis-open.org/cover/dom.html`

DOML1:   Document Object Model (DOM) Level 1 Specification (Version 1),
W3C Recommendation 1 October, 1998.
`http://www.w3.org/TR/REC-DOM-Level-1/`

DOML2:   Document Object Model (DOM) Level 2 Specification (Working Draft).
   http://www.w3.org/TR/WD-DOM-Level-2/

DRAKOSWWW: *From Text to Hypertext: A Post-Hoc Rationalisation of LaTeX2HTML* by
   Nikos Drakos.
   http://www.cbl.leeds.ac.uk/nikos/doc/www94/www94.html

DSSSLCLARK: James Clark's DSSSL information.
   http://www.jclark.com/dsssl/

DSSSLLIST: DSSSL Mailing List.
   http://www.mulberrytech.com/dsssl/dssslist/index.html

DSSSLMML: DSSSL style sheet for MathML.
   http://www.nag.co.uk/projects/openmath/mml-files/

DSSSLONL: DSSSL Online.
   http:
   //metalab.unc.edu/pub/sun-info/standards/dsssl/dssslo/do960816.htm

DSSSLPDF: DSSSL specification online in PDF.
   ftp://ftp.ornl.gov/pub/sgml/WG8/DSSSL/dsssl96b.pdf

DSSSLSUM: Harvey Bingham's DSSSL syntax summary.
   http://www.tiac.net/users/bingham/dssslsyn/index.htm

DSSSLTUTA: Paul Prescod's *Introduction to DSSSL*.
   http://itrc.uwaterloo.ca:80/~papresco/dsssl/tutorial.html

DSSSLTUTB: Daniel M. Germán's *An Introduction to DSSSL*.
   http://csg.uwaterloo.ca/~dmg/dsssl/tutorial/tutorial.html

DTDPARSE: Norman Walsh's SGML DTD parser.
   http://www.ora.com/homepages/dtdparse/

DVIOUT: Windows 9X/NT DVI viewer that supports HyperTeX \specials.
   http://akagi.ms.u-tokyo.ac.jp/dvioute_help.html

DVIPS: Tom Rokicki's DVI to PostScript driver.
   http://www.radicaleye.com/dvips.html

EAD: Encoded Archival Description initiative.
   http://www.loc.gov/ead/ead.html

EC: European Union's Web server.
   http://europa.eu.Int/

ECMASC: Standard ECMA-262, ECMAScript Language Specification.
   http://www.ecma.ch/stand/ecma-262.htm

ELEMATTR: SGML/XML: Using Elements and Attributes.
   http://www.oasis-open.org/cover/elementsAndAttrs.html

ENTIMAN: Entity Management.
   http://www.oasis-open.org/html/a401.htm

EPRINT: Los Alamos e-Print archive of scientific papers preprints.
  http://xxx.lanl.gov/

EPSIG: Electronic Publishing Special Interest Group.
  http://www.oasis-open.org/cover/epsig.html

EPSTOPDF: Perl utility that makes page size equal to BoundingBox for EPS files.
  http://www.tug.org/applications/pdftex/epstopdf

ESIS: ESIS—ISO 8879 Element Structure Information Set.
  http://www.oasis-open.org/cover/WG8-n931a.html

FOP: James Tauber's Formatting Object to PDF Translator.
  http://www.jtauber.com/fop/

FOSI: MIL-M-28001C standard for Formatting Output Specification Instance.
  http://www-cals.itsi.disa.mil/core/standards/28001C.PDF

FPISERVER: Peter Flynn's server to resolve Formal Public Identifiers.
  http://www.ucc.ie/cgi-bin/PUBLIC

FPISYNTAX: Formal Public Identifiers syntax.
  http://www.oasis-open.org/cover/tauber-fpi.html

FRM: Document authoring and publishing system (includes SGML support).
  http://www.adobe.com/prodindex/framemaker/

GROVES: DSSSL Graph Representation of Property Values (groves).
  http://www.oasis-open.org/cover/topics.html#groves

GSHOME: Ghostscript home page.
  http://www.cs.wisc.edu/~ghost/

HOOD: HTML Document Type Definitions.
  http://www.utoronto.ca/webdocs/HTMLdocs/HTML_Spec/html.html

HTML2SPEC: HTML 2.0 Specification.
  http://www.w3.org/MarkUp/html-spec/

HTML4:   HTML 4.0 Specification.
  http://www.w3.org/TR/REC-html40/

HTMLENTS: Character entity references in HTML 4.0.
  http://www.w3.org/TR/REC-html40/sgml/entities.html

HTMLINXML: XHTML 1.0: Extensible HyperText Markup Language.
  http://www.w3.org/TR/WD-html-in-xml/

HTMLTIDY: Dave Raggett's Tidy cleans up HTML pages and converts them to XHTML.
  http://www.w3.org/People/Raggett/tidy/

HTTPNG: W3C and IETF HTTP-NG activity.
  http://www.w3.org/Protocols/HTTP-NG/Activity.html

HTTPRFC: HTTP 1.1 specification.
  http://www.w3.org/Protocols/rfc2068/rfc2068

HYPERLTX: Otfried Cheong's Hyperlatex LaTeX to HTML translator.
    `http://www.cs.ust.hk/~otfried/Hyperlatex/`

HYPERTEX: HyperTeX FAQ.
    `http://xxx.lanl.gov/hypertex/`

HYTIME: Hytime Standard.
    `http://www.ornl.gov/sgml/wg8/docs/n1920/html/n1920.html`

ICE: The Information and Content Exchange (ICE) Protocol.
    `http://www.w3.org/TR/NOTE-ice`

IETF: The Internet Engineering Task Force.
    `http://www.ietf.org/`

IMAGEMAGICK: John Christy's image processing utilities.
    `http://www.wizards.dupont.com/cristy/`

INRIA: Institut national de recherche en informatique et en automatique.
    `http://www.inria.fr/`

ISO8879TC2:   Web SGML adaptations.
    `http://www.ornl.gov/sgml/WG8/document/1955.htm`

ITRANS: A package for printing text in Indian Language Scripts.
    `http://www.aczone.com/itrans/`

JADE: James Clark's DSSSL implementation.
    `http://www.jclark.com/jade/`

JADETEX: JadeTeX macro package for Jade TeX backend.
    `ftp://ctan.tug.org/tex-archive/macros/jadetex/`

JADETEXB: TeXFOTBuilder: a Generic TeX backend for Jade.
    `http://www.jclark.com/jade/TeX.htm`

JAVADOC: Sun's Java documentation page.
    `http://java.sun.com/docs/index.html`

JAVAFAQ: Cafe au Lait Java FAQs, News, and Resources.
    `http://metalab.unc.edu/javafaq/`

JAVASC: Netscape's JavaScript Guide.
    `http://developer.netscape.com/docs/manuals/communicator/jsguide4/`

JPEG: JPEG Frequently Asked Questions.
    `http://www.faqs.org/faqs/jpeg-faq/`

JSML: Java Speech Markup Language Specification.
    `http://java.sun.com/products/java-media/speech/forDevelopers/JSML/`
    `index.html`

JUMBO: JAVA-XML, The JUMBO browser.
    `http://ala.vsms.nottingham.ac.uk/vsms/java/jumbo/`

KEIO: Keio University.
    `http://www.keio.ac.jp/`

KOALAXSL: Koala XSL engine for Java.
    `http://www.inria.fr/koala/XML/xslProcessor/`

KONA: HL7 Kona Proposal (health care).
    `http://www.mcis.duke.edu:80/standards/HL7/sigs/sgml/WhitePapers/KONA/`

L2HCTAN: LaTeX2HTML sources on CTAN.
    `ftp://ctan.tug.org/tex-archive//support/latex2html/sources/`

L2HDOC: LaTeX2HTML online documentation.
    `http://www-dsed.llnl.gov/files/programs/unix/latex2html/manual/`

L2HLIST: LaTeX2HTML mailing list.
    `mailto:latex2html@tug.org`

L2HMML: Generating MathML markup using LaTeX2HTML, WebEQ, and WebTEX.
    `http://www.geom.umn.edu/~ross/webtex/webtex/`

L2HSA: LaTeX2HTML source repository.
    `http://www-dsed.llnl.gov/files/programs/unix/latex2html/sources/`

L2HSC: LaTeX2HTML source repository.
    `http://saftsack.fs.uni-bayreuth.de/~latex2ht/`

LECHE: XML News and Resources.
    `http://metalab.unc.edu/xml/`

LINUXML: UNIX in XML project.
    `http://www.ozemail.com.au/~birchb/linuxml/linuxml.htm`

LTXML: LTXML XML Tools.
    `http://www.ltg.ed.ac.uk/software/xml/`

MALAYALAM: Malayalam-TEX.
    `ftp://ctan.tug.org/tex-archive/languages/malayalam/`

MALEREX: SGML Exceptions and XML.
    `http://www.arbortext.com/Think_Tank/XML__Resources/SGML_Exceptions_`
    `and_XML/sgml_exceptions_and_xml.html`

MAPLE: Waterloo Maple home page.
    `http://www.maplesoft.com/`

MATHEMATICA: Wolfram Research Mathematica home page.
    `http://www.wolfram.com/`

MATHSYMP: National Symposium in Mathematics.
    `http://www-math.mpce.mq.edu.au/texdev/MathSymp/`

MATHTYPE: WYSIWYG equation editor outputting TEX or MathML.
    `http://www.mathtype.com`

MICROPRESS: Micropress home page.
    `http://www.micropress-inc.com`

MIT: Massachusetts Institute of Technology.
    `http://web.mit.edu/`

MMLGUID: A comprehensive guide to MathML maintained by Pankaj Kamthan.
    http://indy.cs.concordia.ca/mathml/

MMLRES: MathML Resource List.
    http://www.webeq.com/webeq/mathml/resources.html

MMLSPEC: MathML specification.
    http://www.w3.org/TR/WD-math/

MPEG: MPEG Frequently Asked Questions.
    http://www.faqs.org/faqs/jpeg-faq/

NDVI: Netscape plugin for viewing DVI files (supports HyperTEX \specials).
    http://norma.nikhef.nl/~t16/ndvi_doc.html

NETPBM: netpbm utilities.
    ftp://ftp.x.org/contrib/utilities/netpbm-1mar1994.p1.tar.gz

NIKNAK: Commercial PostScript to PDF convertor.
    http://www.5-d.com/niknak.htm

NISTHMF: Digital Library of Mathematical Functions.
    http://www.nist.gov/DigitalMathLib/

OASIS: Organization for the Advancement of Structured Information Standards.
    http://www.oasis-open.org/

OFX: Open Financial Exchange.
    http://www.ofx.net

OMEGA: TEX 16-bit implementation based on Unicode.
    http://www.gutenberg.eu.org/omega/

OMGTECH: Object Management Group technical documents.
    http:
    //www.omg.org/techprocess/meetings/schedule/Technology_Adoptions.html

OMNIMARK: SGML environment for managing and delivering personalized content on
    the Web.
    http://www.omnimark.com

PDFMARKD: Pdfmark documentation.
    http://partners.adobe.com/supportservice/devrelations/technotes.html

PDFMARKP: Pdfmark primer.
    http://www.ifconnection.de/~tm/

PDFSPEC: PDF specification.
    http://www.adobe.com/supportservice/devrelations/PDFS/TN/PDFSPEC.PDF

PDFTEXEX: pdfTEX examples.
    http://www.tug.org/applications/pdftex/

PDFTEXS: pdfTEX source.
    ftp://ftp.cstug.cz/pub/tex/local/cstug/thanh/

PDFZONE: The PDF Zone.
http://www.pdfzone.com/

PERL: The Perl source home page.
http://www.perl.com/pace/pub/

PERLSGML: Perl programs and libraries for processing SGMLDTDs.
http://www.oac.uci.edu/indiv/ehood/perlSGML.html

PGML: Precision Graphics Markup Language.
http://www.w3.org/TR/1998/NOTE-PGML

PNG: The Portable Network Graphics home page.
http://www.cdrom.com/pub/png/

PSGML: Emacs Major Mode for editing SGML coded documents.
http://www.lysator.liu.se/projects/about_psgml.html

PSGMLXML: Patches to add XML to PSGML.
http://www.megginson.com/Software/psgmlxml-19980218.zip

QWERTZ: The qwertz HTML to LaTeX Converter.
http://nathan.gmd.de/projects/zeno/qwertz/qwertz.html

RAGHIST: A history of HTML (Chapter 2 of Raggett et al. (1998)).
http://www.w3.org/People/Raggett/book4/ch02.html

RAGHTML: Raggett's 10 minute Guide to HTML.
http://www.w3.org/MarkUp/Guide/

RDF: Resource Description Framework.
http://www.w3.org/RDF/

RFC1630:   Universal Resource Identifiers in WWW.
http://info.internet.isi.edu:80/in-notes/rfc/files/rfc1630.txt

RFC1738:   Uniform Resource Locators (URL) Specification.
http://info.internet.isi.edu:80/in-notes/rfc/files/rfc1738.txt

RFC1866:   Hypertext Markup Language – 2.0.
http://info.internet.isi.edu:80/in-notes/rfc/files/rfc1866.txt

RFC2045:   Multipurpose Internet Mail Extensions (MIME) Part One: Format of Internet
Message Bodies.
http://info.internet.isi.edu:80/in-notes/rfc/files/rfc2045.txt

RFC2141:   Uniform Resource Name (URN) Syntax Specification.
http://info.internet.isi.edu:80/in-notes/rfc/files/rfc2141.txt

RFC2396:   Uniform Resource Identifiers (URI): Generic Syntax.
http://info.internet.isi.edu:80/in-notes/rfc/files/rfc2396.txt

SAMANALA: Samanala Transliteration.
http://www-texdev.mpce.mq.edu.au/l2h/indic/Indica/samanala/

SAX: Simple API for XML.
http://www.megginson.com/SAX/index.html

SAXJAVA: SAX Java distribution.
     http://www.megginson.com/SAX/javadoc/packages.html

SDML: Signed Document Markup Language: W3C note.
     http://www.w3.org/TR/NOTE-SDML/

SGML2XML: SGML to XML.
     http://www.xml.com/xml/pub/98/07/dtd/index.html

SGMLC: Programming language for processing SGML documents on MS Windows.
     http://www.dircon.co.uk/sgml/

SGMLNEW: SGML and XML News.
     http://www.oasis-open.org/cover/sgmlnew.html

SGMLSPM: SGMLSpm source archive.
     http://www.megginson.com/Software/SGMLSpm-1.03ii.tar.gz

SGMLTOOLS: Home page of the SGMLtools project.
     http://www.sgmltools.org/

SINDOC: Sinh-HTML docs.
     http://www-texdev.mpce.mq.edu.au/l2h/indic/Sinhala/lreport/

SINTEX: Sinhala-TEX.
     ftp://ctan.tug.org/tex-archive/language/sinhala/

SMIL: Synchronized Multimedia Integration Language 1.0 Specification.
     http://www.w3.org/TR/REC-smil/

SOTU98:   President Clinton's 1998 State of the Union speech.
     http://www.whitehouse.gov/WH/SOTU98/address.html

SOTU99:   President Clinton's 1999 State of the Union speech.
     http://www.whitehouse.gov/WH/New/html/19990119-2656.html

SOX: Schema for Object-oriented XML.
     http://www.w3.org/TR/NOTE-SOX/

SP: SP SGML parser.
     http://www.jclark.com/sp/

SPDOC: SP parser documentation.
     http://www.jclark.com/sp/nsgmls.htm

SPEECHML: SpeechML markup language.
     http://www.alphaWorks.ibm.com/formula/speechml

STYLECSS: W3C's CSS stylesheet page.
     http://www.w3.org/Style/CSS/

SVGSPEC: Scalable Vector Graphics Specification (Working Draft).
     http://www.w3.org/TR/WD-SVG/

TDTD: tdtd DTD editing Emacs macros.
     ftp://ftp.mulberrytech.com/pub/tdtd/

TEIGUIDE: TEI Lite: An Introduction to Text Encoding for Interchange.
    `http://www.uic.edu/orgs/tei/intros/teiu5.html`

TEIHOME: TEI Text Encoding Initiative home page.
    `http://www.uic.edu/orgs/tei/`

TEILITE: TEI lite DTD.
    `http://www-tei.uic.edu/orgs/tei/p3/dtd/teilite.dtd`

TEIXML: XML version of TEI DTD.
    `http://www.loria.fr/~bonhomme/xml.html`

TEX2HTML: Commercial version of `tth` (adds additional features).
    `http://www.tex2html.com`

TEX4HT: TEX4ht translator.
    `http://www.cis.ohio-state.edu/~gurari/TeX4ht/mn.html`

TEXLIVE: Ready-to-run CD-ROM distribution of TEX-related software (UNIX and Windows 9X/NT).
    `http://www.tug.org/texlive.html`

TEXML: System to typeset XML documents with TEX.
    `http://www.alphaWorks.ibm.com/formula/texml/`

TEXPIDER: MicroPress' version of TEX that writes HTML directly.
    `http://www.micropress-inc.com/webb/wbstart.htm`

TIFF6:   Specification of TIFF, version 6.
    `http://www.adobe.com/supportservice/devrelations/PDFS/TN/TIFF6.pdf`

TTH: TEX to HTML translator.
    `http://hutchinson.belmont.ma.us/tth/`

TUGINDIA: TUGIndia Journal.
    `http://ftp.gwdg.de/pub/dante/usergrps/tugindia/tugindia11.pdf`

TXPL: IBM techexplorer Hypermedia Browser.
    `http://www.software.ibm.com/enetwork/techexplorer/`

UNICODE: Unicode Consortium home page.
    `http://www.unicode.org`

URNIETF: IETF URN Working Group.
    `http://www.ietf.org/html.charters/urn-charter.html`

VISXML: Visual XML.
    `http://www.pierlou.com/visxml/`

VML: Vector Markup Language.
    `http://www.w3.org/TR/NOTE-VML`

W2CMATH: W3C's Math home page.
    `http://www.w3.org/Math/`

W3C: World Wide Web Consortium home page.
    `http://www.w3.org/`

W3CFUTURE: W3C plans for markup after HTML.
   `http://www.w3.org/MarkUp/Activity.html`

W3CGR: W3C Graphics.
   `http://www.w3.org/Graphics/Activity`

W3CSTYLE: W3C's Style Page.
   `http://www.w3.org/Style`

WAI: Web Accessibility Initiative.
   `http://w3.org/WAI/`

WEB3D: The WEB3D (formerly VRML) home page.
   `http://www.web3d.org/home.html`

WEBDAV: Web Distributed Authoring and Versioning (IETF WEBDAV Working Group).
   `http://www.ics.uci.edu/pub/ietf/webdav/`

WEBEQ: WebEQ Equation Editor.
   `http://www.webeq.com`

WEBHIST: Little History of the World Wide Web.
   `http://www.w3.org/History.html`

WIDL: Web Interface Definition Language.
   `http://www.w3.org/TR/NOTE-widl`

XCATALOG: John Cowan's XCatalog proposal.
   `http://www.ccil.org/~cowan/XML/XCatalog.html`

XDVI: Paul Vojta's X Windows TEX previewer.
   `http://math.berkeley.edu/~vojta/xdvi.html`

XLINKSPEC: XML Linking Language Specification.
   `http://www.w3.org/TR/WD-xlink`

XMI: XML Metadata Interchange.
   `http://www.oasis-open.org/cover/xmi.html`

XML4J: XML for Java.
   `http://www.alphaworks.ibm.com/formula/xml/`

XMLDATA: XML-Data, an XML vocabulary for schemas.
   `http://www.w3.org/TR/1998/NOTE-XML-data/`

XMLDEV: XML developers' list.
   `http://www.lists.ic.ac.uk/hypermail/xml-dev/`

XMLEDI: XML/EDI: an E-business framework using XML.
   `http://www.geocities.com/WallStreet/Floor/5815/`

XMLERRATA: XML 1.0 Specification Errata.
   `http://www.w3.org/XML/xml-19980210-errata`

XMLFAQ: Peter Flynn's XML FAQ.
   `http://www.ucc.ie/xml/`

XMLINTRO: XML introduction.
   `http://www.oasis-open.org/cover/xmlIntro.html`

XMLNS: Namespaces in XML.
   `http://www.w3.org/TR/WD-xml-names/`

XMLPAGE: XML page.
   `http://www.oasis-open.org/cover/xml.html`

XMLPARS: List of free XML software.
   `http://www.stud.ifi.uio.no/~larsga/linker/XMLtools.html`

XMLRES: XML resources page.
   `http://capita.wustl.edu/XMLRes/`

XMLSPEC: The XML specification (Version 1).
   `http://www.w3.org/TR/REC-xml`

XMLSTYLE: XML stylesheet.
   `http://www.w3.org/TR/xml-stylesheet`

XPDF: Xpdf, an Independent PDF viewer.
   `http://www.aimnet.com/~derekn/xpdf/`

XPPARS: James Clark's xp XML parser.
   `http://www.jclark.com/xml/xp/index.html`

XPTSPEC: XML Pointer Language Specification.
   `http://www.w3.org/TR/WD-xptr/`

XSL97:   XSL (original 1997 submission).
   `http://www.w3.org/TR/NOTE-XSL.html`

XSLCSS: Using XSL and CSS together.
   `http://www.w3.org/TR/NOTE-XSL-and-CSS/`

XSLMAIL: XSL Mailing List.
   `http://www.mulberrytech.com/xsl/xsl-list`

XSLREQ: XSL Requirements Summary.
   `http://www.w3.org/TR/WD-XSLReq/`

XSLWD: XSL Working Draft (December 1998 version).
   `http://www.w3.org/TR/1998/WD-xsl-19981216`

XTPROC: James Clark's xt XSL transformation engine.
   `http://www.jclark.com/xml/xt.html`

XUL: Extensible User Interface Language.
   `http://www.oasis-open.org/cover/xul.html`

YANDY: Y&Y Inc.
   `http://www.yandy.com/`

YUDIT: Yudit Unicode editor.
   `http://czyborra.com/yudit/`

Bibliography

Abramowitz, M. and Stegun, I. A. 1972. *Handbook of Mathematical Functions*. New York: Dover Publications.

Bienz, T., Cohn, R., and Meehan, J. R. 1996. *Portable Document Format Reference Manual Version 1.2*. San Jose, Calif.: Adobe Systems Incorporated. Available online at [↪PDFSPEC].

Boumphrey, F. 1998. *Professional Style Sheets for HTML and XML*. Chicago: Wrox Press, Inc.

Bradley, N. 1998. *The XML Companion*. Reading, Mass.: Addison Wesley Longman.

Carr, L., Rahtz, S., and Hall, W. 1991. Experiments with T_EX and hyperactivity. *TUGboat*, **12** (1), 13–20.

Drakos, N. and Moore, R. 1998. *The LaTeX2HTML Translator, User's Guide and Manual*. Accompanies the software, 1998. Online version available at [↪L2HDOC].

Flynn, P. 1998. *Understanding SGML and XML Tools*. Norwell, Mass.: Kluwer Academic Publishers.

Foster, K. R. 1999. Math on the Internet. *IEEE Spectrum*, **36** (4), 36–40.

Goldfarb, C. F. and Prescod, P. 1998. *The XML Handbook*. Englewood Cliffs, N.J.: Prentice Hall.

Goossens, M., Mittelbach, F., and Samarin, A. 1994. *The LaTeX Companion*. Reading, Mass.: Addison-Wesley.

Goossens, M., Rahtz, S., and Mittelbach, F. 1997. *The LaTeX Graphics Companion: Illustrating Documents with TeX and PostScript*. Tools and Techniques for Computer Typesetting. Reading, Mass.: Addison-Wesley.

Harold, E. 1998. *XML Extensible Markup Language*. Foster City, Calif.: IDG Books Worldwide, Inc.

ISO:15924 1999. *Codes for the Representation of Names of Scripts*. International Organization for Standardization, Geneva, Switzerland. International Standard ISO 15924:1999.

ISO:3166 1997. *Codes for the Representation of Names of Countries and Their Subdivisions—Part 1: Country Codes*. International Organization for Standardization, Geneva, Switzerland. International Standard ISO 3166-1:1997.

ISO:639 1988. *Code for the Representation of Names of Languages*. International Organization for Standardization, Geneva, Switzerland. International Standard ISO 639:1988.

ISO:639-2 1998. *Code for the Representation of Names of Languages—Part 2: Alpha-3 Code*. International Organization for Standardization, Geneva, Switzerland. International Standard ISO 639:1998.

ISO:8879 1986. *Information Processing—Text and Office Systems—Standard Generalized Markup Language (SGML). First edition, 1986-10-15*. International Organization for Standardization, Geneva, Switzerland. International Standard ISO 8879:1986.

ISO/IEC:10179 1996. *Information Technology—Processing Languages—Document Style Semantics and Specification Language (DSSSL). First edition, 1996*. International Organization for Standardization, Geneva, Switzerland. International Standard ISO/IEC 10179:1996. A PDF version is available online for personal use, see [↪DSSSLPDF].

ISO/IEC:10646-1:1993 1993. *Information Technology—Universal Multiple-Octet Coded Character Set (UCS)—Part 1: Architecture and Basic Multilingual Plane, (with amendments)*. International Organization for Standardization, Geneva, Switzerland. International Standard ISO/IEC:10646-1:1993.

ISO/IEC:11172 1993. *Information Technology—Coding of Moving Pictures and Associated Audio for Digital Storage Media at up to about 1,5 Mbit/s—Parts 1 to 4*. International Organization for Standardization, Geneva, Switzerland. International Standard ISO/IEC 9070:11172.

ISO/IEC:14772-1 1998. *Information Technology—Computer Graphics and Image Processing—The Virtual Reality Modeling Language—Part 1: Functional Specification and UTF-8 Encoding*. International Organization for Standardization, Geneva, Switzerland. International Standard ISO/IEC 14772-1:1998.

ISO/IEC:8839-1 1998. *Information Technology—8-Bit Single-Byte Coded Graphic Character Sets—Part 1: Latin Alphabet No. 1*. International Organization for Standardization, Geneva, Switzerland. International Standard ISO/IEC 8859-1:1998.

ISO/IEC:9070 1991. *Information Processing—SGML Support Facilities - Registration Procedures for Public Text Owner Identifiers. Second edition, 15 April 1991*. International Organization for Standardization, Geneva, Switzerland. International Standard ISO/IEC 9070:1991.

Jelliffe, R. 1998. *The XML and SGML Cookbook: Recipes for Structured Information*. Englewood Cliffs, N.J.: Prentice Hall.

Knuth, D. E. 1986. *The TeXbook*, volume A of *Computers and Typesetting*. Reading, Mass.: Addison-Wesley.

Lamport, L. 1994. *LaTeX: A Document Preparation System: User's Guide and Reference Manual*. 2nd edition. Reading, Mass.: Addison-Wesley.

Leventhal, M., Lewis, D., and Fuchs, M. 1998. *Designing XML Internet Applications*. Englewood Cliffs, N.J.: Prentice Hall.

Lie, H. W. and Bos, B. 1997. *Cascading Style Sheets: Designing for the Web*. Reading, Mass.: Addison-Wesley.

Maler, E. and Andaloussi, J. E. 1996. *Developing SGML DTDs: From Text to Model to Markup*. Englewood Cliffs, N.J.: Prentice Hall.

McGrath, S. 1998. *XML by Example. Building E-Commerce Applications*. Englewood Cliffs, N.J.: Prentice Hall.

Megginson, D. 1998. *Structuring XML Documents*. The Charles F. Goldfarb series on open information management. Englewood Cliffs, N.J.: Prentice Hall.

Merz, T. 1998. *Web Publishing with Acrobat/PDF*. Berlin, Germany: Springer-Verlag.

Murray, J. and vanRyper, W. 1996. *Graphics File Formats*. 2nd edition. Sebastopol, Calif.: O'Reilly & Assoc. Inc.

Raggett, D., Lam, J., Alexander, I., and Kmicc, M. 1998. *Raggett on HTML 4*. Reading, Mass.: Addison-Wesley.

Rahtz, S. 1995. Another look at LaTeX to SGML. *TUGboat*, **16** (3).

Smith, N. E. 1998. *SGML/XML Filters*. Plano, Tex.: Wordware Publishing, Inc.

St. Laurent, S. 1997. *XML: A Primer*. Portland, Ore.: MIS Press.

Tanenbaum, A. S. 1996. *Computer Networks*. 3rd edition. Englewood Cliffs, N.J.: Prentice Hall.

Unicode Consortium 1996. *The Unicode Standard, Version 2.0.* Reading, Mass.: Addison-Wesley.

Wall, L., Christiansen, T., and Schwartz, R. L. 1996. *Programming Perl.* 2nd edition. Sebastopol, Calif.: O'Reilly & Assoc. Inc.

Index

Throughout the index bold face page numbers are used to indicate pages with important information about the entry, for instance, the precise definition of a command or a detailed explanation; page numbers in normal type indicate a textual reference.

Other books from Addison Wesley Longman

PostScript Language Reference Manual, Third Edition, Adobe Systems
The PostScript language is widely recognized as the industry standard for page description. Incorporated into a broad range of printers, imagesetters, and computer displays, PostScript describes exactly how text, sampled images, and graphics will appear on a printed page or on a computer screen.

The **PostScript Language Reference**—known as **the Red Book**—is the complete and authoritative reference manual for the PostScript language. Prepared by Adobe Systems Incorporated, the creators and stewards of the PostScript standard, it documents the syntax and semantics of the language, the Adobe imaging model, and the effects of the graphics operators. This **Third Edition** has been updated to include **LanguageLevel 3** extensions, which unify a number of previous extensions and introduce many new features, such as high-fidelity color, support for masked images, and smoother shading capabilities.

An accompanying CD-ROM contains the entire text of this book in Portable Document Format (PDF) ISBN 0-201-37922-8.

LaTeX: A Document Preparation System, Second Edition, Leslie Lamport.
The definitive LaTeX user's guide and reference manual, written by the system's creator, clearly documenting the latest 2ε release. ISBN 0-201-52983-1

The LaTeX Companion, Michel Goossens, Frank Mittelbach, Alexander Samarin.
A companion to the Lamport book and to any other introduction to LaTeX, this expertly compiled reference answers common user questions left open by the introductions, and describes add-on packages available to solve diverse problems. ISBN 0-201-54199-8

The LaTeX Graphics Companion, Michel Goossens, Sebastian Rahtz, Frank Mittelbach. This handy reference describes techniques and tricks needed to illustrate LaTeX documents, and answers common user questions about graphics and PostScript fonts. ISBN 0-201-85469-4

BUGS in Writing: A Guide to Debugging Your Prose, Lyn Dupré.
What every scientific writer needs to know to write clearly, correctly, effectively. Numerous examples—often hilarious! Comprises 150 easily digestible segments. ISBN 0-201-37921-X

Available where technical books are sold. Or, order directly from Addison Wesley Longman: 1-800-822-6339. http://www.awl.com/cseng